MANAGING E-DISCOVERY AND ESI

MANAGING E-DISCOVERY AND ESI

From Pre-Litigation Through Trial

MICHAEL D. BERMAN
COURTNEY INGRAFFIA BARTON
PAUL W. GRIMM
EDITORS

AMERICAN BAR ASSOCIATION
Section of Litigation

In cooperation with the
Maryland State Bar Association

Cover design by ABA Publishing.

Printed in the United States of America.

15 14 13 12 11 5 4 3 2 1

Library of Congress Cataloging-in-Publication Data

Managing e-discovery and ESI: from pre-litigation through trial/edited By Paul Grimm, Michael Berman and Courtney Barton.

p. cm.

Includes bibliographical references and index.

ISBN 978-1-61632-973-0

1. Electronic discovery (Law)--United States. I. Grimm, Paul W., 1951- II. Berman, Michael, 1948- III. Barton, Courtney Ingraffia.

KF8902.E42M36 2011
347.73'072--dc23

2011026964

Discounts are available for books ordered in bulk. Special consideration is given to state bars, CLE programs, and other bar-related organizations. Inquire at Book Publishing, ABA Publishing, American Bar Association, 321 North Clark Street, Chicago, Illinois 60654-7598.

www.ababooks.org

This publication made possible by agreement with and cooperation of the Maryland State Bar Association.

CONTENTS

PUBLISHER'S NOTE

The ABA Section of Litigation is the premier association for U.S. lawyers involved in litigation and trial practice. More than 50,000 lawyers representing countless areas of practice turn to the ABA Section of Litigation for member-only access to the latest news, information, and thinking on legal strategy, bringing all sides to one place to form a comprehensive view of the profession.

The Book Publishing Board has been helping authors develop litigation-related books since the Section of Litigation was founded in 1973. All board members are current or former litigators. Our mission is to help serve the profession by publishing books with strong practical value to lawyers whose practice includes litigation. Since 2006, the Section of Litigation has also published some types of books under its 'First Chair Press' imprint.

ACKNOWLEDGMENTS

Michael D. Berman
To my parents, Marjory and Fred, and all the Goldmans,
For showing me what is possible;
To Patricia,
For making it possible;
To Annie, Alex, Adam, Aryah, Susan, Asa, Sarah,
and Dafna
To show them what is possible;
and
To SP4 James D. Brown, PFC Alan G. Mandes,
and PFC Donald W. Persinger
April 24, 1973: Taken too soon, but not forgotten.

Courtney I. Barton
To Michael and Josie
and
To my dad, Roy J. Ingraffia, Sr., M.D.
who taught me that the little engine could.

The Hon. Paul W. Grimm
To Lynne, John, Samantha, Gia, and Phoebe
And to all Lawyers who cooperate in the conduct of discovery.

FOREWORD

THE HON. BARBARA JACOBS ROTHSTEIN

Since the adoption of the Federal Rules of Civil Procedure in 1938, discovery has been the touchstone that defines our approach to ensuring that civil cases reach a just resolution. Access to information has become the sine qua non of our judicial process. We are committed to the principle that only full disclosure can assure a dependable foundation for arriving at a fair outcome.

The strain on civil discovery began to show in the 1970s and 1980s. Litigation became more complex and individual claims were often aggregated into class actions that far exceeded the vision of the original drafters of the Federal Rules. Litigation of such dimensions required more extensive discovery. This led to cases in which attorneys faced warehouses of documents in response to discovery requests. The costs could be staggering and the discovery process itself became the focus of litigation.

While judges and attorneys were focusing on problems arising from massive amounts of paper documents, a quiet revolution was taking place that would quickly dwarf the discovery problems related to paper. The warehouses of paper documents were replaced with terabyte disks storing even greater amounts of information in electronic form. Information previously exchanged by phone calls or casual conversations was stored on multiples of electronic mail. Discovery conferences became a venue of odd technical discussions about concepts such as "metadata," "data storage architecture," and the cost of reviving information on data systems that had long been scrapped.

Today the central role of electronically stored information (ESI) is well known. In discussing the 2006 amendments to the Federal Rules of Civil Procedure, the Hon. Lee Rosenthal explained, ESI "has enhanced the parties' ability to uncover the facts of the case" and "serves the fundamental tenet of American jurisprudence in that it permits cases to be resolved based on their merits."[1] But the challenges presented by this new format are less well known. As the Federal Judicial Center Pocket Guide on electronic discovery explains, "ESI discovery presents unique issues including its scope of discovery, the allocation of costs, the form of production, the waiver of privilege and work-product protection, and the preservation of data and spoliation." [2]

The unique issues raised by ESI are often unfamiliar to attorneys. The concepts are daunting and the risk of error is great. Mr. Berman, Ms. Barton, and Judge Grimm provide a much needed synthesis with this ESI sourcebook. Taking a thorough, practical, and easily understandable approach, the authors discuss both the applicable legal principles and technological issues from the pre-litigation planning stage through the discovery and trial stages. A busy practitioner can, within minutes, find authoritative guidance on virtually any ESI issue.

The book begins by setting the ESI stage with Judge Facciola's discussion of the history of ESI, aptly framed "Did anyone get the license plate of the rocket ship that hit me?" This is followed by retired Judge Hedge's description of the governing Federal Rules of Civil Procedure. Judge Grimm provides a synopsis of the all important privilege-protection provisions. Other chapters cover the relevant Civil Rules in clear and concise detail: Rule 26(a)(1) (initial disclosures), 26(b)(2)(B) (not reasonably accessible), 26(b)(5)(A) (privilege logs), 26(f) (conference of parties), and 26(g)(sanctions).

The Civil Rules also encourage the parties to control the costs of ESI. "Those who are educated about the rules and creative in their use will save themselves, their clients and the courts a great deal of time and money. Those who are not will continue to blame the rules, never realizing that 'the fault lies not in our rules, but in themselves.'"[3]

A 2009 survey by the Federal Judicial Center concluded that the current federal rules are working well and are adequate to meet

1. Milberg LLP & Hausfeld LLP, *E-Discovery Today: The Fault Lies Not in Our Rules . . .*, 4 FED. CTS. L. REV. 1, 48 (2011) (citing the Hon. Lee H. Rosenthal, Keynote Address at the Georgetown University Law Center Advanced E-Discovery Institute: Is the E-Discovery Process Broken, and, if So, Can't It Be Fixed? (Nov. 12, 2009)).

2. B. Rothstein, R. Hedges & E. Wiggins, MANAGING DISCOVERY OF ELECTRONIC INFORMATION: A POCKET GUIDE FOR JUDGES 20 (Fed. Jud. Ctr. 2007).

3. Milberg LLP & Hausfeld LLP, *supra* at note 1, 2.

the challenges posed by ESI,[4] but there will always be gaps in the rules and this book provides needed and detailed guidance on how to fill those gaps. This is especially true in dealing with matters of cost. The sourcebook discusses in great detail many legal, technological, and cost-based issues, emphasizing proportionality, preplanning, and cooperation as crucial for counsel.

The sourcebook is especially valuable in discussing areas where the guidance from the Civil Rules and case law is unclear or emerging. It offers practical suggestions about important and often ignored areas, such as the use of ESI depositions, structured databases, the timing of spoliation motions, and ending a litigation hold, along with how to advise clients about prelitigation planning, computer usage, and knowledge management policies.

The editors have assembled a highly qualified group of authors, including federal judges, a state appellate judge, private practitioners, academicians, public-sector attorneys, service providers, and forensic consultants. With each author focusing on an area of special expertise, the assembled chapters provide a comprehensive review of this challenging subject in one concise volume.

"Our entire system of jurisprudence is based on adequate disclosure; take that card from the bottom of the pyramid, and we must be prepared to re-build the entire foundation of that system."[5] There is no chance of putting the digital genie back in the bottle. Attorneys and judges must master and use ESI. "Attorneys and judges—many of who admittedly face a steep learning curve—have to throw out the paper playbook and adapt to the digital world in which we live."[6] This book provides the tools that will allow them to do so.

4. E. Lee & T. Willging, ATTORNEY SATISFACTION WITH THE FEDERAL RULES OF CIVIL PROCEDURE (Fed. Jud. Ctr. 2010), http://www.fjc.gov/public/pdf.nsf/lookup/costciv2.pdf/$file/costciv2.pdf.

5. Milberg LLP & Hausfeld LLP, *supra* note 1, at 5.

6. *Id.* at 4.

EDITOR'S NOTE

The original concept of this book was to assemble the wisdom and work of many accomplished members of the Bench and Bar in addressing issues presented by electronically stored information (ESI), and to compile a practitioners' deskbook, not a treatise. To that end, the editors invited the participation of many people who willingly and generously gave of their valuable time and effort. We are most appreciative of their efforts and their biographical information is included at the end of this book.

In addition to the many authors and contributors noted in the text, we would like to acknowledge the behind-the-scenes efforts of Tim Brandhorst, Deputy Director of Book Publishing at ABA Publishing, for his role in shepherding this effort, and John B. Isbister (Tydings & Rosenberg, LLP), Publications and Content Officer of the ABA Section of Litigation, for helping to bring this project to the American Bar Association. Special thanks are also in order to Spencer Punnett, Co-Chair of the ABA Section of Litigation's Book Publishing Board, for tirelessly reviewing, editing, and improving the entire manuscript. We would like to thank Heather Pike of Rifkin, Livingston, Levitan & Silver, LLC, for her work on this project. We are grateful to our employers for providing us with this opportunity.

We have, in part, tried to present settled principles as settled. There are, however, areas open to debate, discussion, and even disagreement, and we have included that discussion and debate even where one or more of the primary editors disagrees with part of a particular chapter, the opinions expressed, or the conclusions drawn. Each author's chapter represents the personal opinions and views of the author, and not the organizations with which they are affiliated or employed, the editors, publisher, or other authors.

Of course, both the members of the Bench and the private practitioners who have contributed to this work do so solely in their individual capacity and not on behalf of the courts or any other organization, including the American Bar Association. Issues presented by ESI are fact-sensitive and some are in flux, changing rapidly. The editors and authors are not providing legal advice, and each practitioner should conduct independent, jurisdiction-specific[1] research in addressing each ESI issue.

1. As has been noted, "[r]ecent decisions . . . have generated concern throughout the country among lawyers and institutional clients regarding the lack of a uniform national standard governing when the duty to preserve potentially relevant evidence commences, the level of culpability required to justify sanctions, the nature and severity of appropriate sanctions, and the scope of the duty to preserve evidence and whether it is tempered by the same principles of proportionality that Fed.R.Civ.P. 26(b)(2)(C) applies to all discovery in civil cases." Victor Stanley, Inc. v. Creative Pipe, Inc., 269 F.R.D. 497 (D. Md. 2010), aff'd in part and modified in part on unrelated grounds, No. MJG-06-2662 (D. Md. Nov. 1, 2010), subsequent opinion (D. Md. Jan. 24, 2011). In light of the pendency of Victor Stanley before the Hon. Paul W. Grimm, who is one of the writers and editors of this book, Judge Grimm did not contribute to this summary of the case or the conclusions drawn, nor did he contribute to the discussion in this book of any other case pending before him.

INTRODUCTION

By Michael D. Berman

The legal landscape, and litigation, changed markedly in the middle of the last decade. Venerable concepts, like the duty to preserve relevant information, production and review of discoverable information, authentication, and introduction of evidence, had to adapt to email, word processing, spreadsheets, and metadata, as well as the personal computer, hard and thumb drives, smartphones, networks, the Internet, and web pages. Although attorneys long had to master technical concepts ranging from comminuted fractures to generally accepted accounting principles, electronically stored information (ESI) presented unfamiliar terms, such as deleted data, metadata, network architecture, native and static files, and, in some instances, case-dispositive and career-destroying sanctions.

High-visibility decisions such as *Zubulake*[1] and *Qualcomm*,[2] combined with the December 2006 amendments to the Federal Rules of Civil Procedure, blazed across the legal firmament. Continuing legal education programs and webinars blossomed like flowers in spring. While many of the resources were excellent, the explosion of information itself sometimes paradoxically made clear, neutral guidance difficult to find.

---

1. Zubulake v. UBS Warburg LLC (*Zubulake V*), 229 F.R.D. 422 (S.D.N.Y. 2004); Zubulake v. UBS Warburg LLC (*Zubulake IV*), 220 F.R.D. 212 (S.D.N.Y. 2003); Zubulake v. UBS Warburg LLC (*Zubulake III*), 216 F.R.D. 280 (S.D.N.Y. 2003); Zubulake v. UBS Warburg LLC (*Zubulake II*), 230 F.R.D. 290 (S.D.N.Y. 2003); Zubulake v. UBS Warburg LLC (*Zubulake I*), 217 F.R.D. 309 (S.D.N.Y. 2003).

2. Qualcomm, Inc. v. Broadcom Corp., 2008 WL 66932 (S.D. Cal. Jan. 7, 2008), *vacated and remanded in part*, 2008 WL 63810 (S.D. Cal. Mar. 5, 2008), *appeals dismissed*, 327 Fed. Appx. 877, 2008 WL 6400775 (Fed. Cir. Aug. 18, 2008), *on remand*, 2010 WL 1336937 (S.D. Cal. Apr. 2, 2010).

There is, however, a need for such guidance because "[d]iscovery is expensive, and electronic discovery is really expensive."[3] The overriding themes of this book are that (1) with proper planning, transparency, and cooperation, ESI is manageable; and (2) proportionality, not forensic knowledge, is the bedrock principle of handling ESI successfully from an attorney's perspective.

This book identifies the key issues related to ESI—prelitigation management, preservation, collection, processing, review, production, and use in deposition and at trial—and provides practical guidance to litigators. The editors have brought together a knowledgeable, talented, skilled, and respected group of authors who have addressed each stage of the ESI process, from "A" to "Z," in a clear and understandable way.

This is a book for the busy litigator (or judge) who wishes to handle ESI competently, and who also has interrogatories to answer, depositions and hearings to attend, and meetings that demand his or her immediate attention. Courts, lawyers, and litigants are, at the beginning of the twenty-first century, still "writing the book" on the use of ESI in litigation. Therefore, where principles are settled, citation to representative[4] authority is provided. Where principles are unsettled, that is made clear. And the book goes further, addressing novel issues in a practical way.

The purpose of this guidebook is to provide working, practical, cost-effective tools to those who must deal with ESI in disputes of varying magnitude. The book is divided into eight parts that follow the sequence from the prelitigation stage through trial.

Part One: The legal groundwork

"Let's start at the very beginning," so kicks off a classic song, "a very good place to start."[5] Part One lays the groundwork.

In his chapter on the history of electronic discovery, The Hon. John M. Facciola answers the question: "Did anyone get the license plate of the rocket ship that hit me?" Noting that "[t]he revolution in the processing of information in a complicated society brought as dramatic a change in civil procedure and evidence as the Amer-

3. A.L. Brown, *The Manageable Challenge of Electronic Discovery*, ROBINS, KAPLAN, MILLER & CIRESI (formerly posted at http://www.rkmc.com/).

4. This book is intended as a practical guide, not a comprehensive academic treatise, so there has been no effort to cite every authority supporting a point.

5. RODGERS & HAMMERSTEIN, *Do-Re-Mi, on* THE SOUND OF MUSIC (1959).

ican common law courts ever confronted," Judge Facciola then "slow[s] that rocket ship down" with a discussion of major developments in handling ESI in discovery over the past decade, including *Zubulake* and the Sedona Conference.

Next, in his rule-by-rule look at the December 2006 amendments to the Federal Rules of Civil Procedure, retired Judge Ronald J. Hedges does what every ESI litigator must do. He starts with the text of the rules and the Advisory Committee Notes to them, providing a concise description of the fundamental principles.

Then, as a comparison, Robert Dale Klein and The Hon. Joseph F. Murphy, Jr. show how the laboratories of federalism are adapting the federal rules to the unique litigation culture of their various jurisdictions. The chapter focuses "on the uniformity and variations among the states, each of which must fit rules related to ESI into its own unique procedures, customs, systems, and processes. In doing so, [the chapter] also consider[s] the countervailing factor that ESI presents the same technical and cost problems and issues in the north, south, east, and west."

Part Two: A primer on buzzwords, information technology, and corporate management policies

Part Two moves from the legal groundwork to the technological predicates for handling ESI. It provides a primer for the attorney who must act as technical translator between information technology personnel, laypersons, and the legal framework set out by state and federal law. Because ESI presents a tripartite blending of legal, technological, and business issues, it is necessary to have input from all disciplines.

Scott Fischer and Richard E. Davis, both of whom are technical consultants, begin with a layperson's description of topics such as networks, backup tapes, and the various types of email systems. If "zettabytes" and "yottabytes" were not part of "your early-childhood lexicon," this chapter will assist practitioners in communicating about technology.

William A. McComas, an attorney and programmer, then explains how businesses use computer usage and knowledge management policies to structure and control their data in the "free for all" period before litigation is anticipated. The chapter provides a litigation-oriented "road map for the management of corporate ESI."

Kate Paslin, an attorney and service provider, describes metadata, when and why it matters, and how to address it. The metadata chapter describes the different categories of metadata, and when to request it in discovery.

Part Two concludes with a fresh perspective on structured data in e-discovery, by David Kessler and Daniel L. Regard II. After a discussion of what structured data is, the authors discuss the relatively uncharted area of discovery of electronic databases. They note that "at a time when structured data is growing at unprecedented levels, there is either confusion or a lack of knowledge about how to handle it from a legal and practical perspective." The chapter then discusses how the courts have addressed structured data and practical considerations in handling that data.

Oliver Wendell Holmes wrote: "A word is not a crystal, transparent and unchanged, it is the skin of a living thought and may vary greatly in color and content according to the circumstances and the time it in which it is used."[6] Part Two provides the vocabulary and concepts for an attorney to employ when speaking with forensic experts and opposing counsel.

Part Three: The duty to preserve—trigger, scope, limits, termination, and sanctions for breach

In Part Three, we turn to one of the most problematic areas of ESI, the duty to preserve. A recent study noted: "In the 230 cases in which sanctions were awarded, *the most common misconduct was failure to preserve ESI,* which was the sole basis for sanctions in ninety cases. It was also cited as one of the types of misconduct in forty-six cases involving multiple misconduct."[7] Preservation is the sine qua non of e-discovery; for without it, there is nothing.

Part Three addresses the trigger, scope, limits, termination, and sanctions for breach of that duty. Practitioners Leslie Wharton and Stephanie Weirick define the duty to preserve, discuss best practices, and explain sanctions, detailing the basis for sanctions, the analytical framework, and the types of sanctions imposed. They note that "[a]lthough all U.S. jurisdictions recognize a duty to preserve evidence for use in litigation, various federal and state courts take somewhat different approaches to the nature and scope of

6. Towne v. Eisner, 245 U.S. 418, 425 (1918) (citing Lamar v. United States, 240 U.S. 60, 65 (1916)).

7. D. Willoughby et al., *Sanctions for E-Discovery Violations: By the Numbers*, 60 Duke L.J. 789, 803 (2010) (emphasis added).

the duty to preserve and the standards for imposing sanctions for spoliation, the violation of the duty to preserve." The importance of this discussion cannot be overstated: "E-discovery sanctions are at an all-time high."[8]

In exploring these issues, however, Part Three goes beyond the standard duty-to-preserve analysis. In Chapter 9, The Hon. Paul W. Grimm, Conor R. Crowley, and Leslie Wharton present a reasoned mechanism to define what is proportionate to the case, thereby providing a framework for limiting the scope of the duty to preserve to what is reasonable in light of the needs of the case and resources of the parties. In a chapter coauthored by Rachel A. Shapiro, Part Three points to use of the secondary evidence rule as a mechanism for "filling the gap" when ESI is destroyed by an opponent. Part Three also answers the question: "When does a litigation hold end?"

"Preservation," like a fishing net, gathers a mass of sometimes undifferentiated information that may range from the "smoking gun" document to innocuous executable word processing program files. Next, someone has to pick through the net, find what is important, and use it in the lawsuit. While the duty to preserve is triggered when litigation becomes reasonably anticipated, the duty to produce is triggered by the initial disclosure and discovery provisions of the Federal Rules of Civil Procedure.

Part Four: Production—initial disclosures and discovery

Unlike the "free for all" prelitigation preservation period, production is governed by well-established discovery principles and supervised by the courts. "Production" of ESI involves standard litigation skills, like sifting and winnowing information, negotiation, initial disclosures, interrogatories, requests for production of documents, privilege logs, and depositions; however, they are applied in a new context. Production also involves some new skills, like understanding at a high level metadata, structured and unstructured data, email headers and chains, and their risks and benefits. It introduces seemingly new legal constructs, such as "not reasonably accessible because of undue burden or cost."

Thus, on the heels of preservation, a party must begin the arduous process of searching through the data it has collected in order to find responsive information. While preservation has proven to

8. *Id.* at 790.

be one of the most problematic areas of ESI, production has not been trouble-free. A recent study noted: "Failure to produce [ESI] was the sole basis for sanctions in thirty-five [recent] cases and was mentioned in another sixty-seven cases involving multiple types of misconduct. Delay in production was the sole basis for sanctions in sixteen cases and mentioned in forty-five cases involving multiple types of misconduct."[9]

Part Four addresses these issues, including initial disclosures and discovery. Practitioners Catherine L. Muir and Meghan A. Podolny describe the varied responsibilities of information technology and records management personnel, highlight the roles of in-house and merits counsel, and discuss the responsibilities of custodians. They then explain how to set up preservation, collection, review, and production protocols, concluding: "As e-discovery issues continue on their trajectory to the forefront of litigation, it is advantageous for entities to thoughtfully establish well-conceived plans and processes to abate both risks and costs associated with repeatedly responding to increasingly complex demands."

Courtney Ingraffia Barton describes the unique aspects of initial disclosures of ESI. The December 1, 2006, amendments to the Federal Rules of Civil Procedure made clear that these mandatory disclosures include electronically stored information. The "initial disclosure" chapter provides practice tips to comply with the rule.

Scott Fischer and Richard E. Davis next discuss the technological aspects of gathering, reviewing, and producing ESI in light of its fragility, dispersal, and persistence. They explain concepts such as "data mapping" and "de-duplication." The chapter defines bit-by-bit capture, active file retrieval, and the significant operational and cost differences of each, and it explains the various stages of the production process.

Part Five: Unique aspects of privilege

Part Five builds on the premise that ESI is different from paper, especially when it comes to privilege. Melissa E. Goldmeier has coauthored a chapter on the unique aspects of privilege logs relating to email "chains," "threads," or "strings." The goal is to show

9. *Id.* at 803.

how to avoid shooting a mouse with an elephant gun or fighting a dragon with a paper sword.[10]

In the chapter after that, The Hon. Paul W. Grimm, Leslie Wharton, Conor R. Crowley, and Jeanna Beck discuss multiple authorities holding that confidential, attorney-client implementation discussions must be disclosed in certain circumstances, and offer an analytical framework for determining what must be disclosed, and when. They offer practical advice on the segregation of implementation communications from other, case-related, attorney-client communications and work product.

With volumes so large that they cannot be reviewed by humans, ESI presents complex issues related to inadvertent disclosure of privileged communications. Practitioners David D. Cross, Jared S. Hosid, and Courtney Ingraffia Barton describe Federal Rule of Evidence 502, which has particular application to ESI in that context, and provide important practice tips for safeguarding the privilege. The chapter explains that FRE 502 was enacted because privilege review of ESI "has taken document review costs to unprecedented levels and imposed enormous burdens on parties and courts." They conclude that "[o]nly time will tell whether FRE 502 will achieve the cost-savings intended."

Part Five closes with The Hon. Paul W. Grimm highlighting the 10 most important things litigators need to remember about FRE 502, including its scope and important limits to its application. Judge Grimm reviews the cases and cautions, for example, that "the first thing to keep in mind is the limited scope of FRE 502. It applies only to the attorney client privilege, and to work product protection."

Part Six: Discovery—conferences of the parties, search methodology, depositions, and evidentiary issues

Part Six discusses the use of ESI in the discovery process, beginning with the conference of the parties. That conference has been described as the "linchpin" of the use of ESI in litigation.[11] The initial chapter therefore describes that process, puts it in context, discusses mandatory and optional topics, and sets out a protocol for preparing for a successful conference: "With the requisite

10. Anderson v. Beatrice Foods Co., 900 F.2d 388, 395 (1st Cir. 1990), *cert. denied*, 498 U.S. 891 (1990).

11. Craig Ball, *Musings on Meet and Confer*, http://www.craigball.com/Musings_on_Meet_and_Confer.pdf (2007) (Mr. Ball describes the Rule 26(f) conference as "a linchpin of success in electronic discovery."

preparation and cooperation, [the conference of the parties] can provide cost savings, avoid discovery and evidentiary issues, and prevent satellite-sanctions litigation, and it offers trial attorneys the opportunity to exercise control, provide input to the court, and chart the course for the case."

Of course, handling ESI successfully during the discovery process requires that an attorney be able to find what is important, responsive, and privileged. Attorneys David D. Cross and Sanya Sarich Kerksiek comprehensively describe, in clear terms, the important body of case law and sometimes-surprising scholarship addressing search methodology. They note that "[k]eyword searches, used for legal research and surfing the web, are the most basic and most common forms of electronic searches. But keyword searching may not capture all, or even a majority, of the information sought."

Jason R. Baron, a national authority on search methodology, then discusses how to design a reasonable, defensible e-discovery search, providing a commonsense "guide for the perplexed." After describing an 1985 study in which " [the] lawyers and paralegals were convinced that they were retrieving over seventy-five percent of the desired documents" while "in actuality retrieving only twenty percent," and reviewing litigation over the design of Boolean searches, Baron "suggest[s] that the central considerations for keyword searching involve first proportionality, then proper design, followed by an iterative testing, sampling, and refining process, combined with transparent attempts to discuss, in a Rule 26(f) conference or elsewhere, appropriate keyword searches with the opposing litigants, after detailed consultation with the custodians who created the ESI."

Because an attorney cannot search ESI that has not been preserved, processed, and produced, attorney Michael B. MacWilliams describes how to approach and conduct a corporate-designee deposition directed to ESI issues, with the goal of learning whether an opponent's ESI protocols were acceptably designed and employed. The chapter also addresses defending corporate-designee depositions focused on ESI.

Part Six concludes with a discussion of the use of ESI in depositions and a comprehensive chapter by attorneys Kevin F. Brady and Bryant L. Young on how to offer ESI successfully into evidence at trial. As noted in *Lorraine v. Markel American Ins. Co.*,[12] "considering the significant costs associated with discovery of ESI, it makes

12. 241 F.R.D. 534, 538 (D. Md. 2007).

little sense to go to all the bother and expense to get electronic information only to have it excluded from evidence or rejected from consideration during summary judgment because the proponent cannot lay a sufficient foundation to get it admitted."

Part Seven: Costs, cost reduction, cost shifting, and ADR

Part Seven follows up on the costs of ESI. Jared S. Hosid and Courtney Ingraffia Barton describe the concept, unique to ESI, of "not reasonably accessible because of undue burden or cost." The authors provide detailed practice tips for making, supporting, and challenging that objection.

Scott Fischer and Richard E. Davis describe how technological innovations, in this instance "crawling" and "indexing" technologies, have made some previously "inaccessible" ESI accessible, by reducing the costs involved in recovering and using that ESI. They state that "[n]ew high-capacity computer and network data-searching technologies have changed the cost-benefit landscape."

Part Seven also includes a thorough description of the important concept of "cost-shifting" in e-discovery by The Hon. James C. Francis IV. Judge Francis notes that "[a]s courts have confronted the costs generated by e-discovery, they have fashioned a new body of law for dealing with cost allocation." Describing the area as "fluid," Judge Francis describes settled concepts and identifies open questions and procedural issues related to cost-shifting motions.

Part Seven concludes with a discussion of alternative dispute resolution (ADR) as a means of cost control. The chapter notes the advantages and disadvantages of using ADR for ESI issues, concluding that the use of special masters, arbitrators, or mediators should be considered in appropriate circumstances.

Part Eight: Ethics, cooperation, and reasonableness

Because it is unique, ESI also presents some unique ethical issues, which are described in Part Eight. Dennis P. Duffy and Courtney Ingraffia Barton note that "state and local bar associations have been quietly issuing ethics opinions that will no doubt have a tremendous impact on pretrial practice." The chapter explains clearly the duty of competent representation in the information age, the myriad of conflicting ethical rules regarding metadata, and the ethical issues of outsourcing ESI review. It also poses and answers the question: "Electronic files: Who owns them?"

Because of the cost implications of voluminous, fragile, and persistent data, there has been a paradigm shift away from an adversarial model of handling ESI, aptly described in a chapter about the Sedona Conference's "Cooperation Proclamation." More than 100 judges have endorsed that proclamation, making it a must-read for every litigator. The chapter concludes: "There is a clear and steady march of professionalism codes, procedural rules, and discovery decisions away from an adversarial model of, and toward a cooperative approach to, handling ESI in litigation."

Part Eight closes with a description by The Hon. Paul W. Grimm of the ethically based "stop and think" rule in ESI. Judge Grimm reviews the genesis of that rule, its impact on specific discovery issues, the important decisions in *Qualcomm, Inc. v. Broadcom Corp.*, and the use of a "discovery budget" as a tool for defining "how much is enough" in a particular case. Judge Grimm notes that Rule 26(g), enacted in 1983, is "[o]ne of the most important, but apparently least understood or followed, of the discovery rules" and describes the application and import of that rule. The nineteenth-century English jurist Sir Henry Maine said, "Law is secreted in the interstices of procedure."[13] ESI presents a number of procedural issues.

Conclusion

This book is designed to help both novices and experienced litigators learn new vocabulary and techniques, and master and apply important legal principles, for preserving, collecting, processing, reviewing, producing, and using ESI in litigation. It will permit attorneys to act as "translators" between clients, information technology experts, and courts and, by applying principles of proportionality and information technology to the problems presented by voluminous, fragile, and persistent ESI, assist them to "secure the just, speedy, and inexpensive determination of every action and proceeding."[14] It is designed to facilitate the traditional role of the attorney as the one who applies legal principles to help solve clients' problems in a technological area, just as attorneys have handled cases involving other complex scientific issues for decades or more. As members of a learned profession that has been able to master the law applicable to the science of DNA and fingerprints, toxicology and pharmacology, and economics and survey research, litigators and judges are equally capable of adjusting to the information age.

13. Dissertations on Early Law and Custom 389 (1883).

14. Fed. R. Civ. P. 1.

PART ONE

EVOLUTION OF E-DISCOVERY RULES: FROM SEMINAL CASE LAW TO THE 2006 FEDERAL CIVIL PROCEDURE AMENDMENTS AND BEYOND

CHAPTER 1

A HISTORY OF ELECTRONIC DISCOVERY

THE HON. JOHN M. FACCIOLA

Judicial thinking on discovery of electronically stored information (ESI) has undergone a revolution since the turn of the twenty-first century. In this lucid overview, a federal magistrate judge discusses (1) the influential 1999 law review article that questioned the adequacy of traditional approaches in the new electronic environment; (2) a now-famous series of judicial decisions in the Zubulake *case, which broke new ground across a range of important ESI issues; (3) how a consensus on best practices developed under the auspices of the Sedona Conference; (4) the nature and significance of extensive ESI-related amendments to the Federal Rules of Civil Procedure in 2006; and (5) why a failure to adequately address e-discovery issues in criminal procedure "is going to be dangerous to the courts."*

1. Introduction: Did anyone get the license plate of the rocket ship that hit me?

In any society, and particularly one whose legal system is predicated on the common law and its emphasis on following precedent, change is a slow process, following the model that there should be no change unless change is necessary. The revolution in the processing of information in a complicated society brought as dramatic a change in civil procedure and evidence as the American common law courts ever confronted. The revolution was as wide as it was deep. New forms of information management and retrieval have led to entirely new requirements in the search and production of information. Indeed, a complementary revolution took place in establishing the authenticity of information introduced into evidence, with the courts now pondering how to prove that emails, voice messages, and tweets are what they seem to be, and therefore as worthy of consideration by a fact finder as a piece of paper.[1]

The dramatically different nature of the changes that the information technology revolution made can be illustrated by comparing the 2006 amendments to the Federal Rules of Civil Procedure, which dealt with information technology and e-discovery and radicalized the very nature of the rules pertaining to discovery, and the more recent amendments, effective December 1, 2010, which deal with how to calculate the number of days within which a party has to file a responding pleading or other filing. The latter problem has been around in the common law for centuries, while the 2006 amendments dealt with new developments in the past 20 years in a rapidly, ever-changing environment. It is like comparing a rocket ship to a horse-drawn carriage.

We intend to slow that rocket ship down for at least a moment to try to understand the historical forces that shaped the present environment. We expect to show that the process has been unique in the history of American civil procedure in many ways:

- First, the relationship between district court judges and magistrate judges has been significantly altered, with the magistrate judges now producing the vast majority of the opinions and having primary responsibility for the judicial management of e-discovery.
- Second, because so many of the cases filed in federal court settle, there are precious few appellate decisions; and a decision by the Supreme Court, if one ever comes, may be a generation away. This has led to idiosyncratic case law, developed, as it were, from below by magistrate judges with little or no appellate guidance.

1. *See generally* GEORGE L. PAUL, FOUNDATIONS OF DIGITAL EVIDENCE (2008).

- Third, there have been unexpected developments in the demands imposed on lawyers, ethics for which the broad statements of their duties and responsibilities have provided little guidance.
- Fourth, the Sedona Conference, a nonprofit think tank of lawyers, judges, and computer technicians, has had a profound impact on the development of the law.
- Fifth, making money, like nature, abhors a vacuum and, consequently, an entire industry selling services that lawyers engaged in electronic discovery need (or are made to think they need) has emerged. It is now impossible to attend a conference on electronic discovery not sponsored in whole or in part by such vendors, who, if nothing else, produce T-shirts for lawyers, essentially converting them into overeducated sandwich boards.
- Finally, one particular problem, the cost of reviewing electronically stored information to locate potentially privileged information, led to a case that, in turn, inspired a new Federal Rule of Evidence.

We will track all of these developments, but we must first begin with the emergence of a district judge whose influence on this one area of law is unique in American history.

2. The New York judge—Shira A. Scheindlin

The early cases were few and far between, and statements in them seem, in retrospect, almost quaint. But, as has so often been true,[2] the revolution began in a law review article entitled *Electronic Discovery in Federal Civil Litigation: Is Rule 34 up to the Task?*,[3] by Judge Shira A. Scheindlin and her former law clerk, Jeffrey Rabkin.

The central theme of the article was that Rule 34 of the Federal Rules of Civil Procedure, promulgated in 1937, was unequal to the questions that arose in the new world of information technology and that a substantial revision of the rule was in order. The article was remarkably prescient in identifying the problems that the later amendments to the Federal Rules would address; indeed some remain open problems despite the amendments.

2. Samuel D. Warren & Louis D. Brandeis, *The Right to Privacy*, 4 Harv. L. Rev. 193 (1890).

3. Shira A. Scheindlin & Jeffrey Rabkin, *Electronic Discovery in Federal Civil Litigation*, 41 B.C. L. Rev. 327 (1999).

The first problem was the word "documents" in Rule 34. Did it include new and unprecedented types of information buried in the computer's memory but not apparent on the screen, such as backup, cookies, cache, and history files?[4] Rule 34 spoke of the inspection or copying of designated documents.[5] But if the producing party insisted on printing the requested computer files, did that comply with the Rule's other requirement that the documents be produced as they are kept in the ordinary course of business?[6] If the demanding party demanded both hard copy and electronic format, who should bear the cost of producing the duplicate hard copies?

The sheer size of a computer's memory raised other problems: the more that must be kept means the more costly the production might be for what is legitimately demanded. How were courts to strike the appropriate balance between cost and value now that even a small business maintained large computer memories that collected information, both apparent and embedded, indiscriminately? Since this memory also captured files that had been removed from active memory, was a litigant required to search for this material and other data embedded in the computer's capacious memory? How were traditional privileges such as the work-product privilege to be accommodated in this new world? Who was to pay for the search?[7]

Judge Scheindlin and Mr. Rabkin ultimately concluded that Rule 34 would be up to the task of dealing with the new world of information technology only if Rule 34 was amended to (1) include electronically stored information and (2) require that all electronically stored information be produced in the same form in which it is stored.[8] Hence, if the party represented by counsel demanded the production of electronically stored information in printed form in addition to, or instead of, its electronic form, then that party shall bear all costs associated with the requested production.

Since there is no such thing as a coincidence, Judge Scheindlin was forced to cure some of the very deficiencies she had written about when into her courtroom walked Laura Zubulake.

---

4. *Id.* at 347.
5. Fed. R. Civ. P. 34(a)(1).
6. *Id.* at 34(e)(1).
7. Scheindlin & Rabkin, *supra* note 3, at 347.
8. *Id.* at 374.

3. The *Zubulake* decisions

The conventional wisdom now and then was that electronic discovery is reserved for the big cases—the multidistrict antitrust cases involving Fortune 500 companies—but the *Zubulake* case was anything but that. It was a deceptively simple case of gender discrimination. But when it was finished, Judge Scheindlin, who presided, would forge a revolution in how courts consider and resolve the very issues that the judge herself had raised in her article—issues that had to be resolved under Rules of Civil Procedure, like Rule 34, that gave little or no guidance.

The lawsuit. UBS Warburg LLC hired Zubulake to be the director and senior salesperson of its Asian equities sales desk in New York.[9] Whatever her starting salary, Zubulake's salary was $500,000 when she was terminated,[10] and she claimed that she was fired because of her gender in retaliation for her complaining about that discrimination. She had an email that suggested that she be fired as soon as possible after her Equal Employment Opportunity Commission (EEOC) charge was filed, in part so that she would not be eligible for year-end bonuses.[11] She contended that there were other emails relevant to her case that now existed only on backup tapes and, perhaps, other archived media.[12] She demanded that UBS produce those emails at its expense; UBS asserted that the process of producing them would cost $175,000.

Zubulake I *and cost-shifting.* Judge Scheindlin first concluded that Rule 34, as it then read, required the production of electronic documents currently in use, but also the production of documents that may have been deleted and now resided only on backup disks.[13] She then indicated that the presumption that the producing party must pay the cost of production, and the crippling effect that shifting costs to the requesting party would have on discrimination and retaliation cases and all potentially meritorious claims, required that cost-shifting should be considered only when electronic discovery imposes an undue burden or expense on the responding party. Finding that the emails stored on the UBS

9. Zubulake v. UBS Warburg LLC (*Zubulake I*), 217 F.R.D. 309 (S.D.N.Y. 2003).
10. *Id.* at 312 n.9.
11. *Id.* at 312 n.8.
12. *Id.* at 312.
13. *Id.* at 317.

backup tapes were inaccessible, and that UBS would therefore suffer an undue burden, the judge modified an earlier test, articulated in *Rowe Entertainment, Inc. v. The William Morris Agency,*[14] and concluded that a new seven-factor test[15] was to be used to determine whether the presumption that the producing party pays for the costs of production should yield so that some or all of the costs of production are shifted to the requesting party. Applying those factors to ascertain whether the sought-after evidence was important enough to justify its cost,[16] the judge concluded that UBS would be compelled to produce responsive emails from any *five* backup tapes *selected by Zubulake.* Once that was done, and UBS detailed what the process of restoring the backup tapes had cost, the judge would engage in a cost-shifting analysis using the factors she had identified. In *Zubulake III,*[17] Judge Scheindlin then applied those factors to conclude that Zubulake must share in the cost of restoration, although UBS must bear the bulk of that expense.

In *Zubulake IV,*[18] Judge Scheindlin turned from cost to what has proven to be some of the most fractious and complicated issues that lawyers and judges encounter in electronic discovery: what electronically stored information must be preserved, when must it be preserved, and what happens if it is not?

The single most significant difference between litigation in a paper universe and an electronic one is permanence. In a paper universe, the document is created and stored and its permanence is a function of a single decision by a human being: throw it out or keep it. Thus, the document is either going to be stored in its present form in a warehouse or it is going to be destroyed. Computer-generated information is nothing like that. Whether it is preserved is not the product of a single human decision but of the interplay

14. 205 F.R.D. 421, 429 (S.D.N.Y. 2002).

15. *Zubulake I*, 217 F.R.D. at 322 (setting out the test). The factors are 1. The extent to which the request is specifically tailored to discover relevant information; 2. The availability of such information from other sources; 3. The total cost of production, compared to the amount in controversy; 4. The total cost of production, compared to the resources available to each party; 5. The relative ability of each party to control costs, and its incentive to do so; 6. The importance of the issues at stake in the litigation; and 7. The relative benefits to the parties of obtaining the information. *Id.*

16. *Id.* at 322–23.

17. Zubulake v. UBS Warburg LLC (*Zubulake III*), 216 F.R.D. 280 (S.D.N.Y. 2003). *Zubulake v. UBS Warburg LLC* (*Zubulake II*), 230 F.R.D. 290 (S.D.N.Y. 2003), addressed issues not relevant here.

18. Zubulake v. UBS Warburg LLC (*Zubulake IV*), 220 F.R.D. 212 (S.D.N.Y. 2003).

between a person who creates a programming code that will automatically preserve a document or throw it out. Thus, a janitor program may delete all emails that are older than a certain date. Conversely, a well-designed backup program will preserve all information on a network at a moment in time, and that preservation will capture the information no matter what the user does to it thereafter. The user who creates an email on Tuesday in a system that is backed up on Wednesday will find that the email still exists in the backup system even though she deleted it on Thursday. Hence, the computer has kept that which she intended to destroy. Indeed, the very word "delete" is a misnomer. While the computer key may say "delete," what has really occurred is that the information thought to be obliterated has merely been transferred to another portion of the computer's memory, from which it may be retrieved.

To make matters worse, the world has witnessed an extraordinary increase in the storage capacity of computers and other memory-capturing devices, and an equal decrease in their cost. A one-terabyte hard drive costs about $120. The petabyte barrier is about to crumble.[19] We will then graduate to exabyte. Comparisons to paper are ridiculous, so one need only note that as a matter of simple arithmetic, a five-exabyte storage device would contain *every word ever spoken.*[20]

Given this cheap and seemingly inexhaustible capacity, the temptation is to keep everything and let the problem of finding anything await another day. Added to that phenomenon is the idiosyncratic nature of preservation that is dependent on the whim of all the individual users of a computer network. If the person who keeps everything sits next to the person who keeps nothing, an exploration of their hard drives, in addition to what is preserved by the backup of the network they use, will lead to entirely different results.

Obviously, the only solution (if there is one) is a streamlined, well-enforced records management policy that keeps what should be kept and truly eliminates what should not. If there is no such policy, and no consistent implementation, the destruction of what should have been kept can have serious and expensive conse-

19. Curt Monash, *The 1-Pedabyte Barrier Is Crumbling*, Network World, Aug. 25, 2008, http://www.networkworld.com/community/node/31439.

20. Ralph C. Losey, *Hash: The New Bates Stamp*, 12 J. Tech. L. Pol'y 1, 10 (2007).

quences. In the next two *Zubulake* decisions, UBS Warburg was to learn just how expensive.

At first, UBS Warburg seemed ready to prevail. In *Zubulake IV*,[21] Judge Scheindlin articulated the now familiar regimen of preservation of potentially relevant data. First, the producing party must preserve evidence that it knew or should have known was relevant to the litigation. Second, it must do so when it reasonably anticipates litigation.

The judge then refined the scope of relevance to include information created by individuals who are likely to have discoverable information (relevant to a claim or defense or likely to lead to such evidence),[22] and all the information created for them, such as any emails they receive. This obligation extended to at least all the key players in the case, the ones most likely to have the discoverable information.[23] This would exclude what the judge had defined in an earlier opinion as "inaccessible information," which would include backup tapes preserved solely for the purpose of disaster recovery. On the other hand, if backup tapes are accessible (i.e., actively used for information retrieval), then such tapes would likely be subject to the litigation hold.

As to timing, litigation had to be anticipated when Zubulake filed her discrimination and retaliation charges with the Equal Employment Opportunity Commission but, even before that defining moment, almost everyone associated with Zubulake recognized the possibility that she might sue.[24] With that possibility existing, there arose the obligation to create a litigation hold that stopped all processes that could destroy discoverable information.

Applying that principle, and finding that at least as to one backup tape UBS was grossly negligent, the judge nevertheless declined to impose sanctions because Zubulake failed to convince her that the information lost would have supported her claims. The judge did, however, order that certain persons be redeposed, and these redepositions contained the seeds of UBS's ultimate defeat.

Those depositions compelled the judge to conclude:

> The proof is clear: UBS personnel unquestionably deleted relevant e-mails from their computers after August 2001, even

21. *Zubulake IV*, 220 F.R.D. 212.
22. *See* FED. R. CIV. P. 26(b)(1).
23. *Zubulake IV*, 220 F.R.D. at 212.
24. *Id.* at 217.

> though they had received at least two directions from counsel not to. Some of those e-mails were recovered (Zubulake has pointed to at least 45), but some—and no one can say how many—were not. And even those e-mails that were recovered were produced to Zubulake well after she originally asked for them.[25]

But hadn't counsel fulfilled her obligation by directing her clients not to delete the relevant emails? No, because the judge redefined the nature of the counsel's obligation. It is counsel's job to (1) impose the litigation hold; (2) make certain that all sources of potentially relevant information are identified and made subject to the hold; (3) interview all the key players (if possible) and all the potential custodians of discoverable information to ensure all possible sources of information are subject to the hold, and thereby allowing for what may be idiosyncratic decisions by individuals as to what to keep and what to destroy; and (4) make sure that the persons subject to the hold know and clearly understand their preservation obligations and how they apply to information that may come into their possession after the hold is imposed.[26]

The judge then concluded that while UBS's counsel had fulfilled most of these obligations, they had failed to (1) advise one employee of the litigation hold; (2) require another to produce her files; (3) preserve certain backup tapes; and (4) produce certain emails a witness claimed to have turned over to them. The judge concluded that UBS acted willfully and that this finding of willfulness justified in itself the conclusion that the lost information was presumably relevant.

Besides requiring certain payments and restorations, the judge announced that she would give an instruction to the jury that, if it found that UBS could have produced the evidence that was lost and was material, it was permitted, but not required, to infer that the evidence would have been unfavorable to UBS.[27]

Whether due to that instruction or other factors, the jury returned a most substantial verdict in Zubulake's favor. Thus, after it was all over, Ms. Zubulake left the courthouse wiser and appreciably richer. The lawyers and judges, however, were denied the denouement that they expected because the case settled before

25. *Id.* at 429.
26. *Id.* at 432–35.
27. *Id.* at 440.

there could be appellate review of Judge Scheindlin's decisions. Nevertheless, the decisions were to become the single most cited decisions in the area of electronic discovery, and the principles that they established were to serve as the basis of the development of the 2006 amendments to the Federal Rules of Civil Procedure. An equally fecund source for those amendments was the work of the Sedona Conference.

4. The Sedona Conference

Richard Braman, the founder of the Sedona Conference, was a brilliant and hard-charging antitrust lawyer in Minnesota who took a brief break from his practice to start a jazz club. The next break was complete and more significant, if less tuneful.

He had grown more and more dissatisfied with the traditional continuing legal education classes that had a "talking head" lecturing a group of bored lawyers who were there only because they had to be, and who were probably breaking the record for most crossword puzzles completed. Perhaps the greatest loss was the time spent by those, like Braman, doomed to lecture the unwilling. Braman had a different idea with different foundations. First, there would be no single talking head but a diverse faculty of lawyers, judges, and academics who would use a dialogue method that had as its central purpose to encourage all the participants to discuss a single topic. Participation would be limited to a small group, no more than 45, and the setting would be away from their offices to limit the potential for distraction. The participants would be assured that what went on in the room stayed in the room, an idea later stolen by the Las Vegas Chamber of Commerce.

The idea took off and was so well received that Braman decided to make a career of it. In 1998, with wife and dog in tow, he arrived in Sedona, Arizona, and the Sedona Conference was born in a new home. Braman had created the Conference as a § 501(c)(3) organization, knowing that it would be unlikely to attract the kind of lawyers and judges Braman wanted if they thought they were working only to make someone else rich. The underlying idea is that working groups of lawyers, judges, academics, and consultants are to devote their attention to specific problems in the areas of antitrust, complex litigation, and intellectual property. Braman chose these areas because of their crucial connection to the social, intellectual, and economic advancement of the society and its legal culture.

The prestige of the Conference quickly grew because Braman was particularly adept at attracting engaging and intellectually challenging judges, lawyers, and practitioners who did not hesitate to strongly express their views. To Braman's delight, the sparks flew and the participants opened their minds to new ways of doing and thinking about "tipping point" issues, the resolution of which would have a profound impact on the law and consequentially the society at large. Nobody does the crossword puzzle during a Sedona meeting and, as for distractions, if your cell phone goes off you must pay $20, with the money going to a charity.

By 2001, Braman wanted the Conference to have a broader impact than the one created by the publication of the papers that led to the discussions at the meetings. The papers, while excellent scholarship, were written before the meetings and could not reflect the dialogue that took place during it. Braman was reluctant to tape the meetings, for that would break the rule of "what goes on in Sedona stays in Sedona." During a meeting of the Complex Litigation section, the topic of electronic discovery drew hot and heavy dialogue from the participants and Braman asked one of them, Jonathan Redgrave, a skilled antitrust lawyer, to be scrivener, with the idea that he might be able to convert his notes from the meeting into a journal article that captured the dialogue. That did not work, so the participants who were interested decided that the creation of a working group would make more sense. Hence the Sedona Conference Working Group 1 was born from a mutual desire to see if dialogue, devoted to the draft papers discussed at the meeting, could yield guidelines and best practices designed to move the law and the practices of the courts and judges forward in a reasoned way that was both practical and pragmatic.

In 2002, lawyers and judges who would later form the working group began discussing ways of producing "best practices" for lawyers to follow in addressing electronic document production. The obligations upon litigants to preserve electronically stored information were unclear, but the risks of being found to have spoliated evidence were great. At that point, there were not that many judicial opinions that gave guidance, for the result in each case was a prisoner of its facts. The Working Group, then assembled, began the process of providing such guidance in the form of core principles that could be invoked to address the most nettlesome and demanding problems in the discovery of electronically stored information.[28]

A subsection of the Working Group usually prepares a draft of proposed principles that are reviewed by the entire group at its semiannual meetings. The initial draft of the Working Group on Electronic Document Production, published in 2003 for public comment, was then discussed at the Working Group's semiannual meetings. *The Sedona Principles: Best Practices, Recommendations & Principles for Addressing Electronic Document Discovery* (2005) (originally published in 2003 for public comment), was then revised and published in a second edition in June of 2007.

A central principle animating the Working Group has been the fear that the costs of electronic discovery might defeat the purpose of the Federal Rules of Civil Procedure as defined by Rule 1, that is, to secure the just, speedy, and inexpensive determination of every action and proceeding. This fear has led to an insistence that discovery be proportionate to the case at hand and that, when attempting to resolve difficulties, dialogue between litigants occur in good faith from the inception in order to provide the best hope for inexpensive and prompt resolution of discovery problems.[29] The Principles were also designed to complement the Federal Rules of Civil Procedure and their broad standards of "reasonableness" or "likelihood of leading to relevant evidence" with guidelines specifically tailored to address the unique challenges posed by electronic document production.

The 2007 version of the Principles[30] therefore places primary responsibility on the parties to confer early in discovery regarding all their electronic discovery problems. Reduction of costs is achieved by (1) requiring organizations to properly preserve their data in the first place because, as explained above, the lack of such a system can only lead to expensive and often fruitless action by relieving them of any obligation to take every conceivable step to preserve all potentially relevant information, or to produce deleted, shadowed, fragmented, or residual data; (2) requiring dis-

28. *See* The Sedona Principles: Best Practices, Recommendations & Principles for Addressing Electronic Document Production (Sedona Conference Working Group Series 2004), at x (Preface).

29. *Id.* at xi.

30. The Sedona Principles: Best Practices, Recommendations & Principles for Addressing Electronic Document Discovery (2d ed. 2007), *available at* http://www.thesedonaconference.org/dltForm?did=TSC_PRINCP_2nd_ed_607.pdf.

covery demands to be as clear as possible; and (3) emphasizing that production should ordinarily be limited to active data and the demanding party has the burden to justify access to inaccessible data such as backup tapes. According to the Principles, cost-shifting to the producing party is reserved for those situations in which the information sought is not reasonably available to the producing party.

Additionally, the Principles limit the award of sanctions to situations in which there has been a clear violation of a duty to preserve evidence, a culpable violation of that duty, and a reasonable probability that the loss of evidence materially prejudiced the adverse party. The Principles leave open whether a negligent failure to preserve evidence could be the basis for sanctions and whether, as Judge Scheindlin ruled, willful destruction could in itself establish a presumption that the destroyed evidence was relevant and justify, for example, the giving of an adverse inference instruction.

The Sedona Conference,[31] under the guidance of its founder, believes that dialogue is preferable to debate. Indeed, its sessions always begin with its founder reading from a book that contrasts dialogue with debate. More recently, Sedona, building on its dialogue model and insistence that good faith negotiations by litigants can, and should, resolve many electronic discovery problems, took the next step in 2008 when it issued The Sedona Conference Cooperation Proclamation.[32] The Proclamation is nothing less than an attempt to replace the adversarial nature of discovery, particularly as it pertains to electronic discovery, with a cooperation model in which the parties and their counsel use every means at their disposal to resolve their controversies amicably. To that end, Sedona is now preparing judicial and lawyer tool kits that will advance this goal by presenting methods to aid in achieving resolution with surrendering either party's rights or privileges. Among the methods suggested are

- utilizing internal ESI discovery point persons to assist counsel in preparing requests and responses

31. In the interests of full disclosure, the author notes that he is a member of the Judicial Advisory Board of the Sedona Conference and is reimbursed for his expenses when he attends Sedona Conference meetings.

32. The Sedona Conference Cooperation Proclamation (2008), *available at* http://www.thesedonaconference.org/dltForm?did=proclamation.pdf.

- exchanging information on relevant data sources, including those not being searched, or scheduling early disclosures on the topic of ESI
- jointly developing automated search and retrieval methodologies to cull relevant information
- promoting early identification of form or forms of production
- developing case-long discovery budgets based on proportionality principles
- considering court-appointed experts, volunteer mediators, or formal alternative dispute resolution (ADR) programs to resolve discovery disputes

The Proclamation has been endorsed by many judges, and the Conference plans training and other sessions to effectuate it further. The Proclamation has been cited by judges who see it as creating a norm to which counsel may be held if the controversy before the court could have been avoided without compromising either party's interests.[33]

5. 2006 Amendments to the Federal Rules

With the work of the Sedona Conference proceeding apace, and more and more judges and lawyers confronting electronic discovery in their cases, the momentum began to modify the Federal Rules of Civil Procedure. Judge Scheindlin's question in her law

33. *See, e.g.*, Oracle USA, Inc. v. SAP AG, No. C-07-01658 PJF(EDL), 2009 WL 3009059, at *2 (N.D. Cal. Sept.17, 2009); Capitol Records, Inc. v. MP3tunes, LLC, No. 07 Civ. 9931(WHP) (FM), 2009 WL 2568431, at *2 (S.D.N.Y. Aug. 13, 2009); *In re* Direct Sw., Inc., Fair Labor Standards Act (FLSA) Litig., 08-1984-MLCF-SS, 2009 WL 2461716, at *1, 2 (E.D. La. Aug. 7, 2009); Wells Fargo Bank, N.A. v. LaSalle Bank Nat'l Ass'n, No. 3:07-cv-449, 2009 WL 2243854, at *2 (S.D. Ohio July 24, 2009); Dunkin' Donuts Franchised Rests. LLC v. Grand Cent. Donuts, Inc., No. CV2007-4027(ENV) (MDG), 2009 WL 1750348, at *4 (E.D.N.Y. June 19, 2009); Ford Motor Co. v. Edgewood Props., Inc., 257 F.R.D. 418, 424–25, 427 (D.N.J. May 19, 2009); Newman v. Borders, Inc., 257 F.R.D. 1, 3 (D.D.C. Apr. 6, 2009); William A. Gross Const. Assocs., Inc. v. Am. Mfrs. Mut. Ins. Co., 256 F.R.D. 134, 136 (S.D.N.Y. Mar. 19, 2009); S.E.C. v. Collins & Aikman Corp., 256 F.R.D. 403, 415 (S.D.N.Y. Jan. 13, 2009); Covad Commc'ns Co. v. Revonet, Inc., 254 F.R.D. 147, 148–49 (D.D.C. Dec. 24 2008); Gipson v. Sw. Bell Tel. Co., Civ. No. 08-2017, 2008 U.S. Dist. LEXIS 103822, at *4 (D. Kan. Dec. 23, 2008); Aguilar v. Immigration & Customs Enforcement Div. of U.S. Dep't of Homeland Sec., 255 F.R.D. 350, 353–56, 358–59, 362 (S.D.N.Y. Nov. 21, 2008); Mancia v. Mayflower Textile Servs. Co., 253 F.R.D. 354, 359, 363 (D. Md. 2008).

review article of whether the Federal Rules were up to the task of dealing with the unique problems presented by electronic discovery was answered "no," and the Federal Rules Advisory Committee, under the chairmanship of Judge Lee Rosenthal, got to work and ultimately produced the new rules that became effective in 2007. The significance of each of the amendments in creating the actual practices that pertain to electronic discovery are, of course, dealt with elsewhere in this book. From a historical point of view, two points have to be made.

The adoption of rules of civil procedure does not take place in an ivory tower but in a real world. In that world, lawyers' interests are derivative of their clients'; plaintiffs' lawyers think differently from defendants' lawyers for the same reason that plaintiffs think differently from defendants. Understandably, the comments made about the rules as they proceeded from draft to draft are a perfect reflection of this dichotomy.

Whether due to that tension or another cause, even rules of civil procedure, like any other human thing that emerges in a culture where debate is encouraged, are subject to a political process that is conservative in the sense that accommodation of the interests engaged leads to compromise between competing positions. Due to that or perhaps other causes, it is startling how small the changes to the 2006 rules really are. Anyone looking for a revolution in civil procedure will have to look elsewhere. All the new rules do is (1) include electronically stored information within the categories of information that must be initially disclosed (Rule 26(a)(1)(ii)) and that qualify for production during discovery (Rule 34(a)(1)(A)); (2) require a party to specify a form in which electronically stored information must be produced and permit the opposing party to object (Rule 34(b)(1)(C) & (2)(D)); (3) specify the format in which electronically stored information must be produced if a form is not specified; (4) create a limited clawback procedure when one party has produced privileged material to the other (Rule 26(b)(5)(B)); and (5) create a safe harbor, prohibiting sanctions under the rules for the good faith destruction of electronically stored information in the ordinary course of business (Rule 37(e)).

The rules therefore do not speak to the fundamental questions that have proved most intractable, such as: Under what circumstances may costs be shifted, and what is the nature and trigger of the preservation obligation? Perhaps this is so because the fundamental philosophy was to encourage counsel, thought to be more knowledgeable than the judges, to resolve their differences and to create a mechanism for them to create a discovery plan that would run itself. Thus, and most fundamentally, the linchpin of the approach was to require the lawyers to meet and confer and discuss the mandated subjects, such as form of production of electronically stored information or agreements they had achieved or were contemplating pertaining to privilege. There is, therefore, a fascinating convergence between this approach of mandated discussions, ultimately blessed by judicial order adopting the plan, and the Sedona Conference Proclamation on Cooperation.

The long-term significance of the Rules may have to be assessed by considering, perhaps years from now, whether they created an alternative to the traditional adversarial model of discovery in the form of court-enforced cooperation. Whether that comes to pass may be as much a function of economics as attitude; clients, pressed by outrageous bills for electronic discovery, may march with their feet for a more cooperative model to which their lawyers will have to adhere. If that occurs, then the 2006 amendments, dismissed by some as minimalist, may be deemed the beginning of a revolution.

6. E-discovery in the criminal context: The new frontier

Electronic discovery in criminal cases is the forgotten stepchild with precious little attention being given to it. That failure, however, is going to be dangerous to the courts because law enforcement is growing ever more sophisticated in its use of tools to search and secure electronically stored information. It is the experience of magistrate judges that search warrants seeking the production of an object are the exception to the rule of seeking warrants for the intangible, from email accounts to the contents of computers to signals from a cell phone that may permit the user's location to be pinpointed to within a few feet. Indeed, the author of this chapter, a magistrate judge, actually had a month's duty reviewing warrants in a busy urban jurisdiction and did not have a single application for anything tangible. Every application for a warrant or order was for something intangible, such as an email account or the contents of a cell phone. Though the procedures depicted on television shows like *CSI* are unrealistic, the technical capability of law enforcement grows stronger every day.

That growth creates a difficult problem. The more electronically stored information law enforcement gathers, the greater the obligation of the prosecutor to review it and determine what is probative of guilt and what is exculpatory. The latter, of course, fulfills the responsibility of the prosecution, known as its Brady obligation, to produce evidence that would tend to exculpate the defendant. The obligation to review a large amount of data is no less forbidding in a criminal case, and the taxpayers are going to have to pay for it to be done. Moreover, the prosecution may make the evidence (whether probative or exculpatory) available to the defendant in electronic format, raising a whole new set of problems. First, if the defendant is incarcerated and the data is voluminous, how will he or she get access to it? Must the government provide him or her with a computer? Second, if the prosecution produces all the information indiscriminately, without an index or other means of searching it, how does the defendant analyze it? To the defendant with retained counsel, the cost can be forbidding. For the indigent defendant, the cost will have to borne by the taxpayers because the court may have to permit an analysis or search of the data to be done at public expense. Since the funds available are finite, one case could potentially bankrupt a court's entire Criminal Justice Act budget.

The courts have, therefore, already expressed their concern that a data dump does not fulfill the obligations the government has.[34] Thus, in the *Skilling* case, the government recused itself by providing a jointly searchable database to the defendant. In another case, the author of this chapter ordered the government to translate Spanish-language documents it had received from the Colombian government into English, and then had counsel for the parties immediately consult with each other to create a written agreement that had as its purpose to ensure that the translated documents be produced in such a way that they could be marshaled into a

34. *See, e.g.*, United States v. Skilling, 554 F.3d 529, 577 (5th Cir. 2009), *aff'd in part, rev'd in part on other grounds*, 130 S. Ct. 2869 (2010) (dictum that padding a file of turned-over material with useless information to frustrate the defendant's review might violate Brady obligation as would "[c]reating a voluminous file that is unduly onerous to access"); United States v. Hsia, 24 F. Supp. 2d 14, 29–30 (D.D.C. 1998) ("The government cannot meet its Brady obligations by providing [the defendant] with access to 600,000 documents and then claiming that she should have been to find the exculpatory information in the haystack"; government obliged to specifically identify Brady material), *rev'd in part and appeal dismissed in part on other grounds*, 176 F.3d 415 (D.C. Cir. 1999), *cert denied*, 528 U.S. 1136 (2000). *Compare* United States v. Ferguson, 478 F. Supp. 2d 220, 241–42 (D. Conn. 2007), *with* Emmett v. Ricketts, 397 F. Supp. 1025, 1043 (N.D. Ga. 1975).

database that was searchable with software that the defense counsel already owned or was commercially available.[35]

There is presently no movement toward amending the Federal Rules of Criminal Procedure to grapple with electronic discovery in criminal cases. It would be criminal to forget how long and difficult the process of securing amendments to the Civil Rules was, and to pretend that this problem will go away. History, unfortunately, sometimes teaches the truth of what was said of the Bourbons: "They have forgotten nothing and learned nothing."

35. United States v. Mendieta, Crim. No. 04-446 slip op. at 4–6 (D.D.C. Jan. 28. 2009).

CHAPTER 2

THE ESI AMENDMENTS TO THE FEDERAL RULES OF CIVIL PROCEDURE:

A RULE-BY-RULE LOOK

Ronald J. Hedges

As described in the previous chapter, extensive amendments in 2006 to the procedural rules governing federal civil litigation brought significant changes to treatment of electronically stored information during the discovery process. This chapter briefly examines each specific rule and its significance to electronically stored information (ESI).

1. Introduction

On December 1, 2006, the Federal Rules of Civil Procedure were amended to address discovery of electronically stored information. These amendments were the culmination of a long and arduous process that began with the Advisory Committee on Rules of the Judicial Conference of the United States, proceeded through written comments and public hearings to a report of the Judicial Conference Committee on Rules of Practice and Procedure to the Chief Justice of the United States, and saw the proposed amendments adopted by the Supreme Court and transmitted to Congress. This rulemaking process, which derives from the Rules Enabling Act, need not concern us here.[1] What this chapter addresses are the 2006 amendments themselves. Note that the ESI-related amendments to the Rules were themselves subject to amendment effective December 1, 2007. These 2007 amendments, however, were intended to be stylistic only.[2] Unless otherwise noted, any quotations from the Rules in this chapter will be to the 2007 text.

2. Rule 34: Producing ESI for inspection and other purposes

Somewhat paradoxically, this chapter starts with Rule 34, which addresses itself to, among other things: "Producing . . . [ESI] . . . for Inspection and Other Purposes." Why?

As the Advisory Committee Note states, "Rule 34(a) is amended to confirm that discovery of [ESI] stands on equal footing with discovery of paper documents."[3] In a sense, Rule 34(a) introduced the phrase "electronically stored information" into the Rules. The Advisory Committee Note also speaks of the "expansive" nature of the phrase "electronically stored information":

> The wide variety of computer systems currently in use, and the rapidity of technological change, counsel against a limiting or precise definition of [ESI]. Rule 34(a)(1) is expansive and includes any type of information that is stored electronically. A common example often sought in discovery is electronic communications, such as e-mail. The rule covers—either as documents or as [ESI]—information "stored in any medium," to encompass future developments in computer technology. Rule 34(a)(1) is intended to be broad enough to cover all current types of computer-based information, and flexible enough to encompass future changes and developments.[4]

1. For a detailed summary, see R.J. HEDGES, DISCOVERY OF ELECTRONICALLY STORED INFORMATION: SURVEYING THE LEGAL LANDSCAPE (BNA 2007).
2. *See, e.g.*, FED. R. CIV. P. 26 advisory committee's note to 2007 Amendment.
3. FED. R. CIV. P. 34(a) advisory committee's note to 2006 Amendment.
4. *Id.*

Note that "[r]eferences elsewhere in the rules to [ESI] should be understood to invoke this expansive approach."[5] The meaning of the term "ESI" is "broad, but whether material that falls within this term should be produced, and in what form, are separate questions that must be addressed under Rules 26(b), 26(c), and 34(b)."[6] This chapter will return to Rule 34(a) and (b) later but, first, turns to other Rules.

3. Rule 26(a)(1): Initial disclosures by parties

Rule 26(a)(1) concerns "initial disclosure" by parties. The concept of the initial disclosure "without awaiting a discovery request" was first introduced into the Rules in 1993. In 2006, the rule was amended to narrow the scope of disclosure and to "restore nationwide uniformity to disclosure practice."[7] Disclosure is generally beyond the scope of this chapter.[8] Note, however, that the rule was amended in 2006 parallel with Rule 34(a) to recognize that ESI "as well as documents that it [a party] may use to support its claims or defenses" must be disclosed.[9]

The obligation to comply with Rule 26(a)(1) requires parties to collect and analyze ESI at the earliest stage of litigation, as does the attorneys' obligation to comply with the certification requirement of Rule 11(b) when presenting "a pleading, written motion, or other paper." The initial disclosure obligation of Rule 26(a)(1), however, "should not place unreasonable or unnecessary burdens on the parties. . . . In complex litigation, this rule may need modification or suspension."[10] Thus, the scope and timing of initial disclosure of ESI may be the subject of discussion between the parties and, if necessary, the court.[11]

4. Rule 26(f): The "meet and confer" requirement

The "meet and confer" requirement may well be the most important of the 2006 amendments and, indeed, may be the most

5. *Id.*

6. *Id.*

7. Fed. R. Civ. P. 26(a) (2000 Amendment).

8. See chapter 13.

9. Fed. R. Civ. P. 26(a) advisory committee's note to 2006 Amendment.

10. Manual for Complex Litigation (Fourth) § 11.13 (2004).

11. *See* Fed. R. Civ. P. 26(f)(3)(A) (directing parties to consider, among other things, "what changes should be made in the timing, form, or requirement for disclosures under Rule 26(a), including a statement of when initial disclosures were made or will be made").

important electronic discovery rule! Why? "[I]t gives the parties an opportunity to reach agreement on the 'contours' of the civil litigation in which they are engaged and, just as importantly, agree on what they disagree about and present their disputes for early judicial resolution, perhaps even at the Rule 16(b) initial scheduling conference."[12]

Rule 26(f) requires parties in most civil litigation to "meet and confer" among themselves and to submit a discovery plan to the court before any Rule 16(b) initial pretrial conference. Rule 26(f) itself was amended in 2006 to include, among the issues that the parties must consider, these related to ESI:

- "any issues about preserving discoverable information"[13]
- "any issues about disclosure or discovery of [ESI], including the form or forms in which it should be produced"[14]
- "any issues about claims of privilege or of protection as trial-preparation materials, including—if the parties agree on a procedure to assert these claims after production—whether to ask the court to include their agreements in an order"[15]

Rule 26(f) also requires the parties to consider

- "the nature and basis of their claims and defenses and the possibilities for promptly settling or resolving the case"[16]
- "the subjects on which discovery may be needed, when discovery should be completed, and whether discovery should be conducted in phases or be limited to or focused on particular issues"[17]
- "what changes should be made in the limitations on discovery imposed under these rules or by local rule, and what other limitations should be imposed"[18]

12. R. J. Hedges, *Rule 26(f): The Most Important E-Discovery Rule*, N.J. LAW J., Complex Litigation & E-Discovery Supp. at S-6 and -7 (May 18, 2009).
13. FED. R. CIV. P. 26(f)(2).
14. FED. R. CIV. P. 26(f)(3)(C).
15. FED. R. CIV. P. 26(f)(3)(D).
16. FED. R. CIV. P. 26(f)(2).
17. FED. R. CIV. P. 26(f)(3)(B).
18. FED. R. CIV. P. 26(f)(3)(E).

- "any other orders that the court should issue under Rule 26(c) or under Rule 16(b) and (c)"[19]

The issues to be considered at the meet and confer described in Rule 26(f) may be supplemented by local rules or policies of individual U.S. district courts and often have been, particularly with regard to electronic discovery.[20]

As noted above, the 2006 amendments to Rule 26(f) added issues related to electronic discovery. These are touched on below. Readers are directed to specific other chapters that develop the issues in more detail.[21]

Preservation. "Rule 26(f) is also amended to direct the parties to discuss any issues regarding preservation of discoverable information during their conference as they develop a discovery plan. This provision applies to all sorts of discoverable information, but can be particularly important with regard to [ESI]."[22] Note the recognition of the Advisory Committee that "[f]ailure to address preservation issues early in the litigation increases uncertainty and raises a risk of disputes."[23]

Production. "The parties may be able to reach agreement on the forms of production, making discovery more efficient. . . . Early discussion of the forms of production may facilitate the application of Rule 34(b) by allowing the parties to determine what forms of production will meet both parties' needs." Moreover, "[e]arly identification of disputes over the forms of production may help avoid the expense and delay of searches or production using inappropriate forms."[24]

Privilege. The Rules are intended to further the "just, speedy, and inexpensive determination of every action and proceeding."[25] Nowhere is this more apparent than the Advisory Committee

19. FED. R. CIV. P. 26(f)(3)(F).
20. *See, e.g.*, U.S. DIST. CT. FOR THE DIST. OF MD., SUGGESTED PROTOCOL FOR THE DISCOVERY OF ELECTRONICALLY STORED INFORMATION, http://www.mdd.uscourts.gov/news/news/ESIProtocol.pdf.
21. See, for example, chapter 19.
22. FED. R. CIV. P. 26(f) advisory committee's note to 2006 Amendment.
23. *Id.*
24. *Id.*
25. FED. R. CIV. P. 1.

Note to Rule 26(f): "The Committee has been repeatedly advised about the discovery difficulties that can result from efforts to guard against waiver of privilege and work-product protection. Frequently parties find it necessary to spend large amounts of time reviewing materials requested through discovery to avoid waiving privilege."[26] The Advisory Committee also noted that problems associated with privilege "often become more acute when discovery of [ESI] is sought."[27] The Advisory Committee Note encourages parties "to agree to protocols that minimize the risk of waiver" in appropriate actions.

These three "P's"—preservation, production, and privilege—are central to Rule 26(f) and discovery of ESI.

5. Rule 16: Developing a discovery plan

Rule 16(b), in many ways, parallels the meet and confer process of Rule 26(f). The obligation to meet and confer and to submit a discovery plan is triggered by the parties' receipt of notice that the court will conduct a scheduling conference under Rule 16.[28] The purposes of the conference include

- "expediting disposition of the action"[29]
- "establishing early and continuing control so that the case will not be protracted because of lack of management"[30]
- "discouraging wasteful pretrial activities"[31]
- "improving the quality of the trial through more thorough preparation"[32]
- "facilitating settlement"[33]

The amendments to Rule 16 in 2006 were "designed to alert the court to the possible need to address the handling of discovery of [ESI] early in the litigation if such discovery is expected to occur."[34] Optimistically, the Advisory Committee observed that "[i]n many instances, the court's involvement early in the litigation will help

26. Fed. R. Civ. P. 26(f) advisory committee's note to 2006 Amendment.
27. *Id.*; see chapters 15, 17, and 18.
28. Fed. R. Civ. P. 26(f)(1).
29. Fed. R. Civ. P. 16(a)(1).
30. Fed. R. Civ. P. 16(a)(2).
31. Fed. R. Civ. P. 16(a)(3).
32. Fed. R. Civ. P. 16(a)(4).
33. Fed. R. Civ. P. 16(a)(5).
34. Fed. R. Civ. P. 16 advisory committee's note to 2006 Amendment.

avoid difficulties that might otherwise arise."[35] Rule 16(c) describes the content of any scheduling order, and was amended in 2006 to include "disclosure or discovery" of ESI and "agreements the parties reach for asserting claims of privilege or of protection as trial-preparation material after production."[36]

Note the conclusion of the Advisory Committee that "[a]n order that includes the parties' agreement [on privilege] may be helpful in avoiding delay and excessive cost in discovery."[37] Although Rule 16 does recognize that agreements may be incorporated into scheduling orders, "[t]he rule does not provide the court with authority to enter into such a case-management or other order without party agreement, or limit the court's authority to act on motion."[38]

6. Rule 26(b)(5)(B): The clawback provision

The clawback provision of Rule 26(b)(5)(B) is not, on its face, about electronic discovery. Newly adopted in 2006 as part of the package of electronic discovery amendments to the Federal Rules, it focuses on the procedure to address a party's claim that it inadvertently produced privileged materials or protected work product. "Rule 26(b)(5)(B) is added to establish a parallel procedure to assert privilege or protection as trial-preparation material after production, leaving the question of waiver to later determination by the court."[39] The "parallel" is to Rule 26(f)(3)(D), which directs parties to meet and confer about claims of privilege and work product and about agreements to assert claims after production.

The rule requires a party making a claim of inadvertent production to "notify any party that received the information of the claim and the basis for it." The "receiving" party must then promptly "return, sequester, or destroy the specified information and any copies it has." The receiving party may not "use or disclose the information until the claim is resolved" and must take "reasonable steps to retrieve the information." The receiving party may promptly "present the information to the court under seal for a

35. *Id.*

36. FED. R. CIV. P. 16(b)(3)(B)(iii), (iv).

37. FED. R. CIV. P. 16 advisory committee's note to 2006 Amendment.

38. *Id.*

39. FED. R. CIV. P. 26(f) advisory committee's note to 2006 Amendment.

determination of the claim." Interestingly, the rule also imposes a preservation duty on the party that asserts a claim. That party must "preserve the information until the claim is resolved."

Rule 26(b)(5)(B) established a uniform procedure among the U.S. district courts to assert inadvertent production claims. Prior to adoption of the rule, the courts had looked to federal common law or state law. Remember though that Rule 26(b)(5)(B) is a rule of *procedure*. Federal Rule of Evidence 502, which is beyond the scope of this chapter,[40] addresses the *substantive* "side" of inadvertent production.

7. Rule 26(b)(2)(B): "[N]ot reasonably accessible because of undue burden or cost"

Rule 26(b)(2)(B) was also newly adopted in 2006. It stems from the distinction between "accessible" and "inaccessible" ESI recognized in *Zubulake v. UBS Warburg LLC*.[41] The rule is worth quoting in full:

> *Specific Limitations on Electronically Stored Information.* A party need not provide discovery of [ESI] from sources that the party identifies as not reasonably accessible because of undue burden or cost. On motion to compel discovery or for a protective order, the party from whom discovery is sought must show that the information is not reasonably accessible because of undue burden or cost. If that showing is made, the court may nonetheless order discovery from such sources if the requesting party shows good cause, considering the limitations of Rule 26(b)(2)(C). The court may specify conditions for the discovery.[42]

The Advisory Committee Note explains the text.

> In General. Electronic storage systems often make it easier to locate and retrieve information. These advantages are properly taken into account in determining the reasonable scope of discovery in a particular case. But some sources of [ESI] can be accessed only with substantial burden and cost. In a particular case, these burdens and costs may make the information on such sources not reasonably accessible.[43]

40. See chapters 15, 17, and 18.
41. 217 F.R.D. 309 (S.D.N.Y. 2003) (subsequent citations omitted).
42. FED. R. CIV. P. 26(b)(2)(B).
43. FED. R. CIV. P. 26(b)(2) advisory committee's note to 2006 Amendment; see chapter 25.

The rule itself is technologically neutral: "It is not possible to define in a rule the different types of technological features that may affect the burdens and costs of accessing" ESI.[44]

The Advisory Committee Note also speaks of a possible priority for discovery of ESI: "In many circumstances the requesting party should obtain and evaluate the information from such sources [that are reasonably accessible] before insisting that the responding party search and produce information contained on sources that are not reasonably accessible." The Note also draws the attention of parties to the need to confer about discovery from not reasonably accessible sources and to also do so before any motion is made.

Note also that the rule "does not relieve a party of its common-law or statutory duties to preserve evidence. Whether a responding party is required to preserve unsearched sources of potentially responsive [ESI] that it believes are not reasonably accessible depends on the circumstances of each case. It is often useful for the parties to discuss this early in discovery."[45]

"Sources." Note that the rule focuses on the *sources* of ESI rather than on the ESI itself. Why? "Information sources are designed to provide ready access to information used in regular ongoing activities. They also may be designed so as to provide ready access to information that is not regularly used. But a system may retain information on sources that are accessible only by incurring substantial burdens or costs. Subparagraph (b) is added to regulate discovery from such sources."[46]

How should a "source" be identified? The party that invokes the rule in response to a discovery request must do so by identifying, "by category or type," the sources of "*potentially* responsive information that it is neither searching nor producing."[47] Moreover, the identification should, "to the extent possible, provide enough detail to enable the requesting party to evaluate the burdens and costs of providing the discovery and the likelihood of finding responsive information on the identified sources."[48]

---

44. *Id.*
45. FED. R. CIV. P. 26(b)(2) advisory committee's note to 2006 Amendment.
46. *Id.*
47. *Id.* (emphasis added).
48. *Id.*

"Good cause." The responding party has the burden of proof that ESI on a particular source is *in fact* "not reasonably accessible because of because of undue burden or cost." Note that the requesting party "may need to test this assertion" and that discovery "might take the form of requiring the responding party to conduct a sampling of information contained on the sources . . . , allowing some form of inspection of such sources, or taking depositions of witnesses knowledgeable about the responding party's information systems."[49] Thereafter, "[t]he requesting party has the burden of showing that its need for the discovery outweighs the burdens and costs of locating, retrieving, and producing the information." Appropriate considerations include

- "the specificity of the discovery request"
- "the quantity of information available from other and more easily accessed sources"
- "the failure to produce relevant information that seems likely to have existed but is no longer available on more easily accessed sources"
- "the likelihood of finding relevant, responsive information that cannot be obtained from other, more easily accessible sources"
- "predictions as to the importance and usefulness of the further information"
- "the importance of the issues at stake in the litigation"
- "the parties' resources"[50]

In making a good-cause determination, the court may also look to the willingness of the requesting party "to share or bear the access costs" to the sources.[51]

The Advisory Committee Note suggests that "[i]n some cases, the court will be able to determine whether the identified sources are not reasonably accessible and whether the requesting party has shown good cause for some or all of the discovery, consistent with the limitations of Rule 26(b)(2)(C), through a single proceeding or presentation."[52] Unfortunately, the Note recognizes that "the court and the parties may know little about what information the

49. *Id.*
50. *Id.*
51. *Id.*
52. *Id.*

sources . . . might contain, whether it is relevant, or how valuable it may be to the litigation."[53] The Note then recognizes, again, that "focused discovery" may be needed.

Limitations. Even assuming that good cause is found, the limitations on discovery of Rule26(b)(2)(C) apply. This is the so-called "proportionality rule," which applies "to all discovery of [ESI], including that stored on *reasonably* accessible sources."[54] For discovery of ESI from not reasonably accessible sources, conditions "may take the form of limits to the amount, type, or sources of information required to be accessed and produced. The conditions may also include payment by the requesting party of part or all of the reasonable costs. . . ."[55]

8. Rule 33(d): Producing ESI as "business record" in response to interrogatories

Rule 33 governs interrogatories to parties. Subsection (d) describes a party's option to respond to interrogatories by producing business records. That subsection was amended in 2006 to include ESI as a "business record," with the Advisory Committee stating: "Much business information is stored only in electronic form; the Rule 33(d) option should be available with respect to such records as well."[56] Under the rule, and assuming that "the burden of deriving or ascertaining the answer will be substantially the same for either party, the responding party may answer by:

> (1) "specifying the records that must be reviewed, in sufficient detail to enable the interrogating party to locate and identify them as readily as the responding party could; and
>
> (2) giving the interrogating party a reasonable opportunity to examine and audit the records and to make copies, compilations, abstracts, or summaries."[57]

The option to produce ESI has several possible ramifications. First, to satisfy (1) and (2), the responding party may be required

53. *Id.*

54. *Id.* (emphasis added).

55. *Id.*

56. Fed. R. Civ. P. 33 advisory committee's note to 2006 Amendment.

57. Fed. R. Civ. P. 33(d).

to "provide some combination of technical support, information on application software, or other assistance" to the interrogating party.[58] Second, the responding party "may be required to provide direct access to its electronic information system, but only if that is necessary to derive or ascertain the answer to the interrogatory."[59] Interestingly, in the latter situation, the Advisory Committee Note suggests that, given the possible sensitivity of ESI on the system, the responding party may need to "derive or ascertain and provide the answer itself rather than invoke Rule 33(d)."[60]

9. Rule 34: Requests for production of ESI

As noted in the beginning of this chapter, Rule 34 was amended in 2006 to specifically incorporate production of ESI. Rule 34(a) now provides, in pertinent part:

> A party may serve on any other party a request within the scope of Rule 26(b) . . . to produce and permit the requesting party or its representative to inspect, copy, test, or sample the following items in the responding party's possession, custody, or control . . . any designated documents or electronically stored information . . . stored in any medium from which information can be obtained directly or, if necessary, after translation by the responding party into a reasonably useable form.[61]

Pursuant to subsection (b)(1), the requesting party, among other things:

- "must describe with reasonable particularity each item or category of items to be inspected"[62]
- "may specify the form or forms in which [ESI] is to be produced"[63]

Subsection (b)(2) describes how a party must respond or object to a request for production of ESI. The responding party may object to a requested form of ESI. If the responding party does so

58. FED. R. CIV. P. 33 advisory committee's note to 2006 Amendment.
59. *Id.*
60. *Id.*
61. FED. R. CIV. P. 34(a)(1)(A).
62. FED. R. CIV. P. 34(b)(1)(A).
63. FED. R. CIV. P. 34(b)(1)(C).

"or if no form was specified in the request—the party must state the form or forms it intends to use."[64]

Subsection (b)(2) also specifies procedures that apply for production of ESI "[u]nless otherwise stipulated to or ordered by the court."[65] These procedures require a responding party to

- "produce documents as they are kept in the usual course of business or must organize and label them to correspond to the categories in the request."[66]
- "If a request does not specify a form or forms for producing [ESI], . . . produce it in a form or forms in which it is ordinarily maintained or in a reasonably useable form or forms."[67]

Subsection (b)(2) also provides that "[a] party need not produce the same [ESI] in more than one form."[68]

Rule 34 is simple in its text, but incorporates many nuances. Reference to the Advisory Committee Notes shines light on the intent and purpose of the rule.

Testing or sampling. "Rule 34(a)(1) is also amended to make clear that parties may request an opportunity to test or sample materials sought . . . in addition to inspecting and copying them. That opportunity may be important for both [ESI] and hard-copy materials."[69] The Advisory Committee Note recognizes that "issues of burden and intrusiveness raised by requests to inspect or sample can be addressed by Rules 26(b)(2) and 26(c)."[70] The Note also recognizes that inspection or testing "may raise issues of confidentiality or privacy." Moreover, amended Rule 34(a) "is not meant to create a routine right of direct access to a party's electronic information, although such access might be justified in some circumstances."[71]

"Usual course of business." Why should ESI be produced as "kept in the ordinary course of business" or be labeled to correspond to categories of a request? Hard-copy documents must be

64. FED. R. CIV. P. 34(b)(2)(D).
65. FED. R. CIV. P. 34(b)(2)(E).
66. FED. R. CIV. P. 34(b)(2)(E)(i).
67. FED. R. CIV. P. 34(b)(2)(E)(ii).
68. FED. R. CIV. P. 34(b)(2)(E)(iii).
69. FED. R. CIV. P. 34(a) advisory committee's note to 2006 Amendment.
70. *Id.*
71. *Id.*

produced in this manner. So should ESI: "The production of [ESI] should be subject to comparable requirements to protect against deliberate or inadvertent production in ways that raise unnecessary obstacles for the requesting party."[72] The Note does not, however, discuss what something "comparable" might be.

"Form or forms." "This rule recognizes that different forms of production may be appropriate for different types" of ESI.[73] The Advisory Committee Note describes different types of ESI (including, by way of example, electronic spreadsheets and image or sound files) and concludes that "[r]equiring that such diverse types of [ESI] all be produced in the same form could prove impossible, and even if possible could increase the cost and burdens of producing and using the information. The rule therefore provides that the requesting party may ask for different forms of production for different types" of ESI.[74] The Note also recognizes that the requesting party may not have a preferred form of production and that it may not know the form in which the producing party maintains ESI, "although Rule 26(f)(3) is amended to call for discussion of the form of production in the parties' pre-discovery conference."[75]

Responding to requests. Recall that a responding party must identify the form in which it intends to produce ESI absent a specification of form by the requesting party or when the responding party objects to a specification. "Stating the intended form before the production occurs may permit the parties to identify and seek to resolve disputes before the expense and work of the production occurs." Moreover, simple production of ESI without prior identification of form "runs a risk that the requesting party can show that the produced form is not reasonably useable and that it is entitled to production of some or all of the information in an additional form."[76]

Failure to agree on form or forms of production requires parties to meet and confer under Rule 37(a)(1) before any motion practice.[77]

72. FED. R. CIV. P. 34(b) advisory committee's note to 2006 Amendment.
73. FED. R. CIV. P. 34(b)(2) advisory committee's note to 2006 Amendment.
74. *Id.*
75. *Id.*; see chapter 19.
76. FED. R. CIV. P. 34(b) advisory committee's note to 2006 Amendment.
77. *Id.*

If a court must resolve a dispute, it "is not limited to the forms initially chosen by the requesting party, stated by the responding party, or specified in this rule for situations in which there is no court order or party agreement."[78]

"Ordinarily maintained or in a reasonably useable form or forms." The rule requires that, "if necessary, a responding party 'translate' information it produces into a 'reasonably useable' form. Under some circumstances, the responding party may need to provide some reasonable amount of technical support, information on application software, or other reasonable assistance to enable the requesting party to use the information."[79]

Note, however, that the option to produce in a reasonably useable form "does not mean that a responding party is free to convert [ESI] from the form in which it is ordinarily maintained to a different form that makes it more difficult or burdensome for the requesting party to use the information efficiently in the litigation."[80] ESI should not be produced in a form that "removes or significantly degrades" any preexisting ability to search.[81]

10. Rule 45: Subpoenaing ESI

Rule 45 governs subpoenas. It was amended in 2006 "to conform the provisions for subpoenas to changes in other discovery rules, largely related to discovery of [ESI]."[82] The amendments to Rule 45 conform to those of Rule 34. For example:

- Rule 45(a)(1)(A)(iii) incorporates ESI as an "object" subject to being subpoenaed.
- Subsection (a)(1)(C) provides that "[a] command to produce . . . [ESI] may be included in a subpoena commanding attendance at a deposition, hearing, or trial, or may be set out in a separate subpoena."
- Subsection (a)(1)C) also provides that "[a] subpoena may specify the forms or forms in which [ESI] is to be produced."
- Subsection (a)(1)(D) allows a subpoena to call for "inspection, copying, testing, or sampling" of ESI.

---

78. *Id.*
79. *Id.*
80. *Id.*
81. *Id.*
82. FED. R. CIV. P. 45 advisory committee's note to 2006 Amendment.

- Subsection (c)(2)(B) directs that objections be made to, among other things, the form or forms of production specified in a subpoena.[83]
- Subsection (d)(1) establishes procedures to produce ESI:
  - Absent specification of a form of production in a subpoena, ESI must be produced "in a form or forms in which it is ordinarily maintained or in a reasonably useable form or forms."[84]
  - ESI need not be produced in more than one form.[85]
  - ESI residing on sources that are "not reasonably accessible because of undue burden or cost" need not be produced absent good cause and then only subject to the limitations of Rule 26(b)(2)(C).[86]

Mention should be made here of the opportunity to test or sample ESI afforded by amended Rule 45(a)(1)(D). Again, as with Rule 34(a), the Advisory Committee Note observes that this opportunity "may present particular issues of burden or intrusion" such that "the protective measures of Rule 45(c) should be enforced with vigilance when such demands are made."[87] Moreover, those demands "may raise issues of confidentiality or privacy" and the opportunity to sample and test "is not meant to create a routine right of access to a person's electronic information system, although such access might be justified in some circumstances. Courts should guard against undue intrusiveness resulting from inspecting or testing such systems."[88]

Finally, Rule 45 was amended in 2006 to parallel Rule 26(b)(5)(B) and, in so doing, to establish a procedure to address claims for inadvertent production of materials subject to the attorney-client privilege or subject to work-product protection.[89] Indeed, the language of the former rule is almost identical to that of the latter.

83. FED. R. CIV. P. 45(c)(2)(B).
84. FED. R. CIV. P. 45(d)(1)(B).
85. FED. R. CIV. P. 45(d)(1)(C).
86. FED. R. CIV. P. 45(d)(1)(D).
87. *Id.*
88. *Id.*
89. FED. R. CIV. P. 45(d)(2)(B).

11. Rule 37(e): "Safe harbor" or "uncharted minefield" on sanctions for lost ESI?

This is another "new" rule first adopted as part of the 2006 amendments. When adopted it was numbered Rule 37(f). It was renumbered as part of the 2007 amendments.

Rule 37(e) is known as the "safe harbor," as a "lighthouse," and as an "uncharted minefield." It is stark in its simplicity: "Absent exceptional circumstances, a court may not impose sanctions under these rules on a party for failing to provide [ESI] lost as a result of the routine, good-faith operation of an electronic information system."

"Many steps essential to computer operation may alter or destroy information, for reasons that have nothing to do with how that information might relate to litigation. As a result, the ordinary operation of computer systems creates a risk that a party may lose potentially discoverable information without culpable conduct on its part."[90] Rule 37(e) is intended to protect against the imposition of sanctions under that circumstance.

Note that "routine operation" encompasses "the ways in which . . . systems are generally designed, programmed, and implemented to meet the party's technical and business needs."[91] It includes "the alteration and overwriting of information, often without the operator's specific direction or awareness."[92] Note also that "[g]ood faith in the routine operation of an information system may involve a party's intervention to modify or suspend certain features of that routine operation to prevent the loss of information, if that information is subject to a preservation obligation."[93] This language, at least by implication, raises the possibility of "discovery about discovery"[94] should a party assert Rule 37(e) in opposition to an application for sanctions, just as discovery may be sought under Rule 26(b)(2)(B).

The Advisory Committee Note comments on the relationship of Rule 37(e) to Rule 26(b)(2)(B): "Whether good faith would call for steps to prevent the loss of information on sources that the party believes are not reasonably accessible . . . depends on

90. Fed. R. Civ. P. 37(f) advisory committee's note to 2006 Amendment.
91. *Id.*
92. *Id.*
93. *Id.*
94. See chapter 16.

the circumstances of each case."[95] Moreover, the rule only protects against sanctions under the Rules. "It does not affect other sources of authority to impose sanctions or rules of professional responsibility."[96] Finally, the rule only restricts the imposition of "sanctions": "It does not prevent a court from making the kinds of adjustments frequently used in managing discovery if a party is unable to provide relevant information."[97]

12. Conclusion

This chapter provides an overview of the Federal Rules in the context of electronic discovery. Discovery of ESI is now a staple in litigation in the U.S. courts. Other chapters of this book will explore how the Rules have been implemented and interpreted by case law.

95. FED. R. CIV. P. 37(f) advisory committee's note to 2006 Amendment.
96. *Id.*; see chapter 8.
97. *Id.*

CHAPTER 3

THE STATES:
WHAT ARE THE LABORATORIES OF FEDERALISM DOING?

Robert Dale Klein and
The Hon. Joseph F. Murphy, Jr.

Although the federal court system has been in the forefront of developments in the realm of e-discovery, the states have not been far behind. In this overview, a Maryland litigator and a state appellate judge review similarities and differences in the states' approaches compared to the federal system and to each other.

1. Introduction: Laboratories of federalism versus national uniformity and standard

As of the third anniversary of the Federal Rules of Civil Procedure amendments implementing procedures for discovery of electronically stored information (ESI)—December 1, 2009—27 states by rule or statute had adopted state court procedures for ESI discovery. That total increased to 29 in 2010, when two more states adopted ESI rules.[1]

This chapter focuses on the uniformity and variations among the states, each of which must fit rules related to ESI into its own

1. In April 2010, Wisconsin adopted ESI rules effective January 1, 2011, and on August 18, 2010, the State of New York adopted ESI rules that became immediately effective.

unique procedures, customs, systems, and processes. In doing so, we also consider the countervailing factor that ESI presents the same technical and cost problems and issues in the north, south, east, and west. While federalism provides for multiple systems,[2] it is equally significant that there "is concern throughout the country among lawyers and institutional clients regarding the lack of a uniform national standard" governing many ESI issues.[3] Keeping both guideposts in mind, we will address the similarities and differences found in the various court systems, using Maryland's experiences and decisions as illustrative and a comparator.

The procedures of 24 of the 29 states having ESI rules largely mirror the federal e-discovery rules, in whole or in part.[4] For example, New Hampshire has adopted only the Federal Rules' requirement that parties meet and confer early in the case to discuss e-discovery issues.[5] In cases in which a preliminary court

2. "In some instances, the duty to preserve is governed by state law, in others, by federal law." P. Grimm et al., *Proportionality in the Post-Hoc Analysis of Pre-Litigation Preservation Decisions*, 37 U. BALT. L. REV. 381, 390 (2008). Noting the impact of conflict of laws issues, the article states that "there is a need for clear guidance to litigants." *Id.* at 391–92.

3. Victor Stanley, Inc. v. Creative Pipe, Inc. 269 F.R.D. 497 (D. Md. 2010), (*Victor Stanley II*), *aff'd in part and modified in part on unrelated grounds*, No. MJG-06-2662 (D. Md. Nov. 1, 2010) *subsequent opinion*, No. MJG-06-2662 (D.Md. Jan. 24, 2011). For example, there is no uniform standard for preservation of backup tapes. *Id.* at *26. Nor is there agreement about the degree of culpability to support a claim of spoliation. *Id.* at *31. This has "created uncertainty and added to the concern that institutional and organizational clients have expressed regarding how to conduct themselves in a way that will comply with multiple, inconsistent standards." *Id.* at *35.

Indeed, commentators have observed inconsistent approaches to handling e-discovery issues by federal and state courts sitting in the very same state. *See, e.g., Harmonizing the Pre-Litigation Obligation to Preserve Electronically Stored Information in New York State and Federal Courts,* Advisory Group to the New York State-Federal Judicial Council (Sept. 2010) (potential inconsistencies between federal and state law governing prelitigation duty to preserve ESI).

4. As of August 2010, the following 24 states had adopted e-discovery procedures that substantially mirror, in whole or in part, the federal amendments concerning e-discovery: Alaska, Arizona, Arkansas, California, Indiana, Iowa, Kansas, Louisiana, Maine, Maryland, Michigan, Minnesota, Montana, Nebraska, New Jersey, New Mexico, North Dakota, Ohio, Tennessee, Utah, Virginia, Washington, Wisconsin, and Wyoming.

5. By Rules Order dated January 18, 2007, the Supreme Court of New Hampshire adopted Superior Court Rule 62, which, among other things, requires counsel for all parties, or parties if unrepresented, to meet and confer personally or by

conference has been ordered, New York's ESI rules require parties to be prepared to discuss ESI at the preliminary conference, and in certain classes of cases, to have conferred about them in advance of the preliminary conference.[6] Other states do not follow the federal paradigm. For example, three states follow the so-called "Texas model" for handling e-discovery.[7] Currently, two more states are known to be considering adoption of e-discovery procedures.[8] The State of Colorado expressly has declined to amend the Colorado Rules of Procedure to mirror the e-discovery amendments to the

---

telephone to discuss, among other things, "the scope of discovery, including particularly with respect to information stored electronically or in other medium, the extent to which such information is reasonably accessible, the likely costs of obtaining access to such information and who shall bear said costs, the form in which such information is to be produced, the need for and the extent of any holds or other mechanisms that have been or should be put in place to prevent the destruction of such information, and the manner in which the parties propose to guard against the waiver of privilege claims with respect to such information." *See* N.H. SUP. CT. R. 62(I)(C)(4).

6. *See* N.Y. UNIF. R. TRIAL CTS. 202.12(b), (c), and 202.70(g) and related Rule 8 (effective August 18, 2010). Section 202.12(b) provides in pertinent part:

> Where a case is reasonably likely to include electronic discovery, counsel for all parties who appear at the preliminary conference must be sufficiently versed in matters relating to their clients' technological systems to discuss competently all issues relating to electronic discovery: counsel may bring a client representative or outside expert to assist in such e-discovery discussions.

7. In 1999, Texas became the first state to adopt rules explicitly governing e-discovery when it added rules 196.3 and 196.4 to its Rules of Civil Procedure. The Texas Rules differ in some key respects from the Federal Rules of Civil Procedure, as discussed *infra* at nn. 21, 31, 39 & 56. Both Idaho and Mississippi have adopted rules similar to the Texas model, except that they have substituted *discretionary* cost-shifting for the *mandatory* cost-shifting feature of the Texas Rules. *See* discussion, *infra* at nn. 21, 33, 39 & 56.

8. The states of Connecticut and Illinois currently are studying adoption of e-discovery rules similar to the Federal Rules amendments. On February 23, 2009, legislation was introduced in the New York State Assembly (Bill A06000) to amend the New York Civil Practice Law and Rules to explicitly address e-discovery. According to that bill, which does not appear to be under active consideration by the New York legislature in 2010, the "proposed amendments are intended primarily to clarify the treatment of electronically stored information in civil disclosure proceedings conducted prior to the filing of a note of issue." Until the August 2010 amendments to the New York Uniform Rules of Trial Courts discussed *supra* at n.6, e-discovery issues in New York largely had been addressed by case law.

Federal Rules of Civil Procedure,[9] and 18 states do not yet appear to have undertaken development or adoption of e-discovery procedures.[10] The table at the end of this chapter provides a quick overview of the status of e-discovery procedures adoption in each of the 50 states as of August 2010. It is against that backdrop that we examine the various state approaches to key areas of ESI and compare them to the national model.

2. Early discussion of e-discovery issues

Fewer than half of the states adopting e-discovery procedures to date have adopted the Federal Rules' approach of mandating early "meet and confer" discovery conferences between parties or their counsel to discuss discovery of ESI, reach agreement where possible, and submit any disputes remaining to the court for resolution. Specifically, only 13 of the 29 states having some form of e-discovery procedures routinely require such conferences, as opposed to requiring them on a more selective basis.[11]

Presumably this divergence from the federal approach stems from recognition that state trial court dockets tend to include a broader range of litigation, oftentimes involving lesser stakes, than seen in many federal courts, and the Maryland approach typifies

9. At a meeting on January 25, 2008, the Colorado Supreme Court Committee on Rules of Civil Procedure approved a motion to not make changes to the Colorado Rules that would have mirrored the amendments to the Federal Rules of Civil Procedure concerning e-discovery.

10. Those 18 states are Alabama, Delaware, Florida, Georgia, Hawaii, Kentucky, Massachusetts, Missouri, Nevada, North Carolina, Oklahoma, Oregon, Pennsylvania, Rhode Island, South Carolina, South Dakota, Vermont, and West Virginia.

11. As of August 2010, 13 states required parties or their counsel to meet and confer early in the case to address e-discovery issues: Alaska, Arizona, California, Indiana, Iowa, Kansas, Maine, New Hampshire, New Mexico, North Dakota, Tennessee, Utah, and Wisconsin.

Fifteen of the 16 other states that have adopted e-discovery procedures impose "meet and confer" requirements on a selective case-by-case basis, either through the use of scheduling orders or at least by virtue of rules requiring that parties engage in good faith discussion to resolve a discovery dispute before bringing it to the court for resolution: Arkansas, Idaho, Louisiana, Maryland, Michigan, Minnesota, Mississippi, Montana, New Jersey, New York, Ohio, Texas, Virginia, Washington, and Wyoming.

Nebraska appears not to have any requirement that counsel confer regarding ESI issues, either for purposes of framing e-discovery parameters at the outset of litigation or, at a minimum, before bringing an e-discovery dispute to the court for resolution.

the state approach to early discussions. For example, the Maryland e-discovery rules apply solely to civil[12] cases filed in the circuit courts of Maryland, which are trial courts of general jurisdiction. Maryland purposefully did not adopt e-discovery rules for any type of case filed in the District Court of Maryland, which is a court of limited jurisdiction.[13] Thus, a "one size fits all" requirement that parties meet and confer about e-discovery would be neither practical nor necessarily cost-beneficial in all, or perhaps even most, state court cases. Therefore, states such as Maryland, which have trial courts of differing jurisdictional authority, or which, for any given court, employ "differential case management" techniques for assigning their cases to different "tracks" for case management and scheduling purposes, have adopted rules that permit trial courts to selectively impose e-discovery "meet and confer" requirements.

Even within the Maryland circuit courts, e-discovery "meet and confers" are not mandated in every civil case. Like many states, the Maryland circuit courts issue different "form" scheduling orders, depending upon the differentiated case management track to which they assign a given civil case. Maryland Rule 2-504(b)(2)(G) permits, but does not require, such a circuit court scheduling order to contain "provisions for discovery of electronically stored information." Such a scheduling order also is permitted, but not required, to contain "a process by which the parties may assert claims of privilege or of protection after production," thus encouraging the use of court-approved "clawback agreements," "quick-peek agreements," or other agreed procedures for privilege review and postproduction assertion of privilege

12. The Criminal Law Subcommittee of the Standing Committee on the Rules of Practice and Procedure of the Court of Appeals of Maryland is presently studying whether the Maryland circuit court rules governing criminal proceedings should be amended to address e-discovery matters. Currently, there also are no corollary Federal Rules of Criminal Procedure concerning e-discovery. See chapters 1, 6.

13. Although there are a few types of cases in which the District Court of Maryland has exclusive original civil jurisdiction without respect to the amount in controversy (for example, landlord and tenant, distraint, or wrongful detainer actions), with respect to actions in contract or tort, or attachment before judgment, the Maryland district court's exclusive original civil jurisdiction is limited to those cases in which the amount claimed does not exceed $30,000, exclusive of prejudgment or postjudgment interest, and attorney's fees. *See generally* Md. Code Ann., Cts. & Jud. Proc. 4-401 (2009 cum. supp.).

for inadvertently produced information in appropriate cases.[14] In short, based on procedures that differ from the federal rules, Maryland, like many other states, chose not to routinely mandate conferences of the parties.

On the other hand, although parties are not required to attend a court scheduling conference in every Maryland circuit court case, mandatory scheduling conferences do tend to be held in cases assigned to the more "complex" differentiated case management tracks and, hence, in cases having a greater potential for e-discovery issues to arise. Maryland Rule 2-504.1(c) permits a circuit court to require that the parties, at least 10 days before a mandated court scheduling conference, complete sufficient initial discovery to enable them to participate in the conference meaningfully, in good faith, and to make decisions regarding, among other things, "(E) any issues relating to preserving discoverable information, (F) any issues relating to discovery of electronically stored information, including the form in which it is to be produced, [and] (G) any issues relating to claims of privilege or of protection." Further, the court may order the parties to confer in advance, in person or by telephone, and attempt to reach agreement or at least narrow the areas of disagreement regarding the matters to be considered at the scheduling conference.[15] Thus, the conference requirement is dependent on case management decisions.

When a conference is conducted, Maryland generally follows the federal pattern. A Rules Committee Note to Maryland Rule 2-504.1 lists examples of matters that may be considered at, and thus in advance of, a court-ordered scheduling conference when discovery of electronically stored information is expected, including[16]

- its identification and retention
- the form of production, such as PDF, TIFF, or JPEG files, or native form, for example, Microsoft Word or Excel
- the manner of production, such as CD-ROM
- any production of indices
- any electronic numbering of documents and information

14. *See* MD. R. 2-504(b)(2)(H); *see also* MD. R. 2-402(e).

15. MD. R. 2-504.1(c)(2).

16. For additional examples of topics that parties should be prepared to discuss when they meet and confer regarding the discovery of ESI, see chapter 19.

- apportionment of costs for production of electronically stored information not reasonably accessible because of undue burden or cost
- a process by which the parties may assert claims of privilege or of protection after production
- whether the parties agree to refer discovery disputes to a Master or Special Master

The Committee Note further provides that the parties also may need to address any request for metadata, for example, information embedded in an electronic data file that describes how, when, and by whom it was created, received, accessed, or modified, or how it is formatted.[17]

Irrespective of whether court rules mandate that parties meet and confer regarding e-discovery issues early in litigation, the Maryland Rules permit parties to do so voluntarily if they believe that they have a case likely to involve such issues. E-discovery issues such as (1) determining the appropriate scope of litigation "holds" on routine destruction of ESI, (2) defining the appropriate scope of e-discovery, (3) determining accessibility of ESI and the attendant costs of production, (4) specifying the format of production and any attendant metadata, and (5) developing agreed, court-ordered procedures for privilege review and nonwaiver of privilege are among the myriad topics best addressed at the front end of the litigation process, before costly mistakes and false starts are made due to a failure to nip such issues in the bud.

This approach typifies the states. Indeed, although Texas has no procedural rule requiring an e-discovery "meet and confer" on even a selective basis, the Supreme Court of Texas recently imposed, through case law, a duty to confer before engaging in e-discovery, stating:

> A fundamental tenet of our discovery rules is cooperation between parties and their counsel, and the expectation that agreements will be made as reasonably necessary for efficient disposition of the case. TEX. R. CIV. P. 191.2. Accordingly,

17. For a more detailed discussion of metadata and factors to consider in determining the extent to which metadata should be preserved and produced in a particular case, see chapter 6 and The Sedona Conference, The Sedona Principles: Best Practices, Recommendations, and Principles for Addressing Electronic Document Production (2d ed. 2007), Principle 12 & cmt.

> *prior to promulgating requests for electronic information, parties and their attorneys should share relevant information concerning electronic systems and storage methodologies* so that agreements regarding protocols may be reached or, if not, trial courts have the information necessary to craft discovery orders that are not unduly intrusive or overly burdensome. The critical importance of learning about relevant systems early in the litigation process is heavily emphasized in the federal rules. Due to the "volume and dynamic nature of electronically stored information," failure to become familiar with relevant systems early on can greatly complicate preservation issues, increase uncertainty in the discovery process, and raise the risk of disputes. FED. R. CIV. P. 26(f) notes of the advisory committee to the 2006 amendments.[18]

In light of the nature of state court litigation, it appears that there is not, and will likely not be, a uniform national standard regarding early discussion; however, many states have accepted and adopted that process, mandating it where appropriate and recognizing it as an option when desired by counsel.

3. Two-tiered approach where ESI is not reasonably accessible because of undue burden or cost

With the exception of Wisconsin[19] and possibly New York,[20] every state adopting e-discovery procedures has implemented a

18. *In re* Weekley Homes, L.P., 295 S.W.3d 309, 321–22 (Tex. 2009) (emphasis added).

19. Wisconsin's discovery rules do not expressly address information that a party claims is "not reasonably accessible." The Wisconsin rules simply permit a party to object to producing requested information by stating the reasons for objection. *See* WIS. STAT. 804.09(2)(b). The burden then shifts to the requesting party to move to compel the discovery to which an objection has been raised. *See* WIS. STAT. 804.09(2)(c).

20. The New York Uniform Trial Courts Rules do not expressly adopt a two-tiered approach, but do require parties at a preliminary court conference to discuss "anticipated cost of data recovery and proposed initial allocation of such cost." *See* N.Y. UNIF. R. TRIAL CTS. 202.12(c)(3)(f). This provision arguably constitutes at least tacit recognition of a possible two-tiered approach to discovery of ESI. Furthermore, Bill A06000 introduced in the New York State Assembly in 2009, had it been enacted, would have amended Rule 3-122(a) of the New York Civil Practice Law and Rules to expressly clarify that a party need not provide discovery of ESI from sources that the party identifies as "not reasonably accessible because of undue burden or cost."

two-tiered approach, distinguishing ESI that is "not reasonably accessible" from that which is.[21] In every such state, the responding party has the burden of identifying the sources of electronically stored information that the party claims are "not reasonably accessible because of undue burden or cost."[22] There are, however, differences within that uniform approach.

For example, Maryland Rule 2-402(b)(2) goes further than the FRCP 26(b)(2)(B) strictures adopted by most state courts with e-discovery rules, in that the Maryland rule not only requires that the responding party identify the sources alleged to be "not reasonably accessible," but also requires that the responding party *"state the reasons* why production from each identified source would cause undue burden or cost. The statement of reasons *shall provide enough detail* to enable the requesting party to evaluate the burdens and costs of providing the discovery and the likelihood of finding responsive information in the identified sources." If a requesting party in Maryland disagrees with the responding party's claim that ESI is not reasonably accessible, it would be incumbent upon the requesting party to file a motion to compel discovery, whereupon the burden initially would be upon the

21. The "not reasonably accessible" language comes from FED. R. CIV. P. 26(b)(2)(B) and corollary rules adopted by most states with e-discovery procedures. In a conceptually similar but slightly differently worded vein, a responding party subject to the Texas Rules of Civil Procedure must produce requested ESI that "is reasonably available to the responding party in its ordinary course of business." *See* TEX. R. CIV. P. 196.4. If the responding party cannot—through reasonable effort—retrieve the data or information requested or produce it in the form requested, the responding party must state an objection complying with the Texas Rules of Civil Procedure. *Id.*

Both Idaho and Mississippi follow the Texas model with respect to electronically stored information that is not "reasonably available to the responding party in its ordinary course of business." *See* IDAHO R. CIV. P. 34(b)(2); MISS. R. CIV. P. 26(b)(5).

22. Most states adopting e-discovery procedures have adopted the language of FED. R. CIV. P. 26(b)(2)(B), which provides:

> A party need not provide discovery of electronically stored information from sources that the party identifies as not reasonably accessible because of undue burden or cost. On motion to compel discovery or for a protective order, the party from whom discovery is sought must show that the information is not reasonably accessible because of undue burden or cost. If that showing is made, the court may nonetheless order discovery from such sources if the requesting party shows good cause, considering the limitations of Rule 26(b)(2)(C). The court may specify conditions for the discovery.

party from whom the discovery was sought to "first *establish* that the information is not reasonably accessible because of undue burden or cost."[23] Once that showing is made, however, the burden then shifts to the requesting party to "*establish* that its need for the discovery *outweighs* the burden and cost of locating, retrieving and producing the information."[24]

And, in sharp contrast to the mainstream approach of placing the burden on the party requesting ESI to move to compel production of ESI from sources that the responding party identifies as being "not reasonably accessible," the recently enacted California Electronic Discovery Act takes the exact opposite approach.[25] Instead of placing a burden on the requesting party to move to compel the production of ESI identified by the responding party as being "not reasonably accessible," the California e-discovery law requires the responding party to seek a protective order with respect to production of such information.[26] The California Electronic Discovery Act also suggests that a responding party who fails to object to the production of ESI on the grounds that it is not reasonably accessible because of undue burden or expense may waive the right to seek a protective order if the party fails to object on those grounds in its written response to a requesting party's demand for production of ESI.[27]

Maryland typifies the general approach to ESI that is "not reasonably accessible." If persuaded that the need for discovery does outweigh the burden and costs of production, a Maryland circuit court may order the discovery and specify conditions, including

---

23. Md. R. 2-402(b)(2).

24. Md. R. 2-402(b)(2) (emphasis added).

25. California Electronic Discovery Act 2009 Cal AB5.

26. *See* Cal. Code Civ. P. 2031.060(a), (c).

27. The California Electronic Discovery Act amends section 2031.210(d) of the California Code of Civil Procedure to provide as follows:

> (d) if a party objects to the discovery of electronically stored information on the grounds that it is from a source that is not reasonably accessible because of undue burden or expense and the responding party will not search the source in the absence of an agreement with the demanding party or court order, the responding party shall identify in its response the types or categories of sources of electronically stored information that it asserts are not reasonably accessible. By objecting and identifying information of a type or category of source or sources that are not reasonably accessible, the responding party preserves any objections it may have relating to the electronically stored information.

an assessment of costs.[28] As the Committee Note to the applicable Maryland rule points out, the reasonable costs of retrieving and reviewing electronically stored information ordinarily are borne by the responding party. At times, however, the information sought is not reasonably available to the responding party in the ordinary course of business. For example, restoring deleted data, disaster recovery tapes, residual data, or legacy systems may involve extraordinary effort or resources to restore the data to an accessible format. Maryland Rule 2-402(b)(2) empowers the court, after considering the factors listed in Maryland's analog to FRCP 26(b)(2)(C), which is codified in subsection (b)(1) of Maryland 2-402,[29] to shift or share costs between parties if the e-discovery demand is unduly burdensome or costly because of the nature of the effort involved to comply, but the requesting party has demonstrated substantial need or justification for the production of the ESI that is not reasonably accessible.[30]

Compared to the federal courts and virtually every other state that has adopted e-discovery procedures, Texas is unique in its approach to the cost-shifting or sharing issue. In Texas, if a court orders the responding party to produce ESI that is not reasonably available to the responding party in its ordinary course of business, the court "*must* also order that the requesting party pay the reasonable expenses of any extraordinary steps required to retrieve and produce the information."[31] However, in the federal courts

28. MD. R. 2-402(b)(2).

29. MD. R. 2-402(b)(1) provides in pertinent part:

> [T]he court shall limit the frequency or extent of use of the discovery methods otherwise permitted under these rules if it determines that (A) the discovery sought is unreasonably cumulative or duplicative or is obtainable from some other source that is more convenient, less burdensome, or less expensive; (B) the party seeking discovery has had ample opportunity by discovery in the action to obtain the information sought; or (C) the burden or cost of the proposed discovery outweighs its likely benefit, taking into account the complexity of the case, the amount in controversy, the parties' resources, the importance of the issues at stake in the litigation, and the importance of the proposed discovery in resolving the issues.

30. *See* THE SEDONA CONFERENCE, THE SEDONA PRINCIPLES: BEST PRACTICES, RECOMMENDATIONS & PRINCIPLES FOR ADDRESSING ELECTRONIC DOCUMENT PRODUCTION (2d ed. 2007), Principle 13 & cmt.

31. TEX. R. CIV. P. 196.4 (emphasis added).

and all but two other states adopting ESI procedures[32]—including Idaho and Mississippi, which otherwise follow the Texas model of e-discovery—cost shifting or sharing is within the discretion of the trial court for ESI that the court orders to be produced to the requesting party notwithstanding the fact that the ESI is "not reasonably accessible" or "not reasonably available to the responding party in its ordinary course of business."[33]

4. Postproduction assertion of privilege or protection

A. Costs of privilege review

Costs of privilege review in e-discovery can be staggering, due in no small part to the sheer volume of ESI in the form of word processing documents, spreadsheets, databases, email, and so on, and the complex array of places where data can be stored, such as corporate networks, individual user PCs, laptops, Internet "data cloud" storage, cell phones, BlackBerrys, pagers, PDAs, digital cameras, fax machines, and voicemail systems, and a wide variety of backup media including disks, tapes, CD-ROMs, DVDs, thumb drives, and other removable storage devices. According to one technology industry analyst, as of 2009 a corporate employee receives an average of 108 email messages per day at work, which means that in the course of a year, a business employing 100 people would receive on average more than 3.9 million email messages, and this figure does not count the emails sent by those very same employees during the year.[34]

32. New York's and Wisconsin's discovery rules do not expressly address ESI that a party claims is "not reasonably accessible." However, N.Y. Unif. R. Trial Cts 202.12(c)(3)(f) requires parties at a preliminary court conference to discuss "anticipated cost of data recovery and proposed initial allocation of such cost," which arguably constitutes a tacit recognition of a two-tiered approach to discovery of ESI, and at least express recognition of possible cost-shifting with respect to retrieval of some or all data. By way of contrast, Wisconsin's rules do not address cost-shifting relating to e-discovery, or for that matter, discovery of any information, regardless how it is stored or recorded. *See generally* Wis. Stat. 804.01 *et seq*.

33. *Compare* Tex. R. Civ. P. 196.4 *with* Idaho R. Civ. P. 34(b)(2) *and* Miss. R. Civ. P. 26(b)(5).

34. *See* Press Release, Radicati Group, The Radicati Group Releases "Business User Survey, 2009" Study (Nov. 23, 2009), http://www.radicati.com/?p=4579.

The high cost of ESI privilege review often includes the cost of experts used by both the requesting and producing parties.[35] Annual revenues earned by ESI discovery consultants grew from $40 million dollars in 1999 to $430 million dollars in 2003, and were projected to total $2.865 billion dollars by the year 2007.[36] Furthermore, given the volume of ESI and the disparate places in which it can be stored, the risks of inadvertent production of privileged or work-product protected information can be significant. Consequently, parties often incur significant additional costs attendant to the preproduction screening of ESI in order to segregate and withhold privileged or work-product-protected information from disclosure.

B. Postproduction assertion of privilege: Timing of a clawback

In recognition of the high costs and risks of such preproduction screening of ESI, and of the reality that no preproduction screening process is perfect, the federal courts and the majority of states with e-discovery procedures have adopted provisions that expressly provide for postproduction assertion of claims of privilege or protection of information that was inadvertently disclosed during production.[37] For example, Maryland Rule 2-402(e)(2) permits a producing party to assert a claim of privilege or work-product protection after production of the information. Although the rule encompasses information stored or produced in any form, this subsection of Rule 2-402 was adopted primarily because it is increasingly costly and time-consuming to thoroughly review all ESI in advance of production. Subsection (e)(2), in conjunction with subsections (e)(3) and (e)(4) of Rule 2-402, is intended to facilitate

35. The possible need for, and use of, experts in connection with the search methodology for privilege review is discussed in chapters 20 and 21.

36. See annual revenue statistics and projections reported in *Hopson v. Mayor & City Council of Baltimore*, 232 F.R.D. 228 (D. Md. 2005).

37. Of the 29 states with some form of e-discovery procedures, the following 21 have provisions expressly permitting postproduction assertion of privilege or protection similar to that afforded by Fed. R. Civ. P. 26(b)(5)(B): Arizona, Arkansas, California, Idaho, Indiana, Iowa, Kansas, Louisiana, Maine, Maryland, Michigan, Minnesota, New Jersey, New Mexico, Ohio, Tennessee, Texas, Utah, Virginia, Washington, and Wyoming. The other e-discovery procedure states of Alaska, Mississippi, Montana, Nebraska, New Hampshire, New York, North Dakota, and Wisconsin do not have such clawback provisions for inadvertently produced privileged or protected information.

the efficient and cost-effective disclosure of electronically stored information without the risk of draconian consequences, such as potential "subject matter waiver" of privilege or work-product protection, in the event that privileged or protected information inadvertently is disclosed in the process of discovery.

Rule 26(b)(5)(B) of the Federal Rules of Civil Procedure imposes no time limit by which a party must assert a postproduction claim of privilege or protection with respect to inadvertently disclosed information.[38] Some states impose express time limits for such assertions,[39] whereas Maryland Rule 2-402(e)(2) requires that any such claim be asserted within "a reasonable time" after information is produced in discovery that is subject to a claim of privilege or protection.

This differing approach reflects the reality of adapting new rules to an existing corpus juris. The "reasonable time" requirement of the Maryland rule stems from the pre-ESI decision of Maryland's intermediate appellate court in *Elkton Care Center Assocs., Ltd. Partnership v. Quality Care Management*,[40] in which the Maryland Court of Special Appeals held that one factor in determining waiver was whether there were any delays associated with taking measures

38. *Cf.* FED. R. EVID. 502.

39. Some states set specific time limits for postproduction assertion of privilege. *See, e.g.*, ARK. R. CIV. P. 26(b)(5)(A)(i) (requiring that a party who inadvertently produces privileged or protected information must notify the receiving party of that fact "within 14 calendar days of discovering the inadvertent disclosure, . . . by specifically identifying the material or information and asserting the privilege or doctrine protecting it"); TEX. R. CIV. P. 193.1(d) (providing that a party who inadvertently produces material or information without intending to waive a claim of privilege does not waive that claim "if—within 10 days or a shorter time ordered by the court, after the producing party actually discovers that such production was made—the producing party amends its response, identifying the material or information produced and stating the privilege asserted"); IDAHO R. CIV. P. 26(b)(5)(B) (providing that "when a party produces information without intending to waive a claim of privilege, it may, *within a reasonable time*, notify any party that received the information of its claim of privilege" (emphasis added)). Although Idaho generally follows the Texas model with respect to e-discovery, in this regard Idaho's approach is similar to that of Maryland. The e-discovery rules of the other Texas model state, Mississippi, are silent with respect to postproduction assertion of privilege or work-product protection claims.

40. 805 A.2d 1177 (Md. 2002).

to rectify the disclosure, and whether it would be in the interest of justice to find a waiver under the circumstances.[41]

Thus, the Maryland Rules (like those of other states) were drafted against the backdrop of common law precedent and provide that, within a reasonable time after notice of inadvertently produced privileged or protected information, each receiving party must return, sequester, or destroy the specified information and any copies and may not use or disclose the information until the claim is resolved.[42] A receiving party that wishes to determine the validity of a claim of privilege or protection must *promptly* file a motion under seal requesting that the court determine the validity of the claim.[43] A receiving party that disclosed the information before being notified must take reasonable steps to retrieve it. The producing party must preserve the information until the claim is resolved.[44]

C. Substantive principles of waiver

States face unique issues when it comes to rules related to privilege waiver, such as those contained in Federal Rule of Evidence 502. First, there is the initial question of whether to promulgate such a rule. Next, because they are not grounded in the Federal Constitution's Supremacy Clause, there are questions related to the extraterritorial effectiveness of state privilege protection rules.

Thus far, only two states appear to have adopted provisions akin to FRE 502. Maryland was the first, when it adopted its e-discovery rules package effective January 1, 2008 (and thus prior to enactment of FRE 502). Although not styled as "rules of evidence," subsections (e)(2) through (e)(4) of Maryland Rule 2-402 are functionally equivalent to FRE 502, at least within the borders of the State of Maryland. Next, the Supreme Court of Iowa adopted a new Iowa rule of evidence that parallels FRE 502.[45] Whether other states will follow suit remains to be seen.

It seems, however, that everyone on the planet is in agreement that the sheer volume of electronically stored information increases the probability that privileged information will be inadvertently

41. *Id.* at 1183–84.
42. Md. R. 2-402(e)(2).
43. Md. R. 2-402(e)(2).
44. Md. R. 2-402(e)(2).
45. *See* Iowa R. Evid. 5.502 (effective June 1, 2009).

disclosed during e-discovery. The consequences that flow from inadvertent disclosure during "old fashioned" discovery will no doubt be relevant to the issue of what consequences flow from the inadvertent disclosure that occurred during e-discovery and were discussed in *Elkton Care*.[46] While affirming the trial court's ruling that the inadvertent disclosure constituted a waiver of appellant's attorney-client privilege,[47] the appellate court described the three different analytical frameworks that might be applied to an inadvertent disclosure of privileged information. In *Elkton Care*, the producing party copied documents "tabbed" by the requesting party during document review and turned them over to the requesting party. It was agreed that one of those "tabbed" documents was privileged. The waiver issue arose at trial on cross-examination when the requesting party sought to examine the producing party using the privileged document.[48] After the jury was presented with the privileged information, it determined that the producing party had breached the contract and an appeal was noted.

First, the Court noted that: "Following Wigmore,[49] some courts have adopted the 'strict test' or 'waiver' test, under which an inadvertent disclosure constitutes a waiver of the privilege."[50] Next, it wrote that "[s]ome courts have adopted the 'lenient' or 'no waiver' test, under which the attorney's negligence cannot waive the privilege because the client, and not the attorney, is the holder of the privilege."[51] In short, under Wigmore's approach *any* unprivileged disclosure results in waiver, while under the "lenient" approach there is a waiver *only* if the disclosure was intentional.

Faced with two diametrically opposed standards, the Court noted that Professors Mueller and Kirkpatrick[52] have criticized

46. 805 A.2d 1177 (Md. 2002).

47. The *Elkton Care* Court noted that the attorney-client privilege and work product doctrine are "separate and distinct," however, "[w]hen the disclosure is made to the adverse party," that distinction disappears. *Id.* at 1183, quoting *Hartford Fire Ins. v. Garvey*, 109 F.R.D. 323, 328 (N.D. Cal. 1985).

48. The privileged memorandum was introduced for the purpose of impeaching a trial defense by showing that the defense was formulated after the privileged memorandum. Id. at 1181.

49. *See* 8 Wigmore, Evidence 2325 at 633 (McNaughton rev. 1961).

50. Elkton Care, 805 A.2d at 1183 .

51. *Id.*

52. *Id.* at 1184, citing Christopher B. Mueller & Laird C. Kirkpatrick, *Evidence*, 5.29 at 450-52 (4th ed. 1995) (footnotes omitted).

them as inflexible positions and suggested that: "A third intermediate view sensibly holds that the question whether disclosure during discovery results in loss of privilege protection depends very much on the circumstances. . . ." Adopting that "fact specific case-by-case[,]"[53] "intermediate" test, the *Elkton Care* Court concluded:

> The courts that use this approach examine the following factors: "(1) the reasonableness of the precautions taken to prevent inadvertent disclosure in view of the extent of the document production; (2) the number of inadvertent disclosures; (3) the extent of the disclosure; (4) any delay and measures taken to rectify the disclosure; and (5) whether the overriding interests of justice would or would not be served by relieving a party of its error."[54]

The Court then applied the five-factor test to the facts presented, concluding that: "Factors one, two and three -- *the reasonableness of precautions taken to prevent inadvertent disclosure, the number of inadvertent disclosures, and the extent of the disclosure* -- all strongly favor waiver."[55] As to those factors, it explained:

> Here, the privileged document was inadvertently included in a half-full box of documents produced by a lawyer who was then representing appellant. Appellee's counsel tabbed that document, along with others, and returned all of the tabbed documents to the lawyer then representing appellant, who arranged to have the tabbed documents copied and delivered to appellee's counsel. Thus, on two occasions during the pretrial discovery phase of this case, counsel then representing appellant had the opportunity to assert the attorney-client privilege with respect to the memorandum at issue. *This is not a case in which hundreds of boxes and/or thousands of documents were produced.*[56]

53. *Id.*
54. *Id.*, citing *Sampson Fire Sales v. Oaks*, 201 F.R.D. 351, 360 (M.D. Pa. 2001). While delineating the factors to consider, the Court noted: "In most inadvertent disclosure cases, at least one factor is closely related to another factor." *Id.* at 1185.
55. *Id.* (emphasis in original).
56. *Id.* (emphasis added).

Turning to factor four, delay and measures taken to rectify the disclosure, the Court noted that "the inadvertent disclosure occurred during pre-trial discovery, but was not brought to [trial] Judge Thompson's attention until (in the words of appellant's brief) 'the penultimate day of trial. . . .' "[57] It therefore concluded that this factor pointed toward waiver because, for example, it deprived the trial court of preventative remedies such as an *in limine* order. Finally, based on an evaluation of the direct examination that occurred prior to assertion of the privilege, the fifth factor (the overriding interests of justice) strongly favored waiver.[58] *Elkton Care* demonstrates the need for a nuanced approach to the inadvertent production paradigm even in the arguably simpler context of a few boxes of paper documents.[59]

It is with this backdrop that Maryland Rule 2-402(e)(3) was promulgated. It provides that disclosure of a communication or information covered by the attorney-client privilege or work-product protection does not operate as a waiver if the holder of the privilege or work-product protection (1) made the disclosure inadvertently, (2) took reasonable precautions to prevent disclosure, and (3) took reasonably prompt measures to rectify the error once the holder knew or should have known of the disclosure.

"Reasonable precautions to prevent disclosure" may include reasonably crafted "clawback" agreements or "quick peek" agreements that have been approved by a court order (discussed below). In an effort to facilitate the discovery of information, particularly ESI, parties may agree to certain protocols to minimize the risk of waiver of a claim of privilege or protection. These protocols are not risk free. One example is a clawback agreement, that is, an

57. *Id.* at 1184.

58. *Id.* at 1185.

59. *Elkton Care* has been directly applied to inadvertent production of ESI. Cont'l Cas. Co. v. Under Armour, Inc., 537 F. Supp. 2d 761, 767 (D. Md. 2008)("Applying these factors to the present case compels the conclusion that the privilege has been waived by the inadvertent posting of the privileged communications on cnacentral.com."); F.H. Chase, Inc. v. Clark/Gilford, 341 F. Supp. 2d 562, 564 (D. Md. 2004)("The documents were sent to inData via the internet after Defendants' non-attorney assistant created Lotus Notes databases containing all non-privileged and responsive documents. . . . That assistant inadvertently sent inData the original data base, containing both privileged and non-responsive documents."); L. McLain, "Advanced Issues in Electronic Discovery," 37 U.Balt.L.Rev. 315, 318 n. 7 (2008).

agreement that production will occur without a waiver of privilege or protection as long as the producing party promptly identifies the privileged or protected information that has been produced.[60] Another example is a quick-peek agreement, meaning that the responding party provides, *without* first screening it for privileged or protected material, certain requested information for an initial examination by the requesting party, but without waiving any privilege or protection. The requesting party then designates the subset of documents or ESI it wishes to have actually produced, and the producing party may then review that subset and assert any applicable privilege or protection.[61]

Thus, the Maryland Rules for quick-peek agreements have to be analyzed against the existing body of law. One such case is *Hamilton v. Verdow*,[62] in which the Court of Appeals of Maryland held that the State of Maryland was entitled to assert its "executive privilege" when moving to quash a subpoena that sought production of a confidential report prepared by an ad hoc committee established by the governor to advise him of what changes would be needed to prevent escapes by patients at Spring Grove, a state psychiatric hospital. *Hamilton*, however, also involved an important "waiver of privilege" issue that arises whenever counsel are considering quick-peek and/or clawback agreements.

In *Hamilton*, the Court of Appeals answered two questions of Maryland law "certified" to that Court by the U.S. District Court for the District of Maryland, in which a federal diversity action was pending against the superintendent of Spring Grove and two staff psychiatrists. The plaintiff in that action was the personal representative of the estate of a resident of Florida who had been killed in that state by a Spring Grove patient after the patient escaped from the hospital. The holding in *Hamilton* that is relevant to quick-peek and/or clawback agreements is that, while waivers may, in some circumstances, be conditioned and limited, a selective "picking and choosing" will be permitted only in specific factual situations. In *Hamilton*, the patient, a serial killer, had

60. *See* The Sedona Conference, The Sedona Principles: Best Practices, Recommendations & Principles for Addressing Electronic Document Production (2d ed. 2007), cmt. 10.a.

61. *See id.*, cmt. 10.d.

62. 414 A.2d 914 (Md. 1980).

previously authorized the release of medical records to the representative of one victim and then sought to preclude release to the representative of another victim. In both instances, the decedents' representatives were suing the same hospital on similar bases and, therefore, the patient was deemed to have waived the privilege in a second action. The *Hamilton* Court recognized that there could be a conditional waiver, but stated:

> In order to permit a selective waiver, there should be some reasonable basis for distinguishing between two different situations. In this case, however, there is no rational ground for distinguishing between [the patient's] waiver of his entire medical file to [the plaintiff in the first action] when that information is identical to the information requested by the plaintiff [in the second action]. Both [plaintiffs] brought suits that involve substantially the same defendants and that are predicated on virtually identical facts and allegations. Both parties intended to use the information for the same purpose. Accordingly, by expressly authorizing the [first] plaintiff to obtain the medical records, [the patient] has similarly waived his statutory privilege with respect to discovery by the plaintiff in the present action.[63]

While quick-peek and/or clawback *orders* may afford protection to a party who objects to producing e-discovery material to a "similarly situated" adverse party, the implications of *Hamilton* for quick-peek and/or clawback *agreements* are obvious. As states consider rules providing these potentially beneficial procedures, it is important to also consider their possible common law limitations.

Another question regarding state procedural ESI rules is extraterritoriality. For example, Subsection (e)(4) of Maryland Rule 2-402 codifies the well-established proposition that parties can enter into an agreement to limit the effect of waiver by disclosure between or among them.[64] Nonwaiver agreements and orders can be important in limiting the costs of privilege review, especially in

63. 414 A.2d at 920.

64. *See, e.g.*, Dowd v. Calabrese, 101 F.R.D. 427, 439 (D.D.C. 1984) (no waiver where the parties stipulated in advance that certain testimony at a deposition "would not be deemed to constitute a waiver of the attorney-client or work product privileges"); Zubulake v. UBS Warburg LLC (*Zubulake III*), 216 F.R.D. 280, 290 (S.D.N.Y. 2003) (noting that parties may enter into "so-called 'claw-back' agree-

cases involving e-discovery. However, the utility of an agreement or order is substantially diminished if it provides no protection outside the particular litigation in which the order is entered. Parties are not likely to be able to reduce the costs of preproduction review for privilege and work product if the consequence of disclosure is that the privilege is waived and information can be used by nonparties to the litigation.

Of course, a nonwaiver agreement among parties to a case ordinarily can bind only those parties. Therefore, Maryland Rule 2-402(e)(4) makes clear that if parties want protection from a finding of waiver by disclosure in separate litigation involving other litigants, the parties' agreement must be made part of a court order.[65] That rule provides that an agreement of the parties governing confidentiality of disclosures is enforceable against nonparties only if it is incorporated in a court order.

However, there can be no assurance that this enforceability will be recognized by courts other than those of the State of Maryland. That is because there is some dispute as to whether a state-court confidentiality order entered in one case can bind nonparties, especially those in other states, from asserting waiver by disclosure in separate litigation.[66]

It should be noted that the issue of whether FRE 502 is constitutional has not yet been tested in the courts. The same is true with respect to its Maryland and Iowa state court corollaries, which also have not been court-tested in terms of the extraterritorial reach, if any, of Maryland or Iowa court-approved nonwaiver agreements between litigants with respect to their binding effect on nonparties outside the borders of those states.

---

ments that allow the parties to forego privilege review altogether in favor of an agreement to return inadvertently produced privileged documents").

65. For an example of a court order embodying the terms of a clawback agreement between parties to a case, see R. Klein, Maryland Civil Procedure Forms with Practice Commentary, Form 2-402.4 (LexisNexis Matthew Bender, 3d ed. supp. 2010).

66. *See* Md. R. 2-402(e)(4) rules committee note; *see generally* Hopson v. City of Balt., 232 F.R.D. 228 (D. Md. 2005).

5. Sanctions and safe harbors

The majority of states with e-discovery rules[67] have adopted provisions identical or similar to the "safe harbor" provision of FRCP 37(e), which provides: "Absent exceptional circumstances, a court may not impose sanctions *under these rules* on a party for failing to provide electronically stored information *lost* as a result of the routine, good faith operation of an electronic information system."[68]

Maryland's version of the federal safe harbor rule is worded more broadly than FRCP 37(e), in that Maryland Rule 2-433(b) is not limited to ESI that has been "lost," but instead applies to ESI that "is no longer available":

> Absent exceptional circumstances, a court may not impose sanctions *under these Rules* on a party for failing to provide electronically stored information *that is no longer available* as a result of the routine, good faith operation of an electronic information system. (Emphasis added.)

It also should be noted that the "under these Rules" limitation appearing in both FRCP 37(e) and Maryland Rule 2-433(b) is in deference to the fact that courts still retain inherent authority to impose sanctions for a failure to preserve evidence in appropriate circumstances.[69]

---

67. Nineteen states thus far have adopted safe harbor provisions for e-discovery: Alaska, Arizona, California, Indiana, Iowa, Kansas, Louisiana, Maine, Maryland, Michigan, Minnesota, Montana, New Jersey, North Dakota, Ohio, Tennessee, Utah, Wisconsin, and Wyoming.

Of the six other states having at least some e-discovery procedures akin to the federal e-discovery amendments, the following do not appear to have adopted any safe harbor provision analogous to federal Rule 37(e): Arkansas, Nebraska, New Hampshire, New Mexico, Virginia, and Washington. New York's ESI procedures also have no safe harbor provision.

With respect to the three Texas model states with e-discovery provisions (Texas, Idaho, and Mississippi), none has any legislative or rule equivalent to the safe harbor provision of FED. R. CIV. P. 37(e).

68. FED. R. CIV. P. 37(e) (emphasis added).

69. *See, e.g.*, Weaver v. ZeniMax Media, Inc., 923 A.2d 1032 (Md. Ct. Spec. App.), *cert denied*, 931 A.2d 1097 (Md. 2007) (trial court has inherent authority to impose sanctions for spoliation of evidence occurring prior to the commencement of litigation and, hence, outside the reach of the Rules of Procedure); Klupt v. Krongard, 728 A.2d 727 (Md. 1999) (circuit court has inherent authority to impose sanction

Like the Maryland safe harbor rule, California Code of Civil Procedure section 2031.060(i)(1) appears to provide a broader safe harbor from sanctions than FRCP 37(e), because the California provision applies not only to ESI that has been "lost" but also to ESI that has been "damaged, altered or overwritten" as the result of the routine, good faith operation of an electronic information system. Furthermore, the California safe harbor arguably is also deeper than the federal safe harbor rule and its state court corollaries, because the California Act does not limit that the sanctions that are prohibited from imposition to merely those sanctions imposed "under these rules."[70]

On the other hand, considering that California Code of Civil Procedure section 2031.060(i)(2) provides that "this subdivision shall not be construed to alter any obligation to preserve discoverable information," the differences between the wording of California's safe harbor provision and the wording of FRCP 37(e) and its state court counterparts may be more reflective of differences in drafting styles than in intended differences in the scope of a trial court's authority, be it inherent or rule-based, to impose sanctions when a party fails to preserve ESI that it has a reason to believe may be relevant to a claim. In any event, it is at least an open question whether the California legislature intended the California courts to retain any residual inherent authority to impose sanctions if the safe harbor provision of California Code of Civil Procedure section2031.060(i)(1) is triggered.

In short, it appears that the states are accepting of safe harbors, while leaving the contours and depth to be determined in the future.

6. FRCP 26(g) certifications

The Federal Rules of Civil Procedure impose certification requirements under FRCP 26(g). Maryland, like many states, does not have a direct analog.[71] This may be because other rules and common law impose that requirement indirectly.[72]

---

for destruction of evidence); Glynn v. Edo Corp., 2010 WL 3294347 (D. Md. Aug. 20, 2010) (sanctioning "self help" litigant).

70. *See* CAL. CODE CIV. P. 2031.060(i)(1).

71. See chapter 31; P. Grimm and L. Yurwit, *Electronically Stored Information in Maryland and Federal Courts*, (MICPEL 2008), 227.

72. *Id.*

In *Holden v. Blevins*,[73] a case that did not present e-discovery issues, the appellate court made clear that an attorney's ethical obligations preclude the presentation of false testimony, and remanded the case for further proceedings in the trial court. The appellee had testified before a jury that he had been awarded a number of commendations for valor in combat. On appeal, that assertion was challenged and the appellate court noted during oral argument that, when a party offers false testimony, the party's attorney must call upon the client for corrective action or reveal the fraud to the tribunal. Shortly after oral argument, the appellee submitted an affidavit stating that his testimony was false. The appellant contended in part that "because the jury must have assigned significant weight to that portion of appellee's testimony, the verdict should not be permitted to stand."[74]

The appellate court commended counsel for providing the disclosure and held that it required a remand for further proceedings, noting:

> A lawyer's duty of "[c]andor toward the tribunal" is governed by [Model] Rule 3.3 which, in pertinent part, provides:
>
> > (a)(4) . . . If a lawyer has offered material evidence and comes to know of its falsity, the lawyer shall take reasonable remedial measures.[75]

There are, to be sure, clients who will not welcome the news that the lawyer's duty to advocate zealously on behalf of the client does not trump the lawyer's duty to reveal his or her client's false testimony to the tribunal. Whether the case does or does not involve e-discovery, however, the application of these principles to a discovery pleading, even in the absence of a provision such as FRCP 26(g), can be at least be colorably asserted.

7. Conclusion

More than half the states have adopted some rules applicable to ESI. Virtually every state court employing e-discovery procedures has adopted provisions recognizing the critical importance of identifying, resolving by agreement, and teeing up for early

73. 837 A.2d 1053 (Md. App. 2003).
74. *Id.* at 1056.
75. *Id.* at 1055 – 1056 (footnotes omitted)(emphasis added).

court resolution in the litigation process any issues relating to e-discovery.[76]

Other than New York and Wisconsin, every such jurisdiction also expressly recognizes that not all ESI is "reasonably accessible" to the party asked to produce it, and with the exception of California, state courts presumptively permit a party responding to ESI discovery requests to decline to produce ESI that the party identifies as being not reasonably accessible due to undue burden or costs of production.[77] While there are some differences in the degree of specificity required with respect to such assertions, in every jurisdiction, if such an assertion is challenged, the burden is on the responding party to demonstrate that the ESI is in fact "not reasonably accessible" due to undue burden or costs of production. In most jurisdictions, upon such a showing, the burden then shifts to the requesting party to demonstrate substantial need for the information, and the court, if persuaded by that demonstration of need, may order production of the ESI on such conditions as are appropriate, including but not limited to, in the court's discretion, shifting all or part of the costs of production to the requesting party. In Texas, that cost-shifting is mandatory, not discretionary.

Twenty-one of the 29 states with e-discovery rules have provisions dealing with inadvertent production of privileged or work-product protected information, but thus far only Maryland and Iowa have any provisions akin to FRE 502 concerning the binding effect on nonparties of court-approved clawback agreements or other agreements between parties to litigation concerning nonwaiver of privileges or protections with respect to information inadvertently disclosed in the course of the litigation.

---

76. Of the 29 states that have adopted some form of e-discovery procedures to date, only Nebraska appears not to have any requirement that counsel confer regarding ESI issues, either for purposes of framing e-discovery parameters at the outset of litigation, or, at a minimum, before bringing an e-discovery dispute to the court for resolution.

77. California differs from the other states in this regard in that the burden is on the responding party to file a motion for a protective order, rather than opposing a motion to compel discovery filed by the requesting party. Although Wisconsin's rules do not expressly discuss ESI that is "not reasonably accessible," the Wisconsin procedural scheme places the burden on the party requesting information to move to compel discovery of ESI to which the party served with the request has objected on *any* stated ground, including but not limited to, not being reasonably accessible.

Finally, the majority of states implementing e-discovery procedures afford an FRCP 37(e) type of safe harbor for ESI that is "lost,"[78] "lost, damaged, altered, or overwritten,"[79] or otherwise "no longer available,"[80] as the result of the routine, good faith operation of an electronic information system. However, in every such jurisdiction, the otherwise safe harbor will not be available if the court finds that "exceptional circumstances" exist warranting the imposition of appropriate sanctions.

It remains to be seen how the states will resolve the issue of preserving and tailoring their local customs and processes while accommodating the call for a uniform national standard.

78. *See* Fed. R. Civ. P. 37(e).

79. *See* Cal. Code Civ. P. 2031.060(i).

80. *See* Md. R. 2-433(b).

50-State Status of E-Discovery Procedures Adoption as of August 2010

State	ESI Procedures Adopted	Meet and Confer Requirement	Two-Tiered Approach re ESI Accessibility	Postproduction Assertion of Privilege or Protection Allowed	FRE 502 Equivalent Adopted	Safe Harbor Provision
Alabama						
Alaska	✔	✔	✔			✔
Arizona	✔	✔	✔	✔		✔
Arkansas	✔	selective basis	✔	✔		
California	✔	✔	✔	✔		✔
Colorado						
Connecticut	under study					
Delaware						
Florida						
Georgia						
Hawaii						
Idaho	✔	selective basis	✔	✔		
Illinois	under study					
Indiana	✔	✔	✔	✔		✔

State	ESI Procedures Adopted	Meet and Confer Requirement	Two-Tiered Approach re ESI Accessibility	Postproduction Assertion of Privilege or Protection Allowed	FRE 502 Equivalent Adopted	Safe Harbor Provision
Iowa	✓	✓	✓	✓	✓	✓
Kansas	✓	✓	✓	✓		✓
Kentucky						
Louisiana	✓	selective basis	✓	✓		✓
Maine	✓	✓	✓	✓		✓
Maryland	✓	selective basis	✓	✓	✓	✓
Massachusetts						
Michigan	✓	selective basis	✓	✓		✓
Minnesota	✓	selective basis	✓	✓		✓
Mississippi	✓	selective basis	✓			
Missouri						
Montana	✓	selective basis	✓			✓
Nebraska	✓		✓			
Nevada						
New Hampshire	✓	✓	✓			

State	ESI Procedures Adopted	Meet and Confer Requirement	Two-Tiered Approach re ESI Accessibility	Postproduction Assertion of Privilege or Protection Allowed	FRE 502 Equivalent Adopted	Safe Harbor Provision
New Jersey	✔	selective basis	✔	✔		✔
New Mexico	✔	✔	✔	✔		
New York	✔	selective basis	tacit recognition			
North Carolina						
North Dakota	✔	✔	✔			✔
Ohio	✔	selective basis	✔	✔		✔
Oklahoma						
Oregon						
Pennsylvania						
Rhode Island						
South Carolina						
South Dakota						
Tennessee	✔	✔	✔	✔		✔
Texas	✔	selective basis (by case law*)	✔	✔		

State	ESI Procedures Adopted	Meet and Confer Requirement	Two-Tiered Approach re ESI Accessibility	Postproduction Assertion of Privilege or Protection Allowed	FRE 502 Equivalent Adopted	Safe Harbor Provision
Utah	✔	✔	✔	✔		✔
Vermont						
Virginia	✔	selective basis	✔	✔		
Washington	✔	selective basis	✔	✔		
West Virginia						
Wisconsin	✔	✔				✔
Wyoming	✔	selective basis	✔	✔		✔

* *In re* Weekley Homes, L.P., 295 S.W.3d 309, 321–22 (Tex. 2009) ("prior to promulgating requests for electronic information, parties and their attorneys should share relevant information concerning electronic systems and storage methodologies so that agreements regarding protocols may be reached or, if not, trial courts have the information necessary to craft discovery orders that are not unduly intrusive or overly burdensome.").

PART TWO

UNDERSTANDING ESI SYSTEMS AND POLICIES IN THE CONTEXT OF E-DISCOVERY

CHAPTER 4

INTRODUCTION TO INFORMATION TECHNOLOGY FOR THE ATTORNEY ADDRESSING E-DISCOVERY ISSUES

SCOTT FISCHER, RICHARD E. DAVIS, AND MICHAEL D. BERMAN

Intended for nontechies, this chapter offers a crash course in what legal professionals need to understand about information technology for purposes of e-discovery. Among other things, it covers computer networks, backup storage, and email systems (including the new collaborative tools). As the authors write, "Forensic information system technology is as much a part of the twenty-first-century litigator's tool kit as online legal and factual research."

1. Introduction

If you are reading this book, you are probably an attorney, legal assistant, or law student with no more knowledge about information technology than that gained in ordinary life. While you are probably familiar with, and use, email, word processing, and the Internet, "bits," "bytes," "zettabytes," and "yottabytes"[1] were not likely part of your early-childhood lexicon. The differences between "PDF," "TIFF," and "native" files might not have been covered in your middle-school education, and perhaps those intricacies were not the primary factor motivating you to attend law school. "Metadata" and "slack space" are probably relatively new concepts that you first heard about in connection with the December 2006 amendments to the Federal Rules of Civil Procedure. And your eyes may be glazing over and your mind traveling to a weekend at the beach as you read these words.

This chapter is not intended to provide you with sufficient expertise to mirror-image a hard drive, preserve shared folders on a server, or identify and extract metadata fields. It is intended to provide you with a high-level view of information technology so that you can serve as a "translator" between forensic experts, clients, and courts. The lawyer's role is to understand the law as it applies to e-discovery, ensure that clients are properly advised and that forensic efforts are efficiently employed when needed, and assist in preservation and production decisions that can be defensibly made and persuasively presented to courts. You are no more expected to be able to recover deleted data in an e-discovery matter than you would be expected to treat a comminuted fracture in a malpractice or personal injury case.

As an attorney, you must know how to communicate effectively with clients to implement preservation plans; when and how to retain consultants[2] and how to speak "consultant-talk" with them; how to depose experts using their specialized language;[3] how to go "information shopping" in a Rule 26(f) conference of the parties;[4] and how to produce, receive, review, and use electronically stored information (ESI) in connection with litigation. In short, you can drive a car without being an auto mechanic. You need to know when the car's oil needs to be changed, but not how to change it.

1. See appendix E.
2. See appendix A for tips on retaining consultants.
3. See chapter 22.
4. See chapter 19.

In order to "kick the tires" in e-discovery, it is important to learn a new vocabulary and the organizational parameters of computer systems.

2. Overview of computer systems

In common parlance, the term "computer" has become the ubiquitous definition for any electronic device that can run programs to send and receive email, surf the Internet, play games, create and store documents, and perform a host of automated tasks. An X-box, PlayStation, or Wii is, after all, a computer, as is your cable TV box and programmable home thermostat.

In the context of business and e-discovery, however, we are confronted with linked, electronic devices known as a "computer system," "network," or information technology system. A computer system is made up of several key components, some of which play a greater role than others in the e-discovery process. Today's computer systems can generally be classified into three categories:

1. Consumer systems for home use, such as personal desktop and portable computer "stand-alone" systems.
2. Networked "enterprise systems" used by businesses and government, and characterized by powerful servers to which employees connect using office desktop and portable computers. These systems may facilitate the use of email, Internet, word processing, spreadsheets, databases, and websites, and, while they may be tailored and unique, often deploy "off-the-shelf" applications, and store large volumes of data.
3. High-end or specialized computing systems for complex space, military, research, or business applications designed to process massive amounts of data, often encrypted, and to perform highly complex, specialized calculations and modeling. For example, government agencies may have specialized systems for unique services, such as criminal justice systems with home monitoring technology for probationers or offenders; manufacturers may have systems especially designed for tailored functions.

While each of these categories of computer systems may contain myriad differentiating bells and whistles, each having specific functionality geared toward the type of user and function, they all have the same baseline characteristics:

1. *One or more central processing units (CPUs) and the operating system.* The CPU manages the programs, or applications (e.g., Microsoft Word and Microsoft Excel), that run with the computers' operating system (e.g., Windows, Leopard, and Linux). The greater a CPU's processing power and speed, the more concurrent instructions it can execute. Two common brands of CPUs are Intel and AMD.
2. *Storage.* Online, readily accessible data storage is contained on the drives of the computer system. Because these drives are the file cabinets of the computer system, understanding a target user ("custodian") or entity's storage methodology and infrastructure is perhaps the most important aspect of e-discovery. When asked why he robbed banks, Willie Sutton reportedly replied, "Because that's where the money is."[5] So, too, can the lawyer say: "I want the storage drive forensically imaged because that's where the 'smoking gun' data is." The term "online storage" can be synonymous, at its most basic level, with "workstations" connected to "servers." The term "workstation" describes a business computer that has a unique hardware configuration, system access privileges, and/or a distinct role in the business enterprise, and is connected to the computer system. As the name implies, it is where the employee works, that is, inputs and receives data. The server is the heavy-duty hardware that performs storage and other service functions for the workstations, and permits the sharing of data. Both workstations and servers may have hard drives, although the number and characteristics may vary. Typical storage devices include the following:
   a. *Fixed disk space or hard drive.* The "C:" drive of a computer is typically referred to as a "local" fixed disk or hard drive. Most computers can accommodate multiple fixed disks; however, the configuration of these disks on a server can become quite complex, with internal partitions, and can affect the way discovery is conducted. Fixed disk sizes commonly range from under 140 gigabytes (GBs) to multiple terabytes.[6]

5. For a historical description of the Willie Sutton quotation, see http://en.wikipedia.org/wiki/Willie_Sutton.

6. While the majority of the computer systems on which electronic discovery is currently being performed are three to five years old, and therefore generally

b. *External media.* This term encompasses any number of devices including, but not limited to, external hard drives, tape drives, "thumb" or USB drives, DVDs, and CD-ROMs. Large-scale, inexpensive storage has become the norm in both the consumer and business marketplace. For example, external hard drives can store as much as a terabyte for less than a few hundred dollars. And a 16GB thumb drive, costing approximately $30, can hold the equivalent of about 1,040,000 pages of text.

c. *Enterprise storage (SAN and NAS).* SAN (storage area network) and NAS (network-attached storage) devices are typically found in corporate or government environments. While it is worthwhile to be aware of the distinctions in the enterprise storage category, the rationale for, and the functionality of, the tools employed in the data acquisition process have many similar characteristics.

    i. A SAN is a complex group of interconnected storage devices that, when properly implemented, appear to users as a simple storage location. The lack of a true physical location of data means that one cannot rely on imaging a physical device or disk when gathering potentially relevant information in an e-discovery initiative.

    ii. NAS devices, unlike SANs, are typically discrete storage devices attached to a network. Although there is no qualitative difference from the user's perspective, the method by which the hardware stores data is significantly different, and therefore the imaging or copying of data has different technical requirements.

    iii. Because of distinctions between a SAN and a NAS, the initial disclosure process under Rule 26(a)[7] could be construed to require a certain level

have less storage, newer models generally have greater capacity.

7. See chapter 13. FED. R. CIV. P. 26(a)(1)(A)(ii) requires that a party provide "a copy—or a description by category and location—of all documents, electronically stored information, and tangible things that the disclosing party has in its possession, custody, or control and may use to support its claims or defenses, unless the use would be solely for impeachment."

of granularity when it comes to the technical storage infrastructure of an organization.

d. *Redundant array of independent disks (RAID).* Many servers use a RAID configuration to increase the reliability and integrity of data stored on a server. In this configuration, multiple hard disks share similar information about the files stored on the server so that if one of the server's disks fails, the data is not lost. Unlike the single-file storage model that is employed by laptops and desktop computers, RAID systems create greater fault tolerance and redundancy by spreading data across multiple disks. This effectively means that data is constantly being overwritten in available sectors vacated by files that previously occupied those sectors.

3. *Random access memory (RAM).* This is often referred to as "volatile memory." The technical significance of RAM is that the more of it a computer has, the more information it can store before its performance and responsiveness begin to degrade. Think of RAM as a dry-erase board. When the computer is turned on, it begins to write pieces of information on the board that it needs for that particular session, based on the programs or tasks the user submits via the keyboard or mouse. When the computer is turned off, that transitory information is no longer needed by the computer, and it wipes all the information off the dry erase board. This information, which is stored in RAM but never copied to a storage device, is lost when the computer shuts down. The point of the analogy is that it is important to note that information stored in RAM is available only while the computer is turned on. For this reason, RAM is considered to be "volatile storage" and data contained in RAM is often called "ephemeral data." RAM has become important in some cases[8] because information relevant to a particular discovery initiative may be stored only in RAM; however, that is the exceptional situation.[9]

---

8. *See* M. ARKFELD, ELECTRONIC DISCOVERY AND EVIDENCE §7.9(A)(6)(h) (2d ed. 2009) (collecting cases).

9. *See id.* Preserving the information in RAM is technically possible; however, doing so generally requires specialized computer forensics software that is used on a computer while it is powered up. This specialized software will take a

3. "Writing" data on disks

A disk drive is composed of one or more platters, and looks very much like a round, brown phonograph record with a magnetic tone arm. Information is placed on the disk magnetically, in a series of zeroes and ones. These "bits" of information are then grouped into "bytes" of information, which represent individual characters.

Computers randomly place, or "write," data on disks. A single typed memorandum may be fragmented and stored in multiple locations, or sectors, on the disk. A specialized tool, generally called the file allocation table, tells the computer where to find the fragments when the user decides to open a stored file.

When a user deletes a file, only the allocation table entry is removed; the data itself remains, untouched, on the disk. As such, it is forensically recoverable, unless or until the computer randomly overwrites that sector to reuse it for new data.

When a drive is forensically copied, or "mirror imaged," each bit and byte is copied, bringing with it all current active data, all recoverable deleted data, and all empty sectors. The implications of this process are discussed below in chapter 14.

Applications, or programs, such as Microsoft Word and Microsoft Excel, write the data to disks in a manner that the creating program is able to later read and interpret. This stored information is called a native file. It resides on the hard drive or other storage media, with its included metadata, waiting to be called into action by the application. Often, an application's "language" is proprietary; without the proprietary application, a reviewing attorney may not be able to open and review the file.[10]

Other applications may convert a native file to a new format. For example, programs like Adobe Acrobat may be used to convert a native file into a portable document format (PDF). PDF is generally described as a "static" or "petrified" format, because the native application can no longer access and modify it. The two most typical static formats are PDF and tagged image format (TIFF). A static format is much like a photocopy of a paper document and, generally, much or all metadata is stripped out when a native file is converted to a static format. One major advantage of static

snapshot of the RAM, which in some instances will be viewable as "clear text" (human-readable characters).

10. This proprietary-information issue must be considered when negotiating a form of production at a Rule 26(f) conference because it could have a significant impact on cost.

documents is the availability of free "readers" that permit universal access to the document, without the need for purchasing native applications.[11] One should be cognizant of the fact that certain data conversion processes may alter or delete metadata that may be of evidentiary value.

4. Computer networks

The concept of computer networking is fairly well understood by the layperson. In the context of litigation, however, it is important for both parties to have a precise and mutually understood definition of the term "network" to avoid confusion. The most familiar example of a computer network is presented by the local area network (LAN). A simple LAN might consist of three or four computers connected by Ethernet cables through a hub, a device that has a connecting port for each computer cable that is on the network. While not always the case, computers on a LAN can typically share common resources, such as a printer or an Internet connection. Over the years, the functionality and complexity of LANs have afforded computer system users greater ability to collaborate, share, and collectively store information, while concomitantly creating greater complexity in the discovery process.

Wireless LANs are becoming more common. They operate on the same basic LAN principles as a wired LAN; however, connectivity to the network is established using radio frequencies over which data is sent and received by computers on the wireless network. Because of this, security is a serious concern. Unless encrypted, that data can be intercepted by anyone who is within range.

WANs, or wide area networks, are an extension of the LAN principle to much larger networks. WANs can include thousands of users and comprise multiple LANs.

Virtual private networks (VPNs) involve the use of software to create a highly secure "private" network connection within a larger network. VPNs are commonly used to allow computer users who are not in the office to connect to the network via the Internet, using certain software and password credentials. Symantec's pcAnywhere is a typical example of an off-the-shelf application permitting remote access.[12]

11. Static documents are also easily redacted and Bates numbered.

12. Extranets and intranets are becoming more common as networking devices.

Network users typically have access to a variety of data storage locations. On a corporate network, users may have a private data storage location, typically called a home directory. They may also have access to a common, or "shared," directory. VPN users who access corporate data from an outside location may also have the ability to store data on the computer from which they access the VPN. Therefore, if a target custodian's computer is on any type of network, it is imperative that counsel engaging in discovery determine if that target custodian has access to other custodians on the LAN, WAN, or VPN, and determine the location of all home and shared directories.

5. Backup tapes: The paradigm of offline storage

A. General description

While backup tapes were developed as a cheap and reliable way to store large amounts of data and system-configuration information for a variety of purposes, no single purpose has been as important as their use and applicability in ensuring a business entity's recovery from catastrophic system failures (disaster recovery) or unavailability.[13] Their relevance in the e-discovery process has in recent years been discussed in innumerable cases and articles. There are many formats of backup tapes; the most common in use today are DLT and LTO tapes.[14]

Traditionally, the cost, complexity, and operational impact of backup tape e-discovery have been such that courts have been reluctant to order a party to restore data from backup tapes without a showing of good cause, such as a failure to properly implement a litigation hold or spoliation. There was good reason for this reluctance. Backup tapes typically store data in a linear fashion, with rows of data that stretch from end to end. Because the familiar "tree structure" was lacking, the only way to access data was to restore it, by copying the data from tape to an operational computer. This was time-consuming, because of the volume of

13. In addition to disaster recovery, backup tapes are sometimes used for archival purposes. The usage may have important discovery ramifications by, for example, rendering FED. R. CIV. P.26(b)(2)(B) (not reasonably accessible because of undue burden or cost) inapposite. Counsel should always be alert to the possibility that tapes have many potential uses other than disaster recovery.

14. For a comprehensive list of available tape formats as of the printing of this chapter, see RenewData, http://www.renewdata.com/reference-card-request.php.

data, compression, and the transfer rates, and costly, because the restored data still had to be preserved, searched, and reviewed.[15]

B. Backup tape software, partial or incremental backups, tape rotation, and the cost of a litigation hold on backup tapes

Backup tapes often capture much less than the entire computer system. Backup tape software provides computer network administrators with the ability to target certain designated sources of data, such as a network file or email server, for regular or incremental backups. A typical business may back up data daily, weekly, monthly, quarterly, and/or annually. It will likely, pursuant to a records-management or disaster-recovery protocol,[16] "rotate" or reuse the tape media, which generally[17] destroys previously stored information contained on the overwritten tape. For this reason, when a litigation hold is issued, it is important to determine the impact of the cessation of tape rotation on the enterprise and whether cessation is required.[18]

Imposition of a litigation hold on backup tapes may be costly. For example, it may be necessary to preserve the software that created the tape. A typical LTO4 tape costs approximately $35 and, in an organization with a 45-day rotation, plus quarterly and annual backups, it would be necessary to purchase approximately 50 new tapes each time a litigation hold is imposed. While that $1,750 price tag may be substantial, depending on the needs of the case, it is not a complete picture, because businesses often back up multiple servers. Thus, for example, there may be 50 tapes for the email server, plus 50 tapes for the server that contains word processing documents, and more tapes for other servers. Additionally, when the tapes are taken out of rotation, prudent information technology personnel will likely want to create a new, complete backup for disaster recovery, imposing additional costs.

---

15. The development of technology that allows one to gain access to the substantive file or email content and metadata that are stored on a tape, without the need for the software used to back up the data or the software used to create the data, has reduced the cost, complexity, and operational impact of backup tape e-discovery. See chapter 26.

16. See chapters 5 and 12.

17. The word "generally" is used because, for example, if the overwriting data requires less storage capacity than the overwritten data, some data will not be overwritten.

18. For the applicable legal standards governing backup tapes, see chapters 9 and 25.

An often overlooked piece of information generated by backup tape software is the backup software transaction log. A transaction log is effectively a time and data source record of backup, restoration, and cataloging activity. In situations where backup tapes are missing, backup software transaction logs can show evidence of when missing tapes were last "touched." Litigators should be keenly aware of the potentially critical importance of backup tape transaction logs, as they can provide a detailed listing of which servers were backed up and/or restored, which folders and files were backed up and/or restored, and precisely when the actions took place.

Tape, as a storage mechanism, is facing competition from other applications. Email archiving software, for example, is in widespread use. While tape will undoubtedly have significant impact on litigation for the foreseeable future, other technologies such as disk backup are growing in popularity.

When engaging in backup tape discovery, it is always important to know the format of the backup tape and whether or not data compression or encryption was used. Backup software that compresses data to tape can double the tape's capacity and therefore double the amount of storage needed to restore data as well as the price to process the data. It is also important to know whether the data on the tape media is encrypted because if the restoring party does not have the de-encryption key, it is entirely possible that none of the encrypted data will be usable.

6. Email systems

In order to intelligently approach preservation and production of email, it is necessary to understand the most common email applications. Email has become the de facto document management system of the corporate world, and is far and away the most important component of litigation-related discovery.

A. Microsoft Exchange

The most commonly implemented email system, both in business enterprises and for home use, is the Microsoft family of messaging products. They include Microsoft Exchange and various versions of Microsoft Outlook. Initially released in 1996 as Exchange Server 4.0, the program was coupled with Microsoft Outlook in the Microsoft Office 97 suite of products. From that point forward, Microsoft Exchange (the server side of the messaging system) and Microsoft Outlook (the stand-alone side of the messaging system) have been the de facto standard[19] for email collaboration, calendaring, instant messaging, contact management, and a host of related ancillary functions.[20]

It is important to note that Microsoft Exchange can be configured to store user email files in locations other the Microsoft Exchange server. Microsoft Outlook PST files (personal storage files, discussed below) can be stored on a custodian's computer or in a designated folder, such as a user home directory. Thus, for example, Mr. Jones's email may be on the "S," for "shared" drive, as S:\companyname\shared\jones. The Exchange database is discussed more fully in chapter 14.

One particularly noteworthy feature of Exchange servers is that they may be set to retain deleted email for a specified period, for example, 10 days. This feature is designed to permit system administrators to recover inadvertently deleted email when the chief executive officer calls in desperation seeking "that missing message." Counsel should be aware of this temporary storage and mailbox purging activity, which could cause spoliation. Similarly, counsel should be on the lookout for instances where their adversary has failed to curtail system activities that result in the destruction of potentially responsive email data that was stored in a transitory manner.

Except when stored on the Exchange server, Microsoft Outlook generally stores information in personal storage (PST) or offline storage (OST) files. These personal storage files contain email, calendar, contact, and other Outlook information. Great care must be taken when producing these files, because deleted data may remain resident and recoverable in the file; however, "compaction" may be used to reduce that possibility.

---

19. This is, of course, not to say that there are no valid competitors. There are, for example, many specialized software packages designed for specific professions. Amicus Attorney is one example of a package designed for attorneys that performs multiple functions, and there are many others. References in this chapter to commonly available software are illustrative and are not an endorsement of any product.

20. The Windows-based Microsoft Outlook has been available for the Mac systems, but the rapid growth of the Mac platform has resulted in Outlook being supplanted by Entourage for Mac OS X. Microsoft has announced plans to redeploy the Outlook brand to the Mac OS X environment in 2010; the implication for e-discovery is that there will be more uniformity in discoverable metadata across the Mac and Windows operating systems.

B. Server-based email versus PC-based email

For many organizations, email systems double as a type of document management system. Because of its ease of use, document attachments are frequently stored and indexed on an Exchange server. As a result, the great majority of e-discovery issues involve the extraction of mailboxes from Exchange environments. Outlook communicates with Exchange via Microsoft's MAPI protocol and can take advantage of all the Exchange features. In addition, Exchange supports global mailbox standards and can send to and receive mail from all POP3 and IMAP4 client programs (defined below). Exchange also supports web-based access. This means that a custodian who uses Exchange has access to a wide variety of mailboxes for his or her email. Mailbox owners often use their Exchange to connect to their office Outlook and multiple web mail accounts. It is not uncommon to find private information commingled with a corporate mailbox. This is an important point for attorneys to remember when tailoring their discovery requests, because mail can be sitting in myriad repositories and in many forms.

When dealing with e-discovery issues with Microsoft Exchange, it is important to be familiar with the standard email protocols. These protocols govern the interactions between email servers and email clients. There are three basic email protocols: POP, IMAP, and MAPI. Understanding the protocols is important in determining how to extract responsive information from an Exchange server.

(1) POP

POP stands for "Post Office Protocol" and it is the oldest and simplest of the three. At the time of this book's publication, it will appear most frequently as POP3, the current version of the protocol. In the world of email, a POP account is equivalent to an old-style post office box. Emails are sent from a remote server to the POP account on the Exchange server, similar to the way snail mail is sent from a post office in a distant city to the addressee's post office box in his or her home town. When the user connects to the POP account, he or she will download the mail from the server to his or her local machine. Like the post office box, the POP account on the server is emptied when it is downloaded to the local machine and, although the system can be set to retain mail on the server, the primary purpose of a POP account is to transport the email from the server to the user's local machine. In short, in the POP world, information is stored on the Exchange server on a temporary basis, until it can be moved to a client machine.

(2) IMAP

The Internet Message Access Protocol (IMAP) is the yin to the POP account's yang. Where POP was designed in an age of slow connections and dial-up, and where connection to the server was expensive and time-consuming, IMAP was designed to utilize broadband connections. IMAP prefers to leave messages on the server, because the assumption is that a high-speed connection to the Internet is always readily accessible. The user may download his or her emails to a local machine, but that is secondary. IMAP users expect their data to remain on the Exchange server; even though users may copy data down to their workstation, the server is their preferred repository.

(3) MAPI

The Messaging Application Programming Interface (MAPI) is a Microsoft proprietary email protocol that is utilized by Microsoft Outlook to communicate with Microsoft Exchange. It is important to remember that MAPI works only for Outlook-Exchange interactions.

C. Web browsers for email

With Internet use rapidly becoming universal, simpler email solutions that do not require any email client at all abound. In these cases, the server may be accessed through the use of a web browser. Email systems that rely on a web browser for access behave similarly to IMAP because email messages remain on the server until they are deleted. Examples of this type of web-based mail include Gmail, Hotmail, Yahoo! Mail, and many others.

Web-based email poses several preservation and discovery challenges:

1. The data is ephemeral.
2. The email system is not within the control of the individual custodian. Control lies with the third-party provider.
3. The retention polices of the web-based email data are subject to the control and discretion of the hosted-email service third-party provider.

Most of the common web-based mail applications can be integrated with PC-based mail programs like Outlook. In many instances, when counsel needs to have their client preserve web-based email, the custodian can defensibly download web mail into email programs like Microsoft Outlook without adulterating critical, substantive metadata information. The user should consult with the web mail provider to determine the configuration settings that best fulfill this function.

D. Collaborative tools—the new reality of email and documents

Microsoft SharePoint is a platform of Microsoft tools, products, and software components that facilitate, among other things, group collaboration, Internet and intranet functionality, data search, and document management. SharePoint services can also be used to host websites that access shared custodian workspaces, data, and documents. By virtue of combining various and sundry forms of discoverable data, SharePoint has added an additional dimension of complexity to e-discovery and will continue to change the way lawyers need to think about the forms of potentially discoverable data as well as where that potentially discoverable information resides.

E. Lotus Notes

After Microsoft Exchange, Lotus Notes is the most important email provider in the world of e-discovery.[21] It is the client side of a client-server, comprehensive collaborative application offered by IBM as a flagship product for its business market. Lotus Notes provides email, calendaring, instant messaging, and a variety of desktop applications to IBM customers. Just as Microsoft Exchange utilizes its proprietary Exchange server, IBM utilizes its proprietary Lotus Domino server. In much the same way that Exchange uses nonproprietary mail protocols, a Lotus Notes client can use IMAP or POP when working with non-Domino mail servers.

Unlike Microsoft Exchange, which entered the market primarily as an email solution, IBM's Lotus Notes entered into the market primarily as a database solution. Today, however, both Exchange

21. Again, we emphasize the most common products. Many other products, such as Novell's GroupWise, may occupy the e-discovery landscape.

and Lotus Notes have functionality that extends well beyond their initial market entry uses. Both software applications provide highly complex, interactive document management functionality.

For example, the Lotus Notes Domino system is also a platform for developing customized client-server and web applications. Its use of design constructs and code provide capabilities that facilitate the construction of "workflow" type applications (which may typically have complex approval processes and routing of data).

A hallmark of Lotus Notes from its inception has been its understanding and utilization of replication. A key feature of Notes is that many replicas of the same database can exist at the same time on different servers and clients, across dissimilar platforms, and the same storage architecture is used for both client and server replicas. Litigators should be aware that replication may create multiple copies of data throughout the enterprise.

7. Conclusion

Forensic information system technology is as much a part of the twenty-first century litigator's tool kit as online legal and factual research. Winston Churchill wrote: "When I look back on all these worries I remember the story of the old man who said on his deathbed that he had had a lot of trouble in his life, most of which had never happened."[22] ESI can be viewed as "a lot of trouble," much of which will not materialize if attorneys learn the vocabulary and concepts necessary to "kick the tires" and drive the car.

22. WINSTON CHURCHILL, *September Tensions*, ch. 23 *in* II THE SECOND WORLD WAR: THEIR FINEST HOUR (1949), as quoted in http://en.wikiquote.org/wiki/Winston_Churchill.

CHAPTER 5

COMPUTER USAGE POLICIES, RECORDS MANAGEMENT, AND CORPORATE IT INFRASTRUCTURE:

A GUIDE FOR ATTORNEYS BEFORE & DURING LITIGATION

By William A. McComas and Michael D. Berman

Strong, well-designed computer usage policies and records management policies are increasingly essential to the legal well-being of many corporations. This chapter offers detailed guidance to attorneys who need to review their client's policies and corporate IT infrastructure, either before or during litigation. It also serves as a primer for litigators who want to probe an opponent's policy and implementation and operational weaknesses. In their discussion, the authors include a number of potential problems that are often overlooked, as well as issues that are currently emerging.

1. Introduction

As electronically stored information and the transmission of it have become a linchpin in our global economy, so too has the burden of managing and safeguarding electronically stored information (ESI) and the risks and exposure from mismanaging it. Discovery has become a critical crossroad where the proper management of ESI prior to and during litigation is rewarded and where the mismanagement of it prior to or during litigation is exposed in the form of inefficient and costly business processes and reputational[1] and legal risk (often in the form of sanctions).

Given this new reality—a reality in which digital technology is entwined within each and every business decision at all levels—companies must learn to prepare and enforce policies that effectively manage and safeguard what is often one of their most important assets, ESI, through computer usage and records management policies and through technology. To the extent the companies are unable to regulate themselves, one can expect that governments will continue to impose onerous statutory requirements in this arena.

This chapter is intended to provide attorneys with a road map for the management of corporate ESI that can also be used to expose the mismanagement of it in disputes and investigations. This chapter also briefly reviews the history of computer usage and records management policies, explains their purpose, describes how information technology (IT) departments typically operate, and identifies new computer usage issues that have emerged as trouble spots for businesses, attorneys, and litigants in recent years. The focus is not on advising companies and attorneys how to draft and implement policies. Instead, the primary goal is to educate those who are, or will likely be, facing litigation or investigations that involve ESI, so that attorneys can properly respond to a litigation or investigative process, such as by interviewing

1. The Wikileak disclosures are a good example of the reputational risk suffered by the U.S. government as a direct result of it not being able to safeguard its ESI.

their clients, seeking discovery, and deposing their opponents and responding to the same from their opponents.[2]

The importance of managing ESI and properly using computer devices has recently been reinforced by *City of Ontario v. Quon,* wherein the Supreme Court unanimously ruled that the City of Ontario possessed a legitimate interest in determining whether it was paying for its employee to make non-work-related communications through a device issued by the City of Ontario.[3] In that case, the government employee was utilizing a popular text messaging service on a mobile device.

While some aspects of the handling of ESI in connection with legal processes are new, the recognition that there is a need to manage ESI has been around for nearly 20 years. According to a 1998 article in the *New York Times,* Amazon.com instructed its employees, at a time when ESI was just emerging and gaining popularity, "Quite simply put, there are some communications that should not be expressed in written form."[4] The caution found in this quote is clear. Amazon's management recognized that employee communications contained in ESI could be a potential hot spot, and wanted employees to be mindful of what they were committing to in written, permanent, documentable communications.

While most businesses in the past have had as their primary focus safeguarding their data from deletion, it is equally true that some information should not be retained. The government, for example, has statutory obligations to destroy certain information,[5] and the private sector must also be on the alert to balance the costs

---

2. *See* Qualcomm Inc. v. Broadcom. Corp., 2008 WL 66932 (S.D. Cal. Jan. 7, 2008), *vacated and remanded in part,* 2008 WL 63810 (S.D. Cal. Mar. 5, 2008), *appeals dismissed,* 327 Fed. Appx. 877, 2008 WL 6400775 (Fed. Cir. Aug. 18, 2008), *on remand,* 2010 WL 1336937 (S.D. Cal. Apr. 2, 2010) (sanctions over $8 million for failing to meet "case review and enforcement of discovery obligations" and discussing failure to search deponent's email).

3. 130 S. Ct. 2619 (2010).

4. Quoted in A. Harmon, *Corporate Delete Keys Busy as E-Mail Turns Up in Court,* N.Y. Times, Nov. 11, 1998, http://www.nytimes.com/1998/11/11/business/corporate-delete-keys-busy-as-e-mail-turns-up-in-court.html. "Now, Amazon is among the growing ranks of companies that are imposing new restrictions on E-mail." *Id.* "The second-most important question we must face, after choosing to communicate at all, becomes how to deliver what we want to say." J. Freeman, The Tyranny of E-Mail (Scribner 2009).

5. Pursuant to 42 U.S.C. Sec. 3302, the archivist promulgates regulations governing disposal of records and, additionally, some records of criminal activity must be expunged, e.g., 19 U.S.C. Sec. 3607.

of overretention with the risks of improper destruction. Unfortunately, attorneys and their clients tend to forget that just saving everything and/or mismanaging unnecessary documents, paper or electronic, can often constitute a significant danger in terms of cost to the company, and also legal exposure.

Consider the disaster that befell the Boeing Co. In 1997, the world's largest aircraft manufacturer found itself confronted with a class action suit alleging securities fraud.[6] In a deposition, the plaintiffs' attorney learned that Boeing had some 14,000 email backup tapes stored in a Washington, D.C., warehouse. Naturally, the attorney demanded the tapes, and while the company tried unsuccessfully to narrow the scope of discovery, it realized to its horror that due to the technology that was available at the time, it was unable to tell whose emails were on which tapes without fully restoring the backups to a server. The situation was further complicated by the fact that Boeing used several email systems and its technology department was not centralized but scattered throughout the world.

Not only had Boeing retained far more data than what was required, its method of backup was woefully disorganized. In the end, it cost Boeing a fortune to restore all of the tapes, and then cull through all the data to pick out what was necessary for production. The unhappy result was that the content of the tapes was so sufficiently damning that Boeing finally decided to cut its losses and concluded the lawsuit by settling for $92.5 million.[7]

While the technology has progressed in this area,[8] the principle still holds true, and the entire Boeing misadventure should serve as a warning that document retention policies and the organization of retained ESI should be a foundational consideration for all corporate and law firm planning.[9] In fact, similar cases to the Boeing fiasco as well as other cases involving the spoliation (destruction or altering) of evidence over the last decade have fueled many entities to move records management and computer usage to the forefront of their priorities and agenda. The risks of not doing so are substantial.

---

6. See Julius Melnitzer, *Keeping Track of the Invisible Paper Trail: What Legal Departments Can Learn from Boeing's Experience*, Corporate Legal Times, Feb. 2003.

7. *Id.*

8. See Chapter 26.

9. S. Nelson & J. Simek, *Law Firm Document Retention Policies*, Law Prac. Today (July 2004), http://www.abanet.org/lpm/lpt/articles/ftr07046.html.

A. Historical context

Until the first decade of the twenty-first century, computer usage and records management policies often played only a minor role in many corporations because computer use and access were limited by available technology, and the risks of mismanagement were underappreciated. During the 1960s and 1970s, for example, corporations began using mainframe computers to process and store information, but these mainframes were self-contained islands of ESI with minimal interoperability with other computer systems and with very limited storage capacity. Even with the advent of the personal computer in the 1980s, corporations continued to keep computers isolated as individual workstations, which were rarely if ever linked among each other or into a larger network. As a result, the storage of ESI was limited to the physical memory of the computing device or where the storage device was located as was the case with mainframes.

It was not until the late 1980s that networking technology developed by Novell allowed corporations to build local area networks (LANs; networks among computers within a building) and eventually wide area networks (WANs; networks of computers between remote divisions). Yet at the still-early stages of this networking technology, there was little email and ESI was mostly limited to internal documents, or other digital data such as databases, and it was stored within the physical boundaries of the business.

By the late 1990s, and into the twenty-first century, networking protocols were standardized using Internet standards, and the commercialization of technology exploded.[10] Information transmission and storage began to proliferate internally and externally from corporations as the communication protocols were optimized. With this standardization of communication protocols also came increased bandwidth, and this resulted in increased speed. What used to take half an hour to send over the Internet suddenly became possible to send in a minute. ESI, whether small or large, could be transmitted in seconds, making it easier to send and receive large volumes of ESI outside the perimeter of the business. For instance, in the early 1990s, transmitting a 100-megabyte file across a dedicated communication circuit for use in the prepress operation of the printing industry would have taken several hours, but today that same file can be transmitted within seconds using a standard configuration.

10. See Appendix E.

In fact, keeping with the current trends, ESI is increasing at such a fast clip that its rate doubles nearly every four years. The proliferation of ESI, expressed in kilobytes, megabytes, and gigabytes, is illustrated in this table:

Year	Average Disk Space per Person
1983	20K
1996	28MB
2000	472MB
2004	4.2GB
2008	9.6GB

It is this exponential growth of ESI along with the increase in versatility, miniaturization, and portability of computing and storage devices used by employees and individuals that has resulted in the need for corporations to adopt policies and technology to manage their employees' use of their information technology and to manage the creation, use, and storage of their ESI.

The future, too, promises daunting challenges as computing and storage devices continue to be miniaturized, nanotechnology continues to be commercialized, and physical storage devices continue to become more portable, including the new trend toward "cloud," or browser-based, application access, because the ESI for a corporation could be located nearly anywhere in the world.

B. The important players in information technology

Attorneys who are assisting clients with technology usage, ESI storage, or electronic discovery obviously must understand a company's organizational structure and technical infrastructure that guides and manages the client's information technology systems. Four key components of such structure are the records management plan, the computer usage policy, the network "map,"[11] and the organizational chart of the IT department. Once an attorney understands and is familiar with the organization's structure, it will become far easier for the attorney to locate relevant ESI, find knowledgeable parties who can help the attorney understand the system, and identify the appropriate custodians of records, often called "key players." There are critical IT functions in an

11. A network "map" or data plan is a diagram of the computer network, and is beyond the scope of this chapter. For a sample data map, see chapter 14.

organization that may be carried out by one person or several depending on the size of the company, either inside the company or as an outsourced service provided by a third-party entity. This top-to-bottom approach helps an attorney identify ESI and its locations, relevant risks related to the ESI and its locations, and relevant or responsive ESI, whether prior to or during litigation.

The organizational structure and analysis of these roles is generally straightforward when the company is not within the media, publishing, or information technology industries.

(1) Nontechnology companies

In most companies, IT functions are fairly predictable and straight-lined among the staff, managers, directors, and chief technology officers (CTOs).[12] The figure highlights a typical IT department; the number of discrete job classifications normally depends on the size of the entity.

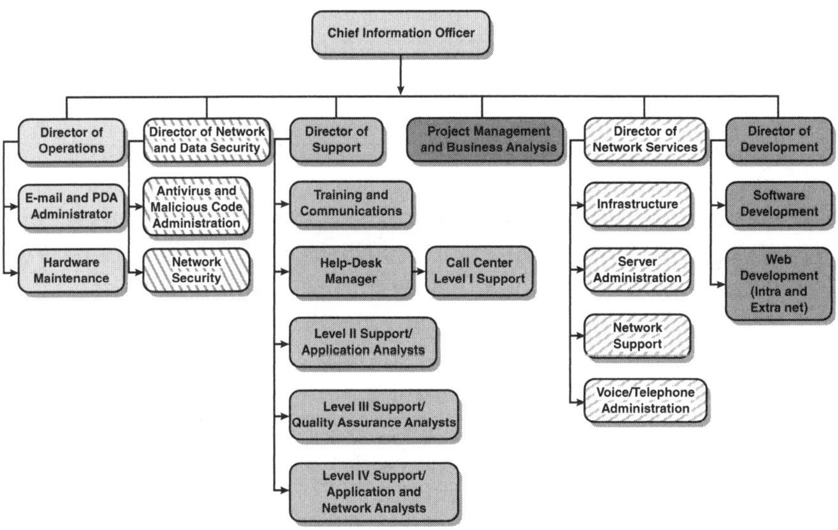

The purpose of the IT department is fairly specific. It keeps the computer systems operational, makes it accessible for end users, tracks and deploys appropriate upgrades to applications as they become available, outlines and advises the company as to what emerging technology would be appropriate to incorporate, and provides security to the network and ESI. In recent years, the IT department has taken on a somewhat larger role with the business,

12. There is no industry-wide uniformity in nomenclature. What one business calls a CTO may be called a chief information officer (CIO) in another.

and will act as an engine of innovation, finding new ways to make business processes more efficient and profitable. In these cases, usually the CTO is more business minded and uses the IT department to drive business initiatives, and the lines between business and IT functions may not be clear because individuals from other departments may be central to such innovation yet not identified within the IT organization.

Because the technology arena is still so relatively new, it can be difficult to identify what the function of each individual is within an organization as standards do not often exist for job classifications within IT. Rather, it is wiser to look at job descriptions within a particular organization to identify who is responsible for what aspect of the technology and workflow. Even so, the job descriptions of each role within the IT department can be complex to a layperson reviewing job specifications; outside observers who are not familiar with IT will sometimes fail to understand what each individual is responsible for on a daily basis. The box offers a brief summary of each job classification within a typical IT department of a non-technology-related industry.

Chief Information Officer—leads the information processing, safeguarding, and creation of the enterprise, and is responsible for all information technology functions of the enterprise, including computer system operations, help desks, data centers, production scheduling functions, computer program development, technical service centers, computer system operations, and communication networks (including both voice and data).

- **Director of Operations**—directs the day-to-day activities of the enterprise's information systems including, but not limited to, supervising the acquisition and maintenance of all hardware systems including servers and portable devices.
    - **Email and PDA Administration**—provides programming and operational support for groupware and software applications, such as Microsoft Exchange, Lotus Notes, and Novell Groupwise, and integrates technologies for devices such as cell phones, PDAs, and Blackberry, smart phones, Android devices, iPhones, and iPad.

- **Hardware Maintenance**—provides operational support for personal computers and for mid-range and large systems for ESI; responsible for storage, operating systems, systems management, performance tuning and optimization, and disaster recovery. Moves and places all hardware within the enterprise.

- **Director of Network and Data Security**—recommends, designs, and develops integrated security solutions that ensure that proprietary/confidential data and systems are protected from intruders; responsibilities include, but are not limited to, configuring and validating secure systems and testing security products and systems to detect security weakness and for compliance assurance.
  - **Antivirus and Malicious Code Administration**—manages the selection, implementation, testing, and maintenance of antivirus and malicious code (spam, spyware, and adware) hardware and software; applies updates and upgrades to such hardware and software and modifies the design of such systems.
  - **Network Security**—manages the selection, implementation, testing, and maintenance of firewalls; applies updates and upgrades to the firewalls and routers and modifies security design to maintain both software and hardware systems.
- **Director of Support**—acts as a liaison between employees and departments within the enterprise to ensure that all online, voice, network, and hardware and software-related problems are processed and resolved in an accurate and timely manner and provides assistance, coordination, and follow-up on user questions.
  - **Training and Communications**—trains users in the general application and use of computer hardware and software and determines the general user training needs; designs, develops, and delivers course curricula, teaching tools, and methodologies that meet both general and specific user needs.

- **Help Desk Manager**—manages the help desk and call center and the escalation process if problems cannot be resolved in a timely manner or within the call center.
- **Level I Support—Call Center**—provides technical assistance to all users within the enterprise through various methods that include answering questions by phone, email, and deskside assistance; maintains the Help Desk database and documentation regarding the end user interaction.
- **Level II Support—Application Analysts**—deploy, upgrade, and maintain applications within the enterprise and the second tier of support beyond the Help Desk/Call Center in the escalation process.
- **Level III Support—Quality Assurance Analysts**—test every application and/or hardware process upgrade or modification that is scheduled to be deployed to the enterprise so as to minimize disruption to the end user population; are the third tier of support beyond the Help Desk/Call Center in the escalation process.
- **Level IV Support—Application and Network Analysts**—investigate and assess services, software, and hardware to solve issues that the business analysts identify regarding the workflow within the enterprise; research and make recommendations regarding new products and trends within the industry; are the fourth tier of support within the Help Desk/Call Center escalation process.

- **Project Management and Business Analysis**—develops queries, analyses, and reports aimed at understanding and documenting enterprise system performance; designs baseline expectations for comparing results to goals; monitors performance metrics and trends.
- **Director of Network Services**—designs, installs, maintains, tests, and manages networks and their

devices (including, but not limited to, bridges, hubs, routers, switches, and gateways), including LANs, WANs, and other networks; supports client server applications and provides telephone support, high-speed or real-time audio, and video support.

- **Infrastructure**—designs, implements, tests, and supports the enterprise's infrastructure for computers, LANs, WANs such as satellite, laser, microwave, and radio links, and/or LANs for wireless devices and stations within buildings or the local geographical area.
- **Server Administration**—designs, maintains, implements, tests, and supports web servers and applications servers.
- **Network Support**—responsible for any network connectivity issues reported by the Help Desk/ Call Center and for the physical wiring of the network, and any wireless hardware that is in use by the enterprise.
- **Voice/Telephone Administration**—designs, develops, and tests telecommunications systems and/or call centers including, but not limited to, software and hardware systems, radio frequency and microwave circuits, assemblies, and subsystems.

- **Director of Development**—designs, specifies, codes, tests, debugs, maintains, and documents computer software programs; helps users by identifying problems and designing integrated solutions.
    - **Software Development**—designs, prototypes, tests, and writes applications and services using a number of application programming languages utilizing third-party software, originally authored software, or software subject to open source standards. These are the actual programmers within the enterprise.
    - **Web Development (Intra and Extra net)**—designs, tests, prototypes, develops, and implements applications and services using a number of web programming languages and services.

(2) *Technology products and services companies*

As mentioned above, job description analysis becomes even more difficult when the company is in the IT, media, publishing, or information technology industries, as not only are the titles of the position sometimes ambiguous, the individual job functions might be as well. For example, some companies in the business of providing a particular technology product and/or service may place a mini-IT department within a division that is identified as a product, yet none of those functions are listed on the IT department's organization chart. The individuals in this product division may often know more of the technical details of the specific product or service than their counterparts in the IT department, who may only provide the back-office tools that facilitate the operations of the product or service, rather than its functionality. To give one example, a product division of an online media company may deploy and maintain a sophisticated digital product that tracks weather and traffic-related data central to corporate revenue, while the IT department will manage core business systems, such as company-wide email, calendaring, word processing, and hosting.

(3) *Other key individuals*

In addition to the IT personnel, there are other individuals who should be considered when preparing a computer usage and information management strategy. Among them are departed employees, legal hold administrators, human resources personnel, management, and outside vendors.

The separation of an individual from a company can be a critical event in the context of ESI management. Departing employees are often the source of trade secret theft (e.g., stealing customer information), and they often take with them their former employer's company computing devices (e.g., smartphones) that store original[13] business ESI that may someday be necessary in connection with litigation and/or investigations. Companies must be vigilant about preventing such theft and have a detailed policy regarding the company's physical devices as well as ESI at the time an employee departs. Departing employees also may be the custodian of critical original business ESI, and mismanaging the

13. The word "original" is not used in an evidentiary sense. For a discussion of the original document rule, see chapters 10 and 24. Rather, the term "original" means that the file is the original file created that may or may not have a duplicate.

transfer of responsibility of the custodian of such records may lead to the loss of critical ESI, the violation of an existing litigation hold, and/or the loss of the integrity of the original ESI. For example, failing to safeguard and preserve the time and date stamp on the ESI while copying it from one computing device to another may cause the ESI to appear as if it was created on a later date than it was originally.[14]

Each level of management within a company is an absolutely essential group to assess in terms of the company's overall approach to ESI, whether an attorney is assisting a client with making necessary policy or is assessing where holes might exist in a client's or opponent's plan in connection with litigation, because it is important to identify the company's culture and view toward ESI as well as how the company is currently managing its ESI. For example, does management look at ESI policies as a necessary end to appease legal requirements or as an absolute necessity toward meeting the goals of the business? Policies for records management and computer usage that are supported by senior management and driven downward through an organization where the leadership leads by example are usually policies that have been identified and implemented universally throughout an organization. On the other hand, policies that are not adopted and driven downward by the leadership are oftentimes inadequate in terms of their scope and implementation and will also likely lead to increased costs in terms of expenses and inefficiencies associated with the mismanagement of ESI and to an increased risk in legal exposure that may result in costly sanctions.

The less the leadership is involved in these policies, the more likely one will find gaps between the policies and practices of their organization. These gaps will likely be exploited by experienced attorneys familiar with technology, seeking spoliation claims against an opponent, or potentially they will be the source of possible loss of evidence that could be pivotal to a claim or defense of the company.[15]

One essential consideration for attorneys considering knowledge management plans is that they need to be aware of clients and opponents that are outsourcing their storage of ESI, or using any business processes that directly result in the storage of original business ESI in the control of a third party. Third-party outsourcers/vendors may store ESI on servers (i.e., cloud computing)

14. See discussion *infra* § 3.
15. See chapter 8.

or they may provide services that enable users to create and store original ESI (email and hosting services) outside the direct control of a client and/or opponent.

Prior to litigation, attorneys should confirm with their clients whether there is a policy in place to govern the use of such third-party vendors. If such use is permitted, or if technology does not prevent such use, attorneys should confirm that the third-party vendor does not retain any original business ESI; if it does, the client should take measures to confirm that such ESI complies with the company policies in terms of retention, preservation, production, and destruction. The attorney should also confirm that there is a policy in place to require the company representatives to negotiate terms in agreements with such third-party vendors that require the third party to comply with litigation holds imposed on the company when there is a threat of litigation.

The quick identification of third-party storage becomes particularly important in the context of litigation as it is essential that the attorneys and/or client immediately notify third-party custodians of any applicable litigation hold and its associated requirements, as they may be responsible for all such data that is stored off-site. Also, during discovery, attorneys should quickly learn whether their opponents use third-party outsourcing vendors. If the opponent uses third-party vendors to store ESI, then the attorney should notify the opponent and/or vendor about its obligation to preserve any and all such ESI. In addition, attorneys should assess whether there is a gap between the opponent's policy and the third-party vendor practices. If there is a gap, then attorneys may be able to seek spoliation claims against the party.

2. Computer usage policies

A. Purpose and role of computer usage policies

A company's computer usage policy is one of the most important tools available to help manage, preserve, archive, safeguard, and produce original business ESI. Properly drafted, computer usage policies will help a company (in addition to safeguarding its assets, protecting its reputation,[16] and increasing its productivity) know where all of its original business ESI is located and where it

16. Claire Swire E-mail, http://en.wikipedia.org/wiki/Claire_Swire_e-mail ("The Claire Swire e-mail of 2000 was supposedly a very personal e-mail from Claire Swire to Bradley Chait, who worked at Norton Rose, a law firm in London. He forwarded it to six friends, one of whom in turn forwarded it further

is physically stored for easy retrieval, preserving, and safeguarding. The intent of these policies is essentially to allow a company to draw a box around all of its original business ESI so that there is a finite perimeter that the company must safeguard as well as a defined search area when retrieving vital ESI. Without such clear boundaries, a company trying to safeguard all of its ESI or trying to find all of its original business ESI will be in the proverbial position of trying to find a needle in a haystack or corking a hole in the boat with a sponge.

To create such boundaries, companies must draft computer usage policies that provide guidance and establish parameters that set clear and concise expectations for employees and anyone accessing the company systems to adhere to while using the company's property, computer systems, telecommunications systems, and/or bandwidth. Companies invest substantial sums in hardware, software, and maintenance of computer systems, and a company that would not think of allowing an employee to operate valuable machinery without adequate training and supervision should exercise no less than the same level of care with the computer systems that permit the company to operate. In short, one aspect of a properly drafted computer usage policy is to control risks and costs by delineating what is, and what is not, permitted usage of business assets.

Organizations routinely adopt computer usage policies to:

- govern employee use and access to computer systems, applications, data, mobile devices, and telephone systems, including whether business systems may be used for personal communications,
- provide guidelines for the use of services offered by third parties—web-based email, blogging software, instant messaging, and social networking sites (e.g., Facebook, MySpace, LinkedIn)—and for the Internet in general, such as whether there is any expectation of privacy and prohibiting accessing of objectionable sites,
- govern the storage of ESI and information on fixed, temporary, or mobile storage devices, whether they are owned, operated, or controlled by the employer, the employee, or a third party,

---

with the subject line of 'Do you know Claire Swire' until it spread worldwide within days, and received wide coverage in newspapers and television.").

- provide procedures to implement litigation holds, and
- provide procedures for controlling ESI when terminating employees[17] and divesting assets.

In the context of litigation, a properly drafted computer usage policy—one that provides clear boundaries where the original business ESI is located and that is followed in practice by the organization—serves two critical functions. First, the cost of litigation will be reduced because the legal department or attorneys will not need to waste time locating the data to be accessed when preparing for the case or producing documents in connection with the case. Second, if the policy accurately reflects the practice of the company, then there will be no gaps for the opposition to find and then exploit by asserting that the gap led to the spoliation of relevant ESI. On the other hand, knowing best practices in this area will enable attorneys to better identify what if any issues may exist with the opposition's policies and procedures that can be exploited with claims that potential spoliation may have occurred or claims about the reliability, authenticity, and/or accuracy of the opponent's ESI evidence.

Corporations that fail either to practice what is stated in their computer usage policies or who implement poorly drafted computer usage policies may be leaving themselves exposed to incur major litigation costs as well as risking the loss or theft of essential ESI, and the stakes likely will get higher and higher as we move further into the digital age. Three examples illustrating implications of computer usage policies follow:

- *Example #1.* Company A allows an employee to serve as an outside director of Charitable Corp. Company A's computer usage policy allows employees to use Company A's email and word processing systems for personal purposes, including in connection with the directorship. When Charitable Corp. is sued, Company A's ESI may be subject to subpoena as well as compliance with very costly discovery obligations. Company A's generosity has resulted in a substantial, unanticipated cost that could have been avoided had it had different computer usage policies in effect. Company A might well be displeased with the legal advice

17. *E.g.*, M. Jaron, *E-Discovery Issues in Business Downsizings and Closings*, Digital Discovery & e-Evidence (BNA) (Feb. 4, 2010).

it had—or had not—received if this cost came as a surprise, rather than as a known and voluntarily assumed risk.

- *Example #2*. Company B's computer usage policy does not prohibit employees from storing information on their local hard drive. Nor does it restrict storage to network drives. When Company B is sued, it may have a costly obligation to preserve some or all of those local drives, at a cost of approximately $750–$1,000 per drive, and sometimes higher depending on the type of data to be mined. Again, the failure of the computer usage policy to restrict storage has imposed a significant, unanticipated cost on Company B.
- *Example #3*. Company C is a nonparty construction manager involved in a number of large construction projects, including the Bronx Courthouse.[18] Its Bronx Courthouse records are subject to a subpoena. None of its other construction projects are involved. The problem presented is how to economically separate project-related ESI from its other ESI. The trial court notes that: "[The construction manager] did not want to produce emails that did not relate to the Bronx Courthouse project. This problem would have been avoided, of course, if [the construction manager] used a standard 'Re' line in its Bronx Courthouse emails to distinguish that project from its other work. It did not do so, however."[19] In short, a computer usage policy could have avoided a complex, costly issue.

The mechanics of implementing a computer usage policy will continue to be developed in the coming years. Although computer usage policies have been around for decades in corporate America, they have not historically played an important role in corporate governance nor have they been a focus or emphasis in litigation. Indeed, in the past they were seldom updated or monitored for compliance once they had been initially adopted by the corporation. As is the case with all corporate policies, the policies and procedures are only as good as the creation, revision, monitoring, and enforcement of such policies. Once a computer usage policy is incorporated into the business, the company must then establish procedures through which it can effectively monitor and enforce

18. William A. Gross Constr. Assocs., Inc. v. Am. Mfrs. Mut. Ins. Co., 256 F.R.D. 134 (S.D.N.Y. 2009).
19. *Id*. at 135.

computer usage, conduct audits, and enforce compliance to the policy, as well as identifying a process to update the policy as new technology becomes available. Now, and even more so as we move forward, these simple policies will play a critical role in corporate governance and litigation and the mechanics for compliance will be at the heart of the success or failure.

B. Content and scope of computer usage policies

The content of a typical computer usage policy has been changing from a stereotypical general corporate policy to one that contains detailed specifications that require careful and coordinated planning when preparing. Even though a policy may begin with general purpose and scope provisions, the policy is intended to provide an enforceable condition of employment for the users of vital business assets. One of the key points in a computer usage policy is whether use of the business's email and Internet systems is restricted to business use, or whether limited, personal use is permitted and, if so, whether there is any expectation of privacy with respect to ESI while using the systems for personal use. Additionally, companies may choose to prohibit email for certain types of communications, such as highly sensitive trade secrets.[20] They may provide different access rights to the various types of ESI within the organization. For example, the system administrator[21] and clerical staff might be prohibited from accessing health care (or other confidential) electronic information subject to the Health Information Portability and Accountability Act (HIPAA). Policies can incorporate password protocols, prohibit or regulate the use of flash drives and external hard drives, and/or require encryption of all sensitive data stored on any portable device; in some cases, sensitive data (credit card data, for instance) may require

20. Some companies have imposed partial email embargos: "Overwhelmed by e-mail? Some professionals are fighting back by declaring e-mail-free Fridays. . . ." M. Kessler, *Fridays Go from Casual to E-Mail-Free*," USA Today, Oct. 5, 2007, http://www.usatoday.com/tech/techinvestor/corporatenews/2007-10-04-no-email_N.htm. According to proponents, "E-mail isn't forbidden, but everyone is encouraged to phone or meet face-to-face. The goal is more direct, free-flowing communication and better exchange of ideas," *Id.*

21. In *Weaver v. Zenimax Media, Inc.*, 923 A.2d 1032 (Md. Ct. Spec. App. 2007), Zenimax's CTO, Weaver, produced certain information in discovery. During incursions into others' offices, he scanned hundreds of emails and printed some. While a computer usage policy would not likely stop a determined intrusion, at least it would make clear the violation of company policy.

encryption regardless of where it is stored. A computer usage policy might prohibit leaving a laptop computer or smartphone in an unattended vehicle and warn employees that if they use their home computer for business purposes, they may need to make it available in litigation. Also, it might remind employees about email etiquette and that email should be drafted as if it will appear on the front page of the newspaper,[22] which, in today's climate, might very well happen.

It is worth noting that restricting the employee's computer usage may conflict with the freedom to which many employees have become accustomed in the workplace as the technology arena has matured. However, while it is important to take this into consideration when implementing new policies, it should be stressed to all employees that these policies and procedures are being implemented to protect not only ESI but also the company itself—which also protects their jobs—and that relaxed policies will likely increase costs, lead to the theft of corporate assets, and/or lead to the tarnishing of a corporation's reputation. For example, many times when companies have allowed employees to use company IT systems for personal as well as business use, the resulting complications for discovery have led to increased hours for the legal team trying to cull through all of the ESI.

Also a common occurrence, especially as more and more companies opt to let employees work from home, is the use of web-based email and home computers, which most people consider a convenient option until litigation arises. In such circumstances, the duty to preserve ESI and produce it in response to discovery requests may be extended to the employee's home computers, and the third-party companies that operate mail service, which markedly increases the cost of preservation, processing, and production in litigation and also increases the likelihood of inconsistencies between the stated policy and the practice. These inconsistencies may lead to spoliation claims asserting that the company has breached its duty to preserve.

---

22. In 2003, one State of Maryland employee sent an email ending: "Please make this note disappear!" In the Appeal of Yellow Transp., MSBCA 2374, 13, http://www.msbca.state.md.us/decisions/pdf/2389yellow.pdf. The Maryland State Board of Contract Appeals noted: "People with nothing to hide do not put phrases such as 'Please make this note disappear!' into their communications." *Id.* at 34.

As was stated before, usage policies are only documents, and they are only as good as the company's ability to ensure compliance. Often well-meaning employees who do not have an adequate understanding of the usage policy in the course of doing business can easily (intentionally or unintentionally) disregard the policies. Even more challenging today is when the implementation of computer usage policies is solely through the use of technology; then attorneys may be required to understand the rules used to drive the technology (by interviewing stakeholders and reviewing technology configurations) before they are able to identify potential inconsistencies in the rules that may lead to further inquiries to find documents or that may require preparing defenses to, or making claims of, spoliation of evidence. If compliance with the policy is under an honor system, then attorneys must interview the custodian of the pertinent records to determine whether the policy reflects the actual business practices before moving forward with litigation strategies.

It also may be necessary to expand a review of a company's computer usage beyond the computer usage policy itself. There may be several other policies that address computer usage, such as (1) human resource policies; (2) marketing policies; and (3) intellectual property policies. For example, a marketing policy may describe how employees should conduct themselves on the Internet while representing the company or when using the company's credentials, as in, for example, posting a blog entry on behalf of the company.[23] Obviously, policies regarding use of racially derogatory, sexually explicit, and other similar materials are important and are typically addressed in general human resource policies regulating all corporate communications in general.

Attorneys should also assess whether there is any general human resource policy that may appear to address other company activities that may apply unknowingly to company ESI or to company services. For example, a company's physical bulletin board in the workplace will likely be subject to certain general human resource policies and laws that may or may not govern an online bulletin board made available by the company to its employees

23. *See* D. Weiss, *Akin Gump Chair Hits Partner's Personal Blog on "Ugly" Indian Prayer*, ABA J., Jan. 19, 2011, http://www.abajournal.com/news/article/akin_gump_chair_hits_partners_personal_blog_post_on_ugly_indian_prayer/ (Akin Gump partner apologizes for a posting made to a third-party blog).

via the company intranet. If such lapses are found during litigation, then it is best to apply the general rule to the specific activity to assess compliance, whether by your client or the opponent. Of course, if the lapse is found prior to a litigation hold, then the policy should be revised and policies corrected.

C. Considerations that one should assess prior to litigation holds or to evaluate the opposition's behavior during litigation

There are several important concepts worth examining when reviewing computer usage policies. Prior to litigation, the biggest issues are whether the policy is comprehensive in scope and whether the company's business process is reflected accurately in the policy. During litigation, the largest concerns are whether the client is complying with the applicable litigation holds and is accurately assessing the scope and locations of possible responsive documents for litigation preparation or opponent's discovery requests. The following are commonly overlooked areas that may lead to an inconsistency between the policy and practice and/or may be problematic for a party during litigation:

(1) Business versus personal use

Most computer usage policies will address whether a company's systems should be used solely for business purposes. Obviously, if the policy bans using company equipment for personal purposes, the risk of uncovering personal ESI, which may increase the cost of discovery or, worse, expose the company to additional liability, will be significantly reduced. Such a policy obviously may conflict with the needs of the employees to perform necessary personal functions such as coordinating car pools for their children. Balancing this conflict is admittedly a challenge for most companies. Whether to take the risk, however, should be an informed business judgment.

Attorneys should thoroughly review computer usage policies and investigate company implementation of such policies if personal use of the company systems is permitted whether directly through policy or indirectly through ineffective technology. If personal use is permitted, then attorneys should determine how extensive personal usage is within the company, how the company stores personal ESI, and whether there is a method internally to quarantine personal ESI from business ESI. In some cases, a company may segregate personal ESI from business ESI by technical measures, such as through folders or document management systems that may or may not require human interaction to tag or label such ESI.

During litigation, attorneys should query their clients to assess how personal ESI is managed and should probe the opponent on the same topic. With respect to clients, attorneys should determine whether personal ESI is collected, stored, and preserved prior to discovery to assess whether employees using the computer systems for personal use will present any additional burdens on the litigation process. If personal use is not isolated from business use or if personal ESI is not isolated from business ESI, the following may likely occur: (1) increased litigation costs because the personal ESI will be processed in connection with production; (2) increased litigation costs because the personal ESI may become obstacles to efficiently producing documents during discovery; and (3) increased legal exposure for the company because statements made in personal ESI (e.g., employee communications with their lawyers) or conduct revealed by the personal ESI may be attributable to the company (e.g., associating individual conduct like downloading and/or distributing pornography or copyrighted material).[24] For example, back in the early days of Napster, many employees downloaded songs from the Internet not realizing that such acts were copyright infringement, and network administrators were horrified to find upon requests for production that much of this illegal content was being stored on company hard drives. In the context of an adversary, the same initial inquiry should be made in terms of personal use. Attorneys should then assess whether the personal ESI is commingled or not, whether personal use is limited, and whether any personal acts or statements can be attributable to the client or the opposition.

A recent Supreme Court case navigated the boundary between personal use of company computer resources and the expectation of privacy for government employees. In *City of Ontario v. Quon*, the Supreme Court overturned a lower court's decision involving a government employee's use of a computing device and the employee's expectation of privacy.[25] The California lower court held that the City's computer usage policy was not sufficient to

24. Martha Neil, *Wrongful Death Suit Against Ex-Partner Creates Document Dilemma for Arent Fox*, ABA J., http://www.abajournal.com/news/article/wrongful_death_suit_against_ex-partner_creates_document_dilemma_for_arent_f/
25. 130 S. Ct. 2619 (2010).

defeat the employee's expectation of privacy even though the policy had a general limitation that stated the City's equipment was intended to be used in business purposes only.[26] In overruling the lower court's decisions, which were more concerned with the government searching its employees, the Supreme Court held that the search was reasonable in that the City had a legitimate interest in determining whether it was paying for its employees to make personal communications through City equipment.[27] In reaching this decision, the Supreme Court refused to address the issue of whether an employee using the City equipment for personal use was in violation of the policy. The Court noted in dicta that the same search would be "regarded as reasonable and normal in the private-employee context."[28]

(2) Prohibitions

It is important that a computer usage policy be easy to enforce and monitor and that it be as specific as possible regarding prohibited activity, as well as what is allowed. In fact, most computer usage policies will list restricted communications, messaging, actions, and activities in order to establish acceptable and unacceptable behavior by employees using the company computer systems.

Computer usage policies that contain a specific list of restricted activities will likely reduce a company's legal risks by distancing the company from employees' misuse of company resources, and will likely reduce its litigation costs by limiting where original business ESI is located. However, while a concise list is easiest to enforce and follow, attorneys must remain aware that any misuse that is not expressly forbidden by the company may likely increase the company's legal risk; thus, with the rate that technology changes, the laundry list should be amended frequently and immediately following any major case law that redefines ESI's parameters.

The company should ensure that all of the employees are informed immediately following any substantive changes to the policy. Some of the typical restrictions cover the following areas:

- personal Internet usage; if permitted, limitations may be placed on time, actions, or substance,
- third-party service or storage of business ESI,

26. *Id.* at 2626–27.
27. *Id.* at 2632–33.
28. *Id.* at 2623.

- storing or transmittal of trade secrets from their original location,
- inappropriate dissemination or use of copyrighted materials, including articles and software, that are not properly licensed or that are in violation of copyright laws or software license agreements,
- sending, receiving, or printing of proprietary data, trade secrets, or other confidential information that belongs to the company and that is outside the ordinary, authorized course of the employee's business activities,
- exchange or printing of messages with content that would reasonably be considered offensive or disruptive to any employee, owner, individual, or group,
- transmittal of offensive, harassing, defaming, threatening, or discriminating statements or language that disparages others including, but not limited to, messages based on race, national origin, gender, sexual orientation, age, disability, religion, or any other characteristic protected by law,
- sending or soliciting of sexually oriented, obscene, or pornographic messages or images,
- sending of disruptive content including the forwarding of chain letters, items for sale, and other non-business-related information that a reasonable person would find to be a nuisance; unreasonable use of products that would use an inordinate amount of bandwidth and thus cause the network to slow down for all users of the system; sending of large attachments through the email system that would slow down the email system for everyone,
- operating a business, usurping business opportunities, or soliciting money for personal gain,
- advancement of individual political or religious views or searching for jobs outside of the company,
- gambling or engaging in any other activity in violation of local, state, or federal law,
- fraudulent transmission of messages using an alias attached to the company domain, or using another company employee's email account to send messages, or any transmission of email that does not clearly display the sender's name, unless the sender is explicitly authorized to send email for another person and the sender's name is clearly rendered on the email,

- expression of personal opinions in blogs, emails, or on the Internet using company credentials unless the user has obtained prior consent from the company,
- solicitation of political, religious, charitable, or outside business interests,
- transmittal of privileged communications between the employee and a third party such as an attorney, accountant, health care provider, or clergy,
- transmittal of content that violates any law, rule, regulation, or company policy or business interest, and
- use of company technology in a manner that is likely to cause network congestion or significantly hamper the ability of other people to access and use the company technology.

(3) Employee Internet usage

One of the more important components of a computer usage policy is whether a company grants its employees access to the Internet. The use of the Internet to perform job functions has become nearly a necessity for most employees. Once a company decides to permit Internet access, however, the lines between personal use and business use of the company computer systems become harder to monitor and regulate.

Access to the Internet will likely permit employees to access third-party vendor services, such as Yahoo mail, which may be used for personal and/or business purposes and which may or may not store original business ESI. The computer usage policies will generally prohibit certain types of these activities such as stating that employees cannot use, or store original business ESI at, these nonsanctioned providers. When users are permitted to access the Internet, additional restrictions required to be included in computer usage policies range from governing the usage and storage of ESI on or through third-party computer systems to governing how users communicate through the use of company computers. Policies may also direct that personal Internet usage be limited to, for example, lunch breaks. They may also include the acquisition of blocking software to limit access to certain types of websites.[29]

29. *Air Force Reportedly Blocks Sites Posting WikiLeaks*, Huffington Post, Dec. 14, 2010, http://www.huffingtonpost.com/2010/12/14/air-force-wikileaks_n_796799.html.

A recent New Jersey Supreme Court decision helped navigate the boundaries of personal Internet use under a computer usage policy that was ambiguous regarding the employees' activities. The court in *Stengart v. Loving Care Agency Inc*[30] had to evaluate the effect that the attorney-client privilege had on a company whose employee was using a third-party email system from work to communicate with her lawyer. Stengart used her employer's laptop to communicate with her attorney through her personal Yahoo email account about an anticipated lawsuit against her employer. After the employee filed the discrimination suit, her then ex-employer found numerous emails on the company computer between Stengart and her attorney. The employer's computer usage policy was nearly identical to the policy in the *Quon* decision, except that the policy provided that "occasional personal use is permitted."

This court found that there were two "ambiguities" with the computer usage policy that "cast doubt over the legitimacy of the company's attempt to seize and review personal emails sent through the company's computer via the employee's personal email account."[31] The court found that the policy did not clearly define the scope of the company computer systems and that a reasonable person could conclude that not all emails are company property because the policy expressly permits the employees to use the systems for occasional personal use.[32] As a result of the decision, the employer incurred greater discovery costs because it had to separate ESI between responsive and nonresponsive ESI, all while honoring the employee's attorney-client-privileged ESI.

30. 990 A.2d 650 (N.J. 2010).

31. *Id.* at 659.

32. *Id.* If an employee has a privilege against an employer reviewing data on the employer's computer system, the cost of preservation and production may be substantially higher because the employer must determine whether a communication is privileged before reviewing it. Thus, a policy that permits employees unrestricted use of the employer's email system with an expectation of privacy may impose unanticipated costs on the employer in the event of litigation. The question of whether such a privilege exists inevitably involves computer usage policies. *E.g.*, Scott v. Beth Israel Hosp., 2007 WL 3053351 (NY. Sup. 2007); Banks v. Mario Indust. of VA., Inc., 650 S.E.2d 687 (Va. 2007); *In re* Asia Global Crossing, Ltd., 322 B.R. 247 (S.D.N.Y. 2005); Curto v. Med. World Commc'ns, Inc., No. 03-CV-6327, 2006 WL 1318387 (E.D.N.Y. 2006); P. RICE, ELECTRONIC EVIDENCE: LAW AND PRACTICE 154 (ABA 2005); J. Gergacz, *Employees' Use of Employer Computers to Communicate with their Own Attorneys and the Attorney-Client Privilege*, 10 COMPUTER L. REV. & TECH. J. 269 (2007).

Even though some companies today prevent Internet access in the workplace either through policy, technology, or both, there are considerably more companies today that permit it. Obviously, if employees do not have access to the Internet, then no additional investigation is needed with respect to Internet usage other than to confirm that the policy reflects the practice. If, however, Internet access is granted to employees, then there are a number of additional queries that are necessary before assessing the company's risk or vulnerabilities arising from employee Internet usage.

If an employer grants Internet access to its employees, the employer will typically address in its computer usage policy whether the Internet use is solely for business use or whether it is for business and personal use. Although the risks are a little different between solely business use versus business and personal use, there are still several additional risks that arise when employers grant employees the right to use the Internet for personal uses.

The *Stengart* court made it abundantly clear that when granting Internet access for personal use, the line between what is considered to be the company computer systems and what is considered to be a third-party computer system may become less clear, unless companies provide detailed specifications outlining the boundaries of what a company deems to be its systems within its policies. More significantly, as the *Stengart* court held, an employee's expectation of privacy may attach to some personal ESI stored on company computers if the restrictions on computer use are not specific enough to prohibit such employee uses.

If the Internet is used for business purposes, then employers typically adopt in their computer usage policy restrictions and procedures for posting content and conducting other business on the Internet. Otherwise, the employer may be at risk because employee actions and statements may be attributed to the company itself if the employee is acting within the employee's scope of employment (i.e., there is no restriction in the employer's policy that prohibited such acts) or if the employee appears to others to be acting within the scope of his or her employment.

The typical usage policies of companies that permit their employees to use the Internet often limit the extent to which employees are permitted to use third-party providers for services or storage. The proliferation of inexpensive, user-friendly web-based services has made the workplace much more efficient, but it has also decentralized the storage of business ESI because many of these service providers are outside of the contracting process for the company.

For example, employees who contract directly with vendors to obtain services like Google Docs or Yahoo email are likely creating islands of original business ESI that most likely will be excluded from the company document and litigation management policies regarding retention, litigation holds, and production. These islands will increase discovery costs, increase the likelihood of mismanaging evidence that may be useful for a defense or claim in litigation, and/or increase the likelihood of mismanaging discovery including implementing litigation holds. For these reasons, companies typically include restrictions in their computer usage policy that outline the extent to which employees are permitted to engage in such activities.

Attorneys reviewing computer usage policies regardless of the purpose of the review should examine whether the company directly or indirectly (i.e., by not having controls) grants Internet use by the employees, and if so, whether use is limited to business or personal use. Upon learning of such use, attorneys must query further to determine the scope and risks, and if it is prior to litigation, attorneys should conform the policy to employees' conduct, or vice versa. If litigation has commenced, attorneys should make the inquiries to confirm that the client is preserving potentially responsive information for the case, as well as complying with litigation holds. If the attorney is reviewing the opponent's policy, an assessment should be made on whether there are any inconsistencies between the policy and the work practices of the employees, and if so, whether this would warrant possible spoliation claims. The key to all of the inquiries on this issue is how extensive the restrictions are on computer use set forth in the computer usage policy, and whether employees complied with them.

(4) Monitoring the computer usage policy and employee compliance

Employers often disclose in computer usage policies whether the company monitors employees while the employees use the computer systems. Sometimes this notification may be made in a more general human resource policy. The majority of the jurisdictions do not require an employer to notify its employees of any surveillance measures it might deploy, but many employers as a matter of practice, courtesy, and ensuring legal compliance in the states where disclosure is required will disclose the practice of surveillance to their employees.

Computer usage policies often address and disclose how the organization intends to monitor employee activity within the computer system as well as inside the company's facilities. While such monitoring efforts may initially lead to tensions between the employees and management, they do provide a company with many benefits, and generally if such policies are explained to the employees, they see the necessity to protect the company, and thus their jobs.

Companies may elect to monitor their employees for various reasons. One popular reason that is critical to many companies is to provide a deterrent against misbehavior, such as preventing trade secret theft. It is estimated that employees account for nearly 60 percent of reported trade secret thefts.[33] Another common reason that companies monitor employees is to identify more efficient ways to complete business processes and optimize workflow, by utilizing the information obtained through monitoring employees to facilitate improving software functionality and/or provide users with more targeted training. By way of example, a company may monitor its computer systems through the use of applications like keyloggers that record keyboard activity and then take this information to assess how users move through a menu structure of an application so that the company can target training programs to users who do not utilize the software efficiently. Companies may also routinely monitor the content of email to prevent employment discrimination.

Within the context of litigation, a company computer usage policy should be reviewed by attorneys to determine if such monitoring is part of a company's stated policy; the security team should be interviewed to determine if such practices are utilized even if not stated in the usage documentation; any litigation holds issued should extend to these activities if applicable; and the information retained by them should be considered in connection with factual development and/or discovery. Such monitoring may be critical.

33. B. Krebs, *Data Theft Common by Departing Employees*, Wash. Post, Feb. 26, 2009, http://www.washingtonpost.com/wp-dyn/content/article/2009/02/26/AR2009022601821.html.

(5) Foreign software

Through computer usage policies, companies often prohibit employees from installing software on their computer systems (or permit it under extremely tight requirements). Companies may prohibit employee software installations for a number of reasons. Among the most common are to obtain operational efficiencies and limit legal risks and exposure.

Companies that prohibit employee software installation will likely improve the efficiency of their operations, because it is easier to track and maintain data integrity of the files and information generated by the users as well as to maintain the standardization of stored ESI through the utilization of approved software applications such as document management systems.

Among the many other reasons that software installation by individual users is discouraged in a corporate environment is that such a policy reduces the costs associated with help desk and other support services; reduces the security risks for the company, including infection of the company systems with malware, spyware and other forms of malicious code and the associated costs of remediating damages once exposed; and reduces the risk of perimeter security breaches because malicious code is one of the sources that makes company systems vulnerable to outside attacks.

Companies that prohibit employees from installing software on their systems may also reduce legal risks, costs, and exposures when such policies are combined with proper document management systems. Among the benefits arising from such policies are that (1) original business ESI will be located more efficiently when generated by company software applications that fall within the company controls and processes; (2) original business ESI will be more likely identified for the purposes of litigation holds and preservation; (3) original business ESI that is more easily located may aid in the development of the company's defenses or claims; and (4) the incidence of unlicensed software making its way into the corporate environment is reduced. The auditing of workstations and controlling of software installations on company systems potentially reduces litigation costs as file formats are standardized between applications, and the processing of the ESI will be consistent and efficient.

When a company allows employees to install software applications on its systems without tight controls, the company is likely creating a number of potential problems for itself. The most significant is that the company may be exposing itself to spoliation claims by its opponents. If the company is unaware of ESI generated by users who use such applications, then litigation hold administrators will most likely fail to preserve such ESI when deploying litigation holds, and ESI will be missed both in the preservation efforts and possibly the collection efforts. Thus, the litigation costs and operation costs will likely rise for the reasons described above, which leads most companies to prohibit such practices, as the costs far outweigh the benefits of allowing such activity.

Attorneys reviewing computer usage policies should examine the policy for how it addresses employee-installed software and should also review the company's practice with respect to such software. Keep in mind that technology controls may prevent such actions even though the usage policies and employees may not address it specifically. Also, it is important to note that while many companies do limit the installation of outside software, many employees figure out how to get around the policy and may in fact have software installed that is not approved by the company.

Obviously, before litigation, the biggest issue is whether the policy, technology, and practice conform to one another. If they do not, then the attorney should help ensure that the policy and practice of the employees are consistent. If you are performing a review of your client's company during ongoing litigation, you should immediately identify whether employees have the capability to install foreign software and then determine the scope of such capability (perhaps by requesting a software audit of workstations that are in question) for the purposes of deploying litigation holds and preparing for evidence collection in your client's case. If you are performing a review on an opponent during discovery, you should also perform a foreign software review to determine the possible locations of responsive documents and, more importantly, to determine whether the opponent is properly preserving and producing original business ESI.

(6) Security and access

In today's climate, companies are making computer security one of their highest priorities, both in the form of safeguarding digital assets from outside intruders and in granting employees controlled access to their systems. Companies have ascertained that it is in their best interest to make security a higher priority as corporate wealth continues to transition from tangible assets to intangible assets, such as trade secrets. Also, in some cases, companies may fall within the scope of federal and state regulations that mandate the levels of intruder security and user access, such as HIPAA and GLBA.[34]

Security and access controls can be attained through several different methods maintained by the technology department. While often these security policies and access controls are delineated within the computer usage policies and procedures documentation, it is important to interview the CTO, senior network administrators, and the senior security officer regarding these issues to obtain a complete picture of how data and perimeter security and ESI access controls are handled within a company.

To assist IT departments in applying access controls to original business ESI, companies will often adopt what is known as a trade secret scale. A trade secret scale groups documents according to who should have access to them, similar to the different security levels utilized by the federal government. At one end of the scale is valuable ESI with limited employee access, and on the other end of the scale is ESI with unlimited employee and public access. ESI in the form of formulas for products, such as beverages and food recipes, would be an example of ESI with limited access and restricted distribution controls. ESI in the form of marketing materials, such as marketing brochures and website pages, would be an example of ESI with open access and unlimited, unrestricted distribution.

When a company has weak security and access controls or the lack thereof, it can find itself facing a number of potentially serious challenges. For instance, if anyone can access the trade secrets of the company, then the trade secrets status could be lost or may be compromised intentionally by theft, or unintentionally by employees who accidently disclose those trade secrets, which could in a worst case scenario put the company out of business. We have seen the impact of such action by employees from the recent disclosures made by WikiLeaks involving the United States' military and foreign affairs records. Also, the potential threat from outside the company can be damaging, as the integrity of all of the ESI contained in company systems can be called into question if intruders

34. The Gramm-Leach-Bliley Act (GLBA) is also known as the Financial Services Modernization Act of 1999.

are able to penetrate the security from outside and tamper with the ESI.

There have been a number of courts that have addressed the scope of security and access controls. The most extensive decisions in this area involve the Computer Fraud and Abuse Act.[35] For some claims, to prove Computer Fraud and Abuse, the federal or state government or the plaintiff must prove data theft. One element of data theft is whether an employee or other individual accessed the data "without authorization" or exceeded "authorized access." This element captures both the third-party intruder into the company's systems and the employee who exceeds his or her access controls. Claims for data theft under the Computer Fraud and Abuse Act often derive from intellectual property theft.

In applying the Computer Fraud and Abuse Act to employee theft of trade secrets and the issue of whether or not the employee properly had access to the company trade secrets, the courts interpreting the phrase "without authorization" or exceeding "authorized access" appear to be splitting. The issue appears headed for resolution by higher courts.

One line of cases follows a Seventh Circuit decision in *International Airport Centers LLC v. Citrin*.[36] The Seventh Circuit held that when an employee breaches his or her duty of loyalty owed to the company, the employee's right to access the company systems is immediately terminated.[37] The Seventh Circuit applied agency principles to the employer and employee relationship. Under agency law, an employee who exceeds his or her agency relationship is not acting within the authorization of the principal, and accordingly, an employee who steals trade secrets from his or her employer's computer systems ceases having access to the employer's computer systems the moment the act commences.[38]

The logic found in *International Airport Centers* and the subsequent line of decisions is under attack. In the Ninth Circuit, the court in *LVRC Holding LLC v. Brekka*[39] refused to apply the agency theories adopted by the *International* court. The Ninth Circuit held that employees cannot be found to act "without authorization"

35. 18 U.S.C. § 1030.

36. 440 F.3d 418 (7th Cir. 2006).

37. *Id.* at 420-21

38. For a recent decision condemning "self help" to an opponent's ESI, see Glynn v. EDO Corp., 2010 WL 3294347 (D. Md. Aug. 20, 2010).

39. 581 F.3d 1127 (9th Cir. 2009).

in terms of accessing the employer's computer systems, because the employer gives employees "permission to use" the company computers at the commencement of their employment. In other words, the employee's purpose for accessing the information did not violate the plain language of the Computer Fraud and Abuse Act. As computer usage policies gain prominence and awareness, the decision in this court is likely to become the majority view.[40]

Attorneys reviewing computer usage policies and practices of their clients and opponents should be certain to perform a full and in-depth query on computer security and access controls whether prior to or during litigation. Prior to litigation, attorneys should be reviewing policies and practices and advising clients on the trade secret scale to confirm that policy mirrors practices, and should be adding restrictions on usage, such as "employees cannot use the company system to steal trade secrets," so that the client does not need to rely on case law to make it clear that computer systems cannot be used for such purposes.

During litigation, attorneys should review computer usage policies and practices to determine how a company utilizes security and access controls for a number of reasons, including whether the company permits proxy rights (as described later in this chapter). One case that highlights the value of this process involved a woman who worked for Oracle and accused CEO Larry Ellison of sexual harassment, based in part on an email that appeared to be authored by her manager. Oracle discovered, however, that the woman used proxy rights to author the email transmitted from her manager's account. The significance of a comprehensive computer usage policy regarding such rights is self-evident.

---

40. In *United States v. Rodriguez*, No. 09-15265, 2010 U.S. App. Lexis 26203 (11th Cir. Dec. 27, 2010), the Eleventh Circuit affirmed a lower court's conviction of a Social Security Agency employee who accessed the SSA's database for purposes unrelated to business and was convicted of a misdemeanor criminal offense under the Computer Fraud and Abuse Act for exceeding the scope of his authorization to access the SSA computer systems. *See also* M. Neil, "Husband Says Wife Cheated, but He's Charged with Felony After Reading Her E-Mail," ABA J. (Dec. 28, 2010), www.abajournal.com/news/article/husband_says_wife_cheated_but_he's_charged_with_felony_after_reading_her_e-m (husband faces a charge under the Computer Fraud and Abuse Act for allegedly gaining unauthorized access to his wife's personal email account during a domestic dispute).

In addition, if any trade secrets must be produced during discovery, the attorney should confirm the existence of the policy and implement appropriate procedures. Attorneys also should request intrusion logs from the security team to ascertain if the client's computer systems have been breached by intruders outside of the company. If in fact the system has been compromised, then the attorney may need to determine whether the intruder tampered with any ESI.

With respect to the opposition during litigation, attorneys should query their opponents on security and access controls to assess the degree of sophistication of such techniques and determine whether the policies are consistent with company practices. Among the many queries and document requests to make, attorneys may wish to query the opposing party regarding any security breaches, whether by outside intruders or by insiders to the organization (i.e., employees) who may have exceeded their authorization, in order to assess the integrity of the ESI on its system. If there have been any security breaches, then the attorney can use such information to challenge the authenticity of the ESI produced as evidence by the opposition.

(7) Remote network access

Typically, computer usage policies inadequately address remote access (access to company systems from a different physical location such as home, Wi-Fi "hot spots," or a hotel when traveling, and the use of portable storage devices such as flash drives and handheld computers) both from a technical and practical perspective, and often rely on documentation and policy from other sources in the organization, including IT, for access controls and fixed assets tracking for portable storage and computing devices. Obviously, the primary concern is that any access point into the company system is a security risk, and the easiest fix is for a company to eliminate remote access. However, in the diverse workplace of the twenty-first century, most companies out of necessity permit users to access the company systems from remote locations or through portable storage and/or computing devices to increase efficiency and accessibility, but in so doing, they face a number of potential security challenges.

In addition to the security threat to company systems by both employees and nonemployees if security and control measures are weak, remote access also may lead to actual tampering with original business ESI. It may also lead to the loss of the integrity of the ESI, either by direct nefarious actions or by indirect means, such as producing an atmosphere of uncertainty as to whether the company's ESI has been compromised.

More significantly in terms of the legal integrity of any ESI, remote access also challenges the company's document management policies because business ESI may become physically located anywhere—often outside the control of the company's document management system. Consequently, companies must rely on an employee honor system to ensure that the original business ESI is within the management and control of the company document management systems, that any data removed from the system is only a copy, and that the original remains with the company.

Remote access will also likely increase litigation costs even if only copies are stored on the remote machines, because the mere fact that ESI is located on these machines may force preservation and review of any drives that contain potentially relevant material. Naturally, if the employee honor system for storing or archiving only copies in remote machines and devices is broken—which frequently happens without employee knowledge because the system does not have any fail-safes built in to warn of potential loss of ESI or ESI being saved outside the control of the company's document management policies—the discovery costs will likely increase twofold. This results from the fact that the remote machines and devices will need to be preserved and reviewed. If there is a break in the employee honor system, or no honor system at all, the company will likely become more vulnerable to spoliation claims because business ESI will likely be outside the company document management and the litigation hold procedures. This could also increase the possibility that a company is unable to preserve or locate a document necessary for its defense and/or claim.

Attorneys reviewing computer usage policies before or during litigation should not only carefully understand the policy and technology, but also investigate and understand the employee practices that utilize the available technology.[41] Obviously, before litigation, the primary goals of an attorney should be to reconcile

41. The need to understand how employees use the system is clear: "This case is just the latest example of lawyers designing keyword searches in the dark, by the seat of the pants, without adequate (indeed, here, apparently without any)

any disparity between the company policies and procedures and to educate the users and management about the following: (1) the security concerns, both from within and outside the organization; (2) the potential hazard of relying on an honor system for original business ESI instead of built-in fail-safes; and (3) the potential impact to the company when employees fail to comply with the policies.

The security education also should extend to any applicable statutory regulations, such as HIPAA and GLBA, and extend to protect and secure portable storage and computing devices, by using encryption and remote-destruction techniques. During litigation, attorneys need to immediately identify the scope of remote access and portable devices and ensure that the litigation hold procedures are extended to all potential sources of original business ESI so as to avoid spoliation. Attorneys also need to understand the scope of remote access so that they can better manage the discovery costs and, when appropriate, make efforts to reduce the costs by being efficient in the process and in reaching an agreement with the opposition. The attorney should also understand each opponent's remote access policies and practices so that the attorney is better positioned to make clear, concise discovery requests and to seek spoliation sanctions, if warranted.

D. Emerging issues

There are a number of emerging issues that, because they stem from the arrival of new technologies and trends, often are not adequately addressed by companies in their current computer usage policies and practices. Nevertheless, as companies improve in technology management and as policies evolve and improve over time, attorneys should inquire as to how a company and its policies address the following:

(1) Proxy rights

Companies need to address proxy rights in their computer usage policies, and if permitted, use technological measures to manage the use of proxy rights. Proxy rights are the use of software features by which one user is able to access and perform functions within an application *in the name of another user*. In email, for example, proxy rights are used frequently by administrative assistants to

discussion with those who wrote the emails." William A. Gross Constr. Assocs., 256 F.R.D. at 135.

send messages in the name of their supervisors. Under a computer usage policy, such actions should be transparent to the recipient and to anyone else who may come in contact with the communication. The same applies if users share their credentials or if a user is an automated computer process such as a "bot" (a computer or digital robot). The use of such functionality will likely confuse the issue of who actually transmitted or stored ESI, or who had knowledge of a transmitted message and/or the contents of a transmission. The best practice is for companies to prohibit the use of proxy rights. If proxy rights or bots are permitted, companies should use tight security and access controls so that a record is created to capture when proxy rights and bots are used.

The use of proxy rights and the ability to identify the actual source of the communication of the message have been critical in some cases. Such was the case mentioned previously that involved CEO Larry Ellison, who was accused of sexual harassment.[42] The female employee relied on an email that her supervisor allegedly sent to Ellison, after she allegedly refused his sexual advances, as a principal piece of evidence in her case against Oracle and Ellison. Oracle was, however, able to determine, based on a forensic review, that the woman had used proxy rights to access her supervisor's email account and send to Ellison the incriminating email that stated that she had been fired immediately after she refused his advances.[43]

Attorneys should review both their clients' and opponents' computer usage policies and practices to assess whether such organizations are using or preventing proxy rights and bots. Obviously, if the policy and technology prohibit it, then an attorney does not need to investigate any further. If, on the other hand, the company policy authorizes it or if the company's technology is not advanced enough to prevent such activities, the attorney investigating proxy rights and bots use prior to litigation must determine whether the company takes measures to preserve and identify each instance of its use. If the review is performed during litigation, attorneys should confirm the clients' and opponents' proxy rights and bots

42. E. Mills, *Ellison's Former Girl Friend on Trial for Faking Email*, COMPUTERWORLD, Jan. 19, 1997, http://computerworld.co.nz/news.nsf/news/CC256CED0016AD1EC C25684C000D619A.

43. *See also* J. Mirkinson, *Tucker Carlson Sent E-mails Posing as Keith Olbermann*, HUFFINGTON POST, last updated Nov. 10, 2010, http://www.huffingtonpost.com/2010/11/09/keith-olbermann-hoax-did-_n_781241.html.

practice so that the attorney can fully understand the scope, when relevant, of an individual who may have knowledge of relevant ESI and to properly identify fraudulent ESI, as was the case in the Oracle matter.

(2) *Instant messaging*

Another emerging issue that companies and attorneys must address with their policies, practices, and technology is instant messaging. Instant messaging (IM) is a type of communication service that enables an individual to create a private, text-based conversation with another in real time. IM has become ubiquitous through tools like Yahoo messenger, MSN, and AOL's AIM. This feature began to attract large numbers of users in the late 1990s with the computer program ICQ and has become widely popular over the last decade. It is estimated that today there are 47 billion IM messages sent daily.[44] Companies, however, have been slow to address instant messaging in their computer usage policies and with technology.

As is the case with any facet of computer usage policies, if the policy permits instant messaging or the technology cannot prevent it, then attorneys and companies must confront how to manage the use of instant messaging. The biggest challenges arising from employees using IM are the following:

1. Is IM being used only for business purposes?
2. Is the content a business record?
3. Is the content of the message being recorded and preserved in accordance with document retention practices?
4. Does the litigation hold procedure extend to IM messaging?

Companies often deploy technology to preserve IM communications or operate on an honor system whereby employees are asked to copy the IM communication into a format that can be managed by the company's document management system. Once it is captured as original business ESI, the ESI then falls into the litigation hold procedure when the time arises. Such manual capture, however, is problematic in the context of rushed and busy employees who are multitasking.

44. *13.9 Bln Instant Messages Are Sent a Day, 46.5 Bln Daily by 2009*, ZDNET, July 21, 2005, http://www.zdnet.com/blog/itfacts/139-bln-instant-messages-are-sent-a-day-465-bln-daily-by-2009/8425.

Attorneys reviewing client computer usage policies and practices should investigate their policies and procedures thoroughly to determine how IM is managed. If the review is prior to litigation, attorneys should be aware of their client's use of IM and the measures used, if any, to preserve original business ESI communicated through, or stored by, IM and to eliminate any gaps between policies and practices. The most common gap is when employees are not preserving the contents of the IM message. Following the commencement of litigation, attorneys should confirm that the litigation hold is attached properly to IM communications and, if relevant, seek IM communications from their clients for factual development purposes. Attorneys should investigate their opponents' IM policies and practices to determine whether IM communications are available for discovery and to determine whether there has been any breach of the opponent's duty to preserve the ESI generated from IM communications.

In addition, companies that permit IM often must reduce their security measures to permit the IM tool to function properly. With the reduced security measures, attorneys should also look at the number of incidences, by interviews and reviewing server logs, of security breaches of their opponents to assess whether the integrity of original business ESI could be called into question on the basis that the opponent is unable to authenticate the accuracy of the ESI due to having any number of intruders who could have manipulated the ESI.

(3) Blogs

Companies and attorneys need to address employee use of blogs and postings in company- and employee-sponsored blogs. Blogs are a type of website that is more interactive than a typical static website, and they are increasingly becoming an issue in electronic discovery because of their rapid adoption among Internet users.[45] Blogs permit interactive, two-way communications between the publishers of the content posted on the blog and the Internet users who read and elect to comment on the post in the blog. This two-way communication raises a concern for attorneys and companies because statements may be attributed, or actions reflected in the published content, that the company does not sponsor and/or authorize.

45. The discussion can extend to online services such as Wiki, Wikibooks, and Google Docs.

There are number of issues for companies and attorneys to assess if a company is publishing a blog or if it is permitting its employees to post content/entries within a blog sponsored by it or a third party. If the company is sponsoring the blog, then it should take measures to ensure that the content that is posted within the blog does not create any legal exposure for the company, such as messages with pornographic or unauthorized content. This is often accomplished through a computer usage policy, by mandating review of all user postings before they are published. If a company authorizes its employees to post content within blogs sponsored by third parties, most such companies implement policies and controls that require the content to be (1) reviewed prior to its posting using the same standards and procedures as a company uses for press releases and (2) posted using controls (i.e., branding or attribution requirements displayed in the content) that indicate the source of the content is the company, such as that the employee must use a company email address or user credentials associated with the company.[46]

These computer usage policies often state that if an employee posts a blog entry or publishes/hosts a blog that is not authorized by the employer, then such posting or blog should not contain any of the employer credentials, branding, and/or "look and feel." A computer usage policy must create bright lines between authorized and nonauthorized employee blog postings and employee-hosted blogs to prevent an employee from posting an unauthorized blog entry in which the content may be attributed as a statement or action made by the employer.

Companies and their attorneys should adopt or review their policies to confirm that blogs and blog entries are not creating liability for themselves. Prior to litigation, companies and their attorneys should review the procedures for posting blog entries in sanctioned blogs and how employees may post sanctioned blog entries. In addition, they should confirm that employees have clear guidance on how they should post nonsanctioned blog entries or publish/host nonsanctioned blogs so that content or actions cannot relate back to the employer.

Also, during litigation, attorneys should confirm that the litigation hold extends to the company blog and employee-sanctioned blog entries at other third-party blogs. They should review their

46. *See supra* note 23.

opponents' practices and determine if there is any disparity between the practices and the requirements of a litigation hold to determine whether spoliation claims can be made. In addition, attorneys should review the opponent's computer usage policy on blogs and its employee blog postings on third-party blogs, to determine whether any statements made and/or acts can be related back to the opponent if applicable. Companies should be prepared to preserve all blog entries made by its employees, even where the blog platform is controlled by third parties.

(4) Portable computing and storage devices

Companies that authorize the use of portable computing and storage devices are often challenged with identifying the scope of where business records are located, for either management or litigation purposes. Portable computing and storage devices, such as laptops, handheld computers, smartphones, and thumb drives, among others, have become indispensable to many people in business and personal lives today. Their portability alone creates havoc for companies because they (1) contribute to the decentralization of the management of original business ESI; (2) increase electronic discovery costs; (3) increase the likelihood of a breach of the duty to preserve; and (4) most likely increase the number of inconsistencies between the record retention policies and company practices, any of which may be used to pursue sanctions by an opponent.

Computer usage policies that prohibit portable computing devices and/or portable storage devices limit company exposure fivefold. The challenge, however, is that these types of policies are few and far between. In our ever-mobile workforce and advancement of telecommuting, most companies are unable to operate or unable to design technology and policies that prevent such usage.

In the more typical scenario, one where companies are permitting portable computing and/or portable storage devices, the challenge to manage original business ESI and the opportunity to mismanage ESI increase significantly. To mitigate the dangers such devices pose and to better manage their ESI, companies often include in their computer usage policy the requirements that portable computing and/or storage devices can only be used to store duplicate copies of original business ESI and that the company must maintain a custodian database that archives who is in possession of each device and where it is located. A company may also limit who uses such devices and specify where the devices must be stored and when they are to be returned. Without a usage policy governing portable computing and storage devices, business ESI may become scattered in servers and devices—perhaps those of a competitor—all over the world.

Another area to consider in the context of portable computing and storage devices is the use of encryption. Encryption is used to limit who has access to ESI and/or the device if, for example, the device falls into the hands of a third party. A company can encrypt on various levels: within the contents of a file (such as a field within a database); at the file level; at the system level; and/or at the device level. In some cases, statutes may require companies to establish specific encryption levels, such as a level for medical records information protected under HIPAA.

Computer usage policies often address other means of preventing unauthorized access to portable computing and storage devices. For example, in addition to password design, protection, and refreshing, being able to remotely disable either a hard drive or a PDA that has been lost or stolen is critical, especially when sensitive ESI could have been compromised. In cases involving the theft of information (identity theft or trade secrets theft, for example), a company that has failed to encrypt key information or take advantage of other similar means to safeguard its ESI will surely come under unwelcome scrutiny by the opposition and/or regulators and will likely be the basis of statutory violations and tort claims including negligence.[47]

Companies and attorneys should review the policies and practices for remote and portable storage devices on a regular basis. Prior to litigation, they should review whether any business ESI can be created, saved, and/or deleted outside of the company document management systems and litigation hold procedures. If technology does not prevent or track the creation and storage of original business ESI on such devices, the company, at the minimum, should deploy an honor system among its employees, along with training on how to properly maintain the ESI. Training should also extend to the proper use of encryption. During litigation, companies and their attorneys should review the policies and

47. A number of statutes, as well as federal regulations, address obligations in connection with prevention of identity theft and reporting the compromise of personal information.

practices, query technology controls if any, and assess whether any business ESI is located on portable computing and storage devices. If so, this ESI may be relevant to a client's claims or defenses and may fall within the scope of the litigation hold. Companies and attorneys should also inquire whether their opponents are using such devices, what policies govern that use, and what measures are used to preserve portable ESI.

(5) Text messages (SMS)

SMS ("short message service") is another popular communication tool that is often overlooked by companies, attorneys, and computer usage policies. SMS messages are the text messages transmitted between telephones or between a telephone and another computing device. Most companies permit SMS messaging or do not have the technical means to prevent it. SMS messages can be transmitted (1) through a company server, in which case the company collects the ESI; (2) through a communications carrier, in which case the carrier collects the ESI; or, (3) from one device to another, in which case each device collects the ESI. Companies permitting options (2) or (3) should take additional measures to preserve ESI, such as retrieving it from the service provider in a routine manner or deploying an honor system whereby the employees must preserve such messages, if they are business records.

Companies that issue cell phones, PDAs, and other SMS-enabled devices to their employees are faced with a number of challenges. Prior to litigation, attorneys who are advising a company should investigate whether SMS messaging is permitted for business purposes, and if so, whether the company takes measures to preserve SMS messages containing original business ESI, as with options (1) and (2) above, or whether the company trains and implements an honor system whereby each employee is obligated to record, preserve, and archive original business ESI if the company and/or employee utilizes option (3) above.

Attorneys who are in the midst of litigation should assess the SMS policies and practices of their client and opponent. A company must act quickly to preserve the SMS messages when the content or action reflected in the message is relevant to the claims, defenses, or subject matter of the action. In addition, once the litigation hold attaches, the company will be required to preserve relevant ESI including SMS messages; having no computer usage policy, or an unclear practice, may create havoc in terms of compliance. On the other hand, the opponent will likely be struggling with some of the same collection and preservation issues that make it an easy target, permitting negotiation of a reasonable compromise, even if there was no adequate computer usage policy.

(6) Voicemail

Contemporary voicemail is often stored as ESI in the form of a .wav file. With the convergence of voicemail and email systems, companies and their attorneys must be careful with their computer usage policies and practices with respect to voicemails. Today, many voicemail messages are stored within an employee's email inbox, or if not in the email, on a computing device that is easily accessible and likely stored along with other original business ESI. After all, voicemail messages are simply an audio file stored on a computer, much like a ring tone or music file. Voicemail messages may also be saved on different systems as well, such as a company server for the phone network located in its office or a provider's system in the case of a portable phone. Voicemail messages also can be attached to email. Prior to litigation, the attorney should ensure that the computer usage policy and practice conform to each other and that there is a policy with respect to collection of voicemail. During litigation, attorneys should review their client's voicemail practices and policies and determine whether there are any inconsistencies, and, if so, correct them immediately. Then they should provide guidance on preservation of voicemails. Attorneys should also look at the practices and policies of their opponent's voicemail collection and preservation to determine if there are inconsistencies and any possible failures to preserve messages that can be used to make claims for spoliation.

E. Conclusion

A computer usage policy is a tool for managing one of a company's most important assets. Computer usage issues stem from advances in technology that make our workplaces more efficient, yet have had the effect of increasing the volume of ESI generated and decentralizing the locations in which ESI is stored. The computer usage policy is the primary tool to limit what ESI is electronically generated and where such information is stored. In the film *Field of Dreams*, Shoeless Joe Jackson said, "If you build it, he will come."[48] In the world of ESI, if the data is created, you may need it for your case, or an opponent will likely ask for the preservation and production of that data. Failure to apply prudent, prelitigation usage controls of ESI will likely increase discovery costs and possibly expose a company to unnecessary risk.

3. Records management policies

The records management policy controls the retention and destruction of what was created under the computer usage policy. Like computer usage policies, records management policies are also increasingly becoming a critical component of the well-being of many corporations. In fact, the value of many corporations today is tied to digital records and their proper collection, preservation, maintenance, and safekeeping. Companies that deploy proper records management strategies will be best situated to protect their trade secrets, be more efficient at retrieving their business records, likely preserve corporate worth and reputation, likely reduce litigation costs through more efficient production, and likely reduce legal exposure by minimizing the possible mistakes arising from improper records management.

This section of the book is not intended to help the reader prepare and draft records management policies, but rather to assist attorneys who are involved with reviewing corporate ESI policies to identify and correct possible issues, whether prior to or during litigation. The basic rule of thumb is that a business should preserve what is necessary to comply with statutory, regulatory, contractual, and business requirements, and destroy what is not, unless it is subject to a litigation hold.[49]

While many forward-thinking companies today have implemented some form of record management policy for their entire system, including the obvious email systems, it is important to note that records management is more complex than simply a policy to govern the storing or deleting of ESI or the securing of an email system. An adequate records management policy encompasses much more than that, and records should be viewed in a much broader scope within the corporate environment. A reason-

48. The Internet Movie Database, http://www.imdb.com/title/tt0097351/quotes.
49. Carlucci v. Piper Aircraft Corp., 102 F.R.D. 472 (S.D. Fla. 1984) (default judgment awarded where the stated purpose of defendant's policy for destroying ESI was the elimination of ESI that might be detrimental to defendant in a lawsuit).

able definition of the phrase "records management" in today's world is the following:

> Records Management is the Field of Management responsible for the efficient and systematic control of the creation, receipt, maintenance, use and disposition of records, including processes for capturing and maintaining evidence of and information about business activities and transactions in the form of records.[50]

Within any corporate environment, a records management policy needs to dovetail with the computer usage policy, and because a majority of data is created electronically, it must operate seamlessly with computer usage policies. While computer usage policies address the use of technology and the creation, safeguarding, and storage of ESI, the records management policy is the primary tool to determine what information should be stored, archived, safeguarded, and/or preserved, and when it should be discarded.

In the past, records management policies were known as "document destruction" or "document retention" policies. Now, they are sometimes called "records and information management" or "knowledge management policies," and their scope often extends well beyond the historical understanding of a records/document management policy. Today, these policies extend to include, among others, disaster recovery, security breaches and mitigation, destruction,[51] and trade secret designations.

Regarding records management and document retention, the Supreme Court has stated: " 'Document retention policies,' which are created in part to keep certain information from getting into the hands of others, including the Government, are common in business. . . . It is, of course, not wrongful for a manager to instruct employees to comply with a valid document retention policy

50. International Standards Organization (ISO) 15489:2001.

51. When destroying ESI, complex policies and procedures must often be followed. For example, if transferring, decommissioning, or selling computers, photocopiers, or other storage devices, a company will often perform a "Department of Defense" format of the hard drive to confirm that no data can be recovered from the storage device by the transferee. The need for such policies is demonstrated by the fiasco in which NASA transferred computers and/or provided access to computers with sensitive information to random individuals. *See* I. Klotz, *NASA Sold Computers with Sensitive Data, Report Says*," REUTERS, Dec. 7, 2010) www.reuters.com/article/idUSTRE6B66UG20101207.

under ordinary circumstances."[52] Similarly, the Sedona Conference noted: "The hallmark of an organization's information and records management policies should be reasonableness."[53] In short, "[d]estruction is an acceptable stage in the information life cycle; an organization may destroy or delete electronic information when there is no continuing value or need to retain it."[54]

A. A brief review of records management

Historically, records management was a humdrum administrative headache that involved considering the preservation and destruction of physical documents and ESI that was relatively low on the corporate priorities list. Typically, it was characterized by a schedule that described what information should be saved and when such information should be discarded. In the past, for each business record and/or class of business records, companies balanced their need to retain the record with a timeline that determined when that record could be discarded based on statutory, regulatory, contract, business, or common law requirements. Often, the lodestar was a desire to avoid storage costs.

Today, while the foregoing principles still largely apply, those humdrum inconsequential days are over, and storage costs have dropped markedly. Not only does today's records management environment require a much broader scope, as discussed in the introduction to this section, it also requires the shift of records management strategies from paper "hard copy" records to ESI. Since technology has become ever more increasingly fluid, portable, and vital to business processes, and with systems burgeoning with massive amounts of

52. Arthur Andersen LLP v. United States, 544 U.S. 696, 704 (2005); Lewy v. Remington Arms Co., Inc., 836 F.2d 1104 (8th Cir. 1988) ("First, the court should determine whether Remington's record retention policy is reasonable considering the facts and circumstances surrounding the relevant documents. For example, the court should determine whether a three year retention policy is reasonable given the particular document. A three year retention policy may be sufficient for documents such as appointment books or telephone messages, but inadequate for documents such as customer complaints. Second, in making this determination the court may also consider whether lawsuits concerning the complaint or related complaints have been filed, the frequency of such complaints, and the magnitude of the complaints. Finally, the court should determine whether the document retention policy was instituted in bad faith.").

53. The Sedona Conference, Best Practices Guidelines and Commentary for Managing Information & Records in the Electronic Age, at 8 (Nov. 2007). [hereinafter Best Practices].

54. *Id* at iv.

sensitive data, proper records management and maintenance have become extremely challenging, and unfortunately not many companies know how to adequately manage their ESI, which has led to the unfortunate reality that electronic data fiascos have become commonplace. These situations oftentimes have far-reaching consequences, mar an otherwise solid reputation, increase the cost of litigation, expose businesses to tremendous liability, tarnish valuable brands, reduce corporate wealth, and compromise security.

It is worth noting that the challenge of competently managing digital records emerges not only from adapting current strategies as they move from the paper to digital world, but also from the cost perspective of how to adequately preserve, search, safeguard, use, and archive ESI.[55] In addition, companies oftentimes have trade secrets to safeguard and have a duty to protect the privacy of employees, clients, and customers. Indeed, in addition to possible contractual duties and obligations, state and federal legislators and regulators have now stepped in and require some companies to implement measures to ensure the protection of certain records that are more readily available and transferrable now that they are digital, such as consumer, financial, and health information. Some statutes even mandate the destruction of certain types of stale information.

Compounding the challenge that most businesses face today is that most digital documents carry within them what is known as "metadata": hidden data containing information regarding the document. Metadata can be helpful and harmful on many fronts, including, but not limited to, its use in authenticating documents and piecing together the complete picture of an action, communication, or business record.[56] But metadata can also get companies into trouble when documents containing confidential metadata are inadvertently disclosed to outside parties during a contracting process or during a litigation production.[57] For example, metadata reportedly indicated that Microsoft's 1999 annual report was at least partially prepared on an Apple computer.[58]

55. In at least one instance, a board member has sued the government to challenge its records management. J. Burris, *Howard School Board Member Files Suit to Prevent Deleted Email*, Balt. Sun, Oct. 31, 2010, http://articles.baltimoresun.com/2010-10-31/news/bs-md-ho-dyer-lawsuit-20101029_1_school-board-member-files-chairwoman-ellen-flynn-giles-e-mail.

56. See chapters 6 and 24.

57. See chapter 29.

58. S. Rosenberg, *Microsoft's Annual Report: Made on Macintosh*, Salon, Oct. 12, 1999, http://www.salon.com/tech/log/1999/10/12/microsoft_report/index.html.

Beyond metadata, there is a host of questions facing companies today that are pursuing good records management practices. For instance, what kind of information should or should not be stored on (easily stolen or lost) laptops, home PCs, and handheld devices that are independent from corporate systems? Will the company block access to expired web pages (web pages that are no longer published by a company/publisher yet remain available on the Internet to any user via a third-party website)? How will it ensure that data it collects from customers is managed and secured in the manner that the company promised to its customers in agreements, such as privacy policies on its website? Understanding how companies address these issues will help attorneys (1) assess the level of importance an organization places on records management; (2) assess vulnerabilities that should be corrected before litigation; and (3) identify deficiencies to exploit if an opponent has faulty policies and procedures.

Many companies, faced with these apparently overwhelming issues, opt to increase storage capacity and adopt a "keep anything and everything" policy without any forethought to constructing storage, retrieval, and protection schematics. In addition, IT personnel unfortunately often view the existence of inexpensive, large-scale storage devices as an open invitation to save information that is no longer needed for simplicity or disaster-recovery purposes.

The trouble, of course, with this "keep it all" approach is that systems can become bloated, disorganized, cumbersome, and confusing for those who use or safeguard them or need to access them to retrieve vital records for business or litigation purposes. And anything that is kept may need to be searched, reviewed, and produced in a lawsuit. If litigation is anticipated and the company has no structured records management program in place, it may be unable to locate information that could prove beneficial to its case, or the information could be too costly to find and/or produce. More problematic still, a company may fail to preserve the required information, subjecting it to claims of spoliation, or a court may order restoration and review without cost sharing.[59]

B. Elements of a records management policy

An attorney reviewing client policies and practices prior to or during litigation, or a litigation opponent's practices and policies

59. See chapter 27.

during discovery, should be familiar with the core principles of record management policies. The scope of records management policies may sound complicated (and it certainly can be[60]), but when you drill down to their essence, records management policies are really all about good communication.[61] Just as good communication is a technological, cultural, and business process, so essentially are records management policies.

First and foremost, a strong records management system will be the product of a thorough review of regulatory and contractual duties, an analysis of business needs, and the product of discussions between counsel, risk management, records managers, the information technology department, and business or transactional personnel. These discussions should include some of the basic questions regarding a company's ESI such as what needs to be retained, what may be destroyed, where the data is stored, who has access to the records, what procedures are currently being used regarding exiting employees and their computers, how the sale or transfer of digital assets to third parties is currently being handled, and what the current policy is regarding disposal of antiquated computers, telephones, portable computing, and storage devices and servers. A company generally uses a data map diagram and its organizational chart to outline the individuals responsible for ESI and the locations of ESI. After these discussions to ascertain what the current policy is, a comprehensive records management policy can be structured to accomplish the following:

(1) Establish policies that will apply to ESI throughout its entire life cycle

A document life cycle begins at its creation; then continues through storage, modification, usage, transmittal, archiving; and ends in its destruction, if ever. A simple guideline to follow to create ESI policies can be created by answering the following questions:

60. "Regulatory and judicial bodies must recognize that this area is enormously complex, that the boundaries of legitimate policies adopted in good faith must be sufficiently elastic, and that an organization that makes good faith efforts in this area should not be penalized for partial performance or an imperfect implementation." Best Practices, *supra* note 43, at 9.

61. In the words of the *Zubulake* court: "The conduct of both counsel and client thus calls to mind the now-famous words of the prison captain in Cool Hand Luke: 'What we've got here is a failure to communicate.'" Zubulake v. UBS Warburg LLC (*Zubulake V*), 229 F.R.D. 422, 424 (S.D.N.Y. 2004) (quoting Cool Hand Luke (Warner Bros. 1967)).

1. Is the ESI a business record?[62]
2. How long should each category of document, including ESI, be retained?
3. Who has access to stored ESI?
4. What are the legal and business requirements to retain and safeguard, or to destroy, the ESI?
5. Where will certain ESI be stored?
6. How will it be labeled?
7. How can users track changes to ESI?
8. What should be done with metadata?
9. How can persistent ESI be economically destroyed?

Such questions should be dealt with at the organizational level so that everyone will always be on the same page, literally and figuratively. Records management policies should also include the requirement that ESI be archived (or saved) in a format that will ensure that the data can be retrieved at least 10 years from the archived date.[63]

(2) Assign responsibilities and authorities

Most organizations have established protocols that govern who can access which parts of their internal systems and ESI. The same kinds of policies should be captured in records management in connection with registration, modification, archiving, and deletion of ESI. In other words, all ESI should be analyzed to determine who should have access rights or authority to change the status of the ESI from its current status, whether it is to make edits, move it to archives, or destroy it. If these access rights are not addressed by an independent policy, the records management documentation should at least designate the individual with the authority to impose (and release) a litigation hold, as well as implementation procedures.

(3) Provide records management tools to employees

Modern records management in large organizations often requires, in addition to policies, new technologies that can technologically deploy a written policy. Thus, IT investments and training may

62. The term "business record" is defined later in this chapter.

63. It is important to save the ESI in a format that can be accessed and viewed years later. There are many examples of vendors no longer producing software that functions with the older ESI, rendering that ESI useless or too expensive to retrieve.

be necessary. For example, if an individual is told to "destroy" or "preserve" certain email, does that employee have sufficient training to accomplish the task; or can the requirements of the policy be an automated function performed by the available technology so that human intervention is not required? This could suggest the need for, for example, email archiving software or sophisticated enterprise-wide document management and archiving software.

(4) Integrate records management into business processes

The policies set in place must become ingrained in the business processes throughout the organization. Ideally, the newly created structure for records management should integrate into the current workflow and business processes, minimizing disruption to the business and making it easier for employees to modify their current work habits. A crucial element of the implementation of these policies is who is driving the policy. Historically, policies that were implemented by IT departments, rather than the corporate leadership, were often not adopted completely by an organization. Thus, it is imperative that when the policies are created, the leadership of an organization publicly support the changes and is actively involved in their implementation, monitoring, and modification.

(5) As with all policies, consistent monitoring, auditing, and enforcement are required

Inconsistent implementation of lawful instructions to destroy ESI may markedly increase costs in later litigation by, for example, requiring the labor-intensive process of searching of backup tapes. The Sedona Guidelines state: "Information and records management policies must be put into practice."[64] Consider, for example, the consequences of destroying outdated, active email while leaving copies of those emails on backup tapes. Ultimately, the existence of the copies could require the production of information that would otherwise not be accessible or *reasonably* accessible because of undue burden or cost as interpreted by courts.

Obviously, each company and industry will have different challenges regarding its records management policies, but by following the guidelines above and evaluating the current workflow process, a proper and comprehensive records management policy can be

64. Best Practices, *supra* note 53, at v.

created. Companies that implement effective, proper records management policies will (i) be more efficient, communicate more effectively between departments, (ii) minimize employee mistakes, (iii) satisfy their legal obligations, (iv) reduce legal exposure by reducing the likelihood of sanctions or reduce the chances of being unable to locate an exonerating document related to a claim or defense, (v) safeguard their assets more effectively, and (vi) preserve their reputation by not being the target of an embarrassing public debacle involving ESI.

C. Attorney's role when assessing records management policies prior to or during litigation

Attorneys should be familiar with the best practices for records management and the challenges of it so that they can properly advise their clients prior to litigation, efficiently manage their client's ESI production during litigation, and effectively seek discovery from their opponents. Prior to litigation, attorneys should review records management policies and correct any disparities that are found between the client's policies and practices. During litigation, attorneys should be proactively deploying the litigation hold and seeking ESI that is responsive to their client's claims and defenses for the case, using the records management policy (along with the computer usage policy) as a guideline or road map. The records management process and procedures are also critical when communicating with other litigants in anticipation of discovery. Attorneys should also be able to identify poor records management policies so that they can assess the consequences.

D. Emerging issues

The following emerging issues should be considered by all attorneys while analyzing records management policies and/or practices:

(1) What is a business record?

As mentioned previously, identifying and properly processing business ESI is a necessary initial step for any client implementing records management policies within an organization and also when filtering responsive documents for litigation. So what is actually considered to be a business record?[65] While the courts

65. Governments often face a similar dilemma in defining what constitutes a public record under access to information statutes.

have not been entirely clear regarding this matter, there are some general guidelines that each business can apply in making the determination for its specific company.

The International Organization for Standardization (ISO) defines a business record as "Information created, received, and maintained as evidence and information by an organization or person, in pursuance of legal obligations or in the transaction of business."[66] The operative language is "in pursuance of legal obligations or in the transaction of business." Navigating the scope of this phrase is a delicate inquiry. This phrase requires one to examine the actual content of the ESI before determining whether it is a business record and, accordingly, one that should fall within the scope of records management. For example, is an email announcing that there are doughnuts in the kitchen a business record? On the one hand, it has nothing to do with business, so it may at first be perceived as excluded from the definition, but, on the other, is it brought back within the scope of the business record definition if, during the break, an individual sexually harasses another, with the email serving as evidence of the meeting? This definition and the corresponding assessment are critical to identifying what ESI should be included in the company's records management process.

Certain electronic business records create issues for records management strategies due to unique issues arising from their creation, handling, control, and ownership: emails, dynamically created web pages, SMS messages, instant messages, and voicemails.

One common mistake made by corporations is that they have policies that are inconsistent between ESI and its hard copy equivalent. Emails in particular are a good example of this; companies frequently delete emails on a regular basis[67] while at the same time stating that hard copy letters containing comparable business data should be saved for three years. Is treating an email differently from a hard copy acceptable, and is this inconsistency a source of possible exposure? Should companies treat an accounting record found in email differently from the same accounting record stored in a spreadsheet application?

Instant messages, text messages, and voicemails also prove to be difficult records to manage. In some cases, the configuration of

66. ISO 15489:2001.

67. For example, IT departments routinely set up protocols to automatically delete emails after a specified period of time, e.g., 90 days. These auto-deletion settings may conflict with document retention requirements.

the communication method may limit the ability of a company to manage the records without intervention and participation by the employees or third parties, as more fully described in the computer usage section above. To the extent these items are business records, companies and litigators need to assess how they comply with the current records management policy; in the context of litigation, they need to ensure that the litigation hold extends to these items; and they must assess on an ongoing basis whether there is any gap between the company's current practices and the duty to preserve with respect to such communications.

Dynamically created web pages are another concern for records management. A dynamically created web page is a web page that is assembled in real time from various web servers around the world. The problem with these web pages is that they may not be reproducible at some time in the future. This obviously presents a challenge if the viewer of the dynamically created web pages takes offense at the content displayed to the user or actions triggered by the website. A company that is unable to produce the web page viewed by the user, or that produces a web page that differs from what the user produces, will likely be viewed unfavorably by a judge or jury for not being able to authenticate, validate, or otherwise secure the evidence derived from the company's records.

(2) Time and date

The accuracy of the time and date associated with ESI is becoming increasingly important in the context of records management, as litigators are more frequently investigating time/date accuracy in the preparation of their cases. When documents were created, accessed, modified, and/or shared can prove to be critical information for litigants, but confirming the accuracy of such information is not always easy. Consider a typical Microsoft Word document. It may have been created in 2003, but if it is duplicated on the same computer or placed on another computer in 2010, the duplicate may appear to have been created in 2010.

It is also true that the time/date associated with documents is determined by the time that is set on the actual *computer* on which the document was created. Should the time on a computer be set to the first Friday in January, when it was really the first Monday in January, the computer will not object; thus, it is remarkably easy to intentionally or unintentionally manipulate the time and date associated with the creation and modification of ESI. While there are some computer networks that will reach out to the Internet to obtain their time and date settings from a certified source, computer clocks are seldom set according to a certified or reliable source, such as an atomic clock, and can be easily overridden even if set by such a reliable process.

It is also important to note that files themselves may have fields in them that read the time and date of the computer and store it in the field until the next time that the file contents are updated. To a party reviewing the documents in a native file format, the document will appear as the current date and time, and if printed, the current date and time will appear on the printout, yet the true creation date of the letter may have been months ago. Companies and litigators should take and document the measures used to maintain the integrity of the time and date of their systems so that the ESI is properly dated, and take measures to capture date and time for documents so that date and time are preserved during the entire life cycle of the ESI.

Because time/date accuracy has become problematic, some companies are taking measures to maintain and preserve the original time and date of ESI through such services as digital notaries. Such measures may prove helpful, because many litigators now appreciate the importance of reliable, ESI-provided time/date data in creating timelines for their cases. Litigators have also learned how to contest the accuracy and authenticity of the time and date of relevant documents when the appropriate measures are not taken. For example, the accuracy[68] of time and date of a web page that has been printed can be easily contested because the web page most likely has been brought into a program that permits it to be edited before it is printed.

(3) Archiving in third-party public websites

Another unique challenge to corporate records management is the proliferation of third-party websites that archive, or "cache," public websites. Most major search engines like Google and Yahoo participate in this copying system to optimize their search capabilities. Obviously, a search engine will return a response much faster if it is actually searching only its own servers, instead of the entire web, for a search term. However, most people do not know that there are

68. The best evidence is the web page as it stands in its natural format with measures taken to prevent modifications to it. Authentication is discussed in chapter 24.

copies or snapshots of their website being taken automatically by these parties often thousands of times a day. The Wayback Machine[69] is another tool that is constantly trolling the Internet, copying web pages and data in order to create an actual archive of the entire Internet from virtually the beginning. If a page has been posted on the Internet at one time, then chances are that the Wayback Machine has a copy of the content on one of its servers. These are only a few of the better-known parties that are creating archives of information from the Internet, and there are many others that often provide images of what websites contained in the past, so deleting an item on a corporate web page no longer means that a third party will not be able to access the item, any more than deleting an email would.

As the legal community has become aware of these practices, archived web pages have become valuable in defamation, libel, intellectual property, infringement, noncompete, and unfair trade competition cases. For example, the Wayback Machine can be useful at establishing first commercial use in the context of trademark infringement claims.

Companies that want to reduce their exposure arising from such archives and tools can apply certain technological techniques to reduce the chance of unwanted ESI from appearing on archival sites like the Wayback Machine. These measures, however, are often unpopular among the marketing personnel because they often require the website to appear lower in search engine results.[70] In addition, such measures will work only to the extent that the search or archive site voluntarily complies (which some of them readily admit that they do not) with certain standards adopted by engineers on the Internet. Those standards, however, are voluntary and they have not been incorporated into legislation yet. In the interim, adequate computer usage and records management policies are the best safeguard.

(4) Third parties in possession of business records

With the onset of cloud computing and outsourcing, more and more companies are permitting third parties to possess and control their business records. These types of relationships create

69. The Wayback Machine, www.internetarchive.org.

70. M. Liedtke, *Texas Attorney General to Investigate Complaints about Google's Search Engine,* Wash. Post, Sept. 3, 2010, http://www.washingtonpost.com/wp-dyn/content/article/2010/09/03/AR2010090305857.html?hpid=topnews.

particular challenges to organizations adopting good records management practices because the original ESI is no longer in the possession and control of the company and its policies. Common issues are (1) the third party does not honor the record retention and destruction protocol of the company and (2) the third party has no obligation to honor, and often no knowledge about, the duty to preserve that may attach to original business ESI in its possession. These challenges often lead to gaps in a company's record management policies that are open vulnerabilities to opposing litigators who learn about them.

One solution to prevent such gaps is for companies to address the issue in their initial contract with the "cloud" provider. At the minimum, attorneys should ensure that their clients properly document and maintain the names and locations of all of the outsourced entities that contain original business ESI so that the moment a litigation hold attaches to ESI in the possession of a third party, the company is able to notify the vendor immediately to preserve the relevant ESI. Of course, if such procedures and actions are not addressed in the original agreement, then the vendor will likely ask for a hefty price to perform such services.

(5) Metadata

Metadata has become the veritable boogeyman for many attorneys, yet it is a necessary component in the digital world, particularly with regard to records management. Metadata is the information contained in a data environment about that information. While it varies from program to program, metadata generally consists of the following:

1. Metadata inside a file;
2. Metadata associated with a file at the operating system level;
3. Metadata in an external file that is linked to the original file; and/or
4. Metadata such as the formulas behind the visible numbers in spreadsheets and values in database fields, which are only displayed or accessible to the user as native files and are not readily accessible to a user not trained in the native application.

Metadata in emails is the technical information in the header, which is the sending and receiving path that the file took from point A to point B; in Microsoft files, it is the information in the file properties; and in Microsoft Word, it also is the "invisible" text created in the track-changes function when the toggle is set so the user is unable to see the edits.[71]

When managing records, companies need to assess how metadata will be handled by the organization. For example, companies that do not archive files in native file formats may be jeopardizing the preservation of important information that could be found in the metadata, preservation of which may be mandated by, for example, statutes. In the context of litigation, litigators need to assess whether metadata exists and whether it is necessary for the case; destroying such information can have dire implications for a company as there might be information contained in that information that could help their case or the loss of which could expose the company to spoliation claims. Litigators also need to be careful of removing metadata when accessing case files, and know how such deletions should be handled in the context of litigation and in relation to the duty to preserve. Metadata can also become a potential liability if a litigator or a business attorney were to inadvertently disclose information to the other side that contains a privileged attorney-client communication within the metadata. Familiarity with metadata by attorneys has now become mandatory.[72]

(6) Tools and utilities to preserve and authenticate data

Another important aspect of a comprehensive records management policy is the establishment of procedures and tools to authenticate and preserve ESI in a manner so that the ESI is trustworthy, accurate, reliable, and tamperproof while maintaining a clear chain of custody. Companies need to plan for the eventuality that ESI will be subject to discovery in litigation, and they need to be prepared so that when such events occur, they can immediately preserve and subsequently produce it in a defensible manner.

There are a number of tools in the marketplace that allow companies to forensically preserve their ESI, and the ones that are the most effective are the ones that are reusable and able not only to

---

71. For a discussion of metadata in Microsoft Office documents, and the built-in "scrubber," see Microsoft Office, Remove Hidden Data and Personal Information from Office Documents, http://office.microsoft.com/en-us/excel-help/remove-hidden-data-and-personal-information-from-office-documents-HA010037593.aspx.

72. See chapter 29.

preserve the evidence but also maintain a chain of custody in a manner that is defensible, trustworthy, reliable, and acceptable in court.[73] These concerns arise frequently in the context of securing and preserving content found online and in the context of producing it to the other side. If someone uses a printed document from an online website, the document can be impeached, because a printed version is not the most reliable or trustworthy method to preserve the ESI since information could be lost or tampered with during the conversion from digital to a printed form. In the context of litigation, producing a document in its native file format[74] must be done in a manner so that if the other side intentionally or unintentionally alters its content, then the producing party is able to demonstrate that the ESI has been modified from its original source and is not authentic.

(7) Tools to respond to third-party subpoenas

In the digital age, a party to litigation may ask a third party to produce documents related to a dispute between it and another party. These types of requests are becoming more and more prevalent, particularly since the Digital Millennium Copyright Act of 1998 (DMCA) permits parties to make such requests to websites to obtain information about the website's users even before litigation is commenced. The more traditional request from a third party is for a party litigant to issue a subpoena duces tecum to seek ESI from that third party during the pendency of litigation.

Either approach may be problematic to third parties who have received such requests and failed to develop an adequate records management policy. For example, if a litigant asks a third party to produce the contents of an adversary's email stored on its servers without qualification, and if the third party produces all of the ESI, including personal email unrelated to the litigation, then the subpoenaed party and its law firm may have exposed themselves to liability pursuant to the Stored Communications Act and Computer Fraud and Abuse Act.[75] In addition, if the subpoena is pursuant to the DMCA, and the party produces information about an individual beyond what is necessary to obtain the identity of the party allegedly infringing on the requesting party's copyright, then the producing party may violate the DMCA and possibly

73. See chapter 24.

74. See chapter 4.

75. Theofel v. Farley Jones, 359 F.3d 1066 (9th Cir. 2003).

breach a contract between its customer and itself regarding the confidentiality of the information it receives from the Internet user.

4. Conclusion

"There is no single standard or universal policy that can be applied as a talisman to guide future conduct or judge the wisdom of prior practices for any given organization. Instead, there is a continuum of possible models, all or many of which may allow an organization to meet its unique business and legal needs, and there are an infinite number of combinations that may fall within the boundaries of reasonable, defensible, and good management practices."[76] Nevertheless, it has been authoritatively stated that "Organizations should consider implementing information and records management policies and practices that specifically address electronic information and records, including the retention, preservation and destruction of electronic information and records."[77]

We have endeavored in this chapter to provide only general and broad considerations that we hope will be useful for attorneys to use in interviewing their clients, planning for discovery, participating in a "conference of the parties,"[78] and requesting information from their opponents. If further detailed guidelines are needed, we suggest consulting specialized resources.[79] "Dramatic events have played out in boardrooms, courts and the media in the last several years, focusing the attention of lawmakers, lawyers, regulators, auditors and investors on one critical aspect of business—the management of information and records. This awakening regarding the intrinsic value of information assets has resulted in a special need to refocus on the processes by which business records are managed, particularly those that are produced and stored electronically."[80]

76. Best Practices at 5.

77. *Id.* at 7.

78. See chapter 19.

79. The American Records Management Association provides a self-assessment for records management and other related information on its web site, www.arma.org.

80. The Sedona Guidelines, Best Practices & Commentary for Managing Information & Records in the Electronic Age App. B, 56 (Sep. 2004 Public Comment Draft).

CHAPTER 6

INTRODUCTION TO METADATA AND FORM OF PRODUCTION UNDER RULE 34

Kate Paslin

Case law and rule revisions over the last five years underscore a practitioner's need to account for metadata from the point of identifying and collecting information through production and the use of evidence at trial. In this chapter, in-house counsel for a legal software maker (and former litigator) explains (1) the nature of metadata; (2) why and how it can be important; (3) its discoverability; (4) some practice advice (including how to scrub metadata from a document, considerations on whether to request metadata in production, and when it is worth retaining an outside expert); and (5) a look ahead at issues related to metadata and its discovery in the "cloud."

1. What is metadata?

A. Definition and types

Most commonly referred to as "data about data," metadata describes the background or structural information inherent to electronic files and media. The Latin and Greek prefix "meta" translates to "among," "about," "with," or even "change," depending on context.[1] True to its meaning, metadata encapsulates information about the creation, movement, alteration, and design of any file. The metadata available for each native file type—that is, files in their original electronic format—varies according to application, default settings, changes made by individual users, and/or settings selected by the system manager or information technology (IT) staff. Metadata exists on all levels, from the individual document or email to Internet web pages, collaboration sites, and enterprise-wide servers and operating systems. Some applications or files contain thousands of pieces of metadata, while others maintain a select few. Simple examples include[2]

- the band across the top of a facsimile, reflecting the sender's phone number, the time and date of transmission, and the number of pages sent
- the information viewable under the "Properties" menu in a Microsoft Word document, including the author or custodian and the date of creation or modification
- the more than 1,200 fields describing email, including sent and received dates, reply, forward, copy, blind copy, and sender address book information
- Internet "metatags" that allow browser searches to locate relevant websites and text file "cookies" that track usage of a website and report information back to the site's owner
- information gathered by digital voicemail systems, including the caller, date, time, and duration of the message

Courts and lawmakers recognize the frequency with which metadata factors into litigation cost and strategy, as common sources of discovery increasingly take electronic form. Case law defines metadata as "information about a particular data set which describes how, when and by whom it was collected, created, accessed and/or modified and how it is formatted."[3] The Federal Rules of Civil Procedure likewise acknowledge the meaning and

---

1. *See, e.g.*, http://ask.reference.com/related/Prefix+Meta; http://www.merriam-webster.com/dictionary/meta?show=1&t=1302401930.

2. *See* THE SEDONA CONFERENCE, THE SEDONA PRINCIPLES: BEST PRACTICES, RECOMMENDATIONS & PRINCIPLES FOR ADDRESSING ELECTRONIC DOCUMENT PRODUCTION 3–4 (2nd ed. 2007).

3. Williams v. Sprint/United Mgmt. Co., 230 F.R.D. 640, 646 (D. Kan. 2005).

- The "Properties" selection[12] notes the creation date of the document, the date that changes or modifications were last applied, the number of times the document was accessed, and the total amount of time spent editing it. One implication of such information involves the transmission of a document reflecting work product from lawyer to client. The metadata above would suggest to the client whether the actual time spent working on the document accurately reflects the time the lawyer billed for that service, or the potentially embarrassing information of who actually drafted it before it received a partner's approval and signature.
- Under the Tools menu in the 2003 version,[13] "Track Changes" creates a record of every alteration or edit made to a document, including deleted words or phrases, commentary between coauthors, and prior revisions assigned to particular users. Since tracked changes can be hidden, a person may not realize the feature is activated. Through tracked changes, a document could reveal a lawyer's or client's thought process throughout, for example, contract negotiations, including the adjustment of settlement dollar amounts up or down.
- A "Comment" option appears under the Insert menu and within the Track Changes toolbar or review ribbon. Like other tracked changes, a user can choose to display or hide Comments, which then carry with the document wherever the lawyer or client transmits it.
- The "Save Options" feature—found by following the File menu to Save As, selecting Tools, then Save Options—enables choices like "Always create a backup copy," "Allow fast saves," and "Allow backup saves." Any of these choices, if selected, could create a saved or additional copy of a previous version of a document with or without the author's knowledge (depending on the author's understanding of available tools). "Fast saves," for example, protects against losing changes to a document in case of hardware failure, by appending the changes at the end of a document file. It does not, however, replace the actual

12. In the 2003 version, "properties" is found under the "file" menu. In the 2007 version, it is accessed using the Office Button and then the "prepare" selection. In Word 2010, "properties" is found in the "info" section of the "file" tab.
13. The "track changes" option was moved to the "review" ribbon in 2007.

edited material—so the document may retain changes in the form of metadata that the author attempted to delete.[14]

- Finally, the "Versions" feature under the File menu saves multiple versions of a document, adding an additional version each time it is saved. If left intact, prior versions of the document would remain for viewing by any recipient, including a client or opposing counsel.

In sum, protection of a lawyer's work product and a client's privilege and confidentiality often rely on a cognizant use of these tools, bearing in mind that metadata not only exists within common applications in multiple forms, but also carries with the document or file when shared, copied, or even converted. The legal profession can learn from the experience of the White House intern who diligently posted one of former President Bush's speeches on Iraq to the White House website in PDF format, in turn publishing sufficient metadata to reveal the actual speech writer's identity to the national press.[15]

(2) Erasing metadata from a document

Under appropriate circumstances, software may be used to "scrub," or delete, metadata from a document or file. A lawyer may choose to scrub firm work product or communications for privilege and client confidentiality reasons. Or, litigants may employ scrubbing during discovery to "clean" a data set of unnecessary metadata prior to production. In the latter situation, experts recommend against the scrubbing of the original documents or files to protect both firm and client from potential spoliation claims later in the course of litigation.

Metadata scrubbing tools remove metadata from files before transmission to another party, for example, in the form of email attachments or web posting. Each file type—documents, spreadsheets, presentations, photos, audio files—contains a unique set of metadata with a corresponding program or tool to erase it. Metadata removal tools fall into four general categories:[16]

14. This option was moved in 2007 to the "Word Options" selection under the Office Button.

15. N. Kane Bennett, *Five Hazards to Avoid While Navigating Metadata*, CONN. LAW TRIBUNE, February 7, 2007, *available at* http://www.law.com.

16. *See* Wikipedia, Metadata Removal Tool, http://en.wikipedia.org/wiki/Metadata_Removal_Tool.

- integral scrubbing tools included within certain applications
- batch scrubbing tools that can process multiple files
- email client add-ins, designed to delete metadata from email attachments just before transmission
- server-based systems, designed to automatically remove metadata at the network level

Although lawyers may find the exploration of all the above categories of scrubbing software worthwhile, Microsoft Word 2003 supplies several simple methods of customizing settings and[17] cleaning unwanted metadata from a Word document. First, the Security tab (Tools—Options—Security) allows encryption of a file,[18] specified privacy settings like the removal of identifying information from the file Properties, and a warning of tracked changes and comments prior to printing, saving, or sending a document.[19] The Summary tab (File—Properties—Summary) lists metadata in individual fields; to remove it, simply highlight and delete unneeded entries and click OK. Next, turn off the Fast Saves feature noted above (Tools—Options—Save—Allow Fast Saves) by unchecking or deselecting the box next to the Fast Saves option. Under Versions (File—Versions), highlight versions of the document not to be shared and select Delete. Finally, a user can download a Remove Hidden Metadata add-in for Microsoft Office to remove metadata even where the document was drafted with one of the above metadata-creating features enabled.[20] Once installed, this add-in creates the additional option "Remove Hidden Data" under the File menu. Under this option, a user can create and name a "clean" version of the document and click "Next" to begin

17. Though Word 2003 has been supplanted by Vista (in 2007) and Word 2010, this discussion focuses on Word 2003 because many companies have not yet adopted Microsoft 2010 because of compatibility issues.

18. In the 2007 version, this function was moved under the Office Button, following the "prepare" command. In Word 2010, the "permissions" option is located in the "file" tab.

19. In the 2007 version, this function was moved under the Office Button, following the "Word Options" command. To select this option in Word 2010, the sequence is "File > Help > Options > Trust Center > Trust Center Settings > Privacy Options."

20. Visit http://www.microsoft.com/downloads and search "remove hidden data."

a scan of the file. The process of scanning the document ensures a copy or version free of hidden metadata.[21]

For other software programs, search Google, Yahoo, Bing, or a similar web browser for commercial software metadata scrubbers. As with all software, when researching scrubbing tools, make sure the specific functionality and integration capabilities match the needs of legal workflow.[22]

2. Why does metadata matter?

A. In general

Just as companies exist to perform, not litigate, metadata exists to help users perform, without regard to future legal ramifications. Metadata can therefore become a help or hindrance to litigation depending on type, usage, location, and cost of production. Beyond its evidentiary use, metadata also permits companies and litigants to organize copious amounts of information by custodian, file type, date, and a number of other useful criteria, not to mention the invaluable ability to search across electronic information by subject matter, with increasing speed and accuracy.

Electronic files and media constitute the vast majority of today's communication and record keeping. Industry experts estimate that worldwide, people send between 30 and 60 billion emails every day.[23] Corporations frequently adapt internal policies and practices to keep pace with the flow of information, including the adoption of new technologies, storage limitations, retention and destruction policies, and routine data recycling. Prelitigation, companies strive to maximize efficiency and budget. Postlitigation, data preservation and spoliation concerns arise. Legal professionals must now mirror the technical savvy of other industries and prepare themselves to advise clients on issues of preservation, spoliation, and appropriate records management practices.

B. In litigation

As noted above, metadata often travels with the file or document it describes, carrying with it a potential treasure trove of

---

21. In the 2007 version, the "scrubber" is found under the Office Button, "Prepare," and then "Inspect Document." In Word 2010, the inspection tool is found under "file," "info," "prepare for sharing."

22. Hricik & Scott, *supra* note 11.

23. Seth E. Pierce, *Navigating the E-Discovery Maze*, Applied Discovery, 2008, http://www.applieddiscovery.com.

organizational, evidentiary, privileged, and/or prejudicial information. Capitalizing on the organizational attributes of metadata throughout the process of preservation, collection, production, and review can save enough time and money to help parties survive protracted, presumptively cost-prohibitive disputes. The evidentiary value of application and embedded metadata, or the ability of system metadata to authenticate evidence and protect against challenge, could foreseeably determine success or failure at trial.

Likewise, the decision to request the production of unnecessary metadata or the unjustified erasure of metadata from discoverable files or documents can invite disaster to a client's case and budget. While valuable in many ways, the production of metadata carries its own inherent costs and risks. Even outside the realm of discovery, an attorney sending or receiving a legal document or communication containing inadvertently disclosed metadata may face serious ethical violations for sending, or seeking out or viewing, that information.

The conversion of virtually all communication and potentially relevant data in civil discovery to electronic format has spawned not only significant revisions to the rules of civil procedure and evidence, but also a flood of new case law outlining previously unknown legal and ethical requirements for counsel. For the first time ever, lawyers must achieve a certain level of technical sophistication to avoid the risk of sanctions and maintain the viability of an action.[24]

3. Metadata in discovery

A. General discoverability and the process of requesting metadata

Like all other forms of electronically stored information, metadata falls within the general scope of discovery and may be requested if (1) relevant to the claims or defenses of either party and (2) not privileged. Due to the technical nature of producing metadata and its potential cost, metadata is discoverable subject to an analysis of burden and expense.[25] Some courts—in addition to considerations of demonstrated relevance, privilege, burden, and expense—require a showing of good cause to justify the burden and expense of production.[26]

---

24. See chapter's 8 and 29.

25. Williams v. Sprint/United Mgmt. Co., 230 F.R.D. at 651–52.

26. U.S. Dist. Ct., Dist. of Md., The Suggested Protocol for Discovery of Electronically Stored Information (2007).

Three main federal court approaches to the production of metadata have emerged. In the first, courts favor the production of electronic documents in their native format, with original metadata intact.[27] The second supports a presumption against the production of metadata, absent a strong showing of particularized need. Under this second approach, the failure to request metadata prior to the production waives any later objection to its absence.[28] The third line of cases strikes a balance between the first two, supporting the production of metadata when relevant and not overly burdensome to the producing party.[29]

The following paragraphs outline the primary federal rules revised to account for the complexities of electronically stored information (ESI) and governing the discovery of metadata. Since their adoption in 2006, a majority of states have enacted rules closely mirroring the federal revisions.[30]

(1) Rule 34: Metadata enters the realm of discoverable information

Under the Federal Rules of Civil Procedure, revised to account for the proliferation of electronically stored information, an analysis of the discoverability of metadata begins with Rule 34.[31] Although Rule 34 does not specifically address metadata, it does provide the right of a party to specify the desired form of production, including the request for ESI with accompanying metadata. The responding party may object to all or part of the request for reasons of cost, burden, irrelevance, or privilege. The requesting party must then provide a showing of good cause or otherwise support its request for metadata by demonstrating its utility in a motion to compel.

If the requesting party fails to specify a form of production, Rule 34 requires the producing party to produce in (1) the form in which the data was "ordinarily maintained," which may include native format and accompanying metadata, or (2) a "reasonably useable" form, which translates to reasonably usable and searchable.

27. *See* Nova Measuring Instruments Ltd. v. Nanometrics, Inc., 417 F. Supp. 2d 1121 (N.D. Cal. 2006).

28. *See* Wyeth v. Impax Labs., Inc., 248 F.R.D. 169 (D. Del. 2006).

29. *See In re* Seroquel Products Liab. Litig., 244 F.R.D. 650 (M.D. Fla. 2007).

30. For a review of e-discovery rules enacted in each state, see chapter 3 or visit eLaw Exchange, http://www.elawexchange.com.

31. The procedure for requesting and producing ESI under Rule 34 is also discussed in greater detail in chapter 2.

Production of metadata is not, however, mandatory. In accordance with Rule 34's parameters, parties commonly pair TIFF (tagged image file format) with OCR (optical character recognition) text files for production. TIFF format, essentially an image or photograph of the original document, preserves the appearance and content of the document without carrying over metadata. OCR technology, run against the TIFF images and typically provided as part of a load file,[32] offers the ability to search across the text of the documents with a relatively small margin of error. The Advisory Committee Notes to Rule 34 elaborate on the searchability requirement: if a business ordinarily maintains its information in an easily searchable electronic form, a party may not significantly degrade or remove that convenience in its form of production.[33] "Documents stripped of metadata allowing searches do not comply with Rule 34(b)."[34]

Although a Rule 26(f) conference (also called "the conference of the parties") plays a central role in guiding the scope, timing, and specificity of a request or objection to the production of metadata, Rule 34 underscores the importance of a timely objection as to the ongoing form a production takes, and specifically whether the opposing party has produced the desired metadata throughout the entire course of discovery. The court addressed this issue involving not the agreement to produce, but rather the *adequacy of production,* in the recent *Ford Motor Co. v. Edgewood Properties* case.[35] In *Ford Motor Co.*, plaintiffs objected to the defendants' request for production in native format with metadata and proceeded to produce in TIFF with searchable text (OCR). Three rolling productions and almost one year later, defendant Edgewood filed a motion to compel re-production in the original requested form. In denying Edgewood's motion, the court explained that the defendant failed to object within a reasonable period of time, allowing multiple rolling productions to occur without checking for adequacy or compliance issues. *Ford Motor Co.* clarifies the obligation of counsel to not only comply with the procedure proscribed by Rule 34 for

32. A load file is a data file that defines the links between multiple records in a database and document images.

33. Fed. R. Civ. P. 34(b) advisory committee's note to 2006 Amendment.

34. *In re* Payment Card Interchange Fee & Merch, Disc., 2007 WL 121426, at *4 (E.D.N.Y. Jan. 12, 2007).

35. Ford Motor Co. v. Edgewood Props., Inc., 2009 WL 1416223 (D.N.J. May 19, 2009).

requesting metadata, but also to monitor the compliance of opposing counsel throughout the discovery process in order to preserve future objections.

(2) Rule 26(f): The requirement for timeliness, specificity, and early cooperation

A prompt request for a party's preferred form of production, including any type of metadata, permits the responding party to make the necessary arrangements for the production or raise any timely objections. The negotiation between counsel as to what form the production will ultimately take occurs at the Rule 26(f) conference of the parties.[36] The Advisory Committee Notes to Rule 26(f) offer a definition of metadata and provide that its discoverability "may be among the topics discussed in the Rule 26(f) conference."[37] Pursuant to the spirit and intent of the conference, parties must be prepared to discuss the type and format of all discoverable electronic data, including any requested metadata for certain documents or file types. The failure of a party to raise these topics in a timely manner or make a specific request may result in the ultimate denial of an otherwise valid request for production with metadata.[38]

In a case illustrating the importance of specificity, the District Court for the District of Columbia held that a plaintiff's request for "any documents stored or maintained in files in the normal course of business . . . in such a manner as to preserve and identify the file from which such documents were taken" lacked sufficient detail to support a request for metadata. Rather, the wording of the request appeared to address "a common concern of paper discovery: the identification of a document's custodian and origin." The court summarized its decision with the basic principle of law that a court will not compel discovery that has not been sought.[39]

In addition to timeliness and specificity, the conference of the parties highlights the need for cooperation among counsel. As the court stated in *Ford Motor Co.*: "this entire problem could have been avoided had there been an explicit agreement between the parties as to production. . . . Parties would be best to heed the

36. For more information on Rule 26(f) conferences, see chapter 19.

37. FED. R. CIV. P. 26(f) advisory committee's note.

38. Ky. Speedway, LLC v. Nat'l Ass'n of Stock Car Auto Racing, Inc., 2006 U.S. Dist. LEXIS 92028 (E.D. Ky. Dec. 18, 2006).

39. D'Onofrio v. SFX Sports Group, Inc., 247 F.R.D. 43 (D.D.C. 2008).

admonition of a recent court that 'the best solution in the entire area of electronic discovery is cooperation among counsel.'"[40]

(3) Rule 26(b)(2)(C): Balancing the benefit against the burden of producing metadata

If contested, a request for metadata must survive Rule 26(b)(2)(C) ("the proportionality rule"), requiring a court to weigh the benefit of the metadata against the potential burden of production. A burden issue arises because the additional review and production of the metadata associated with every potentially relevant document necessarily result in a more complex, time-consuming, and even cost-prohibitive discovery process. The fact that most metadata carries "limited evidentiary value"[41] only compounds the complexity of production concerns. Citing this balancing test, the court in *Aguilar*[42] found the production cost of metadata from email backup tapes "unquestionably high and the likely benefit low," and so declined to order production.[43] On the other hand, cost shifting between parties may tilt the scales back in favor of production: despite the burden outweighing the likely value, the *Aguilar* court permitted the production of system metadata for Word and PowerPoint documents *at the requesting party's expense.*[44]

B. The Sedona Principles: Best practices for the discovery of metadata

Lawyers seeking to obtain—or challenge—the production of metadata in discovery may consult the compiled recommendations of lawyers, judges, and industry experts through the publications of the Sedona Conference. In particular, Principle 12 of *The Sedona Principles: Best Practices, Recommendations & Principles for Addressing Electronic Document Production*[45] explores the legal obligation, if any, to produce metadata for evidentiary, authentication, or organization and searching purposes.

---

40. *Ford Motor Co.*, 2009 WL 1416223 (citing William A. Gross Constr. Assocs., Inc. v. Am. Mfrs. Mut. Ins. Co., 2009 WL 724954 (S.D.N.Y. Mar. 19, 2009)).

41. Wyeth v. Impax Labs., Inc., 248 F.R.D. 169, 171 (D. Del. 2006).

42. Aguilar v. Immigration & Customs Enforcement Div., U.S. Dep't of Homeland Sec., 255 F.R.D. 350 (S.D.N.Y. 2008).

43. *Id.* at 360.

44. *Id.* at 363 (emphasis added).

45. THE SEDONA CONFERENCE, THE SEDONA PRINCIPLES: BEST PRACTICES, RECOMMENDATIONS & PRINCIPLES FOR ADDRESSING ELECTRONIC DOCUMENT PRODUCTION, at Principle 12 (2d ed. 2007).

Federal courts frequently cite the Sedona Principles as an alternate or additional authority on the discoverability of ESI and specifically on the proper basis for production of metadata. In *Autotech Technologies v. Automationdirect.com*,[46] the court denied a motion to compel the production of metadata where the requesting party failed to make its request until after production, relying in part on the 2005 Sedona Principles. The court ruled that absent a special request for metadata (or any reasonable showing of relevance to the claims and defenses), and a prior order of the court based on a showing of need (i.e., good cause), a scanned image production in PDF or TIFF complies with Rule 34. Though the reasons remain unclear, the court rested its opinion on the 2005 Sedona Principles rather than the revised 2007 version. Note the difference in position on the production of metadata between the two versions of Principle 12:

- 2005: Unless material to the resolution of a dispute, there is *no obligation to preserve and produce metadata* absent agreement of the parties or order of the court.
- 2007: Absent party agreement or court order specifying the form or forms of production, production should be made in the form or forms in which the information is ordinarily maintained or in a reasonably usable form, *taking into account the need to produce reasonably accessible metadata that will enable the receiving party to have the same ability to access, search and display the information as the producing party where appropriate or necessary* in light of the nature of the information and the needs of the case.[47]

The Sedona Principles recognize that "the two 'primary considerations' should be the need for and the probative value of the metadata, and the extent to which the metadata will 'enhance the functional utility of the electronic information.'"[48] In other words, metadata's inclusion in the discovery process should rest on its relevance and ability to assist in the organization and review of the documents, including the ability to search them. The Sedona Conference places extra importance on this latter function of meta-

46. Autotech Techs., Ltd. P'ship v. Automationdirect.com, Inc., 248 F.R.D. 556 (N.D. Ill. 2008).
47. Shannon Kirk & Kathryn Hong, *Rule 34: A Cause for Confusion*, LAW TECH. NEWS, Jan. 16, 2009.
48. *Aguilar*, 255 F.R.D. at 356.

data—the provision of contextual and functional information—in its findings. Metadata includes "all of the contextual, processing, and use information needed to identify and certify the scope, authenticity, and integrity of active or archival electronic information or records."[49]

Maintaining their focus on practicality, the Sedona Principles assert the sufficiency of ESI production in TIFF or PDF, together with a load file containing searchable text and selective metadata, over native production. Although courts across the country frequently cite Sedona recommendations, practitioners must bear in mind that the Sedona Principles represent nonbinding practice guidelines.

C. Lessons learned on the discoverability of metadata

1. Rule 34 allows a request for, but does not necessarily require, the production of metadata. Imaged documents, like PDF or TIFF, if produced with searchable text and load files, may constitute "reasonably usable" forms.
2. A request for metadata must be timely and specific; these aspects, together with the early cooperation of counsel, are central considerations for the court when ruling on a motion to compel.
3. If the responding party objects to a request for metadata, the court will weigh the potential cost and burden of production against the technical utility of the metadata and its particularized relevance (evidentiary value) to the litigation.
4. Some metadata may present issues relating to privilege and work product, while most does not.

4. Metadata in practice

A. The decision to request metadata

The decision in any given case to request metadata will depend on the anticipated native file types in the opposing party's possession. Each type of metadata presents unique evidentiary or functional advantages, as well as the potential risk for the inadvertent disclosure of confidential or privileged information. System metadata

49. The Sedona Conference, Best Practices Guidelines & Commentary for Managing Information and Records in the Electronic Age, at app. D: Technical Appendix (Sept. 2004).

may offer important information as to who authored, accessed, or edited key documents in a case, like board minutes. In particular, it can provide key discoverable information that may not carry over into a TIFF or PDF image, like the author or date of internal corporate reports not formatted to display such data. Embedded metadata may shed light on misleading accounting figures by revealing the formulas behind financial spreadsheets, or otherwise explain or clarify discoverable, displayed information. The production of substantive metadata, while useful in its ability to capture the actual text of comments and revisions to a document, may require a cost-prohibitive amount of additional review for privileged content. On the other hand, if there are genuine questions regarding authenticity of documents, a request for metadata may be important.

(1) Advantages to production with metadata

Litigants regularly agree to exchange native files, including metadata, for its utility in tracking email or organizing a database of information. Metadata may also be preserved and produced with static images. Production with metadata allows parties to expedite review and case preparation through batch (objective) coding, keyword searching, filtering, and categorization (by custodian, topic, or date) of substantive case issues, privilege, or confidentiality. Another advantage involves the ability to review full email strings or threads, providing context to each message and enhanced accuracy in coding or "tagging" them. Batch coding likewise applies to the identification of duplicate copies (of the same document, usually to multiple recipients) and "near duplicates" (documents sharing a certain percentage of similarity);[50] by coding such materials together, a firm can vastly reduce the cost of attorney review and more easily meet deadlines.

As noted earlier, litigants commonly exchange TIFF or PDF files, together with an OCR load file to maintain the ability to search across them. The process of scanning native files to images with OCR risks greater inaccuracy than simply leaving the original file intact. OCR builds a text file or "copy" of the text in an image based on its recognition of each character, but only within an industry-accepted margin of error that increases as the document quality

50. Near-duplicates are documents that differ by a few words or paragraphs; following production, near duplicates can be identified according to a selected percentage of similarity and grouped to provide greater efficiency in review.

decreases. Conversion to TIFF removes metadata altogether, while PDF replaces or distorts the original metadata attached to each document. Absent precautions or expertise, conversion of native files can blur the connections between attachments and their parent email or links between documents. In some cases, native production may actually lessen the complexity of large databases or files that do not translate well to imaging (e.g., spreadsheets, digital voice or sound recordings, animated content, websites, video, graphics, or drawings).

Metadata can also play a central role in proving or disproving the authenticity of certain electronic documents, verifying the authenticity of a document's content, source, path, and chain of custody as a whole. "Because metadata shows the date, time and identity of the creator of an electronic record, as well as all changes made to it, metadata is a distinctive characteristic of all electronic evidence that can be used to authenticate it under [Federal Rule of Evidence] 901(b)(4)."[51]

(2) Disadvantages to production of metadata

Production of native, or other, files with metadata carries two significant disadvantages. First, the metadata must be reviewed for relevance and responsiveness. Second, it must be reviewed to protect privileges. Review increases cost and the margin of error.

Exchanging documents in native format, though useful for the production of metadata, can also complicate some basic review and production processes in other ways. The challenges presented by the simple application of production numbers or secure redactions often result in the need to image documents anyway. If a party intends to produce TIFF images in visibly good condition, the relatively small margin of error inherent in OCR may have little or no impact on the quality of the review. Supporting the sufficiency of nonnative production, the Sedona Principles note that "even if native files are requested, it is sufficient to produce [ESI] in PDF or TIFF format accompanied by a load file containing searchable text and selected metadata."[52]

---

51. Lorraine v. Markel-Am. Ins. Co., 241 F.R.D. 534, 547–48 (D. Md. 2007); chapter 24.

52. The Sedona Conference, The Sedona Principles: Best Practices Recommendations & Principles for Addressing Electronic Document Production, at Principle 12 (2d ed. 2007).

If responsive documents are scrubbed of metadata in litigation, that process requires transparency, that is, disclosure, and a copy of the production must be retained in native format with its metadata intact. Litigants can return to the native version, if necessary, to protect against challenges to the authenticity of evidence, charges of spoliation (the accidental loss or alteration of data), or to demonstrate good faith in discovery practices. Both sides stand to save a considerable amount of time and money simply by agreeing, early in the discovery process, to postpone the production of metadata until its use becomes necessary for specified files. The federal rules, in fact, provide for the possibility of phased production, with metadata excluded from phase I and included in a smaller phase II production.[53]

B. Evaluating the need for a specialist

The preservation and collection of metadata present a unique challenge to the discovery process. Not only does a legal advisor need to know when and what type of metadata to request in a particular action, but also the appropriate methods by which to gather and review it. One of the primary complications of exchanging data in native format revolves around forensic preservation and collection. The complexity and cost of obtaining a forensically sound, legally defensible copy of electronic data can outweigh the evidentiary value of metadata to the case. Practitioners must discuss and decide on a case-by-case basis whether the subject of the litigation justifies the cost of such specialized help, asking a few basic questions: Are fraud or dishonesty at issue? Malpractice? Does the need exist for a neutral third party to act as arbitrator or collector of discovery? Anytime a custodian of data or system manager copies, relocates, or converts data—often for routine and justifiable business purposes—the inherent risk of changing the original metadata behind those files arises. For example, simply opening a Word document to confirm its relevance to a case replaces the "Modified" field with new information, updating the time and date stamp automatically recorded by the native application to reflect who last accessed or altered the document. The person opening the document may have just caused spoliation of potential evidence, and depending on the importance of that infor-

53. FED. R. CIV. P. 26(f)(3)(B).

mation to the case, exposed both the client and counsel to potential sanctions or, in egregious cases, an adverse jury instruction.

Another potential hazard involves the wrong choice of software or data processing tool. If a company new to litigation asks its records management or IT staff to copy files requested by opposing counsel, and gives no further instruction on *how* to copy those files, the staff may utilize common "ghosting" software to duplicate the data. Without knowing the evidentiary and authentication value of metadata in civil litigation, the company may fail to realize that ghosting programs not only change certain fields of metadata, but typically copy only active files, as opposed to all files (active and inactive) captured by a professional, forensic collection. The inactive files—deleted from view but still residing on a computer's hard drive until overwritten by new data—can sometimes represent the most valuable or sought-after evidence.

Just as paper records require a basic level of care to avoid tearing or fading, digital records require the safekeeping of basic, commonly referenced metadata fields like the date stamps in a Word document or the formulas built into Excel. Both independent and professional methods exist to safeguard against the inherent preservation and collection risks when handling metadata. For example, tools exist to "write protect" the metadata on a hard drive, ranging in cost from free to about $200.[54] Although the availability of affordable software programs makes the independent preservation and collection of metadata possible and potentially less expensive, lawyers must be cognizant of user error and note the limitations and purpose of each program (e.g., programs designed solely for the management of email or specified file types).

Through the process of forensic imaging, hired specialists can preserve and produce a legally defensible data set, called an "authenticated volume," meaning that the electronic data the collection contains maintains the original attributes and integrity of the information needed for discovery. Specifically, obtaining an authenticated volume guarantees that the copying, conversion, or movement of files from one location to another has not altered the metadata in any way. Forensic specialists provide documentation of the steps taken to create an authenticated volume of the data and can testify in court as to its integrity and chain of custody. Expert assistance may also prove necessary when requesting

54 Craig Ball, *Don't Mess with System Metadata*, Law Tech. News, Apr. 23, 2009.

unusual or specialized forms of metadata. For example, in a case where a live demonstration of defendants' hierarchical databases was ordered as part of discovery, plaintiffs were forced to retain a consulting expert simply to decipher what changes were made to certain records and when.[55]

Before engaging a service provider or specialist, consider the capabilities of the staff and collection tools available to the client. Sizable offices or companies experiencing frequent litigation commonly deploy software specifically designed to collect and preserve metadata forensically or have the budget to do so. A trained staff, together with the increasingly intuitive programs already offered to the market, may mitigate or eliminate the additional cost of third-party support.

In addition, not every situation calls for forensic imaging. Only some cases necessitate the production of metadata for evidentiary purposes, authentication, or organization and searching of large data sets. If, for instance, the merits of a case rest entirely on scientific reports and expert testimony, or if there is no genuine dispute as to authenticity, then neither party will likely require the discovery of metadata. Alternatively, the review and production of metadata may become more important in a case involving fraud or misrepresentation. From a technical vantage point, some requested metadata may no longer exist; native files altered or converted prior to the onset of a litigation hold—due to the routine functioning of a business's preservation and destruction policy—may negate the need for any type of metadata collection, independent or forensic.

In determining whether to forgo the independent collection of metadata in favor of a forensic analysis, consider the following questions:[56]

- Does the custodian of a certain computer or files occupy so central or crucial a position that an accusation of data tampering or destruction could hurt the company?
- Is the user suspected of stealing/misappropriating trade secrets or poaching customers or employees?
- Does the litigation involve the suspected forgery of a computer-generated document or communication?

55. Aguilar v. Immigration & Customs Enforcement Div., U.S. Dep't of Homeland Sec., 255 F.R.D. 350 (S.D.N.Y. 2008).

56. Ball, *supra* note 53 (reproduced with permission of the author).

- Does the inappropriate use of email or the Internet factor into the alleged misconduct?
- Did a departing employee bring a personal laptop, external hard drive, or thumb drive to work?
- Did the size of a user's server email storage suddenly or significantly diminish, or are messages believed to be missing from storage?
- Do server logs or indicators reflect atypical access to data areas?
- Has a user been notably secretive in the use of company computers or been observed using someone else's machine without permission?
- Has the user recently requested that IT reinstall the operating system on his or her machine?
- Has the user inquired into data destruction techniques or been observed with wiping software?[57]

5. Metadata in the clouds

Cloud computing presents the next major hurdle for lawyers attempting to develop legally defensible practices in dealing with electronic evidence. In fact, the speed with which technology companies develop new software and service models far exceeds the law's current ability to keep pace, creating a "no man's land" between the realities of Internet-based business and the remedial capabilities of litigation. This disconnect will likely grow, perhaps exponentially, as the "Millennials"—the newest generation of technically literate youth—flood the professional marketplace.

The "cloud" refers to the scalable, dynamic, and virtually limitless body of resources and services made available over the Internet. Cloud computing encompasses three primary models: infrastructure as a service (IaaS), platform as a service (PaaS), and software as a service (SaaS). As its name implies, IaaS supplies Internet-based data processing, storage, and networking bandwidth. PaaS provides for cloud-based development and testing of custom applications. SaaS pulls local applications into the cloud, like email, word processing, and customer relationship management systems. Cloud computing enables offices to outsource most of

57. The list in the text is derived from *Don't Mess with System Metadata, supra* note 53, with the gracious permission of the author.

their hardware, software, and support while increasing available storage and access to sophisticated tools.

Most importantly, cloud computing fundamentally changes how people perceive, manage, share, and store data. Take, for example, software developers whose company policies, limited server capacity, and laborious approval process frustrates their ability to work efficiently and meet deadlines. These busy engineers can swipe a credit card to test a new application in the cloud and pull the results back into the company. A larger company may not even learn that a portion of development took place off-site until months, or even years, later.

Some dismiss the fervor surrounding the cloud as unnecessary hype. Oracle CEO Larry Ellison quipped, "My objection to cloud computing is the fact that cloud computing is not only the future of computing, it is the present and the entire past. Google's now cloud computing. Everybody's cloud computing. All it is, is a computer attached to a network."[58] Few would argue, however, that the cloud presents real and yet unresolved challenges to traditional litigation. Would most attorneys know, for the purposes of the Rule 26 conference, where their client's cloud-based data resides? Who controls that data? Who ensures defensible preservation and collection procedures once litigation ensues? How does any particular cloud service regard or protect privacy or privilege? How much time will a lawyer require to retrieve the specific form of production requested under Rule 34 by opposing counsel? Does the technology even allow for the customary forms of production? More importantly for purposes of this chapter, how does one identify, preserve, and produce metadata contained on someone else's computer systems in the clouds? Is metadata changed when it moves through the cloud, and what are the consequences if it changes after the duty to preserve arises? Do transactional attorneys need to insert contractual rights into agreements with service providers?

Lawyers and their clients can prepare for some complexities of cloud-based computing by amending service agreements to account for greater control and ownership of data, like access to system metadata. But more important than any other preventative measure may be the willingness of counsel to engage in an open dialogue with their clients and adversaries about these issues. A

58. Yobie Benjamin, *Cloud Computing: Jobs, Good and Bad News, the Future and Larry Ellison*, SF GATE, Sept. 22, 2009.

simple web search reveals a wealth of resources for determining key topics to discuss, beginning with an assessment of data access and security.[59]

6. Conclusion

As the world of metadata grows, lawyers must adapt to the expansion and innovation of other industries, utilizing the tools and mirroring technology practices with their own set of modernized practices in discovery.[60]

59. *See, e.g.*, Jon Brodkin, *Gartner: Seven Cloud Computing Security Risks*, Network World, July 2, 2008.

60. Production of ESI with metadata, or, alternatively, scrubbing of metadata, may present ethical issues that are beyond the scope of this chapter. See chapter 29 for a more detailed discussion of those topics.

CHAPTER 7

THE DISCOVERY OF STRUCTURED DATA

DAVID KESSLER AND DANIEL L. REGARD II[1]

A staggering amount of information is now stored in databases and other structured forms. Here, an electronic evidence expert and a litigation practitioner join to provide a briefing on the nature and form of structured data and its discoverability under current law. The chapter includes a detailed discussion of major cases in this subject area—often followed by specific "practice tips" to be gleaned from them.

1. Introduction

This chapter analyzes the definition, case law, and practical tips for handling structured data, or databases, in civil discovery. The amount of digital information generated annually is increasing at an explosive rate.[2] The dramatic increase in the quantity of information, coupled with the increasing use of electronic data creation

---

1. The authors would like to acknowledge the valuable contributions of Richard Hunter, an attorney at Drinker Biddle & Reath LLP, and Julian Ackert, a director at Intelligent Discovery Solutions.

2. *See* Emily Burns, *E-Discovery: One Year of the Amended Federal Rules of Civil Procedure*, 64 N.Y.U. ANN. SURV. AM. L. 201, 201 (2008) (citations omitted) (highlighting statistics regarding growth rate of the "digital universe" from 5 exabytes in

and storage by corporations, has created myriad challenges to parties conducting discovery in litigation.

Furthermore, of the growth forecasted by the IDC, almost 75 percent is expected to comprise databases and other forms of structured data. The discovery of structured data is not as well understood as the discovery of unstructured data by the Bench, Bar, and parties, and the pertinent case law is just developing. Like much of e-discovery, the discovery of databases can present paradoxes. Many are not static in nature, but instead are interconnected with other data sources, and are often subject to updates and adjustments on an ongoing basis based on automatic processes and user inputs. On the other hand, they can be long lasting and survive independently of any particular employee, function, or even company. Thus, at a time when structured data is growing at unprecedented levels, there is either confusion or a lack of knowledge about how to handle it from a legal and practical perspective. The intent of this chapter is to shed some light on three key elements of structured data:

- What is it?
- How have the courts addressed structured data?
- What are the practical considerations?

2. What is structured data?

Many people label data as either structured or unstructured, as we have in the introduction. The truth, however, is that all data has varying degrees of structure and lies on a continuum between purely structured and purely unstructured—with the overwhelming majority existing in the middle. This continuum can further be described by three different characteristics. The first is the information itself. The second is the container in which data is stored and retrieved. The third is the method in which the data is retrieved.

Thus, an employee's Microsoft Word and PowerPoint documents stored on her desktop—classic unstructured data—may have little structure with respect to any of these three characteristics. On the other side of the continuum, many laypeople use the phrase "structured data" and "database" interchangeably, but there are other highly structured data sets including network log files, electronically printed reports, and document file structures.

2002 to 161 exabytes in 2006). One exabyte is equal to approximately one billion gigabytes.

Furthermore, as described below, certain aspects of a database can be highly unstructured. Some familiar documents, including spreadsheets and email, have both structured and unstructured components.[3]

Understanding these three characteristics has practical applications in the discovery of structured data—especially in the determination of burden and cost, the determination of the scope (or completeness) of the data that will be discovered, and the selection of tools for identifying, preserving, collecting, and producing structured data. This is because the more data is unstructured along any of these three characteristics, the less useful are automated methods of identifying, reviewing, producing and evaluating the data and, hence, the greater the potential burden and cost to both parties.

A. Structured content

The content of data files (or data fields) can be tightly controlled or uniform within a narrow range of values. This is considered structured content. An example of structured content is a U.S. phone number. A phone number in the United States is typically written as the area code in parentheses, followed by a three-digit prefix, a hyphen, and a four-digit suffix, such as (212) 555-1212. If a set of files contained only U.S. phone numbers, they could be analyzed, reviewed, searched, and handled in a uniform and consistent manner.

The opposite of this is unstructured content. The classic example of unstructured content is an email body. The content of the body of an email is free-flowing and unrestricted. It could contain words, numbers, links, pictures, files, and/or tables, all of varying sizes and content.

Databases typically contain some type of structured content. That is to say, at least some data fields (e.g., columns in a spreadsheet) within a database have strict controls regarding the format of individual values (e.g., dates, social security numbers). However,

3. While in some cases email may be stored in the form of structured data, the discovery and handling of email messages are beyond the scope of this chapter. Similarly, individual spreadsheets have highly structured features, but the Bench and Bar have developed methods for handling their discovery as unstructured data and, thus, are beyond the scope of this chapter. However, as shown below, many of these lessons are helpful in understanding how courts have treated databases and other structured data sets.

other fields may be highly unstructured such as text fields (e.g., a comments field in technical help desk database). Importantly, the same data field can be highly structured in one database and highly unstructured in another. For example, an address field could be a simple text field in one database and a series of tightly controlled fields in another where the "State" code must be one of a finite list of two-character choices and the "Zip" code is limited to a five-digit integer.

The more structured the content of a file (or a field) is, the easier it should be to index, search, isolate, export, sort, produce, and receive.

B. Structured container

The locations where data are stored can be structured, even when the data itself is not. For example, a spreadsheet typically has highly uniform columns and rows; that is, the *layout* is uniform, but the contents of the cells at the intersection of columns and rows can be highly variable. So is it with databases. Individual database tables are often compared to spreadsheet tables for good reason. Both have columns (fields) and rows (records). Typically, database tables have uniformly formatted values in a given column, but this may vary as well.

Where the container of a file (or a field) is more structured, it can be easier to search, isolate, export, review, produce, and receive.

C. Structured retrieval

How data is organized and retrieved can also be described in terms of structured or unstructured. Again, databases are the epitome of structured retrieval, but it is important to note that not all aspects of databases are equal in terms of their ability to be retrieved.

Consider a database of invoices where each invoice has a section to capture special instructions. While the invoices may be highly organized by invoice number, purchaser, and date, they may not be organized by those special instructions. In the context of a litigation exercise, a request to produce all invoices with special instructions to leave packages without requiring a signature, for example, may be much more difficult to comply with than a request to produce all invoices for customer XYZ.

Even loose data files, typically considered the most unstructured area of data, can be stored in a data management system that enables a high degree of retrieval, albeit along a restricted set of fields and values. For example, a data management system that compels employees to list the author of a document before it can be saved may allow a party to identify all documents where a particular author was chosen. And as data management systems proliferate, it is likely that we will see an improved ability to retrieve these unstructured data files by a combination of fielded values and full text searches. Hence they may remain unstructured as to content, and likely unstructured as to container, but become more structured as to retrieval.

D. Databases

As described above, the terms "structured data" and "database" appear to be used interchangeably, at least in the case law. Databases are typically highly structured along all three aspects described above. Much of their data is in the form of structured content. Much of their data is also in structured containers. Much of their data is susceptible to structured retrieval. It is also important to recognize, however, that some of the data stored in databases may not seem to be structured at all. Returning to the example of email stored in databases, .wav files (sound files) stored as attachments to emails may fit none of the criteria.

E. Special challenges of databases

Databases present several challenges that are separate and distinct from the normal collection of emails and loose files that are handled in modern litigation. These challenges include

- complex physical structure
- complex digital structure
- multiple methods of establishing structure
- multiple methods of exporting and transferring data
- software and hardware dependencies
- varying degrees of data quality over time
- varying degrees of data quantity over time
- customization
- potential data encryption at the field level

The complex physical structure means that databases may have many tables (some have 5,000 or more) and those dependencies may extend to tables beyond the immediate database.

The complex digital structure means that the way individual records are constructed can vary widely. For example, sometimes all of the information for that record is stored as a single collection. Alternatively, there may be pointers to other locations where components, especially large binary objects (BLOBs), are stored. Record sizes are typically fixed, but can also be variable in length.

The structure (the relationship between the tables) may be fixed, and reflected in relationship tables that the database stores and maintains. The structure may be dynamic, and created by queries and software modules on an as-needed basis. The latter method would leave no permanent traces in the database itself as to how those relationships are to be created.

Software and hardware dependencies means that additional modules, certain operating system versions and/or updates, certain database versions and/or updates, and even specifically named drives and network locations may be needed in order for the database and its applications to function correctly. This is particularly important when copying entire databases.

Varying degrees over time refers to the fact that the quality or even existence of database entries varies. For example, it is not uncommon to have databases expanded over time and for earlier entries to lack values for the expanded fields. It is also not uncommon to have manual inputs eventually replaced with automated inputs, or to have the validation routines for certain fields improved over time, again affecting the quality of the contents.

Many businesses customize their software, some quite substantially. Base familiarity with the original system may lead to incorrect assumptions about the current system. Furthermore, unless there is clear documentation, the current staff may not know of the customizations, or how they actually affect the data.

Field level encryption—for example, for personally identifiable information such as social security number—can hamper or completely frustrate the usage of those fields. If those fields are also used for building the relational table models, then the larger database structure can be adversely affected as well.

Individually, or as a whole, these aspects (and others) of databases can lead to miscommunications between parties as to the nature, behavior, application, and availability of data from databases, and compound the challenges already inherent in the discovery process.

Currently, the sparse opinions that have focused on databases have not focused on these technical challenges, but rather have analyzed them using the framework the courts have developed to scrutinize discovery disputes regarding unstructured electronically stored information (ESI). Practitioners, however, should be cognizant of these challenges as they advise their clients regarding their discovery obligations and make representations to their opponents and the court. As the volume of structured data increases dramatically and, thus, becomes prevalent in more and more discovery disputes, we expect that courts will begin to focus on the challenges in their decisions.

3. How is the discovery of structured data treated under the law?

First and foremost, structured data is electronically stored information. Therefore, it is appropriate to look at how we handle ESI generally for guidance on how to handle structured data. At the same time, because databases present challenges that other types of data may not, practitioners need to be aware when e-discovery rules and methods can have unexpected consequences.

A. The discovery of databases

Although the case law on databases is scant, there is some precedent. We have found it best to organize the legal issues around six questions:

1. *Discoverability:* Are databases discoverable?
2. *Relevance:* How does one determine if all or part of a structured data collection is relevant?
3. *Preservation:* What is the duty to preserve the relevant structured data? What are the limitations on this duty to preserve?
4. *Burden:* How does one calculate the burden of producing structured data and how does this affect a party's duty to produce structured data?
5. *Form of production:* In what formats can structured data be produced? What are the limitations on these forms of production?
6. *Third-party vendors:* What is the boundary of possession and control when a third-party vendor owns and/or operates the underlying database or system?

B. Discoverability of structured data

While discovery of structured data raises certain unique issues, data compilations generally are considered to be within the scope of discoverable material.[4] Provided that an appropriate discovery request is made, data from databases and other forms of structured data must be produced.[5]

C. Determining relevance in discovery of structured data

An important question facing litigants and courts is deciding what parts of a structured data repository are relevant. In some cases, parties may seek only a few records stored in a large database. In other cases, a party may request that the entire database be produced for inspection. Accordingly, in crafting motions to compel production of structured data, courts have taken a range of approaches, from simply declining to order production of a database to ordering full access to the requesting party.[6]

While it is possible that all or almost all of the data in a database would be relevant to a litigation—for example, a special purpose database that was created to store only data for a project that since become the focus of the litigation—the much more common circumstance is that certain data in a database is potentially relevant and most is not. Does this make the entire database relevant and discoverable? No. Just as the fact that a certain number of an employee's emails are relevant does not make all of that person's emails relevant, the fact that specific data in a database is relevant

4. *See, e.g.*, FED. R. CIV. P. 34(a) (2007) ("any designated documents or electronically stored information—including . . . data or data compilations—stored in any medium from which information can be obtained"). The Advisory Committee Notes further indicate that Rule 34(a)(1) "is expansive and includes any type of information that is stored electronically," and that it "is intended to be broad enough to cover all current types of computer-based information, and flexible enough to encompass future changes and development."

5. *See In re* EBay Seller Antitrust Litig., 2009 WL 3613511 (N.D. Cal. Oct. 28, 2009) ("The Federal Rules of Civil Procedure clearly contemplate the production of information from dynamic databases."); Margel v. E.G.L. Gem LAB Ltd., 2009 WL 2224288, at *4 (S.D.N.Y. May 29, 2008); Tulip Computers Int'l B.V. v. Dell Computer Corp., 2002 WL 818061, at *7 (D. Del. 2002) (providing plaintiff's expert data analyst access to corporate defendant's database).

6. *See, e.g.*, Bob Barker Co. v. Ferguson Safety Prods., 2006 U.S. Dist. LEXIS 14789, at *12–13 (N.D. Cal. 2006) (declining to order production of financial services database responsive to discovery request because "it is unclear how a party could go about producing 'a database,' which ordinarily is a dynamic collection of data that changes over time").

does not make the entire database relevant.[7] However, practitioners need to be careful to examine the data relationships within the database. These linkages can connect seemingly irrelevant data to relevant data in a way that makes the irrelevant data probative of an issue in the litigation.

> Practice Tip
>
> Focus on the data relevant to the litigation, not the container of the data.

(1) General standards for relevance in discovery of electronically stored information, including structured data

In crafting discovery orders pertaining to structured data, courts first consider the general standards for relevance in pretrial discovery set forth in the governing rules of civil procedure. While the definition of relevance varies from jurisdiction to jurisdiction, it is substantially similar across most. For simplicity's sake, this chapter focuses on the Federal Rules of Civil Procedure. Rule 26 defines the scope of discovery as follows:

> Unless otherwise limited by court order, the scope of discovery is as follows: *Parties may obtain discovery regarding any non-privileged matter that is relevant to any party's claim or defense*—including the existence, description, nature, custody, condition and location of any documents or other tangible things and the identity and location of persons who know of any discoverable matter. *For good cause, the court may order discovery of any matter relevant to the subject matter involved in the action.* Relevant information need not be admissible at the trial if the discovery appears reasonably calculated to lead to the discovery of admissible evidence. *All discovery is subject to the limitations imposed by Rule 26(b)(2)(C).*[8]
>
> . . .

7. *See In re* Lowe's Cos., Inc., 134 S.W.3d 876, 876 (Tex. App. 2004); *Ex parte* Wal-Mart, Inc., 809 So. 2d 818, 823 (Ala. 2001); Nicholas J. Murlas Living Trust v. Mobil Oil Corp., 1995 WL 124186 (N.D. Ill Mar. 20, 1995) ("Producing an entire computer database would indeed be unduly burdensome on Mobil and the court cannot see how information regarding other contaminated sites would be relevant to this litigation.").
8. FED. R. CIV. P. 26(b)(1) (emphasis added).

(C) *When Required.* On motion or on its own, the court must limit the frequency or extent of discovery otherwise allowed by these rules or by local rule if it determines that
 (i) the discovery sought is unreasonably cumulative or duplicative, or can be obtained from some other source that is more convenient, less burdensome, or less expensive;
 (ii) the party seeking discovery has had ample opportunity to obtain the information by discovery in the action; or
 (iii) the burden or expense of the proposed discovery outweighs its likely benefit, considering the needs of the case, the amount in controversy, the parties' resources, the importance of the issues at stake in the action, and the importance of the discovery in resolving the issues.[9]

Moreover, the Federal Rules specify that a party need not produce electronically stored information if production of such matter is "not reasonably accessible because of undue burden or cost."[10] The discovery rules are to be construed broadly to permit full and fair discovery.[11]

(2) Courts analogize to similar discovery requests of nonstructured data

In *Ex parte Wal-Mart, Inc.*, the Alabama Supreme Court granted a writ of mandamus to limit a lower court's discovery order covering certain structured data contained in a corporate database.[12] A customer allegedly was injured in a Wal-Mart store when a television fell off a shelf and hit him.[13] After filing a negligence suit in state court, the plaintiff customer requested the production of documents contained in a database controlled by CMI, a wholly owned subsidiary of Wal-Mart.[14] The database maintained and controlled by CMI contained reports from accidents causing injury to customers and employees at all Wal-Mart stores.[15] The

9. FED. R. CIV. P. 26(b)(2)(C).
10. FED. R. CIV. P. 26(b)(2)(B).
11. *See* Hickman v. Taylor, 329 U.S. 495, 507 (1947) (highlighting the importance of mutual knowledge as being essential to proper litigation).
12. *Ex parte* Wal-Mart, Inc., 809 So. 2d 818, 823 (Ala. 2001).
13. *Id.* at 819.
14. *Id.* at 819–20.
15. *Id.* at 822.

plaintiff customer requested all incident reports contained in the CMI database pertaining to instances of individuals being injured by falling merchandise in a Wal-Mart store.[16]

Responding to Wal-Mart's contention that the requests were "overbroad, unduly burdensome, and not reasonably calculated to result in the discovery of admissible evidence," the trial court entered an order requiring Wal-Mart to produce all incident reports from Alabama stores for the five-year period preceding the date of the plaintiff's injury.[17] In reviewing the trial court's discovery order under an abuse of discretion standard, the Alabama Supreme Court concluded that the trial judge abused his discretion only to the extent that he failed to narrow the discovery order to incidents involving the type of accident at issue (i.e., injury from falling merchandise) and granted mandamus relief accordingly.[18] In reaching this conclusion, the court analogized to a discovery order in a similar customer injury case involving accident reports not stored in a database or structured data.[19]

Practice Tip

Focus on the appropriate date range and narrowly construed needs of the case.

The Court of Appeals of Texas conducted a similar analysis in *In re Lowe's Companies, Inc.*[20] A customer filed suit against the Lowe's home improvement company after he was allegedly injured by an item falling from a shelf in the store.[21] In response to plaintiff's discovery request, the trial court entered an order compelling Lowe's to produce the database used to compile and maintain records of injuries and accidents occurring in its stores.[22] The trial court also ordered a Lowe's representative to appear at a deposition to testify

16. *Id.* at 819–21.
17. *Id.* at 821.
18. *Id.* at 822–23.
19. *See id.* at 822 (relying on *Ex parte* Heilig-Myers Furniture Co., 684 So. 2d 1292 (Ala. 1996) to determine reasonable temporal range of such request for production of documents); *Ex parte* Wal-Mart Stores, Inc., 682 So. 2d 65, 67 (Ala. 1996) (holding that trial judge did not abuse discretion in ordering substantially similar discovery over nonstructured data).
20. 134 S.W.3d 876, 876 (Tex. App. 2004).
21. *Id.*
22. *Id.* at 877 (describing trial court discovery order).

regarding the database and to be prepared to search, sort, and print data from the database in response to plaintiff's questions.[23] Lowe's objected to the discovery order as being overbroad as to geographic area, time period, and subject matter of the information contained within it, inter alia.[24]

In concluding that the plaintiff's discovery request was overbroad, the court looked first to the general discovery standards of relevance set forth under Texas law. Texas law provides that discovery orders that are overbroad and not reasonably tailored with respect to time, geographic region, or subject matter amount to impermissible "fishing expeditions."[25] The Texas Court of Appeals, relying on cases not dealing with discovery of structured data (or other electronic data), held that the discovery order was overbroad and impermissible because it was not limited by time, geographic region, or subject matter, and granted Lowe's request for mandamus relief.[26]

> Practice Tip
>
> Tailor your requests to the time, focus, and subject matter of the case.

D. Preservation: What is the duty to preserve structured data?

The obligation to preserve evidence arises when the party has notice or should have notice that the evidence may be relevant to litigation.[27] The scope and format of preservation as it relates to structured data, however, are not straightforward, as the data

23. The trial court order read as follows: "Ms. Dagner is ordered to bring with her a computer or have access at the time of her deposition to a computer that is capable of logging onto the database and capable of searching, sorting and printing the data on the computer as requested by Plaintiff's counsel in the deposition. Such data that is requested for printing should be limited to data of accidents prior to the accident made the basis of this suit and should be limited to accidents involving reports of customers injured due to falling merchandise." *In re* Lowe's, 134 S.W.3d at 877.

24. *Id.* at 879.

25. *Id.*

26. *See id.* at 880 (concluding that discovery order requiring access to database and printed data from database was improper due to lack of limitations as to time, place, and subject matter).

27. Best Buy Stores, L.P. v. Developers Diversified Realty Corp., 247 F.R.D. 567, 570 (D. Minn. 2007) (internal citations omitted); see chapter 8.

is generally composed not only of the individual pieces of data, but also a method of interconnecting such data.[28] Dynamic data, or data that can be altered based on other fields or actions, also require special attention throughout the preservation process. Metadata and third-party data are two more components that might require preservation.

> Practice Tip
>
> The preservation of data in databases may be more involved than other types of preservation.

(1) Scope

At the outset of a lawsuit, each party has a duty to "preserve information that is or may be relevant to the lawsuit, or which reasonably may lead to the discovery of admissible evidence."[29] If the information is not discoverable, then the party has no duty to preserve it.[30] Judgment regarding what information to preserve is made by the party in possession of that information; a demand by the requesting party to preserve nondiscoverable information does not trigger a duty to preserve that information.[31] In *Paul*, the plaintiffs demanded that the defendant preserve, among other items, all of the information in every database maintained by the defendant.[32] The parties could not agree on a narrowed scope.[33] The defendant incurred costs over $292,000 in preserving all of the electronic data, and sought reimbursement of these costs citing unreasonable burden.[34] The court held that because the defendant had the sole discretion to make a reasonable judgment about what information must be preserved, the plaintiffs did not have to reimburse the defendant for those costs.[35]

28. Jay E. Grenig & William C. Gleisner, eDiscovery & Digital Evidence § 7.18 (2008).
29. Paul v. USIS Commercial Servs., Inc., 2007 WL 2727222, slip op. at *1 (D. Colo. Sept. 17, 2007).
30. *Id.*
31. *Id.*
32. *Id.*
33. *Id.*
34. *Id.*
35. *Id.*

Practice Tip

Clarify the scope of preservation early during the meet-and-confer process.

As the obligation to preserve is limited to discoverable and thus relevant evidence, a party is obligated only to preserve those parts of a database that are relevant to the litigation. Thus, just as a single relevant email in an employee's inbox does not require a party to preserve the entire inbox, knowing that potentially relevant data exists in a database does not require a party to preserve the entire database, which may be expensive or technically infeasible. That being said, depending on the party and the database, it may be easier to take a snapshot of a small or medium-sized database than to isolate the potentially relevant data within it and preserve it. Also, practitioners need to be aware that if any of the potentially relevant data in a database is dynamic or automatically changes or purges, more intensive preservation steps may be required.

(2) Format

The issue of whether a database must be preserved in the same format as it is used in the ordinary course of business arose in *Best Buy Stores, L.P. v. Developers Diversified Realty Corporation*. The discovery issue in this case centered on a database prepared by Best Buy for a separate case, *Odom v. Microsoft*.[36] The database was downgraded from searchable format beginning on July 27, 2006.[37] The court held that the searchable functionality of the database was not relevant with regard to preservation as of July 2006, even though the complaint was filed previously, in September 2005.[38] Although Best Buy should have been on notice at the time that the defendants would seek some of the information in the Odom database, Best Buy did not have a duty to preserve the Odom database as of July 27, 2006, at a monthly cost of over $27,000, "absent specific discovery requests or additional facts suggesting that the database was of particular relevance to this litigation." The court also

36. *Best Buy*, 247 F.R.D. at 570.

37. *Id.*

38. *Id.*

pointed to the fact that Best Buy did not destroy the information, but merely changed the format to remove search functionality.

> Practice Tip
>
> Databases store (and modify) data differently than individual files and email systems do. As such, there is a multitude of ways to preserve data within them.

(3) Dynamic data

When data is automatically and frequently overwritten, "preservation obligations can be difficult or impossible to execute."[39] There are no cases that speak directly to this issue that involve structured data, but the Federal Rules of Civil Procedure Advisory Committee, along with other parties, have commented on these difficulties.

The Advisory Committee noted in 2005 that "many database programs automatically create, discard, or update information" and that "suspending or interrupting these features can be prohibitively expensive and burdensome."[40] Although Rule 37(e) prohibits (absent extraordinary circumstances) sanctions if dynamically stored information is lost as a result of good faith, routine operation, "a party is not permitted to exploit the routine operation of an information system to thwart discovery obligations by allowing that operation to continue in order to destroy specific stored information that it is required to preserve."[41] One proposed approach to battle the problem of preserving continuously changing data is to preserve snapshots of the information on a database by running and recording queries of the database at certain periods of time.[42] As extracting relevant data from a complex database application in a native format is not always feasible, saving the results in an imaged format is a suggested alternative.[43]

---

39. Thomas Y. Allman, *Managing Preservation Obligations After the 2006 Federal E-Discovery Amendments*, 13 RICH. J. L. & TECH. 9, at ¶ 46 (Spring 2007).
40. *Id.* (internal citations omitted).
41. FED. R. CIV. P. 37(e), advisory committee's note to 2006 Amendment.
42. Allman, *supra* note 38, at ¶ 48.
43. *Id.*

Practice Tip

Where dynamic data within a database is potentially relevant to a matter, a practitioner should move reasonably quickly to preserve such data before it is modified or overwritten including, where appropriate, discussing the issue with opposing counsel.

E. Burden of collecting, processing, and producing structured data

That discovery is not unbounded and that it should be proportionate to the litigation it is meant to support is no less true for discovery from databases and other structured data sets than from any other ESI source. However, the case law is just emerging as to how to determine the cost and burden of collecting and producing structured data.

(1) Ex parte Wal-Mart, Inc.

After the trial judge ordered production of sorted accident reports from all stores within the state occurring during the five years preceding the plaintiff customer's incident, Wal-Mart objected on the grounds that querying the database and producing reports therefrom would be unduly burdensome and costly.[44] The court rejected Wal-Mart's undue burden argument after commenting that because Wal-Mart's database was equipped to "run" searches of incidents similar to the one giving rise to the plaintiff's injuries, conducting such searches would not be unduly burdensome or costly.[45]

(2) Jones v. Goord

In measuring the burden of producing concededly relevant data contained in a prison's inmate status database, the U.S. District Court for the Southern District of New York considered a variety of factors beyond the actual cost of searching and duplicating

44. Note that in the request for production of documents, the plaintiff sought the results from the database to be delivered in several different forms, sorted in order of the date of the injury claim number and store number, respectively.

45. *See Ex parte* Wal-Mart, Inc., 809 So. 2d 818, 822 (Ala. 2001) ("because Wal-Mart or CMI can 'run' a report [listing similar incidents], Wal-Mart's production of the customer incident reports and employee accident review forms about falling-merchandise incidents would not unduly burden Wal-Mart or its attorneys.").

the electronic data.[46] In *Jones*, class members comprising prison inmates filed suit against various New York State officials alleging that certain prisons conditionally violated their First and Eighth Amendment rights.[47] In weighing the costs of producing the electronic information stored on the database, the court considered the costs of compiling and running searches and duplication onto electronic media, but found that these costs likely would be minimal.[48]

In denying discovery, the court credited defendant's expert affidavits and cost projections in finding that "[prison] personnel would need to prepare extensive documentation of the structure of the programs and databases to enable any experts retained by plaintiffs to understand the layout of the data, the meaning of codes, and the sources from which those codes can be derived."[49] Furthermore, the court concluded that production would also cause an undue burden by forcing disclosure of "highly sensitive" information contained in the inmate databases that could have serious negative consequences for the state in the event such information was disclosed.[50]

---

46. Jones v. Goord, 2002 U.S. Dist. LEXIS 8707 (S.D.N.Y. 2002), *dismissed*, 435 F. Supp. 2d 221, 266 (S.D.N.Y. 2006).

47. *Id.* at *2–4 (explaining protracted factual backdrop of inmates' concerns over adverse health effects associated with prison's policy of housing more than one inmate per cell).

48. *Id.* at *28 (postulating that costs of duplication are comparatively low).

49. The court described the interconnectedness and interrelatedness of the data as follows:

> [T]he databases in question are not simply collections of lists or numbers that can be easily extracted and correlated with other numbers; rather, each of the requested databases has been constructed to support the interactions of hundreds of concurrent users rather than to support the analytical activities of a few. Consequently, the databases are integrally connected to a data system that comprises 25 separate but interdependent subsystems that each are comprised of scores of programs, tens of databases and scores of screen and report formats. There are over 3,000 programs containing a total of 1,500,000 lines of program instructions.

Id. at *28 (internal quotations and citations omitted). *See id.* at *31 (concluding defendant's cost of production would be significant, approaching $100,000).

50. *Id.* at *33 (declining to find new prison information privileged, instead relying on system of protective orders to safeguard privileged or sensitive material).

Practice Tip

Be prepared to produce specific facts, including expert reports and testimony, supporting any claims of unreasonable burden.

Practice Tip

Databases may require contextual information about tables, relationships, and code values in order to make the information they contain understandable.

Even in light of the substantial costs associated with production of the inmate database, the court highlighted Rule 26(b)(2)(iii)[51] and noted that if the plaintiff had shown that the benefit outweighed the burden, discovery would be appropriate, notwithstanding substantial public or private cost.[52] Plaintiffs provided the court with only the most general sense of what they planned to do with the data after it was produced.[53] Given the failure to describe in any meaningful fashion how they planned to use the data, the court concluded that discovery would not be proper because plaintiffs had "put[] the virtual cart before the digital horse."[54]

Practice Tip

Be prepared to advise the court on the value of the data sought and how it would be useful to the parties.

(3) When is structured data not reasonably accessible?

One of the most significant changes made to the Federal Rules of Civil Procedure by the 2006 amendments was inclusion of Rule 26(b)(2)(B), which provides that a party does not need to even search, much less produce data from, not reasonably accessible

51. Since this ruling, the rule has been renumbered as Rule 26(b)(2)(C).
52. *Id.* at *38.
53. *Id.* at *39–40 ("Other than very general statistical terms, such as 'regression analysis,' that offer little specific content, plaintiffs do not describe what they hope to find or how they hope to find it.").
54. *Id.* at *40.

data sources identified by a party.[55] However, upon a showing of good cause, a requesting party can require a party to collect and produce data from such a data source.[56] If that showing is made, "the court may nonetheless order discovery from such sources if the requesting party shows good cause."[57] In making such a determination, courts have assessed whether or not the data are reasonably accessible, and if not, whether to limit the discovery or to shift costs to the requesting party. Whether or not structured data is considered reasonably accessible turns on the fact-specific burdens of producing that data in the case at hand. In two cases, the courts have examined whether structured data was not reasonably accessible (though *OpenTV* predates the amendments and applies the *Zubulake I* standard).

(a.) ***OpenTV v. Liberate Technologies***

In a 2003 case, *OpenTV v. Liberate Technologies*, plaintiff OpenTV requested 100 versions of source code for various products during discovery for an infringement action.[58] Liberate offered to make its complete source code database available at its facilities, along with an index to the database, and an engineer to provide technical assistance.[59] It further argued that by doing so, it was providing the database in the order and manner in which it is kept in the ordinary course of business, in compliance with Rule 34.[60] OpenTV argued that this was unwarranted cost shifting.[61]

The court agreed that such an arrangement would indeed shift the costs to OpenTV, but that it might be warranted.[62] "The presumption is that the responding party must bear the expense of complying with discovery requests, but [the responding party] may invoke the district court's discretion under Rule 26(c) to grant protective orders protecting him from 'undue burden or expense' in doing so, including orders conditioning discovery on the requesting party's payment of the costs of discovery."[63] "Whether production of [such] documents is unduly burdensome or expensive

55. FED. R. CIV. P. 26(b)(2)(B).
56. *Id.*
57. *Id.*
58. OpenTV v. Liberate Tech., 219 F.R.D. 474, 475 (N.D. Cal. 2003).
59. *Id.*
60. *Id.* at 476.
61. *Id.*
62. *Id.*
63. *Id.* (quoting Oppenheimer Fund, Inc. v. Sanders, 437 U.S. 340, 358 (1978)).

turns primarily on whether it is kept in an accessible or inaccessible format (a distinction that corresponds closely to the expense of production)."[64] The *OpenTV* court found that the requested electronic data were stored in an inaccessible format for purposes of discovery, because it would take 125 to 150 hours of work to complete the extraction process for the 100 versions of source code.[65]

After determining that the database was inaccessible, the court found that shifting costs to the plaintiff was appropriate. The *OpenTV* court applied the cost-shifting factors set out in *Zubulake I*:

1. the extent to which the request is specifically tailored to discover relevant information;
2. the availability of such information from other sources;
3. the total cost of production compared to the amount in controversy;
4. the total cost of production compared to the resources available to each party;
5. the relative ability of each party to control costs and its incentive to do so;
6. the importance of the issues at stake in the litigation; and
7. the relative benefits to the parties of obtaining the information.[66]

The court found that because the source code was highly likely to contain relevant information that cannot be found in any other source, the first two factors weighed against cost shifting.[67] Although the parties did not state the amount in controversy, the court estimated that the potential for recovery was in the hundreds of thousands of dollars, and "it likely pales to the overall amount in controversy."[68] The court found that neither party lacked resources, but that Liberate was in the better position to control the cost of production because the data was stored in their database, and their offer to help authenticate the code added a step, increasing the overall burden of production.[69] Thus, the court ruled that factors three and five weighed against cost shifting, while factor

64. *Id.* (quoting Zubulake v. UBS Warburg LLC (*Zubulake I*), 217 F.R.D. 309, 318 (S.D.N.Y. 2003)).
65. *Id.* at 477.
66. *Id.*
67. *Id.* at 477–78.
68. *Id.* at 478.
69. *Id.*

four weighed in favor of cost shifting.[70] The court found that there were no novel issues in this case and, therefore, that factor 6 was neutral.[71] The court found that OpenTV stood to benefit more from the requested source code than Liberate, and therefore this factor weighed in favor of cost shifting.[72] Although the court found only two factors out of seven favoring cost shifting, it ordered that the parties split the cost to extract the source code from the database due to the undue burden and expense involved.[73]

(b.) ***Best Buy***

Similarly, the *Best Buy* court found that the Odom database was not reasonably accessible, because the cost to restore the data to a searchable format totaled $124,000 plus monthly maintenance fees of over $27,000.[74] The magistrate court had previously determined that the database was reasonably accessible because it compared the cost of restoration with the potential breach of contract damages, which were in excess of $800,000.[75] In contrast, on appeal, the court did not consider the potential recovery in determining whether the data was reasonably accessible.[76] Because the requesting party was unable to show that the requested data was only available from the Odom database and could not be obtained from any other source, the court dismissed the magistrate judge's order that Best Buy restore the Odom database.[77]

(3) Improper reliance on confusing data systems

While the cost and burden of collecting and producing data has become a well-established factor limiting civil discovery,[78] a line of cases originating with *Kozlowski v. Sears Roebuck & Co.*[79] has found that a party cannot claim burden caused by their own unique document management or information technology (IT) systems.[80]

70. *Id.* at 478–79.
71. *Id.* at 479.
72. *Id.* at 479.
73. *Id.*
74. Best Buy Stores, L.P. v. Developers Diversified Realty Corp., 247 F.R.D. 567, 570 (D. Minn. 2007).
75. *Id.* at 569.
76. *Id.* at 570.
77. *Id.* at 571.
78. *See, e.g.,* Rules 26(b)(2)(B), 26(b)(2)(C)(iii), and 26(g).
79. 73 F.R.D. 73, 76 (D. Mass. 1976).
80. *See, e.g.,* Dunn v. Midwestern Indem., 88 F.R.D. 191, 197–98 (S.D. Ohio 1980) (quoting Kozlowski v. Sears, Roebuck & Co., 73 F.R.D. 73, 76 (D. Mass. 1976)

It should be noted that *Kozlowski* is more than 30 years old and predates the adoption of not only the "not reasonably accessible due to undue burden or cost" clause in Rule 26(b)(2)(B) but also the proportionality clause in Rule 26(b)(2)(C).

F. Production format: In what format should structured data be provided?

The production format for structured data can be a challenging issue for both requesting and producing parties. Rule 34 sets forth the standard for the format of production for ESI:

> The request . . . may specify the form or forms in which [ESI] is to be produced. . . .
>
> If a request does not specify a form for producing [ESI], a party must produce it in a form or forms in which it is ordinarily maintained or in a reasonably useable form or forms; and
>
> A party need not produce the same [ESI] in more than one form.[81]

For structured data, however, the format in which it is ordinarily maintained (its "native" format) may be highly proprietary, difficult to export, or useless to the requesting party because it does not have the tools or space to review and host it. On the other hand, what format is reasonably useable may be difficult to discern for the producing party because the request may not make clear what the producing party intends to do with the data. Of course, the producing party may not know their document request even implicates structured data and may not know themselves what they plan to do with the data. One thing that is relatively clear is that to the extent the database is searchable in the ordinary course, the production should also be searchable.[82]

(noting impracticability is not impossibility); Static Control Components, Inc. v. Lexmark Int'l, 2006 U.S. Dist. LEXIS 16662, at *19–20 (E.D. Ky. 2006) ("The Federal Rules do not permit Lexmark to hide behind its peculiar computer system as an excuse for not producing this information to SCC.")); *see also* Phillip M. Adams & Assoc., L.L.C. v. Dell, Inc., 621 F. Supp. 2d 1173,1193 (D. Utah 2009) (subsequent history omitted).

81. FED. R. CIV. P. 34(b)(1)(C) and FED. R. CIV. P. (34)(b)(2)(E)(ii) & (iii); *see also* Coleman v. Blockbuster, 2007 WL 4084281 (E.D. Pa. Nov. 15, 2007) (outlining parties' formatting obligations to produce its database information).

82. FED. R. CIV. P. 34 advisory committee's note to 2006 Amendment (if the responding party ordinarily maintains the information in a way that makes it

Practice Tip

Work with your technology partners to determine how you can produce and receive structured data in discovery. Remember to include instructions in document requests and objections in document responses regarding production format. As always, where appropriate, meet and confer with opposing counsel regarding production format.

Courts have not come to an agreement as to what form of data is required, nor do they all address the issue with the same levels of specificity. Several cases provide for the review and order for structured data production in vague terms, such as requiring "a complete unedited electronic copy of Defendant's database," with no further discussion of the issue.[83] In contrast, the following cases have each developed an explanation of what format is appropriate for the production of structured data, and the reasons for ordering such format. Special considerations such as metadata and the use of canned reports are reviewed as well.

Practice Tip

Most of the time, prewritten (canned) reports or properly documented flat file exports are the preferred form for producing and receiving structured data.

(1) Native file production

Several courts have found that native file production of databases is appropriate. In the first case, debtor NVMS sought billing data from its previous billing provider, MBP. MBP provided the debtor with a hard copy of its claims as well as an unformatted text file of the claims, but did not want to produce the file in its native format on the basis that its modifications of the underlying software constituted a trade secret.[84] The court weighed the possibility of trade secret disclosure against the cost of reinputting the data and

searchable by electronic means, "the information should not be produced in a form that *removes or significantly degrades* this feature" (emphasis added)).

83. Beardsley v. All Am. Heating, Inc., 2007 WL 869959, at *3 (W.D. Wash. 2007).

84. *In re* NVMS, LLC, 2008 Bankr. LEXIS 2674, at *3 (Bankr. M.D. Tenn. 2008).

concluded that the debtor was entitled to the data in its native format.[85] In this case, the data could be provided in a manner that could be loaded into commercially available software.[86] The court, however, designated a third-party billing company to review the claims to protect the confidential information.[87]

In May 2009, the U.S. District Court for the District of Columbia also held that a database should not be provided in its native format, but in a more intrusive manner—by ordering forensic imaging of the entire database server.[88] This dispute centered on the issue of whether the defendant took data stored in one of its databases and gave it to other customers.[89] The judge recognized that "the database itself, and not just that data that it holds, should be an exhibit in this case."[90] The plaintiff requested a forensic image because it needed access to historical data about the database in addition to the data itself.[91] Expert testimony showed that there might be pieces of information located on the server but outside of the database that "would tend to show what Revonet [the defendant] did with the data because of the way that SQL databases usually work and how the electronically stored information was used."[92] Although the advisory committee cautions against making forensic examination because of the "undue intrusiveness" of such action, the court held that after balancing the burdens against the needs of this case,[93] delivery of the database must be in this format.[94] Because the defendant's salespeople used a web-based interface to access the database, the court also ordered that forensic copies be made of each of the salespeople's hard drives in order

85. *Id.* at *7–8.
86. *Id.*
87. *Id.* at *10.
88. Covad Commc'ns Co. v. Revonet, Inc., 2009 WL 1472345, at *4 (D.D.C. May 27, 2009).
89. *Id.* at *1.
90. *Id.*
91. *Id.* at *5.
92. *Id.*
93. The court balanced the burden on the servers, potential business disruption, and confidentiality issues against the potential benefits of what discovery might find. It did not consider any economic burdens or benefits because "paradoxically 'the amount in controversy,' 'the likely benefit,' and the 'needs of the case' can only be ascertained by permitting the discovery sought." *Id.* at *7.
94. *Id.* at *6.

to look at the temporary Internet cache files that might indicate access to the database.[95]

(2) Duplicate requests: When is a party entitled to receive structured data in a native file format, if it has already received the data in another format?

Rule 34 states that "a party need not produce the same electronically stored information in more than one form."[96] However, on at least two occasions, courts have examined whether a party receiving structured data from another party was entitled to a production in native format.

The first case, *Classicstar*, demonstrates one approach to resolving the burden imposed by a duplicate request—shifting the cost. In this case, the parties had initially agreed that defendants would provide the data either in its native format, which would require the plaintiffs to purchase database software costing $15,000, or provide the data in a generic format, such as .tif.[97] At the time, the plaintiffs had opted not to purchase the software, and to receive the data in .tif format. Although the requested financial data were then provided in such a format, the plaintiffs subsequently requested the same data in its native format, because it would be "so much more usable."[98] Because the parties had a previous agreement in place, the court ordered the defendants to provide the data in its native format, but the costs of copying and delivering the data would be shifted to the plaintiffs, since the data had already been produced once.

> Practice Tip
>
> Understanding up front the likely usage of, and specifying the appropriate format for, structured data productions will be more economical and efficient than having to request duplicate productions later.

The second case, *Jones*, noted *supra*, was a class action case by prisoners against the New York State Department of Correctional

95. *Id.* at *2.
96. FED. R. CIV. P. 34(b)(2)(E)(iii).
97. *In re* Classicstar Mare Lease Litig., 2009 U.S. Dist. LEXIS 9750, 24–25 (E.D. Ky. 2009).
98. *Id.* at 17–22.

Services and a variety of prisons. As part of the discovery process, the plaintiffs sought access to various databases maintained by the prison authorities.[99] The plaintiffs already had hard copies of the sought data records, but argued that the information produced in electronic format would be "more valuable in the form of an electronic database" as opposed to hard copy.[100] The defendants in turn argued that producing the databases would be not only an economic burden (due to the complexity of the requested systems and the required corresponding documentation, the production would cost an estimated $100,000 to complete[101]), but also a security risk, as there was a huge inherent risk of the sensitive data falling into the wrong hands because electronic formats could not as easily be safeguarded as paper documents.[102] The court, in balancing the competing interests of the parties under Rule 26(b)(2), held that the economic burden and security risks outweighed the plaintiffs' desire to obtain the data, particularly since the plaintiffs were unable to specify whether the data sought would be useful.[103] The court further pointed out that by waiting six years after litigation commenced to request this data, the parties had already spent a large sum of time and money reviewing the paper documents, and the cost of the requested discovery must be assessed in the context of the total discovery to date.[104]

(3) Metadata production

Courts recognize that in the world of e-discovery, "metadata has become the 'new black.'"[105] Metadata[106] is frequently requested

99. Jones v. Goord, 2002 U.S. Dist. LEXIS 8707, at *1–2 (S.D.N.Y. 2002).
100. *Id.* at 18.
101. The court pointed out that the databases were integrated with "25 separate but interdependent subsystems that each are comprised of scores of programs, tens of databases and scores of screen and report formats. There are over 3,000 programs containing a total of 1,500,000 of program instructions." *Id.* at *29. The court also gave an example of the complexity of the database systems, showing that one of the requested systems is actually composed of eight separate database tables with 2 million rows. *Id.* at *30.
102. *Id.* at 29–37.
103. *Id.* at 41.
104. *Id.* at 45.
105. Aguilar v. Immigration & Customs Enforcement Div., U.S. Dep't of Homeland Sec., 255 F.R.D. 350, 359 (S.D.N.Y. 2008).
106. Metadata is often defined as "data about data," but courts have used numerous definitions, not all of which are consistent. As this chapter is about discovery of structured data and not metadata, we are using the definitions provided by each court without comment.

because it provides information about the document or data that is not on the face of the document.[107]

The seminal case on the production of metadata is *Williams v. Sprint/United Mgmt. Co.,* which considered it in the context of spreadsheets. The discovery issue arose when the plaintiffs requested that the defendant produce the "active file" versions of Excel spreadsheets so that the plaintiffs could perform statistical analysis without rekeying data.[108] The defendant provided the Excel spreadsheets "scrubbed" of metadata, and with several cells locked.[109]

The *Williams* court held that if an electronic file is requested in the manner in which it was maintained in the ordinary course of business, or as an "active file" or "native file," then the producing party should produce the electronic documents with their metadata intact.[110] The burden to object to the production of metadata is placed on the producing party because that party "is in the best position to determine whether producing it is objectionable."[111] The producing party also has the burden of producing the metadata if it knows or should reasonably know that the metadata is relevant to the dispute, even if not specifically requested.[112]

The *Williams* court also set out guidelines regarding the usefulness of metadata with regard to structured data, particularly as to databases and spreadsheets. "As a general rule of thumb, the more interactive the application, the more important the metadata is to understanding the application's output."[113] Metadata is often critical to understanding a database application.[114] When a "database is a completely undifferentiated mass of tables of data," the metadata is the key to showing the relationships between the data; without such metadata, the tables of data would have little meaning."[115] "A spreadsheet application lies somewhere in the middle" and "the need for its metadata depends upon the complexity and purpose of the spreadsheet."[116] It may be necessary to produce metadata

107. *Id.* at 354.
108. Williams v. Sprint/United Mgmt. Co., 230 F.R.D. 640, 643 (D. Kan. 2005).
109. *Id.* at 644.
110. *Id.* at 652.
111. *Id.*
112. *Id.* at 654.
113. *Id.* at 647.
114. *Id.*
115. *Id.*
116. *Id.*

when the cells contain formulas, because only the values appear on the face of the document.[117]

The metadata in *Williams* was intrinsic to the structure of the Excel spreadsheets at issue. The court found that without the metadata in the spreadsheets the requesting party could not understand the data stored in the spreadsheets or how it interrelated (in essence this is what formulas do—create relationships between data).

> Practice Tip
>
> Metadata can increase the complexity of discovery. After *Williams v. Sprint*, balancing limited production now with greater access reserved for later has become more common.

Another important case is *Aguilar v. Immigration and Customs Enforcement Division of the U.S. Department of Homeland Security*, a 2008 case in the Southern District of New York that provided an opportunity to break down metadata into three distinct categories—substantive, system, and embedded metadata—and to discuss the situations in which such metadata should be produced.[118] *Aguilar* concerned 30 immigrants who brought a civil rights class action suit against the U.S. Department of Homeland Security Immigration and Customs Enforcement Division (ICE). The plaintiffs claimed they were subject to unlawful searches in their homes in violation of the Fourth Amendment.[119]

The parties in *Aguilar* did not have a conference to determine the form of ESI and metadata production until May 2008, when the defendants had already substantially completed their discovery efforts, although the plaintiffs' first request did state that "all documents shall be produced as they are kept in the usual course of business."[120] At the conferences in May and July 2008, the plaintiffs requested that spreadsheets and databases be provided in native format, as well as "meaningful information about the meta-

117. *Id.*

118. *See also* U.S. Dist. Ct., Dist. of Md., The Suggested Protocol for Discovery of Electronically Stored Information (2007).

119. *Aguilar*, 255 F.R.D. at 352.

120. *Id.* at 352–53.

data fields of ICE's hierarchal databases so that the Plaintiffs can determine which database metadata they should request."[121]

The *Aguilar* court established the following guidelines with respect to spreadsheet and database discovery and, in particular, the accompanying metadata. First, substantive metadata indicates substantive changes made by the user, such as prior edits or comments.[122] The metadata is embedded in the document that it describes.[123] It is sometimes referred to as "application metadata" because it is created as a function of the application software used to create the document or file.[124] The court noted that most substantive metadata lacks evidentiary value because it is not evident (readily visible), and it "need not be routinely produced" unless good cause is shown.[125]

The second guideline established by the court in *Aguilar* is that system metadata indicates data such as "the author, date, and time of creation, and the date a document was modified."[126] The metadata is created by the operating system or application.[127] If the authenticity of the document is questioned or if establishing who received what information and when is important to the claims or defenses of a party, then system metadata should be provided.[128] Otherwise, courts have commented that most system metadata lacks evidentiary value because it is not evident.[129]

The third guideline is that embedded metadata indicates "text, numbers, content, data, or other information which is not typically visible to the user viewing the output display."[130] Examples include spreadsheet formulas, hidden columns, externally or internally linked files, hyperlinks, references, and database information.[131] Embedded metadata is information that is directly or indirectly inputted into the native file by a user.[132] As opposed to substantive and system metadata, the court feels that embedded metadata

121. *Id.* at 353.
122. *Id.* at 354.
123. *Id.*
124. *Id.*
125. *Id.*
126. *Id.*
127. *Id.*
128. *Id.*
129. *Id.*
130. *Id.* at 354–55.
131. *Id.* at 355.
132. *Id.*

"should be produced as a matter of course" because "this type of data is often crucial to understanding an electronic document."[133]

> Practice Tip
>
> Metadata can have many definitions, shapes, and sizes. Understanding which type(s) of metadata are present and relevant is important in resolving discovery requests and disputes.

The *Aguilar* court also clarified how the Federal Rules apply to metadata discovery. Generally, metadata is discoverable if it is relevant to the claim or defense of any party and is not privileged.[134] A court may order the discovery of any matter relevant to the subject matter involved in the action.[135] A balancing test requires the court to weigh the probative value of proposed discovery against its potential burden.[136]

If the requesting party specifies the form of production and requests metadata, and if the responding party objects to the request, then the responding party must specify the form it intends to use. If the parties cannot agree on a form, then they must meet and confer before filing a motion to compel.[137]

If the requesting party does not specify the form of production, then under *Aguilar* the responding party must specify the form it intends to use, and "produce it in a form or forms in which it is ordinarily maintained or in a reasonably usable form or forms."[138] "This does not mean 'that a responding party is free to convert electronically stored information from the form in which it is ordinarily maintained to a different form that makes it more difficult or burdensome for the requesting party to use the information efficiently in the litigation."[139] Specifically, "if the ESI is kept in

133. *Id.*
134. *Id.*
135. *Id.*
136. *Id.* (citing FED. R. CIV. P. 26(b)).
137. *Id.* (citing FED. R. CIV. P. 34(b)).
138. *Id.* (citing FED. R. CIV. P. 34(b)(2)).
139. *Id.* (quoting FED. R. CIV. P. 34(b) advisory committee's note to 2006 Amendment).

an electronically-searchable form, it 'should not be produced in a form that removes or significantly degrades this feature.' "[140]

The *Aguilar* court also looked to the Sedona Principles for guidelines. "Absent party agreement or court order specifying the form or forms of production, production should be made in the form or forms in which the information is ordinarily maintained or in a reasonably usable form, taking into account the need to produce reasonably accessible metadata that will enable the receiving party to have the same ability to access, search, and display the information as the producing party where appropriate or necessary in light of the nature of the information and the needs of the case."[141] In selecting production form, two primary considerations should be the need for, and probative value of, the metadata, and the extent to which metadata will "enhance the functional utility of the electronic information."[142] Production in static image form does not work well for spreadsheets and databases.[143]

In reviewing the case with respect to the rules laid out above, the *Aguilar* court's first major emphasis was on the timing of the request. The court's rule concerning metadata is "Ask for it. Up front."[144] The court stressed that the parties should confer and agree prior to involving the court.[145] With this timing issue in mind, the court stated that it was to review the facts with a "heightened burden" because the plaintiffs had not requested metadata until the defendants had basically completed their discovery collection efforts.[146]

With regard to the production of spreadsheets, the court ruled that "when a spreadsheet relies on mathematical formulas, the metadata that discloses those formulas often is necessary for a thorough understanding of the spreadsheet."[147] However, in

---

140. *Id.* (quoting FED. R. CIV. P. 34(b) advisory committee's note to 2006 Amendment)

141. *Id.* at 356 (quoting THE SEDONA CONFERENCE, THE SEDONA PRINCIPLES: BEST PRACTICES, RECOMMENDATIONS & PRINCIPLES FOR ADDRESSING ELECTRONIC DOCUMENT PRODUCTION, at Principle 12 (2d. ed. 2007)).

142. *Id.* (quoting THE SEDONA CONFERENCE, THE SEDONA PRINCIPLES: BEST PRACTICES, RECOMMENDATIONS & PRINCIPLES FOR ADDRESSING ELECTRONIC DOCUMENT PRODUCTION, at Principle 12, cmt. 12b (2d. ed. 2007)).

143. *Id.*

144. *Id.* at 357.

145. *Id.* at 358.

146. *Id.* at 359.

147. *Id.* at 362.

the case at hand, the underlying formulas were not necessary to understand the spreadsheet, because the data was just "lists that could have been created through a word processing program."[148]

Ultimately, the *Aguilar* court held that absent some showing that the sheets were fraudulently modified after the fact to conceal the scope of the operation, or the date that they were created or modified, the metadata is not relevant.[149] Because it was not burdensome to the defendants to provide the spreadsheets, and the defendants had expressed a willingness in the September 2008 conference to provide them in native format, however, the court ordered the production anyway.[150] With regard to the production of the database metadata, the first request was denied. The first database, the Deportable Alien Control System (DACS), was used by ICE operations officers to track the removal proceedings of illegal aliens.[151] When a record was created for an alien, the officer printed a hard copy and placed it in a green file folder.[152] These folders were produced by the defendants.[153] The plaintiffs sought metadata information because they believed they might be able to infer who made changes to the records by comparing who was signed into the database at the time.[154] The court disagreed. "Since the fugitive operations officers apparently used the green folders as their basic resource, the DACS metadata would seem to be of limited usefulness . . . There has been no showing that the information in the file folders does not accurately reflect the state of the fugitive operations officers' knowledge at the time the searches occurred."[155] The second request for metadata information was partially granted.

The ICE agents used two integrated database systems: SEACATS and TECS, the U.S. Treasury Department's Treasury Enforcement Communications System.[156] The ICE agent prepared a "subject record" or "incident report" in SEACATS; the data then became part of the TECS database.[157] The agent "typically prints out the

148. *Id.*
149. *Id.*
150. *Id.*
151. *Id.* at 363.
152. *Id.*
153. *Id.*
154. *Id.*
155. *Id.*
156. *Id.* at 362.
157. *Id.*

relevant screens, which are kept in hard copy in the ICE office."[158] The defendant produced hard copies of these screenshots.[159] TECS is used by 40 federal agencies in real time mode.[160] Plaintiffs sought data architecture (table and field lists) to determine if there was relevant metadata, but defendants cited law enforcement privilege.[161] The defendants also claimed that all data in SEACATS and TECS is displayed on the face of the subject record and that no relevant information exists behind what is displayed on the print-outs.[162] The *Aguilar* court held that the defendant needed to set up a training session to demonstrate the system to the plaintiffs using dummy data, which would allow them to better understand the architecture of the system.[163]

<u>Practice Tip</u>

The more unique the database, the more likely that additional supporting information or education will be appropriate.

(4) Canned reports

Generally speaking, companies create structured data for business purposes, not for litigation. As part of that business purpose, many databases have standard reports that provide data to business users in the ordinary course of business. These reports, otherwise known as "canned reports," have potential value in discovery as they are prevalidated—at some level the party knows what data is collected in the report—and they are easier to run than creating customized searches of the database for information. So far, courts have taken inconsistent positions as to the appropriateness of using canned reports from databases to satisfy document requests.

In *Jinks*, the plaintiff sued the Navy for restructuring its staff in violation of Title VII of the Civil Rights Act.[164] As part of discovery, the court ordered the defendant to provide access to its Facilities

158. *Id.*
159. *Id.*
160. *Id.*
161. *Id.*
162. *Id.*
163. *Id.* at 363.
164. Jinks-Umstead v. Gordon England, Sec'y. of the Navy, 227 F.R.D. 143, 145 (D.D.C. 2005).

Information System (FIS) database for review by plaintiff's counsel.[165] The database contained two sources of information: "(1) pre-written 'canned reports,' and (2) customized data queries."[166] When the plaintiff's supervisor needed information regarding the number of contracts at each office, from which she would base her staffing needs, she would call the technical specialist that developed the FIS database to pull a report.[167] Rather than using a canned work in place (WIP) report, the specialist would formulate a query at the time of each request, because the WIP report did not provide a summary but rather just gave information on each individual contract.[168] The supervisor would receive the requested data informally, generally on a sticky note that she would throw away after using the information.[169] Although the Navy provided the WIP reports for the time period in question, the court ordered that the Navy "re-create the process" by reformulating the relevant queries for the time in which the plaintiff was employed, so that the data would be provided in the same format as the supervisor had received it at the time she made staffing decisions.

Similarly, in *Margel v. E.G.L. Gem Lab*, the court held that "information maintained in an electronic database is necessarily in a form that is not identical to a report based on the basis of that data and should, therefore, ordinarily be produced."[170] Although the defendant had produced reports from the database that it maintained, the court ordered access to the portion of the database relevant to the discovery sought.[171]

In a different vein, in *Aguilar*, hard copy printouts from a database were considered sufficient in one instance, but not in the other.[172] As previously described, the *Aguilar* court held that the hard copies of the DACS records that were printed out at the time a record was created for each alien were considered a reasonably usable form of the data.[173] Due to the evidence that the fugitive operations officers primarily relied upon the file folders

165. *Id.* at 147.
166. *Id.* at 146.
167. *Id.* at 146.
168. *Id.* at 147.
169. *Id.* at 146.
170. Margel v. E.G.L. Gem Lab Ltd., 2008 WL 2224288, at *5 (S.D.N.Y. May 29, 2008).
171. *Id.* at *6.
172. *Aguilar*, 255 F.R.D. at 363.
173. *Id.*

containing those hard copies, and because there was no showing that the information in the file folders did not accurately reflect the state of the fugitive operations officers' knowledge at the time the allegedly illegal searches occurred, the court denied the plaintiffs' request for metadata concerning the DACS database.[174] On the other hand, the court ordered the defendants to set up a training session to demonstrate their TECS database, even though the defendants claimed that all records were "displayed on the face of the record" and no relevant data existed other than what was shown on the printout.[175]

> Practice Tip
>
> Canned reports are typically an early candidate for the extraction and discovery of data from structured data systems, but in certain circumstances they may be insufficient.

(5) Direct access: When is direct access to the structured data source appropriate?

Rule 34 grants production of any electronically stored information "stored in any medium from which information can be obtained either directly or, if necessary after translation . . . into a reasonably usable form."[176] Thus, direct access is allowed under the rules, but generally speaking it is at the discretion of the producing party unless the requesting party can establish good cause for production of data.

The Eleventh Circuit addressed this issue in *In re Ford,* finding that direct access to the requested databases was not appropriate given the relevant facts.[177] In this case, the plaintiff sought direct access to Ford's MOS and CQIS databases to conduct searches for claims related to defective seatbelts, the crux of his claim against Ford.[178] The court held that "Rule 34(a) does not grant unrestricted, direct access to a respondent's database compilations. Instead, Rule 34(a) allows a requesting party to inspect and copy the product—

174. *Id.*
175. *Id.*
176. FED. R. CIV. P. 34(a)(1)(A).
177. *In re* Ford Motor Co., 345 F.3d 1315, 1317 (11th Cir. 2003).
178. *Id.* at 1316.

whether it be a document, disk, or other device—resulting from the respondent's translation of the data into a reasonably usable form."[179] It further explained that Rule 34(a) allows the producing party to search its own records directly to produce the records, not that the requesting party receives the right to directly search the data itself.[180] The court held that while some kind of direct access might be permissible in certain cases, this case was not one of them because the plaintiff's request was too broad in scope, and because the district court made no findings that Ford had failed to comply with discovery requests.[181]

The *Ford* decision was not novel at the time, and has been upheld with regard to structured data in at least one district. In *Cummings v. General Motors Co.*, a previous case with facts similar to *In re Ford*, plaintiffs requested direct access to any databases that in any way related to the seats and seat belts in all "N" model cars.[182] The court denied the request because the scope was overly broad, the subject matter of the proposed searches was duplicative of previous discovery, the plaintiffs had failed to show that the defendant's previous production was deficient, and the proposed searches would create the danger of disclosing privileged work-product or attorney-client communications.[183]

In 2007, the Northern District of Mississippi refused to allow a plaintiff direct access to Kmart's database, citing *In re Ford* and stating that the validity of the *Ford* decision had not been disturbed by the 2006 amendments to the Federal Rules of Civil Procedure related to discovery of ESI.[184] Because the plaintiff had not produced evidence that Kmart had acted improperly during discovery, the request for direct access was denied.[185]

Practice Tip

The courts have held direct access to databases to be at a higher standard than the production of data from

179. *Id.* at 1316–17.

180. *Id.* at 1317.

181. *Id.* (The court, in dicta, did state that in the case where the producing party has conducted itself improperly, direct access might be permissible.)

182. Cummings v. Gen. Motors Co., 2002 U.S. Dist. LEXIS 27627, at *22–23 (W.D. Okla. 2002).

183. *Id.* at 23–25.

184. Butler v. Kmart Corp., 2007 WL 2406982, at *3 (N.D. Miss. 2007).

185. *Id.*

databases.

At least one court has imagined a possible set of facts where direct access to a database would be appropriate, aside from the instance where the producing party is acting inappropriately. In *In re Lowe's*, the plaintiffs requested that Lowe's provide direct access to the database during a deposition of a Lowe's representative such that the representative could log onto the database, search, sort, and print the data requested by plaintiff's counsel.[186] The court held that under Texas law, the request for direct access was too broad in scope as it would allow plaintiffs to access data without any limitation as to time, place, or subject matter.[187] In dicta, however, the court stated that, although the plaintiff's initial discovery request did not specify that the items be produced in electronic data format, the database records do fall within the scope of the original request, indicating that with the appropriate limitation on scope access to the database would be provided.[188]

G. Third-party vendors

When third-party vendors own and/or operate the underlying database or system containing the documents and other material that are the subject of a discovery request, responding appropriately raises unique issues pertaining to the boundaries of possession and control. Procter & Gamble, a manufacturer of household products, filed a Lanham Act suit and state law tort claims against a competitor, alleging that it had disseminated false rumors.[189] To facilitate calculation of damages arising from the alleged acts of the competitor, Procter & Gamble retained the services of a third-party market research company called Information Resources Incorporated (IRI).[190] IRI collected and compiled market research trend data pertaining to mass market retail products, such as those of Procter & Gamble.[191] IRI's database was constantly being adjusted on a "rolling basis" in response to real-time trends in

186. *In re* Lowe's, 134 S.W.3d at 877.
187. *Id.* at 880.
188. *Id.*
189. *See* Procter & Gamble Co. v. Haugen, 427 F.3d 727, 727 (10th Cir. 2005) (plaintiff alleged that defendant harmed plaintiff's business by spreading false rumors that president of plaintiff company supported Church of Satan).
190. *Id.* at 731.
191. *Id.*

retail purchasing activities of consumers.[192] Procter & Gamble retained IRI to provide it with access to IRI data about Procter & Gamble's products that was later used to generate internal reports on consumer behaviors.[193] The competitor made several requests for production of the IRI market share data from Procter & Gamble; and, after issuing four orders for production, the district court sanctioned Procter & Gamble for failure to comply with the discovery orders.[194] The circuit court closely scrutinized the level of possession and control over the data and concluded that sanctions against Procter & Gamble were improper.[195] The court found it compelling that Procter & Gamble did not own or even possess the IRI data that may have been responsive to the discovery order.[196] Moreover, IRI "compiled, possessed and owned" the data and, for a fee, provided Procter & Gamble with access to the data.[197]

Given the lack of ownership and control over the data sought, Procter & Gamble faced a difficult choice regarding how to comply with the broadly worded discovery orders. The court postulated that the most reasonable means of complying would have been (1) provide the competitor with regular access to the database; (2) conduct downloads of the IRI data to Procter & Gamble's computer facilities anytime data was used; or (3) arrange for IRI to provide archival data to the competitor. Reviewing the record, the court found that each of these alternatives carried considerable costs in terms of time and resources.[198] The court found that providing full access to the database would likely not have been satisfactory to the competitor because the database was constantly changing and the competitor was only interested in data from a particular time period. Similarly, both downloading the data and paying IRI to provide archival data were impracticable as well because Procter & Gamble did not have computer facilities adequate to the task of downloading the IRI data, and IRI would have charged some $30 million to provide the competitor

192. *Id.*
193. *Id.*
194. *Id.* at 732.
195. *Id.* at 739 (finding no basis on record for district court finding of willfulness or bad faith in failing to produce documents from database owned and maintained by independent third party).
196 *Id.*
197. *Id.* (noting Procter & Gamble's lack of ownership and control militated against finding of willfulness required to support harsh sanction of dismissal).
198. *See id.* (highlighting significant downsides to each alternative).

with the archived data they sought.[199] Recognizing these difficulties in responding to the discovery order, the court found that the sanctions issued against Procter & Gamble for failure to produce the database documents were improper.[200]

> Practice Tip
>
> Focus on the data, not on the database.

(1) Direct subpoena of third party

Rule 45 of the Federal Rules of Civil Procedure permits a party to serve discovery requests upon a nonparty.[201] In *Tessera v. Micron Technology*, a nonparty was ordered to conduct searches of its database and provide copies of the results of such searches to a party to litigation.[202] The court found that the nonparty's substantial efforts in complying with the discovery order were not unduly burdensome even though it had "collected, reviewed and designated more than 100,000 pages of documents for production" and incurred costs greater than $70,000.[203] Parties seeking discovery of structured data may also consider utilizing Rule 45 to obtain data directly from the third-party vendor if ownership and control issues complicate their efforts to obtain such data from the party to litigation.

(2) Data vendors that are wholly owned subsidiaries of a party do not raise the same issues regarding the boundaries of ownership and control

In *Ex parte Wal-Mart*, a wholly owned subsidiary of Wal-Mart owned and maintained incident reports created after a customer or employee was injured in a Wal-Mart store.[204] Not surprisingly, the mere fact that the data vendor was a separate entity was not sufficient to call into question Wal-Mart's control and possession of the database. The court did not make a distinction between

199. *See id.* (noting that data could have been obtained from IRI directly via Rule 45 subpoena).
200. *Id.* at 741.
201. Fed. R. Civ. P. 45.
202. 2006 WL 733498, at *8 (N.D. Cal.) (granting motion to compel production of results of database search using specified search terms).
203. *Id.* at *10.
204. *Ex parte* Wal-Mart, Inc., 809 So. 2d at 822.

Wal-Mart and its wholly owned subsidiary in determining ownership and control of the database that was the subject of the discovery order.[205]

4. Conclusion

As the volume and importance of structured data increases, its prevalence in discovery and discovery disputes is expected to rise dramatically over the next few years. There are many aspects of standard discovery that are applicable to structured data, but counsel should be alert to specific nuances. Because of the sheer size of certain databases—especially enterprise databases—practitioners need to be aware that no single person, IT or otherwise, may understand how it works and that efforts to preserve or collect data may have significant effects on the system's performance and result in significant business interruptions. Because some databases are highly customized and proprietary (and almost all are specifically configured for their business function), discovery on each database may require specific tools and knowledge (with little overlap from client to client or even database to database within a client). Focusing on the potentially relevant subject matter stored within the database is more prudent than focusing on the database container itself.

Early discussions in the meet-and-confer process to specify the preservation and production format may help control downstream costs associated with database discovery. Preservation of entire databases may be more complex than focusing preservation on the structured data that they contain, and may require supporting information about the container structure. In most matters, production of structured data through canned reports or flat file exports is more appropriate than production of the entire database.

Finally, while the courts' understanding of structured data is evolving, structured data is typically less understood by the court than unstructured data, so be prepared to advise the court on the particularities of your circumstances and how the characteristics of your structured data affects relevance, preservation, and production of information.

205. *Id.*

PART THREE

FOCUS ON THE DUTY TO PRESERVE ESI: NATURE, SCOPE, SANCTIONS, AND LIMITS

CHAPTER 8

DUTY TO PRESERVE: BEST PRACTICES, SPOLIATION, SANCTIONS, AND THE SAFE HARBOR PROVISION

LESLIE WHARTON
AND STEPHANIE WEIRICK

In the field of e-discovery, the duty to preserve electronically stored information is littered with possible pitfalls and mined with potential sanctions. Here, a senior e-discovery counsel and a litigator in private practice look in depth at the duty and its scope, as well as spoliation and sanctions issues.

1. Introduction

Although all U.S. jurisdictions recognize a duty to preserve evidence for use in litigation, various federal and state courts take somewhat different approaches to the nature and scope of the duty to preserve and the standards for imposing sanctions for spoliation, the violation of the duty to preserve.[1] Further, it can be

1. *See, e.g.*, Victor Stanley, Inc. v. Creative Pipe, Inc. (*Victor Stanley II*), 269 F.R.D. 497 (D. Md. 2010) (discussing different standards used by various federal courts

difficult to provide clients with black letter guidelines on the scope of their duty to preserve because the question of when a duty to preserve attaches, the scope of the duty, and the effects of a failure to preserve are heavily dependent on the facts and circumstances of each particular case. This chapter lays out the sources, nature, and scope of the duty to preserve, the courts' power to sanction for failure to preserve, and the factors considered by courts when deciding whether and how to sanction a party for spoliation. In doing so, we address some of the best practices for complying with the duty to preserve, and provide suggestions for how to initiate and monitor a litigation hold.

2. The duty to preserve

In our judicial system, contending parties muster evidence and legal argument in support of their competing positions; then, the ultimate decision-maker, be it judge, jury, or a combination of the two, decides the winner. The ability to obtain evidence through discovery is critical to the integrity of the adversarial decision-making process.

> Aside perhaps from perjury, no act serves to threaten the integrity of the judicial process more than the spoliation of evidence. Our adversarial process is designed to tolerate human failings—erring judges can be reversed, uncooperative counsel can be shepherded, and recalcitrant witnesses compelled to testify. But, when critical documents go missing, judges and litigants alike descend into a world of ad hocery and half measures—and our civil justice system suffers.[2]

As Judge Grimm reminded the parties in *Victor Stanley II*, "the duty to preserve evidence relevant to the litigation of a claim is *a duty owed to the court*, not to a party's adversary."[3]

---

in assessing sanctions for spoliation and providing a table of cases, by circuit, of the key decisions addressing sanctions for spoliation).

2. United Med. Supply Co. v. United States, 77 Fed. Cl. 257, 258–59 (2007); Bradley v. Sunbeam Corp., No. Civ. A. 5:99CV144, 2003 WL 21982038, at *17 (N.D. W. Va. Aug. 4, 2003) ("nothing abuses the judicial process more than when a party refuses to produce or destroys evidence"), *vacated on other grounds*, 378 F.3d 373 (4th Cir. Aug. 6, 2004); *see also* Pension Comm. of Univ. of Montreal Pension Plan v. Banc of Am. Sec., LLC, 685 F. Supp. 2d 456, 461–62 (S.D.N.Y. 2010).

3. 269 F.R.D. at 525 (emphasis added).

A. Source of duty to preserve

The duty to preserve has its roots in the common law duty to avoid spoliation of evidence.[4] That duty is reflected in the rules of civil procedure governing pretrial discovery.[5] State rules of civil procedure governing discovery do likewise.[6]

The duty to preserve is also reflected in the rules of professional ethics governing lawyers.[7] For instance, ABA Model Rule 3.4 provides that "a lawyer shall not unlawfully obstruct another party's access to evidence or unlawfully alter, destroy or conceal a document or other material having potential evidentiary value." Various state rules of professional ethics contain similar injunctions.[8] The American Bar Association's August 1999 civil discovery "standards" prescribe that "[w]hen a lawyer who has been retained to handle a matter learns that litigation is probable or has been commenced, the lawyer should inform the client of its duty to preserve potentially relevant documents and the possible consequences for failing to do so." Rules of ethics and court decisions make it clear that counsel have a duty to instruct their clients on the duty to preserve and actively assist the client in fulfilling that duty. As Judge Scheindlin stated in *Zubulake V*, "Once a 'litigation hold' is in place, a party and her counsel must make certain that all sources of potentially relevant information are identified and placed 'on hold.' . . ."[9] Indeed, courts have sanctioned attorneys based on

---

4. *See* Zubulake v. UBS Warburg LLC (*Zubulake V*), 229 F.R.D. 422, 425 (S.D.N.Y. 2004) (noting the common law source of the duty to preserve); *see also* Danis v. USN Commc'ns, Inc., No. 98 C 7482, 2000 WL 1694325, at *1 (N.D. Ill. Oct. 23, 2000) (the duty of disclosure arises out of both the rules of civil procedure and the rules of professional conduct); *see also Victor Stanley II*, 269 F.R.D. at 521–22.

5. For instance, Rule 26(b) implicitly recognizes a duty to preserve in stating that "[p]arties may obtain discovery regarding any nonprivileged matter that is relevant to any party's claim or defense." Rule 26(f)(2) directs parties to "discuss any issues about preserving discoverable information."

6. *See, e.g.*, Cal. Civ. Proc. Code § 2017.010; N.J. Rule 4:10-2(a); La. Code Civ. Proc. art. 1422.

7. For an excellent discussion, see Judge Paul W. Grimm, *Ethical Issues Associated with the Duty to Preserve Electronically Stored Evidence*, Westlaw SL061 ALI-ABA 199 (Feb. 9–10, 2006).

8. *See, e.g.*, N.Y. Lawyer's Code of Prof'l Responsibility EC 7-27 ("a lawyer should not suppress evidence that the lawyer or the client has a legal obligation to reveal or produce"); Cal. Rules of Prof'l Conduct 5-220 ("A member shall not suppress any evidence that the member or the member's client has a legal obligation to reveal or to produce").

9. *Zubulake V*, 229 F.R.D. at 432.

Rule 26(g) and ethical standards for failing to disclose the client's destruction or withholding of discoverable information.[10]

The rules of civil procedure and Bar ethics rules are not the only basis on which a court may find a duty to preserve. Courts have looked to statutes and regulations in holding that the destruction of records violated a legal duty to preserve.[11] Similarly, courts have relied on custom in the industry or a party's normal course of conduct as a source of the duty to preserve.[12] Where the duty to preserve is derived from substantive law—as opposed to ethical or procedural rules—the duty is governed by state law in state courts and in federal courts exercising diversity jurisdiction, and by federal law in federal courts exercising federal question jurisdiction.

B. When the duty to preserve attaches

A party has a duty to preserve once it "reasonably should know that the evidence may be related to anticipated litigation,"[13] or—stated somewhat differently—when "a party should have known

10. *See, e.g., In re* Rosenthal, 2008 WL 983702 (S.D. Tex. Mar. 28, 2008) (counsel violated the Texas Disciplinary Rules of Professional Conduct for failure to disclose the loss of electronically stored data); Qualcomm Inc. v. Broadcom Corp., 2008 WL 66932, at *18 (S.D. Cal. Jan. 7, 2008) *vacated in part*, 2008 WL 638108 (Mar. 5, 2008) (referring counsel for disciplinary hearings under California rules of professional conduct for intentionally hiding or recklessly ignoring relevant documents in violation of their discovery obligations). *rev'd*, 2010 WL 1336937, at *2 (S.D. Cal. Apr. 2, 2010) (reversing order sanctioning attorneys where, despite "significant mistakes, oversights, and miscommunication on the part of both outside counsel and Qualcomm employees," outside counsel "made significant efforts to comply with their discovery obligations").

11. *See* Byrnie v. Town of Cromwell Bd. of Educ., 243 F.3d 93 (2d Cir. 2001) (finding violation of duty to preserve where documents destroyed before the end of the statutory two-year retention period); Estate of LeMay v. Eli Lilly & Co., 960 F. Supp. 183, 186 (E.D. Wisc. 1997) (finding violation of duty to preserve where NASD rule required preservation of instant messages reflecting securities trading activity); *see also* P. Grimm et al., *Proportionality in the Post-Hoc Analysis of Pre-Litigation Preservation Decisions*, 37 U. BALT. L. REV. 381, 412 (Spring 2008) (discussing sources and scope of the prelitigation duty to preserve) (see chapter 9).

12. *See, e.g.*, Welsh v. United States, 844 F.2d 1239 (6th Cir. 1988) (where standard medical protocol called for the preservation of tissue removed from a patient, postsurgery destruction of tissue sample held to violate the duty to preserve), *overruled on other grounds by* 554 F.3d 650 (6th Cir. 2009).

13. *See, e.g.*, Silvestri v. Gen. Motors Corp., 271 F.3d 583, 591 (4th Cir. 2001).

that the evidence may be relevant to future litigation."[14] Given such an amorphous standard, the specific facts of each case will necessarily dictate when the duty is triggered. Some examples include

- entry of a court order[15]
- the filing of a lawsuit[16]
- receipt of a subpoena or discovery request[17]
- receipt of a demand or preservation letter[18]
- an accident causing injury or property damage[19]
- forming the intent and taking action in preparation for filing a lawsuit[20]

14. Fujitsu Ltd. v. Fed. Express Corp., 247 F.3d 423, 436 (2d Cir. 2001).
15. *See, e.g.*, Victor Stanley, Inc. v. Creative Pipe, Inc. (*Victor Stanley II*), 269 F.R.D. 497, 521 (D. Md. 2010); Lorillard Tobacco Co. v. Yazan's Serv. Plaza, Inc., No. 05-70804, 2007 WL 1834714, at *9 (E.D. Mich. June 25, 2007); Keir v. UnumProvident Corp., No. 02-Civ.-8781, 2003 WL 21997747 (S.D.N.Y. Aug. 22, 2003) (court order to preserve email backup tapes).
16. *See, e.g.*, Danis v. USN Commc'ns, Inc., No. 98 C 7482, 2000 WL 1694325 (N.D. Ill. Oct. 23, 2000) (duty to preserve attached as of the date complaint filed); Joostberns v. United Parcel Servs., Inc., 166 F. App'x. 783 (6th Cir. 2006) (duty to preserve not violated where documents destroyed in accordance with standard document retention program before defendant received notice of the plaintiff's claims).
17. *See, e.g.*, Mosaid Techs. v. Samsung Elecs. Co., 348 F. Supp. 2d 332 (D.N.J. 2004) (receipt of discovery requests triggered duty to preserve email even when requesting party failed to complain about defendant's failure to produce the email until after close of discovery); *In re* Rosenthal, No. H-04-186, 2008 WL 983702 (S.D. Tex. Mar. 28, 2008) (attorney fined and held in contempt of court for failure to ensure preservation of records subject to Rule 45 subpoena).
18. *See* Optowave Co. v. Nikitin, No. 6:05-cv-1083-Orl-22DAB, 2006 WL 3231422 (M.D. Fla. Nov. 7, 2006) (receipt of demand letter triggers duty to preserve); *but see* Cache Le Poudre Feeds, LLC v. Land O'Lakes, Inc., 244 F.R.D. 614, 622–23 (D. Colo. 2007) (ambiguous demand letter held insufficient to trigger defendant's duty to preserve).
19. *See, e.g.*, Garrett v. Albright, No.4:06-CV-4137-NKL, 2008 WL 681766 (W.D. Mo. Mar. 6, 2008) (duty to preserve accident logbooks); Testa v. Wal-Mart Stores, Inc., 144 F.3d 173 (1st Cir. 1998) (duty to preserve attached when institution had notice of potential suit arising out of accident).
20. *See* Rimkus Consulting Grp., Inc. v. Cammarata, 688 F. Supp. 2d 598, 640–41 (S.D. Tex. 2010) (duty to preserve attached when defendants began planning to file a preemptive suit against the plaintiff); Micron Tech., Inc. v. Rambus Inc., 255 F.R.D. 135 (D. Del. 2009) (duty to preserve attached when party formed the intent to enforce its patents through litigation, several years before bringing its first infringement action).

The duty to preserve does not end when a lawsuit is filed.[21] During the course of a lawsuit, as new claims and defenses are identified, the scope of the duty to preserve may change.[22]

C. Who has the duty to preserve?

The duty to preserve applies not only to materials in the possession of the parties to a lawsuit, but may also apply in situations wherein a party does not directly possess the potentially relevant material, but has access to or indirect control over the information.[23] Although jurisdictions vary, this may include reaching out to subsidiaries and affiliates,[24] former employees who may have retained relevant materials,[25] and current and former counsel.[26] If a party does not have control over relevant evidence, that party may be required to provide notice to the opposing party of its existence so that the opposing party can examine the evidence, even if no suit has been commenced.[27]

---

21. *See* Teague v. Target Corp., No. 3:06-CV-191, 2007 WL 1041191 (W.D.N.C. Apr. 4, 2007) (plaintiff had duty to preserve home computer a year after she filed suit because the information on that computer was relevant to the parties' claims and defenses). See chapter 11 for a discussion of when a litigation hold ends.
22. *See, e.g.*, Telecom Int'l Am., Inc. v. AT&T Corp., 189 F.R.D. 76 (S.D.N.Y. 1999) (discussing duty to preserve when new claims asserted several years after lawsuit filed).
23. *See* Silvestri v. Gen. Motors Corp., 271 F.3d 583, 591 (4th Cir. 2001) (plaintiff driver had duty to notify manufacturer before owner had car repaired); Goodman v. Praxair Servs., Inc., 632, F. Supp. 2d 494 (D. Md. 2009) (discussing meaning of "control" for purposes of duty to preserve); World Courier v. Barone, No. C-06-3072, 2007 WL 1119196, at *1 (N.D. Cal. Apr. 16, 2007)); *In re* WRT Energy Sec. Litig., 246 F.R.D. 185, 195 (S.D.N.Y. Sept. 7, 2007) (duty to preserve attached when plaintiffs were advised that relevant documents would be destroyed and were given the opportunity to take custody of them).
24. E-Trade Sec., LLC v. Deutsche Bank AG, 230 F.R.D. 582, 588 (D. Minn. 2005) (defendant NSI had a duty to preserve and produce documents from Nomura Canada because it had "control" over its affiliate Nomura Canada evidenced when "in-house counsel for NSI . . . sought and obtained select documents from Nomura Canada when responding to the SEC investigation").
25. *See* Cache Le Poudre Feeds, 244 F.R.D. at 629 (citing cases).
26. Poole v. Textron, Inc., 192 F.R.D. 494, 501 (D. Md. 2000) (documents in possession of "a party's attorney or former attorney are within the party's 'control' for purposes of Rule 34"); Books Are Fun, Ltd. v. Rosebrough, 239 F.R.D. 532, 556 (S.D. Iowa 2007) (same).
27. *See Silvestri*, 271 F.3d at 595 (lawsuit dismissed as sanction where, more than a year prior to filing suit, driver of automobile had duty to notify defendant General Motors so that it could test vehicle before owner turned over vehicle to insurance company).

D. The scope of the duty to preserve

Courts have described the scope of the duty to preserve in a variety of ways. In *Zubulake IV*, Judge Scheindlin stated that a party "is under a duty to preserve what it knows, or reasonably should know, is relevant in the action, is reasonably calculated to lead to the discovery of admissible evidence, is reasonably likely to be requested during discovery and/or is the subject of a pending discovery request."[28] Other courts have described the scope of the duty as "ensur[ing] that discoverable documents are available to be produced,"[29] or information that "bears on, or . . . reasonably could lead to other matter[s] that could bear on, any issue that is or may be in the case."[30] Courts are in agreement that a party is not required to anticipate every future twist and turn in a case when initiating a litigation hold, but rather must carry out its preservation obligations under a "reasonableness" standard.[31]

Once the duty to preserve attaches, that duty includes the obligation to identify, locate, and maintain documents or other materials containing information that fall within the scope of the duty. For businesses and other organizations, the duty to preserve is normally effectuated through the "legal hold" process.[32] Some of

28. Zubulake v. UBS Warburg LLC (*Zubulake IV*), 220 F.R.D. 212, 217 (S.D.N.Y 2003) (citing Turner v. Hudson Trans. Lines, Inc., 142 F.R.D. 68, 72 (S.D.N.Y. 1991)).

29. Danis v. USN Commc'ns, Inc., No. 98 C 7482, 2000 WL 1694325, at *33 (N.D. Ill. Oct. 23, 2000).

30. Kidwiler v. Progressive Paloverde Ins. Co., 192 F.R.D. 193, 199 (N.D. W. Va. 2000) (quoting Oppenheimer Fund, Inc. v. Sanders, 437 U.S. 340, 350 (1978)).

31. *See, e.g., Zubulake IV*, 220 F.R.D. at 217 ("anyone who anticipated being a party . . . to a lawsuit must not destroy unique, relevant evidence that might be useful to an adversary" but has no duty to keep or retain "every document" in its possession); Abramowitz v. Inta-Boro Acres, Inc., No. 98-CV-4139, 1999 WL 1288942 (E.D.N.Y. Nov. 16, 1999) (where plaintiff's notice of claim for age discrimination stated that his termination for use of vulgar language was a mere pretext, there was no duty to preserve prelitigation tapes of driver/dispatcher conversations); *but see* Griffin v. GMAC Commercial Fin., LLC, Civ. No. 1:05-CV-199-WBH-GGB, 2007 WL 521907 (N.D. Ga. Feb. 15, 2007) (when plaintiff's EEOC letter failed to identify issue, defendant's failure to recognize relevance of destroyed documents was "understandable" but a prudent employer would have anticipated the need to preserve all documents relating to the complaining employee.).

32. *See, e.g.*, THE SEDONA CONFERENCE COMMENTARY ON LEGAL HOLDS: THE TRIGGER & THE PROCESS (Aug. 2007) (setting out recommended practices for defining the scope of and managing the duty to preserve); *see also* Moore v. Napolitano, Civ. No. 00-953, 2010 WL 2780914 (D.D.C. July 15, 2010) (detailing failures in party's implementation of legal hold and document collection process);

the most important steps to prevent the loss of potentially relevant information include (1) notifying all persons who may have custody or control over the information, including departments such as information technology and human resources; (2) suspending normal document destruction procedures; and (3) stopping the programmed automatic deletion of email and other data from computer systems, including (where appropriate) "janitor" programs and the rotation of backup tapes.[33]

Relevance is not the only limitation on the scope of discovery: a party may seek a protective order limiting discovery if "the burden or expense of the proposed discovery outweighs its benefit, taking into account the needs of the case, the amount in controversy, the parties' resources, the importance of the issues at stake in the litigation, and the importance of the proposed discovery in resolving the issues."[34] Rule 1 of the Federal Rules of Civil Procedure describes the purpose of our civil justice system to "secure the just, speedy, and inexpensive determination of every action and proceeding."[35] This principle of proportionality not only supports cost shifting, but may limit the scope of the duty to preserve itself, and therefore, discovery in general.[36] Indeed, courts are granted

---

Qualcomm Inc. v. Broadcom Inc., No. 05cv1958-B, 2010 WL 1336937, at *5 (S.D. Cal. Apr. 2010) (detailing "pervasive miscommunication and incomplete document search . . . compounded by an inadequate follow-up in response to contradictory or potentially contradictory evidence" but reversing order sanctioning attorneys where there was insufficient evidence to establish bad faith).

33. *See, e.g.*, Wingnut Films, Ltd. v. Katja Motion Picture Corp., 2007 WL 2758571, at *14–15 (C.D. Cal. Sept. 18, 2007) (detailing failure to stop auto-deletion for email after anticipation of litigation and ordering sanctions for that and other discovery abuses); *see also Zubulake IV*, 220 F.R.D. at 218 ("As a general rule, th[e] litigation hold does not apply to inaccessible backup tapes (e.g., those typically maintained solely for the purpose of disaster recovery), which may continue to be recycled on the schedule set forth in the company's policy. On the other hand, if backup tapes are accessible (i.e., actively used for information retrieval), then such tapes would likely be subject to the litigation hold").

34. Fed. R. Civ. P. 26(b)(2)(C)(iii).

35. Fed. R. Civ. P. 1.

36. *See, e.g.*, D'Onofrio v. SFX Sports Grp., Inc., Civ. No. 06-687, 2010 WL 3324964, at *9 (D.D.C. Aug. 24, 2010) (holding that it would be an abuse of discretion under court's inherent power to award sanction of attorney's fees where spoliating party has already "expended a veritable king's ransom" in attempting to recover lost evidence); Major Tours, Inc. v. Colorel, Civ. No. 05-3091, 2009 WL 3446761 (D.N.J. 2009) (ordering cost sharing after weighing costs and benefits of restoring backup tapes); Wiginton v. Ellis, No. 02-C-6832, 2003 WL 22439865 (N.D. Ill. Oct. 2, 2003) (where defendant claimed duty to preserve imposed excessive costs,

broad discretion and flexibility "to assess the circumstances of the case and limit discovery accordingly to ensure that the scope and duration of discovery is reasonably proportional to the value of the requested information, the needs of the case, and the parties' resources."[37]

E. Duty to preserve: Best practices

The highly fact- and context-specific nature of the spoliation analysis may make it difficult to predict when a failure to preserve will result in sanctions or what those sanctions may be. However, the time, cost, delay, and distraction of the motion practice and discovery-on-discovery that almost inevitably follow upon the suspicion of spoliation provide strong incentives to ensure against even the inadvertent loss of potentially relevant information. Although the cases cited throughout this chapter provide the best guidance for satisfying the duty to preserve, recognized "best practices" include

- taking immediate action to ensure preservation as soon as the duty to preserve is triggered
- issuing a litigation hold notice to all those who may have possession, custody, or control over information that may be relevant to a foreseeable claim or defense
- following up with each custodian, and with those who control critical organizational processes (such as information technology and human resources), to make sure that the litigation hold notice is understood, to identify the potentially responsive information, and to ascertain that it is being preserved
- suspending automatic document deletion programs and, if necessary, backup tape rotation
- issuing periodic reminders to all custodians, human resources, and information technology personnel of the

---

defendant had duty to use best efforts to search for relevant information before destroying nonrelevant data); Convolve, Inc. v. Compaq Computer Corp., 223 F.R.D. 162, 177 (S.D.N.Y. 2004) ("heroic efforts far beyond those consistent with [defendant's] regular course of business" not required to preserve potentially relevant evidence). For a comprehensive discussion of the problem of proportionality, *see* Grimm, *supra* note 11, at 412.

37. *See* The Sedona Conference Commentary on Proportionality in Electronic Discovery (Oct. 2010) (outlining "principles of proportionality" and suggested considerations to determine the appropriate scope of discovery).

litigation hold, including any changes to the scope of the litigation hold warranted by newly identified issues in the litigation
- where necessary to ensure preservation of electronically stored information (ESI), undertaking a collection of that ESI and securing it in a sound and defensible manner[38]

In addition, for business or other organizations that are frequently involved in litigation, it may be prudent to establish policies and procedures for identifying when the duty to preserve is triggered and providing training to employees so that they are able to alert management when they become aware of events that may trigger that duty.

Finally, although it may not be possible in prelitigation contexts, one of the best ways to avoid allegations of spoliation is to discuss the scope and burdens of preserving potentially responsive information with opposing counsel. Courts increasingly expect parties to treat discovery as a nonadversarial process.[39] By engaging in dialogue with the opposing party and its counsel, one may be able to simultaneously limit the burden of preserving only tangentially relevant or largely duplicative information and create a record that will prevent future allegations of spoliation.

3. Sanctions and evidence spoliation

A. Courts' authority for issuing sanctions

Simply defined, spoliation is "the destruction or material alteration of evidence or the failure to preserve property for another's use as evidence in pending or reasonably foreseeable litigation."[40] Or as one federal district court put it:

38. *See generally* Zubulake V, 229 F.R.D. at 434.

39. *See, e.g.*, Cartel Asset Mgmt. v. Ocwen Fin. Corp., No. 01-cv-01644-REB-CBS, 2010 WL 502721, at *13 (D. Colo. Feb. 8, 2010) (citing Sedona Conference Cooperation Proclamation (2008)) (warning that "'meet and confer' requirement should not be overridden by counsels' decision to approach discovery as a war of attrition"); Oracle USA, Inc. v. SAP AG, No. C-07-01658, 2009 WL 3009059, at *2 (N.D. Cal. 2009) (noting that "the failure to cooperate on defining the contours of appropriate discovery . . . threatens the fair and cost-effective exchange of relevant discovery"). As of September 30, 2010, the Sedona Cooperation Proclamation had been endorsed by 111 sitting and retired judges. *See* http://www.thesedonaconference.org/content/tsc_cooperation_proclamation/endorsements.pdf. See chapter 30 for more detail.

40. Pitney Bowes Gov't Solutions, Inc. v. United States, 94 Fed. Cl. 1, 4 (Fed. Cl. 2010) (quoting United Med. Supply Co. v. United States, 77 Fed. Cl. 257, 263

> By now, it should be abundantly clear that the duty to preserve means what it says and that a failure to preserve records—paper or electronic—and to search in the right places for those records, will inevitably result in the spoliation of evidence.[41]

Rule 37 of the Federal Rules of Civil Procedure permits a court to impose sanctions for discovery-related abuses, including spoliation. For example, under Rule 37 a court can impose sanctions if a party fails to respond to discovery[42] or "fails to obey an order to provide or permit discovery."[43] Similarly, courts may award sanctions under Rule 26(g) of the Federal Rules of Civil Procedure when counsel (or a party) have wrongfully certified the completeness and accuracy of their discovery responses.[44]

However, courts do not need to rely on Rules 26(g) or 37 to impose sanctions for abuse of discovery. Courts have an "inherent power" to manage their own affairs and levy sanctions when a party violates its discovery obligations, such as the duty to preserve.[45] Generally speaking, though, courts will not order sanctions based on their own authority if they can do so under a particular rule or statute.[46]

(2007)); *see also* West v. Goodyear Tire & Rubber Co., 167 F.3d 776, 779 (2d Cir. 1999) (citing BLACK'S LAW DICTIONARY).

41. Pension Comm. of the Univ. of Montreal Pension Plan v. Banc of Am. Sec., LLC, 685 F. Supp. 2d 456, 461–62 (S.D.N.Y. 2010).

42. FED. R. CIV. P. 37(a)(3); *see also* 8A CHARLES ALAN WRIGHT, ARTHUR R. MILLER & RICHARD L. MARCUS, FEDERAL PRACTICE & PROCEDURE § 2283, at 608 (2d ed. 1994); *see also In re* Seroquel Prods. Liab. Litig., 244 F.R.D. 650, 656 (M.D. Fla. 2007); Alexander v. Fed. Bureau of Investigation, 186 F.R.D. 78, 88 (D.D.C. 1998) ("In making the determination of whether to impose sanctions, Rule 37(b)(2) does not require a showing of willfulness or bad faith as a prerequisite to the imposition of sanctions upon a party") (citations omitted).

43. FED. R. CIV. P. 37(b)(2).

44. FED. R. CIV. P. 26(g); Rottlund Co., Inc., v. Pinnacle Corp., 222 F.R.D. 362 (D. Minn. 2004), *rejected in part by* 2005 WL 407860 (D. Minn. Feb. 17, 2005) (discussing Rule 26(g) obligations and awarding sanctions for failure to comply with that rule). See chapter 31.

45. *See, e.g.*, Chambers v. NASCO, Inc., 501 U.S. 32, 43–46 (1991) (discussing the courts' inherent powers which "extend[] to a full range of litigation abuses"); Union Pump Co. v. Centrifugal Tech. Inc., No. 10-30040, 2010 WL 5186616 (5th Cir., Dec. 16, 2010) (discussing court's inherent power to sanction parties for spoliation); *Pension Comm.*, 685 F. Supp. 2d at 469–71; *United Med. Supply Co.*, 77 Fed. Cl. at 263–64.

46. *United Med. Supply Co.*, 77 Fed. Cl. at 268–71 (discussing a court's ability to issue sanctions under its inherent authority and limitations placed thereon).

Just as with the federal rules, state rules of civil procedure provide state courts with the authority to sanction parties for discovery abuses such as spoliation.[47] Many state courts also possess inherent powers, which provide the power to sanction parties for the failure to preserve.[48]

B. The sanctions analysis

Regardless of the specific rule or authority, a court may issue sanctions when a party violates its duty to preserve information potentially relevant to an adversary's claims or defenses. When considering whether and what sanctions are warranted, the court's focus is multifaceted: to ensure the spoliator does not benefit from its actions; to deter future misconduct; to minimize the injury to the aggrieved party; and to preserve the integrity of the judicial process.[49] Although different courts apply somewhat different tests and standards when considering sanctions for spoliation of evidence, under virtually every standard the primary objective is to balance the degree of wrongdoing against prejudice to the aggrieved party to prevent injustice in the underlying action.[50]

Although there may be some variances by jurisdiction, all courts focus their sanctions analysis on three key elements: the duty to preserve—when it attached and its scope; the culpability of the spoliating party; and the relevance of the lost evidence, or, put differently, the degree of prejudice to the nonspoliating party

---

47. *See, e.g.*, N.Y. C.P.L.R. § 3126 (sanctions for refusing to comply with order); MASS. R. CIV. P. 37 (authority for issuing sanctions); MD. RULE 2-433(a)(1)–(3) (authorizing specifically identified sanctions).

48. *See, e.g.*, Weaver v. Zenimax Media, Inc., 175 Md. App. 16, 42 (2007) ("From time immemorial, certain powers have been conceded to courts, because they are courts. Such powers have been conceded, because without them they could neither maintain their dignity, transact their business, nor accomplish the purposes of their existence. These powers are called inherent powers.").

49. *See, e.g.*, *Pension Comm.*, 685 F. Supp. 2d at 475–79; Orbit One Commc'ns, Inc. v. Numerex Corp., Civ. No. 08-CV-0905, 2010 WL 4615547 (S.D.N.Y. Oct. 26, 2010) (evaluating bases for sanctions and disagreeing with presumptions adopted in *Pension Comm.*); Victor Stanley, Inc. v. Creative Pipe, Inc. (*Victor Stanley II*), 269 F.R.D. 497, 534 (D. Md. 2010); *United Med. Supply*, 77 Fed. Cl. at 264; Metro. Opera Ass'n, Inc. v. Local 100 Hotel Emps. & Rest. Emps. Int'l Union, 212 F.R.D. 178, 219 (S.D.N.Y. 2003).

50. Davis v. Grant Park Nursing Home, Civ. No. 1:08-CV-01764, 2010 WL 4642531, at *1 (D.D.C. Nov. 9, 2010).

arising from the loss of that evidence.[51] How a court will apply the various factors, and what weight and presumptions will be given to each, largely will depend on the specific facts before it.

(1) Duty to preserve

If there is no duty to preserve, there can be no violation of that duty and hence no sanctions. It is of no surprise, then, that most of the decisions addressing sanctions for spoliation engage in detailed analysis of when the duty to preserve attached and the scope of that duty.[52] The court's determination of whether there was a duty to preserve and its scope will be strongly influenced by the court's evaluation of the relevance of the missing material and the controlling party's culpability in failing to preserve it.

(2) Culpability

Culpability can come in three different forms: bad faith, willfulness, or knowing destruction; gross negligence; and ordinary negligence.[53] Most, but not all courts, require a showing of willfulness or bad faith before imposing significant sanctions.[54] In jurisdictions where a showing of willfulness or bad faith is required, the movant usually must show that the spoliating party engaged in egregious discovery misconduct, such as violating a court order,

---

51. *Zubulake IV*, 220 F.R.D. at 220. For a jurisdiction-by-jurisdiction review of the various standards for ordering spoliation sanctions, see *Victor Stanley II*.

52. *See supra* notes 13–37.

53. *See Victor Stanley II*, 269 F.R.D. at 529–31; *Pension Comm.*, 685 F. Supp. 2d at 476–78; Rimkus Consulting Grp., Inc. v. Cammarata, 688 F. Supp. 2d 598, 614–15 (S.D. Tex. 2010); *see also Goodman v. Praxair Services, Inc.*, 2009 WL 1955805, at *18 (D. Md. July 7, 2009) (citing *Thompson v. U.S. Dep't of Housing and Urban Dev.*, 219 F.R.D. 93, 101 (D. Md. 2003)); Residential Funding Corp. v. DeGeorge Fin. Corp., 306 F.3d 99, 108 (2d Cir. 2002)).

54. *See, e.g.*, Silvestri v. Gen. Motors Corp., 271 F.3d 583, 593 (4th Cir. 2001) (dismissal is generally appropriate in circumstances of bad faith); *cf. Residential Funding*, 306 F.3d at 108 ("culpable state of mind," not bad faith, required before an adverse inference can issue); Phillip M. Adams & Assoc., LLC v. Dell, Inc., No. 1:05-CV-64, 2009 WL 910801, at *14 (D. Utah Mar. 30, 2009) (declining to impose "extreme sanctions" because of circumstances mitigating culpability); *see also United Med. Supply*, 77 Fed. Cl. at 263–64, 268 (2007) (stating that "'bad faith' need not be shown in order to impose even the most severe of the spoliation sanctions authorized by RCFC 37(b) and (d)" and that "an injured party need not demonstrate bad faith in order for the court to impose, under its inherent authority, spoliation sanctions").

lying to the court, or intentionally destroying evidence.[55] In those jurisdictions where gross or even ordinary negligence is sufficient, a party may be able to obtain a sanctions order by simply showing that the destruction of documents occurred after the duty to preserve attached.[56]

When a party has destroyed data willfully or through gross negligence, a court may use the destruction itself as a basis for finding that the destroyed evidence was relevant and thus that there was a duty to preserve.[57] In every case, the court will inquire closely into the facts and circumstances of the alleged spoliation when assessing culpability.

Courts face inherent tensions when required to calibrate culpability to the ordering of sanctions. As one court noted:

> Requiring a showing of bad faith as a precondition to the imposition of spoliation sanctions means that evidence may be destroyed willfully, or through gross negligence or even reckless disregard, without any true consequences. At least in Hohfeldian terms, in which a duty is the jural correlate of a right, this approach is tantamount to suggesting that the "duty" to preserve evidence is not much of a duty at all.[58]

(3) Relevance and prejudice

For purposes of evaluating spoliation, the test for "relevance" is narrower than that applied under Rule 401 of the Federal Rules of Evidence.[59] The aggrieved party must show that the lost or destroyed information would "have been relevant to an issue

---

55. *See, e.g.*, *Victor Stanley II*, 269 F.R.D. at 542–53 (appendix of cases); *Metro. Opera*, 212 F.R.D. at 224–26; de Espana v. Am. Bureau of Shipping, No. 3 CV 3573, 2007 WL 1686327, at *4 (S.D.N.Y. June 6, 2007).

56. *See, e.g.*, Sampson v. Cambridge, Maryland, 251 F.R.D. 172, 182 (D. Md. 2008) (in the case of negligent destruction, sanctions not warranted where relevance not proven); *Pension Comm.*, 685 F. Supp. 2d at 467.

57. *Zubulake IV*, 220 F.R.D. at 221; *see also Residential Funding*, 306 F.3d at 108–09.

58. *United Med. Supply Co.*, 77 Fed. Cl. at 257; *see also* P. Rice, Electronic Evidence: Law and Practice (ABA, 2d ed. 2008), 141–42.

59. *See* Arista Records LLC v. Usenet.com, Inc., 608 F. Supp. 2d 409, 439 (S.D.N.Y. 2009) (citing *Residential Funding*, 306 F.3d at 108–09). Under Rule 401, "relevance" is defined as "having the tendency to make the existence of any fact that is of consequence to the determination of the action more probable or less probable than it would be without the evidence."

at trial or otherwise would naturally have been introduced into evidence."[60]

Most courts equate "relevance" with the prejudice to the requesting party caused by the spoliation.[61] Relevance and prejudice are inextricably connected in evaluating a spoliator's culpability and determining whether and what sanctions are warranted: in general, the more willfulness or bad faith in failing to preserve evidence, the less prejudice the courts require the injured party to show before ordering sanctions.[62] In most cases, a court will presume relevance of the evidence where spoliation was intentional or willful, because of the permissible inference that any party who intentionally and willfully destroys evidence must be trying to hide unfavorable facts.[63] Some courts have adopted a presumption of relevance where the evidence was lost as a result of gross negligence.[64] The extent of prejudice will be measured by the

60. Vodusek v. Bayliner Marine Corp., 71 F.3d 148, 156 (4th Cir. 1995); *see also* Henning v. Union Pac. RR Co., 530 F.3d 1206, 1220 (10th Cir. 2008) (denying adverse inference instruction and prohibiting plaintiff from informing jury of destruction of dispatcher tapes where plaintiff could not show relevance and therefore prejudice).

61. *See, e.g.*, Silvestri v. Gen. Motors Corp., 271 F.3d 583, 594 (4th Cir. 2001) (conducting a "prejudice" analysis); Consol. Aluminum Corp. v. Alcoa, Inc., 244 F.R.D. 335, 346 (M.D. La. 2006) (to determine whether to order adverse inference sanction, court considers whether the missing evidence is relevant, whether it would have supported the requested adverse inference, and whether the non-spoliating party suffered prejudice from its destruction).

62. *See, e.g.*, Mosaid Tech. Inc. v. Samsung Elec. Co., 348 F. Supp. 2d 332 (D.N.J. 2004); United States v. Philip Morris USA, Inc., 327 F. Supp. 2d 21 (D.D.C. 2004); Metro. Opera Ass'n, Inc. v. Local 100 Hotel Emps. & Rest. Emps. Int'l Union, 212 F.R.D. 178, 178 (S.D.N.Y. 2003); *see also* King v. Am. Power Conversion Corp., 181 Fed. App'x 373, 2006 WL 1344817, at *3 (4th Cir. 2006) (upholding dismissal where plaintiff's negligent spoliation effectively deprived defendant of evidence essential to its defense).

63. *See, e.g.*, Victor Stanley, Inc. v. Creative Pipe, Inc. (*Victor Stanley II*), 269 F.R.D. 497, 531–32 (D. Md. 2010); *Vodusek*, 71 F.3d at 156; *see also* Reynolds v. Crown Equip. Corp., Civ. No. 5:07CV0018, 2008 WL 2465032, at *4 (W.D. Va. June 16, 2008) (although dismissal may be appropriate if the spoliation was "so prejudicial as to substantially deny a defendant the ability to defend against the claim," dismissal not appropriate where plaintiff was not culpable for loss of evidence).

64. *See* Pension Comm. of the Univ. of Montreal Pension Plan v. Banc of Am. Sec., LLC, 685 F. Supp. 2d 456, 467–68 (S.D.N.Y. 2010) (gross negligence in failing to issue litigation hold held sufficient to support permissive adverse inference that missing evidence was favorable to the nonspoliating party); *but see* Orbit One Commc'ns, Inc. v. Numerex Corp., Civ. No. 08-CV-0905, 2010 WL 4615547, at *10–11 (S.D.N.Y. Oct. 26, 2010) (cautioning that presumption of relevance based

availability of other, compensating evidence.[65] If a court concludes that the evidence was relevant, then any sanction imposed must suit "the purpose of leveling the evidentiary playing field and . . . sanctioning the improper conduct."[66]

C. Types of sanctions

There are many different sanctions that a court may award depending on a party's culpability in failing to preserve evidence and on the degree to which the nonspoliating party was prejudiced by the loss of that evidence. These sanctions include

- dismissal or directed verdict[67]
- an adverse inference that the missing evidence would have been favorable to the nonspoliating party[68]
- requiring the sanctioned party to provide additional discovery[69]

---

on gross negligence in failing to follow proper preservation procedures can become a "'gotcha' game rather than a full and fair opportunity to air the merits of the dispute" (quoting *Pension Comm.*, 685 F. Supp. 2d at 471)).

65. *See, e.g.*, Phillip M. Adams & Assocs, LLC v. Dell, Inc., 621 F. Supp. 2d 1173, 1195 (D. Utah 2009); Arista Records LLC v. Usenet.com, Inc., 608 F. Supp. 2d 409 (S.D.N.Y. 2009) (severe sanction of instructing jury to find specific facts unwarranted where there was sufficient evidence on the record to support plaintiff's claims of liability). See chapter 10.

66. *Vodusek*, 71 F.3d at 156.

67. *See, e.g.*, James Hardie Bldg. Prods., Inc. v. GSE Dev. Corp., No. 03-21168-CIV, 2007 WL 2176036, at *7 (S.D. Fla. July 24, 2007) (granting summary judgment on counterclaim in order to avoid "trial by ambush"); Telxon Corp. Sec. Litig. v. PricewaterhouseCoopers, LLP, No. 5:98CV2876, 2004 WL 3192729 (N.D. Ohio July 16, 2004) (default judgment for failure to preserve and produce various versions of documents in database under Rule 37); *Metro. Opera Assoc.*, 212 F.R.D. 178 (default judgment awarded for defendant's discovery abuses, including intentional destruction of computers containing responsive materials).

68. *See Pension Comm.*, 685 F. Supp. 2d at 497, n. 251 (permissive adverse inference); Rimkus Consulting Grp., Inc. v. Cammarata, 688 F. Supp. 2d 598, 618–20 (S.D. Tex. 2010) (permissive adverse inference); Teague v. Target Corp., No. 3:06CV191, 2007 WL 1041191 (W.D.N.C. Apr. 4, 2007) (ordering adverse inference where plaintiff was at least negligent in destroying home computer containing relevant electronic information); Broccoli v. Echostar Commc'ns Corp., 229 F.R.D. 506 (D. Md. 2005) (adverse instruction where defendant failed to issue a company-wide litigation hold and failed to preserve clearly relevant emails after receipt of EEOC complaint); Testa v. Wal-Mart Stores, Inc., 144 F.3d 173 (1st Cir. 1998) (upholding permissive adverse inference).

69. *See, e.g.*, Ajaxo Inc. v. Bank of Am. Tech. & Operations Inc., No. Civ-S-07-0945, 2008 WL 5101451 (E.D. Ca. Dec. 2, 2008); Cache La Poudre Feeds, LLC v. Land

- prohibiting the introduction of specific evidence or cross-examination of a witness[70]
- monetary sanctions[71]
- contempt[72]

In deciding whether dismissal or other case-determinative sanctions are appropriate, courts will consider a variety of factors such as:

> (1) degree of actual prejudice to the opposing party, (2) the degree of interference with the judicial process, (3) the litigant's culpability, (4) whether the litigant was warned in advance that dismissal was a likely sanction, and (5) whether a lesser sanction would be effective.[73]

As at least one court has stated, the objective is to place the "risk" of an error in judgment on the party who wrongfully creates the

O'Lakes, Inc., 244 F.R.D. 614, 638 (D. Colo. 2007) (ordering certified responses to discovery requests).

70. *See* Nelson-Salabes, Inc. v. Morningside Dev., LLC, 284 F.3d 505, 512 n.10 (4th Cir. 2002) (exclusion ordered where evidence not timely disclosed); Storetrax .com, Inc. v. Gurland, 168 Md. App. 50 (2006) (failure to make discovery on eve of trial warranted preclusion of material withheld); *In re* WRT Energy Secur. Litig., 246 F.R.D. 185, 201 (S.D.N.Y. 2007) (plaintiffs who failed to make timely responses to interrogatories and destroyed relevant documents were prohibited from contesting defendants "success rate theory"); Perez v. Hyundai Motor Co., 440 F. Supp. 2d 57 (D.P.R. 2006) (excluding testimony of expert witness); *but see* Travel Sentry, Inc. v. Tropp, No. 06-CV-6415, 2008 WL 2097613 (E.D.N.Y. May 15, 2008) (evidence preclusion not warranted where the prejudice could be remedied by other means).

71. *See* Victor Stanley, Inc. v. Creative Pipe, Inc. (*Victor Stanley II*), 269 F.R.D. 497, 539–40 (D. Md. 2010) (awarding attorney's fees and costs); Capellupo v. FMC Corp., 126 F.R.D. 545 (D. Minn. 1989) (ordering FMC to pay plaintiff two times her fees and costs and make a payment of $1,432 to the Clerk of the Court for the court's time in considering plaintiff's motion for spoliation sanctions); *see also* Union Pump Co. v. Centrifugal Tech. Inc., No. 10-30040, 2010 WL 5186616 (5th Cir. Dec 16, 2010) (upholding district court's refusal to award attorney's fees for spoliation where the court issued permissive adverse inference instruction and found the jury verdict made the nonspoliating party whole).

72. *See Victor Stanley II*, 269 F.R.D at 539–40, *modified*, No. MJG-06-2662, Memorandum and Order Re: Appeal from Order of Magistrate Judge (Nov. 1, 2010) (declining to incarcerate defendant Pappas for possible future failure to pay sanctions).

73. Phillip M. Adams & Assocs., LLC v. Dell, Inc., 621 F. Supp. 2d 1173, 1193 (D. Utah 2009) (citing LaFleur v. Teen Help, 342 F.3d 1145, 1151 (10th Cir. 2003)).

risk, and restore the prejudiced party to the same position it would have been in absent the wrongful destruction of evidence.[74]

Although very reluctant to impose sanctions in general, courts typically divide sanctions between those that are simply punitive, such as an award of costs or attorney's fees, and those that are issue-related, such as an adverse inference.[75] Courts understandably are reluctant to order a punitive default judgment or directed verdict except in the most extreme cases.[76] For instance, in *Sampson v. Cambridge, Maryland,*[77] plaintiff's counsel sent a preservation letter demanding that all emails and other electronic data be preserved; the defendant failed to initiate a system for preserving data and did not back up email communications, and no email could be located on a key custodian's hard drive.[78] Balancing culpability and prejudice, the court found that although the defendant could have done more to ensure preservation, its conduct did not rise to the level of bad faith and that the plaintiff had failed to meet her burden of demonstrating that the emails would have been relevant to her claims. The court awarded only monetary sanctions, denying the plaintiff's request for a directed verdict or adverse inference instruction.[79]

Because an issue-related adverse inference instruction also can be outcome-determinative, the requesting party also faces a high burden in establishing its right to such a sanction. For example, in *Vodusek v. Bayliner Marine Corp.,*[80] the Fourth Circuit held that while bad faith was not a necessary predicate to an adverse inference instruction, there must, at a minimum, be a showing "that

74. *See Pension Comm.*, 685 F. Supp. 2d at 469 (citing *West v. Goodyear Tire & Rubber Co.*, 167 F.3d 776, 779 (2d Cir. 1999)).

75. *See* D'Onofrio v. SFX Sports Grp., Inc., Civ. No. 06-687, 2010 WL 3324964, at *5–7 (D.D.C. Aug. 24, 2010) (classifying specific sanctions); *Victor Stanley II*, 269 F.R.D. at 534–38 (describing remedial and punitive nature of sanctions).

76. *See* Silvestri v. Gen. Motors Corp., 271 F.3d 583, 593 (4th Cir. 2001) ("[T]he district court must consider both the spoliator's conduct and the prejudice caused and be able to conclude either (1) that the spoliator's conduct was so egregious as to amount to a forfeiture of his claim, or (2) that the effect of the spoliator's conduct was so prejudicial that it substantially denied the defendant the ability to defend the claim."); *see also* Chambers v. NASCO, Inc., 501 U.S. 32, 44–45 (1991) (acknowledging that dismissal, while a severe sanction, is within the court's discretionary powers).

77. 251 F.R.D. 172 (D. Md. 2008).

78. *Id.* at 175–77.

79. *Id.* at 182–84.

80. 71 F.3d 148 (4th Cir. 1995).

the party knew the evidence was relevant to some issue at trial and that his willful conduct resulted in its loss or destruction."[81] Following *Vodusek*, the court in *Goodman v. Praxair Services, Inc.*[82] found that an adverse instruction was warranted even though the plaintiff had failed to establish bad faith on the part of the defendant, where a key defense witness had deleted email communications and destroyed key employees' laptops after the duty to preserve was triggered. The court's rationale was that relevant data was willfully destroyed, permitting an inference that the defendant did not want the evidence produced, and thus the inference that the missing evidence would have been unfavorable to the defendant.[83]

The court in *Arista Records*[84] balanced the issues of culpability, relevance, and prejudice somewhat differently, holding that even though the defendant engaged in willful spoliation of highly relevant evidence, an adverse inference was not warranted where a less severe sanction—precluding defendants from challenging plaintiff's statistical evidence on damages—would restore the nonspoliating party to the same position he would have been absent the spoliation. As *Arista Records* illustrates, where sanctions are or may be outcome determinative, courts generally will impose such sanctions only if lesser sanctions are insufficient to ensure that the nonspoliating party's position is not unfairly prejudiced on the merits.[85]

D.Who is subject to sanctions?

Although in most cases the spoliating party will be held responsible for the loss or destruction of relevant evidence, counsel may

81. *Id.* at 156.

82. 2009 WL 1955805 (D. Md. July 7, 2009).

83. *Id.* (quoting Vodusek v. Bayliner Marine Corp., 71 F.3d 148, 148 (4th Cir. 1995)) (citation and internal quotation marks omitted).

84. Arista Records LLC v. Usenet.com, Inc., 608 F. Supp. 2d 409 441–44 (S.D.N.Y. 2009).

85. *See also, e.g., In re* Napster, Inc. Copyright Litig., 462 F. Supp. 2d 1060 (N.D. Cal. 2006) (default judgment inappropriate where "lesser sanctions" such as evidence preclusion, adverse inference instruction, and attorney's fees were effective and adequate); Metro. Opera Ass'n, Inc. v. Local 100 Hotel Emps. & Rest. Emps. Int'l Union, 212 F.R.D. 178, 178 (S.D.N.Y. 2003) (finding that discovery abuse was so extensive that the "evidentiary balance" could not be restored, necessitating entry of judgment of liability against defendants).

also be subject to sanctions under both the rules of civil procedure and the rules of professional conduct.[86]

E. Rule 37(e)—the "safe harbor" provision

Despite the pitfalls that seem to go hand in hand with electronic discovery, litigants may have some protection from sanctions in limited circumstances. Federal Rule of Civil Procedure 37(e) provides a "safe harbor" when relevant electronic data is inadvertently destroyed due to the standard document management processes that are part of a party's information technology program. Rule 37(e) applies only to sanctions that a court may issue under the rules, so a court's inherent and other authority to sanction is unaffected by this provision.[87]

The language of the rule is straightforward:

> Absent exceptional circumstances, a court may not impose sanctions under these rules on a party for failing to provide electronically stored information lost as a result of the routine, good-faith operation of an electronic system.

What is the "routine, good-faith operation of an electronic system" and when does this "safe harbor" apply? The Advisory Committee Notes to the 2006 Amendments provide insight into the meaning of this phrase and offer a two-part test for applying subsection (e): first, a court must determine whether the information was lost due to the "routine operation"; and second, whether the "routine operation" was conducted in good faith.

The Committee Notes define "routine operation" to include

> the alteration and overwriting of information, often without the operator's specific direction or awareness, a feature with

86. *See supra* notes 6 & 8; *see also* Travel Sentry, Inc. v. Tropp, No. 06-CV-6415, 2008 WL 2097613, at *6 (E.D.N.Y. May 15, 2008) (upholding monetary sanction of outside counsel for failing to disclose existence of withheld documents); *but see* Books Are Fun, Ltd. v. Rosebrough, 239 F.R.D. 532 (S.D. Iowa 2007) (declining to sanction counsel for failure to produce critical document in its possession where court found counsel's failure to produce was not due to bad faith or other misconduct).

87. Fed. R. Civ. P. 37(e) advisory committee's note to 2006 Amendment. Further, the Committee Notes make clear that while a party may be protected from sanctions under this subsection, a court may still order that party to produce *other available* relevant information through written discovery or even depositions.

> no direct counterpart in hard-copy documents. *Such features are essential to the operation of electronic information systems.*[88]

Most businesses have standard document retention programs in place providing for the deletion of old material no longer useful to the business. All computers, as part of their operating systems, provide for the automatic overwriting of electronic data on a regular basis. Under the Rules Committee's definition, such programs would be "routine operation" for purposes of managing data.

The key question is whether such "routine operations" are carried out in "good faith." According to the Rules Committee,

> [T]he good faith requirement . . . means that a party is not permitted to exploit the routine operation of an information system to thwart discovery obligations by allowing that operation to continue in order to destroy specific stored information that it is required to preserve.[89]

Thus, one of the main considerations in assessing a party's good faith in operating a "routine system" is what steps were taken to comply with the party's duty to preserve, such as suspending or modifying features of the system that delete, overwrite, or recycle data, if that data is subject to the duty to preserve.[90]

As with the other aspects of the sanctions analysis, whether the "safe harbor" of Rule 37 applies is very fact-specific. An examination of recent reported judicial decisions addressing Rule 37's "safe harbor" reveals that safe harbor protection is rarely granted.[91] As one scholar has noted: "It will take several years of judicial consideration before a producing party can rely on Rule 37 as a defense

88. FED. R. CIV. P. 37(e) advisory committee's note to 2006 Amendment (emphasis added).

89. *Id.*

90. *Id. See supra* notes 1–11 regarding the duty to preserve.

91. *See, e.g.*, Phillip M. Adams & Assocs., LLC v. Dell, Inc., 621 F. Supp. 2d 1173, 1191–92 (D. Utah, 2009) (denying protection under 37(e) due to inadequacies in expert's supporting declaration); Keithley v. Homestore.com, Inc., No. C-03-04447, 2008 WL 3833384, at *5–6 (N.D. Cal. Aug. 12, 2008); Doe v. Norwalk Cmty. Coll., 248 F.R.D. 372 (D. Conn. 2007); Peskoff v. Faber, 244 F.R.D. 54, 60–61 (D.D.C. 2007); Disability Rights Council v. Wash. Metro Transit Auth., 242 F.R.D. 139, 146–47 (D.D.C. 2007); *but see* Mintel Int'l Grp., Ltd. v. Neergheen, No. 08-CV-3939, 2010 WL 145786, at *8 (N.D. Ill. 2010) (laptop's automatic defragmentation and antivirus programs had minimal impact on content of hard drive and thus did not support sanction for spoliation).

to the destruction of ESI."[92] Thus, parties should be cautious about relying on Rule 37(e) as a possible defense, and instead focus on taking measures to preserve relevant electronic data even if those measures require interrupting or altering the normal operation of a computer system.

4. Conclusion

Sanctions motions arising out of a failure to preserve are not new in civil cases, but due to the increased focus on electronically stored evidence, the fragility of that information, and the complexity and cost of implementing preservation decisions there has been an enormous increase in the number of spoliation sanctions rulings in the last few years. Only some of those rulings reflect egregious discovery abuses.

The only way to ensure that you and your client avoid a motion for spoliation, and the time-consuming, expensive, and risky discovery-on-discovery that almost always accompanies such a motion, is to be alert to events that trigger the duty, know the scope of the duty, be diligent in preserving potentially relevant electronic information, and be as transparent as possible with opposing counsel and the court so that there can be a shared understanding of the scope of your duty to preserve and the steps you are taking—and are not taking—to satisfy that obligation.

92. PAUL RICE, ELECTRONIC EVIDENCE (ABA 2d ed. 2008).

CHAPTER 9

PROPORTIONALITY LIMITS ON THE SCOPE OF PRESERVATION

THE HON. PAUL W. GRIMM,
MICHAEL D. BERMAN, CONOR R. CROWLEY,
AND LESLIE WHARTON

The law review article[1] *from which this chapter was adapted discusses how to define reasonable, cost-effective limits on the scope of the pre-litigation duty to preserve. The article was cited in* Victor Stanley, Inc. v. Creative Pipe, Inc.[2] *and* OTO Software, Inc. v. Highwall Technologies, LLC,[3] *as well as the influential Sedona Conference* Commentary on Proportionality in Electronic Discovery.[4] *It is offered here because of its importance in suggesting how the concept of*

1. Abridged and adapted from P. Grimm et al., *Proportionality in the Post-Hoc Analysis of Pre-Litigation Preservation Decisions*, 37 U. BALT. L. REV. 381 (2008) (hereinafter, "P. Grimm, et al., 'Proportionality in the Post-Hoc Analysis,' 37 U.Balt.L.Rev. at ___"). Used by permission.
2. Victor Stanley, Inc. v. Creative Pipe, Inc. (*Victor Stanley II*), 269 F.R.D. 497 (D. Md. 2010), *affirmed in part and modified in part on unrelated grounds*, No.MJG-06-2662 (D.Md. Nov. 1, 2010), *subsequent opinion*, No. MJG-06-2662 (D.Md. Jan. 24, 2011).
3. 2010 U.S. Dist. Lexis 101516, at *23 n.4 (D. Colo. Aug. 6 2010).
4. 11 SED. CONF. J. 289, 296 n.20 (2010) [hereinafter *Proportionality*].

"proportionality" should be applied to actions taken by a potential party during the period before litigation commenced.

1. Introduction

A recent study of 230 sanctions cases concluded that "the most common misconduct was failure to preserve ESI."[5] While the definition of the duty to preserve is well accepted, its application to specific situations is often difficult and costly, and the proportionality limits on the scope of the duty are ill-defined. This chapter suggests application by analogy of the cost-benefit provisions of the Federal Rules to guide prelitigation preservation decisions and provide additional specificity to the proportionality limits on the duty to preserve electronically stored information (ESI). The Federal Rules of Civil Procedure and common law principles present creative litigators with tools and opportunities to establish a framework for the just, speedy, and inexpensive resolution of disputes.[6] Courts and commentators have, in authorities too numerous to cite, stated that the ultimate standard is reasonableness and proportionality. For example, as noted in the recent *Pension Committee* decision:

> In an era where vast amounts of electronic information is [sic] available for review, discovery in certain cases has become increasingly complex and expensive. Courts cannot and do not expect that any party can meet a standard of perfection. Nonetheless, the courts have a right to expect that litigants and counsel will take the necessary steps to ensure that relevant records are preserved when litigation is reasonably anticipated. . . .[7]

Information has changed,[8] and adapting to that change is not problem-free. It requires new approaches to dynamic issues: "It was neither a comet nor a dramatic climactic change that killed

5. D. Willoughby et al., *Sanctions for E-Discovery Violations: By the Numbers*, 60 Duke L.J. 289, 803 (2010).
6. See Fed. R. Civ. P. 1. Rule 1 has been described as "[t]he most important rule of all" because it "gives all the other rules life and meaning." M. Mazza et al., *In Pursuit of FRCP 1: Creative Approaches to Cutting and Shifting the Costs of Discovery of Electronically Stored Information*, 13 Rich. J.L. & Tech. 11 (2007).
7. Pension Comm. of Univ. of Montreal Pension Plan v. Banc of Am. Sec., LLC, 685 F. Supp. 2d 456, 461 (S.D.N.Y. 2010).
8. George Paul & Jason Baron, *Information Inflation: Can the Legal System Adapt?*, 13 Rich. J.L. & Tech. 10 (2007) ("lawyers must understand that information, as a cultural and technological edifice, has profoundly and irrevocably changed").

off the dinosaurs. They perished because they could not adapt to the digital age."[9] Cases imposing substantial sanctions, including criminal prosecution, adverse inference instructions, restrictions on testimony, and monetary penalties, as well as the attendant ethical implications,[10] demonstrate that a misstep in determining the scope of the duty to preserve may have serious consequences.

The application of concepts such as "reasonable" and "proportionate" remains difficult,[11] and the serious consequences of an error may compel a risk-averse potential litigant to exercise extraordinary care in preserving "everything" at enormous cost and effort, although such extraordinary effort is not required by law.[12] Because the duty to preserve often arises before a lawsuit is filed, there is no judicial umpire,[13] no opposing counsel available to negotiate the scope, and no way to determine the applicable source of law, that is, statutory, regulatory, federal, or state, and, if state, which one. This lack of guidance may cause cautious counsel to expend enormous sums to preserve ESI that need not be preserved, that will never be produced in discovery or offered into evidence, and that may exceed the economic value of the claims presented, in contravention of the fundamental principle

9. Martin A. Redish, *Electronic Discovery and the Litigation Matrix*, 51 DUKE L.J. 561, 563 (2001) (quoting Jerold S. Solovy & Robert L. Byman, *Digital Discovery*, NAT'L L.J., Dec. 27, 1999, at A16).

10. *See* MODEL RULES OF PROF'L CONDUCT R. 3.4(a) (2008).

11. The duty "should not be analyzed in absolute terms; it requires nuance, because the duty cannot be defined with precision." Victor Stanley, Inc. v. Creative Pipe, Inc. (*Victor Stanley II*), 269 F.R.D. 497, 522 (D. Md. 2010) (citations and quotations omitted). Although "reasonableness" is a "common standard," it is lacks "a precise and specific meaning." D. Bassett, *Reasonableness in E-Discovery*, 30 CAMPBELL L. REV. 435, 436 (2010). "As a relatively recent concept, e-discovery's reasonableness standards are still developing." *Id.*

12. *See, e.g.*, Zubulake v. UBS Warburg LLC (*Zubulake IV*), 220 F.R.D. 212, 217 (S.D.N.Y. 2003) ("Must a corporation, upon recognizing the threat of litigation, preserve every shred of paper, every e-mail or electronic document, and every backup tape? The answer is clearly, 'no.'"); OTO Software, Inc. v. Highwall Techs., LLC, 2010 U.S. Dist. Lexis 101516, at *23 (D. Colo. Aug. 6, 2010) ("it is generally accepted that a litigant's duty to preserve does not obligate that party to retain every document in its possession"); *Victor Stanley II*, 269 F.R.D. at 524.

13. *See* Steven C. Bennett, *Electronic Materials and Other Discovery Considerations*, *in* INSURANCE COVERAGE 2006: CLAIM TRENDS AND LITIGATION 111, 117–18 (PLI Litig. & Admin. Practice, Course Handbook Series No. 8412, 2006), WL 742 PLI/Lit 111 at 127 (noting that the preservation obligation occurs before there is a chance for a "meet and confer" and before there is "a chance to approach the court for a ruling on the reasonableness of the preservation approach").

established in Rule 1, "to secure the just, speedy, and inexpensive determination of every action and proceeding."

With the exception of *Rimkus*,[14] however, "courts have tended to overlook the importance of proportionality in determining whether a party has complied with its duty to preserve evidence. . . ."[15] This chapter suggests an approach for bridging the gap between the cost-benefit protections provided a litigant under the Federal Rules and the broad scope of the prelitigation duty to preserve. It proposes application by analogy of the protections of Rules 26(b)(2)(C) and 37(e) (or comparable state-law provisions) to guide and limit preservation efforts before a lawsuit is commenced.[16]

Rule 26(b)(2)(C) provides:

> On motion or on its own, the court must limit the frequency or extent of discovery otherwise allowed by these rules or by local rule if it determines that:
>
> (i) the discovery sought is unreasonably cumulative or duplicative, or can be obtained from some other source that is more convenient, less burdensome, or less expensive;
>
> (ii) the party seeking discovery has had ample opportunity to obtain the information by discovery in the action; or

14. Rimkus Consulting Group, Inc. v. Cammarata, 688 F. Supp. 2d 598, 613 (S.D. Tex. 2010).

15. *Victor Stanley II*, 269 F.R.D. at 523.

16. Many Federal Rules in addition to Rules 26(b(2)(C) and 37(e) contain cost-benefit, or proportionality, provisions. *Victor Stanley II*, 269 F.R.D. at 523. For example, Rule 1 calls for the "inexpensive" resolution of cases and "[p]arties, lawyers, and judges have an opportunity today to begin taking creative new approaches to the discovery of ESI, with a renewed focus on the important (yet often neglected) mandate of FRCP 1." Mazza, *In Pursuit of FRCP* 1, 13 RICH. J.L. & TECH. at *7. Additionally, Rule 26(b)(2)(B) addresses ESI that is not reasonably accessible "because of undue burden or cost" and Rule 26(c) protects against "undue burden or expense." Rule 26(f) implicitly incorporates similar concerns and Rule 26(g) prohibits discovery that "needlessly increase[s] the cost of litigation" or that is "unduly burdensome or expensive, considering the needs of the case, prior discovery in the case, the amount in controversy, and the importance of the issues at stake in the action." Similarly, Rule 11 prohibits pleadings or motions that "needlessly increase the cost of litigation" and Rule 45(c)(1) mandates that a party serving a subpoena "take reasonable steps to avoid imposing undue burden or expense." The textual reference to Rules 26(b)(2)(C) and 37(e) is illustrative, not exclusive.

(iii) the burden or expense of the proposed discovery outweighs its likely benefit, considering the needs of the case, the amount in controversy, the parties' resources, the importance of the issues at stake in the action, and the importance of the discovery in resolving the issues.

Rule 37(e) provides: "Absent exceptional circumstances, a court may not impose sanctions under these rules on a party for failing to provide electronically stored information lost as a result of the routine, good-faith operation of an electronic information system."

2. The federal rules, and the protections of Rules 26(b)(2)(C) and 37(e), do not directly apply to prelitigation conduct, presenting an anomaly

The Federal Rules do not directly govern prelitigation conduct. Rule 1 provides: "These rules govern the procedure in the United States district courts in all suits of a civil nature whether cognizable as cases at law or in equity or in admiralty, with the exceptions stated in Rule 81." Rule 1 applies "in" the courts, not to matters that predate initiation of litigation.[17]

The Federal Rules of Civil Procedure are promulgated under the Rules Enabling Act.[18] That statute provides: "The Supreme Court shall have the power to prescribe general rules of practice and procedure and rules of evidence for cases in the United States district courts (including proceedings before magistrate judges thereof) and courts of appeals." It states that the rules may not abridge, enlarge, or modify any substantive right. Again, the statute provides that Federal Rules may be prescribed "for cases in" court, and not prior to the commencement of cases. A lawsuit or action is commenced when a complaint is filed.[19]

Many authorities note the limits on application of the Federal Rules. For example, "Rule 37 does not, by its terms, address sanctions for destruction of evidence prior to the initiation of a lawsuit

---

17. *See generally* 4 CHARLES ALAN WRIGHT & ARTHUR R. MILLER, FEDERAL PRACTICE AND PROCEDURE § 1012 (2002) ("The language of Rule 1 limits the applicability of the federal rules to the United States district courts. . . .").

18. 28 U.S.C. § 2072 (2000).

19. FED. R. CIV. P. 3. "The Federal Rules do not apply until litigation has commenced." *Proportionality, supra* note 4, at 296.

or discovery requests."[20] This limitation was likely a jurisdictional constraint imposed on the drafters: "The Advisory Committee on Civil Rules debated whether it could specify preservation obligations in the Federal Rules of Civil Procedure but ultimately decided it could not do so."[21] In fact, "[a] major criticism of Rule 37(f) [now Rule 37(e)] is that it addresses only sanctions under the federal rules, which generally do not apply prior to commencement of litigation."[22] Similarly, Rule 26(b)(2)(C) is directed toward events occurring during litigation. For example, the title of Rule 26 is "General Provisions Governing Discovery; Duty of Disclosure." Rule 26(b) is captioned "Discovery Scope and Limits." Also, Rule 26(b)(2)(C) addresses the "frequency or extent of discovery otherwise allowed by these rules." The term "discovery" refers to a process that begins, at the earliest, with the filing of a complaint.[23]

Because the duty to preserve may, and often does, arise before commencement of a case, neither the cost-benefit protections of Rule 26(b)(2)(C) nor the "safe harbor" of Rule 37(e) directly apply to a potential party attempting to comply with its preservation obligation, even though that obligation may be defined by the scope of discovery that will apply the moment after litigation is commenced. A potential litigant may be unfairly exposed to excessive costs or, alternatively, a motion for the imposition of sanctions, even if it acted in good faith in attempting to comply with its prelitigation duty to preserve.

In light of the significant sanctions that courts may impose because of a prelitigation failure to preserve ESI, the contours of the prelitigation duty to preserve need to be clear so that informed

20. Capellupo v. FMC Corp., 126 F.R.D. 545, 550–51 (D. Minn. 1989); ABC Home Health Servs., Inc. v. Int'l. Bus. Machs., 158 F.R.D. 180, 182 (S.D. Ga. 1994).

21. THE SEDONA CONFERENCE COMMENTARY ON LEGAL HOLDS: THE TRIGGER & THE PROCESS (Aug. 2007 Public Comment Version) at 5 n.13, http://www.thesedonaconference.org/content/miscFiles/Legal_holds.pdf; *cf. The Sedona Conference Commentary on Legal Holds: The Trigger & the Process*, 10 SEDONA CONF. J. 265, 267 n.10 (2010) [hereinafter *Legal Holds*].

22. Thomas Y. Allman, *Managing Preservation Obligations After the 2006 Federal E-Discovery Amendments*, 13 RICH. J.L. & TECH. 9, ¶ 43 (2007), http://law.richmond.edu/jolt/v13i3/article9.pdf. It should be noted that criticism cannot be directed at the drafters of the Rule, because the drafters were limited by the Rules Enabling Act, 28 U.S.C. § 2072. *Id.* ¶ 45.

23. *See* B & C Tire Co. v. IRS, 376 F. Supp. 708, 712, 714 (N.D. Ala. 1978) (stating general rule; yet noting exception for discovery to perpetuate evidence); *In re* Royal Bank of Can., 33 F.R.D. 296, 299, 302 (S.D.N.Y. 1963).

judgments may be made and subsequently presented to the court. The protections afforded by Rules 26(b)(2)(C) and 37(e) are one mechanism to provide those contours. In the ESI context, the cost-benefit protections of Rule 26(b)(2)(C) and Rule 37(e)'s "safe harbor" should apply by analogy to define prelitigation preservation conduct that is not directly governed by those rules.[24] It would, for example, be anomalous to conclude that a good faith failure to preserve information after a lawsuit is commenced should be afforded greater protection than an identical failure before suit is filed simply because the Rule 37(e) "safe harbor" cannot apply prior to litigation. It would be equally anomalous to sanction a party because it failed to preserve information that, under Rule 26(b)(2)(C), is later determined by the court not to be discoverable.

3. Source of the duty to preserve

The duty to preserve electronic data can arise from a wide variety of sources. It may arise from statutes, regulations, ethical rules, court orders, or the common law.[25] A duty to preserve may also arise through an agreement, a contract, or another special circumstance.[26] State or federal criminal law may also define a duty to preserve, within constitutional constraints.

The duty was not created by the Federal Rules of Civil Procedure or the Federal Rules of Evidence. "As noted in the September 2005 Report of the Standing Committee of the Judicial Conference recommending adoption of the 2006 Amendments, preservation obligations 'arise from independent sources of law' and are dependent upon 'the substantive law of each jurisdiction.'"[27] In some

24. *See* E.E.O.C. v. Jacksonville Shipyards, Inc., 690 F. Supp. 995, 997 (M.D. Fla. 1988); *see also* Thomas Y. Allman, *Rule 37(f) Meets Its Critics: The Justification for a Limited Preservation Safe Harbor for ESI*, 5 Nw. J. Tech. & Intell. Prop. 1 (2006), http://www.law.northwestern.edu/journals/njtip/v5/n1/1/.

25. Dale M. Cendali et al., *Potential Ethical Pitfalls in Electronic Discovery, in* Ethics in Context 2007: Ethics and Electronic Discovery 111, 113 (PLI N.Y. Practice Skills, Course Handbook No. 10960, 2007), WL 171 PLI/NY 105.

26. Boyd v. Travelers Ins. Co., 652 N.E.2d 267, 271 (Ill. 1995) ("[A] duty to preserve evidence may arise through an agreement, a contract, a statute or another special circumstance. Moreover, a defendant may voluntarily assume a duty by affirmative conduct" (citations omitted)).

27. Thomas Y. Allman, *Managing Preservation Obligations After the 2006 Federal E-Discovery Amendments*, 13 Rich. J.L. & Tech. 9, ¶ 1 (2007), http://law.richmond.edu/jolt/v13i3/article9.pdf (quoting Report of the Judicial Conference Committee on Rules of Practice and Procedure Rules 32, 34 (2005).

instances, the duty to preserve is governed by state law; in others, by federal law.[28] Regardless of its source, the existence of the duty is well established. Its scope, however, is not.

4. Scope of the duty to preserve

"Proceeding chronologically, the first step in any discovery effort is the preservation of relevant information."[29] Just as they did not create the duty to preserve, the Federal Rules of Civil Procedure do not define the scope of the prelitigation duty to preserve.[30] Although "[t]he broad contours of the duty to preserve are relatively clear,"[31] it is not always straightforward in application and "[t]he obligation to preserve relevant evidence cannot be defined with precision."[32]

The scope of the duty to preserve information was described in *Zubulake v. UBS Warburg LLC (Zubulake V)*,[33] where Judge Scheindlin noted: "[A] party and her counsel must make certain that all

28. In state courts, and in federal courts exercising diversity jurisdiction, the rule appears to be that state law governs the prelitigation duty to preserve, while federal rules govern the procedure of a case after it is commenced in federal court. *See, e.g.*, Thomas v. Bombadier-Rotax Motorenfabrik, GmbH, 869 F. Supp. 551, 553 (N.D. Ill. 1994) (citing Hanna v. Plumer, 380 U.S. 460, 465 (1965)). Where a federal court exercises federal subject-matter jurisdiction, however, the duty to preserve appears to be governed entirely by federal law. *See* Estate of LeMay v. Eli Lilly & Co., 960 F. Supp. 183, 186 (E.D. Wis. 1997).

29. Pension Comm. of Univ. of Montreal Pension Plan v. Banc of Am. Sec., LLC, 685 F. Supp. 2d 456, 464 (S.D.N.Y. 2010).

30. Recently an e-discovery panel at the Duke University conference proposed consideration of a preservation rule. That proposal is one that is under consideration by the Rules Committee. The introductory note stated: "Panel members disagree as to whether such a rule can or should apply, along the lines of Rule 27 [Depositions to Perpetuate Testimony], prior to the commencement of an action." *See* Elements of a Preservation Rule, http://www.americanbar.org/content/dam/aba/publishing/litigation_news/ediscovery_panel_preservation.authcheckdam.pdf. John M. Barkett has noted: "Attempting to articulate a uniform preservation rule raises a number of concerns, beginning with how to impose prelitigation preservation duties while still acting within the authority of the Rules Enabling Act." K. Lambert, *Is It Time for a Federal Rule on Preservation?*, ABA LITIG. NEWS, Aug. 2, 2010.

31. Zubulake v. UBS Warburg LLC (*Zubulake IV*), 220 F.R.D. 212, 217 (S.D.N.Y. 2003).

32. SHIRA A. SCHEINDLIN, MOORE'S FEDERAL PRACTICE E-DISCOVERY: THE NEWLY AMENDED FEDERAL RULES OF CIVIL PROCEDURE 7 n.28 (2006).

33. 229 F.R.D. 422 (S.D.N.Y. 2004).

sources of potentially relevant information[34] are identified and placed "on hold,' to the extent required in *Zubulake IV*."[35] In *Zubulake IV*, the court held:

> "While a litigant is under no duty to keep or retain every document in its possession . . . it is under a duty to preserve what it knows, or reasonably should know, is relevant in the action, is reasonably calculated to lead to the discovery[36] of admissible evidence, is reasonably likely to be requested during discovery and/or is the subject of a pending discovery request."[37]

34. The duty is often described as a duty to preserve relevant "evidence." China Ocean Shipping Group v. Simone Metals Inc., No. 97 C 2694, 1999 WL 966443, at *3 (N.D. Ill. Sept. 30, 1999); *Pension Comm.*, 605 F. Supp. 2d at 466. The *Zubulake IV* court, however, described the duty in terms of "relevant information," 220 F.R.D. at 218, and the Sedona Conference similarly states that the duty to preserve extends only to "relevant information." *Legal Holds, supra* note 21, passim. The word "information" may lead to different conclusions than the word "evidence," and the former is likely the more accurate term. *See* FED. R. CIV. P. 26(b)(1) ("Relevant information need not be admissible at the trial if the discovery appears reasonably calculated to lead to the discovery of admissible evidence.").

35. *Zubulake V*, 229 F.R.D. at 432.

36. The scope of discovery is set forth in FED. R. CIV. P. 26(b)(1) ("Parties may obtain discovery regarding any nonprivileged matter that is relevant to any party's claim or defense—including the existence, description, nature, custody, condition, and location of any documents or other tangible things and the identity and location of persons who know of any discoverable matter. For good cause, the court may order discovery of any matter relevant to the subject matter involved in the action. Relevant information need not be admissible at the trial if the discovery appears reasonably calculated to lead to the discovery of admissible evidence. All discovery is subject to the limitations imposed by Rule 26(b)(2)(C).") Rule 26(b)(1) sets a minimal threshold for discovery. Thompson v. U.S. Dep't of Hous. & Urban Dev., 219 F.R.D. 93, 97 (D. Md. 2003). Special circumstances may provide justification for narrowing the amount of discovery. *See* Bell Atl. Corp. v. Twombly, 550 U.S. 544, 558–59 (2007) (considering cost of discovery in antitrust action); Cheney v. U.S. Dist. Court for D.C., 542 U.S. 385, 388 (2004) (holding that respect for the Executive Office informs the "entire proceeding"); Clinton v. Jones, 520 U.S. 707 (1997); Hoffman LaRoche, Inc. v. Sperling, 493 U.S. 165, 179 (1989) (citing FED. R. CIV. P. 26(b)); Oppenheimer Fund Inc. v. Sanders, 437 U.S. 340, 351–52 (1978).

37. *Zubulake IV*, 220 F.R.D. at 217 (emphasis added) (citing Turner v. Hudson Trans. Lines, Inc., 142 F.R.D. 68, 72 (S.D.N.Y. 1991)).

Similarly, in *In re Napster, Inc. Copyright Litigation*,[38] the district court ruled that the duty encompassed all material that the party "knows or reasonably should know is relevant to the action."[39]

Descriptions of the scope of the common law duty to preserve are virtually coextensive with the scope of discovery. For example, one commentator asked: "What must be retained and preserved? The simple answer is potentially relevant evidence. This includes any evidence that could be helpful in proving or disproving a claim or defense."[40] In short, the link between the scope of the duty to preserve and the scope of discovery is clear: "Preservation duties do not exist in the abstract, but to serve a purpose: that is, to ensure that discoverable documents are available to be produced."[41]

Under the Federal Rules of Civil Procedure, however, the scope of discovery cannot be definitively ascertained before suit is commenced. For example, although the December 2007 amendments limit discovery to matters related to the parties' "claims or defenses," the court has discretion to expand discovery to all facts related to the "subject matter involved in the action."[42] Counsel faced with determining the scope of the prelitigation duty to preserve cannot know which discovery standard will subsequently apply. While prudence may suggest application of the broader standard, doing so may unnecessarily increase the cost of preservation of ESI.[43]

---

38. 462 F. Supp. 2d 1060, 1067 (N.D. Cal. 2006), *rev'd*, 479 F.3d 1078 (9th Cir. 2007), *vacated*, Nos. C-MDL-00-1369(MHP), C-04-1166 (MHP), 2007 WL 844551 (N.D. Cal. Mar. 20, 2007).

39. *Id.*; accord *Thompson*, 219 F.R.D. at 100 (quoting *Zubulake IV*, 220 F.R.D. at 216 (noting that a litigation hold applies to "relevant" documents)).

40. P. RICE, ELECTRONIC EVIDENCE: LAW AND PRACTICE 106 (ABA, 2d ed. 2008).

41. Danis v. USN Commc'ns, Inc., 2000 WL 1694325, at *33 (N.D. Ill. Oct. 23, 2000).

42. FED. R. CIV. P. 26(b)(1).

43. The preservation of ESI presents special concerns, including the dynamic, often ephemeral nature of some ESI. *See* Conor R. Crowley, *A Shifting View of Preservation: How Ephemeral Are Current Views on Shifting the Costs of Preservation*, DIGITAL DISCOVERY & E-EVIDENCE REP. (BNA) 1, 2–4 (Jan. 1, 2008). For example, Sedona Guideline No. 7 provides: "Factors that may be considered in determining the scope of information that should be preserved include the nature of the issues raised in the matter, the accessibility of the information, the probative value of the information, and the relative burdens and costs of the preservation effort." *See Legal Holds*, supra note 21, at 270. The duty to preserve extends only to "unique" information. *Id.* at 278–79. It is, however, difficult to determine what information is "unique" prior to preserving it for examination.

5. Generic proportionality limits on the scope of the duty to preserve

There is ample authority holding that principles of proportionality limit the scope of the duty to preserve.[44] In short, while all unique, potentially discoverable information falls within the scope of the duty to preserve, there is an implicit notion that the scope of preservation should be proportional to the amount in controversy, the resources of the litigants, and the costs and burdens of preservation.

There is, however, little guidance in applying that generic concept. In fact, "case law is not consistent across the circuits, or even within individual districts."[45] While many decisions and commentators state that preservation should be proportionate, none has been found applying the cost-benefit limitations of Rule 26(b)(2)(C) or the "safe harbor" of Rule 37(e) by analogy.[46] In fact, the Sedona Conference has recently stated that "there is no case law that applies proportionality factors set forth in the Federal Rules in the pre-litigation context."[47]

This leaves a dangerous void for the prelitigation practitioner.[48] "Clearly, one person's trash is another's treasure."[49] A practitioner operating without judicial supervision or court rules must either

44. *E.g.*, Rimkus Consulting Group, Inc. v. Cammarata, 688 F. Supp. 2d 598, 613 (S.D. Tex. 2010). The principle of proportionality holds that the burdens imposed by the duty to preserve should be proportionate to what is at stake in the litigation. Proportionality is often stated in terms of the duty to preserve being one requiring only "reasonable" efforts. *See* Wiginton v. Ellis, 2003 WL 22439865, at *4 (N.D. Ill. Oct. 27, 2003). *See generally* Thompson, 219 F.R.D. at 97–99.

45. Victor Stanley, Inc. v. Creative Pipe, Inc. (*Victor Stanley II*), 269 F.R.D. 497, 523 (D. Md. 2010).

46. In one decision, involving ephemeral data, an early, proposed version of then Rule 37(f) was relied upon to excuse a failure to preserve. Allman, *supra* note 22, at ¶ 46 & n.110 (citing Convolve, Inc. v. Compaq Computer Corp., 223 F.R.D. 162, 177 (S.D.N.Y. 2004)).

47. *Legal Holds,* supra note 21, at 296. The Sedona Conference also suggests applying Rule 26(b)(2)(C) factors to the prelitigation duty to preserve. The Sedona Conference Commentary on Preservation, Management and Identification of Sources of Information that are Not Reasonably Accessible 14–15 (July 2008), http://www.thesedonaconference.org/content/miscFiles/publications_html?grp=wgs110 [hereinafter Sedona Preservation].

48. The situation has been described as "preserve or perish." R. Brownstone, *Preserve or Perish; Destroy or Drown—eDiscovery Morphs Into Electronic Information Management,* 8 N. Car. J.L. & Tech. 1 (2006).

49. Maria Perez Crist, *Preserving the Duty to Preserve: The Increasing Vulnerability of Electronic Information,* 58 S.C. L. Rev. 7, 9 (2006); *accord,* United Med. Supply Co. v. United States, 77 Fed. Cl. 257, 258 (2007).

"overpreserve," wasting scarce resources contrary to Rule 1, or risk "underpreserving" and allegations of spoliation coupled with motions seeking sanctions.

The need for guidance is clear.[50] For example, compare the varying comments regarding the duty to preserve backup tapes. "[T]he parameters of [the duty to preserve's] application to backup tapes have not yet been fully defined."[51] "[R]equesting parties consider backup tapes to be a wealth of information. Producing parties consider them to be the equivalent of a vast waste dump. Thus, not surprisingly, the courts have offered inconsistent guidance as to how they will be treated."[52] There is "generally" no duty to preserve such tapes;[53] however, if the backup tapes pertinent to key players can be identified, there may be a duty to preserve them.[54]

---

50. *See Victor Stanley II*, 269 F.R.D. at 523 (discussing need for uniform, national standard).

51. Grant J. Esposito & Thomas M. Mueller, *Backup Tapes, You Can't Live with Them and You Can't Toss Them: Strategies for Dealing with the Litigation Burdens Associated with Backup Tapes Under the Amended Federal Rules of Civil Procedure*, 13 RICH. J.L. & TECH. 13, ¶ 10 (2007), http://law.richmond.edu/jolt/v13i3/article13.pdf; *Victor Stanley II*, 269 F.R.D. at 524–25.

52. Bennett, *supra* note 13, at 133; *see generally* Withers, *Computer-Based Discovery in Federal Civil Litigation*, 1 FED. CTS. L. REV. 65, 74–75 (2006) (noting unique problems presented by backup tapes).

53. Zubulake v. UBS Warburg LLC (*Zubulake IV*), 220 F.R.D. 212, 217 (S.D.N.Y. 2003). After stating the "general" rule, the *Zubulake IV* court noted the exceptions and stated: "One can question whether the *Zubulake IV* 'exceptions' swallow the rule. For example, backup tapes are always 'accessible' to some degree, and companies may use backup tapes (at least recent ones) for nonemergency document retrieval on occasion. Moreover, it is almost always *possible* for a company to 'identify where particular employee documents are stored on backup tapes,' provided it spends enough time and money to restore and search the tapes. . . ." *See* Jeffrey S. Follett, *Hold Everything? Litigation Response in the Electronic Age, in* ELECTRONIC DISCOVERY AND RETENTION GUIDANCE FOR CORPORATE COUNSEL 2006, at 237, 249 (PLI Litig. & Admin. Practice, Course Handbook Series No. 9006, 2006), WL 747 PLI/Lit 237, 248–50.

54. *See id.* at 217–18; Pension Comm. of Univ. of Montreal Pension Plan v. Banc of Am. Sec., LLC, 685 F. Supp. 2d 456, 464 n.14, 471 (S.D.N.Y. 2010) ("preserve backup tapes when they are the sole source of relevant information or when they relate to key players, if the relevant information maintained by those players is not obtainable from readily accessible sources"); *see also* Cache La Poudre Feeds, LLC. v. Land O'Lakes, Inc., 244 F.R.D. 614, 623 n.10 (D. Colo. Mar. 2, 2007); Daniel Renwick Hodgman, Comment, *A Port in the Storm?: The Problematic and Shallow Safe Harbor for Electronic Discovery*, 10 NW. U. L. REV. 259, 271 (2007) ("Backup tapes probably fall under the litigation hold if they are accessible, not obsolete due to technological advances, and currently used to retrieve information."); Withers,

And one recent decision concluded that the "reasonableness and proportionality" standard "may prove too amorphous to provide much comfort to a party deciding what files it may delete or backup tapes it may recycle. . . . Until a more precise definition is created by rule, a party is well advised to 'retain all relevant documents (but not multiple identical copies). . . .' "[55]

Given the multiple uncertainties surrounding the duty to preserve, a potential civil litigant must guess at the scope of the prelitigation duty to preserve: "A producing party can face a Hobson's choice between the burden and cost of preservation and the risk of sanctions for failing to do so."[56] The party will not know if it made the correct choice until months later, when a court decides the issue.

While the courts and commentators may be wholly correct in their analysis, this situation is directly at odds with the philosophy behind the Federal Rules of Civil Procedure.[57] In 1938, amendments to those rules introduced the concepts of interrogatories and document requests to federal civil litigation. From this modest start, the scope of discovery expanded to encompass the virtually open-ended discovery of all facts related to the "subject matter" of the litigation. In the 1990s, studies demonstrated that the costs attendant with such a standard had become prohibitive, and the 2000 amendments to the Federal Rules scaled back the scope to discovery pertaining to the claims and defenses in the action,[58] with judges being directed to take an active role in supervising the discovery process.[59] One purpose of the 2000 amendments was to emphasize the need for active judicial intervention to ensure the proportionality of discovery through Rule 26(b)(2).[60] In December

supra note 52, at 71 ("In *Linnen v. A.H. Robins Co.*, the defendant faced sanctions in the form of costs and a spoliation inference stemming from counsel's failure to completely investigate stored computer backup tapes, while representing to the court that all relevant computer files had been produced" (footnote omitted)).

55. Orbit One Commc'ns, Inc. v. Numerex Corp., 2010 U.S. Dist. Lexis 123633, at *21 (S.D.N.Y. Oct. 26, 2010), citing Zubulake v. UBS Warburg, LLC, 220 F.R.D. 218, 212 (S.D.N.Y. 2003)(*Zubulake IV*).

56. SEDONA PRESERVATION, *supra* note 47, at n.10.

57. FED. R. CIV. P. 1 provides: "[These rules] shall be construed and administered to secure the just, speedy, and inexpensive determination of every action and proceeding."

58. The Rules confer discretion to permit "subject matter" discovery. *See* FED. R. CIV. P. 26(b)(1) ("For good cause, the court may order discovery of any matter relevant to the subject matter involved in the action.").

59. *See* FED. R. CIV. P. 26 advisory committee's note (b)(1) to the 2000 Amendments.

60. *See id.*

2006, new Federal Rules regarding ESI went into effect. There is no indication that the 2006 amendments were designed to undercut the philosophy behind the 2000 amendments.

At present, however, there can be no assurance that any court will apply the cost-benefit protections of Rule 26(b)(2)(C) and the "safe harbor" of Rule 37(e) to implementation of the prelitigation duty to preserve.[61] As one court recently commented: "[p]roportionality is particularly tricky in the context of preservation" and it "seems unlikely" that "a court would excuse the destruction of evidence merely because the monetary value of anticipated litigation was low."[62] If the common law preservation standard were to differ from the litigation-based proportionality standard, anomalous results might occur. For instance, the absence of clear proportionality guidelines could give rise to coercive demands and settlements, a risk that applies to both plaintiffs and defendants.[63]

Consider also the preserving party's choice-of-law dilemma. Faced with reasonably anticipated litigation and a duty to preserve, the preserving party's decisions may be governed by the source of the duty. If the duty arises under statute, regulation, court order, or contract, the source document may define the duty. If the duty arises under common law, the duty may be a state duty for state courts and diversity cases, or a federal one for federal-question cases. Where federal and supplemental state claims are joined in a single action,[64] there could be differing duties. And the consequence of a breach—whether spoliation is a free-standing tort or a discovery and evidentiary doctrine—may differ depending on the forum. Absent clear guidance regarding limits on the scope of the duty to preserve, a party engaged in a good faith effort to preserve

61. A leading commentator noted only that it was "unlikely" that courts would "invoke their inherent power in order to reach a different result on the same facts as would exist under Rule [37(e)]." Allman, *supra* note 22, at ¶ 45. Mr. Allman correctly suggests that "the natural tendency of most courts will be to use Rule [37(e)] as a "'guidepost' or reference point in exercising their inherent powers." *Id.* In view of the serious sanctions that may be imposed for breaching the duty to preserve, potential litigants need greater certainty.

62. Orbit One Commc'ns, Inc. v. Numerex Corp., 2010 U.S. Dist. Lexis 123633, at *21 (S.D.N.Y. Oct. 26, 2010).

63. The duty to preserve applies to plaintiffs. *See, e.g.*, Silvestri v. Gen. Motors Corp., 271 F.3d 583, 592 (4th Cir. 2001); *see also Legal Holds*, supra note 21, at 267 ("This duty [to preserve] arises . . . whether the organization is the initiator or the target of litigation.").

64. *See* 28 U.S.C. § 1367 (2006); Zubulake v. UBS Warburg LLC (*Zubulake IV*), 220 F.R.D. 212, 216 (S.D.N.Y. 2003) (discussing generally the duty to preserve).

evidence prior to litigation may prove the military maxim that any ship can be a minesweeper—once.[65]

6. Giving meaning to "proportionality"

A court's power to sanction a prelitigation failure to preserve ESI is based on the court's inherent powers, not the Federal Rules.[66] That power, although broad, is not unlimited.[67]

Some courts have squarely held that, although the Rule 37 does not directly apply to prelitigation conduct, it may be applied by analogy. For example, in *United Med. Supply Co. v. United States*, the court noted:

> Several courts have held that Rule 37 sanctions are available even where evidence is destroyed before the issuance of a discovery request, with a few going so far as to apply the rule to conduct that occurred before the lawsuit was filed, provided the party was on notice of a claim. But, the majority view—and the one most easily reconciled with the terms of the rule—is that Rule 37 is narrower in scope and does not apply before the discovery regime is triggered.[68]

Capellupo v. FMC Corp.[69] is representative of the majority view.

> Rule 37, Fed.R.Civ.P., is applicable to the "normal" disputes, delays, or difficulties occurring in civil litigation. Its sanctions are appropriate in instances of a litigant's failure to make or cooperate in discovery. Rule 37 enables a court to punish the litigant who has not responded adequately to discovery requests of an opposing party or to orders of the court compelling discovery. Rule 37 does not, by its terms, address sanctions for destruction of evidence prior to the initiation of a lawsuit or discovery requests.

65. Posting of Brian to http://www.bimmerfest.com/forums/archive/index.php/t-53510.html (Feb. 24, 2004, 06:35 EST) (quoting Anonymous).
66. *E.g.*, Roadway Express v. Piper, 447 U.S. 752, 764–67 (1980); Silvestri v. GMC, 271 F.3d 583, 591 (4th Cir. 2001); *Zubulake IV*, 220 F.R.D. at 216; *see also* D. Willoughby et al., *Sanctions*, 60 Duke L.J. at 800 (most prevalent bases for sanctions are Rule 37 and inherent power).
67. *Chambers v. NASCO, Inc.*, 501 U.S. 32, 43–46 (1991); Rimkus Consulting Group, Inc. v. Cammarata, 688 F. Supp. 2d 598, 615 (S.D. Tex. 2010).
68. 77 Fed. Cl. 257, 268 (2007) (footnote omitted).
69. 126 F.R.D. 545, 551 n.14 (D. Minn. 1989).

However, courts have looked to Rule 37 to guide the exercise of their inherent powers. Thus, even though Rule 37 is not directly applicable to prelitigation conduct, when sanctions are imposed, Rule 37 may guide the court's discretion:

> Prior to the selection of sanction, if any, the Court notes the source of its authority. Defendant challenges the Court's power to impose sanctions pursuant to Fed.R.Civ.P. 37. EEOC agrees that Rule 37 does not directly apply, but insists that the rule is a guide for the exercise of the Court's inherent authority to deal with discovery abuses. The Court agrees with EEOC's analysis. Conduct of the kind which ordinarily would be sanctionable under Rule 37, but falls outside the express terms of the rule, can be sanctioned by proper exercise of this Court's inherent powers. Although Rule 37 does not apply by its terms, the Court looks to that rule as a guide to determine the proper level of response to defendant's offense. This reliance on the principles of Rule 37 is particularly appropriate in the light of the conduct at issue. Defendant destroyed records for which it was on notice that it had a legal duty to preserve, and that duty is imposed, in part, to ensure that those records are available for litigation of a discrimination charge. Rule 37 deals with similar conduct when the legal duty to preserve evidence is imposed in the course of a lawsuit. The present case logically extends Rule 37 principles to the situation in which the legal duty to preserve evidence arises by force of administrative regulation prior to the commencement of a lawsuit. Two of the policies underlying Rule 37—the elimination of profit from failure to comply with the legal duty to preserve evidence and the general deterrent effect that sanctions for an offense will have on the instant case and on other litigation—particularly justify the Court's decision to extend Rule 37 principles to the present case. Encouraging compliance with the administratively imposed duty to preserve evidence in pending discrimination complaints shares these common goals with Rule 37 and therefore the Court should exercise its inherent powers to reach the case in which evidence is destroyed prior to trial in violation of 29 C.F.R. § 1602.14.[70]

70. E.E.O.C. v. Jacksonville Shipyards, Inc., 690 F. Supp. 995, 997–98 (M.D. Fla. 1988) (citations omitted). In short, the result should be identical regardless of

In short, courts have used their inherent powers to reach pre-litigation conduct and have informed their use of those powers by looking to the Federal Rules of Civil Procedure for guidance.

There is no reason why courts could not do the same with the cost-benefit provisions of Rule 26(b)(2)(C) and the "safe harbor" of Rule 37(e). The proportionality rules can and should be applied by analogy to provide guidance to potential litigants operating in the uncertain time before litigation has commenced. Doing so would be consistent with the spirit and terms of the proportionality and cost-benefit rules and provide additional guidance in a costly, important, and ill-defined process. Said differently, potential litigants—and the civil justice system—will benefit if they receive the same protections and guidance that will apply should they become actual litigants.

How would the application of Rules 26(b)(2)(C) and 37(e) factors assist a potential litigant? The potential litigant would have a readily available source of guidance, the body of case law interpreting Rule 26(b)(2)(C) and its predecessor. Based on that rule, the potential litigant might decide that it would be reasonable to spend a specified number of hours[71] and funds performing preservation tasks, and that additional efforts would not be reasonable based on the information then available about the potential nature and scope of the litigation.[72]

Application of the rules' cost-benefit principles will permit parties to articulate reasoned bases for decisions to limit the scope of their preservation obligations or, alternatively, to challenge an opposing party's unreasonably limited efforts to preserve ESI. Faced with a spoliation motion,[73] for example, counsel may persuasively argue that the common law duty to preserve ESI should not be interpreted to mandate that a potential litigant spend $25,000 preserving ESI to defend against a potential $5,000 claim.[74] Simi-

---

whether conduct occurred before or during litigation.

71. Marens v. Carrabba's Italian Grill, Inc., 196 F.R.D. 35 (D. Md. 2000) (litigant required to expend up to 40 hours to search for documents).

72. For additional, more detailed examples, see P. Grimm, et al., "Proportionality in the Post-Hoc Analysis," 37 U.Balt.L.Rev. at 407-11.

73. The first element of a spoliation claim is that the allegedly spoliating party breached its duty to preserve information. Boyd v. Travelers Ins. Co., 652 N.E.2d 267, 270 (Ill. 1995). If, under Rule 26(b)(2)(C)'s application by analogy, there was no duty to preserve, there has not been spoliation.

74. "At some point the adversary system needs to say "enough is enough' and recognize that the costs of seeking *every* relevant piece of discovery is not

larly, faced with a $15 million claim, a potential party may find it difficult to assert that it was not required to expend $100,000 to preserve ESI.

It is recognized that the cost-benefit limits on discovery may be amorphous and difficult to apply to prelitigation preservation decisions. Application of those concepts, however, will provide the most detailed standard available to guide discretion, and may provide preserving parties with a good faith defense to spoliation claims, or alternatively, may strip them of an unreasonable defense. Application of the rules' principles will permit parties to articulate reasoned bases for decisions to limit the scope of their preservation obligations or, alternatively, to challenge unreasonably limited efforts to preserve ESI. Faced with a spoliation motion, if it is correct to state that "the scope of the duty to preserve evidence is not boundless,"[75] Rule 26(b)(2)(C) should assist in defining the boundary.

7. Conclusion

The uncertain scope of preservation obligations before litigation is filed, coupled with the risk of serious sanctions when it is later determined that relevant and unique ESI was not preserved, encourages overbroad prelitigation preservation efforts, resulting in the sometimes disproportionate expenditure of vast sums. Given that a party is provided far more detail concerning the range of potentially discoverable information after litigation is commenced, a party's prelitigation duty to preserve should be as clear and well defined as its duties after a lawsuit is commenced. Application by analogy of Rules 26(b)(2)(C) and 37(e) to the prelitigation duty to preserve provides an improved mechanism for defining the limits of the duty to preserve and providing litigants with practical guidelines in a perilous area where a misstep could have significant ramifications.

---

reasonable." Esposito & Mueller, *supra* note 51, at ¶ 28 n.88 (citing Cognex Corp. v. Electro Scientific Indus. Inc., No. Civ.A. 01 CV10287RCL, 2002 WL 32309413, at *5 (D. Mass. July 2, 2002)).

75. RICE, *supra* note 40, at 118 (citation omitted). The writer made this comment in the context of assessing the duration of the duty to preserve.

CHAPTER 10

THE SECONDARY EVIDENCE RULE IN AVOIDANCE OF SPOLIATION SANCTIONS

BY MICHAEL D. BERMAN
AND RACHEL A. SHAPIRO

As discussed in chapter 8, a breach of the duty to preserve ESI can result in judicial sanctions. May the breaching party avoid such sanctions in whole or part through an application of the "secondary evidence rule" in FRE 1004? According to the authors of this chapter, under some circumstances the answer may be yes.

1. Introduction

This chapter discusses whether, and if so, when, spoliation sanctions would be mitigated or precluded because secondary evidence under Federal Rule of Evidence 1004(3) sufficiently obviates prejudice caused by the opponent's destruction of electronically stored information (ESI). In short, if FRE 1004(3) permits an innocent, nonspoliating party to offer satisfactory secondary evidence of the contents of the spoliated ESI, has the innocent party been prejudiced? While in most instances, the innocent party will not be made whole through secondary evidence, there are situations where such evidence may or should be sufficient. If secondary evidence can completely "fill the gap" caused by the destruction of the primary evidence, then sanctions, or at least the most severe sanctions, may be inappropriate.

2. Definitions of primary and secondary evidence

At least in theory,[1] the Federal Rules of Evidence incorporate the "original writing rule."[2] FRE 1004 is the "primary rule that identifies when secondary evidence is admissible" and it "identifies four circumstances in which secondary evidence may be introduced instead of an original."[3] Secondary evidence "is any proof of the contents of a writing, recording or photograph other than an original or duplicate."[4] Examples of secondary evidence include "testimony from the author of the writing, or someone who read it, earlier drafts, copies, or an outline used to prepare the final."[5] Specifically, the evidence rule provides:

> **Rule 1004. Admissibility of Other Evidence of Contents**
> The original is not required, and other evidence of the contents of a writing, recording, or photograph is admissible if—
> (1) Originals lost or destroyed. All originals are lost or have been destroyed, unless the proponent lost or destroyed them in bad faith; or
> (2) Original not obtainable. No original can be obtained by any available judicial process or procedure; or
> (3) Original in possession of opponent. *At a time when an original was under the control of the party against whom offered, that party was put on notice, by the pleadings or*

1. *See* Jonathan L. Moore, *Time for an Upgrade: Amending the Federal Rules of Evidence to Address the Challenges of Electronically Stored Information in Civil Litigation*, 50 JURIMETRICS J. 147, 189 (2010) ("In modern society, technological changes have rendered the best evidence rule meaningless.").
2. *See* Lorraine v. Markel Am. Ins. Co., 241 F.R.D. 534, 576–77 (D. Md. 2007) (explaining the structure of the original writing rule, and the role of FED. R. EVID. 1004).
3. *Id.* at 579.
4. *Id.* at 576–77.
5. *Id.* Secondary methods may, in addition to testimony, include copies that do not qualify as duplicates but which were made by one with personal knowledge (such as a transcript), secondhand copies, or summaries. KENNETH S. BROUN, MCCORMICK ON EVIDENCE § 238, at 109 (6th ed. 2006).

otherwise, that the contents would be a subject of proof at the hearing, and that party does not produce the original at the hearing; or

(4) Collateral matters. The writing, recording, or photograph is not closely related to a controlling issue. [Emphasis added.]

3. Use of secondary evidence under FRE 1004(1)

FRE 1004(1) has been used to oppose sanctions where secondary evidence will mitigate prejudice caused by nonpreservation of original documents.[6] Secondary evidence of destroyed documents may eliminate, or at least reduce, the prejudice caused by their destruction.[7] And parol evidence has been used to supply information from missing documents.[8]

6. *In re* Terrorist Bombings of U.S. Embassies in E. Afr. v. Odeh, 552 F.3d 93, 147 (2d Cir. 2008) ("The only question before the District Court here was how to mitigate any arguable prejudice to El Hage. The District Court adequately addressed this question by 'permit[ing] . . . El-Hage to offer in evidence transcripts of those [communications] which, because of the destruction of the originals, will constitute the best evidence.' ") (citation omitted). Notably, however, admission of secondary evidence under FRE 1004(1) does not necessarily relieve the spoliating party of all sanctions. In *Vagenos v. LDG Financial Services, LLC,* 2009 WL 5219021 (E.D.N.Y. Dec. 31, 2009), plaintiff sued under the Fair Debt Collections Practices Act, based on telephone communications from the defendant collection agency. Plaintiff, however, deleted a prerecorded message that was left for him on his cell phone answering machine, after making a duplicate. Plaintiff sought to offer the duplicate into evidence. The court analyzed the issue under FRE 1004(1), determining that the deletion was not done in bad faith under that rule. It permitted introduction of the duplicate; however, it also sanctioned plaintiff by holding that "an appropriate sanction for the spoliation of the evidence is an adverse inference instruction." In other words, the plaintiff avoided a "death knell" order excluding the recording at the expense of an adverse inference instruction. *Id.* at *6. *See also* Vodusek v. Bayliner Marine Corp., 71 F.3d 148, 155 (4th Cir. 1995) ("Even if a court determines not to exclude secondary evidence, it may still permit the jury to draw unfavorable inferences against the party responsible for the loss or destruction of the original evidence.").

7. Bell *ex. rel.* Albert R. Bell Living Trust v. Rotwein, 535 F. Supp. 2d 137, 145 (D.D.C. 2008).

8. Diplomat Homes, Inc. v. Comm. Standard Ins. Co., 394 F. Supp. 558, 566 (W.D. Mo. 1975) (explaining that FRE 1004(1) authorizes parol evidence of the contents of document). In *United States v. Marcantoni,* 590 F.2d 1324 (5th Cir.), *cert. denied,* 441 U.S. 937 (1979), a police officer investigating a bank robbery viewed, but did not seize, "bait money" in defendants' possession. When the officer returned with a warrant, the bills were gone. The officer testified to the serial numbers on the bills, and the Fifth Circuit held that the secondary evidence was permissible

In its most common application, FRE 1004(1) permits a party that has lost or destroyed original documents, without bad faith, to offer secondary evidence to prove the contents of those documents. The Advisory Committee Notes state that the rule is "a rule of preference" and "if failure to produce the original is satisfactorily explained, secondary evidence is admissible." In the ESI context, where ESI was destroyed by the routine, good faith operation of an information system, the "safe harbor" of Federal Rule of Civil Procedure 37(e) would preclude sanctioning the party responsible for the destruction and FRE 1004(1) would permit the destroying party to prove its contents through secondary evidence. For example, the destroying party (the "proponent") might be permitted to orally describe the contents of the material it destroyed or lay a foundation for introduction of other secondary evidence. FRE 1004(1) "may be particularly suited for electronic evidence,"[9] but is not the focus of this chapter.[10]

4. Use of secondary evidence to "fill the gap" under FRE 1004(3)

This chapter focuses instead on FRE 1004(3). FRE 1004(3) may assist and protect an innocent party that is disadvantaged by the *opposing* litigant's failure to preserve relevant evidence,[11] by permitting the introduction of secondary evidence, if "[a]t a time when

under FRE 1004(1) and FRE 1004(3). *Id.* at 1329–30. With respect to FRE 1004(3), the court stated that "a legitimate argument can be made on this record that the [defendants] were 'put on notice' that the serial numbers of the two $10 bills 'would be a subject of proof' at the trial, and that, having not produced them at trial, [the defendants] could not object to the use of the [officer's] notes." *Id.* at 1330.

9. Lorraine v. Markel Am. Ins. Co., 241 F.R.D. 534, 579 (D. Md. 2007).

10. FRE 1004(2) permits either party to prove the contents of an unavailable document. Thus, for example, the rule permits oral description, or other secondary evidence, of the contents of material that still exists, but is beyond the subpoena power and "any" other available process or procedure of the trial court. That provision is also beyond the scope of this chapter. *See generally* Broun, *supra* note 5 § 237, at 105–06.

11. The rule is designed to provide an option to the party that is *not* in possession of the writing. For example, the Advisory Committee Note states: "A party who has an original in his control has no need for the protection of the rule if put on notice that proof of contents can be made. He can ward off secondary evidence by offering the original." Fed. R. Evid. 1004 advisory committee's note. A stipulation may, in some circumstances, serve the same purpose. In *Reynolds v. Commissioner of Internal Revenue*, 79 T.C.M. (CCH) 1376 (2000), the Tax Court determined that the parties' stipulation that the 1993 and 1994 tax returns

an original was under the control of the" opponent, "that party was put on notice, by the pleadings or otherwise, that the contents would be a subject of proof at the hearing, and that party does not produce the original at the hearing." Unlike subsection (1), which permits an innocent proponent to describe the contents of writings *it* failed to preserve, subsection (3) permits an innocent *opponent* to describe the contents of writings that the *other* litigant failed to provide.

The impact, if any, of FRE 1004(3) on spoliation sanctions has not been fully explored. In *Bell v. Rotwein*,[12] a trustee asserted that the opposing litigant had destroyed certain documents. The spoliation claim was "rooted in plaintiff's allegation that defendant took possession of and destroyed the original assignment document."[13] However, the court rejected the spoliation claim "because plaintiff has a photocopy of the document that may be admissible in the litigation," citing FRE 1004, without identifying the subsection of the rule that it applied.[14] The court reasoned that spoliation requires a showing that the loss or destruction significantly prejudiced the plaintiff trustee by impairing his ability to prove his claim and, "[b]ecause plaintiff has a photocopy, he cannot make this showing."[15] In short, the application of FRE 1004 permitted the potentially prejudiced litigant to "fill the gap" with secondary evidence, thus ameliorating any prejudice occasioned by the destruction.

Similarly, FRE 1004 was used to "fill the gap" caused by failure to preserve information in an unreported employment discrimination case. There, one of the plaintiffs testified in deposition that she had seen "an email message from a customer in which the customer complained that there were too many African-American employees at [the] Defendant's" store.[16] She asserted that the email was evidence of racial animus by the employer. The plaintiff did not have a copy of the email,[17] and, although requested,

were authentic obviated the taxpayer's objection that the commissioner failed to produce the tax returns.

12. 535 F. Supp. 2d at 137.

13. *Id.* at 145.

14. *Id.*

15. *Id.*

16. King v. Kirkland's Stores, Inc., No. 2:04-cv-1055-MEF, 2006 WL 2239203 (M.D. Ala. Aug. 4, 2006), *related opinion*, No. 2:04-cv-1055-MEF, 2006 WL 2239208 (M.D. Ala. Aug. 4, 2006).

17. *Id.* at *4.

the defendant did not produce it in discovery.[18] Defense counsel represented to the court that the "Defendant has no record that the alleged email ever existed or was sent" to it or its employees.[19] The court held, however, that the plaintiff's testimony was admissible, citing FRE 1004 (1)–(3). "From the record before this court, it would seem that these provisions allow King's testimony about the contents of the email."[20] Again, secondary evidence was used to "fill the gap" under FRE 1004.

In *Wine Corners, Inc. v. Castel Wines International, Ltd.*,[21] a plaintiff was unable to produce a written memorandum satisfying the statute of frauds. Instead, in opposing a motion for summary judgment, it was permitted to "fill the gap" and offer an affidavit "to the effect that certain telex communications in the possession of [its opponent] do in fact contain the elusive twenty-five year term."[22] The court relied on FRE 1004(3).

Other decisions have suggested a similar result without reliance on FRE 1004. For example, in *Rimkus Consulting Group, Inc. v. Cammarata*,[23] the court noted that "in many cases—including the present case—there are sources from which at least some of the allegedly spoliated evidence can be obtained."[24] And, the court continued, "in many cases—including the present case—the party seeking discovery can also obtain extrinsic evidence of the content of at least some of the deleted information from other documents, deposition testimony, or circumstantial evidence."[25] The court noted that because Rimkus was able to obtain "other evidence of the contents of deleted lost records, Rimkus has extensive evidence that it can present."[26] In short: "The loss of evidence prejudiced Rimkus, but not irreparably."[27]

18. *Id.* at *5.
19. *Id.* at *5 n.3.
20. *Id.*
21. 1984 U.S. Dist. Lexis 15547 (N.D.N.Y. 1984).
22. *Id.* at *6, 8–9.
23. 688 F. Supp. 2d 598, 616 (S.D. Tex. 2010).
24. *Id.* at 616.
25. *Id.*
26. *Id.* at 643.
27. Managed Care Solutions v. Essent Healthcare, Inc., 736 F.Supp.2d 1319 (S.D. Fla. 2010), suggested a similar result without reliance on FRE 1004. There, the court denied a plaintiff 's motion for sanctions, reasoning in part that "the allegedly spoliated evidence [was] not crucial to the plaintiff's claims because the plaintiff would still be able to prove its case through additional already obtained

Parallel points were made in *Pension Committee of the University of Montreal Pension Plan v. Banc of America*,[28] where the court discussed "what can be done when documents are no longer available," noting: "At best, their content can be inferred from existing documents or recalled during depositions."[29] In *Pension Committee*, as to certain information, the nonspoliating party "suffered no prejudice because all [of the missing documents] were eventually obtained from other sources."[30]

The application, if any, of FRE 1004(3) in the context of ESI sanctions has not yet been determined. Can it be used in some circumstances to "fill the gap" with secondary evidence where an opponent breaches the duty to preserve unique and relevant ESI? If the court permits secondary evidence to "fill the gap" under FRE 1004(3), should the court relieve the opponent of some or all sanctions under the theory that the party moving for sanctions is no longer prejudiced by the breach?

5. A hypothetical example of "filling the gap" under FRE 1004(3)

Consider this hypothetical: XYZ Corp. seeks sanctions against ABC Corp., asserting that ABC destroyed ESI after a duty to preserve had arisen; the lost ESI was unique and relevant; and XYZ is unable to obtain a copy of the destroyed ESI. XYZ contends that, on June 2, 2009, it orally ordered green widgets from ABC; however, ABC shipped olive-drab widgets. XYZ asserts a claim for damages, and ABC responds that its olive-drab product conformed to the order.[31] On January 1, 2010, XYZ sends a preservation letter to ABC demanding that ABC preserve all email related to the ABC–XYZ transaction from June 1, 2009, through December 31, 2009. ABC is in possession of that email when it receives the January 1, 2010, letter; and the email is relevant and unique; however, ABC

---

evidence," consisting of "deposition testimony and documents received from third parties." *Id.* at 1327.

28. Pension Comm. of Univ. of Montreal Pension Plan v. Banc of Am. Sec., LLC, 685 F. Supp. 2d 456 (S.D.N.Y. 2010).

29. *Id.* at 466.

30. *Id.* at 478.

31. Commercial disputes often turn on the meaning of a word. *See, e.g.*, Frigaliment Importing Co. v. B.N.S. Int'l Sales, 190 F. Supp. 116, 117–18 (S.D.N.Y. 1960) (deeming the word "chicken" alone ambiguous, and holding for the seller on the grounds that the buyer, as plaintiff, failed to meet its burden of proving which of the two plausible meanings the parties intended).

fails to preserve it, and it is overwritten or otherwise destroyed after receipt of the preservation letter.

In this situation, under FRE 1004(3), ABC was "put on notice." That notice was "by the pleadings or otherwise." And ABC was, at least arguably,[32] notified that the "contents would be a subject of proof at the hearing."

The next event in our hypothetical is that XYZ propounds a proper request for production of documents, seeking all email between XYZ and ABC from June 1, 2009. The requested email is relevant to the claims or defenses, and the request is proportional to the needs of the case. ABC candidly and forthrightly admits to destruction of the ESI after receipt of XYZ's preservation letter.[33]

XYZ now moves for sanctions, alleging[34] that ABC had a duty to preserve the relevant email; ABC breached the duty; ABC did

---

32. Because the scope of the duty to preserve is often broader than the duty to produce and admissibility at trial, it may be argued that a preservation request does not constitute notice that the contents will be subject of proof at a hearing and that FRE 1004(3) is not triggered by a preservation request. See chapters 8 and 9.

The same question could also arise after a complaint is filed and a request for production of documents is served. Again, because the scope of discovery is not coextensive with the admissibility at trial, an open issue is whether the complaint and document request suffice to provide notice that the contents of the ESI will be the subject of proof at the hearing.

The Advisory Committee Note states: "The notice procedure here provided is not to be confused with orders to produce or other discovery procedures, as the purpose of the procedure under this rule is to afford the opposite party an opportunity to produce the original, not to compel him to do so." If the notice provision in FRE 1004(3) is construed so as to exclude preservation and discovery demands, the rule may be inapposite.

For purposes of the hypothetical in this chapter, assume that the preservation letter and any subsequent complaint were specific enough in their reference to ABC's internal email to provide ABC with actual notice that the contents of the ESI will be the subject of proof at the hearing. Assume, for example, that XYZ wrote: "Based on statements of ABC's sales personnel, made to XYZ on a date certain, ABC is in possession of a confirming email that demonstrates that XYZ orally ordered green widgets." Although undecided, it would appear that such a statement would be sufficient notice under FRE 1004(3).

33. Such an admission is not a stretch of the imagination, as set forth in appendix B.

34. For a discussion of procedure under FRE 104 and 1004, *see* Lorraine v. Markel Am. Ins. Co., 241 F.R.D. 534, 582 (D. Md. 2007) (stating that the trial judge determines "whether the original is in the possession, custody or control of the opposing party under Rule 1004(3)"). Under FRE 1008, "when an issue is raised" as to "whether the asserted writing ever existed . . . the issue is for the trier of fact to determine."

so with the requisite culpable state of mind in the jurisdiction; and XYZ was prejudiced by the loss or destruction. XYZ asserts in its motion that ABC's email would contain a description of the oral order specifying XYZ's desire for "green" widgets.

It would appear that ABC, having admittedly failed to preserve relevant and unique ESI after the duty to preserve arose, is in jeopardy of at least some sanction. Its failure to preserve relevant information has prejudiced XYZ, which can no longer obtain the critical email that contains the only written description of the terms of the transaction.

If, however, FRE 1004(3) is applicable, it may in some circumstances diminish or eliminate that prejudice. The rule might permit XYZ to prove the contents of the material that ABC failed to preserve using secondary evidence. If XYZ is permitted to prove the actual contents of the ESI lost or destroyed by ABC, then XYZ is less prejudiced, or perhaps not prejudiced at all,[35] and prejudice is generally a prerequisite to the imposition of sanctions.[36]

The operation of this scenario requires some additional facts. Let's say that XYZ orally purchased "green" widgets from ABC. At that time, ABC's sales force told XYZ that ABC's standard operating procedure was that the sales personnel would send an email containing the terms of the order to ABC's manufacturing and accounting personnel, and that the factory would then confirm the details with ABC's chief operating officer via a separate email. XYZ placed the order on June 2, 2009. On June 10, 2009, XYZ called ABC's sales representative to confirm that the representative had followed standard procedure. ABC confirmed that the email reciting the terms of the oral order had been sent to the manufacturing and accounting divisions of ABC. The confirmation was not sent to XYZ. Thus, ABC's internal email is both *unique* and relevant. XYZ is generally aware of its content; however, XYZ does not have a copy.

Has XYZ actually been prejudiced by ABC's failure to preserve the email, when (1) XYZ arguably knows the contents of the email; and (2) FRE 1004(3) permits XYZ to prove the contents through secondary evidence (i.e., through testimony from XYZ and ABC's

35. *Cf.* Hoffman v. Balt. Police Dep't, No. WMN-04-3072, 2009 WL 167144, at *10 (D. Md. Jan. 21, 2009) (permitting nonspoliating party to argue that spoliating party destroyed handwritten notes because contents of notes were harmful, but barring spoliating party from describing contents).

36. See chapter 8 for a discussion of sanctions.

sales personnel)? In other words, if FRE 1004(3) allows XYZ to establish the contents of the email through testimony, may ABC avoid sanctions by asserting that XYZ has not been prejudiced?

Imagine that, in opposition to the sanctions request, ABC asserts that XYZ can testify that it orally ordered green widgets; that ABC's course of conduct was to send a confirming email to its internal divisions; and that both ABC and XYZ will orally confirm the contents of that email through secondary evidence (i.e., oral testimony that an email reciting the terms of the oral order had been sent to the two internal divisions). On these grounds, ABC asserts that XYZ is not prejudiced by ABC's breach of the duty to preserve and that sanctions should not be imposed on ABC.[37]

In some instances, ABC's argument should carry the day. If ABC admits that the internal email recited that XYZ's order was for "green" widgets, it would appear that there is no dispute over the facts of the confirmation and the issue is a purely legal question of whether or not olive-drab widgets conform. If, however, ABC does not admit that the confirmation used the word "green," then FRE 1004(3) would not entirely eliminate the prejudice created by ABC's breach of the duty to preserve.

6. Conclusion

FRE 1004(3) will not be applicable in all, and perhaps in most, spoliation situations. There are impediments to its application as a defense to a motion for sanctions. Chief among them are that (1) the spoliated information is not in existence at the time that the secondary evidence is offered and (2) it may be difficult to demonstrate that "[a]t a time when an original was under the control of the party" that "party was put on notice" that the evidence would be a subject of proof at the hearing. A court may also be skeptical of the spoliator's attempt to avoid sanctions by asserting that the innocent and injured opponent can "fill the gap" by merely describing the contents of the missing document to the finder of

37. Under FRE 1007, "[c]ontents of writings, recordings, or photographs may be proved by the testimony of deposition of the party against whom offered or by that party's written admission, without accounting for the nonproduction of the original." FRE 1007 "does not call for excluding evidence of an oral admission when nonproduction of the original has been accounted for and secondary evidence has become admissible." *Lorraine*, 241 F.R.D. at 581 n.57 (quoting Fed. R. Evid. 1007 advisory committee's note). For a more complete discussion of FRE 1007, *see Lorraine*, 241 F.R.D. at 581–82.

fact. For example, the secondary evidence may be significantly less reliable or probative than the missing original.[38] And, of course, in many, if not most, situations, the nonspoliating party may not know what was contained in the destroyed ESI or, as noted above, there may be a dispute over the secondary evidence.

Nevertheless, the imposition of sanctions, and especially outcome-determinative sanctions, can be a drastic measure.[39] Courts and litigants are well served by having many tools in their tool kit, and FRE 1004(3) may be worthy of consideration in

38. For instance, in *Peschel v. City of Missoula,* the court found prejudice to a plaintiff's case against city police for unlawful arrest and excessive force where the police recklessly lost a video of the arrest. 664 F. Supp. 2d 1137 (D. Mont. 2010). The loss resulted from "glitches in [the department's] newly installed digital video system" and the department's failure "to have any type of back-up system in place to ensure the preservation of the video recordings." *Id.* at 1146. The court found that spoliation sanctions were warranted because the city had a duty to preserve the video, but recklessly lost it. *Id.* at 1143–44, 1147. The city argued that the plaintiff was not prejudiced by the loss because eyewitnesses to the arrest could testify as to what happened at the scene. *Id.* at 1144. The court disagreed, reasoning that "the obvious inherent value of the video recording is that it would have allowed the jury . . . to see the actual events unfold and make its own collective assessment as to whether the force used . . . was or was not reasonable under the circumstances. The jury would not be forced to rely on the conclusions drawn by the various witnesses. . . ." *Id.* at 1145. The court thus found that loss of the video "hindered the most accurate determination of [the] case upon its merits and weigh[ed] in favor of the selected sanction." *Id.* at 1147.

39. Courts should consider imposing *less severe* sanctions where secondary evidence at least decreases the degree of prejudice caused by loss of the original. Spoliation sanctions can range from negative inferences against the spoliating party, to monetary or criminal sanctions, Victor Stanley, Inc. v. Creative Pipe, Inc., 269 F.R.D. 497 (D. Md. 2010), *aff'd in part and modified in part,* No. MJG-06-2662 (D. Md. Nov. 1, 2010), to default judgments and dismissal (in extreme cases). PAUL R. RICE, ELECTRONIC EVIDENCE: LAW AND PRACTICE 159–60 (ABA 2008). Ultimately, the court should fashion a sanction that, among other things, "sufficiently cures any prejudice to an affected party by restoring that party to the position it would have been in but for the spoliation . . . [and] sufficiently restores the accuracy of the fact-finding process." *Peschel,* 664 F. Supp. 2d, at 1143. In *Peschel,* the court was "not convinced that an outright default judgment against the City . . . [would be] appropriate." *Id.* at 1145. Instead, the court "designat[ed], for purposes of the case, that the arresting officers used unreasonable force to effect the arrest of [the defendant]." *Id.* The court rejected the City's request that a lesser sanction (specifically, an adverse inference) be imposed, reasoning that lesser sanctions would not sufficiently "cure the prejudice to [the plaintiff] resulting from the loss of the best evidence of what occurred during his arrest." *Id.* at 1148. *Peschel* shows that courts may consider the quality of secondary evidence in determining the severity of sanction to impose.

appropriate circumstances. If a nonspoliating litigant is able, and permitted, to present undisputed testimony (or other secondary evidence) describing material that should have been, but was not, preserved, in some circumstances that proof may render the imposition of some or all sanctions inapposite.

CHAPTER 11

WHEN DOES A LITIGATION HOLD END?*

BY MICHAEL D. BERMAN

Litigation holds regarding electronically stored information are not intended to be immortal—but when should the duty to preserve finally end? The answer is not always clear. This chapter discusses applicable standards for analysis and applies them to a series of hypotheticals.

Quite understandably, much has been written about when the duty to preserve is triggered and a litigation hold must be initiated. "The duty to preserve attaches at the time that litigation is reasonably anticipated. Although this commonly occurs at the time a complaint is filed, it can also arise earlier, for instance where relevant individuals anticipate becoming parties in imminent litigation."[1]

Decisions such as *Zubulake v. UBS Warburg LLC* (*Zubulake IV*)[2] brought the issue to the forefront, especially in connection with electronically stored information (ESI). The fragility, persistence, and volume of ESI increased the importance of early recognition

---

1. Green v. McClendon, 2009 WL 2496275 (S.D.N.Y. 2009) (citations omitted).
2. 220 F.R.D. 212, 216 (S.D.N.Y.2003).

of the duty to preserve, and proper and prompt imposition of a litigation hold that is proportional to the needs of dispute.

There is, of course, nothing new about the basic concept of the duty to preserve.[3]

When the terminus is clear. Much less attention has been paid to the mirror-image issue of when the duty to preserve ends and the litigation hold may be lifted. In some circumstances, that termination date may be clear. Issuance of a final mandate, with expiration of the date for further appellate review, would generally be the final date for preservation that commenced because litigation was reasonably anticipated.

A plaintiff, whose duty to preserve was triggered because he or she anticipated filing suit, should no longer retain that duty when a firm decision not to file suit is made, absent other circumstances triggering the duty.

A defendant, whose duty was triggered because litigation was threatened, should no longer undergo the burden of that duty when all applicable statutes of litigation and repose have run, without the commencement of litigation.

Similarly, settlement agreements may expressly provide for termination of the duty to preserve and all litigation holds.[4]

1. Some hypotheticals

As the following examples illustrate, however, there are many situations that are not as clear, or where an earlier termination of the duty should be recognized:

Business contracts. Assume that XYZ Corp. receives a letter from ABC Corp., threatening suit for breach of a contract allegedly under seal, in a jurisdiction with a six-year statute of limitations for contract actions and a 12-year statute for documents under seal. The letter unequivocally makes litigation over the assertedly sealed

3. *E.g.*, Bd. of Justices v. Fennimore, 1 N.J.L., 1794 WL 507 (N.J. 1794) ("The excuse is futile; unless the book is produced, every presumption must be made against the defendant.").

4. *See generally* S. Olson, *The Fine Art of Safely Lifting Litigation Holds*, LJN's PROD. LIAB. & LAW & STRATEGY, Apr. 2009; I. MAHONY, CORPORATE COMPLIANCE ANSWER BOOK 232 (PLI 2009); A. Anderson, *Issuing and Managing Litigation-Hold Notices*, 64 BENCH & BAR MINN. 20 (2007); S. GIBSON, LITIGATION HOLDS: TURNING ON—AND OFF—THE SWITCH TO AVOID SANCTIONS AND COSTLY E-DISCOVERY BLUNDERS 151, 160–61 (PLI 2007).

contract reasonably anticipated. Assume further that no lawsuit is filed for seven years, and there are no further communications or transactions between ABC and XYZ.

Must XYZ continue to preserve ESI and documents related to the contract for the full 12 years? Does litigation remain reasonably anticipated, because it is legally possible?

Domestic relations. Alternatively, assume that John tells his wife, Mary, that he intends to sue for divorce based on adultery. Because litigation is reasonably anticipated, that statement triggers the duty to preserve.

Assume the couple separates for three months, reconciles, and resumes the marriage in a state where that resumption is a defense to adultery under the applicable substantive law. Assume further that the couple lives together for several years and then separates and commences divorce proceedings.

Did the duty to preserve, triggered by the earlier threat of a divorce proceeding, continue in effect after resumption of the marriage? If, after resumption of marital relations, John destroys all of the preserved information, can Mary assert spoliation years later in the divorce proceeding?

Third-party production. Imagine that Company DEF is served with a subpoena for ESI under Federal Rule of Civil Procedure 45. It produces the requested information. Is it under an obligation to preserve that information through trial and appeal of litigation to which it is not a party?

Multiple claims. Finally, assume that GHI Corp. receives notice of intent to sue from A, institutes a proper preservation regime and litigation hold, and, a week before it settles with A and obtains a general release of all obligations (expressly including the duty to preserve information), the corporation receives a claim letter from B, asserting related claims. Does the settlement with A release the duty to preserve imposed as a result of A's claim, notwithstanding the related claims of B?

Why is this important? First, if preserved data is prematurely destroyed, and then litigation commences, a strong argument may be presented that intentional destruction occurred after litigation was anticipated, and therefore the destruction was presumptively prejudicial and sanctionable.

Second, the more data that is available, the more data there is that must be potentially preserved, processed, searched, and produced, in connection with other claims or issues. And because information that has been preserved in anticipation of litigation must be securely stored and a litigation hold must be periodically monitored, unnecessary preservation imposes substantial costs.

Governmental wrinkle. Additionally, the question of when a litigation hold terminates may be particularly acute in the government context, or where regulations or statutes prohibit retention beyond a certain date. A public agency might have conflicting duties to preserve information pursuant to a litigation hold, and to delete, for example, expunged data, or confidential financial disclosure reports after a date specified by law. In short, an improperly lengthy litigation hold might conflict with citizens' rights that government not maintain information longer than authorized by law.

2. In search of a standard

In light of these factors, there must be a way to define a time that a litigation hold can be safely brought to an end. In *Cache La Poudre Foods Inc. v. Land O'Lakes Inc.*,[5] the court wrote that a potential dispute did "not crystalize into litigation for nearly two years." This, combined with other factors, was too long:

> Any other conclusion would confront a putative litigant with an intractable dilemma: either preserve voluminous records for a indefinite period at potentially great expense, or continue routine document management practices and risk a spoliation claim at some point in the future.[6]

Guidance from Sedona. The Sedona Conference has provided guidelines explaining when a hold may be terminated.[7]

5. 244 F.R.D. 614, 623 (D. Col. 2007).

6. *Id.* at 623.

7. *See* THE SEDONA GUIDELINES: BEST PRACTICE GUIDELINES AND COMMENTARY FOR MANAGING INFORMATION & RECORDS IN THE ELECTRONIC AGE (Nov. 2007) [hereinafter SEDONA BEST PRACTICES]; THE SEDONA CONFERENCE COMMENTARY ON LEGAL HOLDS: THE TRIGGER & THE PROCESS (Aug. 2007 Public Comment Version) [hereinafter SEDONA LITIGATION HOLD]; THE SEDONA CONFERENCE COMMENTARY ON NON-PARTY PRODUCTION AND RULE 45 SUBPOENAS (Apr. 2008) [hereinafter SEDONA NON-PARTY PRODUCTION].

The Sedona Best Practices suggest: "When the circumstances that gave rise to the hold cease to exist, the organization should determine whether the hold can be lifted in whole or in part, in order to alleviate further costs of preservation."[8]

In short: "Legal holds are exceptions to ordinary retention practices and when the exigency underlying the hold no longer exists (i.e., there is no continuing duty to preserve the information), organizations are free to lift the legal hold."[9]

Comment 5.i provides:

> An organization's policy and procedures can explain not only who in the organization has authority for determining that the need for a legal hold no longer exists, but also what factors or information should be considered, and what procedures should be followed, to remove the legal hold. Considerations may include:
>
> - The form and content of notice that the legal hold has been lifted;
> - Whether there is a post-case obligation to maintain some records or other information pursuant to normal retention schedules or otherwise;
> - Whether the records or other information that can now be destroyed are subject to another legal hold, or may be needed for another special purpose (e.g., needed in whole or in part for other litigation);
> - Whether the underlying litigation that has been resolved gives rise to the reasonable anticipation of other similar litigation;
> - Whether records or information in third-party custody can be destroyed; and
> - Whether the records or other information can be disposed of as soon as the legal hold is lifted, or whether the organization should wait until the next scheduled disposition.[10]

Guideline 11 to the Sedona Litigation Hold analysis provides: "The legal hold process should include provisions for the release

8. Sedona Best Practices, *supra* note 7, at 47.
9. *Id.* at 51.
10. *Id.*

of the hold upon the termination of the matter at issue." The Commentary to that Guideline states:

> An organization creating a legal hold process should include procedures for the release of the information subject to the holds once that organization is no longer obligated to preserve that information. These release procedures should include a process for conducting a custodian and data cross-check to allow the organization to determine whether the information to be released is subject to any other ongoing preservation obligations. Organizations may wish to consider the use of legal holds automation software that can perform custodian, system, and data cross-checking and provide for efficient legal holds management. When the organization is satisfied that the information is not subject to other preservation obligations, notice that the legal hold has been terminated should be provided to all recipients of the original legal hold notice (and any modifications or updated notices), and to records management, IT, and other relevant personnel. Organizations may wish to conduct periodic audits to ensure that information no longer subject to preservation obligations is not unnecessarily retained.[11]

Similarly, the Sedona Non-Party Production analysis addresses the issue vis-à-vis third parties served with subpoenas. It suggests that litigants discuss the end of the duty to preserve, noting that 70 percent of those surveyed reported difficulty in determining when a matter is resolved so that Rule 45 obligations are at an end.[12] The Sedona Conference suggests that a third party's duty should end with the termination of the review period under a subpoena.

Perhaps the simplest technique to determine whether it is permissible to destroy information subject to a litigation hold is to negotiate with the opposing litigant[13] and seek a stipulated court order or a provision in a settlement agreement lifting the hold.

Absent such agreement, the comprehensive Sedona analysis may be summarized to provide that a litigation hold and the coextensive duty to preserve terminates when, even though litigation once was reasonably anticipated, due to intervening events

---

11. SEDONA LITIGATION HOLD, *supra* note 7, Guideline 11.
12. SEDONA NON-PARTY PRODUCTION, *supra* note 7, at 8, 10.
13. *See* THE SEDONA CONFERENCE COOPERATION PROCLAMATION (2008). See Chapter 30.

(such as the passage of time, judicial resolution, or acts or inaction inconsistent with reasonable anticipation of litigation), it is no longer reasonable to anticipate litigation.

3. Other considerations

Organization knowledge management plans should designate an individual to be tasked with performing that analysis in a consistent manner. Once the decision has been supportably made, prior to any destruction, there must also be an analysis of all other threatened or reasonably anticipated claims, litigation holds, and statutory, regulatory, and contractual obligations to ascertain whether they impose a separate preservation obligation.

Additionally, standard organizational retention policies should be consulted prior to destruction, both for consistency and because the information may still be necessary for ordinary business purposes, separate and apart from litigation holds.

Finally, there must be an established mechanism for giving notice that the hold has been lifted, consistent application of destruction policies, guidance regarding the mechanism of destruction, and audit of the destruction process. It does little good, for example, to inadequately destroy the information that is no longer subject to a litigation hold, only to find out months or years later that it remains preserved on disaster recovery or other media.

4. Hypotheticals resolved

Application of these principles provides the following results:

Business contracts. XYZ, having received a demand and preservation letter from ABC seven years earlier, may engage in a reasoned analysis and conclude that litigation is no longer reasonably foreseeable, even though under the applicable statute of limitations, ABC's claim may not be time-barred. The test for continuation of the duty to preserve should be one of reasonableness, not whether it remains legally possible to assert a claim under the statute of limitations.

Domestic relations. Similarly, John should be permitted to destroy the preserved information, after the grounds for divorce have been eliminated under substantive law of domestic relations, by resumption of marital relations and/or by the passage of several years during which the marriage was resumed.

Third-party production. DEF, having produced information subject to the subpoena, should no longer be under any duty to preserve the "original" information through any trial and appeal; that duty has now been shifted to the discovering party that has obtained whatever information it was legally entitled to under Rule 45, and there is no valid reason to impose continuing costs on a nonparty.

Multiple claims. GHI, however, is in a different posture. Although the claims of A triggered the duty and have been settled, B has asserted related claims. While GHI's duty to preserve as to A has been terminated, B's claim imposes a new duty.

Of course, the scope of all such duties is subject to the limits of proportionality or court orders.[14]

5. Back to basics

Because the duty to preserve ESI and impose a litigation hold is easily triggered, and because it may be expensive to continue to maintain a litigation hold, it is important to also identify the circumstances under which the duty ends. In some instances, such as issuance of a final mandate or settlement of all claims, that time is clear. In others, it is both necessary and appropriate to analyze what is reasonably anticipated, an endeavor that, while hardly risk-free, is supported by The Sedona Conference and the intent of Rule 1: "[The Rules] should be construed and administered to secure the just, speedy, and inexpensive determination of every action and proceeding."

14. P. Grimm et al., *Proportionality in the Post-Hoc Analysis of Pre-Litigation Preservation Decisions*, 37 U. Balt. L. Rev. 381, 392–97 (2008). See chapter 9.

PART FOUR

DISCLOSING AND PRODUCING ESI TO ANOTHER PARTY

CHAPTER 12

LITIGATION PREPAREDNESS THROUGH THE E-DISCOVERY PROCESS

BY CATHERINE L. MUIR
AND MEGHAN A. PODOLNY

In any company or other organization, good litigation preparedness requires establishing sound record management systems and e-discovery protocols—regardless of whether any particular legal dispute is on the horizon. When production of electronically stored information (ESI) is actually required during litigation, organized execution of such protocols is essential to avoid various kinds of "ghastly results." This chapter begins by discussing the ESI-related roles and responsibilities of various corporate officers and units within an organization. The authors then outline solid, detailed protocols for ESI preservation, collection, review, and production.[1]

1. See also chapter 14, which sets forth an eight-stage process for gathering, reviewing, and producing ESI in discovery.

1. Introduction

An effective records and information management program is an important component to achieving meaningful reduction of risk and cost associated with litigation preparedness. Entities that develop, implement, and train their employees on carefully developed records retention and destruction policies are better prepared to execute procedures when litigation arises. These policies should usually include, but not be limited to, sections governing the following areas:

- treatment of company/entity records vital to business operations and sensitive information
- compliance with legal holds
- handling of departing and transferring employees' records and documents subject to legal hold
- employee on-boarding processes
- ownership of entity information
- use of entity-owned equipment with respect to use, communications, and privacy
- applicable international retention requirements and repositories
- records of self-assessments/audits
- consequences of noncompliance with any policy or entity directive regarding proper preservation or retention of documents and other information

Many entities unadvisedly use decentralized data storage without effective management mechanisms, typically resulting in the proliferation of duplicative data that incurs unnecessary expenses through the collection, search, review, and production of documents that could otherwise have been discarded pursuant to the entity's retention schedule. Such action raises the risk that the data needlessly being stored in contravention of a records retention schedule may become subject to a subsequent legal hold, thereby making defensible destruction problematic and more costly to substantiate.

The more information an entity has about its electronic data, such as the systems in which data is stored, how long it ultimately resides in the systems, and where copies may exist in the same or other formats, the better armed it will be to create and enforce records retention and destruction policies and locate information necessary to respond to litigation and other information requests.

In-house and outside counsel representing the entity in litigation and regulatory actions must be able to quickly locate potentially responsive data and make accurate representations to opposing parties, opposing counsel, and the court about the systems they intend to search to identify, collect, and produce the relevant evidence. Not only must these representations be consistent and timely, but also counsel likely will be required to compile and assess information regarding the system operations, relative accessibility of the data, and the estimated cost and burden involved at the preservation and retrieval steps to make early strategic decisions in the matter. This knowledge can be used to avoid making costly mistakes in representing the actions they will take or the information they commit to produce.

For example, consider *In re Fannie Mae Securities Litigation*,[2] where the Office of Federal Housing Enterprise Oversight spent more than $6 million complying with a *third-party* subpoena and was sanctioned by the court for failure to timely produce documents. The basis for the sanction rested upon the office's agreement to review and produce documents based upon a set of search terms without any investigation as to the adequacy and yield of those terms or an attempt to negotiate in lieu of a blanket agreement. The stipulated order to which the parties agreed basically reserved to the individual defendants unrestricted discretion to "specify the search terms to be used."[3] This decision should remind entities to take the time and expend the effort to know their data and to not stipulate to any actions of which they do not fully understand the consequences or that they are not prepared to undertake.

Data mapping—the activity of identifying and documenting the locations where an entity's data is stored—purports to solve many information management issues. Indeed, having a general inventory of data types and locations and formats in which data resides can be beneficial for any entity for multiple reasons, such as providing a starting point for identifying potentially responsive data and the points of contact responsible for managing or maintaining such data. Unfortunately, entities can expend vast time, energy, and money in creating extensive and detailed "data maps," only to find that by the time their data maps are deemed complete, old systems and applications have been retired, new storage

2. 552 F.3d 814 (D.C. Cir. 2009).
3. *Id.* at 817.

systems have been employed, departments and their records have been reorganized, or departments have made alternative determinations, such as storing images in lieu of hard copies or summary reports instead of raw data. To be useful, data maps need to be refreshed on a frequent basis.

2. Roles and responsibilities

Representatives from several functions each play a role in an entity's litigation preparedness plan. An ideal, cohesive plan typically will comprise representatives from the legal department, information technology (IT), records management, and possibly compliance or information security. For consistency and cost-effectiveness, the plan should be communicated to all outside counsel who represent the entity in litigation.

A. Legal

Because issues involving e-discovery are legal in nature, initiatives to address an entity's practice are usually driven by the legal department with a complement of other organizational areas to assist in execution. Typically someone within the legal department (e.g., a senior litigation attorney or nonattorney with e-discovery, project management, and/or technical background or skills), or an outside e-discovery counsel or consultant engaged by the entity, is tasked with developing and implementing the protocol, processes, and templates that form the foundation of the e-discovery plan. They also may be responsible for evaluating service vendors and litigation support, processing, review, production, and other tools to choose those most appropriate to help manage the e-discovery workflow, assist in the performance of each step of the lifecycle, and aid in the administrative functions of capturing and tracking corresponding data.

This role typically is also responsible for training in-house counsel and outside counsel on the protocol, acting as a liaison with the IT team, and funneling requests and information between functions.

B. Information technology

Representatives from the IT department may be responsible for preserving data in place, migrating data to a repository, or collecting data to provide for processing. It is essential that for each medium (e.g., email servers or archival repositories, file servers, desktop, backup tapes, and other ESI repositories), the individual identified to assist in e-discovery execution has adequate training and understands the requirements and impacts of collection methods (e.g., the level of metadata and specific fields that must be preserved as generally required by the protocol and also by the specific case). Once an entity has designed the protocol necessary to channel requests for preservation and/or collection, all members of an IT "core team" should be adequately trained to carry out such data requests.

Many entities also put in place a quick response team, often referred to as a SWAT team, to respond to more complex requests to preserve and/or collect data that are subject to a legal hold, particularly when the request covers items from systems that are beyond the ken of the general IT core team processes. The SWAT team generally comprises members from the IT department who are intimately familiar with the operations and idiosyncrasies of entity systems and, if necessary, may reach out to external contacts with knowledge of the IT system when a data request is beyond their purview and knowledge. This extended team or the SWAT team should hold status meetings regularly with the core IT team to share the knowledge gained from recent data requests and help ensure synchronization of all participants' activities.

The best e-discovery plan is one in which there is frequent communication between the legal, IT, and operational departments. An entity cannot rely on its IT department to understand the relevancy of particular data, applications, or systems to pending or anticipated litigation without instigating a joint informative process with the legal department.

As shown by the *Keithley v. Homestore.com, Inc.*,[4] decision, unwitting action by an entity's IT department to destroy or migrate data relevant to a pending or anticipated legal matter will not be excused by courts as a reasonable oversight when data is affected in the absence of continued and thorough communication between the legal and IT departments. An IT department's lack of knowledge regarding what data or systems might be relevant to a pending or anticipated litigation, or failure to communicate with the legal department prior to migrating or changing the controls around an information system, will not serve as an excuse to combat

4. 2008 WL 3833384, at *16 (N.D. Cal. Aug. 12, 2008) (finding the destruction of relevant data "reckless" and "egregious" conduct sufficient to form grounds for sanctions).

allegations of spoliation if the entity makes a decision to retire, decommission, or otherwise destroy the system and the data it contains. Hence, detailed information regarding the data that the legal department considers relevant, and the actions that IT plans to take, should be frequently communicated and documented.

C. Records and information management

Depending upon how this function is organized within an entity, representatives from the records and information management (RIM) department also will likely be involved in coordinating the requested preservation, typically of archived paper records, and suspending the normal destruction policies when such records become subject to a legal hold. This function also may maintain archived copies of frequently requested company information, documents, board minutes, retention schedules, and the like. A well-orchestrated e-discovery plan also will encourage frequent discussions between the RIM department and IT, particularly regarding electronic retention cycles and repositories to store electronic documents subject to retention schedules promulgated by the RIM department. Similarly, the legal department provides a service in communicating with the RIM department regarding any legal developments that would require a type of information or document set to be retained for a longer or shorter period than the entity currently maintains it.[5]

D. Employees and other custodians

Many entities do not have formal enterprise-wide document management systems and, consequently, leave the governance of

5. For example, the expanded state cause of action provided by Maryland's Lilly Ledbetter Fair Pay Restoration Act of 2009 allows an employee showing injury from discriminatory practices—essentially any employment decision having the potential to affect pay—to recover back pay for up to two years prior to the filing of the complaint, based upon discriminatory pay practices that may have occurred decades earlier. The effect of this legislation on document retention cycles would be carefully analyzed by the legal department and communicated to the RIM department to ensure that all relevant records that might be subject to such claims that can be reasonably retained without negatively affecting business operations are, in fact, preserved. *See also* Phillip M. Adams & Assoc., LLC v. Dell, Inc., 621 F. Supp. 2d 1173 (D. Utah 2009) (court reprimanded defendants for their lack of any centralized storage mechanisms to ensure maintenance of documents important to the defendants' business operations, and thus responsive material to the litigation).

the vast majority of their unstructured data up to the individual employees. This places great responsibility not only on the employee to effectively manage the lifecycle of entity information that is generated by that employee, but also on the legal department. The legal department maintains the responsibility for ensuring that employees (1) are adequately trained regarding their obligations should the documents over which they exercise control and possession become subject to a legal hold and (2) execute these obligations pursuant to the entity's defined policy.

The developed e-discovery protocol must reflect the entity's tolerance for risk, including the level of confidence that the legal department has in its employees to adhere to the policy and to execute their preservation obligations.[6] This determination ultimately shapes the roles and responsibilities of the IT group, as the entity evaluates the optimum combination of methods to be used by both "employee custodians"[7] and "system custodians"[8] in reducing costs and risks associated with the preservation of data.

For instance, if the entity has reason to believe that employees are not complying with legal hold notifications issued by the legal department, then it may be prudent or even necessary to supplement or even supplant employee-centric preservation efforts with those initiated and performed by the various IT system custodians. Examples of system custodian preservation might include systemically preserving active emails from a server, pulling a set of backup tapes from routine rotation cycle, or collecting from desktops and other media for preservation purposes. For example, in *Zubulake v. UBS Warburg LLC*, the evidence that potentially relevant email was deleted by its custodian factored into the decision

6. *See, e.g.*, United States v. PMUSA, 327 F. Supp. 2d 21 (D.D.C. 2004) (company relied upon employees to preserve electronic data, but failed to ensure that employees understood their obligations in light of how internal preservation and email deletion systems operated within the company). *See also In re* Intel Corp. Microprocessor Antitrust Litig., 258 F.R.D. 280 (D. Del. June 4, 2008) (company issued timely legal hold notices and relied upon employees to preserve email but did not suspend the system's auto-delete function). *See also* Phillip M. Adams & Assoc., LLC v. Dell, Inc., 621 F. Supp. 2d 1173 (D. Utah 2009) (defendant's reliance on individual employees to determine and retain emails of "long-term value" deemed an inadequate information management practice).

7. Employee custodians are targeted for preservation if the documents that they create or have received are relevant to pending or anticipated litigation.

8. System custodians are those individuals who are responsible for maintaining the systems or applications in which relevant data is stored, but they do not directly author, create, or receive relevant documents.

to restore the backup tapes likely to contain that email.[9] Similarly, in *Forest Laboratories v. Caraco Pharmaceutical Laboratories, Ltd.*, the court's determination that relevant email once stored on an active server had been destroyed after the duty to preserve arose but remained on backup media led it to order a hearing to determine whether that information was subject to an exception that would have required the tapes to be preserved.[10] These decisions indicate that an entity should consider the likelihood that systemic preservation before a discovery dispute is brought by the opposing party may alleviate the necessity of court orders and the threat of sanctions when employee-centric preservation may not be reasonably relied on.

E. Merits counsel

Most entities involved in various types of litigation or investigations tend to engage multiple law firms for the different subject matters or specialties required across their portfolio of cases, and these outside law firms will handle the "merits" of each case or type of case. As a consequence, the trial attorneys or "merits counsel" retained to handle the various cases may possess vastly different levels of knowledge, experience, and sophistication regarding current e-discovery practices and legal standards, not to mention familiarity with an entity's complex information systems. Without a standard, uniform approach to discovery, controlled ultimately by the entity, the entity runs the risk of its merits firms performing discovery pursuant to their own "reasonableness" standards, making inconsistent representations on behalf of the entity, and needlessly duplicating efforts, increasing both risk and cost. Moreover, providing merits counsel with a standard protocol and information about the entity's data and systems that have been developed and approved by the entity enables merits counsel to focus on the zealous representation of the merits of the case.

The alternative can reap ghastly results. Consider the recent, shocking saga of *Qualcomm Inc. v. Broadcom Corp.*[11] Failure to communicate and understand what actions the company had taken to preserve and collect relevant information resulted in the court

9. 216 F.R.D. 280, 287 (*Zubulake III*) (S.D.N.Y. 2003).

10. 2009 WL 998402 (E.D. Mich. Apr. 14, 2009).

11. Qualcomm Inc. v. Broadcom Corp., No. 05cv1958-RMB (BLM), 2008 WL 66932, 88 U.S.P.Q. 2d 1169 (S.D. Cal. Jan. 7, 2008), *vacated in part*, 2008 WL 638108 (S.D. Cal. Mar. 5, 2008).

initially holding merits counsel liable for discovery misconduct based on its failures to adequately monitor its client's discovery. While the court recently softened its harsh ruling by dissolving the sanctions order as further evidence came to light,[12] the lasting legacy of *Qualcomm* urges merits counsel, in order to meet its Rule 26(g)[13] (or state equivalent) reasonable inquiry obligation, to request full information regarding its client's preservation and collection practices. The good client will not wait for merits counsel to make the first move, but rather will provide its e-discovery protocol to the counsel promoting or defending the entity's rights and interests.

3. E-discovery protocol, generally

As a result of the e-discovery amendments to the Federal Rules of Civil Procedure in December 2006, entities have realized the value of developing a litigation readiness strategy that may better facilitate responding to discovery requests in a streamlined, consistent, and cost-effective manner. In addition to the system profiles described elsewhere in this book,[14] many entities have found that creating an e-discovery protocol or playbook that describes the various roles and responsibilities, the entity's standard response to litigation discovery requests, and processes from preservation through production (which also may include information management) will help the entity maintain a consistent, defensible discovery response that will provide repeatable, leveraged answers and help control costs. Each protocol is specifically unique to the entity's systems, litigation portfolio expanse, and tolerance for risk.[15]

12. Namely, that there was a fundamental problem in breakdown of communication between the employees and the attorneys, but that the attorneys made significant efforts to comply with their discovery obligations and did not evidence bad faith. Qualcomm Inc. v. Broadcom Corp., No. 05cv1958-B (BLM) (S.D. Cal. Apr. 2, 2010).

13. "By signing [a disclosure, discovery request, response, or objection], an attorney or party certifies that to the best of the person's knowledge, information, and belief formed after a reasonable inquiry: (a) with respect to a disclosure, it is complete and correct as of the time it is made. . . ." See also chapter 31 on Rule 26(g).

14. *See* chapter 4.

15. What do we mean by risk tolerance? While pulling an entire set of backup tapes and imaging all custodian computers may preserve all potentially relevant information, an entity's size and a case's low profile may render this action "preservation overkill" and result in an ever-increasing pile of data that could be retired were it not for expanded preservation obligations. Alternatively, a

Frequently, the protocol will contain form templates and checklists or other helpful tools to facilitate execution of and compliance with the written protocol. Additionally, the protocol may contain a legal framework or case citations as rationale for the various processes described therein. If updated on a regular basis, this serves to help define current best practices and establish legal defensibility for the processes. Further, if prepared by or at the request of counsel, and disseminated carefully to only legal personnel, the protocol may also help the entity maintain privilege over its e-discovery strategies to the extent it wishes to shield its processes from automatic disclosure.[16]

A comprehensive litigation readiness protocol may be composed of a series of discrete protocols that address specific phases of the overall e-discovery process, yet work in concert to yield a consistent, thoughtful, and repeatable response. Ideally, the protocol and emanating best practices are developed as a product of (1) extensive research of current applicable case law and other legal resources; (2) a close study of industry trends, practices, and tools; (3) an evaluation of litigation service providers and their offerings to help inform, enhance, and execute the protocol (including process and technology vendors and consultants and even outside counsel); and perhaps most important, (4) an assessment and understanding of the entity's current culture, business operational needs, information technology infrastructure, and the policies, budgets, and available human resources of the records and information management, risk management, IT, and corporate security groups that are devoted to executing the protocol.

---

protocol directing preservation of active and foldered email for all key custodians, suspended auto-delete for those same custodians, and thorough and refreshed legal holds to a larger group of employees might be the plan chosen by an entity that determines such action is reasonably likely to capture all relevant, accessible information, and any information lost outside of these methods is an acceptable risk because it is unlikely to be relevant.

16. *See* P. Grimm, et al., *Discovery About Discovery: Does the Attorney-Client Privilege Protect All Attorney-Client Communications Relating to the Preservation of Potentially Relevant Information?*, 37 U. BALT. L. REV. 413 (2008) (see chapter 16); *see also* Major Tours, Inc., v. Colorel, 2009 U.S. Dist. LEXIS 68128 (D.N.J. Aug. 4, 2009). *Accord* Capitano v. Ford Motor Co., 831 N.Y.S.2d 687 (N.Y. Sup. Ct. 2007) (finding that litigation hold notice was protected by the attorney-client privilege and could not be compelled to combat plaintiffs claim that documents that were not produced were either intentionally or negligently destroyed).

The protocol is useful not only for internal members of litigation and IT teams involved in the performance of e-discovery tasks, but also for outside counsel handling the matters. Establishing standard procedures, defining roles and responsibilities, and training all employees and retained consultants involved in executing the protocol at the outset of any particular litigation aids in predictability and can help control associated costs.

4. Preservation protocol

A. When does the duty to preserve accrue?

An entity is required to notify its employees believed to have possession, custody, or control of documents potentially responsive to the subject of a litigation or investigation.[17] In fact, if the entity has a contractual relationship with a third party, such as a consultant or independent contractor, the entity also may have to notify the third party that any documents within its possession, custody, or control are also subject to preservation obligations.[18] Documents are considered under the control of the entity, and thus must be preserved, if the entity has "the right, authority, or practical ability to obtain the documents from a non-party to the action."[19] The distinction between whether or not documents held by a third party are within the "possession, custody, or control" of the entity is important, because if they are, the entity will be held liable for the spoliation of these documents by the third party.[20] As part of its litigation preparedness plan, an entity would be wise to carefully define and identify any such third-party relationship, particularly as it relates to the generation and control of documents that are prepared or maintained by the third party on behalf of or in furtherance of the entity's business.

17. *See* Nursing Home Pension Fund v. Oracle Corp., 254 F.R.D. 559 (N.D. Cal. Sept. 2, 2008).

18. *See* United States v. Maxxam, Inc., 2009 WL 817264 (N.D. Cal. Mar. 27, 2009) (holding defendants responsible for any spoliation of evidence, mainly data inputs, in the possession of a consulting company hired by the defendants' law firm to perform related computer modeling).

19. Goodman v. Praxair Servs., Inc., 632 F. Supp. 2d 494, 515 (D. Md. July 7, 2009) (quoting *In re* NTL, Inc. Sec. Litig., 244 F.R.D. 179, 195 (S.D.N.Y. 2007)).

20. *See, e.g.*, Silvestri v. GMC, 271 F.3d 583, 591 (4th Cir. 2001) (holding that if a party does not have control sufficient to preserve information, it must notify the opponent so that the opponent may attempt to secure the information).

Determining the optimum time for issuing a legal hold notice to custodians and the appropriate scope is critical in order to avoid issues associated with spoliation of evidence.[21]

(1) Timing

Determining the point in time at which the duty to preserve potentially responsive documents is triggered is a very fact-specific analysis. The Sedona Principles regarding legal holds[22] provide a set of general factors to consider when deciding whether the duty to preserve has been triggered. These include considering the nature and specificity of the claim; the party making the claim; the strength of the potential claim; whether the threat of potential litigation is direct, inferred, or implied; and whether there has been media or industry coverage of the potential claim.[23]

For one frequent and specific example, consider the situation where an entity receives demand letters from opposing parties or counsel regarding potential claims. These letters may or may not trigger a preservation obligation, depending on the facts and circumstances. Absent an explicit intent to seek declaratory judgment, the assessment of whether a demand letter constitutes a credible threat of litigation that triggers the duty to preserve may include the presence of a justiciable controversy;[24] the tenor and tone of the communication; the history, if any, with the opposing party or opposing counsel; and the likelihood of obtaining a

21. In fact, courts generally are recognizing the issuance of a legal hold as one of the key primary actions that litigants should employ to protect against the negligent spoliation of relevant data. *See* Pension Comm. of Univ. of Montreal Pension Plan v. Banc of Am. Sec., No. 05-9016, 2010 WL 1843212, at *3 (S.D.N.Y. Jan. 15, 2010). *See also* Jones v. Bremen High Sch., Dist. 228, 2010 WL 2106640 (N.D. Ill. May 25, 2010) (holding that issuing legal hold to only a few key players rather than all employees who had dealings with plaintiff constituted reckless and gross negligence under the circumstances).

22. THE SEDONA CONFERENCE COMMENTARY ON LEGAL HOLDS: THE TRIGGER AND THE PROCESS (Aug. 2007 Public Comment Version).

23. *Id.* at 9.

24. *See* Texas v. City of Frisco, No. 4:07cv383, 2008 WL 828055 (E.D. Tex. Mar. 27, 2008) (dismissing a state-filed declaratory judgment seeking clarification of the state's duty under Federal Rules of Civil Procedure 26 and 37 to preserve evidence in light of an overly broad and general demand letter, on the basis that the City of Frisco's claim of potential litigation in the demand letter was too general to pose justiciable controversy). *See also Goodman*, 632 F. Supp. 2d at 510–11 (finding that duty to preserve was triggered by receipt of a letter that openly threatened litigation).

business resolution.[25] When a demand letter or request for preservation is too general, the duty to preserve has not been wholly triggered.[26] Yet, that means that a potential defendant has notice of some type of potential litigation claim. At this point, doing nothing in the face of a general threat of litigation could be viewed by a court as ignoring the duty to preserve. The potential defendant entity should use resources at its disposal to narrow any potential claims and then consider preserving information that is likely to be highly relevant to the narrowed issues.

A duty to preserve potentially responsive information can arise many years before litigation commences.[27] The imminence of litigation is sufficient, rather than necessary, to create a preservation obligation.[28] The future litigation must be "probable," which has

---

25. *See* Cache La Poudre Feeds, LLC v. Land O'Lakes, Inc., 244 F.R.D. 614, 621–22 (D. Colo. 2007). In *Cache La Poudre*, the court concluded that, under different circumstances, a demand letter alone from one party to another may be sufficient to trigger an obligation to preserve evidence. Yet such a letter would require more explicit wording than the letters that plaintiff sent to the defendants, which not only did not threaten litigation and did not demand preservation of potentially relevant materials, but even offered commercial resolution to the dispute.

26. Texas v. City of Frisco, 2008 WL 828055, at *3. The court found that a justiciable controversy could not exist where the demand/preservation letter did not articulate a "'substantial controversy of immediacy and reality.'" *Id.* at *3 (quoting Shields v. Norton, 289 F.3d 832, 835 (5th Cir. Tex 2002)). The letter at issue only alluded to impacts from the tollway project that could result in potential litigation. There were no specific claims or any indication when the potential litigation may commence. The letter asked the State to preserve "any and all" documents related to the project without specifying the potential claims or the expected timeframe of preservation. *Id.* Yet the *Frisco* court's admonishment for the parties to act in accordance with Rule 26 is an indication that the court feels the duty to preserve has been at least partially triggered. This decision could be interpreted to place the burden on the potential defendant to ferret out the scope of its duty to preserve in the face of a general demand.

27. *See, e.g.*, Phillip M. Adams & Assoc., LLC v. Dell, Inc., 621 F. Supp. 2d 1173, 1191 (D. Utah 2009) (finding that the duty to preserve was triggered more than five years before an infringement letter was received by the defendant because of the industry activity related to the patented item at issue).

28. *See* A. Farber & Partners, Inc. v. Garber, 234 F.R.D. 186, 193 (C.D. Cal. 2006); Kronisch v. United States, 150 F.3d 112, 126 (2d Cir. 1998); UMG Recordings, Inc. v. Hummer Winblad Venture Partners (*In re* Napster, Inc. Copyright Litig.), 462 F. Supp. 2d 1060, 1068 (N.D. Cal. 2006); Quintus Corp. v. Avaya, Inc (*In re* Quintus Corp.), 353 B.R. 77, 83–84 (Bankr. D. Del. 2006). *But see* Phillip M. Adams & Assoc., LLC v. Dell, Inc., 621 F. Supp. 2d 1173 (D. Utah 2009).

been held to mean "more than a possibility."[29] Accordingly, the point in time at which an entity contemplates filing a lawsuit as a plaintiff also must be carefully considered.

A relevant benchmark for assessing whether a preservation obligation has been triggered is whether the entity would assert attorney work-product privilege over documents created at that time. The standard for attorney work product—"reasonable anticipation of litigation"—is generally viewed as the same as the standard for when a preservation obligation arises.[30] Likewise, a court may consider the point in time in which outside counsel is engaged as an indication of when the duty to preserve would accrue.

(2) Scope

To reduce the costs, burdens, and risks associated with preservation, an entity should try to limit the scope of its obligations. Just as it may be a prudent legal and operational strategy to preserve broadly and narrowly tailor a collection (depending on several factors, including the method of processing the data for review), it also would be beneficial to either seek agreement from or define for the opposing party and its counsel the parameters of an entity's search for relevant documents, based on the accessibility and volume of documents and data reasonably calculated to lead to the discovery of admissible evidence.[31] Depending on the particular case strategy, this may include either (1) negotiating with opposing counsel to limit the number and seniority level of custodians, the applicable date range of the hold, other substantive issues involved in the hold, the media or file types or locations from which the entity intends to produce documents, and the form of production, or (2) sending a letter to opposing counsel stating the entity's intentions as to the previously mentioned topics and state what actions

29. Hynix Semiconductor Inc. v. Rambus, Inc., 591 F. Supp. 2d 1038, 1061 (N.D. Cal. 2006).

30. Samsung Elecs. Co. v. Rambus, Inc., 439 F. Supp. 2d 524, 542 (E.D. Va. 2006) (noting that the work product definition of anticipation of litigation can also be used to highlight the preservation trigger when assessing intentional spoliation), *vacated on other grounds*, 523 F.3d 1374 (Fed. Cir. 2008). For this reason, counsel responsible for submitting a privilege log is advised to consider when preservation began in the case when asserting work product. Asserting work-product privilege in a period before preservation instituted could lead to spoliation claims and should only be done after careful consideration of the possible consequences.

31. FED. R. CIV. P. 26(b)(1).

the entity does not plan to take. This sort of transparency serves to clarify an entity's obligations up front and provide a record of cooperation should a discovery dispute arise later in the matter.[32]

If warranted by the facts and circumstances of an individual case, the entity in its discretion may undertake additional, perhaps extraordinary, steps to preserve information. These additional steps may include making forensic images[33] of selected hard drives or suspending the overwriting of backups if information cannot be secured within more accessible sources.[34] If a case may implicate active entity databases, additional systemic steps may need to be taken to preserve the relevant portions of data in its current form. Note that data that comes from media containing the additional data of multiple employees can often be associated with (and thus available for) other existing and future matters associated with those employees. Because such actions potentially have significant associated risk and costs, the choice to preserve on a broader scope must be weighed carefully in the context of preservation efforts for all open and reasonably anticipated matters and becomes a risk-based decision.

Once an entity has considered its tolerance for risk and made a determination of the appropriate time within the sequence of events for which it has a duty to preserve documents and should issue a legal hold notice to custodians, the entity must make decisions about the processes or methods whereby it will administer legal holds.

The proper execution, tracking, and documentation of legal hold notices, responses from recipients, reminder and release notices,

32. William A. Gross. Constr. Assocs., Inc. v. Am. Mfrs. Mut. Ins. Co., 256 F.R.D. 134 (S.D.N.Y. 2009) ("Electronic discovery requires cooperation between opposing counsel and transparency in all aspects of preservation and production of ESI."). Transparency avoids sanction-seeking claims of misrepresentation later in the matter. *See, e.g.*, Maggette v. BL Dev. Corp., 2010 WL 2010816 (N.D. Miss. May 17, 2010) (where party failed to adequately and honestly represent the extent of its search for relevant data); see Chapter 30.

33. "A forensic copy is an exact copy of an entire physical storage media (hard drive, CD-ROM, DVD-ROM, tape, etc.), including all active and residual data and unallocated or slack space on the media. Compresses and encrypts to ensure authentication and protect chain of custody. Forensic copies are often called 'image' or 'imaged copies.'" THE SEDONA CONFERENCE GLOSSARY: E-DISCOVERY & DIGITAL INFORMATION MANAGEMENT 23 (2d ed. Dec. 2007); *see generally* chapter 4.

34. See chapter 25 for a discussion of information that is not reasonably accessible.

escalations, decision points, custodian interview and collection activities, chain of custody, and information about the data itself (such as date ranges and volume) can create a significant administrative burden. Therefore, it behooves an entity to design defensible, repeatable processes for each step of the overall e-discovery process workflow. Depending on an entity's litigation profile (i.e., the volume of litigation, average number of custodians and data volumes, typical matter types, exposure levels, and resources), an entity may opt for a less costly, manual process of sending out notices and tracking the pertinent data on spreadsheets or may decide to automate as much of the process as possible to make it more manageable. Regardless of the litigation profile, without some level of automation and a tracking repository to capture such information as distribution dates, recipients, responses, and decisions regarding why certain potential custodians or groups were not included in the preservation and/or collection efforts, companies run the risk of nonuniform execution and gaps in documentation. This flaw likely would cause the entity to incur administrative costs due to inefficiencies and duplication of efforts.

Most currently available legal hold or e-discovery workflow tracking tools enable entities to automatically create and capture the necessary documentation through the processing of a number of helpful data points so that, at a quick glance, the in-house attorneys and legal personnel can assess crucial information such as (1) which custodians may be subject to multiple legal holds (and, thus, which subsets of their documents may or may not be released); (2) what data has been collected from whom, and covering what date range; and (3) which custodians have not acknowledged receiving, understanding, and complying with legal hold obligations. Additionally, such tools can serve as a form template repository for legal hold and collection efforts. Documentation such as actual hold notices and completed custodian interview memoranda can originate from and be stored within these tools. More rudimentary workflow tracking tools may be homegrown (such as an Access database). Alternatively, more intricate and functionally integrated tools may be purchased "off the shelf" from third-party vendors. Some have modules that extend into records management to help provide a repository map of data system containers.

Reminder notices should be sent periodically (perhaps every three months) to custodians to help ensure that employees remember their obligations and remain in compliance with the legal hold until the hold is released after the matter has been closed. Opinions may vary as to when a matter is defined as "closed" with respect to releasing the legal hold obligation[35] and when and how collected and produced data should be returned to its owner or disposed of under its original retention and destruction schedule. Milestones for releasing data under this concept of "closed" may include, but are not limited to, the points in time at which an appeal period has passed, the matter has been adjudicated or otherwise dispositioned, discovery has closed, all responsive evidence has been produced, and all potentially responsive evidence has been collected (a less prudent option), and also may depend on the circumstances of the case and the operations, business needs, and culture of an entity. When the matter is determined to be "closed," a legal hold release should be issued to all individual custodians and system custodians to instruct them to no longer preserve the subject data solely for this matter but to return it to its original retention schedule.[36]

B. In preparation for the meet and confer

At the outset of discovery in federal and many state cases, pursuant to Rule 26(f) (or the state equivalent), the parties will be required to meet and confer regarding discovery plans.[37]

It is essential that the entity's representatives perform an early case assessment to understand the scope of the substantive claims, the relevant custodians, and the likely places of potentially relevant data in order to decide on and prepare a defensible strategic position regarding intended preservation, collection, and production of data (which will likely be different depending on whether the entity is the plaintiff or defendant). Here, parties provide a roadmap of what they intend to produce, and any barriers of which they are aware that may hinder that production. They may

35. For a discussion of the point in time at which a matter should be considered closed, see chapter 11.

36. *Id.*

37. "[T]he parties must confer as soon as practicable—and in any event at least 21 days before a scheduling conference is to be held or a scheduling order is due under Rule 16(b). In conferring, the parties must consider the nature and basis of their claims and defenses and the possibilities for promptly settling or resolving the case; make or arrange for the disclosures required by Rule 26(a)(1); discuss any issues about preserving discoverable information; and develop a proposed discovery plan." Fed. R. Civ. P. 26(f). *See* chapter 19.

decide details such as the precise custodians to be searched, date ranges to be applied, and metadata fields required; request a specific format of production; and disclose sources that may contain potentially responsive data but that are not reasonably accessible.[38]

Attorneys and other persons making representations and requests for production may not be technically savvy about the entity's systems and data, and thus should be fully informed by the entity regarding what the entity can be prepared to do to mirror what it is requesting of its opponent.

5. Collection protocol

Once the potentially responsive data has been preserved, some or all of the data may be collected. A protocol may establish a standard baseline method for collections, such as stating that all collections, unless otherwise required, must be a logical collection.[39] Despite the somewhat manufactured angst surrounding the capture of metadata,[40] there are a number of technology tools and service vendors that are able to capture sufficient metadata to ensure that data itself and relevant metadata fields are not altered during collection.

38. "A discovery plan must state the parties' views and proposals on: (A) what changes should be made in the timing, form, or requirement for disclosures under Rule 26(a), including a statement of when initial disclosures were made or will be made; (B) the subjects on which discovery may be needed, when discovery should be completed, and whether discovery should be conducted in phases or be limited to or focused on particular issues; (C) any issues about disclosure or discovery of electronically stored information, including the form or forms in which it should be produced; (D) any issues about claims of privilege or of protection as trial-preparation materials . . . ; (E) what changes should be made in the limitations on discovery imposed under these rules or by local rule, and what other limitations should be imposed; and (F) any other orders that the court should issue under Rule 26(c). . . ." FED. R. CIV. P. 26(f).

39. For example, either custodian- or attorney-directed to capture the actual space occupied by a file on a hard drive, including its full file path.

40. Commonly referred to as "data about data," metadata tracks and reveals data about document attributes, such as name, size, type, where it is located, and ownership. Metadata for an email includes items such as addressees and received date. Metadata for other electronic documents reveals "[p]roperties about the file stored in the file, as opposed to document content," including author and creation and revision dates. THE SEDONA CONFERENCE GLOSSARY: E-DISCOVERY & DIGITAL INFORMATION MANAGEMENT (2d ed. Dec. 2007); *see* chapter 6.

Typically it is not necessary for an entity to collect data "forensically"[41] from an employee's entire hard drive or other sources of ESI as part of its normal preservation protocol.[42] Many entities mistakenly believe that they must use or purchase forensic tools to ensure a defensible collection. Not only do such tools require extensive appropriate training, but also the entities employing them need to understand the ramifications that can result from their use, such as the potential overcollection of data. To that end, the misapplication of software can create as many problems as the software purports to solve.

The preservation obligation, and its subsequent collection effort, requires reasonable and good faith efforts to preserve information that may be relevant to pending or threatened litigation, but parties do not necessarily need to take every conceivable step to preserve and collect all potentially relevant ESI.[43] This obligation does not require the "freezing" of all ESI, but rather reasonable preservation action. Even though it can be technically possible to preserve all information through a forensic image, it usually can be done only at a high cost, often approaching or exceeding the amount in controversy.[44] In an ordinary matter, the obligation is met by limiting preservation to "those steps reasonably necessary to secure evidence for the fair and just resolution of the matter in dispute."[45]

Nevertheless, special circumstances in a given case may warrant narrow, targeted forensic collection of information. Counsel should consider whether to use forensic imaging for preservation

41. That is, taking a bit-by-bit image, including slack or unallocated space. *See supra* note 32.

42. In determining whether forensic images and experts are necessary, courts will evaluate five factors: (1) the needs of the case; (2) the amount in controversy; (3) the resources of the parties; (4) the importance of the issues at stake; and (5) the importance of the discovery to the issue in litigation. Peskoff v. Faber, 244 F.R.D. 54 (D.D.C. 2007).

43. The Sedona Conference, The Sedona Principles: Best Practices, Recommendations & Principles for Addressing Electronic Document Production, Principle 5 (2d ed. June 2007).

44. *Id.* at cmt. 5.g.

45. *Id. See* Memry Corp. v. Ky. Oil Tech., 2007 WL 832937, at *3 (N.D. Cal. Mar. 19, 2007) (concluding that the suit at bar did not involve a situation where "computer content was intricately related to the very basis of the lawsuit," and denying the request to order forensic imaging).

purposes (to avoid potential spoliation of evidence) in certain types of cases, such as the following:

- Internal investigation of employee or third-party misconduct.
- Criminal or regulatory matters where the entity is under investigation or is responding to a grand jury subpoena related to entity data.
- Civil litigation where there exist facts to place the entity on notice that relevant information has been deleted prior to the legal hold notice being issued.
- The entity reasonably believes that potentially relevant information may be lost due to the transfer or departure of a custodian.
- There are allegations of dishonest conduct related to the ESI at issue, such as "I never got it," or "I did not read it."
- The entity learns of facts that place it on reasonable notice that an individual employee has failed to follow the terms of a legal hold notice and information has been deleted.

The entity's collection protocol should be designed to ensure the integrity of the collection process, satisfy the entity's obligation to undertake a "reasonable inquiry" in locating all relevant documents and responding to discovery requests,[46] and provide

46. FED. R. CIV. P. 26(g); *see supra* note 12 and accompanying text. Under Federal Rule of Civil Procedure 26(g)(1), a party responding to discovery must certify that the response was made after a reasonable inquiry. Mancia v. Mayflower Textile Servs. Co., 253 F.R.D. 354, 357–58 (D. Md. 2008) (citing FED. R. CIV. P. 26(g) advisory committee's note to 1983 Amendments) ("[T]he certification duty . . . requires that the attorney make a reasonable inquiry into the factual basis of his response, request, or objection . . . [A]n objection to requested discovery may not be made until after a lawyer has paused and consider[ed] whether, based on a reasonable inquiry, there is a factual basis [for the] . . . objection.") (internal quotations and citations omitted). *See also* Poole v. Textron, Inc., 192 F.R.D. 494, 503 (D. Md. 2000) (discussing the duty of reasonable inquiry under the totality of the circumstances); Jones v. Am. Gen. Life and Accident Ins. Co., No. 101-003, 2002 WL 32073037, at *4 (S.D. Ga. Dec 4, 2002) (citing *Poole*). Thus, Rule 26(g) leaves to counsel for the responding party to craft a reasonable inquiry under the circumstances. *See* FTC v. Foster, No. 07-00352, 2007 WL 1827099 (D.N.M. June 11, 2007) (confirming that a party has no obligation, or right, to direct the conduct of the other party's discovery process, such as defining the number or identity of custodians to be searched, but if the responding party fails to conduct a reasonable inquiry in the course of responding to requests for production, the court may fashion an appropriate response to ensure that the injured party is not further harmed from the other's inaction).

an adequate chain of custody so that any evidence collected will be admissible in court.[47]

The collection protocol should be flexible enough to accommodate strategic decisions regarding the timing and method of collection, based on considerations such as

- *Whether any of the circumstances set forth above are present (internal investigation, awareness of previously deleted information, etc.).* This may warrant performing a targeted forensic collection of documents and data in concert with initial preservation efforts.
- *Whether the obligation to preserve relevant documents is ongoing.* Performing a collection too early may result in overcollection of nonrelevant documents or necessitate going back to the same custodian(s) to refresh the initial collection.
- *Whether the matter has a large number of custodians or volume of documents.* If so, then waiting to perform collections until a point in time closer to document review may create a strain on resources.

While permitting employee self-collection of documents was perhaps a common practice until recently, experienced e-discovery practitioners consider it imprudent under most circumstances. First, entity employees, while familiar with the facts of a particular matter, may not understand the full scope of the discovery obligations in a case or the importance of broadly collecting relevant information to be narrowed later. Second, although many entities have utilized employee self-collection methods in the past, recent evolving case law questions that practice.[48]

---

47. For a full discussion on ESI admissibility, see The Sedona Conference Commentary on ESI Evidence & Admissibility (Mar. 2008) and chapter 24. *See also* Lorraine v. Markel, 241 F.R.D. 534 (D. Md. 2007) (illustrating various methods of admitting electronic information as evidence under the Federal Rules of Evidence); P. Grimm, M. Ziccardi & A. Major, *Back to the Future:* Lorraine v. Markel American Insurance Co. *and New Findings on the Admissibility of Electronically Stored Information*, 42 Akron L. Rev. 357 (2009).

48. *See, e.g.*, Phx. Four, Inc. v. Strategic Res. Corp., 2006 WL 1409413 (S.D.N.Y. 2006) (employees failed to inquire or discover relevant documents on a partitioned section of a server taken from a former building); *see also* Goodman v. Praxair Servs., Inc., 632 F. Supp. 2d 494 (D. Md. 2009) (to defendant's argument that it did not violate its duty to preserve evidence because its CEO had printed "relevant" emails and discarded only "irrelevant" information, responding that "the ultimate decision of what is relevant is not determined by a party's subjective assessment filtered through its own perception of self-interest"); Phillip M.

Rather, the collection protocol should specify the actor tasked to perform document collections for specific media type (e.g., legal staff, IT personnel, corporate security, or outside vendors) and how typical collections, notwithstanding the extraordinary circumstances that may warrant or necessitate forensic collection, will be performed, also taking into account the potential need for outside resources to assist with high volume, complex structured data, forensic issues, or time-sensitive collections.

The collection protocol also should address the extent to which the entity will employ custodian questionnaires or interviews to help identify potentially responsive ESI and the locations in which the information resides. Similarly, the protocol should discuss the need for documentation of the decisions made by either in-house or merits counsel regarding whether or not to collect documents from specific custodians.[49] While in certain instances it may not be necessary to interview or collect from every employee who received a legal hold notice, any decision not to collect from an employee should be noted and a record of that decision recorded in the case file.

To that end, the entity should develop a standard collection form template to assist the individual assigned to conduct the interview and undertake the collection. This template would record relevant information about what (1) has been collected, (2) may be relevant but needs collection at a later date, and (3) was not collected because the collector and custodian deemed it nonrelevant. This form should be designed to provide an important, and possibly crucial, audit trail should any questions arise later in a matter, and as such, should be employed consistently in every case.

Adams & Assoc., LLC v. Dell, Inc., 621 F. Supp. 2d 1173 (D. Utah 2009) (finding defendant's reliance on individual employees to determine and retain emails of "long-term value" an inadequate information management practice). More recently, Judge Scheindlin's *Pension Committee* opinion reprimanded plaintiffs for a preservation strategy that placed total reliance on the employee to search and select what the employee believed to be responsive records without supervision from counsel, without an affirmative request to preserve all relevant records, and without a mechanism for collecting the preserved records. Pension Comm. of Univ. of Montreal Pension Plan v. Banc of Am. Sec., No. 05-9016, 2010 WL 1843212, at *8 (S.D.N.Y. Jan. 15, 2010).

49. *See* Zubulake v. UBS Warburg LLC (*Zubulake V*), 229 F.R.D. 422 (S.D.N.Y. 2004) (placing on counsel the burden to interview employees to determine whether *all* potential sources of information have been inspected and guarantee that relevant data was both preserved and produced); *see also* Qualcomm Inc. v. Broadcom Corp., 2008 WL 66932 (S.D. Cal. Jan. 7, 2008), and *supra* notes 10–12 and accompanying text.

6. Review and production protocol

The review and production phase includes processing of electronic documents, loading of the electronic documents to a litigation database or repository, design of a review pane (a checkbox list of tags and/or issues that reviewers select from to categorize a document in an electronic review system), review of the documents for relevance and privilege, and production of documents to opposing counsel, third party, or governmental entity.

The review and production process generally should be coordinated by the entity's in-house counsel or e-discovery counsel, either of whom will work closely with merits counsel to address the facts and circumstances of each individual matter. While each case is substantively different, a thoughtful baseline process should be designed to provide standardization where possible to maximize efficiency and reduce costs in responding to discovery.

A. Processing and limiting the scope

In order to take electronic documents from their native state and convert them into a format that can be readily reviewed by attorneys for relevance and privilege, the collected data must be processed to expand email attachments, remove system files, and de-duplicate where necessary. Any service providers engaged to "cull" the data should have robust data filtering capabilities so that the culling targets the data that is likely to be relevant to the matter, rather than bulk-loading all data into the review system. Data filtering (e.g., by date range, file and document type, and key words) can significantly reduce the amount of data that must be reviewed. Any use of keywords, though, must be carefully constructed with the subject matter of the claim and other custodial knowledge in mind.[50]

---

50. *See* chapters 20 and 21; William A. Gross. Constr. Assocs., Inc. v. Am. Mfrs. Mut. Ins. Co., 256 F.R.D. 134 (S.D.N.Y. 2009) ("This Opinion should serve as a wake-up call to the Bar in this District about the need for careful thought, quality control, testing, and cooperation with opposing counsel in designing search terms or 'keywords' to be used to produce emails or other electronically stored information."); Clear One Commc'ns, Inc. v. Chiang, 2008 WL 920336 (D. Utah Apr. 1, 2008) ("If documents are discovered suggesting that *other* documents exist, which were not identified as potentially responsive, or if a surprisingly small or unreasonably large number of documents is identified as potentially responsive, refinement may be needed."). *See also In re* Fannie Mae Sec. Litig., 552 F.3d 814 (D.C. Cir. 2009), and *supra* notes 1 and 2 and accompanying text. Therefore, it is prudent to seek agreement from opposing counsel up front not only

B. Review platform

By evaluating many review platforms (otherwise known as "litigation support databases") and choosing one to use, license, or purchase that best fits the entity's protocol, human review resources, and budget, attorneys or reviewers will have to learn the system only once, thus saving time and expense on trainings and learning curves. Many platforms have features that enable in-house counsel to monitor the review status and metrics of the review as it progresses. Many entities are considering outsourced review, shifting the management risk and burden to outside entities with contract reviewers or facilities in less expensive locations or even abroad. Outsourcing reviews abroad may not be appropriate for all subject matters, and the entity also must consider any ethical implications that could arise from such an arrangement.[51]

When considering technology functionality, the e-discovery software or service provider chosen should offer the following options, all of which can dramatically reduce attorney review time and ultimately reduce the costs of review:

- *De-duplication:* to enable true duplicates to be reviewed only once
- *Bulk tagging:* for consistent treatment of duplicate documents to cut down on review time and help preserve privilege
- *Family groups:* to facilitate review of like document content in context
- *Exceptions reporting:* receiving information about data that could not be processed or needs special processing resulting in increased time and cost
- *Concept searching:* used primarily for a "first cut" review to help organize the data by analyzing relationships between each word and every other word in sets of documents[52]

Regardless of who performs the review, typically the entity's in-house or merits counsel will provide appropriate training and quality control of the review. To maximize efficiency through consistency, the entity or special e-discovery counsel should develop

on the keywords to be applied, but also the circumstances under which further refinement of keywords would be appropriate and not opposed.

51. Catherine Muir & Courtney I. Barton, *Corporate Strategies for Reducing Ediscovery Costs*, 26(1) ACC Docket 39–40 (Jan./Feb. 2008).

52. *Id.* at 40; *see* chapters 20 and 21.

a default review pane to be applied to all cases absent specific reason to deviate from the default. Then as an individual case may require, merits counsel should work closely with the entity's in-house counsel to design and add any case-specific coding fields to the review pane, considering that the more complex the review pane is, the slower the review may be. This default rationality should also apply to the characterization of coding protocol for document family members.

The entity should determine early in the review process who will prepare the privilege log, as this is often a costly and time-consuming task that should not wait until the end of the review to begin. Depending on the review tool being used, the entity may be able to take advantage of customized coding fields, drop-down options, and metadata population to speed up the process.[53] Taking time to provide clear training and guidance to the review team will result in much more efficient and effective review and will decrease costs on the back end in narrowing down the population of documents to only those that are responsive to the merits, or, alternatively, a larger set of documents that are nonresponsive but are relevant and useful for other reasons.

C. Production

The final step in the process is to produce documents to the opposing side. The exact form of the production generally will have been resolved between the parties in advance pursuant to Rule 34.[54] Generally, the entity should produce documents in the manner in which they are kept in the normal course of business and not produce by document request.[55]

53. *See* chapter 15; The Hon. John Facciola & Meghan O'Donnell (now Podolny), *Innovative Ways to Approach Privilege Logs* (podcast discussion, June 16, 2009), www.ESIBytes.com; Jeanne Thomas, David D. Cross & Courtney Barton, *Reducing the Costs of Privilege Reviews and Logs*, Nat'l L.J., Mar. 23, 2009, http://www.crowell.com/documents/Reducing-the-costs-of-privilege-reviews-and-logs.pdf; The Hon. John M. Facciola & Jonathan M. Redgrave, *Asserting and Challenging Privilege Claims in Modern Litig.: The Facciola-Redgrave Framework*, 4 Fed. Courts L. Rev. 19 (2009).

54. Rule 34(b) states that the discovery request may request the form of production, but the responding party can object and "state the form or forms it intends to use." *See* chapter 2.

55. *Id.* Rule 34(b) also states "[a] party must produce documents as they are kept in the usual course of business or must organize and label them to correspond to the categories in the request; [i]f a request does not specify a form for producing electronically stored information, a party must produce it in a form or forms in

In determining the form of production that will be used in a particular case, local court rules, any discovery orders entered in the case, the entity's written discovery responses, and any agreement between the parties should all be considered and given weight.

7. Conclusion

As e-discovery issues continue on their trajectory to the forefront of litigation, it is advantageous for entities to thoughtfully establish well-conceived plans and processes to abate both risks and costs associated with repeatedly responding to increasingly complex demands. The goal of an e-discovery practitioner should be to continue to find solutions to minimize discovery issues, costs, and risks so that parties may focus on the merits.[56] There are some cases that simply must be litigated, whether to preserve important rights, protect significant proprietary interests, or set good precedent. The philosophical ideal (irrespective of the fiscal reality) is that these outcomes should not be affected or inhibited by the costs and burdens of discovery, and settlement should be driven by the perceived strength of the facts and legal arguments available to the parties. Discovery is a means to an end—an intertwined strategy and process that, to a great extent, can be routinized with authorized protocols to facilitate bringing about the right outcomes. Therefore, it is incumbent on those engaged in the practice of e-discovery to design and employ sound strategies and processes to facilitate those results.

which it is ordinarily maintained or in a reasonably usable form or forms; and [a] party need not produce the same electronically stored information in more than one form."

56. FED. R. CIV. P. 1.

CHAPTER 13

INITIAL DISCLOSURES

BY COURTNEY INGRAFFIA BARTON

This chapter looks closely at the duty to make certain unprompted initial disclosures related to electronically stored information in federal civil cases. The chapter begins with a detailed examination of the applicable rule. It then discusses issues of timing and scope of disclosure, as well as the duty to supplement, ending with a "Duty to Disclose" checklist.

1. Introduction

Except in the case of certain actions, parties to a lawsuit in federal court must, without waiting for a discovery request, provide certain initial disclosures to other parties. This is the duty to disclose imposed by Federal Rule of Civil Procedure 26(a) (see box).[1] On December 1, 2006, this rule was amended to make clear that these disclosures included electronically stored information (ESI). But how, exactly does this work in practice? What has to be disclosed, when does it have to be disclosed, and, how, practically, should it be disclosed? Even more importantly, what happens when there is a failure to disclose by either party?

1. This chapter examines the duty to disclose in federal court under Federal Rule of Civil Procedure 26(a)(1)(A). Some, but not all, state courts also impose a duty to disclose that may or may not follow the Federal Rules. For practice in state courts, please refer to that state's rules of civil procedure. A more detailed discussion of state practice may be found in chapter 3.

Although the duty to disclose is not a new concept under the amended Federal Rules of Civil Procedure, ESI poses some unique challenges to its implementation and fulfillment. Primarily, the duty to disclose requires early, prelitigation attention to sources of electronically stored information and coordination with a parties' duty to investigate as required by Rule 26(g).[2]

Rule 26(a)(1)(A)

(a) Required Disclosures.

(1) *Initial Disclosure.*

(A) In General. Except as exempted by Rule 26(a)(1)(B) or as otherwise stipulated or ordered by the court, a party must, without awaiting a discovery request, provide to the other parties:

(i) the name and, if known, the address and telephone number of each individual likely to have discoverable information—along with the subjects of that information—that the disclosing party may use to support its claims or defenses, unless the use would be solely for impeachment;

(ii) a copy—or a description by category and location—of all documents, electrically stored information, and tangible things that the disclosing party has in its possession, custody, or control and may use to support its claims or defenses, unless the use would be solely for impeachment;

(iii) a computation of each category of damages claimed by the disclosing party—who must also make available for inspection and copying as under Rule 34 the documents or other evidentiary material, unless privileged or protected from disclosure, on which each computation is based, including materials bearing on

2. See chapters 12 and 31 for more on litigation preparedness and Rule 26(g).

the nature and extent of injuries suffered; and

(iv) for inspection and copying as under Rule 34, any insurance agreement under which an insurance business may be liable to satisfy all or part of a possible judgment in the action or to indemnify or reimburse for payments made to satisfy the judgment.

Notes of Advisory Committee on 2006 amendments. *Note to Subdivision (a).* Rule 26(a)(1)(B) is amended to parallel Rule 34(a) by recognizing that a party must disclose electronically stored information as well as documents that it may use to support its claims or defenses. The term "electronically stored information" has the same broad meaning in Rule 26(a)(1) as in Rule 34(a). This amendment is consistent with the 1993 addition of Rule 26(a)(1)(B). The term "data compilations" is deleted as unnecessary because it is a subset of both documents and electronically stored information.

2. History of Rule 26(a)(1)(A)

A. History of the Rule 1993–2000

Rule 26(a) was added in 1993 as an attempt to curb litigation costs though an informal information-sharing process. The thought was that exchanging information early in the case would eliminate the paperwork involved in the formal request process and expedite resolution of the matter through early discovery. This had been the experience of several courts that had local disclosure requirements in place prior to the Rule 26 amendments.[3] Early disclosure, coupled with the Rule 26(f) conference, was thought to ease the discovery burden on the parties.

3. FED. R. CIV. P. 26(a) advisory committee's note to 1993 Amendment. For an interesting review of the initial disclosure process and a proposal for strengthening the purposes of Rule 26(a), see Final Report on the Joint Project of the American College of Trial Lawyers Task Force on Discovery and the Institute for the Advancement of the American Legal System (Mar. 11, 2009) [hereinafter Final Report].

The original rule allowed individual courts to opt out of the Rule 26(a) requirements, providing courts the ability to control the flow of information in their courts. This flexibility also comported with the directive to courts under the Civil Justice Reform Act of 1990 to experiment with policies that might be more efficient.[4] But by 2000, the Rules Committee noted that the inconsistency among district courts was creating confusion. The rule was therefore amended to "establish a nationally uniform practice." Such uniformity was also consistent with the Rules Enabling Act of 1934.[5] However, courts were still permitted to exempt parties from initial disclosures on a case-by-case basis or through stipulation of the parties.[6] The rule was also revised in 2000 to limit the scope of disclosures so that only the information that a party intended to use to support its claims and defenses had to be disclosed.

B. 2006 Amendments: Electronically stored information (ESI)

In 2006, the Federal Rules were amended to reflect that ESI was fair game for discovery. Rule 26(a) was amended accordingly so that currently, a party must provide a copy or provide a description by category and location of all ESI that it plans to use to support its claims or defenses.

When the rule applied primarily to paper, complying with Rule 26(a) was fairly straightforward. A party could either provide copies of paper documents or describe categories and locations, typically a witness's offices or a company warehouse.

With ESI, the duty to disclose has become much more of a challenge as ESI comes in many different formats and its exact location can often be a moving target. Providing copies of ESI requires that parties discuss the form of production with opposing counsel, and identifying, collecting, and copying ESI under the disclosure deadlines can create an enormous burden on the disclosing party.

The copying option under Rule 26(a) is therefore not practicable for ESI. Parties will most likely want to use the second option under Rule 26(a), which allows for a description of ESI by category or location. While this can be less burdensome than providing actual documents, it does require that counsel know and understand a client's information infrastructure, including its information technology (IT) systems, early in the case. While general knowledge

4. Final Report, *supra* note 3.

5. FED. R. CIV. P. 26(a) advisory committee's note to 2000 Amendment.

6. *Id.*

of this kind is required for a party to meet its obligations under Rule 26(f) to confer, Rule 26(a) requires a bit more specificity. For this reason, parties should work with their clients to prepare for litigation.[7] Through a comprehensive litigation preparedness plan and custodian interviews, counsel should be able to have all of the information they need to comply with the rule.

3. Timing and scope of disclosure

A. Timing

Initial disclosures occur after the parties have met and conferred under Rule 26(f), as provided by Rule 26(d): "A party may not seek discovery from any source before the parties have conferred as required by Rule 26(f)."[8] Typically the timing of the initial disclosures is governed by the requisite scheduling order that is provided to the court after the Rule 26(f) conference. Again, this is why it is crucial that a party understand its clients' information management systems and policies early in the case.

B. Scope: Information that is not reasonably accessible does not need to be disclosed

Rule 26(a) requires parties to provide information that the disclosing party may use for its claims and defenses. A prior version of the rule had required the "identification of potential evidence 'relevant to disputed facts alleged with particularity.'"[9] However, after 2000, "a party is no longer obligated to disclose witnesses or documents that it does not intend to use."[10] For purposes of Rule 26(a)(1) initial disclosures, then, a party need not disclose information it plans to claim is not reasonably accessible due to undue burden or cost under Rule 26(b)(2)(B):

> A party need not provide discovery of electronically stored information from sources that a party identifies as not reasonably accessible due to undue burden or cost. On motion to compel discovery or for a protective order, the party for whom discovery is sought must show that this information is not reasonably accessible due to undue burden or cost. If that showing is made, the court may nonetheless order discovery

7. See chapters 5 and 12.
8. FED. R. CIV. P. 26(d).
9. FED. R. CIV. P. 26(a) advisory committee's note to 1993 Amendment.
10. FED. R. CIV. P. 26(a) advisory committee's note to 2000 Amendment.

> from such sources if the requesting party shows good cause, considering the limitations of Rule 26(b)(2)(C). The court may specify conditions for discovery.

Although when responding to discovery a party must identify sources of ESI that are not reasonably accessible, this is not a requirement of Rule 26(a), because if in fact those sources are not reasonably accessible, a party will not know what information is contained therein. As such, if a party does not plan to search those sources, that material will not be used for a party's claims or defenses. However, to the extent a party is aware of these sources, they should be addressed at the Rule 26(f) conference.

C. Scope: Sufficiency of disclosures

As stated above, parties can disclose by copy (which can be difficult with ESI) or by describing the information by location and category. But how detailed does a party need to get? Although there is not a lot of guidance on this from the courts, the issue was addressed in *3M Co. v. Kanbar*,[11] where plaintiff 3M sued the defendant for infringement of two of its trademarks. The defendant moved to compel more specific initial disclosures after 3M had described its documents as follows:

> Such documents relate to the POST-IT trademark, the development, marketing, and sales of products offered under or in connection with the POST-IT trademark, 3M's enforcement of the trademark, the development, marketing, and sales of products offered under or in connection with the Canary Yellow trademark, and 3M's enforcement of the Canary Yellow trademark.[12]

The defendant's motion requested the court order the plaintiff to produce more specific descriptions with Bates numbers and alternatively, an order preventing plaintiff from using at trial, any information not specifically disclosed under Rule 26(a)(1). The defendant complained that the broad description above "made it impossible" to determine which documents plaintiff 3M planned to use.[13] 3M argued that its disclosures were adequate and that the defendant was improperly demanding a trial exhibit list. The court

11. 2007 U.S. Dist. LEXIS 45232 (N.D. Cal. 2007).
12. *Id.* at *3.
13. *Id.*

agreed, stating that "although [p]laintiff's disclosures were lacking in specificity, they were adequate to meet the requirements of Fed. R. Civ. P. 26. An itemized listing of each document is not required under Rule 26(a)."[14]

Citing the Advisory Committee Note, the court stated that "[u]nlike pretrial exhibit disclosure . . . the disclosing party need not provide an itemized listing of each document, item of electronically stored information, or tangible thing."[15] Although sufficiency of Rule 26(a) disclosures will be determined on a case-by-case basis, some courts may not be as generous as the *3M* court. Parties should therefore be aware of their obligations under the rule, which according to the Advisory Committee Notes require that disclosures must allow opposing parties

> (1) to make an informed decision concerning which documents might need to be examined, at least initially, and
> (2) to frame their document requests in a manner likely to avoid squabbles resulting from the working of the requests.[16]

For ESI, these requirements can only be sufficiently met when a party understands both the content and the sources of the information; and while a detailed description may not be required at this stage, an in-depth knowledge of a client's IT systems is required under Rule 26(g), which requires a party to certify that a disclosure has only been made "to the best of the person's knowledge, information, and belief formed after a reasonable inquiry,"[17] and, with respect to a disclosure, "it is complete and correct as of the time it is made"; Sanctions for a violation are mandatory under Rule 26(g).[18]

4. Duty to supplement and failure to disclose

Parties that fail to properly disclose run the risk that the evidence will not be admitted at trial. Rule 37(c)(1) provides that parties that failed to disclose are "not allowed to use that information or

14. *Id.* at *4.
15. *Id.*
16. FED. R. CIV. P. 26(a) advisory committee's note to 1993 Amendment.
17. FED. R. CIV. P. 26(g); *see also* Mancia v. Mayflower Textile Servs. Co., 253 F.R.D. 354 (D. Md. 2008); Qualcomm v. Broadcom, 2008 U.S. Dist. LEXIS 911 (S.D. Cal. Jan. 7, 2008), 2008 U.S. Dist. LEXIS 16897 (S.D. Cal. Mar. 5, 2008).
18. FED. R. CIV. P. 26(g)(3). For more on Rule 26(g), see chapter 31.

witness to supply evidence on a motion, at a hearing, or at a trial, unless the failure was substantially justified or is harmless."[19] The sanction, according to the Advisory Committee Note to Rule 37, provides "a strong inducement for disclosure of material that the disclosing party would expect to use as evidence at any hearing, including the trial, by the deadline."[20] It is crucial, then, that any newly discovered evidence be disclosed in a timely fashion. Indeed, supplementation of disclosures is required by Rule 26(e) if a party learns that its disclosures are materially incomplete or incorrect.[21]

Duty to Disclose Checklist

- Prepare client for litigation and learn about their information management systems.
- In state court, check to see if the rules of civil procedure require initial disclosures.
- In federal court, prepare for and participate in a Rule 26(f) conference.
- Ensure that scheduling order states the timing of initial disclosures.
- Prepare and serve initial disclosures.
- Supplement disclosures as necessary.

19. Fed. R. Civ. P. 37(c)(1).
20. EEOC v. Mazzanti, 2009 U.S. Dist. LEXIS 39350 (N.D. Miss. 2009).
21. Fed. R. Civ. P. 26(e).

CHAPTER 14

GATHERING, REVIEWING, AND PRODUCING ESI: AN EIGHT-STAGE PROCESS

By Scott Fischer, Richard E. Davis, and Michael D. Berman

In this chapter, two e-discovery consultants and a litigator provide clear step-by-step instructions on production of electronically stored information in response to discovery obligations—from initiating a litigation hold to final review before release. The chapter includes several illustrative graphics.

1. Overview

When the Federal Rules of Civil Procedure were amended in December 2006 to more specifically address e-discovery, the issue caused many a heart rate to jump within the legal community. Attorneys were forced to take the time to understand the ramifications of preservation, collection, culling, and production in the electronic age. And because electronic data contains many more "moving parts" than paper data, getting up to speed on the

Figure 14-1
The Unified Legal Data Discovery Lifecycle

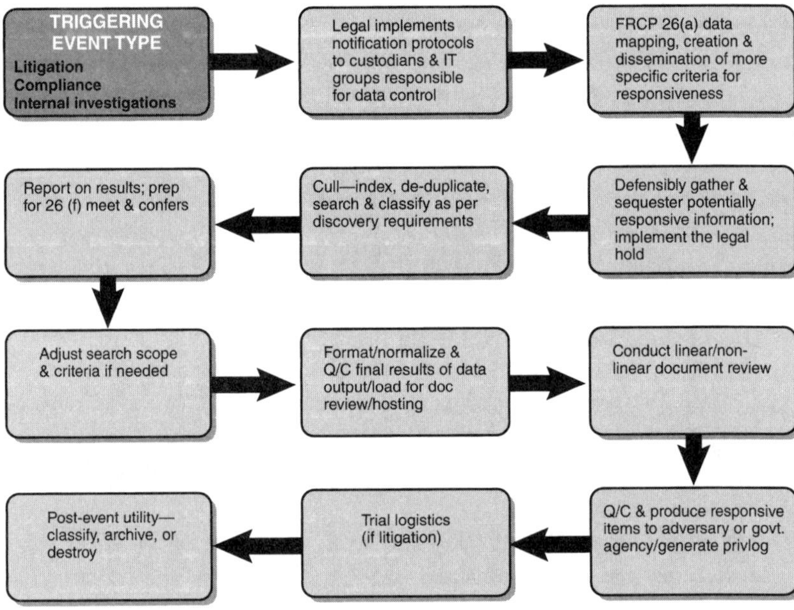

Courtesy of Litigation Logistics, LLC

process was formidable indeed. For this reason, we begin with a description of the e-discovery process itself.

From an information technology perspective, the critical stages shown in Figure 14-1 can be described as follows:

1. Counsel notifies the parties of their duty to preserve potentially relevant information; all normal deletion activities are suspended. The litigation hold is implemented.
2. Data mapping is initiated.
3. Responsive information is gathered, collected, and preserved.
4. Culling, indexing, and de-duplication are implemented.
5. Preparation for the 26(f) conference.
6. Processing for first review.
7. Processing for second review.
8. Second review and production.

2. Stages 1 and 2: The litigation hold and data mapping

A. The litigation hold

Because of its fragility and dispersal, electronically stored information (ESI) presents the possibility of inadvertent spoliation.

Paper evidence is final and static; what you see is truly what you get. A paper letter dated August 1, 2008, is generally accepted as such, barring different information arising from depositions, interrogatories, or witness testimony. While forgery is possible, under normal circumstances there is no way for the paper document to dispute the information that appears on its surface. Short of fire, flood, or mold, it cannot be inadvertently altered.

Electronic information differs markedly. It may be altered by the routine operation of an information technology system. Therefore, it is imperative that the e-discovery process begin with imposition of a litigation hold, preservation, and collection. The nonforensic steps in imposing and monitoring a litigation hold are discussed elsewhere.[1]

The first forensic step is to determine the location of responsive information. This process is known as "data mapping," and it is discussed in the following section. That may be followed by data capture, through bit-by-bit imaging or active file retrieval. Then, the preserved information must be sifted and winnowed to separate the wheat from the chaff. For example, imaging of a hard drive will capture a copy of the word processing program that is entirely superfluous to the matter at bar.

One of the most important aspects of gathering information in the litigation context is determining the likely location, form, and volume of responsive information. This is especially important when dealing with data-intensive, complex discovery in large organizations with equally complex organizational hierarchies. Understanding the organizational structure is often a time-consuming proposition, but well worth the effort.

B. Data mapping

While we break down the increasingly important factors of organizational dispersal and structure in the following categories, it is important to note that the list is by no means exhaustive. Data mapping involves obtaining the following:

1. *Organizational hierarchy.* One key tool is the organizational chart with the names and addresses of the different business units, and their heads and line manager roles and responsibilities within the business units. Human resources departments are often a good source of this

1. *See* chapter 8.

Figure 14-2
Organization Chart

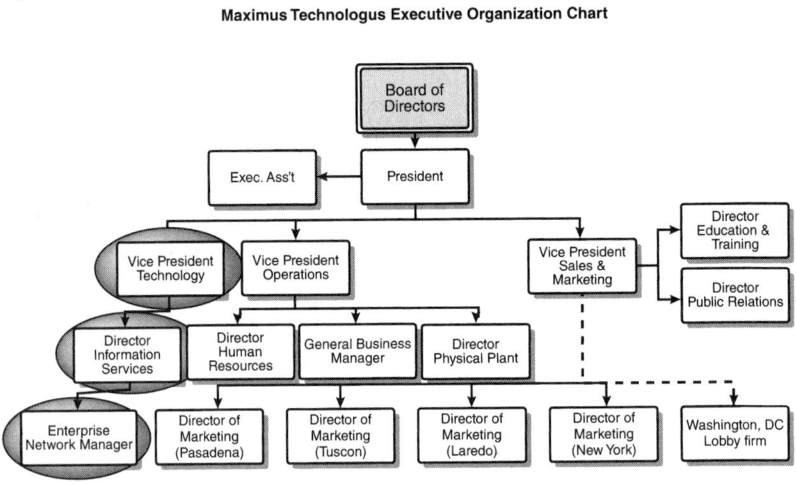

type of information. A typical organization chart may appear as in Figure 14-2.

2. *Geographic dispersal.* A data map will show the physical locations of relevant offices, plants, and facilities. This may highlight on-site and archival storage locations and additional legal issues, such as those presented by application of the European Data Protection Act.
3. *Logical and physical technology infrastructure.* A data map will itemize hardware and software platforms used by and within the enterprise and its different business units and present diagrams of various network topologies and schemas. The information technology arms of the various offices, divisions, or subsidiaries are probably the best source for this type of information.
4. *Departmental policies and procedures.* A key aspect of data maps is an inventory of internal policies and procedures such as document retention and computer usage policies.[2]
5. *Risk management protocols.* A final element of a comprehensive data map is the organization's data backup, storage, archival, restoration, and media rotation protocols.

For litigators, the data map will help in identifying the *sources* of potentially relevant information, including but not limited to the following:

2. *See* chapter 5.

Figure 14-3
Sample Data Map in Graphic Format

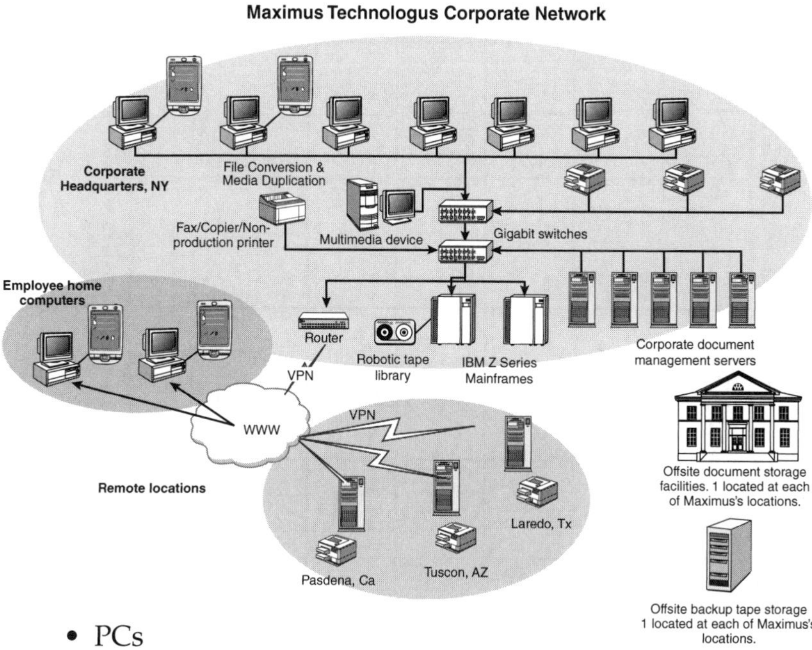

- PCs
- Servers
- Backup tapes
- PDAs
- BlackBerry servers
- Voice over Internet protocol (VOIP) systems
- USB drives and thumb drives
- Loose CDs and DVDs

Data maps can be represented graphically or by simply describing the above categories in general terms. Figures 14-3 and 14-4 represent two data map displays, one in graphic format, the other in tabular format.

3. Stage 3: Responsive information is gathered, collected, and preserved

Because electronic information is ephemeral and dynamic, and because it contains information within itself that can contradict the information on its surface, it is extremely important for counsel to understand the electronic infrastructure of their client and that of their adversary. The underlying importance of this is that the interaction of programs that create and manage electronic files and the hardware platforms on which they are stored creates

Figure 14-4
Sample Data Map in Tabular Format

Device Name	Device Description	IP Address	Location	Administrator	Operating System	CPU (MHz)	Memory (MB)	Manufacturer	Status	Files/ Records	Data Size
sql-sales-01	Database server	10.0.1.51	Row 1 Rack 2	Anna Misiec	Windows Server 2003, Data Center Edition	3	2048	Contoso, Ltd.	OK	45000343	NA
sql-sales-02	Database server	10.0.1.52	Row 1 Rack 2	Anna Misiec	Windows Server 2003, Data Center Edition	3.2	2560	Contoso, Ltd.	OK	34583458	NA
sql-sales-03	Database server	10.0.1.53	Row 1 Rack 2	Anna Misiec	Windows Server 2003, Data Center Edition	3	2048	Contoso, Ltd.	OK	3435554	NA
web-sales-01	web server	10.0.1.12	Row 1 Rack 1	Don Hall	Windows Server 2003, Web Edition	2.4	1536	Contoso, Ltd.	OK	345344543	NA
web-sales-02	web server	10.0.1.13	Row 1 Rack 1	Don Hall	Windows Server 2003, Web Edition	2	1024	Contoso, Ltd.	Unavailable	43535	NA
web-sales-03	web server	10.0.1.15	Row 1 Rack 1	Don Hall	Windows Server 2003, Web Edition	2.4	1024	Contoso, Ltd.	OK	3344534	.007TB
ftp-sales-01	FTP server	10.0.1.14	Row 1 Rack 1	Anna Misiec	Windows Server 2003, Standard Edition	2	1536	Contoso, Ltd.	OK	55645656	.05TB
filestore-sales-01	file server	10.0.1.5	Row 1 Rack 2	Anna Misiec	Windows Storage Server 2003	1.4	1024	Contoso, Ltd.	Unknown	45346645456	.07TB
filestore-sales-02	file server	10.0.1.6	Row 1 Rack 2	Anna Misiec	Windows Storage Server 2003	1.26	768	Contoso, Ltd.	OK	65546547654	27TB
rt-073-1000	1 Gb router	10.0.1.27	Row 1 Rack 1	Don Hall			512	A Datum Corporation	OK		34TB

"metadata." In the context of e-discovery, common file metadata information is represented by the following:

- *System metadata:* information generated and maintained by a computer operating system. Examples of system metadata fields include file creation, file modification, and file access times.
- *Application metadata:* information generated and maintained by specific computer software applications. Examples include the following fields: author, recipient, organization, title, and subject.
- *User metadata:* user-created information to describe files or aid in their classification, or to keep track of changes and comments in a document. Examples include document profile information that is required by a document management system such as Interwoven, Hummingbird, or Worldox, as well as tracked changes, comments, and spreadsheet formulas.

Metadata is critical to managing an evidentiary chain of custody and authenticating[3] electronic files. For example, two documents containing the same human-readable text, created at exactly the same time on two different systems, will have different metadata properties. They may even have different file sizes. The implications here are that electronic documents will inherit some of their metadata characteristics from the system (e.g., workstation, laptop, or PDA) they were created on. These characteristics can be used to authenticate a document's source and substantiate chain of custody protocols, or conversely to dispute the forensic soundness with which an item has been collected.

Some types of electronic file metadata can be altered with the slightest of manipulation. For instance, copying a file from one location to another can change a file's access date. Other types of metadata can be embedded in a file and can reveal information that contradicts what the document purports to be. For example, an electronic letter may be dated "August 1, 2008" on its surface, but the "date created" field contained within its structure might be stamped "September 15, 2008," and the "date last accessed" field may be stamped "December 1, 2008." And if the attorney reviews the letter on his or her computer on April 15, 2009, then the "date

3. *See* chapter 24.

last accessed" field automatically changes to "April 15, 2009." If the attorney's client wished, he or she could open the letter, backspace over the "1" in "August 1, 2008," and type in a "5." With just a few keystrokes, "August 1, 2008" would become "August 5, 2008." Unlike paper, on the surface the document's changes would be completely undetectable. But also unlike paper, the underlying metadata would reveal the changes.

This leads to the requirement of sound preservation and collection techniques. Before *Zubulake* and the December 2006 amendments to the Federal Rules of Civil Procedure, attorneys often paid scant attention to issues of proper collection of electronic evidence and metadata preservation. *Zubulake* and the December 2006 rules[4] emphasized the importance and fragility of electronic information, including metadata, and that proper preservation was expected.

Because the appearance of electronic documents can be changed so easily, and because of the volatile nature of metadata, methods had to be found that could freeze the preservable information in place so that an exact snapshot, or copy, could be created of the ESI and metadata. This is called a "forensic copy" or "mirror image," and it is an exact byte-by-byte duplicate of the original information, in which the source information and metadata have been preserved exactly as they exist on the system, and which was obtained by a methodology that can be documented and defended at a court hearing. Responsive electronic evidence must be forensically frozen in time so that its metadata—the data about the data[5]—is not compromised.

In order to facilitate this process, once there is a reasonable anticipation of litigation, an attorney must alert the client to immediately cease any and all procedures that may delete or alter any electronic files related to the case. This obligation is not limited to simply ensuring that documents are not deleted or visibly altered; it extends to the metadata about the document itself. For example, a key metadata field is "date last accessed." The litigation hold must ensure that critical documents are not opened; the mere act of opening a Word document, for example, will change the "date last accessed," thus altering the metadata.

It is important that the documents and files in question be preserved as soon as possible, for two primary reasons. First, preservation will ensure that metadata, as well as deleted and fragmented

4. For an overview of the Federal Rules, see chapter 2.

5. For a more comprehensive discussion of metadata, see chapter 6.

data, is not compromised. Second, it can be extremely burdensome for a business to have its active systems under a continuing litigation hold; only after the ESI is properly copied and preserved can the business once again use its information systems without restriction, and, in effect, get back to work.

4. Stage 3 (continued): Preservation and collection—Methodologies

There are two distinct methods of forensic collection and preservation: (1) bit-by-bit or byte-by-byte capture and (2) active file retrieval.

A. Bit-by-bit capture

With a bit-by-bit[6] capture (also called "byte-by-byte," "forensic imaging," or a "mirror image"), the entire file server, workstation, or attached storage device is copied, including empty and slack space, as well as deleted data. "Empty space" is space on a drive that has not yet been utilized for document storage. "Slack space" is space on the drive that has been designated for overwriting, but upon which no new data has yet been written. "Deleted data" is data that a user has deleted, but that has not been purged or overwritten by the computer.

Forensic imaging provides a complete copy of the storage device, and is particularly useful in preserving deleted information for later recovery. It is important to remember that the deletion process in a Windows environment does not actually delete the data in question, but rather makes the location on the device (the "slack space") available for new data to be written. Therefore, if one has a complete, forensic copy of a drive, a technician can analyze the "slack space" on the drive for fragments of previously deleted documents. If the computer has not chosen that location for new data and randomly overwritten it, the older, deleted information will still be on the drive and can be restored.

Forensic imaging may be very useful on, for example, workstations and laptops. Assume that a divorcing spouse deleted email related to adultery or a commercial litigant deleted prior drafts of a contract that would show an unfavorable interpretation of a key clause. The deleted data might still reside on a hard drive and be recoverable. Absent prompt creation of a forensic image, however,

6. Generally speaking, a "bit" is the smallest measure of data on the computer's media. Bits are clustered into bytes.

the computer may overwrite that data. Once a forensic image is created, the data are preserved and cannot be later erased.

Bit-by-bit capture of servers, as opposed to workstations or laptops, is often not a viable option, for a variety of reasons. First, file servers must be powered down for an effective forensic copy to be made. This causes a major disruption of business for the owner of the server. In many cases, the loss of business resulting from the powering down of a critical server makes the process simply too burdensome to consider.

More ominously, servers often run for months, or even years, without being powered down. Not infrequently, technicians find to their dismay that older servers, once powered down, are not capable of being powered back up. One must consider whether the risk is worth the effort.

Additionally, as discussed above, many servers use what is called a "redundant array of independent disks" (RAID) configuration to increase the reliability and integrity of data stored on a server. This configuration requires multiple hard disks that share similar information about the files stored on the server so that if one of the server's disks fails, the data is not lost. Unlike the single-file storage model that is employed by laptops and desktop computers, RAID systems create greater fault tolerance and redundancy by spreading data across multiple disks. This effectively means that data is constantly being overwritten in free and slack spaces vacated by files that previously occupied that space. While fault tolerance is achieved, in RAID configurations the way that a system writes data to the hard disks greatly reduces the likelihood that the free and slack spaces, which are often the sources of deleted file information in other media, can be retrieved or imaged. In a RAID configuration a single file's slack space information may exist in so many different locations that reconstruction is difficult to perform. This applies to Exchange servers as well, because data is stored in myriad locations throughout the server, making reassembly problematic.

And finally, bit-by-bit capture is only the first step in acquiring the data. After the bit-by-bit capture is completed, file culling must be performed to retrieve the documents responsive to the discovery request, and exclude superfluous pieces of information. Because a bit-by-bit capture copies an entire drive, the large volume of servers makes this costly. The forensic vendor, having captured the images, must transport them to its lab, and then run file type and keyword searches to narrow down and extract the relevant files from the much larger nonresponsive ocean of data.

Stand-alone PCs and laptops, however, are prime candidates for forensic imaging when called for by applicable legal principles. First, they can be powered down easily without disruption to anyone but the single user. Second, data is stored in files in a foldered environment, so that reconstruction of fragmented data is relatively simple. And third, the drives are generally smaller and simpler, and hence require much less time to image.

Bit-by-bit capture is necessary when the deletion or spoliation of evidence could be an issue. If a party believes that evidence has been deleted, either deliberately or inadvertently, then a forensic examination of a forensic copy may reveal deleted information. However, most cases do not require such a level of detail.[7]

B. Active file retrieval

Active file retrieval is the process in which all the active files within the broad boundaries of a potential litigation request are collected with all metadata information preserved intact. It is particularly well suited to preservation of servers; however, its one most significant shortcoming is that it does not make a bit-by-bit copy and will not preserve deleted or fragmented data, or data in slack space.

There are many programs that claim to perform forensically sound active file retrieval, but it is critical that users understand the underlying methodologies utilized and are able to explain the features in court. The fundamental issue is the way the programs handle metadata. In a forensic preservation, absent agreement to the contrary, it may be critical that none of the file history metadata fields be affected by the preservation software. This applies particularly to the "date last accessed," "date modified," and "date created" fields. Individuals who perform active file retrieval must ensure that methods are in place to prevent changes to these three fields. For this reason, forensic specialists will make use of "write blocking" software or hardware, which are programs and/or devices that prevent files from being touched while they are copied to

7. It is very helpful for all parties to discuss the method of preservation prior to, or at the very beginning of, litigation to avoid costly early efforts and arguments down the road. For example, if all parties agree that there are no issues of improperly deleted information, then the more costly and problematic process of bit-by-bit capture can be avoided.

another location. They do this by permitting read commands to pass, but preventing, or "blocking," write commands from affecting the files in question.

Active file retrieval also guarantees a much smaller document universe for searching and culling. Whereas a bit-by-bit image capture acquires the entire universe (including program files, other active files, and deleted files on hard drive segments that have not been overwritten), active file retrieval is performed within the requested parameters. Consequently, if there is no need to preserve deleted files, the next stage of the process, the culling by keyword and custodian, is performed against a much smaller target area. And because cost is based on the volume of ESI, the cost of processing actively captured ESI can be significantly less.

C. Cost differential between bit-by-bit image capture and active file retrieval

Active file retrieval is far less costly than bit-by-bit capture. Table 14-1 shows a cost-by-cost comparison of the two approaches. In this example we are capturing five custodians whose data is located on one Microsoft Exchange server, one Microsoft Windows file server, and five workstations. Each file server is 1TB (terabyte); each workstation is 250GB.

In the first example, bit-by-bit capture, the entire device has been copied, thereby requiring a second stage for searching the universe of data for responsive information. In the second example, active file retrieval, discovery parameters are being applied during the retrieval of responsive files. Therefore, the second stage for searching required in bit-by-bit capture is not necessary.

Because of the cost, the operational disruptions involved in "taking down" servers, and the fact that it is unlikely to find deleted, responsive data on servers due to the rapid exchange of data, active file capture is the generally preferred technique for preservation of information on servers. In actuality, it is essentially creating a backup of the server's active data.

5. Stage 4: Culling, de-duplication, and indexing

Bit-by-bit image capture and, to a lesser degree, active file retrieval will result in a large data universe. Much of the preserved data will, however, be outside the scope of the duty to preserve or produce ESI. This is especially true for bit-by-bit image capture because system files and program files will be copied during

Table 14-1 **Forensic File Collection Cost Comparison**			
Bit-by-Bit Image Capture—Per GB and Hourly Basis (as of January 2010)			
Item	Action Comment	Item Cost	Total Cost
Microsoft Exchange Server	Imaging not appropriate	N/A	N/A
Windows File Server—non-RAID	Full bit-by-bit image capture	$2,000 + 6 hours @ $300/hour	$3,800
5 workstations	Full bit-by-bit image capture	$500 per workstation + 1 hour @ $300/hour	$3,000
Keyword searching of 3.25TB of data	Search the acquired data for responsive text and/or metadata	$35 per GB	$113,750
Total for imaging and file retrieval			$120,550
Active File Retrieval			
Item	Action Comment	Item Cost	Total Cost
Microsoft Exchange Server	Technician time to perform action	7 hours @ $300/hour	$2,100
Windows File Server	Technician time to perform action	7 hours @ $300/hour	$2,100
5 workstations	Technician time to perform action	1 hour @ $300/ hour for 5 computers	$1,500
Total for file collection			$5,700

the preservation process. It is important to reduce the volume of material by excluding unnecessary information, because processing and review of irrelevant information are wasteful and costly, while also maintaining the original set to guard against spoliation allegations.

For this reason, the next step is a culling process to exclude nonresponsive data, locate potentially responsive information, and create a new information set that will be used in later stages of the litigation. To give one example, ESI experts often maintain file lists generated by the National Institute of Standards (NIST). These lists include known system file types that are typically generated by computer systems and thereby likely to be designated as nonresponsive to a discovery request. This process of removing known nonresponsive file types is termed "de-NISTing." Typical examples of "de-NISTed" information include software programs such as Windows and Adobe Reader, which may be removed from the preserved data in an automated culling process.

The litigation-support marketplace offers many high-speed indexing programs specifically designed to provide immediate access to data sets, allowing attorneys to access the preserved data in order to build a keyword and key custodian list in preparation for the culling process. Companies such as DT Search, EMC Kazeon/SourceOne, Clearwell, Index Engines, and others offer extremely efficient indexing products to the vendor community, which may then provide fast access to the data in a searchable and reviewable format.[8] Some of the tools offer additional features such as tagging,[9] email threading,[10] and concept searching.[11]

The preprocessing step allows attorneys to browse through the preserved and collected data to assist with developing and testing the keywords and date filters to ascertain the volume of data that will be generated with a particular keyword list and, if necessary, make modifications to the search. It also allows them to identify any false positives in advance so that the search can be modified to significantly reduce the volume of data to be processed.

---

8. For a more comprehensive discussion of indexing as it applies to backup tapes, see chapter 26.

9. Tagging is used to indicate that a specific piece of information is related to a specified legal issue. For example, each email that relates to the issue of primary negligence could be tagged as such, and then the database can be searched to retrieve all tags related to that issue.

10. For a discussion of email strings, or threads, see chapter 15. When a software tool performs email threading, it links all messages in a string or thread of email.

11. For a more comprehensive discussion of concept searching, see chapters 20 and 21.

Data de-duplication is an important step to facilitate document review cost containment. It is the process of removing duplicate items from a document collection before it is reviewed. With loose electronic files, de-duplication is typically accomplished by creating a "file fingerprint" or "hash value" that is unique to the file itself. This alphanumeric hash value is generated by applying an algorithm to the metadata and data contained in the file. Hash values (MD-5 or SHA-1) are accepted by courts as unique document identifiers and a defensible basis for de-duplication.[12] Hash values are typically generated by applying the hash algorithm to a combination of metadata fields such as "To," "From," "CC," "BCC," "Date sent," "Date received," and "Subject." If documents have the same hash value, they are duplicates and only one copy need be produced for review.

Once the keyword terms, date filters, and custodians are determined by counsel,[13] the attorneys provide this information to the vendor and the vendor runs the searches. This culling process is used to gather the potentially responsive documents and eliminate unnecessary files and documents from the to-be-created attorney-review set. ESI responsive to the searches is extracted from the universe of preserved data and a new data set is created.

6. Stage 5: Processing for first review

A. Formatting data for review with automated litigation support tools

Up to this point, all of the electronic data has been collected in its original or "native" format. Loose files are preserved and culled in the format in which they were created. For example, a Word document is in Microsoft Word format, an Excel file is in Microsoft Excel format, and a WordPerfect file is in WordPerfect format.[14]

Email is more problematic. Different collection methods or export processes will result in email files being generated in different formats. Some present Outlook emails as hypertext markup, or "html," files, with the attachments stored in separate directories;

12. For a description of hash values, see R. Losey, *Hash: The New Bates Stamp*, 12 J. Tech. L. & Pol'y 1 (2007).

13. For a discussion of searching ESI, see chapters 20 and 21. For a discussion of keyword negotiations in Rule 26(f) conferences, see chapter 19.

14. A native file's format is absolute; even if the file extension is changed, the vendor's software will pull the file information from the document header itself and ignore the file extension.

some present Outlook emails in a proprietary Microsoft message format called ".msg," with the email and its attachment in one file; still others present Outlook emails in an ".eml" format, which is an Outlook Express format that also maintains the email and its attachment in one file. And still others present Outlook files in their classic personal storage table (PST).[15] Lotus Notes mail files are presented in a different format known as NSF. IBM Lotus Notes stores email information in multiple tables, each of which contains data that may be presented in a "view." The way one views email in Lotus Notes is highly customizable.

For this reason, it is imperative that all parties to a litigation discovery initiative understand the nature and character of the data to be collected and the implications of the chosen data collection methodology well before collection and processing are under way so that decisions made at the Rule 26(f) conference do not have undesired consequences. Once collected, it will be necessary for the information to be processed for the specific litigation support tools that will be employed in the document review process. This processing involves creating a "load file." At that point the document review should go in one of two directions: (1) online native and/or TIFF review through simple tagging; or (2) in-house native and/or TIFF review for advanced tagging.

B. Stage 5 (continued): Document review workflow

Online native review is conducted when document culling yields a large volume of documents for review. Many law firms do not have an internal infrastructure capable of a timely review of hundreds of thousands, or even millions, of pages. Consider the following hypothetical:

Let us imagine that the Smith firm conducted an active file retrieval of its client's servers and workstations for a class action litigation. Smith's client is a large pharmaceutical company and the case involves an initial collection of 1,000,000 documents totaling 200GB. The documents are a combination of email, Adobe PDF files, Microsoft Word documents, Microsoft Excel spreadsheets,

15. Microsoft Outlook can also create "OST" files. According to Microsoft, files with the .ost extension are used to keep a local copy of an exchange mailbox on a computer. The OST file synchronizes with the network when the computer is connected to the network. See Microsoft, Create an Offline Folder File (.ost), http://office.microsoft.com/en-us/outlook/HP052422611033.aspx.

Microsoft PowerPoint presentations, drawings, and audio files. The Smith attorneys must review the documents for privilege and responsiveness.

The Smith firm uses AD Summation iBlaze, a popular document review tool; however, the law firm lacks sufficient storage capacity, and Summation iBlaze is not designed to handle native document productions of this size. And considering that the Smith firm does not possess a very fast network to begin with, it is clear that the firm's internal infrastructure cannot handle such a volume.

The firm could decide to process the files to convert the native files to TIFF images, which would speed up the document review; however, TIFF review is far more costly than native review, and is usually used for the final production set. Smith must decide if it is worth converting 1,000,000 documents to TIFF when only 100,000 will be necessary for production.

Given these options, the Smith firm might turn to an online solution, sometimes called an application service provider (ASP). Online-review products provide a hosted solution to the law firm for a set-up fee and monthly charge based on volume. The documents are loaded in their native state onto the hosting company's more powerful infrastructure, where highly efficient, often proprietary, software packages index the text and metadata of the documents. Attorneys may then log into the hosting company via a secure Internet connection, where they are presented with very simple review screens for privilege and relevancy reviews. Firms use such online tools to narrow the document collection further before performing full processing of the final document set for production to the other side.

In addition to the faster and more comprehensive search capabilities, hosted solutions offer 24/7 support and a full-time staff to perform any required ancillary service, such as document loading or burning data to removable media.

Table 14-2 shows a sample of the cost of online native or TIFF review.

Attorneys can review the documents linearly, assessing each document individually, or they may run keyword or metadata searches on the documents. They may then tag the documents according to privilege, issues, and relevance. When they are finished, the hosting vendor will export the tagged documents in native format for final processing. A 200GB preservation may be reduced by 90 percent following the first pass review. The resulting

Table 14-2 Sample Cost of Online Native or TIFF Review (as of January 2010)			
Item	**Action Comment**	**Item Cost**	**Total Cost**
Processing of data for online review, including loading of data	Performs full-text and metadata extraction; loads natives into easily reviewable format	200GB @ $400 per GB	$80,000
Licenses for online review	10 users for two months	$100 per user per month	$2,000
Total			$82,000

hypothetical data set will be reduced to 100,000 documents and 20GB, a volume that is suited to the law firm's in-house hardware and software.

7. Stage 6: Preparation for the 26(f) conference

The Rule 26(f) conference, including needed preparation, is discussed in chapter 19 of this book. It will not be further discussed in this chapter.

8. Stage 7: Preparation for second review

The second review is a process that is akin to document review in the days of paper-based litigation. The selected ESI is provided to the law firm with a load file and imported into a review platform. Table 14-3 shows sample costs.

Typically, law firms request TIFF conversion as well for the second review, because most document productions are in TIFF, rather than native, format. TIFF production allows for Bates stamping and redactions. Native production does not support any form of stamping or endorsement, and cannot be redacted. The cost for TIFF production is shown in Table 14-4.

What the law firm receives at this juncture is a collection of ESI that has been narrowed down from the original collection, together with the load file that permits copying of the ESI to an in-house software program for review by attorneys and legal assistants. This is a mechanical or technical process performed by a vendor.

Table 14-3
Cost of Processing for Second Review—
Natives Only (as of January 2010)

Item	Action Comment	Item Cost	Total Cost
Extract native files, including separation of emails and attachments, metadata extraction, full-text extraction, OCR of nontext native files, and load file for AD Summation iBlaze	20GB of data	20GB @ $500	$10,000
Total			$10,000

Table 14-4
Cost of Processing for Second Review—
Natives and Tiffs (as of January 2010)

Item	Action Comment	Item Cost	Total Cost
Extract native files, including separation of emails and attachments, metadata extraction, full-text extraction, OCR of nontext native files, TIFF conversion, and load file for AD Summation iBlaze	20GB of data	20GB @ $1,000	$20,000
Total			$20,000

9. Stage 8: Second review and production

Second, or final, review and production is where the vendor's role is markedly reduced or ends and counsel's traditional "document review" role predominates. The vendor provides the law firm with the final results of the preservation, collection, processing, and culling process, and a load file that permits the law firm to load the produced electronic information into its internal document review platform, such as Concordance or Summation, where the attorneys perform their final reviews, redact where necessary, tag documents as privileged or nonresponsive, issue-code them, and determine what endorsements, such as "confidential," "subject to protective order," or "attorneys' eyes only," are required.

The document review software generates a "production set" that is then provided to opposing counsel. To the extent the law firm has the infrastructure and staff to support document productions to requesting parties, the firm may produce them internally. Otherwise the final production process may be handled by a vendor. Most commonly, smaller productions are produced in-house, while larger ones (exceeding 10,000 pages) are sent out to a vendor.

10. Summary

Litigation attorneys need not be forensic experts any more than they need to be practitioners in any other technical field presented in litigation. It is, however, important to learn the vocabulary and understand the forensic stages that are involved in preserving and producing ESI. When, for example, there is a legal requirement to preserve information, the technical concepts of network architecture, data mapping, mirror-imaging, and active capture, applied to active, deleted, and disaster recovery data, provide a road map for a cost-effective approach that satisfies legal and ethical obligations.

PART FIVE

PRIVILEGE AND WAIVER ISSUES IN E-DISCOVERY

CHAPTER 15

PRIVILEGE LOGS AND EMAIL CHAINS

BY MICHAEL D. BERMAN
AND MELISSA E. GOLDMEIER

Email chains present thorny problems for legal professionals seeking to protect privilege claims through privilege logs. Some approaches to email logging can result in enormous expense, while less expensive alternatives can present a risk of waiver. In this chapter, the authors look at both extremes, propose a middle-ground solution, and end with practice tips.

1. The requirement of a privilege log

The privilege log is a venerable, necessary, and oft-used tool. It is sometimes called a "Vaughn index," having received that name from the seminal decision in *Vaughn v. Rosen*.[1] The Vaughn index was developed in response to *EPA v. Mink*,[2] and is used as a substitute for the production of documents for in-camera review. It is intended to provide a discovering party with sufficient information to evaluate a claim of privilege or work-product protection, and to allow a court to rule on a claim of privilege without having to review the allegedly protected document itself.[3] In short, its

1. 484 F.2d 820 (D.C. Cir. 1973).
2. 410 U.S. 73 (1973).
3. P. GRIMM, ET AL., DISCOVERY PROBLEMS AND THEIR SOLUTIONS 89 (ABA 2d ed. 2009) (citations omitted).

purpose is to expedite and simplify evaluation of, and litigation over, privilege[4] issues.

Under *Vaughn*, when a party refuses to disclose information pursuant to a claim of privilege, it must provide a detailed explanation of the facts supporting nondisclosure. Conclusory and generalized allegations are not acceptable. *Vaughn* mandated "a relatively detailed analysis in manageable segments" that "could ordinarily be composed without excessive reference to the actual language of the document." The Vaughn index, however, does "not have to contain factual descriptions that if made in public would compromise the secret nature of the information." This indexing system is intended to permit courts to examine and rule on each element of the itemized list.[5]

Federal Rule of Civil Procedure 26(b)(5)(A) formalized the privilege log doctrine:

> (A) *Information Withheld.* When a party withholds information otherwise discoverable by claiming that the information is privileged or subject to protection as trial-preparation material, the party must:
> (i) expressly make the claim; and
> (ii) describe the nature of the documents, communications, or tangible things not produced or disclosed—and do so in a manner that, without revealing information itself privileged or protected, will enable other parties to assess the claim.

Subsection (b)(5)(A) was added in the 1993 amendments to the Federal Rules. The Committee Notes state one of its primary purposes: "Providing information pertinent to the applicability of the privilege or protection should reduce the need for in camera examination of the documents."

Rule 26(b)(5)(A), however, does not specify the method for effectuating that purpose. The Committee Notes state: "The rule does not attempt to define for each case what information must be provided when a party asserts a claim of privilege of work product protection." The Note states that the rule provides for flexibility

4. For ease of reference, and at the risk of oversimplification, the work-product doctrine is subsumed in the term "privilege" in this chapter.

5. The amount of detail necessary to include in a proper Vaughn index was discussed in *Ethyl Corp. v. EPA*, 25 F.3d 1241, 1245 (4th Cir. 1994).

in the privilege log: "Details concerning time, persons, general subject matter, etc., may be appropriate if only a few items are withheld, but may be unduly burdensome when voluminous documents are claimed to be privileged or protected, particularly if the items can be described by categories."

Long before electronically stored information (ESI) emerged, many disputes arose over the adequacy of privilege logs and a body of case law developed addressing how to assert that documents were protected against disclosure.[6]As production of ESI became more frequent, its unique attributes presented new challenges to the old concept. For example, how should privileged metadata be described on a privilege log? How can privilege be protected in an era of terabytes of information?[7]

Because of the ubiquitous presence of email in litigation, email "strands" or "chains" soon became central to privilege issues.[8] Itemization of email in privilege logs has been "frequently discussed in continuing legal education seminars and among lawyers attempting to deal with electronic discovery issues."[9] For example,

---

6. *E.g.*, United States v. Chevron Texaco Corp., 241 F.Supp.2d 1065, 1070, 1078, 1083 n. 15 (N.D.Cal. Mar. 25, 2002)("Privilege disputes have generated a hearty body of case law. . . . There are three distinct apparently unrelated documents that comprise number 48. However, Chevron's privilege log describes only the first document. . . . Number 48 of the log makes no reference to the other two documents. . . ."), amending prior decision, 241 F.Supp.2d 1065 (N.D.Cal. Jun. 18, 2002), subsequent opinion adopting magistrate's report, 241 F.Supp.2d 1065 (N.D.Cal. Sept. 12, 2002); Williams v. Sprint/United Mgmt., 230 F.R.D. 640, 653 (D. Kan. 2005), subsequent opinion, 2006 U.S. Dist. LEXIS 65485, *19-20 (sanction of waiver too harsh, given the totality of the circumstances, for Defendant's failure to assert attorney-client privilege over documents that were similar to inadvertently produced documents), subsequent opinion, 2006 U.S. Dist. LEXIS 81574, *11 (discussing the factors the Court considers when deciding whether to order a party to return inadvertently produced privilege documents to the producing party), remanded, 2007 U.S. Dist. LEXIS 768, *19 (case remanded to a magistrate judge to decide whether a party's intentional but mistaken disclosure of a privileged document constitutes waiver as to redacted portions of that document); *see generally* GRIMM, *supra* note 3, at 88–92.

7. *See, e.g.*, FED. R. EVID. 502; William A. Gross Constr. Assocs., Inc. v. Am. Mfrs. Mut. Ins. Co., 256 F.R.D. 134 (S.D.N.Y. 2009); Victor Stanley, Inc. v. Creative Pipe, Inc. (*Victor Stanley I*), 250 F.R.D. 251 (D. Md. 2008); Hopson v. Mayor & City Council of Balt., 232 F.R.D. 228 (D. Md. 2005).

8. *See, e.g.*, Gregory S. Kaufman & Jennifer M. Moore, *Discovery Can Get Tangled Up in "Strings,"* NAT'L. L.J. (2006).

9. Rhoads Indus., Inc. v. Bldg. Materials Corp. of Am. (*Rhoads II*), 2008 U.S. Dist. LEXIS 96404, at *8 (E.D. Pa. 2008).

Discovery Guideline 10.d.v of the U.S. District Court for the District of Maryland suggests: "The parties are encouraged to confer and reach agreement regarding how to assert privilege/protection claims with respect to Email 'chains' or 'strings,' and if unable to do so, to bring to the attention of the Court their disagreement for prompt resolution."

2. Differing schools of thought regarding email chains or strands present a dilemma to practitioners: Substantial cost versus risk of waiver

There are two diametrically opposed schools of thought, with at least one middle-ground approach. On the one hand, there is authority that every email and attachment in a chain generally needs to be described separately. On the opposite end, it is asserted that only the chain itself need be described in a privilege log, at least if the underlying, nonprivileged information is both responsive to discovery requests and disclosed. In the middle, courts and commentators have looked at a nuanced, tailored approach. Not fully considered in this context, however, has been a rules-based, "categorical" approach.[10]

The preliminary step in understanding the problem is to define an "email chain," "thread," or "email strand." "[A]n e-mail strand (or string) occurs where the printed e-mail actually consists of more than one message, usually formatted with the most recent message first."[11] An email chain or strand is "a series of email mes-

10. For a description of the categorical approach, see GRIMM, *supra* note 3, at 90. Stated directly, "[a]nother approach is for parties to agree that certain categories of documents that are unquestionably privileged, such as communications between inside and outside counsel, need not be identified on a privilege log or may be identified in an abbreviated way." Jeanne Thomas, David D. Cross & Courtney Barton, *Reducing the Costs of Privilege Reviews and Logs*, NAT'L L.J., Mar. 23, 2009, http://www.crowell.com/documents/Reducing-the-costs-of-privilege-reviews-and-logs.pdf. *See also* J. Facciola & J. Redgrave, *Asserting and Challenging Privilege Claims in Modern Litigation*, 4 FED. CTS. L. REV. 19 (2009) (rules-based, categorical approach); THE SEDONA CONFERENCE, THE SEDONA PRINCIPLES: ADDRESSING ELECTRONIC DOCUMENT PRODUCTION 24 (2d ed. 2007).

11. *In re* Universal Serv. Fund Tel. Billing Practices Litigation, 232 F.R.D. 669, 671 n. 2 (D. Kan. 2005). This chapter addresses how email chains or strands that are privileged should be described on a privilege log. It does not address the situation, mentioned in *Rhoads Industries, Inc. v. Building Materials Corp. of America* (*Rhoads I*), 2008 U.S. Dist. LEXIS 9333, at *9 (E.D. Pa. 2008), *subsequent opinion*, 2008 U.S. Dist. LEXIS 96404 (*Rhoads II*) (E.D. Pa. 2008), where a privileged communication "creeps" into an email chain and remains unnoticed when a privilege log

sages by and between various individuals."[12] Often, one or more emails in the chain contain attachments, such as word processing documents or spreadsheets. In short, an email chain occurs when sequentially created electronic communications and documents are tied together.[13]

If an email chain is viewed as a single document, listing only the most recent email on a privilege log should comply with Rule 26(b)(5)(A). On the other hand, the chain may be viewed as a mixture of multiple privileged and unprivileged documents that must be separately logged.[14]

The impact of the "single v. multiple" document decision has been starkly described by the courts. "[A]s a practical matter, requiring each e-mail within a strand to be listed separately on a privilege log is a laborious, time-intensive task for counsel. And, of course, that task adds considerable expense for the clients involved. . . ."[15] In short, a litigant must either choose to expend considerable resources on an email-by-email privilege log, or risk waiver of the privilege by failure to "describe the nature" of the privileged documents on the log.

3. The "separate document, separate listing" solution to avoid "stealth" claims of privilege

In *In re Universal Service Fund Telephone Billing Practices Litigation*,[16] the U.S. District Court for the District of Kansas commendably and

---

is prepared. That situation is one for the application of FRE 502. Nor does this chapter address the issue of keyword searches to locate privileged documents, discussed in *Rhoads, Victor Stanley I, William A. Gross Construction*, and cases cited therein. For a discussion of search methodology, see chapters 20 and 21.

12. *See Rhoads II*, 2008 U.S. Dist. LEXIS 96404, at *2; Facciola & Redgrave, *supra* note 10, at 36, 38.

13. P. RICE, ELECTRONIC EVIDENCE: LAW AND PRACTICE 252–53 (ABA 2d ed. 2008).

14. *E.g.*, Kaufman & Moore, *supra* note 8.

15. *In re* Universal Serv. Fund Tel. Billing Practices Litig., 232 F.R.D. 669, 674 (D. Kan. 2005); *accord* Muro v. Target Corp., 243 F.R.D. 301, 307 n.5 (N.D. Ill. 2007); *Rhoads II*, 2008 U.S. Dist. LEXIS 96404, at *3 n.1. "Although there are some technical solutions to help automate the creation of privilege logs, there currently is no automated or other technical solution for logging distinct e-mails within an e-mail chain. Doing this manually is extremely tedious and time-consuming, and the costs can be substantial." Thomas, Cross & Barton, *supra* note 10.

16. 232 F.R.D. at 671 n.2; *accord* Naik v. Boehringer-Ingelheim Pharms., Inc., 2008 U.S. Dist. LEXIS 47567 (N.D. Ill 2008) (requiring an email privilege log to list each separate document, stating: "A claim of privilege cannot be a blanket claim but

cautiously entered the fray, concluding that an itemized log is preferable. AT&T had submitted a privilege log, and it argued that an email chain is analogous to a conversation, and should be treated as a single document, with only the most recent email listed on the privilege log.

The court, noting that ESI is a rapidly evolving area in which courts and litigants have little guidance, disagreed. It deemed AT&T's decision, "although arguably reasonable, very risky." The court rejected AT&T's single document theory for several reasons. Unpersuaded by the authorities on which AT&T relied, the court believed that the well-established case law on itemized privilege logs provided superior guidance in this arena. Most importantly, the court expressed concern that "the obvious and unavoidable byproduct of the rule advanced by AT&T would be stealth claims of privilege which, by their very nature, could never be the subject of a meaningful challenge by opposing counsel or actual scrutiny by a judge; this in turn, would render Fed.R.Civ.P. 26(b)(5) a nullity."[17]

The court, understandably and properly, stopped short of a bright line rule and "strongly encourage[d]" that counsel "list each

---

must be made and established on a document-by-document basis.") (citations omitted); Novelty, Inc. v. Mountain View Mktg., Inc., 265 F.R.D. 370 (S.D. Ind. 2009) ("blanket assertions"), *subsequent opinion*, 2010 WL 1490416*3 (S.D. Ind. Apr. 12, 2010) (willful failure to provide privilege log).

17. *In re* Universal Serv. Fund Tel. Billing Practices, 232 F.R.D. at 673. While the *Universal Serv. Fund Telephone Billing Practices* opinion noted that itemized descriptions were necessary to avoid stealth claims, *U.S.A. v. Chevron Texaco Corp.*, 241 F. Supp. 2d 1065, 1074 n.6 (N.D. Cal. 2001), *subsequent opinion*, 241 F. Supp. 2d 1065, 1075 n.6 (N.D. Cal. 2002), pointed to the problems with separation of linked email. *Chevron* noted that "[w]ith respect to each series of e-mails for which Chevron asserts protection under the privilege, Chevron breaks the series down into each discrete e-mail message. In our view, such a representation of the documents is misleading. Each e-mail/communication consists of the text of the sender's message as well as all of the prior e-mails that are attached to it. Therefore, Chevron's assertion that each separate e-mail stands as an independent communication is inaccurate." Thus, the court indicated that disturbing the parent-child relationship was misleading.

Practitioners should exercise great care with linked email. If linked, parent and child emails are separated, it can be extremely costly to attempt to put Humpty Dumpty together again. A pristine copy of the email chain, with parent-child links intact, should always be preserved and the failure to do so may implicate spoliation issues. *See* Coleman (Parent) Holdings, Inc., v. Morgan Stanley & Co., Inc., 2005 WL 679071 (Fla. Cir. Ct. 2005) (finding that Morgan Stanley's "failure to produce all e-mail attachments was negligent").

e-mail within a strand as a separate entry."[18] Thus, as a general rule, subject to exceptions, the court recommended itemization of each email in a chain, tipping the scale in that direction to further the goal of full disclosure.

Following this approach, one leading treatise states: "Each e-mail is a separate communication (like separate letters and memoranda) and should be described separately in the privilege log."[19] In perhaps the most eloquent description of the separate-listing approach, the treatise describes the *Microsoft Corp. Antitrust Litigation*. There, Microsoft's privilege log listed only the last chronological message in the chain. The author noted that this may have been sufficient for the requesting party, under a "balance of terror" approach.[20]

Nevertheless, "what was described in Microsoft's privilege logs was quite different from what was actually produced for judicial examination."[21] As a result, the briefs were "far afield from the actual concerns raised by the documents in question."[22] Based on this experience, the treatise concludes: "For the adversarial system to function properly, each message needs to be identified and described in a manner that fairly permits the opposing side to assess whether the claim of privilege is valid."[23]

18. 232 F.R.D. at 674. The court also noted an exception where "each and every separate e-mail within a strand is limited to a distinct and identifiable set of individuals, all of whom are clearly within the attorney-client relationship in which legal advice is being sought or given." *Id.* at 673. In that circumstance, the court indicated, a single entry in the privilege log would not violate Rule 26(b)(5); *Id.* Tri-State Truck Ins., Ltd. v. First Nat'l Bank of Wamego, 2011 WL 117222 (D. Kan. Jan. 13, 2011) ("In this District, Judge O'Hara has held that litigants *generally* must list each email within a string as a separate entry on the privilege log, rather than listing the email string as a single entry, or risk the possibility that the privilege will be deemed waived. . . .") (citation omitted) (emphasis added).

19. Rice, *supra* note 13, at 253. The author also points out that where there are common subjects and recipients, one affidavit may suffice to support claims of privilege for each of the separate communications.

20. *Id.* at 254 ("Of course, it remains just as plausible that because each side is being asked to produce the same type of materials, each wants to enjoy the same convenience.").

21. *Id.*

22. *Id.* at 255.

23. *Id.*; *accord* Helm v. Alderwoods Group, Inc., 2010 WL 2951871, at *2 (N.D. Cal. July 27, 2010) ("the better approach in this case is to required Alderwoods to supplement the log by itemizing each email within the strings.").

4. The "cost-saving approach": Comparing an email chain to an oral conversation

In *Muro v. Target Corporation,*[24] the court reached the opposite conclusion. In *Muro I,* Target Corp. was ordered to supplement its privilege log for 89 documents. Target had "merely copied the information contained in the subject line of the underlying e-mail document." The court concluded that "Target's method of cutting and pasting does not satisfy its obligation to describe the nature of the document adequately." The court noted that "[s]everal documents identified on the log consist of chains of e-mails where portions are expressly designated as privileged: 'Attorney-Client Privileged Communication. Do Not Forward Without Author's Consent.'" The *Muro I* decision concluded that Target needed to establish the identity of the recipients included in the chain of communication to show that distribution to them did not compromise confidentiality.

In *Muro II,* the court considered Target's revised privilege log. It noted: "The log identifies 89 documents. The documents at issue are chains of e-mail communications among Target employees." It stated that Target had now included the job titles of the authors and recipients, and whether the person was an attorney. "With respect to documents consisting of a string or chain of e-mail communications, *Target simply identified those individuals who were party to the last message in time.*"[25] The court stated that application of the principles of attorney-client privilege "in the context of e-mail communications in a large corporation like Target is a relatively new challenge." It wrote: "Only a few reported opinions have addressed, either directly or implicitly, the issue of how e-mail chains should be disclosed on a privilege log."[26] It concluded: "Listing only the most recent e-mail as Target did, fails to disclose important information about what is being withheld from production. . . ." The court pointed to Target's Document 3, which was described on the privilege log as "Email string sent August 12, 2004 at 8:22 AM" to 11 people regarding "potential VAPR Issue with Autosub." Document 3 consisted of five different

24. Muro v. Target Corp., 2006 U.S. Dist. LEXIS 86030 (N.D. Ill. 2006) (*Muro I*), *subsequent opinion,* 243 F.R.D. 301 (N.D. Ill. 2007) (*Muro II*), *subsequent opinion,* 250 F.R.D. 350 (N.D. Ill. 2007) (*Muro III*), *aff'd,* 580 F.3d 485 (7th Cir. 2009). For a critique of *Muro,* see RICE, *supra* note 13, at 256–57.

25. 243 F.R.D. at 304 (emphasis added).

26. *Id.* at 306 (citations omitted).

messages, including two that were simply business communications. The magistrate judge held that the log must identify each communication, "whether that communication is the entire strand (as might occur in a situation where, unlike Target's Document 3, a distinct and identifiable number of individuals have exchanged e-mail on a single privileged topic), or only one part of the strand." Thus, *Muro II* was consistent with *Universal Service Fund Telephone Billing Practices Litigation*, and it required separate itemization of email contained in an email string.

Muro II, however, did not stand the test of further review, and the district judge disagreed with the magistrate judge. In *Muro III*, the court noted: "Authorities are divided on whether a privilege log should include separate entries for multiple e-mails within the same string. Some courts have held that one e-mail string should receive only a single entry. Other courts have concluded that each e-mail should be listed separately to enable the opposing party to determine whether each e-mail in the strand is entitled to privilege, on the theory that this inquiry is necessary if the court is to determine that the entire strand is to receive protections. There is currently no binding authority on this issue."[27]

Muro III analyzed Rule 26(b)(5)(A) in light of *Upjohn Co. v. United States*.[28] It concluded that "even though one e-mail is not privileged, a second e-mail which forwards that prior e-mail to counsel might be privileged in its entirety. In this respect, the forwarded material is similar to prior conversations or documents that are quoted verbatim in a letter to a party's attorney." It stated that "the fact that those documents were attached may be privileged, even if the originals are not."

The *Muro III* decision concluded: "A party can therefore legitimately withhold an entire e-mail *forwarding* prior materials to counsel while also disclosing those prior materials themselves."[29] The court reasoned that it would be confusing to log documents on a privilege log and also produce them to opposing counsel. "More

27. 250 F.R.D. at 362–63 (citations omitted). It has been noted that there is not a uniform approach among the courts. Tri-State Truck Ins., Ltd. v. First Nat'l Bank of Wamego, 2011 WL 117222 (D. Kan. Jan. 13, 2011) ("Courts in other districts have followed a different approach. . . .") (citations omitted); Helm v. Alderwoods Group, 2010 WL 2951871, at *2 (N.D. Cal. July 27, 2010) ("the question of how to apply privilege principles to email communications is a matter of disagreement among district courts.").

28. 449 U.S. 383, 395–96 (1981).

29. *Muro II*, 250 F.R.D. at 363 (emphasis added).

troublingly, the disclosure of this information could very well be a breach of the attorney-client privilege. If the opposing party can gather enough material from the log and already produced materials to discover the topic or contents of material forwarded to counsel then a privileged communication has been revealed to that party. Rule 26(b)(5)(A) requires only that a party provide sufficient information for an opposing party to evaluate the applicability of a privilege, 'without revealing information itself privileged.' "[30]

Muro III stands for the proposition that if the underlying emails in the chain are responsive to discovery requests, nonprivileged, and disclosed, they need not be listed on the privilege log.[31] While *Universal Service Fund Telephone Billing Practice Litigation* found the need to protect against "stealth" claims to be compelling, *Muro III* emphasized that the selection and ordering of documents is itself protected.

5. The middle ground between Scylla and Charybdis

If *Universal Service Fund Telephone Billing Practices Litigation* and *Muro III* demonstrate the ends of the continuum, there is also middle ground. *Universal Service Fund Telephone Billing Practices Litigation,* while encouraging individualized listings, recognized instances where an email-by-email log was not required.[32]

This case-by-case approach was also described in *Rhoads Industries, Inc., v. Building Materials Corp. of America,*[33] where the plaintiff inadvertently disclosed more than 800 privileged electronic documents. The defendant contended that the privilege was waived by careless production and an inadequate privilege log. In *Rhoads II,* the court stated that, after reviewing the authorities, "I have some hesitancy in adopting a broad black-letter rule."

30. The selection and ordering of documents by counsel may be work product. *E.g., In re* Allen, 106 F.3d 582 (4th Cir. 1997).

31. "*Muro* says that a court cannot force a party to individually list emails that appear in a privilege log . . . *Muro* suggests that an email which forwards to counsel information contained in a previous email might be privileged." Flagstar Bank, FSB v. Freestar Bank, N.A., 2009 WL 3756898, at *5 (D.N.H. Nov. 9, 2009); *accord* Cont'l Cas. Co. v. St. Paul Surplus Lines Ins. Co., 265 F.R.D. 517 n. 9 (E.D. Cal. 2010).

32. *See supra* note 18.

33. *Rhoads I,* 2008 U.S. Dist. LEXIS 9333, at *9, *subsequent opinion, Rhoads II,* 2008 U.S. Dist. LEXIS 96404.

Rhoads I described the privilege waiver implications of an inadequate privilege log.[34] Rhoads had used software to screen privileged email and, after producing the nonprivileged messages, it learned that privileged documents had been inadvertently produced. Rhoads then prepared a new privilege log listing 812 inadvertently produced privileged documents. The discovering party asserted waiver. The court reviewed the earlier privilege logs and the log listing the 812 documents. In short, the court was faced with a situation where a party had employed sophisticated screening software and a forensic expert, inadvertently produced privileged ESI that was not described on a privilege log, and then amended the privilege log to describe the privileged email. Rhoads then performed further inspection and prepared a fourth privilege log. For purposes of this chapter, the discussion will focus on the privilege log issue, and not the substantive question of whether Rhoads had employed reasonable precautions.[35]

Rhoads I stated that "the obligation to log privileged documents is mandatory under the specific terms of Rule 26(b)(5)." It held that Rhoads's log of the privileged documents was inexcusably delayed, and that documents that were not logged must be produced. Rhoads sought clarification "because of the manner in which some of the privileged material appear in so-called 'email chains' or 'email strings.'" In short, Rhoads, having been ordered to produce unlogged material, asked the court whether it considered an email that was embedded in a chain to be unlogged material.

The *Rhoads II* decision reviewed *Muro* and other opinions, and concluded:

> A situation may arise where a number of email messages by themselves not privileged, but eventually sent to an attorney for the purpose of securing legal advice, become privileged. If they are not produced, they must be logged individually in order to claim the privilege, but they do not have to be detailed in the log entry describing the email message sent to the attorney.[36]

The *Rhoads II* decision viewed an email chain as "analogous to a meeting that takes place in a conference room between attorney and client for the purpose of seeking legal advice. The facts

34. 2008 U.S. Dist. LEXIS 9333, at *13–14.
35. FRE 502 is discussed in chapters 17 and 18.
36. *Rhoads II*, 2008 U.S. Dist. LEXIS 96404 at *8–9.

discussed at the meeting must be disclosed in discovery, but the communications that take place at the meeting are privileged." It reasoned that, in the electronic world, email "can replace the meeting" and a subsequent letter summarizing the meeting. The court concluded:

> If the purpose of the email string was to gather facts and communicate those facts to the attorney for legal advice, then a good argument exists that the email communications served the functional equivalent of a face-to-face meeting, and although the facts contained in the emails are discoverable, all of the messages, not only the compilation of messages sent to the attorney, are privileged. If that is the case, all of the separate email messages must be disclosed under Rule 26(b)(5), which is usually done by a privilege log. However the client's log need not disclose that all of these emails were forwarded to the attorney.[37]

The *Rhoads II* decision continued:

> On the other hand, if the email messages are part of routine business affairs, and not for the purpose of securing legal advice, then the underlying emails would be discoverable. If a party asserts that, because they are eventually sent to the attorney, the messages become privileged, then each must be entered on the privilege log.[38]

In short, *Rhoads II* and *Universal Service Fund Telephone Billing Practices Litigation* state that there are instances where itemization is required, and situations where it is not.

6. How to avoid shooting a mouse with an elephant gun or fighting a dragon with a cardboard sword

Each of these decisions and treatises is well reasoned and represents a thoughtful attempt to adapt the decades-old privilege log to the realm of ESI.[39] The many iterations of email, as well as the volume of data involved, present challenging and complex issues. As noted above, courts have been concerned that an item-by-item

37. *Id.* at *10–11.

38. *Id. Rhoads II* noted that while *Muro II* did not require that each message in a string sent to an attorney be logged, it did require that each version of an email string be listed. *Id.* at *7.

39. Facciola & Redgrave, *supra* note 10, at 21–22.

listing of email in a chain may drive the cost of litigation to unreasonable levels, while a blanket assertion of privilege may obscure failures to produce nonprivileged email. Counsel and litigants, faced with the choices of expending enormous sums of money or risking waiver of the privilege, need guidance.

On the one hand, universally mandating an item-by-item privilege log may be akin to hunting a mouse with an elephant gun, while permitting stealth claims is much like requiring that the discovering party fight a dragon with a cardboard sword.[40] Does this mean that litigants are aboard the Andrea Gail, sailing into the "perfect storm"?[41]

A. The just, speedy, and inexpensive determination of an action—a rules-based approach[42]

The current requirement for a privilege log is found in Rule 26(b)(5)(A). Of course, Rule 1 provides: "[These Rules] should be construed and administered to secure the just, speedy, and inexpensive determination of every action and proceeding." The "stop and think" rule, Rule 26(g)(1)(B),[43] imposes a good faith duty of reasonable inquiry, analogous to Rule 11, on an attorney signing a discovery pleading (including a response to a document request, and the related privilege log).

Rule 26(b)(2)(C)(iii) can be used to limit discovery where the burden or expense outweighs its likely benefit, and Rule 26(b)(2)(C)(i) may limit it where the discovery sought can be obtained from some other source that is more convenient, less burdensome, or less expensive. Finally, Rule 26(c) protects against

40. Anderson v. Beatrice Foods Co., 900 F.2d 388, 395 (1st Cir. 1990), *cert. denied*, 498 U.S. 891 (1990).

41. Wolfgang Petersen directed the movie *The Perfect Storm*, in which three storms combined near Gloucester, Mass. The movie's web site describes the combination of events as an "almost apocalyptic situation." See *supra* note 27, citing split of authorities.

42. Facciola & Redgrave, *supra* note 10, at 40.

43. Rule 26(g)(1)(B) provides that "with respect to a discovery request, response, or objection, [a signature certifies that] it is: (i) consistent with these rules and warranted by existing law or by a nonfrivolous argument for extending, modifying, or reversing existing law, or for establishing new law; (ii) not interposed for any improper purpose, such as to harass, cause unnecessary delay, or needlessly increase the cost of litigation; and (iii) neither unreasonable nor unduly burdensome or expensive, considering the needs of the case, prior discovery in the case, the amount in controversy, and the importance of the issues at stake in the action." Rule 26(g) is discussed in more detail in chapter 31.

undue burden or expense, authorizing orders that forbid certain "disclosure," forbid inquiry into specified matters, or limit "the scope of disclosure." In fact, the 1993 Committee Note to the privilege log rule, Rule 26(b)(5), states: "A party can seek relief through a protective order under subdivision (c) if compliance with the requirement for providing this [privilege log] information would be an unreasonable burden."

Because email and other ESI must generally[44] be requested under Rule 34, in addressing the email chain issue, Rules 1, 26(b)(2)(C), 26(b)(5), 26(c), and 26(g) should be viewed in combination with Rule 34(b)(2)(B). Rule 34 permits requests by item or category of items, and Rule 34(b)(2)(B) provides that "[f]or each item *or category*, the response must either state that inspection and related activities will be permitted as requested or state an objection to the request, including the reasons."[45]

The concept of categorical privilege logs in connection with ESI is not new.[46] For example, in *Orbit One Communications, Inc. v. Numerex Corp.*,[47] the court wrote: "To lessen the burden posed by reviewing and recording a large quantity of protected communications, Lowenstein may provide *a categorical privilege log* rather than a traditional, itemized privilege log. . . . However, Lowenstein must justify its assertion of privilege with regard to each category, and the description of each category must provide sufficient information for Numerex to assess any potential objections to the assertions of attorney-client privilege." In short, there is authority that Rule 37(b)(2)(B) permits a categorical response to a request for production of documents, and that it also permits a categorical privilege log, provided that the log contains information sufficient to fulfill the purposes of Rule 26(b)(5)(A).[48]

44. ESI may also need to be produced under the initial disclosure rule, FED. R. CIV. P. 26(a)(1), the subpoena rule, FED. R. CIV. P. 45, in deposition, FED. R. CIV. P. 30(b)(2), or as part of answers to interrogatories, FED. R. CIV. P. 33(d).

45. FED. R. CIV. P. 34(b)(2)(B) (emphasis added).

46. GRIMM, *supra* note 3, at 90–91; Facciola & Redgrave, *supra* note 10 at 45.

47. *Id.*; Orbit One Commc'ns, Inc. v. Numerex Corp., 255 F.R.D. 98, 109 (S.D.N.Y. 2008) (emphasis added).

48. The information needed for a categorical assertion of privilege was described in *Imperial Corporation of America v. Durkin*, 174 F.R.D. 475 (S.D. Cal. 1997). In that case, which did not involve ESI, the court noted that "blanket objections" based on privilege are "improper." *Id.* at 477. It then continued: "However, nowhere in Fed.R.Civ.Pro. 26(b)(5) is it mandated that a document-by-document privilege log is required, if a party seeks to withhold documents based on privilege or

In combination, the goal of speedy and inexpensive determination of the action, the "stop and think" obligation of good faith, the cost-benefit balancing process, the discretionary power to limit "disclosure," the permission to respond by objecting to a category of information, and the minimal requirement that an objection state the "nature" of the withheld communications should operate to avoid what the *Universal Service Fund Telephone Billing Practices Litigation* described as "a laborious, time-intensive task for counsel" that "adds considerable expense for the clients involved," unless that labor and task are justified by the specific facts presented in the case before the court. One important goal of the Federal Rules of Civil Procedure is that discovery costs should be *proportionate* to the needs of the case.[49]

Consider, for example, the situation in which a privileged email chain includes nonprivileged, responsive emails that are separately disclosed. Rule 26(b)(2)(C)(i) authorizes limits on relevant discovery where the information may be obtained from another less expensive or less burdensome source. It would seem that there should be no requirement for a costly, itemized privilege log in that circumstance. Of course, rules such as Rule 1, 26(b)(2)(C), 26(c), and 34(b)(2)(B) may not be self-operating and it may be necessary to involve the court in any application of their protections.

Universal Service Fund Telephone Billing Practices Litigation was correctly concerned with "stealth" claims of privilege, and the

---

work product. In fact, the Advisory Committee Notes following Rule 26 indicate that a document-by-document privilege log is not required in certain circumstances." *Id.* The court concluded that a document-by-document log "has been, undoubtedly will, and should remain, the traditional format. However, that paradigm is not rigid and inflexible. Just as in other areas of the law, cases and the rules themselves recognize that there are circumstances in which other solutions or approaches are also appropriate. This is one." *Id.* The *Durkin* court held: "Plaintiffs' counsel shall therefore produce a privilege log as to documents for which a privilege or protection is claimed; that contains the following information: 1. An aggregate listing of the numbers of the withheld documents; 2. An identification of the time periods encompassed by the withheld documents; 3. An affidavit containing the representation(s) that: (a) the withheld documents were: (1) either prepared to assist in anticipated or pending litigation, or (2) contain information reflecting communications between (i) counsels or counsels' representatives, and (ii) plaintiffs or plaintiffs' representatives, for the purpose of facilitating the rendition of legal services to plaintiffs; and, (b) intended to be confidential communications." *Id.* at 479.

49. Mancia v. Mayflower Textile Servs. Co., 253 F.R.D. 354, 358 (D. Md. 2008); *accord* Facciola & Redgrave, *supra* note 10, at 22.

problems described in the *Microsoft Antitrust Litigation* are significant.[50] It may be illusory to hope that the "stop and think" due diligence requirements of Rule 26(g) will obviate all such problems and improper tactics. Notwithstanding that risk, Federal Rule of Evidence 502, and the "clawback" and "sneak peek" provision of Rule 26(b)(5)(B), demonstrate that in the ESI context, perfect resolution of privilege issues must sometimes yield to the economic realities presented by voluminous ESI.[51]

Courts and commentators addressing email chains have done so in a careful, thoughtful, and fact-specific manner. Clearly, there is no bright-line rule. Nevertheless, the guiding principle should be "proportionality" and the costs of protecting the privilege cannot be permitted to swallow the case and drown the litigants.

It is suggested that, absent countervailing circumstances, there should be a modest presumption that the *Muro III* approach should govern or, at least, not result in a waiver if it is employed in good faith, subject to further order of the court. For example, under a rules-based approach, a litigant faced with voluminous email chains might employ the *Muro III* approach, if it is proportionate to the needs of the case. Under the circumstances of a particular case, this might be satisfactory to the discovering party. If, however, the discovering party reasonably sought additional information, a more detailed itemization of some or all of the withheld ESI might be required, *without threat that the initial log waived any privilege.* This two-phase approach, while running some risk of delay and obfuscation, operates under the safeguard of Rule 26(g) sanctions and furthers the goal of Rule 1.

B. The cooperative, front-loaded model, using a Rule 26(f) conference of the parties

There is another solution.[52] The Sedona Conference Cooperation Proclamation suggests a paradigmatic change in discovery.[53]

50. Rice, *supra* note 13.

51. Facciola & Redgrave, *supra* note 10, at 52 (dealing with "cheaters"). *See* Pension Comm. of the Univ. of Montreal Pension Plan v. Banc of Am. Sec., LLC, 685 F. Supp. 2d 456, 461 (S.D.N.Y. 2010) ("In an era where vast amounts of electronic information is [sic] available for review, discovery in certain cases has become increasingly complex and expensive. Courts cannot and do not expect that any party can meet a standard of perfection.").

52. Grimm, *supra* note 3, at 90; Facciola & Redgrave, *supra* note 10, at 44.

53. The Sedona Conference Cooperation Proclamation (2008); Mancia v. Mayflower Textile Servs. Co., 253 F.R.D. 354 (D. Md. 2008); The Sedona

Similarly, the Sedona Principles provide that, in order to "reduce motion practice regarding log deficiencies," parties should confer and consider agreeing "to accept privilege logs that will initially classify categories or groups of withheld documents, while providing that any ultimate adjudication of privilege claims, if challenged, will be made on the basis of a document-by-document review."[54]

Because the issue was not presented, courts have understandably and properly not discussed the role of a Rule 26(f) Conference of the Parties in addressing the issues presented by email chains. "One of the matters that parties should be prepared to address during this initial discussion is the assertion of privilege claims as to e-mails that are part of larger 'strings' comprising both privileged and nonprivileged e-mails."[55] Rule 26(f) directs that parties discuss ESI privilege issues during that conference.[56] An agreement between the parties, submitted to the court for approval, when combined with the protections of FRE 502, can avoid all or almost all of the problems that have been presented by email chains.[57]

7. Practice tips

Consider, for example, whether the outcome might have differed if AT&T had, in *Universal Service Fund Telephone Billing Practices Litigation*, approached the opponent and the court for guidance prior to submitting what the court later found to be a defective privilege log.[58]

In addressing the issues of email chains in privilege logs, counsel should consider the following course of action:

CONFERENCE, COMMENTARY ON ACHIEVING EQUALITY IN THE E-DISCOVERY PROCESS 23 (2009). For a discussion of the Cooperation Proclamation, see chapter 30.

54. THE SEDONA CONFERENCE, THE SEDONA PRINCIPLES: ADDRESSING ELECTRONIC DOCUMENT PRODUCTION 24 (2d ed. 2007).

55. Kaufman & Moore, *supra* note 8; *accord* Muro v. Target Corp. (*Muro II*), 243 F.R.D. 301, 307 n.5 (N.D. Ill. 2007) (citing Kaufman & Moore); *see* chapter 19.

56. *Id.*

57. The impact of FRE 502 on privilege logs is beyond the scope of this chapter. For a discussion of that topic, see chapters 17 and 18; Facciola & Redgrave, *supra* note 10, at 30, 40; Thomas, Cross & Barton, *supra* note 10. It is clear that "[w]hile Rule 502 provides many forms of blessed relief, it does not speak to counsel's obligation after having discovered privileged information to claim that it is exempt from disclosure by specifying why it is privileged." Facciola & Redgrave, *supra* note 10, at 31.

58. There may have been other countervailing factors in that case, as well as a lack of applicable authority, and no criticism of counsel is intended. The point is illustrative only.

- Perform a reasonable, defensible privilege review.
- Prior to preparing a privilege log, seek agreement regarding email chains during a Rule 26(f) Conference of the Parties. Attempt to negotiate the terms and contours of the log with the opposing parties, as well as a "clawback" agreement.
- If negotiations are unsuccessful, the next step could be to seek early judicial assistance. One of the purposes of the amendments to the Federal Rules of Civil Procedure is to "front load" resolution of discovery disputes, *before* parties waste their resources, and to encourage judicial intervention to ensure the proportionality of discovery.[59] By way of example, this process is suggested in Maryland's Discovery Guideline 10.d.v.[60]
- Consider a two-phase approach to email chains, with phase one being a cost-conscious listing of email chains, dates, subjects, and recipients, without itemization, as long as responsive, nonprivileged underlying attachments are produced, and phase two being a more detailed log, in whole or in part, if reasonably requested, without any assertion of waiver due to the prior log.
- The analytical framework should be governed by a panoply of proportionality rules relating to a cost-benefit analysis, as set forth above, keeping in mind the Rule 26(g) obligations of signing counsel;
- Consider, and be prepared to factually address, cost-benefit and proportionality issues related to email chains. Rule 26(b)(5)(A) should be interpreted and applied to further both its goal of efficient resolution of privilege issues, without the need for in camera review, and in light of Rule 1's mandate of the just, speedy, and inexpensive resolution of actions.[61]

---

59. P. Grimm, et al., *Proportionality in the Post-Hoc Analysis of Pre-Litigation Preservation Decisions,* 37 U. BALT. L. REV. 381, 404 (2008).

60. *See* LOCAL RULES FOR THE U.S. DISTRICT COURT, DISTRICT OF MARYLAND 89–90 (amended Dec. 1, 2009), http://www.mdd.uscourts.gov/localrules/localrules August09v3.pdf.

61. It may also be appropriate to consider a request for a nonwaiver order pursuant to FRE 502. *See* n. 55, above. Application of Rule 502 may, in the majority of cases, avoid "the traditional document-by-document privilege log process." Facciola & Redgrave, *supra* note 10, at 44, 49.

CHAPTER 16

ARE ATTORNEY-CLIENT COMMUNICATIONS IMPOSING A LEGAL HOLD AND IMPLEMENTING PRESERVATION EFFORTS PRIVILEGED?

BY THE HON. PAUL W. GRIMM, MICHAEL D. BERMAN, LESLIE WHARTON, JEANNA BECK, AND CONOR R. CROWLEY

Abridged and adapted from P. Grimm et al., *Discovery About Discovery: Does the Attorney-Client Privilege Protect All Attorney-Client Communications Relating to the Preservation of Potentially Relevant Information?*, 37 U. BALT. L. REV. 413 (2008). Used by permission.

As a legal dispute emerges, issues regarding an organization's duty to preserve documents may find expression in attorney-client communications that culminate in a document imposing a hold on destruction of electronically stored information (ESI) or other records. This chapter looks in depth at the potential ability of an opponent to obtain such communications in connection with a spoliation claim, despite assertions of attorney-client privilege. The authors conclude with practical advice as to how preservation communications should be couched in order to minimize risk.

1. Introduction

A. Overview

This chapter examines whether certain attorney-client communications may be considered by a court in connection with a spoliation claim based on an alleged breach of the duty to preserve information. The steps taken by a client to fulfill the duty to preserve information, even if taken in response to privileged communications, have been held to be discoverable, although related attorney communications have not been routinely discoverable. Where there is a preliminary showing of a breach of the duty to preserve information, at least some attorney-client implementation[1] communications have not been protected by courts faced with the issue. The courts' decisions have been supported by a number of different theories, including that the communications

- are in furtherance of a common law duty, and not for the purpose of seeking legal advice;
- fall under the crime, fraud, or tort exception to the privilege;
- are fact work product and disclosable pursuant to established work-product rules;
- are put in issue by an "advice of counsel" defense; or
- fall under the attorney "self-defense" doctrine.

1. When "implement," "implementation communications," and other similar terms and phrases are used in this chapter, they refer to what was said and done in the course of issuing a litigation hold notice, interviewing records custodians, information technology personnel, key players, computer forensic experts, and generally monitoring the preservation process.

These examples fall within two alternative paradigms. Under one, the communications are not privileged at all. Under the other, they are treated as exceptions to the privilege.[2]

Under the first rationale, because preservation communications are made pursuant to a duty imposed by law, they are not communications seeking legal advice and, absent a preliminary showing of breach of the duty to preserve, are wholly irrelevant to the claims, defenses, and subject matter of the action, and therefore not discoverable. Under the second theory, attorney-client preservation communications are inherently privileged or work product. The communications become relevant when there is a preliminary showing of a failure to preserve information that should have been preserved. Upon such a preliminary showing, attorney-client communications become discoverable under either an exception to, or waiver of, those protections.

The outer boundary of a reviewing court's inquiry into attorney-client preservation communications remains to be determined. Courts may distinguish between legal advice related to preservation, on the one hand, and implementation communications, on the other, with the former remaining protected by the privilege in all but the most egregious circumstances, and the latter open to discovery upon a preliminary showing of breach of duty.

B. Background

The duty to preserve is one of the fundamental common law foundations of the adversarial system of justice. In today's litigation environment, it is counsel who most often notify clients of the duty to preserve and oversee the preservation process; draft litigation hold notices; interview records custodians, key persons, and information technology personnel; and take other steps to ensure that the duty to preserve is not breached.[3]

The attorney-client privilege and work-product protection are likewise fundamental underpinnings of the adversarial system of justice. The attorney-client privilege exists to encourage

2. Although the attorney-client privilege is separate and distinct from the work-product doctrine, for simplicity, on occasion this chapter merges the two under the umbrella of "privilege."

3. The contours of the duty to preserve are discussed in chapters 8 and 9 of this book.

full and frank communication between counsel and client.[4] The work-product doctrine recognizes that in the adversarial system of justice, attorneys' deliberative processes should generally be protected.[5] Under Federal Rule of Civil Procedure 26(b)(3), discovery of an opposing party's work product is permitted only upon a showing "that the party seeking discovery has substantial need of the materials in the preparation of the party's case and that the party is unable without undue hardship to obtain the substantial equivalent of the materials by other means."[6] When discovery of fact work product is permitted, courts are enjoined to "protect against disclosure of the mental impressions, conclusions, opinions, or legal theories of an attorney."[7]

In the absence of a breach of the duty to preserve, courts have not hesitated to hold that attorney-client preservation communications are not discoverable; but when faced with a preliminary showing of a breach of that duty, courts have required disclosure of some attorney-client communications implementing the duty to preserve.[8] For example, attorneys and clients have been deposed or otherwise required to disclose their actions in preserving—or

4. *E.g.*, Upjohn Co. v. United States, 449 U.S. 383, 389 (1981) ("Its purpose is to encourage full and frank communication between attorneys and their clients and thereby promote broader public interests in the observance of law and administration of justice. The privilege recognizes that sound legal advice or advocacy serves public ends and that such advice or advocacy depends upon the lawyer's being fully informed by the client."); Fisher v. United States, 425 U.S. 391, 403–04 (1976) ("Confidential disclosures by a client to an attorney made in order to obtain legal assistance are privileged. The purpose of the privilege is to encourage clients to make full disclosure to their attorneys." (citations omitted)). The attorney-client relationship, however, is not always harmonious. The privilege belongs to the client and the client may, at some later date, choose to disclose attorney-client communications. *See, e.g.*, Exact Software v. Infocon, 2006 WL 3499992 (N.D. Oh. 2006) (client filed affidavit stating that attorney failed to properly inform client).

5. Hickman v. Taylor, 329 U.S. 495, 510–11 (1947).

6. FED. R. CIV. P. 26(b)(3).

7. *Id.*

8. *See, e.g.*, Major Tours, Inc. v. Colorel, 720 F. Supp. 2d 587, 618 (D.N.J. 2010), *reconsideration denied*, 2010 U.S. Dist. LEXIS 104006 (D.N.J. Sep. 29, 2010); Peskoff v. Faber, 244 F.R.D. 54 (D.D.C. 2007); Am. Gen. Life Ins. Co. v. Billard, 2010 U.S. Dist. LEXIS 138570, at *18 (N.D. Iowa Dec. 29, 2010), *subsequent opinion on other grounds*, 2010 U.S. Dist. LEXIS 137804 (N.D. Iowa Dec. 30, 2010); Zubulake v. UBS Warburg LLC (*Zubulake V*), 229 F.R.D. 422 (S.D.N.Y. 2004); Zubulake v. UBS Warburg LLC (*Zubulake IV*), 220 F.R.D. 212 (S.D.N.Y. 2003); United Med. Supply Co. v. United States, 77 Fed. Cl. 257 (2007).

failing to preserve—relevant material.[9] What do these decisions mean for counsel and their clients when faced with actual or potential litigation? Can they move forward with confidence that their implementation communications will be protected from disclosure? Or must they now assume that, at least with respect to the preservation and production of discoverable materials, some, or perhaps all, of their communications are themselves subject to discovery?

2. The privilege, work product, and the duty to preserve

A. The attorney-client privilege: Communications related to legal advice

It is generally assumed that confidential communications involving legal advice between an attorney and client are privileged.[10] This privilege is firmly grounded in public policy.[11]

Nevertheless, not all communications between counsel and client are privileged.[12] In *Fisher v. United States*,[13] for example, the Supreme Court wrote that the privilege "protects *only* those disclosures necessary to obtain informed legal advice *which might not have been made absent the privilege*."[14] For a communication to be privileged, it must be for the purpose of seeking or providing legal advice,[15] and the privilege protects the client's communication of information to the lawyer for the purpose of obtaining that

9. *See, e.g.*, Capellupo v. FMC Corp., 126 F.R.D. 545 (D. Minn. 1989).

10. Upjohn Co. v. United States, 449 U.S. 383, 389 (1981) ("The attorney-client privilege is the oldest of the privileges for confidential communications known to the common law." (citing 8 John Henry Wigmore, Treatise on Evidence § 2290 (McNaughton rev. vol. 1961))).

11. *Id.* at 389; Hunt v. Blackburn, 128 U.S. 464, 470 (1888) (noting the privilege is based on the "necessity, in the interest . . . of justice, of the aid of persons having knowledge of the law and skilled in its practice, which assistance can only be safely and readily availed of when free from the consequences or the apprehension of disclosure"); *see also* Ehrlich v. Grove, 396 Md. 550, 576 (2007) (stating that the attorney-client privilege is a "cornerstone" of the legal system).

12. Diversified Indus., Inc. v. Meredith, 572 F.2d 596, 602 (8th Cir. 1977).

13. 425 U.S. 391 (1976).

14. *Id.* at 403 (emphasis added).

15. *See* Upjohn Co. v. United States, 449 U.S. 383, 394–95 (1981); *Meredith*, 572 F.2d at 601–02; McCafferty's, Inc. v. Bank of Glen Burnie, 179 F.R.D. 163, 166 (D. Md. 1998); *see also* Rambus, Inc. v. Infineon Techs. AG, 220 F.R.D. 264, 272 (E.D. Va. 2004).

legal advice.[16] Thus, by extension, when the lawyer interviews client personnel and gathers information that is "part and parcel of legal advice given by the lawyer,"[17] those communications are privileged.[18]

B. The work-product doctrine: Counsel's communications and activities undertaken because of litigation

The work-product doctrine has its origins in *Hickman v. Taylor*,[19] where the Supreme Court held that "lawyer" materials prepared in anticipation of litigation should not be subject to discovery by the opposing party,[20] stating:

> It is essential that a lawyer work with a certain degree of privacy, free from unnecessary intrusion by opposing parties and their counsel. Proper preparation of a client's case demands that he assemble information, sift what he considers to be the relevant from the irrelevant facts, prepare his legal theories and plan his strategy without undue and needless interference.[21]

However, the Supreme Court did not grant absolute protection for the "work product of [a] lawyer," noting that relevant, non-privileged facts could not be hidden by an attorney and that there could be circumstances under which an adversary could establish adequate reasons to justify intruding into that work product.

In the federal courts, the work-product protection is embodied in Rule 26(b)(3), which distinguishes fact from opinion work product. Fact work product can be discoverable upon a showing of substantial need and that the same information cannot be

16. *See, e.g.*, Fed. Trade Comm'n v. Glaxo Smith Kline, 294 F.3d 141, 148 (D.C. Cir. 2002).

17. EDNA SELAN EPSTEIN, THE ATTORNEY-CLIENT PRIVILEGE AND THE WORK-PRODUCT DOCTRINE 244 (ABA 4th ed. 2004).

18. *See, e.g.*, *Upjohn*, 449 U.S. at 390–91; United States v. Rowe, 96 F.3d 1294, 1297 (9th Cir. 1996); *see also* Prudential Ins. Co. v. Massaro, No. CIV. A. 97-2022, 2000 WL 1176541, at *8 (D.N.J. Aug. 11, 2000) (enjoining in-house counsel from disclosing client confidences and privileged information, including the shredding of documents that led to an investigation of the client).

19. 329 U.S. 495 (1947).

20. The duty to preserve relevant materials is a duty that arises because of pending or anticipated litigation. The duty to preserve and the work-product doctrine share this common basis.

21. *Hickman*, 329 U.S. at 510–12.

obtained from another source without undue hardship.[22] Opinion work product, on the other hand, is almost always protected from disclosure.[23]

C. The duty to preserve incorporates a duty to communicate

In our adversary system, characterized by broad discovery in civil litigation, the duty to preserve relevant information is critical to the truth-finding function and the integrity of the judicial process.[24] As a result, parties have long had a common law duty to preserve information relevant to the litigation. The duty rests on both the attorney and the client. The duty to preserve potentially relevant information includes, and is effectuated by, a reciprocal duty to communicate.[25]

Counsel's duty to communicate with clients about the preservation of discoverable materials has been articulated by the American Bar Association,[26] and in a variety of court decisions. For example, in *Zubulake v. UBS Warburg LLC* (*Zubulake V*),[27] the court examined "counsel's obligation to ensure that relevant information is preserved by giving clear instructions to the client to preserve such information and, perhaps more importantly, a client's obligation to heed those instructions;" and, noted that counsel and their clients "need to communicate clearly and effectively with one another to ensure that litigation proceeds efficiently."

The duty runs both ways, and clients have a duty to communicate with their attorneys. In *Wachtel v. Guardian Life Insurance*,[28] the court found that the defendants "violated the integrity of this

22. Fed. R. Civ. P. 26(b)(3); *e.g.*, Maertin v. Armstrong World Indus., Inc., 172 F.R.D. 143, 150 (D.N.J. 1997).

23. *See* Duplan Corp. v. Moulinage et Retorderie de Chavanoz, 509 F.2d 730, 734 (4th Cir. 1974); Trustmark Ins. Co. v. Gen. & Cologne Life Re of Am., No. 00 C 1926, 2000 WL 1898518, at *3 (N.D. Ill. Dec. 20, 2000) (finding that protection of an attorney's opinion work product is almost absolute).

24. For a discussion of the scope of the duty to preserve, see chapters 8 and 9.

25. *See Zubulake V*, 229 F.R.D. at 424 ("The conduct of both counsel and client thus calls to mind the now-famous words of the prison captain in *Cool Hand Luke*: 'What we've got here is a failure to communicate.'" (citation omitted)).

26. ABA Civil Discovery Standards, No. 10 (Aug. 2004) ("When a lawyer who has been retained to handle a matter learns that litigation is probable or has been commenced, the lawyer should inform the client of its duty to preserve potentially relevant documents. . . .").

27. 229 F.R.D. 422, 424.

28. Nos. 01-4183 (FSH), 03-1801(FSH), 2007 WL 1752036, at *10 (D.N.J. June 18, 2007).

court's judicial processes by: . . . (10) keeping even their own outside counsel . . . unaware of their e-mail procedures that resulted in widespread dereliction of their discovery obligations." In *Qualcomm Inc. v. Broadcom Corp.*,[29] the court noted:

> For the current "good faith" discovery system to function in the electronic age, attorneys and clients must work together to ensure that both understand how and where electronic documents, records and emails are maintained and to determine how best to locate, review, and produce responsive documents. Attorneys must take responsibility for ensuring that their clients conduct a comprehensive and appropriate document search.

In short, the duty to preserve incorporates a duty to engage in attorney-client communication.

3. Discoverability of a client's actions implementing the duty to preserve

It is well established that an opponent may obtain discovery of a client's actions taken to implement the duty to preserve information. It is of no moment that the search for responsive information (whether paper or electronic) was conducted at the direction of counsel. Parties are permitted to inquire into an opponent's efforts to preserve relevant information through interrogatories and in depositions directed to the opposing client.[30] For instance, in *In re eBay Seller Antitrust Litigation*,[31] the parties were locked in acrimonious "discovery about discovery,"[32] in which the plaintiffs demanded the production of defendant's litigation hold notices (termed "document retention notices," or DRNs, by eBay) to determine whether eBay had preserved relevant electronic information. Although the court ruled that eBay did

---

29. Qualcomm, Inc. v. Broadcom Corp., 2008 WL 66932 (S.D. Cal. Jan. 7, 2008), *vacated and remanded in part*, 2008 WL 63810 (S.D. Cal. Mar. 5, 2008), *appeals dismissed*, 327 Fed. Appx. 877, 2008 WL 6400775 (Fed. Cir. Aug. 18, 2008), *on remand*, 2010 WL 1336937 (S.D. Cal. Apr. 2, 2010).

30. *See, e.g., In re* Triton Energy Ltd. Sec. Litig., No. 5:98CV256, 2002 WL 32114464, at *3 (E.D. Tex. Mar. 7, 2002) (noting Triton's witnesses testified in deposition that they had not been asked by Triton's counsel to produce or preserve documents).

31. No. C 07-01882 JF (RS), 2007 WL 2852364 (N.D. Cal. Oct. 2, 2007); *accord Zubulake V*, 229 F.R.D 422 (S.D.N.Y. 2004).

32. *eBay*, 2007 WL 2852364, at *1 n.1. "Discovery about Discovery" is sometimes called "culpability discovery" or "satellite discovery."

not need to disclose its litigation hold notices, which had been drafted by in-house counsel, it held that plaintiffs were "entitled to inquire into the facts as to what the employees receiving the DRNs have done in response; *i.e.*, what efforts they have undertaken to collect and preserve applicable information."[33] The court went on to define the appropriate boundaries for plaintiff's Rule 30(b)(6) deposition on eBay's steps to identify and preserve relevant evidence:

> Although plaintiffs may not be entitled to probe into what exactly eBay's employees were told by its attorneys, they are certainly entitled to know what eBay's employees are doing with respect to collecting and preserving ESI. Furthermore, because it would neither be reasonable nor practical to require or even to permit plaintiffs to depose all 600 employees [who received the litigation hold notice], it is appropriate to permit plaintiffs to discover what those employees are supposed to be doing. Even though such inquiry may, indirectly, implicate communications from counsel to the employees, the focus can and should be on the facts of what eBay's document retention and collection policies are, rather than on any details of the [litigation hold letter]. . . . Plaintiffs are entitled to know what kinds and categories of ESI eBay employees were instructed to preserve and collect, and what specific actions they were instructed to undertake to that end.[34]

The *eBay* case stands for the proposition that the actions taken by a client to implement a litigation hold are discoverable and not privileged. As noted, however, the *eBay* court did not, on the facts presented, permit discovery of counsel's litigation hold instructions to the client.

4. Discoverability of counsel's communications in fulfilling the duty to preserve

Although courts generally refuse to permit discovery of counsel's communications related to the preservation of information,[35]

33. *Id.* at *1.

34. *Id.* at *2 (footnote omitted).

35. *E.g.*, Major Tours, Inc. v. Colorel, 2009 U.S. Dist. LEXIS 68128 (D.N.J. Aug. 4, 2009), *aff'd*, 720 F. Supp. 2d 587, 618 (D.N.J. 2010), *reconsideration denied*, 2010 U.S. Dist. LEXIS 104006 (D.N.J. Sep. 29, 2010); Gibson v. Ford Motor Co., 510 F. Supp. 2d 1116, 1123–24 (N.D. Ga. 2007) (refusing discovery of litigation hold notice as

courts have permitted or ordered disclosure when confronted with a showing of a failure to preserve.[36]

A. General rule: No discovery of counsel's communications related to preservation of information

As noted above, in *eBay*, the court ruled that "eBay need not produce copies of the DRNs [drafted by counsel] nor any information about matters contained therein that are privileged or constitute work product,"[37] but left open the question of whether the litigation hold notice was protected by the privilege or work-product doctrine.

In *Muro v. Target Corp.*,[38] the court examined the litigation hold notices at issue in camera and found:

> Each seem to be communications of legal advice from corporate counsel to corporate employees regarding document preservation. As the litigation hold notices, on their face, appear to be privileged material, there is no . . . need to address Muro's argument that work product protection is overcome here by her showing of need.[39]

Similarly, in *Gibson v. Ford Motor Co.*,[40] the court explained why litigation hold notices are protected as attorney work product:

> In the Court's experience, these instructions are often, if not always, drafted by counsel, involve their work product, are often overly inclusive, and the documents they list do not necessarily bear a reasonable relationship to the issues in litigation. This is not a document relating to the Defendant's business. Rather, the document relates exclusively to this litigation, was apparently created after this dispute arose, and exists for the sole purpose of assuring compliance with discovery that may be required in this litigation. Not only is the

---

work product); *see also* India Brewing, Inc. v. Miller Brewing Co., 237 F.R.D. 190, 194 (E.D. Wis. 2006) (holding document retention policy irrelevant in absence of showing of failure to preserve).

36. *See, e.g.*, *Major Tours*, 720 F. Supp. 2d at 618; Capellupo v. FMC Corp., 126 F.R.D. 545, 551–53 (D. Minn. 1989).

37. *eBay*, 2007 WL 2852364, at *1.

38. Muro v. Target Corp., 250 F.R.D. 350 (N.D. Ill. 2007), *aff'd*, 580 F.3d 485 (7th Cir. 2009).

39. *Id.* at 360.

40. 510 F. Supp. 2d 1116 (N.D. Ga. 2007).

> document likely to constitute attorney work-product, but its compelled production could dissuade other businesses from issuing such instructions in the event of litigation.[41]

Other recent decisions recognize the protected status of litigation hold notices, including *Kingsway Financial Services, Inc. v. Price Waterhouse-Coopers LLP*,[42] *Turner v. Resort Condominiums International*,[43] and *Capitano v. Ford Motor Co.*[44] In these decisions, with greater or lesser analysis, courts declined requests to order that litigation hold notices be produced.

B. Showing breach of the duty to preserve may result in some discoverability

Faced with allegations of spoliation, courts have examined attorney-client communications relating to the duty to preserve. For instance, in a series of decisions in *Zubulake v. UBS Warburg*,[45] Judge Shira Scheindlin permitted detailed inquiry into the communications between UBS and its counsel, as illustrated in the following passage:

> Fully aware of their common law duty to preserve relevant evidence, UBS's in-house attorneys gave oral instructions in August 2001—immediately after Zubulake filed her EEOC charge—instructing employees not to destroy or delete

41. *Id.* at 1123. It is noteworthy that in *Gibson*, unlike *Zubulake V*, 229 F.R.D 422, 426 (S.D.N.Y. 2004), the requesting party did not make a preliminary showing that ESI had not been preserved. *Gibson*, 510 F. Supp. at 1123.
42. No. 03 Civ. 5560 RMB HBP, 2006 WL 1520227, at *2 (S.D.N.Y. June 1, 2006) (denying motion to compel production of litigation hold notice and holding that failure to list the notice on privilege log did not waive the privilege); *accord* Major Tours, Inc. v. Colorel, 2009 U.S. Dist. LEXIS 68128 (D.N.J. Aug. 4, 2009), *aff'd*, 720 F. Supp. 2d 587, 618 (D.N.J. 2010), *reconsideration denied*, 2010 U.S. Dist. LEXIS 104006 (D.N.J. Sep. 29, 2010).
43. No. 1:03-cv-2025-DFH-WTL, 2006 WL 1990379, at *7–8 (S.D. Ind. July 13, 2006) (denying motion to compel production of litigation hold notice that defendant claimed was privileged).
44. 831 N.Y.S.2d 687, 688–89 (N.Y. App. Div. 2007) (noting that "'suspension orders' may lead to the production of admissible evidence and are, therefore, relevant" but holding that they "are privileged communications from attorney to client which relate to legal advice given by counsel to client and, as such, are protected as attorney-client privileged documents").
45. Zubulake v. UBS Warburg LLC (*Zubulake I*), 217 F.R.D. 309 (S.D.N.Y. 2003); Zubulake v. UBS Warburg LLC (*Zubulake II*), 230 F.R.D. 290 (S.D.N.Y. 2003); Zubulake v. UBS Warburg LLC (*Zubulake III*), 216 F.R.D. 280 (S.D.N.Y. 2003); Zubulake v. UBS Warburg LLC (*Zubulake IV*), 220 F.R.D. 212 (S.D.N.Y. 2003).

> material potentially relevant to Zubulake's claims, and in fact to segregate such material into separate files for the lawyers' eventual review. This warning pertained to both electronic and hard-copy files, but did not specifically pertain to so-called "backup tapes," maintained by UBS's information technology personnel. In particular, UBS's in-house counsel, Robert L. Salzberg, "advised relevant UBS employees to preserve and turn over to counsel all files, records or other written memoranda or documents concerning the allegations raised in the [EEOC] charge or any aspect of [Zubulake's] employment." Subsequently—but still in August 2001—UBS's outside counsel met with a number of the key players in the litigation and reiterated Mr. Salzberg's instructions, reminding them to preserve relevant documents, "including e-mails." Salzberg reduced these instructions to writing in e-mails dated February 22, 2002—immediately after Zubulake filed her complaint—and September 25, 2002. Finally, in August 2002, after Zubulake propounded a document request that specifically called for e-mails stored on backup tapes, UBS's outside counsel instructed UBS information technology personnel to stop recycling backup tapes. Every UBS employee mentioned in this Opinion (with the exception of Mike Davies) either personally spoke to UBS's outside counsel about the duty to preserve e-mails, or was a recipient of one of Salzberg's e-mails.[46]

The *Zubulake V* court considered the fact that UBS's counsel "instructed UBS's information technology personnel that backup tapes were also subject to the litigation hold";[47] "advised UBS's information technology personnel to locate and retain all existing backup tapes for employees identified by plaintiff"; and "re-emphasized that directive and confirmed that these tapes continued to be preserved both orally and in writing on several subsequent occasions."[48] The court referred to specific conversations between UBS's outside counsel and key UBS employees by date,

46. *Zubulake V,* 229 F.R.D 422, 425 (S.D.N.Y. 2004) (alterations in original) (footnotes omitted).

47. *Id.* at 427. "In August 2002, after Zubulake specifically requested e-mail stored on backup tapes, UBS's outside counsel orally instructed UBS's information technology personnel to stop recycling backup tapes." *Zubulake IV,* 220 F.R.D. at 215.

48. *Zubulake V,* 229 F.R.D. at 425 n.15 (citation omitted).

and reviewed other attorney-client communications in detail sufficient to permit it to conclude that there were "clear and repeated warnings of counsel."[49]

Zubulake V does not stand alone. For example, in *Cache La Poudre Feeds, Inc. v. Land O'Lakes*,[50] the court considered the communications and actions of counsel and authorized a deposition of Land O'Lakes's counsel "to explore the procedures Land O'Lakes took to identify, preserve and produce . . . responsive documents."[51] Similarly, in *United Medical Supply Co. v. United States*,[52] the U.S. Court of Federal Claims, faced with the government's inadequate document retention and undisputed destruction of documents in violation of the duty to preserve, engaged in a comprehensive examination of the preservation communications between the two government attorneys responsible for identifying and preserving relevant materials. It then closely analyzed discussions between another government attorney, Mr. Chadwick, and a government paralegal, Mr. Brown, about "collecting responsive documents from all the facilities involved in this matter," and secured the affidavit testimony of Mr. Chadwick that he had instructed Mr. Brown "to gather and produce all available records of the medical treatment facilities relating to alleged diverted purchases of medical and surgical supplies."[53]

These decisions are in accord with Guideline No. 9 of the Sedona Legal Hold Guidelines, which notes that a legal hold policy and the process of implementation of that policy "may be subject to scrutiny by the opposing party and review by the court."[54] The Commentary for Guideline No. 9 advises:

> Considering issues regarding work product and attorney-client privilege, the [litigation hold] documentation need not disclose strategy or legal analysis. However, sufficient documentation should be included to demonstrate to opposing

49. *Id.* at 426.

50. 244 F.R.D. 614 (D. Colo. 2007).

51. *Id.* at 634. In reviewing the evidence, the court noted that "Mr. Janzen [the attorney] did not have a full understanding of his company's computer systems or the process for creating computer back-up tapes. . . ." *Id.* at 628.

52. 77 Fed. Cl. 257, 264, 273–74 (2007).

53. *Id.* at 260–61.

54. The Sedona Conference, *Commentary on Legal Holds: The Trigger & the Process*, 11 SEDONA CONFERENCE J. 265, 270 (Fall 2010) [hereinafter *Legal Holds*]. Guideline No. 5 of the *Commentary on Legal Holds* discusses judicial evaluation of "an organization's legal hold decision." *See id.*

parties and the court that the legal hold was implemented in a reasonable, consistent and good faith manner should there be a need to defend the process.[55]

The Commentary goes on to note:

While it may never be necessary to disclose this [litigation hold] information, or disclosure may be made only to the court *in camera* to preserve privileged legal advice and work product information, the availability of documentation [of creation and implementation of the litigation hold] will preserve the option of the party to disclose the information in the event a challenge to the preservation efforts is raised and may provide a valuable resource when responding to discovery requests.[56]

In short, when there is a need to defend the preservation process, the Sedona Legal Hold Guidelines contemplate that courts may inquire into implementation of the legal hold and that the inquiry may require the disclosure of some attorney-client communications. For this reason, the Sedona guidelines suggest that parties and their counsel not include legal strategy or legal advice in the legal hold notice, so as to ensure continued protection for that information.

As reflected in the Sedona guidelines, when faced with evidence that a party had failed to preserve relevant ESI, courts may consider attorney-client communications in resolving whether the duty to preserve had been violated. In so doing, courts generally have not provided the rationale for their consideration of attorney-client communications.

C. The crime, fraud, or tort exception to the privilege

The crime, fraud, or tort exception to the privilege will abrogate claims of privilege where the client consulted with counsel in order to commit a crime, fraud, or tort, and the challenged communications or attorney work product were "in furtherance" of that alleged crime or fraud.[57] Courts also have applied the crime, fraud, or tort exception where counsel committed fraud on the court by

55. *Id.* at 284.

56. *Id.* at 285.

57. *See* RESTATEMENT (THIRD) OF THE LAW GOVERNING LAWYERS § 82 (2000); Leslie Wharton, Cheryl G. Ragsdale & Marc Firestone, *Attorney-Client Privilege and Attorney Work Product Protections, in* ASSOCIATION OF CORPORATE COUNSEL,

engaging in a cover-up of the client's prior misconduct and document destruction. For instance, in *In re Grand Jury Investigation*,[58] the court held that certain attorney-client communications fell within the crime-fraud exception where the client used counsel's legal advice to destroy electronic information. The court stated:

> If, with knowledge of the Government's interest in retrieving any remaining emails, Jane Doe continued to receive emails that were arguably responsive to the subpoena and failed to use her position as an executive of the Organization to direct that all email deletions stop immediately, she may be viewed as furthering the obstruction of the grand jury's investigation or the obstruction of justice. . . . In any event, if Jane Doe learned of the Government's interest in certain documents from her conversation with Attorney on January 20, 2005 and subsequently acquiesced in the deletion and destruction of those documents, the second prong of the crime-fraud exception would be satisfied.[59]

The court's reasoning here is significant because it demonstrates that the crime-fraud exception can be used to abrogate the privilege even when counsel advised the client to fulfill its duty to preserve. In this case, because the government was able to show consultation with the attorney, and a subsequent improper deletion of email, the Third Circuit affirmed an order enforcing the subpoena for attorney-client communications.

In *Rambus v. Infineon Technologies AG*,[60] Rambus destroyed relevant materials at a time when it had a duty to preserve the evidence, organized a "shred day," and destroyed 20,000 pounds of documents. The court held that "the crime/fraud exception extends to materials or communication created for planning, or in furtherance of, spoliation."[61] In resolving the resulting dispute

---

Successful Partnering Between Inside and Outside Counsel § 33:80–33:88 (Robert L. Haig ed., West 2009).

58. 445 F.3d 266 (3d Cir. 2006), *cert. denied*, Doe v. United States, 549 U.S. 997 (2006).

59. *Id.* at 297.

60. 220 F.R.D. 264 (E.D. Va. 2004).

61. *Id.* at 283; *accord* Wachtel v. Guardian Life, 2007 WL 1752036, at *2 (citing Rambus v. Infineon, 220 F.R.D. at 283); Wachtel v. Health Net, 239 F.R.D. 81, 103 (D.N.J. 2006) (noting that "when outside counsel asked employees to search for emails in response to Plaintiffs' document requests and Court Orders, that counsel did not know from Health Net that these employees could not access

over Rambus's duty to preserve, the court considered attorney-client communications: "It is self-evident . . . that any communication between lawyer and client respecting spoliation is fundamentally inconsistent with the asserted principles behind the recognition of the attorney-client privilege, namely, 'observance of law' or the 'administration of justice.' "[62]

Other courts have applied the crime, fraud, or tort exception where counsel's advice or work product is used to destroy relevant evidence or otherwise "undermine[] the adversary system itself."[63] In *Capellupo v. FMC Corp.*,[64] attorneys had directed destruction of evidence after the duty to preserve had arisen. In resolving the discovery dispute, attorneys were deposed, their calendar entries were entered into evidence, and their thoughts explored.

D. Other exceptions

Although the crime, fraud, or tort exception may provide justification for permitting discovery of attorney-client preservation communications in the context of a failure to preserve, that exception is not the only one that may be applicable. Attorney-client communications implementing the duty to preserve may also be discoverable under a number of waiver doctrines. For example, by putting counsel's actions and advice "in issue," the client waives any privilege or work-product protection it would otherwise have for those communications.[65]

A client can knowingly choose to waive any privilege. Similarly, a party may inadvertently waive privilege and work-product protection for counsel's involvement in the preservation process,

'historic' e-mail beyond the most current three month period."); PAUL R. RICE, ELECTRONIC EVIDENCE: LAW AND PRACTICE 289–91 (ABA 2d ed. 2008).

62. *Id.* at 284. *See also* Samsung Elecs. Co. v. Rambus, 439 F. Supp. 2d 524, 532–36 (E.D. Va. 2006) (noting that that the *Infineon* decision was grounded on the crime, fraud, or tort exception to the privilege).

63. *See, e.g.*, Madanes v. Madanes, 199 F.R.D. 135, 149 (S.D.N.Y. 2001); *see In re* Sealed Case, 676 F.2d 793, 812 (D.C. Cir. 1982); Wachtel v. Guardian Life Ins., No. 01-4183, 2007 WL 1752036, at *7 (D.N.J. June 18, 2007) (finding prima facie support for in camera review of privileged materials where counsel and client failed to comply with discovery orders).

64. 126 F.R.D. 545, 546–50 (D. Minn. 1989).

65. *See, e.g.*, *Infineon*, 220 F.R.D. at 288–89 (holding that disclosure of a document retention policy and "some of the reasons for adopting [that] policy" in defending against spoliation and crime-fraud allegations put at issue and waived all advice of counsel that went into the preparation of the document retention policy).

if and to the extent the party claims that its preservation efforts were adequate as a defense to claims of spoliation.[66] For instance, given the traditionally restricted scope of attorney-client privilege in the corporate setting, a number of courts have held that the attorney-client privilege can be waived where counsel's internal investigation had the effect of shielding critical facts from discovery and preventing effective examination of witnesses.[67]

At the same time, a client might defend its actions in failing to preserve information by asserting that counsel's advice or actions were negligent. In these circumstances, under the "self-defense" doctrine, counsel might be relieved of their ethical obligation to preserve client confidences and permitted to disclose attorney-client communications in their own defense.[68]

There are thus a number of doctrines that would, in certain circumstances, support a decision to consider attorney-client implementation communications where there has been a failure to preserve ESI.

5. Basis of court's power to consider the content of some attorney-client communications where duty to preserve was breached

When there has been a breach of the duty to preserve, courts have not applied a consistent analytical framework for addressing when an inquiry into attorney-client communications is permissible.

A. The differing views

In the view of some courts, attorney-client communications, such as the legal hold notice, are privileged and/or subject to the work-product protection.[69] As such, they are not discoverable unless an

66. *See* McKenna v. Nestle Purina Petcare Co., No. 2:05-cv-0976, 2007 WL 433291, at *3–4 (D. Ohio Feb. 5, 2007) (noting that the defense of "adequate investigation" will waive privilege claims for documents prepared by attorneys involved in conducting an investigation).

67. *See, e.g.*, Baker v. GMC, 197 F.R.D. 376, 391 (W.D. Mo. 1999); *In re* S. & E. Dist. Asbestos Litig., 730 F. Supp. 582, 585 (S.D.N.Y. 1990).

68. *See, e.g.*, *Qualcomm*, 2008 WL 638108, at *2–3; Model Rules of Prof'l Conduct R. 1.6(b)(5) (2007) (permitting an attorney to disclose confidential client information "to establish a claim or defense on behalf of the lawyer in a controversy between the lawyer and the client . . . or to respond to allegations in any proceeding concerning the lawyer's representation of the client").

69. *See, e.g.*, Gibson v. Ford Motor Co., 510 F. Supp. 2d 116, 123–24 (N.D. Ga. 2007).

exception to the privilege is applicable, as in *Rambus v. Infineon*.[70] Other courts appear to treat attorney-client communications in carrying out the duty to preserve as not privileged. Those communications become relevant and discoverable upon the showing of a failure to preserve required information. This is apparently the view taken in *Zubulake V*[71] and *Land O'Lakes*.[72]

These differing approaches present more than an academic distinction, because the scope of the communications that may be considered is not the same under each of these theories. If consideration of the attorney-client communications implementing the duty to preserve is grounded on the assumption that the communications are neither privileged nor work product, once found relevant, there might be no limitation to the scope of discovery into those implementing communications and actions taken in carrying out the duty to preserve.[73]

If attorney-client communications are privileged and considered under a waiver analysis, the disclosing party must factor the governing jurisdiction's substantive law of waiver into the mix.[74] A party would not, for example, be likely to voluntarily disclose privileged information to defeat a spoliation motion if the collateral effect of that disclosure was a broad privilege waiver, especially one that went beyond implementation communications.

If the allegedly spoliating party asserts an "advice of counsel" defense, by pointing to counsel's advice in defense of the alleged spoliation, the scope may be determined under a separate rule.[75] In this circumstance, under the doctrine of "in issue" waiver, all

70. *Infineon*, 220 F.R.D. at 283.

71. 229 F.R.D. at 435–36.

72. 244 F.R.D. 614, 623 (D. Colo. 2007).

73. The text refers to implementing communications and actions, drawing a distinction between those events and attorney-client communications that constitute pure legal advice or counsel's opinion work product relating to the duty. That distinction may be difficult to draw in practice.

74. *See, e.g.*, FED. R. EVID. 502.

75. *See* Glenmede Trust Co. v. Thompson, 56 F.3d 476, 486 (3d Cir. 1995) ("The attorney-client privilege may be waived by a client who asserts reliance on the advice of counsel as an affirmative defense. . . . The party opposing the defense of reliance on advice of counsel must be able to test what information had been conveyed by the client to counsel and vice-versa regarding that advice. . . ." (citations omitted)).

attorney-client communications on the same subject matter may become discoverable.[76]

And if a client attempts to place blame for a failure to preserve on counsel, counsel may be able to invoke the "self-defense" doctrine to disclose privileged information or to disclose work product to defend themselves, as was ultimately permitted by the court in *Qualcomm*.[77]

Application of the crime, fraud, or tort exception would likely open the door only to consideration of a more limited set of facts. That exception may be invoked only upon a prima facie showing that the client has engaged in the requisite misconduct in failing to preserve relevant documents.[78] Because the crime, fraud, or tort exception is interpreted narrowly and the court's proper inquiry would be limited to those communications "in furtherance of" the alleged spoliation, not all attorney-client communications made in connection with fulfilling the duty to preserve would be discoverable.[79]

Thus, to understand the scope of permissible discovery once the door is opened, it is necessary to determine the justification for obtaining discovery of the attorney-client communications. In some circumstances more than one rationale may be applicable.

B. Resolution of the differing views: A duty-based approach

In *Fisher v. United States*, the Supreme Court wrote that the privilege "protects only those disclosures necessary to obtain informed legal

76. *See id.* at 486–87 (holding that where client relies on advice of counsel, client cannot "define selectively the subject matter of the advice of counsel on which it relied in order to limit the scope of the waiver"); United States v. Skeddle, 989 F. Supp. 917, 918–20 (N.D. Ohio 1997) (discussing factors considered in evaluating scope of waiver).

77. *Qualcomm*, 2008 WL 638108, at *3.

78. *See, e.g.*, Rabushka *ex rel.* United States v. Crane Co., 122 F.3d 559, 566 (8th Cir. 1997) (holding that to apply crime-fraud exception to a particular document, the challenging party must make a threshold showing that the legal advice was made in furtherance of the alleged fraud or closely related to it); *In re* Int'l Sys. & Controls Corp. Sec. Litig., 693 F.2d 1235, 1243 (5th Cir. 1982) (holding plaintiffs must establish that corporate management had "specific intent" to commit fraud through development of the challenged work-product documents for the crime-fraud exception to apply); Loustalet v. Refco, Inc., 154 F.R.D. 243, 246 (C.D. Cal. 1993) (holding crime-fraud exception does not apply where client sought advice of counsel regarding the legality of his conduct prior to submitting false statement to SEC but counsel was not used "to further" the illegal activity).

79. *See* Rambus, Inc. v. Infineon Techs. AG, 220 F.R.D. 264, 288–91 (E.D. Va. 2004).

advice which might not have been made absent the privilege."[80] If the duty to preserve ESI was imposed solely on the client, and counsel's job was limited to advising the client on the nature and scope of that duty, attorney-client communications relating to the duty to preserve would fall squarely within the privilege protection under the *Fisher* rule. But decisions such as *Zubulake V* have held that the duty is not the client's alone, and that counsel has an independent duty to ensure that relevant information is preserved. That duty runs to the court and the justice system.[81]

It appears that the *Zubulake V* court may have considered attorney-client communications because those communications were relevant in light of the preliminary showing of breach of the duty to preserve, and because they were exchanged pursuant to a common law duty imposed on counsel, not in connection with the client voluntarily seeking legal advice.[82] Under this analysis, the duty to preserve, and the related duty to communicate in furtherance of that duty to preserve, are considered obligations of counsel, and, under *Fisher,* those communications are outside the penumbra of the privilege and work-product protections. They become relevant and thus discoverable upon a preliminary showing of failure to preserve information that should have been preserved. Under this view, communications that make up the process of identifying and preserving relevant information are not privileged at all. They constitute neither the giving nor receiving of "legal advice," and the privilege was not intended to cover routine communications between counsel and client when engaged in fulfilling this

80. 425 U.S. 391, 403 (1976).

81. "[T]he duty to preserve evidence relevant to the litigation is a duty owed to the court, not to a party's adversary." Victor Stanley, Inc. v. Creative Pipe, Inc., 269 F.R.D. 497 (D. Md. 2010), *aff'd in part and modified in part on unrelated grounds,* No.MJG-06-2662 (D.Md. Nov. 1, 2010), *subsequent opinion,* No. MJG-06-2662 (D.Md. Jan. 24, 2011). "That the duty is owed to the court, and not to the party's adversary is a subtle, but consequential, distinction." *Id.* at 526.

82. A corollary to the duty to preserve information by effective communications is the court's power to allocate sanctions between attorney and client. A court faced with a failure to preserve or failure to produce relevant evidence may need to determine whether the duty was breached by counsel, by the client, or by both. *See Zubulake V,* 229 F.R.D. at 430, 432–34. One leading commentator has noted that "the analysis of the duty of preservation at the beginning of litigation and throughout the discovery process focuses on the intent and behavior of the parties and counsel." Kenneth J. Withers, *Electronically Stored Information: The December 2006 Amendments to the Federal Rules of Civil Procedure,* 4 NW. J. TECH. & INTELL. PROP. 171, ¶ 62 (2006), http://www.law.northwestern.edu/journals/njtip/v4/n2/3/.

duty to the adversary system. Under *Fisher,* because these communications are mandated, they would have occurred even in the absence of a privilege and therefore they are not protected by the privilege.[83]

This analysis is also consistent with many of the decisions permitting discovery of attorney-client communications implementing legal holds. *Zubulake, Rambus, Cache La Poudre Feeds, Capellupo, United Medical Supply Co.,* and other decisions support the proposition that where there is a preliminary showing of failure to comply with the duty to preserve, some preservation communications between attorney and client become relevant and, therefore, discoverable.[84]

C. Advantages of a duty-based approach

Treating communications implementing legal holds as not privileged can provide counsel and client with a number of very significant benefits. It facilitates the resolution of discovery disputes by removing the risk of subject matter waiver from the disclosure of what counsel has done and learned in the back and forth with the client on what there is, where it is, what should be preserved, and how it should be preserved.[85] If the communications were unprivileged, but irrelevant in the absence of an allegation of breach of duty, a litigant could disclose them without concern that it would be waiving the privilege.

Treating these communications as not privileged, but irrelevant absent a preliminary showing of spoliation, would not be inconsistent with the purposes of the privilege and the work-product doctrine. The duty to preserve goes to the heart of the adversary

83. *See* Fisher v. United States, 425 U.S. 391, 403 (1976) ("Since the privilege has the effect of withholding relevant information from the fact-finder, it applies only where necessary to achieve its purpose. Accordingly it protects only those disclosures necessary to obtain informed legal advice which might not have been made absent the privilege." (citation omitted)).

84. This duty-based approach does not make the communications automatically discoverable. Just as the document retention policy was irrelevant in *India Brewing, Inc. v. Miller Brewing Co.,* 237 F.R.D. 190, 194 (E.D. Wis. 2006), in the absence of any showing of a loss of ESI, the attorney-client implementation communications are not relevant to any claim, defense, or the subject matter of the action.

85. Under FRE 502(a), an intentional disclosure would present a subject-matter waiver. An FRE 502(e) party agreement would provide some protection; however, an FRE 502(d) order would be required for full protection. It would be a prudent precaution to consider, wherever possible, requesting an order pursuant to FRE 502(d) before any intentional disclosure of implementation communications.

system and the attorney's ethical responsibilities. If relevant information may be destroyed when litigation is anticipated, the underlying premises of the judicial system are brought into question. Just as the crime, fraud, or tort exception is grounded on the need to protect the integrity of the justice system, and on common-sense limits to the attorney-client privilege, a duty-based analysis furthers the same goal.[86] Just as there is no need to protect communications relating to a future crime or fraud, there is no need for implementation communications to be protected by a privilege.

Another practical advantage of this approach is that it is grounded on conditional relevancy. Because discoverability is triggered only by a preliminary showing of loss of discoverable information, rather than the showing of attorney misconduct, this approach, unlike the crime-fraud exception, would permit inquiry into such communications upon the negligent loss of discoverable information and could therefore mitigate otherwise acrimonious and protracted discovery disputes.

D. Summary

The "duty" rationale appears best suited to effectuate the purposes of both the privilege and the duty to preserve. In the absence of a loss of discoverable information, adequate protection would be provided to attorney-client preservation communications because disclosure of those communications would be irrelevant to the claims, defenses, and subject matter of the action. Thus, where counsel has performed properly, and the client has done what it should do, so that the requesting party is unable to make a preliminary showing of a breach of the duty to preserve ESI, attorney-client communications would not be discoverable, because they would be irrelevant to any claim or defense and to the subject matter of the action. The communications also would not be discoverable under the crime, fraud, or tort, fact work product, or attorney "self-defense" exceptions, because there has been no wrongdoing. And the opposing litigant's interests are fully protected because that party has the right to ask the client in discovery what steps the client took to comply with the duty to preserve. In contrast, where the requesting party is able to make a preliminary showing of a failure to preserve, because the attorney-client communications

86. *See* Rambus, Inc. v. Infineon Techs. AG, 220 F.R.D. 264, 284 (E.D. Va. 2004) (noting that consulting an attorney to commit a crime or fraud is inconsistent with the purpose of the attorney-client privilege).

were exchanged in furtherance of a legal duty to preserve information and the preservation of potential evidence is necessary to fair and equitable civil litigation, courts may permit discovery into the litigation hold, the steps taken or not taken by counsel, and the client's response to those steps.

6. The outer limit: "Pure" legal advice

The outer limit, if any, of the power to consider attorney-client communications in the context of a breach of the duty to preserve remains to be determined. Decisions such as *Keir v. UnumProvident Corp.*,[87] as well as Commentary to Sedona Guideline No. 9, demonstrate that even in cases of spoliation, some communications may remain privileged.[88] Under a duty-based approach, only implementing communications and actions are not privileged. Courts would not permit discovery of counsel's legal advice, even advice on the duty to preserve, the scope of required preservation, and the legal risks of failing to preserve. To go beyond the non-privileged actions and routine communications involved in the actual process of implementing preservation, a party alleging spoliation would be required to show much more, such as a waiver, a prima facie showing that the opposing party's failure to preserve falls within the crime, fraud, or tort exception to the privilege, or some other basis for intruding upon the privilege or work-product doctrine.

Thus, the investigation into a party's compliance with its duty to preserve should be a multistep process that in most situations will go no further than consideration of implementing communications. As illustrated in *eBay*, the first step is discovery of facts from the client demonstrating how the litigation hold was implemented. If it then becomes necessary or appropriate to proceed more deeply into the nature of attorney-client communications to determine the magnitude of, and prejudice caused by, the failure to preserve, courts may cautiously expand that inquiry and consider some of the routine attorney-client communications involved in satisfying the duty to preserve. This might include when a litigation hold was issued, whether and when a forensic expert was

87. Keir v. UnumProvident Corp., No. 02 Civ. 8781(DLC), 2003 WL 21997747 (S.D.N.Y. Aug. 22, 2003).

88. *See id.* at *11 n. 3. The Commentary to Sedona Guideline 9 states that disclosure may be in camera to protect privileged legal advice and work product. *Legal Holds, supra* note 54, at 285.

retained, what persons were identified as "key players," whether ESI storage facilities were searched, whether "janitor" programs[89] were suspended, what keywords were employed in performing searches, what was preserved, what was not preserved, and whether the lost information was unique, relevant, and significant. If, however, counsel advised a client that litigation holds involve decisions as to whether litigation is reasonably anticipated, choice of law, and proportionality considerations, there appears to be no cogent reason for requiring disclosure of that advice, absent application of an exception to the privilege.

Nothing contained in this analysis would prohibit a litigant from making a voluntary disclosure and the entry of an order under Federal Rule of Evidence 502(d) could simplify and protect that process. Such disclosures would be facilitated if the party had taken steps to engage in communications implementing the process of preservation with the express understanding that they were not confidential and did not incorporate legal advice, so that they could easily be disclosed without the need for "redaction" to refute any allegations of failure to preserve that might later be raised. That disclosure of nonprivileged information would not extend the outer boundary of discovery to encompass pure legal advice.

7. Practical considerations

In today's practice, counsel and their clients are well advised to think early and often about the potential for discovery on communications relating to legal holds and preservation efforts. Especially in the complex world of e-discovery, even those acting in the utmost good faith can lose or fail to preserve relevant information, and even the inadvertent loss of relevant data may lead to probing questions into the conduct of counsel and client.

For this reason, when drafting preservation documents and engaging in implementation discussions, counsel and client should

89. A "janitor program" is "[a]n application that runs at scheduled intervals to manage business information by deleting, transferring, or archiving on-line data (such as email) that is at or past its scheduled active life. Janitor programs are sometimes referred to as 'agents'—software that runs autonomously 'behind the scenes' on user systems and servers to carry out business processes according to predefined rules. Janitor programs must include a facility to support disposition and process holds." The Sedona Conference Glossary: E-Discovery & Digital Information Management (3d ed. 2010), http://www.thesedonaconference.org/publications_html.

be aware that those documents and discussions may ultimately be presented to a court in connection with a spoliation motion. Prudence suggests, for example, that litigation hold letters should not contain tactical and strategic discussions, and should be no more expansive than necessary to effectively accomplish the preservation task.[90] It may be advisable to circumscribe preservation discussions and segregate notes regarding the implementation of preservation efforts from substantive communications involving the merits of the dispute. Even absent a breach of the duty to preserve, the steps taken by a client to preserve information are likely discoverable, and that discovery may indirectly disclose attorney-client communications.

The preserving party may desire to disclose information about its preservation efforts, without disclosing strategic information, in order to attempt to dissuade or defeat a spoliation motion.[91] On the other hand, the opponent may seek such information to support a spoliation argument.

As a tactical or strategic matter, attorney and client may intentionally draft some or all preservation documents in a manner that would create the option of disclosing them without waiving any privilege. If implementation discussions are viewed as communications that are unprivileged because they are compelled by a legal duty, nothing would prohibit voluntary disclosure and such disclosure could be made without concerns relating to waiver of privileges. Thus, careful drafting may make it easier to respond to a spoliation motion.

8. Conclusion

Certain facts—such as what steps a litigant took, or failed to take, to preserve material—are deemed routinely discoverable. Other facts, such as the contents of a litigation hold letter, and attorney-client implementation discussions, should require a greater showing to support disclosure. Actual legal advice, if disclosable at

---

90. *See* Major Tours, Inc. v. Colorel, 2009 U.S. Dist. LEXIS 68128 (D.N.J. Aug. 4, 2009), *aff'd*, 720 F. Supp. 2d 587, 618 (D.N.J. 2010) (ordering partial production of sections of litigation hold notices), *reconsideration denied*, 2010 U.S. Dist. LEXIS 104006 (D.N.J. Sep. 29, 2010).

91. *See* The Sedona Conference, The Sedona Principles: Best Practices Recommendations & Principles for Addressing Electronic Document Production 50 (2d ed. 2007), http://www.thesedonaconference.org/content/miscFiles/TSC_PRINCP_2nd_ed_607.pdf. The course of action suggested in the text would be much safer under an FRE 502 order.

all, should be discoverable only upon a more compelling showing and, perhaps, after in camera review. Although, where there is evidence of a breach of the duty to preserve, there are multiple bases for seeking discovery of some attorney-client preservation communications, the least problematic approach is to assert that implementation communications are unprivileged, compelled exchanges that are only conditionally relevant.

CHAPTER 17

PROTECTION FROM ESI WAIVER UNDER FRE 502

BY DAVID D. CROSS, JARED S. HOSID, AND COURTNEY INGRAFFIA BARTON

Federal Rule of Evidence 502 gives major aid to parties seeking to protect privilege claims while holding down the cost of e-discovery. Even so, there are potential pitfalls. This chapter discusses FRE 502's key provisions, explores the rewards and risks of relying on it, and ends with practice tips.

1. Introduction

The risk of privilege waiver has long been one of the principal drivers of cost and inefficiency in litigation, because of the traditional need to carefully review every document to be produced to identify any privileged information that should be redacted or withheld. These costs and burdens were manageable when documents were collected from file drawers and reviewed by the hundreds or even thousands. The dramatic and persistent increase in electronically stored information, however, has taken document review costs to unprecedented levels and imposed enormous burdens on parties and the courts.

With the rapid proliferation of electronically stored information (ESI) came document review facilities staffed with dozens or even hundreds of attorneys tasked with manually reviewing countless documents for a single matter. And while electronic searches could reduce manual review for identifying relevant documents to be produced, they could not assuage parties' fears of inadvertently producing a privileged document—nor were they widely accepted by courts as appropriate for protecting privilege. Thus, traditional manual review of millions of pages of documents was expected and even routine, until Congress offered some much-needed help.

On September 19, 2008, President Bush signed into law a bill that amended the Federal Rules of Evidence to add FRE 502, intended to provide a remedy for the increasing costs of protecting privilege. FRE 502 is as follows:

> The following provisions apply, in the circumstances set out, to disclosure of a communication or information covered by the attorney-client privilege or work-product protection.
>
> (a) Disclosure made in a Federal proceeding or to a Federal office or agency; scope of a waiver.—When the disclosure is made in a Federal proceeding or to a Federal office or agency and waives the attorney-client privilege or work-product protection, the waiver extends to an undisclosed communication or information in a Federal or State proceeding only if:
> (1) the waiver is intentional;
> (2) the disclosed and undisclosed communications or information concern the same subject matter; and
> (3) they ought in fairness to be considered together.
>
> (b) Inadvertent disclosure.—When made in a Federal proceeding or to a Federal office or agency, the disclosure does not operate as a waiver in a Federal or State proceeding if:
> (1) the disclosure is inadvertent;
> (2) the holder of the privilege or protection took reasonable steps to prevent disclosure; and
> (3) the holder promptly took reasonable steps to rectify the error, including (if applicable)

following Federal Rule of Civil Procedure 26(b)(5)(B).

(c) Disclosure made in a State proceeding.—When the disclosure is made in a State proceeding and is not the subject of a State-court order concerning waiver, the disclosure does not operate as a waiver in a Federal proceeding if the disclosure:
  (1) would not be a waiver under this rule if it had been made in a Federal proceeding; or
  (2) is not a waiver under the law of the State where the disclosure occurred.

(d) Controlling effect of a court order.—A Federal court may order that the privilege or protection is not waived by disclosure connected with the litigation pending before the court—in which event the disclosure is also not a waiver in any other Federal or State proceeding.

(e) Controlling effect of a party agreement.—An agreement on the effect of disclosure in a Federal proceeding is binding only on the parties to the agreement, unless it is incorporated into a court order.

(f) Controlling effect of this rule.—Notwithstanding Rules 101 and 1101, this rule applies to State proceedings and to Federal court-annexed and Federal court-mandated arbitration proceedings, in the circumstances set out in the rule. And notwithstanding Rule 501, this rule applies even if State law provides the rule of decision.

(g) Definitions.—In this rule:
  (1) "attorney-client privilege" means the protection that applicable law provides for confidential attorney-client communications; and
  (2) "work-product protection" means the protection that applicable law provides for tangible material (or its intangible equivalent) prepared in anticipation of litigation or for trial.

FRE 502 generally does not change federal or state law of attorney-client privilege or the work-product doctrine, but rather limits the consequences when privileged information is disclosed. The rule generally provides the following:

- When waiver has occurred, subject matter waiver will not result unless the disclosure was intentional and the material was produced for an unfair advantage.
- Inadvertent disclosure will not result in waiver as long as reasonable steps were taken to protect the privilege and rectify the error.
- Nonwaiver agreements signed by the parties will be given their full effect with respect to those parties in the proceedings in which the agreements are entered.
- Nonwaiver agreements entered as an order of a federal court will be given full effect in both federal and state proceedings including against nonparties in later, unrelated proceedings.[1]

Parties may use FRE 502 to alleviate much of the cost and burden of both privilege review and logging. Parties generally need not conduct page-by-page document reviews any longer in order to avoid privilege waiver, as long as they take other reasonable steps to protect privilege. FRE 502 enables parties to enter into agreements and even obtain court orders protecting privilege without any privilege review at all. If a privileged document is produced, the producing party can demand its return or destruction and the receiving party can be barred from using it. Perhaps most significantly, if disclosure results in waiver, even for intentional disclosures, FRE 502 limits the waiver only to the specific materials disclosed—thus eliminating the much-dreaded subject matter waiver—unless fairness requires that related documents ought to be produced as well.

Invoking these protections is not without risks, however. It is difficult to predict with any certainty what a court may (or may not) consider to be "reasonable" steps to prevent disclosure of privileged information. In particular, several cases suggest that courts may scrutinize the design and accuracy (and thus the "reasonableness") of advanced methodologies used to identify and withhold privileged documents—and even seemingly extensive steps taken to protect privilege may not be enough for some courts. There also exists an open question as to whether such advanced methodologies, allowed under FRE 502 if reasonable, prevent counsel from properly certifying the completeness of a production under

1. Courtney I. Barton & David D. Cross, *Protecting the Privilege: New Federal Rule of Evidence 502*, 23 ABA In House Litigator 8 (Winter 2009).

Federal Rule of Civil Procedure 26(g). Similarly, disclosing client confidences to an adversary may be protected from waiver under FRE 502 yet forbidden by rules of professional conduct.

This chapter will look at this recently enacted rule and provide some practical guidance for its utilization.

2. History of FRE 502

FRE 502 was first contemplated in March 2006 by House Judicial Committee Chair F. James Sensenbrenner, who recognized the need to address the rising costs of litigation due in part to the privilege review required of vast amounts of electronic information.[2] A new rule of evidence was sought to mitigate these costs by substantially limiting subject matter waiver, restricting waiver to intentional or unreasonable disclosures, and giving full effect to nonwaiver agreements, which were then the subject of proposed amendments to FRCP 26(b)(5). These issues were raised by The Hon. Paul W. Grimm in *Hopson v. Mayor & City Council of Baltimore*,[3] a decision cited in the notes to FRE 502.

The original draft of the rule was the subject of hearings at Fordham University in April 2006, which were moderated by the Hon. Jerry E. Smith, U.S. Court of Appeals for the Fifth Circuit, and Dan Capra, Fordham School of Law, and attended by several distinguished speakers, including Judge Grimm, to testify about the need for the proposed rule.[4]

From the Fordham hearings, a series of recommendations were made by the Advisory Committee on Evidence Rules in May 2006 to the chair of the Federal Standing Committee on Rules of Practice and Procedure. On June 22, 2006, the Standing Committee approved a proposed amendment that incorporated input from the Fordham hearings with a recommendation that it be published for public comment. After a public comment period from August 2006 to February 2007, which included 70 public comments and two additional hearings, the Advisory Committee issued a revised rule that was approved by the Standing Committee and the Judicial Conference.[5]

2. *See* S. Rep. No. 110-264, at 4 (2008).

3. 232 F.R.D. 228, 237 (D. Md. 2005).

4. *See* Fordham University School of Law Advisory Committee on Evidence Rules: Hearing on Proposal 502 (Apr. 24, 2006).

5. *See* U.S. Judicial Conference's Letter to Congress on Evidence Rule 502 (Sept. 26, 2007), http://www.uscourts.gov/uscourts/RulesAndPolicies/rules/Hill_Letter_re_EV_502.pdf (last visited Jan. 4, 2011).

On September 26, 2007, the Hon. Lee H. Rosenthal, the chair of the Committee on Rules of Practice and Procedure, submitted the final proposed amendment to the Senate Committee on the Judiciary.[6] And on December 11, 2007, Sen. Patrick Leahy (D-VT) introduced S. 2450 to the Senate Judiciary Committee, which incorporated the language forwarded by the Judicial Conference.

Upon introducing the bill, Sen. Leahy noted: "Billions of dollars are spent each year in litigation to protect against the inadvertent disclosure of privileged materials. With the routine use of email and other electronic media in today's business environment, discovery can encompass millions of documents in a given case, vastly expanding the risks of inadvertent disclosure. . . . Our proposed legislation would set clear guidelines regarding the consequences of inadvertent disclosure of privileged material and provides that so long as reasonable steps are taken in the prevention of such a disclosure . . . no waiver will result."[7]

Sen. Leahy was joined in his support of the bill by Sen. Arlen Specter (R-PA), the ranking member of the committee, who noted that "the proposed rule enjoys wide support from parties on both sides of the 'v.' Both plaintiffs and defendants want this rule because it makes litigation more efficient and less costly; it ensures that the wheels of justice will not become bogged down in the mud of discovery."[8] Both senators urged the Senate to pass the proposal.

On February 27, 2008, the Senate passed the bill without amendment by unanimous consent, and the next day, it was received in the House, where Rep. Sheila Jackson-Lee (D-TX) stated that "the plaintiff bar and the defendant bar have come together in a unanimous voice, indicating that this will in fact enhance their ability to represent their clients and to ensure that they may have the broadest based discovery possible."[9] The House then passed the bill on September 8, 2008,[10] and President Bush signed the bill into law on September 19, 2008.

6. *Id.*
7. 153 Cong. Rec. S15,140, S15142 (daily ed. Dec. 11, 2007).
8. *Id.*
9. 154 Cong. Rec. H7817 (daily ed. Sept. 8, 2008).
10. *Id.*

3. Applicability of FRE 502

FRE 502 applies to proceedings initiated after September 19, 2008, and to earlier-initiated proceedings "insofar as is just and practicable."[11] For cases initiated on or before September 19, 2008, courts may apply FRE 502[12] or conduct an analysis under both FRE 502 and prior law.[13]

The rule's protections generally are applicable to disclosures in both federal and state proceedings, or a court-annexed or court-ordered arbitration, as described below.[14] Only attorney-client privilege and work-product protection are covered by FRE 502.[15]

Courts "must determine whether the material in question is privileged" prior to applying FRE 502.[16] FRE 502 is silent as to which party has the burden of proving waiver, leading at least some courts to assign the burden as they did before the rule's enactment—usually to the proponent of privilege.[17]

---

11. Fed. R. Evid. 502.
12. *See, e.g.*, Heriot v. Byrne, 257 F.R.D. 645, 654 (N.D. Ill. 2009) ("This matter was pending on [the date of enactment], and this Court finds no reason, and Defendants have pointed to none, that precludes the application of FRE 502.").
13. *See, e.g.*, Am. Coal Sales Co. v. Nova Scotia Power Inc., No. 2:06-cv-94, 2009 WL 467576, at *17 n.1 (S.D. Ohio Feb. 23, 2009) (holding that although Rule 502 should have been applied by the lower court, its application of prior law "was not contrary to law" and led to the same conclusion as under Rule 502); Rhoads Indus., Inc. v. Bldg. Materials Corp., 254 F.R.D. 216 (E.D. Pa. 2008) (acknowledging the enactment of Rule 502 but continuing to analyze the effect of an inadvertent disclosure under prior law because the result would be the same).
14. *See* Fed. R. Evid. 502(f) advisory committee note.
15. Fed. R. Evid. 502(g) advisory committee's note. *Cf. id.* ("The operation of waiver by disclosure, as applied to other evidentiary privileges, remains a question of federal common law. Nor does the rule purport to apply to the Fifth Amendment privilege against compelled self incrimination.").
16. *Heriot*, 257 F.R.D. at 655–56. *See also* United States v. Sensient Colors, Inc., No. 07-1275, 2009 WL 2905474, at *3 (D.N.J. Sept. 9, 2009) ("It is axiomatic that FRE 502 does not apply unless privileged or otherwise protected documents are produced.").
17. *See, e.g.*, Amobi v. D.C. Dep't of Corr., 262 F.R.D. 45, 53 (D.D.C. 2009) (implementing the district's preenactment rule that the proponent of privilege had the burden of showing that there had been no waiver); Callan v. Christian Audigier, Inc., 263 F.R.D. 564, 566 n. 3 (C.D. Cal. 2009) ("Rule 502 does not alter" the standard practice of placing the burden on the party claiming inadvertent disclosure); *Sensient Colors*, 2009 WL 2905474, at *3 ("Plaintiff, the disclosing party, has the burden to prove that the elements of FRE 502(b) have been met.").

4. Key Provisions of FRE 502

A. Subject matter waiver

Under FRE 502(a), subject matter waiver in federal and state proceedings can occur only when a disclosure made in federal proceedings or to federal offices or agencies is intentional and "ought in fairness to be considered together" with undisclosed information concerning the same subject matter.[18] In practice, subject matter waiver will occur only if a "party intentionally puts protected information into the litigation in a selective, misleading and unfair manner."[19]

In *Chick-fil-A v. ExxonMobil Corp.*, for example, the defendant was accused of tortiously interfering with the business relationship between the plaintiff and a third party.[20] An attorney for the defendant testified at a deposition that she had spoken with the third party, who had explained that the relationship with the plaintiff had ended for reasons having nothing to do with the defendant.[21] The attorney's notes describing one such conversation were offered at the deposition and cited by the defendant in its motion for summary judgment.[22] The court found that under FRE 502, the disclosure of the attorney's notes should result in a subject matter waiver because it would be "unfair to permit [the defendant] to produce work product supporting its [case] while at the same time withholding other [of its] work product documents (if any) that may undermine this contention."[23]

B. Inadvertent disclosure

Under FRE 502(b), disclosure of privileged information does not operate as a waiver in federal or state proceedings if (1) the disclosure was inadvertent; (2) the holder of the privilege "took reasonable steps to prevent disclosure"; and (3) the holder of the privilege "promptly took reasonable steps to rectify the error."

---

18. Fed. R. Evid. 502(a). *But see* Chick-fil-A v. ExxonMobil Corp., No. 08-61422-CIV, 2009 WL 3763032, at *7 (S.D. Fla. Nov. 10, 2009) (holding that a subject matter waiver under Rule 502(a) does not extend to opinion work product, which historically has been discoverable only in extraordinary circumstances).
19. Fed. R. Evid. 502(a) advisory committee's note.
20. No. 08-61422-CIV, 2009 WL 3763032, at *5 (S.D. Fla. Nov. 10, 2009).
21. *Id.* at *2.
22. *Id.* at *5.
23. *Id. Cf.* Adams v. United States, No. 03-0049-E-BLW, 2009 WL 1117392, at *2 (D. Idaho Apr. 23, 2009) ("There is no evidence that [the partial disclosure of privileged information was made] to obtain some tactical advantage.").

1. *Inadvertence*

Disclosure of privileged information must be inadvertent to avoid waiver under FRE 502(b).[24] Inadvertence is undefined by the rule but has been interpreted to mean "mistaken" or "unintended."[25]

At least one court has taken a different approach to "inadvertence," however. In *Degeer v. Gillis*,[26] a party sought protection of nine emails and attachments under FRE 502. The court found that six of the emails had been inadvertently produced and were protected from waiver under a court-ordered nonwaiver agreement.[27] The court found no waiver as to the other three emails—under a common law test applicable to use of an employer's email systems—but did so only after finding that they had not been inadvertently produced.[28] There seemed to be no dispute that the producing party had not intended to produce those three emails, but the court nonetheless found that the production was not inadvertent under FRE 502(b) because the producing party had known the documents existed at the time of the production.[29] This is an unusual interpretation of inadvertence under 502(b) that one can only hope will not be adopted by other courts.

Courts have found disclosures to be inadvertent based on a declaration from the party responsible for the purported mistake,[30] the presence of disclosed documents on a privilege log produced prior to the disclosure,[31] and "the actions of producing party after

24. FED. R. EVID. 502(b)(1).

25. *See, e.g.*, Amobi v. D.C. Dep't of Corr., 262 F.R.D. 45, 53 (D.D.C. 2009); Multiquip, Inc. v. Water Mgmt. Sys. LLC, No. 08-403-S-EJL-REB, 2009 WL 4261214, at *4 (D. Idaho Nov. 23, 2009) (question of inadvertence is "whether the party intended a privileged document to be produced or whether the production was a mistake."); Coburn Group, LLC v. Whitecap Advisors LLC, 640 F. Supp. 2d 1032, 1038 (N.D. Ill. 2009) (inadvertence is determined by "asking whether the party intended a privileged or work-product protected document to be produced or whether the production was a mistake.").

26. 2010 WL 3732132 (N.D. Ill. Sept. 17, 2010).

27. *Id.* at *8.

28. *Id.* at *9.

29. *Id.*

30. *See* Luna Gaming-San Diego, LLC v. Dorsey & Whitney, LLP, No. 06cv2804, 2010 WL 275083, at *3 (S.D. Cal. Jan. 13, 2010); *Multiquip*, 2009 WL 4261214, at *4.

31. *See* Preferred Care Partners Holding Corp. v. Humana, Inc., 258 F.R.D. 684, 694 (S.D. Fla. 2009).

discovering that the documents had been produced," including the party's speed and diligence in reacting to the disclosure.[32]

2. *"Reasonable steps to prevent disclosure"*

The proponent of privilege must take reasonable steps to prevent disclosure in order to avoid waiver under FRE 502(b).[33] Parties facing a claim of privilege waiver and seeking to invoke the protection of FRE 502(b) should provide the court with a detailed showing of the efforts taken to prevent disclosure of privileged information.[34] The Advisory Committee set forth nonexclusive considerations to guide a court's determination of whether reasonable steps were taken to prevent disclosure, including

- time taken to rectify the error
- scope of discovery and the extent of disclosure[35]
- overriding issue of fairness

32. *See* Heriot v. Byrne, 257 F.R.D. 645, 658–59 (N.D. Ill. 2009) (citing Wunderlich-Malec Sys., Inc. v. Eisenmann Corp., No. 05 C 4343, 2007 WL 3086006, at *4 (N.D. Ill. Oct. 18, 2007)).

33. Fed. R. Evid. 502(b)(2).

34. "It is rare that a Court will not find that a waiver occurred in an instance where a party presents only minimal evidence that it exercised reasonable precautions to prevent a waiver." Peterson v. Bernardi, 262 F.R.D. 424, 431 (D.N.J. 2009). *See, e.g.*, Amobi v. D.C. Dep't of Corr., 262 F.R.D. 45, 54 (D.D.C. 2009) (burden not met where defendant described its efforts minimally as follows: "several reviews of the documents to be disclosed were undertaken, [and] this document was inadvertently produced."); *Peterson*, 262 F.R.D. at 429 ("[P]laintiff does not state when his review occurred, how much time he took to review the documents, what documents were reviewed, and other basic details of the review process. The Court does not accept plaintiff's bare allegation that he conducted a 'privilege review' as conclusive proof that he took reasonable steps to prevent an inadvertent production.").

35. *Heriot*, 257 F.R.D. at 659 ("These two factors should work on a sliding scale: the broader the scope of the discovery, the more extensive a party's disclosure of confidential materials may be without waiving the privilege, and vice versa."). *See, e.g.*, United States v. Sensient Colors, Inc., No. 07-1275, 2009 WL 2905474, at *4 (D.N.J. Sept. 9, 2009) (describing inadvertent disclosure of 214 out of 45,000 produced documents as "relatively speaking[,] not a large number"); *Preferred Care*, 258 F.R.D. at 693 (only five out of 10,000 documents inadvertently produced); Rhoads v. Young Women's Christian Ass'n of Greater Pittsburgh, No. 09-261, 2009 WL 3319820, at *3 (W.D. Pa Oct. 14, 2009) (approvingly noting that "[o]ut of over 1600 pages provided to Plaintiff on April 23, 2009 only four pages of privileged documents were produced.").

- number of documents reviewed or produced[36]
- time constraints for production[37]
- use of advanced analytical software applications and linguistic tools in screening for privilege and work product[38]
- implementation of an efficient system of records management, including the use of privilege designations[39]

Subsequent cases have considered other factors such as the types of resources and techniques used to identify and withhold privileged documents,[40] whether the disclosed documents were so

36. *See, e.g.*, DJ Coleman, Inc. v. Nufarm Ams., Inc., No. 1:08-cv-051, 2010 WL 731110, at *4 (D.N.D. Feb. 25, 2010) (one inadvertently produced document in 850-page production was "not a case in which the document was produced as part of a voluminous production"); *Sensient Colors*, 2009 WL 2905474, at *4 (describing as "substantial" a production of 45,000 documents, and noting that "mistakes were bound to occur"); Coburn Group, LLC v. Whitecap Advisors LLC, 640 F. Supp. 2d 1032, 1039 (N.D. Ill. 2009) (describing "72,000 pages of potentially responsive documents, from which 40,000 pages of documents were produced" as substantially large); *Heriot*, 257 F.R.D. at 659 ("This amount [reviewed and produced 1499 documents comprising 6952 pages] is neither apologetically large nor astonishingly small.").

37. *But see Peterson*, 262 F.R.D. at 430 ("The time constraints about which plaintiff now complains were self-imposed and do not excuse his careless actions.").

38. *See, e.g., Sensient Colors*, 2009 WL 2905474, at *4–5 ("Plaintiff's production was made in the midst of a commendable effort to employ a sophisticated computer program to conduct its privilege review. Unfortunately, mistakes occurred. Plaintiff should not be unduly punished for occasional mistakes that occurred while it started to use new software to organize and sort its documents . . . the Court is satisfied that plaintiff employed diligent efforts and safeguards when it set up and used its analytical software."). *But see* Victor Stanley, Inc. v. Creative Pipe Inc., 250 F.R.D. 251, 259–64 (D. Md. 2008) (producing documents without at least some manual review of both the documents produced and the documents withheld and without relying on qualified persons to design the search protocol may not satisfy the reasonableness requirements of Rule 502(b)).

39. Fed. R. Evid. 502(b) advisory committee's note. *See, e.g.*, Kumar v. Hilton Hotels Corp., No. 08-2689 D/P, 2009 WL 1683479, at *3 (W.D. Tenn. Jun. 16, 2009) (including a privilege designation in bold letters at the top of a privileged email was a reasonable step taken to prevent inadvertent disclosure). *But see Sensient Colors*, 2009 WL 2905474, at *4 (inadvertent disclosure of documents that are self-evidently privileged may indicate lack of reasonable care).

40. *See, e.g., Sensient Colors*, 2009 WL 2905474, at *4 (plaintiff "invested substantial resources to prevent inadvertent production" by employing 12 trained reviewers and employing systematic quality control); *Preferred Care*, 258 F.R.D. at 692–93 (S.D. Fla. 2009) (four attorneys conducted extensive privilege review of 10,000 documents over limited time period). The use of paralegals is not necessarily unreasonable. *See, e.g., Coburn*, 640 F. Supp. 2d at 1039 (use of "experienced paralegals who were given specific direction and supervision by a lawyer who

clearly privileged that heightened care was appropriate,[41] whether sampling was used to test the production,[42] and whether the producing party increased its vigilance as a result of prior inadvertent disclosures.[43] No single consideration is dispositive.[44]

The rule does not necessarily require the producing party to engage in a postproduction review to determine if there had been an inadvertent disclosure, but the producing party cannot ignore any "obvious indications" that disclosure occurred.[45]

---

is lead counsel in the case was not unreasonable" in light of large size of review); *Heriot*, 257 F.R.D. at 660 n.10 ("[T]his Court declines to hold that a procedure is unreasonable in every case that a paralegal or non-lawyer reviews documents for privilege."). The use of a copy vendor after a review is not unreasonable, even where the vendor is responsible for the disclosure; to hold otherwise would "chill the use of e-vendors." *Id.* at 660–61.

41. *See, e.g.*, *Sensient Colors*, 2009 WL 2905474, at *4 (inadvertent disclosure of documents that are self-evidently privileged may indicate lack of reasonable care); *Peterson*, 2009 WL 2243988, at *4 ("Although on a total percentage basis the number of disclosures is small (approximately 135 out of thousands produced), the nature of the disclosures is relevant. Most of the documents in question are exchanges between plaintiff and his counsel. These communications warranted a significant level of scrutiny.").

42. *See, e.g.*, Mt. Hawley Ins. Co. v. Felman Prod., Inc., No. 3:09-cv-00481, 2010 WL 1990555, at *11–12 (S.D.W.Va. May 18, 2010) (although the producing party hired a vendor, tested various search terms, and conducted "eyes-on" review of all documents identified as relevant and potentially privileged, the court nonetheless found it failed to conduct "critical quality control sampling to determine whether their production was appropriate and neither over-inclusive nor under-inclusive").

43. *See, e.g.*, *Sensient Colors*, 2009 WL 2905474, at *5 n.13 ("Plaintiff's Declarations are silent on what it did immediately after it [became aware of the initial inadvertent disclosure] to assure the accuracy of its complete document production, not just the documents" initially disclosed.); *Preferred Care*, 258 F.R.D. at 700 (producing party acted unreasonably in not being more vigilant in light of prior incidents of inadvertent disclosure).

44. *See, e.g.*, Infor Global Solutions (Michigan), Inc. v. St. Paul Fire & Marine Ins. Co., No. C 08-02621, 2009 WL 2390174 (N.D. Cal. Aug 3, 2009) (inadvertently disclosed documents represented only 4 percent of total production, but lack of precautionary steps carried more weight); *Heriot*, 257 F.R.D. at 660 ("[A]lthough Plaintiffs disclosed 13 percent of their privileged documents, the weight of the factors tips the balance in favor of inadvertent disclosure.").

45. Fed. R. Evid. 502(b) advisory committee's note.

3. *"Reasonable steps to rectify the error"*

The producing party must promptly take reasonable steps to rectify an inadvertent disclosure if it is to obtain protection under FRE 502(b).[46]

With regard to the promptness of efforts to rectify the error, courts have disagreed as to whether the starting point is the disclosure itself or the producing party's discovery of the disclosure.[47] Because a court may look to the date of disclosure rather than the date of notice of the disclosure, parties may find it prudent to perform some postproduction review to ensure that any inadvertent disclosures are promptly discovered and addressed.[48]

The amount of time that will be considered reasonable will vary according to the facts of the case.[49] The *steps* a party takes to

---

46. Fed. R. Evid. 502(b)(3). *See* Luna Gaming-San Diego, LLC v. Dorsey & Whitney, LLP, No. 06cv2804 , 2010 WL 275083, at *6 (S.D. Cal. Jan. 13, 2010) (plaintiff failed to object to defendant's use of inadvertently disclosed documents at two depositions and in two summary judgment motions, yet "the most important factor that weigh[ed] in favor of waiver" was plaintiff's failure to take "prompt and diligent steps to reassess its [defective] document production" after being put on notice).

47. *Compare* Coburn Group, LLC v. Whitecap Advisors LLC, 640 F. Supp. 2d 1032, 1041 (N.D. Ill. 2009) ("[T]he relevant time . . . is how long it took the producing party to act after it learned that the privileged or protected document had been produced.") *with Preferred Care,* 258 F.R.D. at 700 (citing dates of disclosure in analyzing whether prompt steps were taken to rectify errors), *and* N. Am. Rescue Prods., Inc. v. Bound Tree Med. LLC, No. 2:08-cv-101, 2010 WL 1873291, at *8 (S.D. Ohio May 10, 2010) (same), *and* Victor Stanley, Inc. v. Creative Pipe Inc., 250 F.R.D. 251, 263 (D. Md. 2008)3 (the "more important period of delay" was the one week that passed between production of the documents and identification of the disclosure by the plaintiff).

48. *See Hopson,* 232 F.R.D. at 244–46 (observing that where "less than full preproduction privilege review" is warranted under the "cost-benefit balancing factors listed in Rule 26(b)(2)," some pre- and postproduction privilege review is nonetheless required to reasonably safeguard privilege by avoiding, and promptly rectifying, inadvertent disclosure). Note that *Victor Stanley* and *Hopson* predate the enactment of Rule 502.

49. *See, e.g., Sensient Colors,* 2009 WL 2905474, at *5 (eight business days was reasonable amount of time between becoming aware of disclosure and seeking the return of the disclosed documents); *Heriot,* 257 F.R.D. at 659 (acting within 24 hours of discovering inadvertent disclosure was reasonably prompt); Rhoads v. Young Women's Christian Ass'n of Greater Pittsburgh, No. 09-261, 2009 WL 3319820, at *3 (W.D. Pa Oct. 14, 2009) (defendants sought return of inadvertently disclosed documents "immediately" where they sent plaintiffs a letter five days after production). *Cf.* Amobi v. D.C. Dep't of Corr., 262 F.R.D. 45, 55 (D.D.C. 2009) (describing as "debatable" the proposition that a party took prompt action

rectify an inadvertent disclosure have been held by at least one court to be more important than the *time* it takes to undertake those efforts.[50] Reasonable steps include lodging an objection at a deposition when a privileged document is offered,[51] sending a letter to the receiving party to assert privilege and request the return of the inadvertently disclosed document,[52] and filing a motion for a protective order.[53] When invoking the protections of FRE 502(b), the producing party may need to comply with FRCP 26(b)(5)(B) by notifying any party that received the information of the privilege claim and the basis for it.[54]

---

where 55 days passed from its identification of the disclosure to any efforts to rectify the error); *N. Am. Rescue,* 2010 WL 1873291, at *8 (producing party did not raise issue of inadvertent disclosure until after the opposing party filed a motion to compel, five months after disclosure); *Preferred Care,* 258 F.R.D. at 693, 700 (in one instance, notifying plaintiff of privilege claim within one week of disclosure was reasonable; in another instance, it was unreasonable to wait two months after disclosure and two weeks after privileged information was used in opponent's motion to compel, especially where there had been prior disclosure problems).

50. *Heriot,* 257 F.R.D. at 662 ("[H]ow the disclosing party discovers and rectifies the disclosure is more important than when after the inadvertent disclosure the discovery occurs.").

51. *See, e.g.,* Laethem Equip. Co. v. Deere & Co., 261 F.R.D. 127, 134 (E.D. Mich. 2009); B-Y Water Dist. v. City of Yankton, No. CIV. 07-4142, 2008 WL 5188837, at *2 (D.S.D. Dec. 10, 2008) (Defendant "immediately asserted its privilege when the two documents were referenced during a deposition[,] the first time that counsel for [defendant] realized he may have accidentally produced the privileged information. The Court is satisfied.").

52. *See, e.g., Laethem,* 261 F.R.D. at 134; *Heriot,* 257 F.R.D. at 659 (within 24 hours of discovering inadvertent disclosure, plaintiffs sent a letter to defendants that claimed attorney-client privilege and requested that the documents be destroyed; "[t]hose actions can be described only as responsible").

53. *See* Kumar v. Hilton Hotels Corp., No. 08-2689 D/P, 2009 WL 1683479, at *3 (W.D. Tenn. Jun. 16, 2009) (defendant "took immediate steps to notify the court of this claim by filing the emergency motion."). Note that it is reasonable for the producing party to notify and negotiate with opposing counsel prior to filing a motion. *See, e.g., Laethem,* 261 F.R.D. at 134 (reasonable steps taken where disclosure came to light at a deposition, an objection was immediately lodged, a letter to opposing counsel was sent the same day, and a protective order was sought soon thereafter); *Coburn,* 640 F. Supp. 2d at 1041 ("As for the delay in filing the motion, the facts recited above show that counsel for both sides acted reasonably and civilly in dealing with the disputed documents and the associated deposition transcripts.").

54. Fed. R. Evid. 502(b)(3).

4. *The common law five-factor test and FRE 502(b)*

Prior to the enactment of FRE 502, courts often applied the following five-factor test described in *McCafferty's, Inc. v. Bank of Glen Burnie*[55] to determine whether privilege had been waived by an inadvertent disclosure:

(1) The reasonableness of the precautions taken to prevent inadvertent disclosure in view of the extent of the document production.
(2) The number of inadvertent disclosures.
(3) The extent of the disclosure.
(4) Any delay and measures taken to rectify the disclosure.
(5) Whether the overriding interests of justice would or would not be served by relieving the party of its errors.[56]

Some courts have relied on this five-factor test even after the enactment of FRE 502.

In *Rhoads*, to determine whether an inadvertent disclosure constituted a waiver, the court first determined whether the plaintiff met a threshold level of reasonableness under FRE 502(b), and then in a second step determined whether the plaintiff's actions were reasonable under the five-factor test.[57]

The court appeared to apply this test based on the Advisory Committee Note to FRE 502, which states that the rule is not inconsistent with the five-factor common law test:

> The stated factors (none of which are dispositive) are the reasonableness of precautions taken, the time taken to rectify the error, the scope of discovery, the extent of disclosure, and the overriding issue of fairness. The rule does not explicitly codify that test, because it is really a set of non-determinative guidelines that vary from case to case. The rule is flexible enough to accommodate any of those listed factors.[58]

---

55. 179 F.R.D. 163, 167 (D. Md. 1998).

56. *Id.*

57. Rhoads Indus., Inc. v. Bldg. Materials Corp., 254 F.R.D. 216, 218–19 (E.D. Pa. 2008).

58. *Id.* (quoting Fed. R. Evid. 502 advisory committee's note). *See also* Am. Coal Sales Co. v. Nova Scotia Power Inc., No. 2:06-cv-94, 2009 WL 467576, at *17 n.1 (S.D. Ohio Feb. 23, 2009) (district court, in reviewing a magistrate judge's decision decided before enactment of Rule 502, noted that the magistrate judge's application of the common law factors was not inconsistent with what the analysis should be under Rule 502).

The *Rhoads* court appeared to interpret this passage to mean that in applying FRE 502(b), a court should first decide whether a litigant has met a threshold level of reasonableness, and if that is the case, the court then should apply this five-factor test in completing the analysis:

> In approaching a conclusion, and recognizing that Rule 502 is a recent addition to the law, I believe that the most appropriate approach is to first determine whether the producing party has at least minimally complied with the three factors stated in Rule 502, i.e., that the waiver was inadvertent, the party took reasonable steps to prevent disclosure, and attempted to rectify the error.
>
> In this case, there is no dispute that the production of the privileged documents was inadvertent; the dispute is over whether the steps taken by Rhoads were "reasonable." Consistent with the Committee Note to Rule 502, I conclude that once the producing party has shown at least minimal compliance with the three factors in Rule 502, but "reasonableness" is in dispute, the court should proceed to the traditional five-factor test discussed above.[59]

The problem with the *Rhoads* court's interpretation of FRE 502 is that neither the Advisory Committee Note nor the language of FRE 502 suggests that application of FRE 502(b) entails a two-tiered analysis. Instead, it appears that Congress's intent was for the common law five-factor test to simply assist courts in applying the rule's reasonableness factor as part of a single analysis.[60]

Other courts applying FRE 502(b) have not interpreted it or applied it in the same manner as did the *Rhoads* court.[61] In fact,

59. *Id.* at 226.

60. FED. R. EVID. 502 advisory committee's note, http://federalevidence.com/node/185 (last visited Jan. 4, 2010). The application of this five-factor test under Rule 502(b), as the *Rhoads* court applied it, is especially curious given that two of the five factors—namely, (1) the reasonableness of the precautions taken to prevent inadvertent disclosure and (4) any delay and measures taken to rectify the disclosure—are nearly identical to 502(b)(2) and (3). Thus, it is unclear whether Congress intended for courts to consider the other three factors under 502(b).

61. *See, e.g.*, N. Am. Rescue Prods., Inc. v. Bound Tree Med. LLC, No. 2:08-cv-101, 2010 WL 1873291, at *9 (S.D. Ohio May 10, 2010) (five-factor test "not mandatory and merely serves to guide a court's analysis when appropriate under the particular circumstances of each case"); Laethem Equip. Co. v. Deere and Co., No. 2:05-CV-10113, 2008 WL 4997932, at *8 (E.D. Mich. Nov. 21, 2008) (straightforward

a court in the Northern District of Illinois criticized the *Rhoads* court's interpretation and application of FRE 502(b) as "peculiar," noting that application of the common law factors would "eliminate[] any need to consult the elements required under FRE 502," and that "[s]uch an approach would ignore a Congressional mandate and substitute judicial holdings for legislation."[62]

Despite this negative view of the *Rhoads* decision, at least one other court later took a similar approach to FRE 502. In *Mt. Hawley Insurance Co.*, the court applied the common law five-factor test under FRE 502(b) and found waiver as to nearly 400 documents for failure to take reasonable steps to protect the privilege.[63] The *Mt. Hawley* court's application of the five-factor test was particularly odd because of the circumstances of the case.

First, the parties had entered into a stipulated clawback agreement, yet the court applied FRE 502(b) rather than 502(e).[64] It is not entirely clear from the decision why the court did this, but it appears that the clawback agreement may not have included a nonwaiver agreement; in other words, the clawback agreement required the return or destruction of inadvertently produced privileged documents upon request but perhaps did not provide that inadvertent disclosure did not constitute waiver.[65] Thus, the court analyzed waiver under the "reasonableness" test of 502(b).

Second, the stipulated clawback agreement also provided that the timeliness requirement of 502(b)(3) was satisfied once the request was made for the return or destruction of inadvertently produced privileged documents.[66] The court thus found FRE 502(b)(3) satisfied under this agreement. The court then went on, however, to reassess the very same element in applying the common law five-factor test, which includes as one of its factors "any delay and measures taken to rectify the disclosure."[67] And not only did the court reassess this element, it stunningly reached the opposite conclusion, finding that the producing party had not

---

application of three factors listed in Rule 502(b), without any discussion of "two-tiered" analysis).

62. Heriot v. Byrne, No. 08 C 2272, 2009 WL 742769, at *7 n.7 (N.D. Ill. Mar. 20, 2009).

63. *Mt. Hawley Ins. Co.*, 2010 WL 1990555, at *13.

64. *Id.* at *9.

65. *Id.* at *10.

66. *Id.* at *9.

67. *Id.*

acted promptly enough in rectifying the disclosure.[68] In so doing, the court effectively disregarded the parties' stipulated clawback agreement on this element, in violation of FRE 502(e).

The *Mt. Hawley* decision is odd in a few additional respects. First, the court found that the producing party had taken some two dozen steps to protect the privilege, but these were not enough.[69] The court found that the producing party did not "perform critical quality control sampling to determine whether the production was appropriate and neither over-inclusive nor under-inclusive" and did not perform "simple keyword searches" that could have identified the key privileged document at issue.[70] Second, the court found that the inadvertent productions resulted at least in part from a software failure, yet the court found waiver as to all the documents because the disclosures were "not *solely* attributable" to the software failure.[71] Third, the 377 purportedly privileged documents at issue accounted for a tiny fraction of the overall production, which totaled nearly 350 GB.[72] Thus, the error rate for the privilege protocols applied—that is, the number of privileged documents inadvertently produced as a percentage of the total documents produced—was extremely small. Finally, one of the bases for the waiver finding was the court's conclusion that "[c]onfidentiality cannot be restored" in the inadvertently produced documents—but of course this likely will always be the case with inadvertently produced privileged documents.[73] These circumstances and the court's findings suggest a very high threshold for "reasonableness" under FRE 502(b).

It remains to be seen whether courts will follow the likes of *Rhoads* and *Mt. Hawley*. Such interpretations and applications of FRE 502 are likely to stymie the efficiencies and cost savings Congress intended for the rule. Hopefully these decisions will remain outliers and the courts will bring a more practical and forgiving perspective to FRE 502 and those seeking its protections.

68. *Id.* at *13.
69. *Id.* at *11–12.
70. *Id.* at *12.
71. *Id.* (emphasis added).
72. *Id.*
73. *Id.* at *13.

C. Disclosures made in state proceedings

FRE 502(c) enables parties to a prior state proceeding to belatedly avail themselves of the protections of FRE 502 or to invoke the protections of state law if they later find themselves defending privilege in a federal proceeding. In essence, the federal court will "apply the law that is most protective of privilege and work product."[74]

Under FRE 502, the disclosure of privileged material in a state proceeding, if not subject to a court order in that proceeding, will not cause a waiver in a federal proceeding if one of two conditions is met: (1) the disclosure would not have been a waiver under FRE 502, thereby retroactively applying FRE 502 to the disclosure; or (2) the disclosure is not a waiver under the applicable state law, thereby applying state law in a federal proceeding even where federal law would find waiver.[75]

D. Nonwaiver agreements and court orders

FRE 502(d) provides that a federal court may order that attorney-client privilege or work product protection is not waived by disclosure connected with the litigation pending before the court,[76] and that any such order will apply with full force and effect in any other federal or state proceeding, even as to third parties. FRE 502 does not require that the order memorialize an agreement between the parties, which suggests that a court can act sua sponte or upon motion for a protective order by a party over the objection of one or more parties.[77]

FRE 502(e) provides that parties to a federal proceeding can enter into a nonwaiver agreement that will be binding on the parties to the agreement, but the agreement would not be binding in state court or as to third parties unless it were made part of a court order.[78]

These provisions validate so-called "clawback" and "quick-peek" agreements that have become popular cost-saving devices

---

74. Fed. R. Evid. 502(c) advisory committee's note.
75. Fed. R. Evid. 502(c).
76. The court cannot "enter an order determining the waiver effects of a separate disclosure of the same information in other proceedings, state or federal." Fed. R. Evid. 502(d) advisory committee's note.
77. Fed. R. Evid. 502(d) advisory committee's note.
78. Fed. R. Evid. 502(e).

in e-discovery.[79] Parties entering into these types of agreements should be sure to set forth the intended protections in clear and specific terms, although the legalese that lawyers so often favor is not necessary.[80]

5. The rewards (and risks) of FRE 502

A. Doing away with page-by-page reviews

Invoking the protections of FRE 502 can result in significant cost savings. Perhaps most significantly, subsection (d) enables parties to produce documents with little or no privilege review as long as they obtain and comply with a court-ordered nonwaiver agreement. If privileged documents are disclosed, they can be clawed back and other parties will be barred from using them. Under subsection (b), parties should not need to do a page-by-page privilege review to avoid waiver even in the absence of a nonwaiver agreement, so long as other reasonable steps are taken to protect privilege. For example, parties instead could use electronic search tools to identify potentially privileged materials.

Even if waiver is found, subsection (a) provides a safety net limiting the scope of the waiver. Whether inadvertent or intentional, the most an adversary generally will be able to retain is the particular privileged document that was disclosed, unless fairness requires that related documents also ought to be produced. Thus,

79. A "clawback" agreement is an agreement between the parties that the production of privileged information does not constitute a waiver. It typically sets forth a process for retrieval of inadvertently produced privileged information. A "quick-peek" arrangement allows a requesting party to see a responding party's entire data collection before production and to designate those items that they believe are responsive to the discovery requests. The parties typically agree that any privileged information disclosed to the requesting party's counsel in the quick-peek review does not constitute a waiver. *See, e.g.,* Tremont LLC v. Halliburton Energy Servs., Inc., No. H-08-1063, 2009 WL 959456, at *2 (S.D. Tex. Mar. 31, 2009).

80. S.E.C. v. Bank of Am. Corp., No. 09 Civ. 6829, 2009 WL 3297493, at *1 (S.D.N.Y. Oct. 14, 2009) ("Although the text of the proposed Protective Order is draped in legalese—with the complete first sentence extending over two-and-a-quarter single-spaced pages and featuring no fewer than nine recitations of the word 'Whereas'—the thrust of the proposal is simple enough."); United States v. Sensient Colors, Inc., No. 07-1275, 2009 WL 2905474, at *2 (D.N.J. Sept. 9, 2009) (in deeming that language in a discovery plan concerning waiver did not amount to a clawback agreement, the court noted that the parties were represented by "sophisticated counsel [and i]f they intended to implement a 'clawback' provision this would have been specifically mentioned.").

FRE 502's protections, at least in theory, afford parties the option to conduct limited or even no privilege review—but only if parties are willing to bear certain risks.

B. Understanding the risks

One of the most significant risks of FRE 502 lies with the requirement that to obtain protection for inadvertent disclosure, reasonable steps must have been taken to prevent and rectify the disclosure. Although the rule allows for the use of keyword searches and other methodologies to identify and withhold privileged documents, and some courts have viewed the use of advanced methodologies as evidence of reasonableness,[81] several cases suggest that courts may scrutinize the design and accuracy (and thus the "reasonableness") of these methods.[82] If the courts set a high threshold for "reasonable steps" under FRE 502(b)(2), the costs of developing and defending a privilege protocol, including an electronic search methodology, could swallow the cost savings of limiting or eliminating manual review. Worse, parties could forgo the intended cost-saving protections of FRE 502(b) for fear of a finding of unreasonableness and privilege waiver.

The reasonable inquiry requirement of FRCP 26(g) presents another risk. Even if some protocol short of manual review, such as electronic searches, would satisfy FRE 502, a court nonetheless could find that counsel failed to conduct a reasonable inquiry under FRE 26(g) on the ground that counsel cannot reasonably certify the completeness of a document production when no attorney

81. Rhoads Indus., Inc. v. Bldg. Materials Corp., 254 F.R.D. 216, 222 (E.D. Pa. 2008) ("The fact that Rhoads retained a consultant who recommended and used a fairly sophisticated screening device shows that Rhoads substantially complied with . . . Rule 502.").

82. Victor Stanley, Inc. v. Creative Pipe Inc., 250 F.R.D. 251, 259–64 (D. Md. 2008) (producing documents without at least some manual review of both the documents produced and the documents withheld and without relying on qualified persons to design the search protocol may not satisfy the reasonableness requirements of Rule 502(b)); United States v. O'Keefe, 537 F. Supp. 2d 14, 24 (D.D.C. 2008) (suggesting that those tasked with developing the search methodology may be required to satisfy the expert requirements of Federal Rule of Evidence 702, should they be required to defend the reasonableness of the methodology before the court); Equity Analytics, LLC v. Lundin, 248 F.R.D. 331, 333 (D.D.C. 2008) (same). These cases were issued prior to the enactment of Rule 502, but the authors—Magistrate Judges Paul Grimm and John Facciola—contributed to efforts to design and implement the rule. Chapters 20 and 21 discuss search methodology.

actually looked at the documents that were collected, searched, and produced.[83]

The rules of professional conduct present yet another possible hurdle for FRE 502. FRE 502 effectively permits the disclosure of client confidences to an adversary, but ethical rules do not. To avoid running afoul of ethical duties, counsel would be wise to clearly identify for clients the risks associated with producing potentially privileged information without a traditional manual review, including the disclosure of client confidences to an adversary, and counsel should discuss with the client—and obtain the client's approval—for the specific steps taken to protect privilege.

Even assuming that a party and its counsel could disclose privileged information to an adversary without violating any rules—procedural or ethical—an important problem still remains: once the bell is rung, it cannot be unrung. In other words, once an adversary learns privileged information, that information cannot be stripped from the adversary's mind. And while an adversary can be barred under FRE 502 from using the document containing that information, nothing—not even FRE 502—can undo the potential harm of the privileged information itself having become known to an adversary.

6. Conclusion and practice tips

Only time will tell whether FRE 502 will achieve the cost savings intended. This will depend in large part on what "reasonable steps" courts require to protect the privilege and to rectify inadvertent disclosures under FRE 502(b). If parties can satisfy the rule with less than a manual document-by-document review, then cost savings should be forthcoming. On the other hand, parties may want to wait and see how the rule is tested in the courts before abandoning traditional review, and many may see manual review as the only way to avoid the harms of exposing their client's confidential and privileged information to their adversary. Moreover, if parties are required to retain experts to design and defend electronic search protocols in lieu of painstaking manual review, review costs may be replaced by expert costs.

83. *See* Qualcomm Inc. v. Broadcom Corp., No. 05CV1958-B, 2008 WL 66932, at *3–6 (S.D. Cal. Jan. 7, 2008), *vacated on other grounds*, No. 05CV1958-RMB, 2008 WL 638108 (S.D. Cal. Mar. 5, 2008) (finding that counsel failed to satisfy FRCP 26(g) with the search methodology used to locate and produce relevant documents).

If nothing else, however, the substantial erosion of subject matter waiver and the security provided by court-ordered nonwaiver agreements under FRE 502 are material changes in the law that should provide significant solace to counsel and clients dealing with the overwhelming burden of searching, retrieving, reviewing, and producing millions of electronic records in a timely fashion.

The following are some practice tips for working with FRE 502:

- Negotiate a nonwaiver agreement with opposing counsel and request that the court enter the agreement as an order. If a nonwaiver agreement cannot be reached, move the court to enter a nonwaiver order pursuant to FRE 502(d).[84]
- Be sure that any nonwaiver agreement or order sets forth the desired protections with specificity to avoid disputes later about the propriety or reasonableness of measures taken. State clearly what steps, if any, need to be taken to protect privilege, and identify the trigger—date of discovery or date of production—to start the clock for the timeliness element of FRE 502(b)(3). And remember that FRE 502(b) is silent on whether and when intentional disclosure constitutes privilege waiver, so consider addressing this in the nonwaiver agreement or order, perhaps eliminating subject matter waiver entirely.
- Conduct at least some preproduction manual privilege review even if there is a court-ordered nonwaiver agreement. Manual review may be best for especially sensitive information that a party would not want an adversary to learn, and a party can use technological tools to cull and produce documents that are unlikely to contain privileged information or that may contain privileged information but would not harm the case if disclosed to the other side.
- Utilize experienced professionals to develop and implement technologies used to identify and withhold privileged documents, and coordinate closely with those at the client most knowledgeable about the relevant documents

84. Rajala v. McGuire Woods, Inc., 2010 U.S. Dist. LEXIS 73564 (D. Kan. July 22, 2010) (The court entered a nonwaiver order proposed by the defendant over the plaintiff's objection and observed: "To deny entry of such a clawback provision merely because Plaintiff would be deprived of the opportunity to demonstrate that the producing party had not taken reasonable care to prevent disclosure would defeat the purpose behind Rule 502 (d) and (e).").

and data as well as the electronic systems in which these reside. Be prepared to defend the use and accuracy of any such technologies with a detailed showing of the efforts taken and the knowledge of those responsible for those efforts; to that end, document every step taken. And ensure appropriate supervision throughout the process.

- Seek an agreement with opposing counsel concerning search terms. Utilize sampling or some other measure to ensure that search protocols are neither underinclusive nor overinclusive, within reason.[85]
- Seek an agreement with opposing counsel that certain categories of documents that are unquestionably privileged, such as communications between inside and outside counsel, need not be reviewed or identified on a privilege log or may be identified in an abbreviated way.[86]
- Conduct at least some postproduction review or sampling to ensure that any inadvertently produced privileged documents are quickly identified and measures are promptly taken to rectify the error.
- If made aware of an inadvertent disclosure, quickly contact opposing counsel to assert privilege (in accordance with the requirements of FRE 26(b)(5)) and request the return of the disclosed material. If unsuccessful, promptly file a motion for a protective order.
- Approach privileges other than attorney work-product and attorney-client (such as the physician-patient privilege, spousal privilege, and executive privilege) in the same manner as before the enactment of FRE 502.

85. A common problem with using electronic searches to identify potentially privileged documents that causes such searches to be overinclusive arises from the routine use of legal disclaimers in attorney communications today. Attorneys regularly include automatically generated language posted within emails and on fax cover sheets regarding the "confidential" and "privileged" nature of the communications. Of course, many emails attorneys send today are neither confidential nor privileged, yet electronic filters tend to identify emails with such language as privileged. An effective solution to this problem is to identify words or phrases that are likely unique to the automatically generated disclaimer and to use that language to isolate those documents that are caught by the electronic filter based solely on the inclusion of the disclaimer; this subset of documents then can be manually reviewed or filtered in another way or perhaps logged with greater detail than other documents.

86. See chapter 15.

CHAPTER 18

THE 10 MOST IMPORTANT THINGS YOU NEED TO REMEMBER ABOUT FRE 502

BY THE HON. PAUL W. GRIMM

Chapter 17 provided a comprehensive overview and discussion of recently enacted Federal Rule of Evidence 502, its unique legislative history, and how it has been interpreted by the courts in the first two years of its existence. In this chapter, a federal magistrate judge—on the front lines of e-discovery disputes in the federal courts—offers his "top 10" list of what lawyers should always keep in mind about this crucial rule protecting electronically stored information (ESI) privilege claims.

As chapter 17 of this book makes clear, Rule 502 of the Federal Rules of Evidence had to be affirmatively enacted by Congress, as opposed to adopted by the regular rulemaking process of the Rules Enabling Act, because it altered the common law of the United States regarding waiver of the attorney-client privilege and the work-product doctrine. At the time of its enactment, it was viewed as essential to fulfill the promise of the 2006 changes to the Federal Rules of Civil Procedure addressing discovery of

ESI, particularly FRCP 26(b)(5)(B), which created a procedure for asserting attorney-client privilege or work-product claims even after a producing party discovered that it already had disclosed to its adversary privileged or protected information. Without FRE 502, FRCP 26(b)(2)(B) was an empty promise, because it provided a procedure for asserting a claim of privilege or work-product protection in circumstances where the outcome of the claim would likely be a determination of waiver by the court.

Looking back on the cases decided in the years since FRE 502's enactment, it is doubtful whether the rule has achieved one of its two primary objectives: the reduction of the cost of ESI discovery by eliminating the need for painstaking, document-by-document review of all digital documents before producing them during discovery. And, although the Advisory Committee Notes to FRE 502 make it clear that the use of computer-based search methodology[1] would be an example of reasonable preproduction precautions against inadvertent production of privileged or protected ESI, courts that have interpreted the new rule have not rendered sufficiently consistent opinions regarding the effect of using such digital search methodology to encourage lawyers and clients to expansively use it, instead of conducting more expensive document-by-document review. As chapter 17 notes, some courts have gotten it right, others have not, and it is hoped that in the future, as more lawyers become familiar with FRE 502, and more courts interpret it consistently with its underlying purpose, the goals of the rule will be realized.

One way in which this may come about is for lawyers and judges to quickly grasp the essential provisions of FRE 502, so that it may be more readily understood and applied. In the hope of facilitating this result, I offer this list of the 10 essential facts to remember about the rule.

1. FRE 502's scope is limited

The first thing to keep in mind is the limited scope of FRE 502. It applies only to the attorney-client privilege and to work-product protection. It has no bearing at all on the plethora of other evidentiary privileges such as the spousal communications privilege, governmental privileges, accountant-client privilege, priest-penitent privilege, or psychotherapist-patient privilege. This

1. See chapters 20 and 21 for a discussion of search methodology and privilege.

is not to diminish the importance of the rule, as all experienced litigators know that the frequency with which attorney-client privilege and work-product doctrine are evoked as the basis for refusing to provide requested discovery dwarfs the assertion of any other privilege.

2. FRE 502 applies only in the context of actual disclosure of privileged information

FRE 502 applies only to whether a waiver of the attorney-client privilege or work-product protection has occurred as a consequence of actual disclosure of privileged or protected information. Thus, it is inapplicable to circumstances where a waiver may occur even without disclosure, such as when a party puts at issue in litigation its reliance on attorney advice as a defense to a claim, or when a defendant in a patent claim argues that it may not be found to have willfully infringed on another's patent because it had obtained an opinion letter from a patent attorney that there was no infringement on another's patent.

3. FRE 502 does not define when information is privileged

Importantly, the rule has no effect on the common law regarding whether a communication or information qualifies for protection as an attorney-client privilege or work-product protection. In essence, it starts with the assumption that the privilege or protection applies, and focuses on the effect of its disclosure. Lawyers seeking the protection of the rule, therefore, must first demonstrate that the information disclosed meets the elements of an attorney-client communication, or work-product protection, by whatever common law test is applicable to the jurisdiction where the disclosure was made, or the forum that will decide the dispute.

4. FRE 502 applies across the board

The protections afforded by FRE 502 apply not only to disclosures during discovery in federal civil suits, but also in federal criminal cases, administrative proceedings, or to federal offices or agencies. In addition, the rule applies to federal court-annexed and court-mandated arbitration proceedings.

5. FRE 502 has important legislative history

Unlike routine rulemaking, FRE 502 was affirmatively enacted by both houses of Congress, because it modified the common law regarding privilege waiver, and thus the Rules Enabling Act, 28 U.S.C. § 2074(b), would have prevented its enactment without specific action by Congress. This means that in addition to the Advisory Committee Notes, which explain the origin and purpose of the rule and are crucial in correctly interpreting it, so too is the statement of congressional intent regarding the rule that is attached as an addendum to the Advisory Committee Notes. It is impossible to overstate the importance of reading the Committee Notes and the statement of congressional intent when interpreting FRE 502, and the necessity for applying it to achieve the goals underlying its enactment.

6. FRE 502 has two primary purposes

There are two primary purposes for FRE 502. First, it intended to resolve the splits of opinion among the federal circuit and district courts regarding the effect of disclosure of attorney-client privileged communications or work-product protected information, particularly disagreements among the courts regarding the effect of inadvertent disclosure of privileged or protected information. Having accomplished this, FRE 502 sets a uniform national standard that supersedes any prior federal decisional authority that is contrary to the rule, if it was decided prior to the effective date of the rule. Further, when the result required by FRE 502 is contrary to the privilege law of a state, FRE 502(f) provides that the rule "trumps" that state law.

Second, FRE 502 was intended to address and ameliorate the widely held complaint that the cost of civil litigation, particularly when it involves discovery of ESI, has become disproportionately expensive to what is at issue in many cases. Critics, for example, frequently pointed out that of all the phases of e-discovery (preservation, processing, privilege review prior to production, and ultimate production to the requesting party), preproduction review for privilege—often on a document-by-document basis—has become prohibitively expensive. It is as a consequence of this second purpose of FRE 502 that the Advisory Committee Note specifically singles out use of computer-based search methodology as a reasonable means to employ to undertake preproduction review for privilege and protection.

Regrettably, however, as the discussion in chapter 17 lamentably demonstrates, courts have been slow to get this message and interpret FRE 502(b) in a clear and consistent manner that would promote the use of computer-based search methodology as an important component of preproduction review for privilege and protection. Until courts are willing to do so, FRE 502 will never fulfill its second objective, and litigants are well served to make this point forcefully when arguing about the reasonableness of computer-based privilege review as a component of reasonable preproduction precautions when there is an issue of inadvertent production of privileged or protected information.

7. FRE 502 establishes a "default" rule against subject matter waiver

FRE 502(a) establishes a "default" rule that when there has been disclosure of privileged or protected information under circumstances that constitutes a waiver (either under FRE 502 itself, or the common law of privilege waiver), the waiver is limited to the specific privileged or protected information disclosed, and does not constitute subject matter waiver. This is a great departure from the pre-Rule 502 common law of waiver in many federal circuits, which found subject matter waiver.

FRE 502(a) further provides, however, that a limited subject matter waiver may occur, the scope of which extends to undisclosed privileged or protected information that deals with the same subject matter of that which was disclosed, but only if (1) the waiver was intentional, and (2) the related undisclosed privileged/protected information "ought in fairness be considered together" with that which was disclosed.[2]

One example of when fairness requires a finding of subject matter waiver is when the party that intentionally disclosed the privileged or protected information selectively disclosed only some of the privileged or protected information dealing with the same subject matter, and the failure to disclose the remainder would be unfair or misleading. Note that even when FRE 502(a) results in a finding of subject matter waiver, it is still narrower than the waiver that many courts would have found prior to the enactment of FRE 502. Under prior law, many courts would have found that intentional disclosure of privileged or protected information constituted a waiver of *all* related undisclosed information, without the need to establish that fairness required the additional disclosure.

2. FED. R. EVID. 502(a)(1)–(3).

As a necessary corollary to FRE 502(a)'s requirement that disclosure of privileged or protected information cannot result in subject matter waiver unless it was intentional, it follows that if the disclosure of privileged or protected information was inadvertent, as discussed in FRE 502(b), then there can never be subject matter waiver. For inadvertent disclosures of privileged or protected information, the waiver always is limited to the privileged or protected information actually disclosed.

8. FRE 502 incorporates the concept of preproduction and postproduction reasonableness

FRE 502(b) deals with the consequences of inadvertent disclosure of privileged or protected information, and states that such disclosure does not result in a waiver if the disclosing party took reasonable steps to prevent disclosure ("preproduction reasonableness"), and also promptly took reasonable steps to rectify the inadvertent disclosure once it learned it had occurred ("postproduction reasonableness").

Examples of preproduction reasonableness include use of computerized search and information retrieval technology to "digitally" search for privileged or protected ESI (including keyword searches, Boolean searches, concept searches, and related computerized search methods). Search methodology is discussed in more detail in chapters 20 and 21.

Examples of postproduction reasonableness include compliance with the postproduction procedures for asserting privilege or protection provided by FRCP 26(b)(5)(B). The Advisory Committee Notes to FRE 502(b) make it quite clear that a producing party is not required to do a "postproduction" review of what was produced to meet the requirement of postproduction reasonableness; rather, its duty to take prompt and reasonable remedial action is triggered by knowledge of the inadvertent disclosure of privileged or protected information, or of circumstances that would put a reasonable person on notice that an inadvertent production had occurred. Thus, the key time period is not how much time elapsed between inadvertent production and initiation of reasonable remedial action, but rather how much time elapsed from discovery of the inadvertent disclosure to the commencement of reasonable remedial action. The Advisory Committee Note also makes it quite clear that it was intended that FRE 502(b) does not require perfection, or even taking "all reasonable" preproduction and postproduction measures, merely that what was done in a particular case was reasonable.

While many courts have interpreted FRE 502(b) as it was intended, a regrettably large number of courts, as chapter 17's discussion illustrates, have declined to afford the protection intended by FRE 502(b) for inadvertent disclosure because the producing party's preproduction or postproduction action was deemed to be insufficiently "reasonable." Such a hard-line interpretation was quite common under pre-Rule 502 waiver law, but FRE 502(b) was enacted to change that, and reviewing courts should keep that in mind when interpreting FRE 502(b) "reasonableness."

9. FRE 502 provides for court orders that expand its protection

FRE 502(d) authorizes a federal court to order that privilege or protection is not waived by the disclosure connected with a case pending before that court, and if this is done, that order is binding on the parties to that litigation, and, crucially, also on nonparties, and such a nonwaiver order is binding on all other federal and state courts. As the Advisory Committee Note to FRE 502(d) provides, this is one of the most important features of FRE 502, because it enables the parties in a federal case to enter into nonwaiver agreements, such as "clawback" or "quick-peek" agreements, under which little, or even no, preproduction review for privilege or protection is done.

Further, FRE 502(d) permits a court to issue a nonwaiver order even if the parties to the litigation have not requested it, or if one party has requested it but the other has objected. The reason is that FRE 502(d) is intended to help reduce the enormous costs associated with document-by-document preproduction review of ESI, and to encourage the parties to agree to nonwaiver agreements so that they may provide documents in response to a document production request in a cost-effective manner that is not disproportionately expensive, given what is at issue in the case.

While a court may issue an FRE 502(d) nonwaiver order on its own initiative, or over the objection of the parties, a court may not order that information that is covered by the attorney-client privilege be produced (absent a finding of waiver) or that work-product information be produced (except as contemplated by FRCP 26(b)(3)).

Finally, FRE 502(d) only allows a court to enter a nonwaiver agreement with respect to privileged or protected information that is disclosed "in connection with litigation pending before the court." As chapter 17 noted, some courts seem to have been reluctant to find that an FRE 502(d) order could entirely excuse the producing party from conducting any preproduction review for privilege or protection, but this is entirely inconsistent with the express purpose of FRE 502(d), as explained in the Advisory Committee Notes.

10. It is important to read the entire rule

Finally, FRE 502(e) is closely related to FRE 502(d). FRE 502(e) provides that the parties in a federal case may enter into a nonwaiver agreement as part of a confidentiality agreement or stipulated protective order. As with FRE 502(d), they are free to determine whether they must undertake any preproduction review for privilege or work product, and may agree that none be undertaken, to keep expenses down.

FRE 502(e) provides that these agreements are binding "only on the parties to the agreement." Thus, it is vitally important for a party who wants protection against nonparties to the litigation, to obtain an order from the court pursuant to FRE 502(d). It is hard to imagine why a litigant would not do so as a matter of course, since courts have not appeared to be reluctant to do so when asked. However, as chapter 17 notes, extreme care must be exercised when drafting nonwaiver agreements under FRE 502(e), because some courts have interpreted them very narrowly, finding waiver even in instances where such an agreement had been negotiated but did not cover the specific circumstance in which the disclosure had occurred. This is unfortunate because it undermines the important goal of FRE 502 of reducing the costs associated with discovery, particularly ESI.

PART SIX

SEEKING AND USING ELECTRONICALLY STORED INFORMATION

CHAPTER 19

THE RULE 26(F) CONFERENCE OF THE PARTIES

BY MICHAEL D. BERMAN*

What is a Rule 26(f) conference? What does Rule 16 have to do with it? What should be discussed at the conference? How do you prepare for the conference? This chapter answers all these questions and more.

1. What is a Rule 26(f) conference?

A revitalized procedure known as the "conference of the parties" is central to the entire electronically stored information (ESI) process.[1] The conference of the parties is partially analogous to two simultaneous depositions. While party A seeks information from

*The author appreciatively acknowledges the assistance of Melissa E. Goldmeier, a 2010 graduate of the University of Baltimore School of Law and a 2007 graduate of Wright State University.

1. *See* Craig Ball, Musings on Meet and Confer, http://www.craigball.com/Musings_on_Meet_and_Confer.pdf (2007) (describing the Rule 26(f) conference as "a linchpin of success in electronic discovery"); M. Cowper & J. Rosenthal, *Not Your Mother's Rule 26(f) Conference Anymore*, SEDONA CONFERENCE J., Fall 2007 ("Perhaps no change in the Federal Rules is more dramatic than the one associated with the changes to the meet and confer requirement of Rule 26(f)."); G. Paul & J. Baron, *Information Inflation: Can the Legal System Adapt?* 13 RICH. J.L. & TECH. 10 (2007) ("If early meet and confer obligations result in a body of case law better defining cooperative behavior, it will likely be the most profound, 'emergent' aspect of legal practice under the December 2006 changes to the Federal Rules of

party B, party B is simultaneously "deposing" party A in an effort to obtain information. Unlike a discovery deposition, however, the ultimate goal is to reach agreement, or to identify areas of disagreement for prompt presentation to the court as a cost-saving measure. Therefore, the conference is also a negotiation and it has been noted, in connection with a Federal Rule of Civil Procedure 26(f) conference, that: "To get something, you have to be willing to give up something—in this case, information about your ESI."[2] While deponents are often urged to "volunteer nothing," the primary tool of a Rule 26(f) conference is transparency.

Courts have written that failure to communicate is a central, recurrent problem in the e-discovery process.[3] The "conference of the parties" mechanism has been "cynically" described as a process in which two lawyers who do not trust each other discuss matters that neither understands.[4] Just as Georges Clemenceau said that war is too important to be left to the generals,[5] attorneys frequently cannot "go it alone," and it is important to have a multidisciplinary approach to a conference of the parties. "The overriding theme of the recent amendments to the discovery rules has been open and forthright sharing of information by all parties to a case with the aim of expediting case progress, minimizing burden and expense, and removing contentiousness as much as practicable."[6] As the Sedona Conference Cooperation Proclamation[7] points out, this is a paradigmatic change in the practice of civil litigation.

Civil Procedure."); P. RICE, ELECTRONIC EVIDENCE: LAW AND PRACTICE 21 (ABA 2d ed. 2008) (Rule 26(f) is "[p]erhaps" the "most significant" change).

2. *See* Cowper & Rosenthal, *supra* note 1.

3. *See, e.g.*, Zubulake v. UBS Warburg LLC (*Zubulake V*), 229 F.R.D. 422 (S.D.N.Y. 2004) ("The conduct of both counsel and client thus calls to mind the now-famous words of the prison captain in Cool Hand Luke: 'What we've got here is a failure to communicate.'"); *accord* William A. Gross Constr. Assoc., Inc., v. Am. Mfrs. Mut. Ins. Co., 256 F.R.D. 134 (S.D.N.Y. 2009).

4. *See* Ball, *supra* note 1.

5. *See* M. Berman, *Tips to Avoid Mistakes with ESI Vendors* (ABA 2009), http://www.abanet.org/ . . . ROLE=lt&AREATYPE=premium&URL=%2Flitigation%2Fmo%2Fpremium%2Dlt%2Fnewsletters%2Ftechnology%2F0709%5Fberman%2Ehtml, reprinted in appendix G.

6. Bd. of Regents of Univ. of Neb. v. BASF Corp., 2007 WL 3342423 (D. Neb. 2007).

7. THE SEDONA CONFERENCE COOPERATION PROCLAMATION (2008), *available at* http://www.thesedonaconference.org/dltForm?did=proclamation.pdf.

Rule 26(f) provides (italics added):

(f) Conference of the Parties; Planning for Discovery.

(1) Conference Timing. Except in a proceeding exempted from initial disclosure under Rule 26(a)(1)(B) or when the court orders otherwise, *the parties must confer as soon as practicable*—and in any event at least 21 days before a scheduling conference is to be held or a scheduling order is due under Rule 16(b).

(2) Conference Content; Parties' Responsibilities. In conferring, the parties must consider the nature and basis of their claims and defenses and the possibilities for promptly settling or resolving the case; make or arrange for the disclosures required by Rule 26(a)(1); discuss any issues about preserving discoverable information; and develop a proposed discovery plan. *The attorneys of record and all unrepresented parties that have appeared in the case are jointly responsible for arranging the conference,* for attempting in good faith to agree on the proposed discovery plan, and for submitting to the court within 14 days after the conference a written report outlining the plan. The court may order the parties or attorneys to attend the conference in person.

(3) Discovery Plan. A discovery plan must state the parties' views and proposals on:

(A) what changes should be made in the timing, form, or requirement for disclosures under Rule 26(a), including a statement of when initial disclosures were made or will be made;

(B) the subjects on which discovery may be needed, when discovery should be completed, and *whether discovery should be conducted in phases* or be limited to or focused on particular issues;

(C) *any issues about disclosure or discovery of electronically stored information, including the form or forms in which it should be produced;*

(D) *any issues about claims of privilege*[8] or of protection as trial-preparation materials, including—

8. See chapter 15 regarding ESI privilege logs.

if the parties agree on a procedure to assert these claims after production—whether to ask the court to include their agreement in an order;[9]

(E) what changes should be made in the limitations on discovery imposed under these rules or by local rule, and what other limitations should be imposed; and

(F) any other orders that the court should issue under Rule 26(c) or under Rule 16(b) and (c).

(4) Expedited Schedule. If necessary to comply with its expedited schedule for Rule 16(b) conferences, a court may by local rule:

(A) require the parties' conference to occur less than 21 days before the scheduling conference is held or a scheduling order is due under Rule 16(b); and

(B) require the written report outlining the discovery plan to be filed less than 14 days after the parties' conference, or excuse the parties from submitting a written report and permit them to report orally on their discovery plan at the Rule 16(b) conference.

A Rule 26(f) conference of the parties is often called a "meet and confer"; however, that is a misnomer. The GAP Report to Rule 26(f) states: "The rule is amended to require only a 'conference' of the parties, rather than a 'meeting.' There are important benefits to a face-to-face discussion of the topics to be covered in the conference, and those benefits may be lost if other methods of conferring were routinely used when face-to-face meetings would not impose burdens. Nevertheless, geographic conditions in some districts may exact costs far out of proportion to these benefits. The amendment allows the court by case-specific order to require a face-to-face meeting, but 'standing' orders so requiring are not authorized."[10]

Rule 26(f)(1) mandates that the parties must "confer as soon as practicable." The comments to Rule 26(f) illustrate the goal of "front

9. *See* Fed. R. Evid. 502.

10. FED. R. CIV. P. 26 GAP report, *available at* http://www.law.cornell.edu/rules/frcp/ACRule26.htm.

loading" discussions about, and disputes over, ESI so that they can be identified and discussed, and an agreement can be reached, or, if necessary, presented for judicial resolution before litigants' assets are wasted on futile or ill-designed efforts. For example, the Committee Notes to Rule 26 state that in cases involving ESI, the 2006 amendment to Rule 26(f) directs the parties to discuss ESI and that "discussion at the outset may avoid later difficulties or ease their resolution." The Notes reemphasize that point: "Early identification of disputes over the forms of production may help avoid the expense and delay of searches or production using inappropriate forms." The Notes then redouble that emphasis: "Failure to address preservation issues early in the litigation increases uncertainty and raises a risk of disputes." In short, "it is no longer acceptable for the parties to defer good faith discussion."[11]

Rule 26(f)(2) places the burden on counsel to initiate and conduct a conference.[12] Where parties have failed to communicate, however, courts have not hesitated to order that they do so.[13] Commitments made, and agreements reached, during a Rule 26(f) conference are likely binding, absent exceptional circumstances.[14]

---

11. Hopson v. Mayor & City Council, 232 F.R.D. 228, 245 (D. Md. 2008); *In re* Seroquel Prods. Liab. Litig., 244 F.R.D. 650, 655 (M.D. Fl. 2007) (quoting MANUAL FOR COMPLEX LITIGATION §11.446). The Committee Notes to Rule 16(b) are in accord, alerting "the court to the possible need to address the handling of discovery of electronically stored information early in the litigation if such discovery is expected to occur. . . . In many instances, the court's involvement early in the litigation will help avoid difficulties that might otherwise arise. . . ."

12. It has been noted that the Rule 26(f) conference may occur long after the duty to preserve has arisen. *See* INSTITUTE FOR THE ADVANCEMENT OF THE AMERICAN LEGAL SYSTEM FINAL REPORT ON THE JOINT PROJECT OF THE AMERICAN COLLEGE OF TRIAL LAWYERS TASK FORCE ON DISCOVERY AND THE INSTITUTE FOR THE ADVANCEMENT OF THE AMERICAN LEGAL SYSTEM 13 (Univ. of Denver 2009). There is nothing that precludes voluntarily conducting a conference prior to the commencement of litigation.

13. Mancia v. Mayflower Textile Servs. Co., 253 F.R.D. 354 (D. Md. 2008); Victor Stanley, Inc. v. Creative Pipe, Inc. (*Victor Stanley I*), 250 F.R.D. 251, 254 (D. Md. 2008) ("following a hearing, the court ordered the parties' computer forensic experts to meet and confer in an effort to identify a joint protocol to search and retrieve relevant ESI responsive to Plaintiff's Rule 34 requests"); *In re Seroquel Prods. Liab. Litig.*, 244 F.R.D. at 652 ("the Court requested that the parties meet and confer").

14. *In re* Fannie Mae Sec. Litig., 552 F.3d 814 (D.C. Cir. 2009) (court deadlines are not "moveable goal posts"); Kay Beer Distrib., Inc. v. Energy Brands, Inc., 2009 WL 1649592 (E.D. Wis. 2009) ("Energy Brand asserted that Kay Beer's request that documents, information, and or data be produced in their original electronic

2. What does Rule 16 have to do with it?

The importance of Rule 26(f) cannot be understood without a detour into Rule 16, because the two work in tandem.[15] The end product of a conference of the parties is a proposed discovery plan that will be submitted at the Rule 16 pretrial scheduling conference.

"At the Rule 16 pretrial conference, the parties meet with the court to discuss, among other matters, the proposed discovery schedule and any anticipated discovery disputes. After the Rule 16 conference, the court issues a scheduling order. . . ."[16] Rule 16(a) states that the purposes of a pretrial scheduling conference are "(1) expediting disposition of the action; (2) establishing early and continuing control so that the case will not be protracted because of lack of management; (3) discouraging wasteful pretrial activities; (4) improving the quality of the trial through more thorough preparation; and (5) facilitating settlement."

Rule 16(b)(1)(A) provides that a court must issue a scheduling order "after receiving the parties' report under Rule 26(f)." Rule 16(b)(3)(B) provides that the order may "(iii) provide for disclosure or discovery of electronically stored information; (iv) include any agreements the parties reach for asserting claims of privilege or of protection as trial-preparation material after information is produced; . . . and (vi) include other appropriate matters."

Rule 16(f) provides that a court may impose sanctions, sua sponte or on motion, if a party "is substantially unprepared to participate—or does not participate in good faith—in the [Rule 16] conference." Judge Scheindlin and Mr. Capra note: "The importance of the Rule 26(f) meet and confer is indirectly underscored by Rule 16(f)(1)(B), which authorizes a court to impose sanctions on a party or its attorney if either 'is substantially unprepared to

format was unduly burdensome and noted that the parties had agreed at their Rule 26 conference that either a hard copy or electronic copy would be produced depending on what was most cost-effective."); *In re Seroquel Prods. Liab. Litig.*, 244 F.R.D. at 661 (litigant argued that it should not be sanctioned because discovery requests had not been served; court, however, evaluated duty based on order arising out of conference of parties; "AZ stopped participating in the process to confer on the databases despite its explicit agreement to produce them and to cooperate in providing personnel. . . .").

15. *See* S. SCHEINDLIN & D. CAPRA, ELECTRONIC DISCOVERY AND DIGITAL EVIDENCE: CASES AND MATERIALS 197 (West 2009). The discussion above is based on this text.

16. *Id.*

participate—or does not participate in good faith—in the [Rule 16] pretrial conference."[17]

In combination, Rules 16 and 26(f) provide that the parties must confer in good faith on a number of ESI topics that are designed to impose a cost-benefit analysis and simplify the litigation, and they must do so early in the litigation process. They must be well prepared for the Rule 26(f) conference or they will likely not be well prepared for the Rule 16 conference. If the litigants are unprepared for the Rule 16 conference, sanctions may be imposed. The following sections address the topics that may be discussed in a Rule 26(f) conference and how to prepare for such a conference.

3. What should be discussed at the conference?

Like all of the ESI rules, Rule 26(f) provides flexibility, and the Committee Notes state that "the issues to be addressed during the Rule 26(f) conference depend on the nature and extent of the contemplated discovery and of the parties' information systems." One court has noted:

> Indeed, the newly revised Civil Discovery Standards for the American Bar Association Section on Litigation contain detailed information about the issues that the parties should discuss in their effort to agree upon an electronic records discovery plan. At a minimum, they should discuss: the type of information technology systems in use and the persons most knowledgeable in their operation; preservation of electronically stored information that may be relevant to the litigation; the scope of the electronic records sought (i.e. e-mail, voice mail, archived data, back-up or disaster recovery data, laptops, personal computers, PDAs, deleted data) the format in which production will occur (will records be produced in "native" or searchable format, or image only; is metadata sought); whether the requesting party seeks to conduct any testing or sampling of the producing party's IT system; the burdens and expenses that the producing party will face based on the Rule 26(b)(2) factors, and how they may be reduced (i.e. limiting the time period for which discovery is sought, limiting the amount of hours the producing party must spend searching, compiling, and reviewing electronic

17. *Id.*

records, using sampling to search, rather than searching all records, shifting to the producing party some of the production costs); the amount of pre-production privilege review that is reasonable for the producing party to undertake, and measures to preserve post-production assertion of privilege within a reasonable time; and any protective orders or confidentiality orders that should be in place regarding who may have access to information that is produced.[18]

Similarly, the ESI Protocol of the U.S. District Court for the District of Maryland and many articles provide detailed checklists of discussion topics.[19]

Chapter 15 addresses the unique problems presented by privilege logs in connection with email chains and provides detailed recommendations for avoiding those serious problems through a Rule 26(f) conference. Specifically, counsel should consider discussing whether an email-by-email itemization of messages and attachments in an email chain is required on the privilege log, and also consider a two-phase approach to logging email contained in email chains. A related topic might be how to redact privileged information from ESI and how to identify and protect privileged metadata. Similarly, the parties may define what constitutes a reasonable privilege search[20] so that any production of privileged information would be deemed inadvertent under FRE 502.

Chapter 29 describes the ethical issues presented with review of metadata. At least one jurisdiction, Maryland, does not require that a party receiving metadata provide notice if it discovers inadvertently produced privileged information.[21] Ethics opinions from

18. Hopson v. Mayor & City Council, 232 F.R.D. 228, 245 (D. Md. 2008).

19. U.S. DIST. CT., DIST. OF MD., SUGGESTED PROTOCOL FOR DISCOVERY OF ELECTRONICALLY STORED INFORMATION (2007), http://www.mdd.uscourts.gov/news/news/ESIProtocol.pdf (last visited Oct 21, 2009) [hereinafter MARYLAND PROTOCOL]; *accord* Ball, *supra* note 1 (providing the checklist of topics); Paul & Baron, *supra* note 1 (describing the process); M. Lange & K. Nimsger, ELECTRONIC EVIDENCE AND DISCOVERY: WHAT EVERY LAWYER SHOULD KNOW 42 (ABA 2d ed. 2009) (Rule 26(f) does "not dictate a precise formula for electronic discovery planning"; instead, it provides a "high-level checklist.").

20. *See Victor Stanley I*, 250 F.R.D. at 260 (party designed a defective keyword search for privileged documents).

21. MD. STATE BAR ASS'N, INC., ETHICS DOCKET NO. 2007–09: ETHICS OF VIEWING AND/OR USING METADATA, http://www.icw.lexisnexis.com/applieddiscovery/ . . . /MarylandEOonMetadata.pdf (last visited Oct. 21, 2009).

other jurisdictions require that notice be given after discovery;[22] however, they do not specify time parameters. Because FRE 502 mandates that a party seeking to "claw back" inadvertently produced information under Rule 26(b)(5)(B) do so promptly, parties could use a Rule 26(f) conference to discuss an agreement that they must notify their opponent, within a specified time frame, after they become aware of the receipt of any privileged information and also establish agreed-upon parameters for determining whether a request for sequestration, destruction, or return of that information under Rule 26(b)(5)(B) and FRE 502 will be deemed timely.

Another topic for discussion can be suggested milestone deadlines for certain motions. The Federal Rules do not provide deadlines for spoliation motions and there is a body of common law that provides timeliness guidelines for spoliation motions.[23] In short, if a motion is deemed untimely, the spoliation issue may be waived. Rather than leaving that decision to a somewhat unpredictable, after-the-fact determination, parties could agree that, for example, all spoliation motions shall be filed within 15 days after the moving party knew or should have known of the spoliation and, in any event, at least a specified period of time prior to the discovery cut-off or trial, absent exigent circumstances justifying a later-filed motion.

A Rule 26(f) conference may also be used to "cure" a prelitigation failure to preserve ESI. For example, assume that a duty to preserve arose prior to litigation, on January 1, 2009, and the obligated party should have preserved a January 1, 2008, word processing document, but failed to do so. If the parties conduct a conference of the parties, they may define the scope of the duty to preserve.[24] That agreement might establish the time parameters of relevancy and the parties might agree, for example, that material to be preserved includes only documents created after February 1, 2008. Because the elements of sanctionable spoliation are breach of the duty to preserve, a culpable state of mind, and prejudice, by defining the duty to preserve in a Rule 26(f) conference, parties

22. *E.g.*, ABA Comm. on Ethics & Prof'l Responsibility, Formal Op. 06-442: Review and Use of Metadata (2006).

23. Goodman v. Praxair Servs. Inc., 632 F. Supp. 2d 494 (D. Md. 2009) (discussing authorities); see appendix C.

24. Preservation is specifically included as a topic for Rule 26(f) conferences. FED. R. CIV. P. 26(f)(2); *see* RICE, *supra* note 1, at 21.

may avoid spoliation issues by limiting the scope of the duty to preserve.[25]

Decisional and other authority[26] highlighting the problems associated with keyword searching makes search techniques and technology a topic that is virtually mandatory for Rule 26(f) conferences. In *In re Seroquel Products Liability Litigation*,[27] the court noted:

> "[W]hile key word searching is a recognized method to winnow documents from large repositories, use of this technique must be a cooperative and informed process. Rather than working with Plaintiffs from the outset to reach agreement on appropriate and comprehensive search terms and methods, AZ undertook the task in secret. Common sense dictates that sampling and other quality assurance techniques must be employed to meet requirements of completeness. . . . In this case, AZ never discussed with Plaintiffs which search terms to use as part of the search. There was no dialog to discuss the search terms, as required by Rules 26 and 34.[28]

Despite that guidance and the passage of time, the message has not gotten out.[29]

A Rule 26(f) conference may also serve as a vehicle for defining reasonable efforts to preserve ESI. It is less than clear whether or

---

25. Parties may be able to disclose implementation discussions without waiving the attorney-client privilege. See chapter 16.

26. See chapters 20 and 21; Paul & Baron, *supra* note 1, at 89 (collecting cases).

27. 244 F.R.D. 650 (M.D. Fl. 2007).

28. *Id.* at 664.

29. *See* William A. Gross Constr. Assoc., Inc., v. Am. Mfrs. Mut. Ins. Co., 256 F.R.D. 134, 134 (S.D.N.Y. 2009) ("This Opinion should serve as a wake-up call to the Bar in this District about the need for careful thought, quality control, testing, and cooperation with opposing counsel in designing search terms or 'keywords' to be used to produce emails or other electronically stored information ('ESI'). While this message has appeared in several cases from outside this Circuit, it appears that the message has not reached many members of our Bar."); *Victor Stanley I*, 250 F.R.D. at 260–62; United States v. O'Keefe, 537 F. Supp. 2d 14, 24 (D.D.C. 2008); *accord* Equity Analytics, LLC v. Lundin, 248 F.R.D. 331, 333 (D.D.C. 2008). The contours of Rule 26(g)'s certification and reasonable inquiry requirements are beyond the scope of this chapter. Suffice it to say that an improperly designed search could result in a Rule 26(g) violation and the imposition of sanctions. This provides a significant incentive for discussing keyword or other searches and attempting to reach agreement. See chapters 20 and 21 regarding search methodology and chapter 31 regarding Rule 26(g).

when backup tapes must be preserved.[30] Counsel may use Rule 26(g) to discuss tape-rotation protocols and whether any or all tapes need to be sequestered. Agreements regarding preservation and production of home computers that employees use for working away from the office may be reached. In *Phoenix Four, Inc. v. Strategic Resources Corp.*,[31] defense counsel was held to be grossly negligent for not finding an unmapped, hidden partition on a server. A prior Rule 26(f) agreement might have avoided this by defining away the need to search for hidden partitions or, alternatively, making that obligation clear and unambiguous so that it would not have been overlooked. In the unique situation presented by *Columbia Pictures, Inc. v. Bunnell*,[32] ephemeral data came within the scope of the duty to preserve. A Rule 26(f) agreement could establish proportionality metrics and specify how much time, cost, or effort is reasonable to expend on an ESI task or tasks.[33]

Evidentiary issues are frequently overlooked in Rule 26(f) conferences. In *Lorraine v. Markel American Insurance Co.*,[34] the court noted that "considering the significant costs associated with discovery of ESI, it makes little sense to go to all the bother and expense to get electronic information only to have it excluded from evidence or rejected from consideration during summary judgment because the proponent cannot lay a sufficient foundation to get it admitted." Consider the problems that may arise in deposition and at trial if the Rule 26(f) conference results in an agreement that no metadata need be produced and there later arises a genuine question over authenticity of the ESI. Or, consider the potential problems if ESI is converted from native to static format by a Rule 26(f) agreement, without any discussion of admissibility, and an authenticity issue is later presented. Parties should ensure that any

30. Zubulake v. UBS Warburg LLC (*Zubulake IV*), 220 F.R.D. 212, 217 (S.D.N.Y. 2003) (stating that there is no general duty to preserve backup tapes, but also noting a significant exception to that duty).

31. 2006 U.S. Dist. Lexis 32211 (S.DN.Y. 2006) (as described in R. Losey, e-Discovery Current Trends and Cases 58–59 (ABA 2008)).

32. 245 F.R.D. 443 (C.D. Cal. 2007).

33. Marens v. Carraba's Italian Grill, Inc., 196 F.R.D. 35 (D. Md. 2000) (limiting the number of hours for document discovery); *Victor Stanley I*, 250 F.R.D. at 260–62 (discussing a "discovery budget").

34. 241 F.R.D. 534, 537–38 (D. Md. 2007); P. Grimm, *et al.*, *Back to the Future:* Lorraine v. Markel American Insurance Co. *and New Findings on the Admissibility of Electronically Stored Information*, 42 Akron L.Rev. 359 (2009).

agreement reached at a Rule 26(f) conference does not result in evidence being rendered inadmissible or subject to viable challenge.[35]

Mediation of ESI disputes, use of special masters, referral to another member of the Judiciary for informal resolution, and other alternative dispute resolution of ESI disputes may be concepts that should be addressed at a conference. After all, even with good faith efforts, if the parties could "get along" they would not be in litigation and the assistance of a neutral might help achieve cost saving.[36]

In a federal case, parties might want to discuss whether discovery will be limited to "claims and defenses" or expanded to the "subject matter of the action" under Rule 26(b)(1). That decision could have substantial ramifications on the scope of preservation and production efforts.

Because Rule 26(f)(4)(B) mandates that the parties submit a report to the court after the Rule 26(f) conference, the form and content of the report and the mechanics of preparation should be discussed. For example, a report might specify areas of agreement; areas where parties agree but a court order remains necessary, such as in connection with privilege; and areas of disagreement that require judicial attention. Rather than engaging in an expensive exchange of confirming letters, the parties may appoint an initial drafter and agree to exchange drafts until the report is finalized.

The possibilities of a Rule 26(f) conference are endless. No checklist can anticipate all of the issues that may be appropriate for discussion. There is an old joke that a lawyer once said to a judge who was questioning a witness before the jury, "Your Honor, I don't mind you trying my case; just please don't lose it for me." The Rule 26(f) conference provides a valuable opportunity. It allows the attorneys to prepare a road map for the litigation, and submit it to the court for approval. It permits lawyers to develop the solution and "drive the train."[37]

---

35. For a discussion of the use of ESI in depositions, see chapter 23; for a discussion of admissibility, see chapter 24.

36. For a discussion of alternative dispute resolution of ESI issues, see chapter 28.

37. *See* Scheindlin & Capra, *supra* note 14, at 198 ("The Rule 26(f) discovery conference is not merely a perfunctory exercise. Rather, it is an opportunity for the parties to educate themselves and their adversaries, anticipate and resolve electronic discovery disputes before they escalate, expedite the progress of their case, and assess and manage litigation costs.").

As was recently noted,[38] "the best solution in the entire area of electronic discovery is cooperation among counsel"; and "[e]lectronic discovery requires cooperation between opposing counsel and transparency in all aspects of preservation and production of ESI." The Rule 26(f) conference is often the first opportunity for such interaction after a case has been commenced.

4. How do you prepare for the conference?

Prior planning prevents poor performance in a Rule 26(f) conference.[39] "The obvious place to start preparing for the conference is to think about the end game."[40] The goal is to exchange information in a manner that will permit cost-effective litigation of a client's claims or defenses. This requires preservation of potentially responsive information in a manner that is proportionate to the needs of the case; processing of that information; review for responsiveness, privilege, and importance; and presentation in discovery and at trial in a manner that is consistent with the theme of the case.

In what is likely an understatement,[41] the Committee Notes to Rule 26(f) suggest: "It may be important for the parties to discuss [information technology] systems, and accordingly important for counsel to become familiar with those systems before the conference." Gaining an understanding of a client's information technology system, information technology department, network architecture or data map, and knowledge management (often called

38. William A. Gross Constr. Assoc., Inc., v. Am. Mfrs. Mut. Ins. Co., 256 F.R.D. 134, 136 (S.D.N.Y. 2009).

39. *See* Cowper & Rosenthal, *supra* note 1; RICE, *supra* note 1, at 21 (conference requires "substantial" preparation). The District of Maryland Protocol for the Discovery of ESI states: "Insofar as it relates to ESI, prior planning and preparation is essential for a conference of parties. . . ." MARYLAND PROTOCOL, *supra* note 18, at ¶ 5.

40. R. Raetner, *Preparing for the Rule 26(f) Scheduling Conference and Other Practical Advice in the Wake of the Recent Amendments to the Rules Governing E-Discovery*, FED. LAW., Aug. 2007. In the movie *Charlie Wilson's War*, the Congressman is reported to have said the following about America's early policy in Afghanistan: "These things happened. They were glorious and they changed the world . . . and then we [messed] up the end game." M. Nichols (Universal Studios). With ESI, it is important to always have the "end game" in sight.

41. *In re* Seroquel Prods. Liab. Litig., 244 F.R.D. 650, 653 (M.D. Fl. 2007) ("The failure of the Defendant to investigate and understand its own records and documents and to prepare them for production has not met the expectations of the Court as discussed at the September 2006 Conference").

document management, document retention, or document destruction) policy[42] is an important first step in the process.

On a general level, preparation for a conference of the parties is much like preparation for deposition or trial. In fact, it may be advisable to use the "trial notebook" approach.[43] Prior to attending a conference, it is important to develop a theory of the case and a preliminary trial plan, outline and research applicable substantive and procedural legal issues, develop a factual chronology, and identify key people and documents. It is important to understand what preservation efforts have been undertaken, what has not been undertaken, and the cost and burden of additional preservation efforts. It would be helpful to run test searches on the client's data to determine the efficacy and cost of those searches. It is equally important to develop a detailed "shopping list" identifying areas of inquiry about the opponent's systems and preparedness.

As in any trial-related endeavor, you need to identify strengths and vulnerabilities. For example, what do you need to know about the opponent's information technology, preservation efforts, and knowledge management policies? Do you need to know who key players are? Is there "smoking gun" ESI that is of top priority? Is it important to inquire into automatic deletion policies? A rudderless ship will not likely reach port, at least not in a timely and efficient manner.[44]

---

42. The concepts listed in the text are discussed in more detail in chapters 4, 5, and 12. In *India Brewing Co. v. Miller Brewing Co.*, 237 F.R.D. 190, 193 (E.D. Wis. 2007), the court held that a document retention policy did not have to be produced because it was not relevant to the "claims or defenses." Of course, FED. R. CIV. P. 26(b)(1) provides: "For good cause, the court may order discovery of any matter relevant to the subject matter involved in the action." That issue was not presented and *India Brewing* should not be read as a ringing endorsement for refusing to produce document retention policies. *Cf.* Acorn v. Cnty. of Nassau, 2009 U.S. Dist. Lexis 19549 (E.D.N.Y. 2009) (discussing the request for production of document retention policies); Newman v. Borders, Inc., 2009 U.S. Dist. Lexis 29020 (D.D.C. 2009) (discovery on document retention policies and practices); *see* J. BARKETT, E-DISCOVERY: TWENTY QUESTIONS AND ANSWERS 71 (ABA 2008) (discussing discovery of litigation hold notices).

43. The "trial notebook" is described in J. McElhaney, *Put Away the Accordion*, ABA J., May 2009, at 24, 25.

44. "Any ship can be a minesweeper—once." Anon., cited in P. Grimm, *et al.*, *Proportionality in the Post-Hoc Analysis of Pre-Litigation Preservation Decisions*, 37 U. BALT. L. REV. 381 n.96 (2008).

It may be advisable and appropriate to prepare and provide the opponent with a physical notebook containing key items, such as a data map, document management/retention/destruction policy, and an organizational chart of the information technology department, together with a list of steps taken, or that will not be taken, to preserve ESI. The book could contain sample proposed search terms and show the number of "hits" generated by each term against a live or sample database. Equally advisable is to consider requesting the same information from the opponent.

The ESI Protocol of the U.S. District Court for the District of Maryland makes a number of suggestions regarding preparation for a Rule 26(f) conference.[45] First, the Protocol emphasizes the need for preplanning and suggests that parties consider conducting a discussion to plan for the conference, and exchanging information prior to a Rule 26(f) conference. Reasonable requests for things such as organizational charts, records/information management policies, and network design should not be resisted. Parties might also discuss the time parameters for discovery,[46] identities of key persons, and running sample searches on part or all of the ESI using sample search terms.

The Federal Rules of Civil Procedure do not specify who may attend a Rule 26(f) conference. The parties should discuss, prior to the conference, who should, must, or may participate. Obviously, trial counsel and a client representative with appropriate authority should attend. It may be beneficial for information technology personnel from each litigant be present, as well as an ESI coordinator for each party.[47] Parties may want to agree that they may (or must) have forensic information technology personnel present and that those retained experts will not automatically be viewed as "testifying experts" under Rule 26(a)(2) and 26(b)(4)(A, B) simply because they participated.[48] As a general rule, it is probably not beneficial to have a court reporter present. Although debatable,

45. The discussion in the text is based on the Maryland Protocol; however, it is generic and applicable to any state or federal matter.

46. RICE, *supra* note 1, at 21.

47. For a discussion of the advantages and disadvantages of having an ESI coordinator present at a Rule 26(f) conference, see BARKETT, *supra* note 40, at 95–96.

48. The Maryland Protocol provides: "Identification of an expert for use in a FED. R. CIV. P 26(f) conference of parties does not, in and of itself, identify that person and an expert whose opinions may be presented a trial within the meaning of FED. R. CIV. P. 26(b)(4)(A,B)." MARYLAND PROTOCOL, *supra* note 18, at ¶ 9.B.

some commentators note that "people play nicer" when they are off the record.[49] On the other hand, given the sanctions available under Rule 16(f)(1)(B), there may be times when a verbatim transcript would be appropriate and, perhaps, even necessary. The Maryland Protocol provides that if one party believes that the other should have information technology personnel present, and the opponent refuses, this may be confirmed in a letter a reasonable time prior to the conference, and considered in connection with any request for sanctions.

Parties may also want to discuss inviting a mediator or other alternative dispute resolution neutral to participate. The goals of the conference are to reach agreement or, if that is not possible, to identify disputes that need judicial resolution. A mediator may be of considerable assistance.[50]

Before the conference, counsel should confer with his or her client regarding the anticipated course and topics of the conference and discuss the respective roles of counsel, client, and information technology personnel at the conference. For example, it is helpful to define in advance who will address certain issues. Efforts should be made to identify key persons, and assistants of those people who may store and manage their ESI. The litigation hold should be reviewed and refreshed.

Counsel should review the factual and legal issues presented and make efforts to study the information technology system and identify likely potential sources of responsive ESI. For example, do businesspeople at the client's workplace use short messaging systems and text messages? Is a website involved and, if so, was it dynamic and how was it preserved? Are there unusual or industry-specialized databases that use proprietary software? Are there legacy systems? Do employees use their home computers for business purposes? Are disaster recovery tapes used when an employee accidentally deletes a message, thereby becoming accessible, off-line storage? Have "janitor" and automatic deletion programs been suspended?

Preparing actual cost estimates for various scenarios may be very helpful in an upcoming Rule 26(f) conference. Assume, for example, that it is anticipated that an opponent will be overreaching in its requests. The other party might want to be able to

49. *See* Cowper & Rosenthal, *supra* note 1.
50. See chapter 28.

respond with specific examples of the costs of various tasks, such as preserving and using backup tapes. Because proportionality is central to the Rule 26(f) discussions, preparation may include a "discovery budget."[51]

Just as prior preparation is necessary, parties should leave time for a second Rule 26(f) conference and preparation of a report for the court. Parties should not approach the conference "in a fashion equivalent to hosting a one-of-a-kind, global 'summit meeting.'"[52] Instead, it may be necessary to have "iterative feedback loops where multiple, iterative meet and confer sessions occur for information exchange and discussion of issues to research, negotiate, and agree."[53] In short, parties should exchange information before the Rule 26(f) conference to assist in preparation, conduct the conference, and schedule a follow-up conference, if appropriate, to "close the deal" and submit a report to the court.

5. Conclusion

The Rule 26(f) conference of parties should take place as soon as practicable. With the requisite preparation and cooperation, it can provide cost savings, avoid discovery and evidentiary issues, and prevent satellite-sanctions litigation, and it offers trial attorneys the opportunity to exercise control, provide input to the court, and chart the course for the case. Properly used, the conference(s)—or, if possible, meeting(s)—results in the tailoring of the overriding legal standard of proportionality to the facts of the case.

"Information is fundamental to the legal system."[54] The explosion of information has, however, "stressed" the system.[55] The Rule 26(f) conference presents a chance to apply cost-benefit principles in a judicially governed procedure before a court has imposed a structure on the litigation. "It cannot be emphasized enough that the goal of the meeting to discuss discovery is to reach an agreement that then can be proposed to the court. The days when the requesting party can expect to 'get it all' and the producing party

51. *Mancia*, 2008 U.S. Dist. Lexis 83740 (D. Md. 2008) ("The goal is to attempt to quantify a workable 'discovery budget' that is proportional to what is at issue in the case.").

52. *See* Paul & Baron, *supra* note 1.

53. *Id.*

54. *Id.*

55. *Id.*

to produce whatever they feel like producing are long gone."[56] Through cooperation and a multidisciplinary approach, parties may use Rule 26(f) to approach the target of Rule 1, the just, speedy, and inexpensive resolution of the action.[57]

56. Hopson v. Mayor & City Council, 232 F.R.D. 228, 245 (D. Md. 2008).

57. In some circumstances, self-preservation can be a cost-saving measure and it could be topic for discussion at the conference. For a discussion of the benefits and risks of self-identification and self-preservation, please see M. Berman, *Self-Identification and Self-Preservation: A Fool for a Client?*, http://www.esi-mediation.com/2011/05/26/self-identification-and-self-preservation-a-fool-for-a-client/.

CHAPTER 20

USING ELECTRONIC SEARCH TOOLS AND SEARCH-METHODOLOGY EXPERTS IN E-DISCOVERY: A DISCUSSION OF RECENT CASE LAW AND OTHER AUTHORITIES

BY DAVID D. CROSS
AND SANYA SARICH KERKSIEK

With the huge volumes of information typically involved in e-discovery, litigants increasingly have turned to electronic searches as an alternative. This chapter surveys emerging case law and research on the subject of electronic search methodology, distilling concrete advice from important judicial opinions including Seroquel, O'Keefe, Equity Analytics,

Victor Stanley I, *and* Rhoads.[1] *It ends with a description of steps to design, implement, and document an effective search protocol.*

1. Introduction

Many attorneys are all too familiar with the painful task of manual document review—those long days or even weeks turning the pages of a seemingly endless supply of documents to identify those that are responsive to discovery requests or may be potentially privileged. The advent of document review software (along with scanners and OCR[2] for hard-copy documents) enabled attorneys to gladly move from dusty file rooms (and sometimes warehouses) full of precariously stacked bankers' boxes to the relative comfort of their offices where they could review documents on their computers. But this new approach did little to reduce the time and cost consumed by manual review. As companies and individuals continue to create and store more and more documents and data, the time and cost needed for manual review have become a substantial, if not overwhelming, burden for those in litigation.

Some litigants have sought to save cost and expedite review by using professional document review shops, some of which operate overseas at rates significantly lower than those charged by the typical junior associate or contract attorney at a firm in the United States.[3] But even this solution, which relies on traditional manual review, is costly and time-consuming when millions of pages of documents are involved, as is all too common in complex litigation today.

Like most industries looking to save time and money, lawyers and their clients have turned to technology for a solution. Litigants are increasingly relying on electronic searches, both for collecting

1. *In re* Seroquel Prods. Liab. Litig., 244 F.R.D. 650 (M.D. Fla. 2007); Victor Stanley, Inc. v. Creative Pipe, Inc. (*Victor Stanley I*), 250 F.R.D. 251 (D. Md. 2008); United States v. O'Keefe, 537 F. Supp. 2d 14 (D.D.C. 2008); Equity Analytics, LLC v. Lundin, 248 F.R.D. 331 (D.D.C. 2008); Rhoads Indus., Inc. v. Bldg. Materials Corp. of Am., 254 F.R.D. 216 (E.D. Pa. 2008).

2. OCR stands for optical character recognition, which is an electronic process by which non-searchable text images can be translated into searchable text.

3. *See, e.g.*, Pete Engardio, *Let's Offshore the Lawyers*, BUSINESSWEEK, Sept. 18, 2006 (reporting that DuPont partnered with an offshore document review shop called Office Tiger (now owned by R.R. Donnelley) and that "[b]y going offshore, DuPont aims to save 40% to 60% on document work and cut up to $6 million from its annual $200 million-plus in legal spending. It also hopes to shave months off the discovery process in court cases.").

and producing documents in response to discovery requests and for identifying and culling out potentially privileged documents.

This increasing use of electronic search tools has given rise to a seemingly simple question that has proved to have anything but a simple answer: How does one design an effective search? This question seems simple on the surface because lawyers, of course, have been well accustomed to formulating electronic searches ever since Westlaw and Lexis pulled attorneys out of the libraries and into their massive online databases of cases, statutes, and countless other authorities and reference materials. In fact, anyone with a computer and Internet connection likely has formulated innumerable electronic searches, stringing together words in a little box in a search engine in the hope of finding some particular bit of information buried in a distant corner of the web. But do these day-to-day search skills qualify an attorney (or anyone) to design a search protocol sufficient to satisfy counsel's and client's discovery obligations? Evolving case law concerning electronic searching suggests that the answer is—at least under some circumstances—*likely not.*

In 2008, three decisions addressing important considerations concerning the use of electronic tools for searching, collecting, culling, and producing documents in discovery were issued: *United States v. O'Keefe,*[4] *Equity Analytics, LLC v. Lundin,*[5] and *Victor Stanley, Inc. v. Creative Pipe, Inc. (Victor Stanley I).*[6] These three decisions remain the leading authority from the federal courts on devising and defending an effective electronic search methodology for discovery purposes.

The most significant considerations addressed in these decisions concern the knowledge and competence needed to design effective search protocols and to defend them if challenged by an adversary. *O'Keefe* and *Equity Analytics* suggest the need for an *expert* to design and defend electronic search protocols—and specifically, an expert who meets the requirements of Federal Rule of Evidence 702.[7] *Victor Stanley I* does not go so far as to explicitly impose the requirements of FRE 702 upon experts in discovery disputes, but nonetheless warns against attorneys designing electronic search protocols without the requisite qualifications to

4. 537 F. Supp. 2d 14 (D.D.C. 2008).
5. 248 F.R.D. 331 (D.D.C. 2008).
6. *Victor Stanley I,* 250 F.R.D. 251.
7. *O'Keefe,* 537 F. Supp. 2d at 24; *Equity Analytics,* 248 F.R.D. at 333.

do so.[8] This warning is particularly significant given that in *Victor Stanley I*, the court held that the party's failure to effectively design and defend its electronic search protocol resulted in waiver of more than 150 purportedly privileged documents.[9]

The key question highlighted by these three decisions is how one designs an effective, defensible search. A related question is what qualifications are needed to do so. In light of the exponential increase in the amount of documents and data that must be culled during discovery, what standard can litigants, lawyers, and courts apply to determine whether any particular search protocol is reasonably effective in identifying responsive or privileged documents?

The cited decisions suggest the need for at least some requisite expertise to design and defend electronic search protocols.[10] But the use of experts in conducting discovery raises its own questions and is fraught with its own potential problems, not the least of which is the propriety of applying FRE 702 to discovery disputes. Experts can be expensive, and imposing such a requirement could add significant cost to a discovery process that already suffers from unexpected delays and is prone to being over budget. Also, what qualifications would such experts be required to possess? *O'Keefe* suggests expertise in topics such as computer technology, statistics, and linguistics.[11] But does this mean that litigants must, for example, hire a linguist to develop an effective keyword search? Or a statistician to evaluate various search methods? The answer is unclear and of course would depend upon the circumstances. But such requirements, even in limited circumstances, could have enormous practical consequences for lawyers and litigants in conducting discovery.

Below, we start with a discussion of the background of the legal landscape before the three recent decisions. We focus on the use of keyword searches by attorneys in conducting electronic discovery and on recent research regarding the relative efficacy of such methods in locating relevant documents. This research suggests that simple keyword searching often fails to identify a potentially significant number of responsive documents and that "alternative"

8. *Victor Stanley I*, 250 F.R.D. at 262.
9. *Id.* at 259–60.
10. *O'Keefe*, 537 F. Supp. 2d at 24; *Equity Analytics*, 248 F.R.D. at 333; *Victor Stanley I*, 250 F.R.D. at 262.
11. *O'Keefe*, 537 F. Supp. 2d at 24.

search methods are likely more effective than simple Boolean searching.[12] We then discuss the fact patterns and holdings of the three decisions in more depth. We also discuss a fourth opinion, *Rhoads Industries, Inc. v. Building Materials Corp. of America*,[13] that, like *Victor Stanley I*, addresses the propriety of using automated searches in conducting a privilege review. We then suggest the broad strategies of (1) negotiating an agreement with opposing counsel regarding electronic search protocols and (2) carefully developing, documenting, and executing search protocols, regardless of whether an agreement is reached with opposing counsel. In conclusion, we offer specific practice tips for litigators in conducting discovery in cases involving enormous quantities of documents and data.

2. Background

A. Existing legal authority regarding the propriety of electronic searches in e-discovery is limited

While the use of electronic searches has become fairly commonplace, up until a few years ago there were very few cases that offer guidance on the reasonableness of search protocols or otherwise address their propriety. The 2006 "ESI" amendments to the Federal Rules of Civil Procedure did not address the propriety and use of electronic searches. Decisions addressing traditional manual review offer only nominal guidance because they do not—and of course cannot—address the technological complexities of electronic searches.[14]

---

12. Keyword searching allows a user to search for documents containing particular words identified in a search. Boolean searching allows a user to combine these particular words in more sophisticated searches using the operators "and," "or," "not," and "near" to restrict or broaden a search.

13. 254 F.R.D. 216 (E.D. Pa. 2008).

14. Courts have analyzed the reasonableness of manual review through a balancing test. For example, one court held that a party would not be required to review 19,000 boxes of documents where both the issues and the resources of the parties were limited. Am. Int'l Specialty Lines Ins. Co. v. NWI-I, Inc., 240 F.R.D. 401, 412 (N.D. Ill. 2007). In protecting the parties from unduly burdensome or expensive discovery requests, the court considered "what has been dubbed the proportionality test of Rule 26(b)(2)(iii)[now Rule 26(b)(2)(C)]: the needs of the case, the amount in controversy, the resources of the parties, the importance of the issues at stake in the litigation, and the importance of the proposed discovery in resolving the issues." *Id.* The court required the parties to work together to develop a search protocol and to split the cost of the review. *Id.* at 412–13. Similarly, another court held that it was sufficient for a party to search

In the fall of 2007, the Sedona Conference sought to fill the void by publishing its *Best Practices Commentary on the Use of Search and Information Retrieval Methods in E-Discovery*,[15] the stated goal of which is to provide best practices for judges, lawyers, and clients regarding the nature of the search and retrieval process in the context of civil litigation.[16] This commentary describes many of the challenges of e-discovery, including exponential growth in informational records[17] and the imperfections of both manual and electronic review.[18] Significantly, it also challenges the use of simple keyword searching.[19] While it recognizes that keyword searches can be useful "when the legal inquiry is focused on finding particular documents and when the use of language is relatively predictable,"[20] it notes that "the experience of many litigators is that simple keyword searching alone is inadequate in at least some discovery contexts."[21] As discussed below, *O'Keefe*, *Equity Analytics*, and *Victor Stanley I* also suggest, or at least imply, that simple keyword searching may not be sufficient[22] and *Victor Stanley I* expressly suggests that the use of more sophisticated electronic search methods "can enhance the accuracy and reliability of the

---

for responsive documents only within a company's public affairs department and one individual's office, where the party had demonstrated that the burden of searching other departments greatly outweighed the relative likelihood that responsive documents would be found in those departments. Tavoulareas v. Piro, 93 F.R.D. 24, 27–28 (D.D.C. 1981). Another court held, however, that a search of indices of about 60 boxes of documents, rather than reviewing each document, was inadequate. Alexander v. FBI, 194 F.R.D. 305, 313–14 (D.D.C. 2000). The court based its decision on a failure of proof—the party had failed to make an evidentiary showing regarding why reviewing each individual document was overly burdensome.

15. The Sedona Conference, *Best Practices Commentary on the Use of Search and Information Retrieval Methods in E-Discovery*, 8 SEDONA CONF. J. 189 (Fall 2007) [hereinafter *Sedona Search Commentary*].

16. *Id.* at 191.

17. *Id.* at 194, 197–98.

18. *Id.* at 194–95.

19. *Id.* at 201–04.

20. *Id.* at 201.

21. *Id.*

22. United States v. O'Keefe, 537 F. Supp. 2d 14, 24 (D.D.C. 2008); Equity Analytics, LLC v. Lundin, 248 F.R.D. 331, 333 (D.D.C. 2008); Victor Stanley, Inc. v. Creative Pipe, Inc. (*Victor Stanley I*), 250 F.R.D. 251, 260 (D. Md. 2008).

search."[23] And indeed, more and more courts have been addressing issues surrounding the use of keywords in recent years.[24]

As discussed below in section 2.C, a large project (the TREC Legal Track) has been under way for the last several years to test the theory that alternative search methods are superior to simple or Boolean keyword searching. The results to date suggest that alternative methods are indeed superior. Notwithstanding that such methods may not be readily available or cost effective for attorneys to start using immediately, the broad lesson to take away from the Sedona paper, recent case law, and the TREC project is that an attorney can do much to improve the keyword search methods he or she already is using. Thus, before getting to the cases, we first explore the reasons why simple keyword searching is thought to be inadequate, and then discuss the TREC Legal Track project and results in more detail.

B. Simple keyword searching may not be sufficient

Keyword searches, used for legal research and surfing the web, are the most basic and most common forms of electronic searches. But keyword searching may not capture all, or even a majority, of the information sought. The Sedona paper cites the following reasons to explain why:

(i) a single word may have a number of different meanings, some of which are relevant to a lawsuit and some of which are not;

(ii) a single word or idea may have many synonyms, one or more of which may go overlooked in the keywords because of the difficulty of identifying them all;

(iii) acronyms, shorthand, and slang are routine, particularly in electronic communications, and they may not be captured in the keywords;

(iv) documents sometimes contain multiple languages, particularly in electronic documents such as emails where foreign language is automatically translated but certain words are not translated by the software,

23. *Victor Stanley I*, 250 F.R.D. at 261 n.9.

24. *See, e.g.*, William A. Gross Constr. Assocs., Inc. v. Am. Mfrs. Mut. Ins. Co., 256 F.R.D. 134, 134–35 (S.D.N.Y. 2009) (criticizing party's selection of thousands of search terms, and requiring parties to use alternative search protocol).

and foreign words may not be considered among the keywords; and

(v) even where every conceivable keyword is considered and included, written work often contains errors, such as misspellings, typos and incorrect translations, which cannot necessarily be contemplated and thus may undermine the efficacy of keyword searches.[25]

As a result, it might be the case that keyword searches can be overinclusive or underinclusive, or even both.[26]

The Sedona paper and other sources suggest that there may be more advanced electronic search methods that are superior to simple keyword searching.[27] An oft-cited article classifies such advanced information retrieval methods into three general categories. The first category, "set-theoretic," refers to keyword searching and includes the use of Boolean strings, supplemented by "fuzzy search" methods,[28] which are techniques that attempt to capture all forms of a word rather than relying on exact word matches.[29] The next two categories are both referred to as "concept" or "conceptual" search methods.[30] These methods aim to retrieve documents related to an idea, rather than simply to a specific word or words.[31] They rely on mathematics and statistics to better identify groups of responsive documents.[32] The first category of conceptual methods uses mathematics to find patterns in language usage in communications, and then groups documents accordingly.[33] The second category of such methods relies on input from an attorney or the client (or even a linguist) to

25. *Sedona Search Commentary*, *supra* note 15, at 201–02.

26. *Id.*; G. Paul & J. Baron, *Information Inflation: Can the Legal System Adapt?*, 13 Rich. J. L. & Tech. 10, *38 (Spring 2007), http://law.richmond.edu/jolt/v13i3/article10.pdf.

27. *Sedona Search Commentary*, *supra* note 15, at 202–03, app., includes detailed descriptions of various categories of alternative search methods; *see also* Matus & Davis, *Does Your Search Pass Judicial Scrutiny?*, 10/27/2008 S6 (col. 1) (2008) (for descriptions of probabilistic, rule-based (or "clustering"), and linguistic (or "fuzzy") search models).

28. Paul & Baron, *Information Inflation*, *supra* note 26, at *42.

29. *Sedona Search Commentary*, *supra* note 15, at 219.

30. Paul & Baron, *Information Inflation*, *supra* note 26, at *43.

31. *Id.*

32. *Sedona Search Commentary*, *supra* note 15, at 202–03, app., 219.

33. *Id.* at 203; Paul & Baron, *Information Inflation*, *supra* note 26, at *42.

identify groups of related terms used to find documents concerning a particular topic.[34] The terms are organized into a structure, and groups of documents are collected and organized based on that structure.[35] The premise of each type of conceptual approach is that patterns exist in the way in which humans communicate, orally as well as on paper, and there are ways of identifying those relationships that do not involve simple keyword or Boolean searches.[36]

C. TREC Legal Track study of effectiveness of Boolean search methods compared with alternative search methods

As noted above, there is currently a massive, multiyear study under way that is testing the theory that alternative search methods, such as concept search methods, are superior to keyword or Boolean searching. Results to date suggest that they are.

The TREC Legal Track project is sponsored in part by the U.S. government's National Institute of Standards and Technology (NIST), with the support of the Sedona Conference.[37] The Legal Track is just one of many "tracks" that make up NIST's broader TREC project, or the "Text Retrieval Conference," which was started in 1992. The primary purpose of TREC is to "support research within the information retrieval community by providing the infrastructure necessary for large-scale evaluation of text retrieval methodologies" in a variety of different contexts, such as

34. Paul & Baron, *Information Inflation, supra* note 26, at *42; *See also Sedona Search Commentary, supra* note 15, at 221–222.

35. *Sedona Search Commentary, supra* note 15, at 222–23.

36. *Id.* at 202–03.

37. *See* Jason R. Baron, *The TREC Legal Track: Origins and Reflections on the First Year,* 8 SEDONA CONF. J. 251, 252, 254 (Fall 2007) (describing how the author and his colleague Professor Douglas W. Oard submitted the initial proposal to TREC "[w]ith the backing of the Sedona Conference®," and that the initial participants in the 2006 track included individuals "from Sedona Conference® member law firms"); *see also* Sedona Conference, An Open Letter to Law Firms and Companies in the Legal Tech Sector Re: Invitation to Participate in the TREC Legal Track 2009 (Apr. 22, 2009), http://www.thesedonaconference.org/content/miscFiles/TREC_OPEN_Letter.pdf (inviting participation in the 2008 TREC Legal Track); Stephen Tomlinson, *et al., Overview of the TREC 2007 Legal Track* 1 (Apr. 30, 2008), http://trec-legal.umiacs.umd.edu/legal07t.pdf (noting that the Sedona Conference Working Group on Electronic Document Production helped to create the new mock complaints for 2007).

blogs and the web.[38] The goal of TREC's Legal Track, which began in 2006, is to assess the relative effectiveness of Boolean searching and alternative search methods in the context of civil discovery.[39]

For the 2006 project, the Legal Track planners chose a public collection of about seven million documents, which was available as the result of the settlement of a number of lawsuits by the attorneys general of several U.S. states against seven major tobacco organizations, to use as a test database.[40] The project coordinators then developed topics that would serve as discovery requests.[41] Several institutions were enlisted to run whatever search methodology they chose, and to then submit their respective "runs" of responsive documents.[42] The planners also produced runs using Boolean search queries developed through a mock negotiation, whereby one project planner took on the role of plaintiff's counsel and negotiated with another planner, who had taken on the role of defendant's counsel.[43] The assistance of volunteer document reviewers—including one "expert manual searcher," an individual who had significant experience with searching tobacco-related materials and was familiar with the particular database used—was enlisted for the actual manual review of the various runs that resulted from the automated searches.[44] Finally, the planners' runs were compared with those submitted by the volunteer institutions.[45]

The most significant result of the 2006 study was that none of the automated methods performed any better than the baseline

38. Nat'l Inst. of Standards & Tech., TREC Overview, http://trec.nist.gov/overview.html (last updated Aug. 28, 2008); Nat'l Inst. of Standards & Tech., TREC Tracks, http://trec.nist.gov/tracks.html (last updated Jan. 7, 2009).

39. Jason R. Baron, David D. Lewis & Douglas W. Oard, *TREC-2006 Legal Track Overview* § 1 (2007), http://trec.nist.gov/pubs/trec15/papers/LEGAL06.OVERVIEW.pdf.

40. *See* Baron, *The TREC Legal Track*, *supra* note 37, at 252–53 ("[T]he main strength of the collection consists of its wide range of document genres, including letters, memos, budgets, reports, agendas, minutes, plans, transcripts, scientific articles, and some email—where document length varies from one to many thousands of pages.").

41. *Id.* at 253.

42. *Id.* at 254.

43. *Id.*

44. The reviewers included eight lawyers, 10 law students, three paralegals, one professional archivist, one historian, and several individuals with degrees in science or finances. Baron, *The TREC Legal Track*, *supra* note 37, at 254.

45. *Id.* at 253–54.

negotiated Boolean run.[46] In addition, the expert manual searcher outperformed all of the automated methods.[47] And, as the 2006 TREC Overview paper notes, "[p]erhaps the greatest accomplishment of the TREC 2006 Legal Track is that it happened at all."[48] It was certainly a significant undertaking. But ultimately the results did not establish that alternative automated search methods were any more effective than Boolean searching in locating responsive documents.

The results from subsequent years have been more promising, however. In contrast to the 2006 results, the 2007 results did show that alternative automated search methods resulted in a greater number of "hits" of responsive documents than did the Boolean search.[49] Indeed, up to 78 percent of the total number of relevant documents identified were *not* found by the reference Boolean queries, but were instead found only by the participants' alternative research methods.[50]

Unfortunately, however, "no single alternative method has yet been shown to consistently outperform Boolean Search without increasing the number of documents to [manually] review."[51] Thus, while the alternative automated methods resulted in a greater number of responsive documents, they also resulted in a greater number of documents in the "run," which, in turn, resulted in a greater number of documents that required manual review for the purpose of determining relevance. That said, the 2007 results ultimately did confirm that basic keyword searching often "misses" a potentially significant number of responsive documents.

The 2008 TREC Legal Track project proceeded on an even larger scale than either of the two previous years.[52] The researchers once again succeeded in showing that alternative search methods, when considered together, are more successful in identifying relevant documents than negotiated Boolean searches, although they still did not identify any one particular automated search method that is consistently superior to Boolean searching.[53] Nevertheless, the project produced other interesting results, particularly with

46. *Id.* at 256.
47. *Id.*
48. Baron, Lewis & Oard, *TREC-2006 Legal Track Overview, supra* note 39, § 6.
49. Tomlinson, *et al., Overview of the TREC 2007 Legal Track, supra* note 37, § 1.
50. *Id.* § 6.
51. *Id.* § 1.
52. Douglas W. Oard, *et al., Overview of the TREC 2008 Legal Track* 1(2009), http://trec.nist.gov/pubs/trec17/papers/LEGAL.OVERVIEW08.pdf.
53. *Id.* §§ 2.8.2, 5.

respect to the effects of varying degrees of human effort on the automated procedures. Specifically, the researchers redesigned the project's "Interactive Task" to better fulfill its goal of "model[ing] as accurately as possible the real-world conditions in which companies and law firms, and the e-discovery firms they engage, must meet their document-retrieval objectives and obligations."[54] A "Topic Authority," who takes on the role of a senior partner supervising the review, was assigned to each review team.[55] The Topic Authority was required to form a conception of what is and is not responsive to a topic, and to communicate that conception to the team, just as a supervising attorney would do for document reviewers in the real world.[56] The Topic Authority also assisted the teams in clarifying topics as the teams conducted their reviews, and in adjudicating disputes regarding relevance calls.[57] The teams were permitted a maximum of 10 hours of the Authority's time.[58] The teams used a wide range of their respective Authority's time, from just five minutes to 485 minutes. Interestingly—and perhaps not surprisingly—the team that used the most of its Topic Authority's time located substantially more relevant documents than did the other teams.[59] This result supports the notion that increased interaction between reviewers and supervising attorneys can dramatically increase the effectiveness of a review.[60] In other words, increased human effort can affect the quality of the results achieved by automated methods.

In 2009, the Legal Track project continued its work with the tobacco document database, and also started research on a new database consisting of email messages and attachments that were produced by Enron in response to requests by the Federal Energy Regulatory Commission.[61] The broad goal of the 2009 project was to get even closer to approximating real-world conditions of document review than in earlier years. For example, in continuing their work with the tobacco database, the researchers also took into consideration the fact that there can be considerable variation in

54. *Id.* § 4.1.
55. *Id.*
56. *Id.*
57. *Id.*
58. *Id.*
59. *Id.* § 4.4.4.
60. *Id.* § 4.6.
61. *Interactive Task Guidelines: TREC 2009 Legal Track* § 4.2 (June 19, 2009), http://trec-legal.umiacs.umd.edu/LT09_ITG_final.pdf.

relevance calls depending on the individual reviewer.[62] Thus, they worked with some of the same topics but with a new set of relevance determinations by new volunteer reviewers. Similarly, the Topic Authority continued to play a significant role in the Interactive Task.[63] The volunteer reviewers again had a total of 10 hours of a Topic Authority's time, to ask him or her anything from clarifying a topic to judging the relevance of questionable documents to arranging for conference calls to discuss aspects of their review.[64] In addition, the number of participating private legal services companies increased from just a few to a total of 10.[65]

Results for the 2009 project confirm both that automated search methods outperform simple Boolean search queries and that increased involvement by the Topic Authority leads to better search results.[66] In addition, the Topic Authorities suggested that the quality of the team's interaction with the Topic Authority was ultimately more important than the quantity.[67] Teams that invested time to become familiar with the document collection and the general subject matter of the litigation before interacting with their Topic Authorities were able to formulate questions that helped them "to clarify the topic's scope or to arrive at a common conception of relevance," which, in turn, helped them to better structure their search methodology.[68] These findings suggest that investment of human time and energy can have a significant effect on the results produced by automated search methods. In other words, it generally will not be sufficient to simply run an electronic search and rely on the search tool to automatically and accurately identify all the relevant documents and cull out all the irrelevant documents; rather—and perhaps not surprisingly—even the most

62. *See TREC 2009 Legal Track: Batch Task Guidelines*, at "Overview of the Batch Task" (June 1, 2009) http://trec-legal.umiacs.umd.edu/batch09a.html.

63. *Interactive Task Guidelines: TREC 2009 Legal Track*, at 2 (June 19, 2009), http://trec-legal.umiacs.umd.edu/LT09_ITG_final.pdf.

64. *Id.*

65. Bruce Hedin, *et al.*, *Overview of the TREC 2009 Legal Track* § 1 (July 19, 2010), http://trec-legal.umiacs.umd.edu/LegalOverview09.pdf.

66. Jason R. Baron, What Do I Do with a Billion Emails? The Future of E-Discovery Text Analytics, Presentation at 6th Annual Text Analytics Summit (Boston, Mass., May 25, 2010), at slides 39–40.

67. Maura R. Grossman, *Reflections of the Topic Authorities about the 2009 TREC Legal Track Interactive Task*, at 1 (July 18, 2010), http://trec-legal.umiacs.umd.edu/2009TaReflections.pdf.

68. *Id. See also* Jason Krause, *Human-Computer Assisted Search in EDD*, LAW TECH. NEWS, Dec. 20, 2010, http://www.law.com/jsp/article.jsp?id=1202476197639.

sophisticated electronic searches, like most things in this world, require a significant human touch to be most effective.

The project continued in 2010, with continued focus on evaluating the effect of both the nature and the quantity of the interaction between the teams and their respective Topic Authorities.[69] New for 2010 were the addition of a "privilege" topic, which would cover documents subject to the attorney-client, work product, or other applicable privileges, and the allowance for a fully manual review of a subset of the test database.[70] It will be interesting to see what the complete results from 2010 (due to be published sometime in 2011) will reveal. The project has been approved for its sixth year in 2011.

In sum, while the TREC Legal Track results have not yet identified one particular alternative search method that is superior to keyword and Boolean searching, the results *have* shown that alternative electronic search methods are generally more successful in identifying greater percentages of the relevant documents that were estimated to exist in the collections.[71] And though the project coordinators are careful to couch their results in preliminary and sometimes even uncertain terms, much can be learned from the project, which is the only large-scale study to date that has brought together experts in the fields of e-discovery and information retrieval to examine, scientifically and statistically, the efficacy of electronic search tools in e-discovery.[72]

The results generally support the theory that Boolean or keyword searching is far from ideal, and also support the view that attorneys should be both cautious and creative in employing that type of searching. As a practical matter, of course, keyword searching is likely still the most convenient (and perhaps the most cost-effective) option for most attorneys, but that does not mean that attorneys should simply run a keyword search and think that they are done with their discovery obligation to conduct a reasonable search for responsive documents.[73]

69. *See TREC—2010 Legal Track Interactive Task Guidelines* 2 (2010), http://trec-legal.umiacs.umd.edu/itg10_final.pdf.

70. *Id.* §§ 3.2, 3.3.

71. *See* Tomlinson, *et al.*, *Overview of the TREC 2007 Legal Track*, *supra* note 37, § 6.

72. *See* Oard, Baron & Lewis, *Some Lessons Learned to Date from the TREC Legal Track (2006–2009)*, at 2, http://trec-legal.umiacs.umd.edu/LessonsLearned.pdf.

73. *See* H. Christopher Boehning & Daniel J. Toal, *In Search of Better E-Discovery Methods*, N.Y.L.J., Apr. 23, 2008, http://www.law.com/jsp/legaltechnology/pubArticleLT.jsp?id=900005509469.

Again, investment of human time and energy can have a significant impact on search results, regardless of whether Boolean or some other method is employed. And while no one alternative automated method has yet been proven to be more reliable, cost effective, or efficient than simple keyword searching, and while we may still be a long way from the use of alternative electronic search methods as a matter of course, there are certain things attorneys can and should be doing in conducting electronic discovery, as illustrated by the cases discussed in the next section and as set forth in the suggested strategies and practice tips in section 5.

3. Guidance from the bench on electronic searches in three key decisions: *O'Keefe, Equity Analytics*, and *Victor Stanley I*

While investigations into the "best" search methods continue, litigation marches on, and lawyers must meet their discovery obligations and defend the decisions they made when challenged. In addition, while keyword searching may currently be the best available option, it nevertheless is possible to employ a "bad" keyword search: as noted in *Victor Stanley I*, "all keyword searches are not created equal."[74]

Before 2007, the Sedona paper was about the only significant legal guidance for the courts and practitioners concerning the reasonableness of electronic search protocols. More recently, the *O'Keefe, Equity Analytics*, and *Victor Stanley I* opinions have provided additional guidance—although little additional guidance has been provided by the federal courts since. In each case, a party moved to compel the production of documents or data, arguing that the responding party's search methodology was inadequate.[75]

Victor Stanley I differs from the other two cases in that it addresses the use of electronic searches to identify privileged documents as opposed to documents responsive to discovery requests, but this distinction has little bearing on the factors to be considered when designing an electronic search protocol for either purpose.[76] *Victor Stanley I* suggests that simple keyword searching may not be

74. Victor Stanley, Inc. v. Creative Pipe, Inc. (*Victor Stanley I*), 250 F.R.D. 251, 256–57 (D. Md. 2008).

75. United States v. O'Keefe, 537 F. Supp. 2d 14, 16 (D.D.C. 2008); Equity Analytics, LLC v. Lundin, 248 F.R.D. 331, 332 (D.D.C. 2008); *Victor Stanley I*, 250 F.R.D. at 253.

76. *Victor Stanley I*, 250 F.R.D. at 259–62.

sufficient and that more sophisticated electronic search methods may be needed in some cases.[77]

Most notably, all three decisions emphasize that in any event, attorneys must be prepared to defend their search methods if challenged and that such preparation may involve the use of a technical expert, or at least someone with the qualifications needed to design and implement an effective search methodology.[78] The *O'Keefe* and *Equity Analytics* opinions go so far as to assert that in order to defend the reasonableness of a particular search protocol, a party *may* need to produce an expert who meets the qualification requirements of FRE 702.[79] *Victor Stanley I*, although defending this aspect of those opinions, seems to offer a less stringent standard, opining only that the search protocol must be designed by a qualified person, who could be an attorney, and that the requisite qualifications of the person designing the search protocol depend on the needs and circumstances of each case.[80]

A. *O'Keefe* suggests that FRE 702 expert evidence may be required to evaluate the efficacy of a keyword search in identifying responsive documents

In *O'Keefe*, the earliest of the three decisions, the court found a number of inadequacies in the government's search for records and concluded that it had failed to comply with a discovery order.[81] Notwithstanding the government's deficiencies, the court rejected defendants' argument that the defendants made regarding the adequacy of the search terms used by the government.[82] The court held that, to lodge an objection that the court would consider, the defendants would be required to specifically contend that the search terms used by the government were insufficient in a separate motion to compel, which "must be based on evidence that meets the requirements of Rule 702 of the Federal Rules of

---

77. *Id.* at 260.
78. *O'Keefe*, 537 F. Supp. 2d at 24; *Equity Analytics*, 248 F.R.D. at 333; *Victor Stanley I*, 250 F.R.D. at 262; *see also Sedona Search Commentary*, *supra* note 15, at 204 (noting that, absent an agreement regarding search methodology, parties should be prepared to "prove up" the adequacy of a particular search technology, which may result in "a difficult and expensive battle of experts").
79. *O'Keefe*, 537 F. Supp. 2d at 24; *Equity Analytics*, 248 F.R.D. at 333.
80. *Victor Stanley I*, 250 F.R.D. at 262.
81. 537 F. Supp. 2d at 17–22.
82. *Id.* at 24.

Evidence."[83] Citing, inter alia, the Sedona Conference *Commentary on the Use of Search and Information Retrieval Methods*, the court noted the inherent limitations of keyword searches, but went on to explain that proper evaluation of a particular search is not an easy assessment:

> Whether search terms or "keywords" will yield the information sought is a complicated question involving the interplay, at least, of the sciences of computer technology, statistics and linguistics. . . . *Given this complexity, for lawyers and judges to dare opine that a certain search term or terms would be more likely to produce information than the terms that were used is truly to go where angels fear to tread.* This topic is clearly beyond the ken of a layman and requires that any such conclusion be based on evidence that, for example, meets the criteria of Rule 702 of the Federal Rules of Evidence.[84]

Thus, the *O'Keefe* court essentially refused to consider the question of the efficacy of the challenged search method absent a formal motion to compel supported by *expert evidence* that met the requirements of Federal Rule of Evidence 702.

B. *Equity Analytics* suggests that FRE 702 expert evidence may be required to evaluate the efficacy of the means of collecting documents

Issued less than a month after the *O'Keefe* decision, the court in *Equity Analytics* similarly opined that "determining whether a particular search methodology, such as keywords, will or will not be effective certainly requires knowledge beyond the ken of a lay person (and a lay lawyer) and *requires expert testimony that meets the requirements of Rule 702 of the Federal Rules of Evidence*."[85] In *Equity Analytics*, the court was asked to resolve the impasse between the parties in their attempt to develop a search protocol for a forensic examination of the defendant's computer.[86] The plaintiff alleged that the defendant, a former employee, had gained illegal access to the plaintiff's electronically stored information after he was fired.[87] The defendant's computer contained a wide range of materials,

83. *Id.*
84. *Id.* (internal citations omitted) (emphasis added).
85. *Equity Analytics*, 248 F.R.D. at 333 (emphasis added).
86. *Id.* at 332.
87. *Id.*

many of which had nothing to do with the lawsuit, including personal medical records.[88] Because of the sensitive nature of the personal information stored on the computer, the defendant opposed production of all the data and proposed that certain file types be searched, but the plaintiff found this to be inadequate.[89] The parties also disputed the impact that loading a new operating system onto the computer would have on the search.[90]

As in *O'Keefe*, the court declined to determine the adequacy of the proposed search based on the arguments of counsel alone. Instead, it required the plaintiff to submit an affidavit from an expert explaining why the narrow search proposed by the defendant was inadequate and what impact the new operating system had on the data on the computer.[91] The court reasoned that such expert testimony, as well as an evidentiary hearing at which the expert could be cross-examined, if necessary, would provide the information that was needed to "make the best possible judgment as to how to balance [the plaintiff's] need for information against [the defendant's] privacy."[92]

The *O'Keefe* and *Equity Analytics* decisions together suggest that expert evidence may be necessary to evaluate the efficacy of electronic searches, in the contexts of both collection and production. These conclusions suggest, in turn, that experts may be needed up front to design search protocols to ensure that the searches will be defensible later.[93]

C. *Victor Stanley I* requires "persons qualified to design effective search methodology" but does not go so far as to require an expert

The decision in *Victor Stanley I* by Judge Grimm offers a comprehensive discussion of the use of electronic searches and suggests

---

88. *Id.*

89. *Id.* at 333.

90. *Id.*

91. *Id.*

92. *Id.*

93. *But see* Eurand, Inc. v. Mylan Pharm., Inc., 266 F.R.D. 79, 84–85 (D. Del. 2010), in which the court acknowledged Judge Facciola's warning in *O'Keefe* and *Equity Analytics* that "[n]either lawyers nor judges are generally qualified to opine that certain search terms or files are more or less likely to produce information than those keywords or data actually used or reviewed," but nevertheless went on to analyze the reasonableness of the plaintiffs' search, and held that the terms failed to include those that would have produced documents relevant to the inventors' knowledge of the materiality of certain prior art.

what could be considered a more practical standard for assessing the efficacy of search protocols.[94] The particular issue before the court was whether defendants had waived the attorney-client privilege with respect to 165 documents that had been inadvertently produced.[95] The defendants had used electronic searches to identify nonprivileged documents that were text-searchable.[96] They did not manually review any of the results of that search for privilege.[97] In addition, the defendants did a manual privilege review of the titles, rather than of the full contents, of some documents that were reportedly not text-searchable.[98]

Because *Victor Stanley I* was decided before the enactment of FRE 502,[99] which limits the consequences of waiver when privileged documents are disclosed, the court applied the five-factor test described in *McCafferty's, Inc. v. Bank of Glen Burnie*[100] to determine whether the privilege had been waived. The court, however, did not ignore FRE 502 in conducting its analysis. Instead, it discussed the then-pending rule extensively in a footnote.[101] One of the factors in the test from *McCafferty's* is the "reasonableness of the precautions taken to prevent inadvertent disclosure."[102] This factor is similar to the requirement in FRE 502(b)(2), which requires analysis of whether "the holder of the privilege or protection took reasonable steps to prevent disclosure" to determine whether a disclosure results in a waiver of privilege. It was within this framework that the court evaluated the adequacy of the defendants' search method.

94. Victor Stanley, Inc. v. Creative Pipe, Inc. (*Victor Stanley I*), 250 F.R.D. 251, 261 nn. 9 & 10 (D. Md. 2008).

95. *Id.* at 253, 255.

96. *Id.* at 256.

97. *Id.* at 257 ("[I]t appears from the information that they provided to the court that they simply turned over to the Plaintiff all the text-searchable ESI files that were identified by the keyword search Turner performed as non-privileged. . . .").

98. *Id.* at 256–57.

99. Federal Rule of Evidence 502 became effective on Sept. 19, 2008.

100. 179 F.R.D. 163, 167 (D. Md. 1998).

101. *Victor Stanley I*, 250 F.R.D. at 259 n.5.

102. *Id.* at 259. The five factors listed in *McCafferty's* are (1) the reasonableness of the precautions taken to prevent inadvertent disclosure; (2) the number of inadvertent disclosures; (3) the extent of the disclosures; (4) any delay in measures taken to rectify the disclosure; and (5) overriding interests in justice. *Id.* (citing *McCafferty's*, 179 F.R.D. at 167).

Ultimately, the *Victor Stanley I* court held that defendants waived privilege, finding they had failed to meet their burden to establish that their search was adequate.[103] The specific deficiencies of proof included the failure to identify the keywords they used to conduct the searches and the failure to explain the rationale for the selection of the keywords.[104] The defendants also failed to explain what type of search was conducted—for example, whether it was a simple keyword search or one using Boolean operators.[105] Noting that keyword searches have inherent limitations, the court summarized, in a lengthy footnote, the alternative search methods that are described in the Sedona paper, including the conceptual search methods described above in section 2.B.[106]

While the court implied that these alternative methods may be superior, it is important to recognize that the waiver here was ultimately based on a failure of *proof*—the defendants had relied on electronic searches for privileged information without conducting a manual review and failed to offer sufficient proof that those searches were reasonably effective.[107]

Another aspect of the defendants' failure of proof was their failure to demonstrate the qualifications of the defendant and his attorneys to design the search that they employed and to "analyze[] the results of the search to assess its reliability, appropriateness for the task, and the quality of its implementation."[108] The court observed that the "proper selection and implementation [of keyword searches] obviously involves technical, if not scientific, knowledge."[109] It is this portion of the *Victor Stanley I* holding that arguably has garnered the most attention in the e-discovery community.[110] *Victor Stanley I* does not go as far as *O'Keefe* and *Equity*

103. *Id.* at 256–57.

104. *Id.* at 260.

105. *Id.* at 261 n.9.

106. *Id.*

107. *Id.* at 256–57.

108. *Id.* at 259–60 (citing United States v. O'Keefe, 537 F. Supp. 2d 14, 24 (D.D.C. 2008); Equity Analytics, LLC v. Lundin, 248 F.R.D. 331, 333 (D.D.C. 2008)); *see also In re Seroquel Prods. Liab. Litig.*, 244 F.R.D. 650, 660 n.6, 662 (M.D. Fla. 2007); *Sedona Search Commentary, supra* note 15, at 194–95, 201–02.

109. *Victor Stanley I*, 250 F.R.D. at 260.

110. *See, e.g.*, Dean Gonsowski & William Uppington, *Managing the Sea Change in E-Discovery Search: Rethinking Current Search Protocols and Tools*, 193 N.J.L.J. 533 (2008); Craig Ball, *Grimm Prognosis*, 7/08 LAW TECH. NEWS 36 (col. 1) (2008); Matus & Davis, *Does Your Search Pass Judicial Scrutiny?*, 10/27/2008 N.Y.L.J. S6 (col. 1).

Analytics do in suggesting that the person who designs or defends a search protocol must meet the expert qualification requirements of FRE 702. But *Victor Stanley I* nevertheless holds that for a contested search to withstand judicial scrutiny, a party must be prepared to justify the steps it took. Such justification includes a showing that the search was performed by "persons qualified to design effective search methodology" and that the method was properly executed and tested:

> Selection of the appropriate search and information retrieval technique requires careful advance planning by persons qualified to design effective search methodology. The implementation of the methodology selected should be tested for quality assurance; and the party selecting the methodology must be prepared to explain the rationale for the method chosen to the court, demonstrate that it is appropriate for the task, and show that it was properly implemented.[111]

Interestingly, in discussing the *O'Keefe* and *Equity Analytics* opinions, *Victor Stanley I* notes first that neither opinion expressly held that FRE 702 was "engrafted" into the rules of discovery in civil proceedings.[112] Instead, the court concludes that *O'Keefe* and *Equity Analytics* "made the entirely self-evident observation that challenges to the sufficiency of keyword search methodology unavoidably involve scientific, technical and scientific subjects, and *ipse dixit* pronouncements from lawyers unsupported by an affidavit or other showing that the search methodology was effective for its intended purpose are of little value to a trial judge who must decide a discovery motion aimed at either compelling a more comprehensive search or preventing one."[113] *Victor Stanley I* went on to agree with *O'Keefe*'s conclusion that such information is necessary for a trial judge faced with making factual determinations in the context of a discovery dispute, and that the Federal Rules of Evidence are simply a logical place to turn for the standards a judge should employ in making those determinations:

> Viewed in its proper context, all that *O'Keefe* and *Equity Analytics* required was that the parties be prepared to back up their positions with respect to a dispute involving the

111. *Victor Stanley I*, 250 F.R.D. at 262.
112. *Id.* at 261 n.10.
113. *Id.*

> appropriateness of ESI search and information retrieval methodology—obviously an area of science or technology—with reliable information from someone with the qualifications to provide helpful opinions, not conclusory argument by counsel. The goal of Federal Rule of Evidence 702 is to set standards to determine whether information is "helpful" to those who must make factual determinations involving disputed areas of science, technology or other specialized information. The rule is one of common sense, and reason—opinions regarding specialized, scientific or technical matters are not "helpful" unless someone with proper qualifications and adequate supporting facts provided such an opinion after following reliable methodology. That these common sense criteria are found in the rules of evidence does not render them off-limits for consideration during discovery. It is not unusual for pretrial factual determinations in civil cases to look to the Federal Rules of Evidence for assistance in resolving fact disputes.[114]

In other words, according to *Victor Stanley I*, the key lesson to take away from *O'Keefe*, *Equity Analytics*, and *Victor Stanley I* is that parties and their counsel should "expect to support their position with affidavits or other equivalent information from persons with the requisite qualifications and experience, based on sufficient facts or data and using reliable principles or methodology."[115] Thus, while litigants and counsel should be aware of and open to alternative search methods, it is unlikely, at least for now, that courts would require their use, particularly without the evidence establishing that such methods are indeed reliable. And perhaps more importantly, whatever search methodology a party elects to use, it had better be prepared to defend the design and implementation of that methodology with adequate *proof*, which may include testimony from an expert or at least someone who can demonstrate the requisite knowledge and experience with respect to the methodology used.

4. The *Rhoads* decision

As in *Victor Stanley I*, the issue in *Rhoads Industries, Inc. v. Building Materials Corp. of America* was whether the plaintiff had waived the

114. *Id.*
115. *Id.*

privilege with respect to a set of documents—in this case, about 800—in using an electronic search protocol to identify and cull out privileged documents. The court considered many of the same factors addressed in *Victor Stanley I*.[116] The *Rhoads* decision is perhaps most significant because, unlike *Victor Stanley I*, it was decided after the enactment of FRE 502 and is one of the few cases that applies the rule in the context of assessing the reasonableness of a search protocol involving search methods using keywords.

In *Rhoads*, the court held an evidentiary hearing with testimony by both the lawyer who planned and conducted the review and the information technology consultant who was hired to perform the searches used to identify potentially privileged documents.[117] Like *Victor Stanley*, the *Rhoads* court considered the search terms used and the efforts taken to verify the accuracy of the searches, along with certain other factors.[118] And as in *O'Keefe*, *Equity Analytics*, and *Victor Stanley I*, the court acknowledged the significance of using an expert to design the search protocol, remarking that "[t] he fact that Rhoads retained a consultant who recommended and used a fairly sophisticated screening device shows that Rhoads substantially complied with . . . Rule 502."[119] The court also shared the concern for the limitations of keyword searches, particularly when used for a privilege filter, and attributed at least some portion of the inadvertent production to these limitations:

> Keyword and name searches are frequently employed as an initial method to screen and sort documents, but they are not foolproof. For instance, privileged communications frequently creep into e-mail "chains," but may appear only to some participants in the chain depending on a user's application of the "reply" and "forward" commands. These issues inferably led to at least some of Rhoads' inadvertent disclosures.[120]

In the end, the court found that the privilege had not been waived as to at least some of the documents at issue.[121]

116. Rhoads Indus., Inc. v. Bldg. Materials Corp. of Am., 254 F.R.D. 216, 226 (E.D. Pa. 2008).
117. *Id.* at 226–27.
118. *Id.* at 222–24.
119. *Id.* at 222.
120. *Id.* at 220.
121. *Id.* at 226–27.

5. What attorneys can do

The case law to date suggests two general strategies that attorneys are well advised to employ in designing a search. The first is cooperation with opposing counsel. The second includes careful supervision, planning, and documentation of the plan as it is executed. As a practical matter, counsel should keep these broad strategies in mind as they prepare for and proceed through the search process.

A. Cooperating with opposing counsel in developing a search protocol

First, lawyers should attempt as best they can to cooperate with opposing counsel to agree on a discovery plan that sets forth a specific search protocol for identifying responsive and privileged documents, as well as, in some instances, a search protocol for collecting potentially responsive documents. The theme of cooperation has been growing exponentially in the case law and the literature, and, put simply, must be taken seriously.[122]

Indeed, the failure to cooperate brings with it serious risks, including the possibility that control over the search methodology is taken out of the hands of the parties and their counsel and into the hands of the court. For example, in *D'Onofrio v. SFX Sports Group, Inc.*, the court held: "Since I have gotten so little help from counsel, I will create a protocol of my own using as best I can my understanding of the limited agreement that the parties reached when plaintiff's counsel reacted to defendants' proposal."[123] In *William A. Gross Construction Associates*, the court observed that the parties' failure to agree had "left the Court in the uncomfortable position of having to craft a keyword search methodology for the parties, without adequate information from the parties (and Hill) [a nonparty]."[124] Citing *Victor Stanley I, O'Keefe*, and *Equity Analytics*, the court proceeded to impose a search protocol on the parties.[125] The court stated that the opinion "should

122. *See, e.g.*, Paul & Baron, *Information Inflation*, *supra* note 26, at **3, 25, 56; *Sedona Search Commentary*, *supra* note 15, at 211 ("Practice Point 6. Parties should make a good faith attempt to collaborate on the use of particular search and information retrieval methods, tools and protocols (including as to keywords, concepts, and other types of search parameters."); *see also* appendix A.

123. 254 F.R.D. 129, 131 (D.D.C. 2008).

124. 256 F.R.D. at 135.

125. *Id.*

serve as a wake-up call to the Bar in this District about the need for careful thought, quality control, testing, and cooperation with opposing counsel in designing search terms or 'keywords' to be used to produce emails or other electronically stored information ('ESI')."[126]

If the risk that the court may impose its own search protocol is not enough to motivate parties and counsel to cooperate, perhaps the risk of cost shifting is. In *Surplus Source Group, LLC v. Mid America Engine, Inc.*, the court shifted the costs of conducting a third search of the defendant's documents to the plaintiffs on the ground that, while the defendants showed "a persistent willingness to aide the Plaintiffs in crafting an ESI search,"[127] plaintiff's counsel had unreasonably delayed in responding to the defendant's counsel's attempts to negotiate.[128]

Cooperation can be particularly important in developing and defending a search protocol because it helps avoid disputes that may later arise about the appropriateness and sufficiency of the search efforts taken by either side. This, in turn, will help avoid the cost and inconvenience of unnecessary motions practice as well as reduce each side's exposure to a possible finding of discovery deficiencies and corresponding sanctions. Given that even the best search protocol is likely to miss at least some relevant documents[129] and thus be subject to attack by the opposing side, reaching agreement with the opposing side before proceeding with electronic searches generally will be the best practice.

But what exactly should the parties agree on regarding electronic searches and how should they go about reaching agreement? Agreement on the specific search terms to be used by each side is obvious, but choosing search terms is only part of a comprehensive search protocol—and reaching that agreement may not be as simple as agreeing on a static list of keywords to be used.

(1) What will the search terms be used for?

Search terms can be used for a variety of purposes in litigation. Search terms can be used to identify potentially relevant documents for collection that later will be manually reviewed for

126. *Id.* at 134.

127. Surplus Source Group, LLC v. Mid Am. Engine, Inc., No. 4:08-cv-049, 2009 WL 961207, at *2 (E.D. Tex. Apr. 8, 2009).

128. *Id.*

129. Tomlinson, *et al.*, *Overview of the TREC 2007 Legal Track*, *supra* note 37, §§ 1, 6.

production. They can be used to identify potentially responsive documents from a broader collection, and only those documents captured by the search terms will be manually reviewed for production. They can be used to identify documents that are likely responsive to discovery requests and that will not be manually reviewed at all before production. Search terms even can be used to identify potentially privileged documents that may or may not be manually reviewed before production.

The purpose for which the search terms will be used is a significant factor in determining the appropriate terms and search protocol. For example, search terms used for collection typically should be broad and overinclusive to ensure that reasonable efforts are made to capture all potentially relevant documents. On the other hand, search terms used to identify documents for production, especially without manual review, typically should be narrower and more focused—and more robust—to help limit production to those documents most likely to be responsive (without being unreasonably underinclusive, of course). In some—perhaps many—cases, it may be best to use search terms for multiple purposes, which may necessitate developing multiple sets of search terms and multiple phases to the search protocol.

(2) What should the search terms be?

Once the purpose has been determined, the obvious question becomes what search terms should be used. This, of course, requires someone to develop a list of proposed search terms. One approach is for each side to propose search terms to be used in searching its own documents. Another is for each side to propose search terms to be used for searching the other side's documents. Unfortunately, neither approach is perfect for every case, and both pose certain problems or concerns. Additionally, a party may find itself facing conflicting duties when negotiating search terms with an opposing party.

(a) Who should propose the initial set of search terms?

As discussed below, a threshold determination in identifying effective search terms is identifying categories of relevant facts and data, locations where those facts and data are reasonably likely to be located, and the individuals and entities likely to have relevant materials in their possession or who otherwise may have relevant knowledge. Because it will be necessary to include search terms, including individual names and words likely to be used in relevant documents, that will capture the right facts and data, any list of proposed search terms may provide a glimpse into the drafter's thinking about the matter—much like identifying documents used to prepare a witness for deposition.[130] A party proposing search terms may alert an adversary to the relevance of a particular person or category of facts or data that otherwise may not have occurred to the other side.

Another concern arises from the fact that in the early stages of litigation before any discovery has been conducted, the parties often know very little about the other side's documents. Even in cases in which the parties cooperate well and exchange extensive details regarding their respective ESI in advance of discovery, each side still generally is not conversant in the content of the other side's ESI. This can make the task of determining effective search terms for the other side to use a difficult one because each side may overlook search terms that would be important for capturing responsive, or even key, documents. This is especially problematic with acronyms, euphemisms, code words, jargon, or other terminology that might be used by and known to one side but not the other.

For example, imagine a scenario where the members of a price-fixing cartel refer to their conspiracy by the code name "Kapa Red" to avoid detection, and only they are aware of its use.[131] A plaintiff in a civil suit seeking to recover damages from unlawful overcharges imposed by members of the cartel would have no way of knowing to include this term among proposed search terms for use by the defendant cartel members for collecting or identifying relevant documents for production. As a result, highly relevant documents might never get collected or produced.

One means for helping determine search terms, especially for use by the other side, is to request a concordance once the data has been loaded. A concordance is an alphabetical list of every

130. *See* Disability Rights Council of Greater Wash. v. Wash. Metro. Transit Auth., 242 F.R.D. 139, 142 (D.D.C. 2007) (citing Sporck v. Peil, 759 F.2d 312, 316 (3d Cir. 1985)).

131. "Kapa Red" is taken from an actual, international price-fixing case that resulted in numerous corporate and individual guilty pleas and related civil matters. The code name purportedly used for the conspiracy allegedly was taken from the German term "kapazitaet reduzierung," or capacity reduction, which is a means by which price-fixing cartels fix prices.

word, or term, that appears anywhere in the data, along with a count of the number of times each term appears in the data (the "hit count"). Although the list can be very long, depending on the size of the data at issue—potentially containing tens of thousands of terms—it nonetheless can be very useful. Counsel can, for example, locate variations on key terms, such as misspellings and abbreviations, and add those variations to the search terms. The concordance can also help counsel spot unusual or unusually frequent terms that might otherwise be difficult, if not impossible, to identify in the abstract. For example, something like "Kapa Red" appearing in a concordance, especially with a relatively high hit count, might appear sufficiently unusual to spark investigation into its meaning and use. Finally, the hit counts can help counsel assess the other side's burden claims regarding any particular words as search terms, because counsel will know how often each proposed search term appears in the data. Note, though, that the concordance gives only a total hit count for the data as a whole and generally will not identify how many documents each term appears in within the data.

In short, where only one side will use search terms, it may be preferable to have the opposing side propose a list of terms first to try to gain some insight into opposing counsel's views on the matter and to avoid disclosing one's own views or inadvertently excluding relevant ESI. This approach also affords the producing party additional protection against a challenge to the sufficiency of the terms by the requesting party, particularly since it would be difficult for a party to effectively challenge the very search terms that it proposed. Where both sides will use search terms, the same preference may apply, but it is unlikely that the opposing side would agree to propose both sets of search terms. Rather, each side more likely will have to propose an initial set of search terms—either for its own use or for use by the other side. Therefore, one will have to determine whether proposing one's own search terms or proposing search terms for the other side presents the greater risk (or benefit) for the particular circumstances of the matter at hand.

(b) How do the parties identify appropriate search terms?

The next step is the practical task of identifying the search terms to be used. Part of that process includes gaining a thorough understanding the facts and the issues of case, and picking an initial set of terms based on that understanding. In learning about the case, counsel should not only interview the client about the substance of the case, but should also determine what terminology, jargon, and abbreviations were used in discussing the subject matter of the litigation. Counsel should also identify the key individuals involved, on both the client's and the other side.[132] And it is very important to determine whether any foreign languages are used in the data. Counsel should not assume that running search terms in the language most commonly used will be effective. It may be necessary to run some or all of the terms—against some or all of the data—in one or more other languages.

It is also necessary to identify the various categories of the client's documents and data, to determine where that data is located or stored, and—importantly—to learn the search capabilities of the data systems. There exist many categories of data that go far beyond the email and word processing documents that might initially come to mind, including, for example, images, instant messages, voicemail, audio and video files, computer logs, and text messages.[133] Identifying search terms will depend not only on the substantive issues of the case, but also on the ways in which the categories of data are capable of being searched. At this stage, technical consultants may be consulted to work out the practicalities of designing and running the search or searches. Regardless of whether consultants are used, however, whoever designs the search should be prepared to demonstrate that he or she is qualified to do so, as illustrated by *Victor Stanley I* and the cases discussed above.[134]

Once the initial set of search terms is chosen, it may be prudent to pick a few key custodians to run some initial test searches. The consultants can assist in determining a method for testing the

132. As part of this process, counsel should ensure that the client implements a litigation hold, and should also ensure compliance with the hold throughout the litigation. Zubulake v. UBS Warburg LLC (*Zubulake V*), 229 F.R.D. 422, 431 (S.D.N.Y. 2004); *see also* Pension Comm. of the Univ. of Montreal Pension Plan v. Banc of Am. Secs., LLC, No. 05 CIV 9016, 2010 WL 93124 (S.D.N.Y Jan. 11, 2010).

133. U.S. DIST. CT., DIST. OF MD., SUGGESTED PROTOCOL FOR DISCOVERY OF ELECTRONICALLY STORED INFORMATION § 7(A)(2) (2007), http://www.mdd.uscourts.gov/news/news/ESIProtocol.pdf.

134. Victor Stanley, Inc. v. Creative Pipe, Inc. (*Victor Stanley I*), 250 F.R.D. 251, 261 n.10 (D. Md. 2008); United States v. O'Keefe, 537 F. Supp. 2d 14, 24 (D.D.C. 2008); Equity Analytics, LLC v. Lundin, 248 F.R.D. 331, 333 (D.D.C. 2008).

efficacy of the search terms, including determining whether known sets of relevant data or information were not identified through the terms. If there are significant recall problems with any party's chosen set of terms, the parties should follow up and communicate with one another about the possibility of changing the terms or some other aspect of the search protocol to obtain more accurate results. Once a final set of terms and search design has been tested and shown to be sufficiently reliable for all parties, the final collection can be completed.

(c) What must a party do when it knows proposed search terms are underinclusive?

Take the "Kapa Red" scenario again. The defendants and their counsel know—or arguably should know—the relevance of "Kapa Red," but they also know that the plaintiff almost certainly does not know of its relevance or even its use. So what do the defendants do in negotiating search terms—do they propose "Kapa Red" or not? Suddenly the defendants and their counsel find themselves facing seemingly conflicting obligations. On the one hand, they may have an obligation to include "Kapa Red" as a search term for searching their own ESI because they are duty-bound to ensure that a reasonably diligent search is conducted for relevant documents,[135] and they know that without that term, key documents may be improperly excluded from collection and production. On the other hand, the defense counsel has an ethical obligation to protect their clients' confidences,[136] and by voluntarily proposing "Kapa Red" as a search term when that term is almost certainly unknown to the plaintiff, the defense counsel would be disclosing to the plaintiff a highly relevant client confidence to the extreme detriment of their clients by alerting the plaintiff to very damaging documents that might otherwise go unnoticed by the plaintiff. The defendants, of course, are under no obligation to voluntarily divulge damaging information to the other side. So what does the defense do?

One commentator, Jason Baron, has opined: "As applied in this brave new world of ESI, my argument is that failure to disclose special knowledge of the relevant characteristics of the ESI universe of your client, that would knowingly fail to optimize and impair an otherwise reasonable-sounding search strategy or

135. *See* Fed. R. Civ. P. 26(g).

136. *See* Model Rules of Prof'l Conduct R. 1.6(a) ("A lawyer shall not reveal information relating to the representation of a client. . . .").

protocol request is tantamount to the suppression or concealment of evidence in conflict with one's ethical obligations under Rule 3.4."[137] Baron argues that counsel generally has an "ethical duty" to inform the opposing side that proposed search terms may not capture relevant documents because a key term is not included among the search terms or may be routinely misspelled within relevant documents.[138] But Baron also recognizes the "ethics conundrum" that can arise and acknowledges that this "ethical duty" at times may be at odds with a competing ethical obligation to protect client confidences.[139] Baron observes: "On the other hand, ABA Model Rule 1.6 states that a lawyer shall not reveal information relating to the representation of a client unless the client gives informed consent. Cooperation is fair and good, *but there are perceived limits in the rules where one may bump up against competing considerations*."[140]

Recognizing these potentially "competing considerations" between counsel's ethical obligations, Baron ultimately concludes that it would be a mistake *not* to proffer a key term omitted from an adversary's proposed search terms, such as a synonym for a proposed term known to be used by the responding party. But importantly, Baron's conclusion is premised upon two significant conditions: first, that the deficiency in the proposed search terms "bore greatly on a material issue in the litigation," and second, "there is no outcome-determinative difference perceived" by proffering the omitted term.[141] Baron contends that upon these two conditions, proffering the omitted term would best serve the responding party by gaining credibility and reducing the risk of having to redo the search later.[142] Baron also acknowledges the potential need to obtain the client's consent before proffering the disclosed term to ensure compliance with the ethical duty not to disclose information relating to the representation of the client without the client's informed consent.[143]

137. Jason R. Baron, *E-discovery and the Problem of Asymmetric Knowledge: A Symposium of the Mercer Law Review*, 60 MERCER L. REV. 863, 877 (2009). *See also* The Sedona Conference, *The Case for Cooperation*, 10 SEDONA CONF. J. 339, 344 (2009).

138. Baron, *E-discovery and the Problem of Asymmetric Knowledge*, *supra* note 138, at 876.

139. *Id.*

140. *Id.* at 874 (emphasis added).

141. *Id.* at 876.

142. *Id.*

143. *Id.*

Baron offers sound guidance on how to resolve the question of whether to disclose an omitted, material search term where that disclosure is not potentially outcome-determinative and where the client consents to the disclosure. But what about a situation in which the disclosure *could* be outcome-determinative, a situation like the "Kapa Red" hypothetical where proffering that term could result in identification of highly damaging documents that might otherwise have gone unnoticed by an adversary? Or what if the client simply refuses to consent to the disclosure, leaving counsel caught between what Baron properly characterizes as "competing considerations" in counsel's ethical duties? How does a party resolve such a conflict?

One way is by reaching agreement with the opposing side on search terms without identifying the underinclusiveness of the terms for the other side and then taking whatever reasonable efforts need to be taken to identify potentially relevant ESI that may not be captured by the agreed-upon search terms. This could be achieved by using additional search terms, such as "Kapa Red," not shared with the opposing side or by conducting more traditional searches through interviews with custodians and manual review of targeted ESI. Just because a party agrees to employ a negotiated electronic search protocol for identifying potentially relevant documents does not prevent that party from augmenting that effort with additional search efforts—electronic or manual—not agreed upon by the parties or disclosed to the other side.

It is important to remember that long before the days of e-discovery, parties typically conducted document collection and production with little discussion or agreement regarding the steps each side would take or had taken. While the courts have made clear that discovery in the dark is no longer favored, there generally is nothing wrong with a party taking measures *beyond* those agreed to by the parties. And by employing *additional* efforts not disclosed to an adversary, a party can satisfy its discovery obligations without risking disclosure of client confidences that might result from identifying shortcomings in negotiated search terms and proposing terms to fill those gaps.

(3) What else should the parties consider in crafting an electronic search protocol?

There are additional factors parties may want to consider when developing a search protocol beyond simply negotiating and agreeing upon search terms to be used. We highlight four key considerations here.

(a) What is the scope of the parties' search and production obligations?

An important consideration for the parties once search terms are agreed upon for use by either side is what those terms mean for that party's discovery obligations. The parties may agree that any party using the search terms fully satisfies its discovery obligations by collecting and reviewing for production all ESI captured by those terms, and therefore the party need not collect, review, or produce any other ESI. But this generally may not be the best approach because of the risk that the agreed-upon terms could be underinclusive.

The parties may instead want to make clear in the discovery plan setting forth the search protocol that any party using the search terms still has an obligation to *produce* any ESI that it identifies as relevant and that was not captured by the search terms or otherwise produced. Such a provision would help to ensure that a party could not exploit known deficiencies in agreed-upon search terms by withholding particular documents or data it has identified as relevant and that have not been produced.[144] This approach, for example, would unambiguously require the defendants in the "Kapa Red" cartel to *produce* any conspiratorial documents if it were to identify any apart from those captured by the search terms, including those with the term "Kapa Red." The defendants would not be required, however, to *search* for any potentially relevant ESI that would not be captured by the search terms.

In some cases, the parties (or a party) may want to go further and require any party using the negotiated search terms to separately *search* for any ESI that it believes may be relevant and may

144. *See, e.g.*, Rule 26(f) Stipulation and Order Regarding Discovery Protocols, Docket #312, at 17, *In re* Rail Freight Fuel Surcharge Antitrust Litig., Misc. No. 07-489 (PLF/AK/JMF) (D.D.C. filed Oct. 8, 2009) ("[A] party shall have no obligation to produce any documents, except as otherwise agreed to in writing by the parties, that are not either (a) captured by one or more of the agreed-upon search terms to be applied to ESI of agreed-upon custodians and identified as non-privilege and responsive to a specific propounded discovery request or (b) otherwise identified by the party as non-privileged and responsive to a specific propounded discovery request.").

not be captured by the search terms. Returning again to the "Kapa Red" cartel: were the plaintiff to insist on this requirement for the defendants in that scenario, this would require the defendants to actively search for and produce conspiratorial documents containing the term "Kapa Red."

Regardless of the approach the parties agree to take regarding their respective search and production obligations in light of agreed-upon search terms, the parties generally will be well served to state clearly their intentions and respective understandings as to what each party is required to do, or not do, to satisfy its discovery obligations. It is important to remember that electronic searches are intended as a *means* for a party to comply with its discovery obligations; they do not, in and of themselves, *satisfy* or *substitute for* a party's discovery obligations, unless perhaps the parties clearly agree to that. Avoiding ambiguity or uncertainty regarding the extent of any party's search or production obligations beyond what is required by the electronic search protocol will help to avoid a claim later that the search protocol was not intended to alleviate any party of certain of its discovery obligations or to limit those obligations in any way.

(b) What do the parties do with nonsearchable materials?

In developing an electronic search protocol, parties should keep in mind that not all potentially relevant materials will be capable of being searched. Even ESI may not be searchable, such as image files without associated text. For example, hard-copy documents scanned as PDF or TIFF images without extracted text would not be searchable. Parties generally may be well served by setting forth in the discovery plan a protocol for identifying potentially relevant materials that are not text-searchable. One approach would be to rely on OCR for such materials, including generating OCR for any nonsearchable ESI or hard-copy materials. Another approach would be to rely on more traditional means of identifying potentially relevant materials through interviews with relevant custodians and review of targeted ESI or documents.

In determining how best to proceed, the parties should consider the quality of OCR and the nature of the materials for which OCR would be used. Handwritten materials, for example, generally cannot be effectively OCRed, and even ESI or hard-copy materials with computer-generated or typed text still may not be OCRed effectively if the quality of the text or the materials themselves is poor.[145] Parties may conclude that a hybrid approach, combining both OCR and manual searches and review, is best in many cases.

(c) What particular search syntax will be used?

The exact search syntax to be used is extremely important in designing an effective search protocol and ensuring that the search terms capture what is intended. Not all search tools are the same. They have different search functionalities and capabilities, and perhaps most importantly, they use different search commands—or perhaps even more importantly, they can use the same search commands but with different functionality. For example, including an asterisk at the end of a search term in one search tool may operate as an unlimited expander on the root search term, such that running "disparage*" would capture "disparage," "disparaged," "disparagement," and any other term beginning with the root "disparag." But in another search tool, that same exact command—an asterisk—may operate as only a single character expander, such that "disparage*" would capture "disparages" and "disparaged" but not "disparagement." Thus, counsel needs to know what particular tool will be used, what particular search commands are available, what each search command does, and, finally, what particular search commands will be used with the agreed-upon search terms.

When negotiating search terms, especially to be used by the other side, counsel should agree on the precise syntax to be used, including each term, each search command, and the exact order of both in each search string. Running two search terms together in a single string conjunctively (i.e., with "and") rather than disjunctively (i.e., with "or") can be a far narrower search and thus capture far fewer documents. So it is crucial that the parties consider, discuss, and agree on, if possible, the syntax—based on the particular tool to be used—and ensure that that precise syntax is used in the searches.

(d) What about documents in the same "family" as those captured by search terms?

Finally, parties should consider what to do about documents that are in the same document "family" as those captured by search

145. *See* SHIRA A. SCHEINDLIN & DANIEL J. CAPRA, ELECTRONIC DISCOVERY AND DIGITAL EVIDENCE IN A NUTSHELL 696 (2009).

terms but that are not themselves separately captured by the search terms. For example, the agreed-upon search terms might capture a cover email but not the attachment to that email, or vice versa. The attachment to the email and the cover email itself would be considered within the same document family—the cover email would be the "parent" and the attachment would be the "child." Parties may want to specify whether family documents not separately captured by emails should be reviewed and, if responsive and not privileged, produced. In the absence of an express indication on whether such documents need to be reviewed and produced, a party relying on agreed-upon search terms might reasonably conclude that it bears no such obligation.

A requesting party may find it prudent to insist that family documents be reviewed and produced given that a parent or child document that may appear benign on its face can be extremely relevant when put together with the other documents in the family. In a price-fixing case, for example, an internal confidential price list standing alone in a document production that was captured by search terms might look unuseful to the plaintiff. But if that price list was an attachment to a cover email indicating that it had been sent to a competitor before it was released to customers, it takes on extreme importance to the plaintiff's claims. The cover email might not be captured by the search terms because it, for example, might be an internal email that refers to the competitor by initials or some other cryptic term not included among the search terms.

Regardless of whether the parties ultimately agree to review and produce documents in the families of those captured by search terms, the parties generally would be well served to make clear what their obligations are as to those documents to avoid disputes and possibly even sanctions later.

B. Devising a defensible electronic search protocol: Supervision, planning, and documentation

Developing and documenting a thoughtful plan that includes quality checks and that is well supervised are central to a well-constructed search methodology, especially in the absence of cooperation with or by opposing counsel.[146] Close supervision of the whole process is crucial.

146. *See Sedona Search Commentary*, *supra* note 15, at 212 ("Practice Point 7. Parties should expect that their choice of search methodology will need to be explained, either formally or informally, in subsequent legal contexts (including

The importance of planning, documentation, and supervision is stressed in a recent publication by the Sedona Conference, *The Sedona Conference Commentary on Achieving Quality in the E-Discovery Process*.[147] That paper discusses the use of electronic search tools, but notes that "[t]echnologically advanced tools, however 'cutting edge' they may be, will not yield a successful outcome unless their use is driven by people who understand the circumstances and requirements of the case, as guided by thoughtful and well-defined methods, and unless their results are measured for accuracy."[148] The results of the TREC Legal Track also support the notion that increased human effort and involvement can dramatically improve the effectiveness of automated search methods.

To that end, a discovery plan should include a method for testing and evaluating the search protocol's effectiveness, such as by sampling the discard pile for missed relevant or privileged documents or by a supervising attorney re-reviewing a representative sample of the documents reviewed by primary document reviewers.[149] Another suggestion by the Sedona Conference is independent testing by third-party professionals, such as testing whether all emails were successfully extracted from a hard drive.[150] Additional possibilities include other technical checks, like reconciliation techniques (such as by comparing what volumes of ESI entered a process and what volumes exited the process) and statistical sampling to check the effectiveness of search terms.[151] A discovery plan should also include consulting the client regarding terminology and abbreviations used concerning the subject matter of the litigation. And it may even include the involvement of an

in depositions, evidentiary proceedings, and trials."); Debra R. Bernard & Mary Rose Hughes, *Much Ado About Text Searching*, 8/25/2008 NAT'L L.J. S1 (Col. 2) (2008) (noting that counsel "should have a solid rationale for the [search] method selected, whether that method involves keywords, concepts or other text mining techniques").

147. *The Sedona Conference Commentary on Achieving Quality in the E-Discovery Process*, 10 SEDONA CONF. J. 299, 303–04 (Fall 2009) [hereinafter *Sedona Conference Commentary on Achieving Quality*].

148. *Id.* at 306.

149. *See* Bernard & Hughes, *supra* note 147; *Sedona Conference Commentary on Achieving Quality*, *supra* note 148, at 310.

150. *Id.*

151. *Id.* at 311–12.

"expert," who would assist in either developing the search protocol or executing it, or both.[152]

The aim of this strategy is not only to be prepared to defend the reasonableness of a search protocol in the event a dispute arises, but also to assure quality control and quality assurance in the e-discovery context. The *Sedona Conference Commentary on Achieving Quality* defines "quality control" as "involv[ing] the specific procedures, tools and techniques that ensure high quality is maintained throughout various stages of the e-discovery process (*i.e.*, while people are conducting specific tasks)."[153] "Quality assurance" is defined as "the methods and metrics used at the end of the process to assess and ensure that an e-discovery process is complete and accurate."[154] Potential consequences for ignoring quality control and assurance include the failure to preserve, uncover, or disclose relevant evidence, the possibility that privileged or confidential information may be inadvertently produced, and saving potentially significant cost and burden in the event that initial deficiencies "ultimately require that e-discovery must be redone."[155]

Again, the practical consequences of failing to institute quality checks on the process can be severe. In *Felman Products, Inc. v. Industrial Risk Insurers*, the district court judge affirmed the magistrate judge's decision to allow waiver of privilege with respect to numerous privileged documents—including two key documents harmful to the plaintiff's case—based on the party's failure to institute quality control sampling.[156] Among other things, the magistrate judge found that the party and its counsel "failed to perform critical quality control sampling to determine whether their production was appropriate and neither over-inclusive nor under-inclusive."[157] In affirming, the district judge did not even go that far—he simply based his decision on the high percentage of

152. United States v. O'Keefe, 537 F. Supp. 2d 14, 24 (D.D.C. 2008); Equity Analytics, LLC v. Lundin, 248 F.R.D. 331, 333 (D.D.C. 2008); Victor Stanley, Inc. v. Creative Pipe, Inc. (*Victor Stanley I*), 250 F.R.D. 251, 262 (D. Md. 2008); *see also* Angeline G. Chen & Michael E. Lackey, Jr., *Using E-Discovery Experts to Assist in Discovery Under the Federal Rules of Civil Procedure*, 783 PLI/LIT 251, 260 (2008).

153. *Sedona Conference Commentary on Achieving Quality*, *supra* note 148, at 302.

154. *Id.*

155. *Id.* at 302, 309.

156. No. 3:09-0481 2010 WL 2944777, at *4 (S.D.W.Va. July 23, 2010).

157. Mt. Hawley Ins. Co. v. Felman Prod., Inc., No. 3:09-CV-481, 2010 WL 1990555, at *12 (S.D.W. Va. May 18, 2010). The judge took special note that the law firm representing the producing party here was the same as the law firm representing

irrelevant and privileged documents that had been inadvertently produced: at least 30 percent of more than one million pages produced were either irrelevant or privileged. Based on that fact, the district judge held that it was not necessary for him to "consider the details of [plaintiff's] pre-production document review process—or the unexplained technical glitch that led to the fourth volume of [plaintiff's] e-discovery being not properly screened for potentially privileged materials—to find that [plaintiff's] screening precautions were not reasonable."[158]

The broad point is that parties and their attorneys should avoid falling into the trap of simply running a set of search terms and believing they have satisfied their discovery obligations.

6. Conclusion

The discussions of electronic search methods by courts and commentators and the increasing reliance upon them by clients and counsel suggest that they, and possibly experts too, are becoming common, and perhaps even expected, as the Bar and Bench continue to grapple with the substantial costs and burdens imposed by e-discovery.[159] The further spread of the use of such tools for

---

the producing party in *Victor Stanley I*, albeit after the events relevant to that decision had taken place. *Id.*

158. *Felman Prod.*, 2010 WL 2944777, at *3.

159. *See, e.g., In re Vioxx Prods. Liab. Litig.*, Nos. 06-30378, 06-30379, 2006 WL 1726675, at *2 n.5 (5th Cir. May 26, 2006) (suggesting use of a "statistically sound protocol for sampling documents" that are a part of an in camera review, and requiring the parties to "provide expert assistance to the district court in constructing any protocol"); Treppel v. Biovail Corp., 233 F.R.D. 363, 374 (S.D.N.Y. 2006) (plaintiff's refusal to agree to defendant's proposed search methodology for searching electronically stored information did not excuse defendant from producing documents at all; once plaintiff indicated its disagreement, defendant was nevertheless obligated to unilaterally proceed with the search and provide plaintiff with a detailed explanation of the search protocol); Disability Rights Council of Greater Wash. v. Wash. Metro. Transit Auth., 242 F.R.D. 139, 148 (D.D.C. 2007) (noting that scholarship has suggested that concept searching is more efficient and more likely to produce comprehensive results than keyword searching) (citing Paul & Baron, *Information Inflation*, *supra* note 26); *In re Seroquel Prods. Liab. Litig.*, 244 F.R.D. 650, 660 n.6 (M.D. Fla. 2007) (criticizing party's failure to explain search protocol, stating "AZ's decision to offer only the testimony of a junior level attorney, only somewhat versed in technical issues and one who came late to the process is puzzling. AZ provided essentially no information as to how it organized its search for relevant material, what steps it took to assure reasonable completeness and quality control. Its efforts at finding solutions to technical problems are likewise unilluminated.").

conducting privilege and responsiveness reviews appears to be inevitable, as it is highly unlikely that the quantity of documents and data that litigants and attorneys must manage will decrease anytime soon, if ever.

In the end, only time will tell how the courts will address the question of the reasonableness of electronic search protocols. As the court remarked in *Victor Stanley I,* attorneys would be wise to remain informed by reviewing the literature on the electronic search solutions available and by keeping apprised of the standards the courts may apply in assessing the reasonableness of search protocols.

CHAPTER 21

DESIGNING A "REASONABLE" E-DISCOVERY SEARCH: A GUIDE FOR THE PERPLEXED

BY JASON R. BARON AND MICHAEL D. BERMAN

Despite the utility of electronic searches to sift through masses of electronically stored information (ESI) in discovery, they carry drawbacks and dangers of their own. This builds on the discussion in chapter 20, offering practical advice on designing advanced e-search methodologies at a time when most approaches resemble a "child's game of go fish."

1. Introduction

The preceding chapter surveys the emerging cottage industry of case law and research developing on the subject of "search methodology" used in e-discovery, including a discussion of such important recent cases as *Seroquel, O'Keefe, Equity Analytics, Victor Stanley I,* and *Rhoads.*[1] It is certainly fair to say that there is no

1. *In re* Seroquel Prods. Liab. Litig., 244 F.R.D. 650 (M.D. Fla. 2007); Victor Stanley, Inc. v. Creative Pipe, Inc. (*Victor Stanley I*), 250 F.R.D. 251 (D. Md. 2008); United

single, "fail-safe"[2] search or search methodology that guarantees that all or even most relevant documents will be found. This wasn't ever true in last century's world of paper-based document review, and it remains elusive in the age of terabytes and petabytes of data that increasingly must be dealt with in twenty-first century litigation. Nevertheless, as is becoming increasingly evident to both the Bench and Bar, virtually every significant case now involves the need for litigants to conduct searches for electronically stored information, and thus the question of what constitutes a reasonable, defensible "search protocol" has become a central element of e-discovery case law and practice.

The question of "search" arises in multiple e-discovery contexts. For example, when instituting a litigation hold, it is first necessary to locate and preserve potentially responsive information, a process that involves deciding on initial search parameters, including at a minimum how many custodians and what date restrictions are involved, and that may also involve applying keyword or other filtering techniques to eliminate clearly nonresponsive data. Primarily in response to Federal Rule of Civil Procedure 34 requests for production, the collected material must be further culled, initially at least by the use of automated search techniques using keywords coupled with other means (e.g., clustering techniques as employed in early case assessment), to separate responsive and unresponsive data.

Next, privilege review involves additional searching, which, while it still necessarily involves manual elements, increasingly is being automated. So too, a client's data set must be searched to provide specific Rule 26(a)(1) initial disclosures and, later, specific searches may end up being conducted in response to specific litigation demands, including answering interrogatories and requests for admissions, and preparing for and taking depositions. Additionally, ESI received from the opponent must be searched to determine the thoroughness of the responses, eliminate unim-

---

States v. O'Keefe, 537 F. Supp. 2d 14 (D.D.C. 2008); Equity Analytics, LLC v. Lundin, 248 F.R.D. 331 (D.D.C. 2008); Rhoads Indus., Inc. v. Bldg. Materials Corp. of Am., 254 F.R.D. 216 (E.D. Pa. 2008).

2. The term "fail-safe" was popularized in a 1964 Cold War movie directed by Sidney Lumet, based on the 1963 novel of the same name by Eugene Burdick and Harvey Wheeler. It tells the fictional story of a nuclear crisis, and the president's attempt to end it. *See* http://en.wikipedia.org/wiki/Fail-Safe_(1964_film).

portant data, and locate material information of importance to the claims and defenses in the pending suit.

To all of this, the question arises: how should a practicing litigator best apply the principles described out of this emerging body of case law, commentary, and research, to ESI data sets presented in a specific lawsuit? In the following sections, the authors briefly step through a few of the most salient issues confronting the practitioner in thinking through what constitutes a reasonable, defensible search in today's world of e-discovery. In doing so, we draw on the work of the Sedona Conference, which has produced useful commentaries giving good, practical guidance to e-discovery practitioners in the area of search protocols. This guide is not intended to be comprehensive, but is rather both a starting point and a "snapshot" (as of publication date) as to what constitutes, at least at a high level, best practices in a fast moving area of the law.

2. The cost of manual review and the growing necessity of using automation

Manual review is, in many instances, a dead letter. Assume a dispute with one billion emails, 25 percent of which have attachments. Reviewed at a rate of 50 messages per hour, it would take 100 reviewers, working 10 hours per day, seven days a week, 52 weeks per year, approximately 54 years to complete the review! At $100 per hour, the cost would be $2 billion. Even if manual review were limited to 1 percent of the total universe, the hypothetical time and cost would still amount to $20 million for a first-pass review by 100 junior or contract attorneys over the course of 28 weeks, prior to privilege review.[3]

Recent case law underscores that this isn't an unrealistic scenario—it is rather all too common, and increasingly so. For example, in *In Re Fannie Mae Securities Litigation*, the government

3. *See* George L. Paul & Jason R. Baron, *Information Inflation: Can the Legal System Adapt?*, 13 RICH. J.L. & TECH. 10, at *20 (2007), http://law.richmond.edu/jolt/v13i3/article10.pdf. For a recent example of huge volumes confronting the legal profession, see Report of Anton R. Valukhas, Examiner, at vol. 7, app. 5, *In re* Lehman Bros. Holdings Inc., Chapter 11 Case No. 08-13555 (U.S. Bankruptcy Ct. S.D.N.Y. Mar. 11, 2010) (reporting that out of a universe of 350 billion pages—three petabytes—the examiner narrowed the collection by selecting key custodians and using dozens of separate Boolean searches to collect for review in excess of five million documents, representing 40 million pages, for two further levels of manual review by 70 contract attorneys supplemented by others), http://lehmanreport.jenner.com.

stipulated to undertake a keyword search of ESI on backup tapes, followed by a manual review of the "hits" obtained:[4]

> Pursuant to the stipulated order, the individual defendants submitted over 400 search terms, which covered approximately 660,000 documents. . . . OFHEO undertook extensive efforts to comply with the stipulated order, hiring 50 contract attorneys solely for that purpose. The total amount OFHEO spent on the individual defendants' discovery requests eventually reached over $6 million, more than 9 percent of the agency's entire annual budget.[5]

The reward for being tardy in this effort was, regrettably, the agency being held in contempt, with the added indignity of the contempt citation being affirmed by the D.C. Circuit. Beyond this especially dramatic example, however, stand a growing legion of cases where parties are having to undertake an unexpectedly large manual document review process due to the failure to plan for, think through, and anticipate how an automated review process should work.

Practice Point 1 of the Sedona Conference's *Best Practices Commentary on the Use of Search and Information Retrieval Methods in E-Discovery* states:

> In many settings involving electronically stored information, reliance solely on a manual search process for the purpose of finding responsive documents may be infeasible or unwarranted. In such cases, the use of automated search methods should be viewed as reasonable, valuable, and even necessary.[6]

The problem of volume and the associated complexity in having to search voluminous amounts of ESI is fundamental to e-discovery. Automated methods of search, starting with applying more sophisticated approaches to keyword searching, are the wave of the future. In this regard, the opening words expressed in the *Sedona Conference Commentary on Achieving Quality in E-Discovery* sound a bell:

4. 552 F.3d 814 (D.C. Cir. 2009).

5. *Id.* at 817

6. The Sedona Conference, *Best Practices Commentary on the Use of Search and Information Retrieval Methods in E-Discovery*, 8 SEDONA CONF. J. 189 (Fall 2007) [hereinafter *Sedona Search Commentary*].

> The legal profession is at a crossroads: the choice is between continuing to conduct discovery as it has "always been practiced" in a paper world—before the advent of computers, the Internet, and the exponential growth of [ESI]—or, alternatively, embracing new ways of thinking in today's digital world.[7]

Or, as separately summed up by a recent commentator, "Business has migrated to computers because they are efficient, and the legal system has no alternative but to adjust to this changing paradigm."[8]

3. Using "common sense" and applying proportionality principles in deciding on a search methodology

In *Victor Stanley I*, the court wrote:

> "[W]hile it is universally acknowledged that keyword searches are useful tools for search and retrieval of ESI, all keyword searches are not created equal; and there is a growing body of literature that highlights the risks associated with conducting an unreliable or inadequate keyword search. . . ."[9]

The court went on to say, "Common sense suggests that even a properly designed and executed keyword search may prove to be over-inclusive or under-inclusive . . ."[10] Thus, it seems apparent that lawyers should start by using "common sense" in evaluating how to conduct a particular search in a specific case.[11] Both the requesting and producing parties have a further responsibility to supplement notions of common sense with a sound, defensible process in showing that they have exercised due diligence in exercising their obligation to search for relevant evidence.

At the most basic level, a simple keyword search consists of using software to search a database to find out if that keyword exists. Each responsive document is called a "hit." Thus, for

7. 10 SEDONA CONF. J. 299, 302 (2009).

8. Lynn McLain, Foreword, Symposium Issue, *Advanced Issues in Electronic Discovery: The Impact of the First Year of the Federal Rules and the Adoption of the Maryland Rules*, 37 U. BALT. L. REV. 315, 318 (2008).

9. *Victor Stanley I*, 250 F.R.D. at 256–57.

10. *Id.* at 257.

11. Unfortunately, when it comes to searching ESI, "[c]ommon sense is not so common." Voltaire, http://thinkexist.com/quotation/common_sense_is_not_so_common/145875.html.

example, Windows software enables a user to rapidly search an entire computer for a single word, and Word and WordPerfect have similar capabilities. A Boolean search is more sophisticated, combining "operators" such as "and," "or," and "not," and proximity operators, such as "within the same sentence" or "within 10 words."[12] There are many variants, such as "fuzzy searching" that will look for words that are 30 percent or 90 percent similar to the search term, and natural language searches.[13] While simple keyword searches are likely a bare minimum requirement,[14] the shortcomings to the naïve and simplistic use of these techniques have been demonstrated.[15] And litigation over designing appropriate Boolean searches has occurred.[16]

The next generation of search technology, "[i]n contrast to strict set-based Boolean techniques," is called "concept searching," and it involves "algebraic and probabilistic categories of search methods."[17] Loosely described, these technologies amplify search terms by mathematically selecting conceptually related terms, and

12. *See Sedona Search Commentary, supra* note 6, at 197.

13. *See id.* at app.

14. Qualcomm v. Broadcom Corp., 539 F. Supp. 2d 1214 (S.D. Cal. 2007) (sanctions opinion involving underlying failure to disclose 200,000 emails prior to trial, where court found "incredible that Qualcomm never conducted such an obvious search" using certain keywords) (citation to other decisions omitted), *rev'd in part*, 2010 WL 1336937 (Apr. 2, 2010).

15. Paul & Baron, *Information Inflation, supra* note 3, at *4 n.6 (citing DAVID BLAIR, WITTGENSTEIN, LANGUAGE AND INFORMATION: "BACK TO THE ROUGH GROUND!" 302 (2006) (summarizing 1985 Blair & Maron study in which retrieval effectiveness was measured for 40,000 documents captured in a large corporate litigation, where results of the study showed a large amount of indeterminacy of meaning in natural language in light of the fact that "while [the] lawyers and paralegals were convinced that they were retrieving over seventy-five percent of the desired documents, they were, in actuality retrieving only twenty percent!")). It was also recently noted in SEC v. Collins & Aikman Corp., 2009 WL 94311 (S.D.N.Y. Jan. 23, 2009), that "the inaccuracy of [keyword] searches is by now relatively well known."

16. ClearOne Commc'ns Inc. v. Chiang, 2008 WL 920336 (D. Utah Apr. 1, 2008) (court adjudicated dispute over Boolean conjunctive versus disjunctive operators—"and" versus "or"—as used between search terms).

17. *Sedona Search Commentary, supra* note 6, at 202; Paul & Baron, *Information Inflation, supra* note 3, at *37 *et seq.*; Mia Mazza, Emmalena K. Quesada & Ashley L. Stenberg, *In Pursuit of FRCP 1: Creative Approaches to Cutting and Shifting Costs of Discovery of Electronically Stored Information,*13 RICH. J.L. & TECH. 11 (2007), http://law.richmond.edu/jolt/v13i3/article11.pdf.

they are commercially available.[18] At the same time, there are an increasing variety of early case assessment tools including clustering technologies that clump "like" documents together, to speed the ability to perform document review for responsiveness and privilege.[19]

Much of the problem with searching is caused by the variability of language. "Synonymy" is the variation in describing the same person or thing in a multiplicity of ways, for example, "diplomat," "consul," "official," "ambassador," and so on. "Polysemy" is the use of ambiguous terms, for example, "George Bush" (referring to one of two American presidents) or "strike" (as used in the context of labor union tactics, military actions, options trading, and baseball).[20] Failure to select synonyms will result in false negatives, while use of ambiguous terms will result in false positives. Synonymy and polysemy in a database may be complicated by misspellings, abbreviations, poor records management, and many other factors.

For example, consider a business that employs a diverse workforce ranging from those with a graduate school education to those who lack formal education, and some of whose primary languages may be other than English. Further consider a workforce stratified by age, where the younger cohort of workers is now communicating by use of text messaging, using abbreviations for common English language words and phrases. Additional complications arise where, in the culture of the corporate or institutional client, a variety of abbreviations, slang, and even code words have come to be used over time for various activities and projects undertaken within the enterprise, but not widely known in the outside world. And, of course, deliberate obfuscation by a custodian also may make the search more complex.

---

18. *Sedona Search Commentary*, *supra* note 6, at 206 (citing Anne Kershaw, *Automated Document Review Proves Its Reliability*, 5 DIGITAL DISCOVERY & E-EVIDENCE 11, 11 (2005)).

19. Debra Cassems Weiss, *Predictive Coding Software Helps Morgan Lewis Review Millions of Pages in 1 Month*, ABA J., Nov. 29, 2010, http://www.abajournal.com/news/article/predictive_coding_software_helps_morgan_lewis_review_millions_of_pages_in_1; *see also* Jason R. Baron, Law in the Age of Exabytes: Some Further Thoughts on 'Information Inflation' and Current Issues in E-Discovery Search, 17 RICH. J.L. & TECH. 9, at *32 (2011), http://jolt.richmond.edu/v17i3/article9.pdf.

20. *See generally Sedona Search Commentary*, *supra* note 6, at 201–02.

Against these obstacles, even if one were particularly good at dreaming up bags of words corresponding to search requests, there is necessarily an asymmetry of knowledge between opposing parties—a thumb on the scale—in that the requesting party almost invariably has less knowledge regarding the data set than does the producing party. This has led one prominent legal commentator, Ralph Losey, to characterize current methods of going about formulating search terms as equivalent to a "child's game of go fish."[21] According to Losey,

> The game as played now forces the blind man to make hundreds of guesses at a time, hundreds of key words, hoping that a few might be right. This hurts the respondent who has to review all of the junk generated by the blind guesses. It hurts the requestor too, who eventually has to review all of the relevant and marginal calls.[22]

In Losey's view, a better "game" would be one controlled by the responding party, who knows "their data, their IT systems, their data custodians, their employees, their agents, their attorneys, their language, their retention policies, their retention practices, etc."[23]

Such common sense was not on apparent display in the case of *Kipperman v. Onex Corp.*[24] In *Kipperman*, the court previously had made known its intent that the defendants were to conduct a search of backup tapes to produce meaningful discoverable information and that that the plaintiff should be more "artful with its search terms," including that the plaintiff "utilize a list of the people provided by" the defendants "to review whether all [email] boxes needed to be searched."[25] The court further granted the defendants the opportunity to narrow the plaintiff's search terms; however, the defendants neither narrowed the list of people nor narrowed the plaintiff's terms. Instead, they agreed to search and restore all the email mailboxes with the terms provided by the plaintiff.

---

21. Ralph C. Losey, "Child's Game of `Go Fish' Is a Poor Model for E-Discovery Search," in ADVENTURES IN ELECTRONIC DISCOVERY, 204 (West 2011).
22. *Id.*
23. *Id.*
24. 2008 WL 4372005 (N.D. Ga. Sept. 19, 2008). This example is taken from a lecture by Jason R. Baron, E-Discovery and the Problem of Asymmetric Knowledge, Ethics in the Digital Age Symposium, *in* 60 MERCER L. REVIEW 863, 873 (2009).
25. 2008 WL 4372005, at *7–8.

The *Kipperman* defendants subsequently moved for a protective order seeking relief from having to review and produce all the results of the required search. The defendants contended that the plaintiff's "broad search terms resulted in thousands and thousands of irrelevant hits. For example, the Plaintiff's search terms included the word 'republic.' "[26] They included the word "republic" because there the term "Republic builders" was part of the case. But the "defendants claim that the search captured thousands of irrelevant pages due to one occurrence of the word 'republic' often related to . . . business interests having nothing to do with" the defendants due to the presence of the Republic of France, the Republic of Ireland, and the Czech Republic.[27] So they had to weed through all that, the noise and the junk.

In its ruling, the *Kipperman* court said it was not "unsympathetic to the massive amount of discovery involved in this matter, the considerable burden of working with it, and the overproduction that often comes with e-mail production," and "[t]herefore, the court gave the Defendants numerous tools by which to reduce the burden of e-mail discovery, including an opportunity to limit [the] plaintiff's search terms," but "the Defendants did not take advantage of these opportunities. The Defendants must now lie in the bed that they have made."[28]

Ideally, parties should cooperate with respect to the approach to crafting a proper search methodology, in terms of both the substance of the terms and the process to be employed. In 2008, the Sedona Conference Cooperation Proclamation,[29] signed as of the date of this writing by over 100 state and federal judges, declared that "cooperation by all parties in the discovery process" promotes achievement of the goal embodied in Federal Rule of Civil Procedure 1, to achieve a "just, speedy and inexpensive determination of every action." To that end, the Sedona Cooperation Proclamation suggests cooperation by counsel in two ways relevant to the discussion here: First, "exchanging information on relevant data sources, including those not being searched."[30] And second,

26. *Id.* at *7.
27. *Id.*
28. *Id.* at *8.
29. 10 Sedona Conf. J. 331 (2009 supp.).
30. *Id.* at 332.

"jointly developing automated search and retrieval methodologies to cull relevant information."[31]

A Sedona Conference article entitled "The Case for Cooperation" further elaborates on the theme:

> [W]orking cooperatively with opposing counsel to identify a reasonable search protocol, rather than making boilerplate objections to the breadth of a requested protocol or unilaterally selecting the keywords used without disclosure to opposing counsel, may help avoid sanctions or allegations of intentional suppression. Indeed, because knowledge of the producing party's data is usually asymmetrical, it is possible that refusing to "aid" opposing counsel in designing an appropriate search protocol that the party holding the data knows will produce responsive documents could be tantamount to concealing relevant evidence.[32]

Recent case law has taken to embodying the prescriptions laid out in Sedona's Cooperation Proclamation.[33] As a practical matter, cooperation may often mean allowing the responding or producing party the deference and discretion to take the first stab at developing search terms, as Ralph Losey argues. On the other hand, there would also appear to be good reasons to consider adopting or at least partially adopting a requesting party's proposed search protocols:

> A requesting party may have a legitimate, good faith belief that they are sufficiently informed regarding the causes of action at issue and underlying facts so as to be able to propose well-formed search queries, including through the use of keywords. As the propounder of the eventual discovery requests, the requesting party is in the best position to know what it believes are the most salient aspects of the case that

31. *Id.*

32. The Sedona Conference, *The Case for Cooperation*, 10 SEDONA CONF. J. 339, 344 (2009 supp.) (citing Baron, E-Discovery and the Problem of Asymmetric Knowledge, *supra* note 24).

33. *See, e.g.*, Dunkin' Donuts Franchised Rests., Inc. v. Grand Cent. Donuts, Inc., 2009 WL 1750348 (E.D.N.Y. June 19, 2009) (parties "are directed to meet and confer on developing a workable search protocol" (citing the Sedona Cooperation Proclamation)); *see generally* Ralph C. Losey, Mancia v. Mayflower *Begins a Pilgrimage to the New World of Cooperation*, 10 SEDONA CONF. J. 377 (2009 supp.) (summarizing cases citing to the Sedona Cooperation Proclamation).

> are in need of discovery in the first place. To the extent the producing party is willing to allow the requesting party to control all or some of the keyword search, without raising a threshold objection, doing so holds out the possibility of significantly reducing the level of conflict and subsequent motion practice in discovery. An early agreement on search protocols also may be strategically valuable in diminishing the other side's ability to object to terms and methods that have been made subject to prior agreement (especially if they entail large resources or workloads). Cooperation in the form of reaching agreement on search terms ultimately reduces the legal risk in having to undertake new or different searches through large collections of data.[34]

The emerging "common sense standard" on negotiating search protocols is further buttressed by a growing body of decisional authority on the subject of "proportionality." One consistent, overriding theme of their decisions and writings is that discovery of ESI—indeed, all discovery—must be proportionate to the needs of the case, in accordance with Rules 1, 26(b)(2)(C)(iii), 26(c), and 26(g).[35] This contextual analysis is critical in evaluating decisions such as *O'Keefe*, *Equity Analytics*, and *Victor Stanley I*, and in developing a defensible search methodology. It is inconceivable that jurists who have held that discovery must be reasonable and proportionate to the needs of the case have imposed a different standard when it comes to search methodology.

Thus, what we here choose to term the "Goldilocks principle" applies in proposing search terms as part of an overall search protocol. One court was certainly correct to be incredulous at one party's request that "thousands of additional search terms" be used in a multimillion-dollar lawsuit over defects and delays in

34. Jason R. Baron & Edward C. Wolfe, *A Nutshell on Negotiating Search Protocols in eDiscovery*, 11 SEDONA CONF. J. 229 (2010).

35. *See, e.g.*, Rimkus Consulting Group, Inc. v. Cammarata, 688 F. Supp. 2d 598, 613 (S.D. Tex. 2010) ("Whether preservation or discovery conduct is acceptable in a case depends on what is *reasonable*, and that in turn depends on whether what was done—or not done—was *proportional* to that case and consistent with clearly established applicable standards"); Mancia v. Mayflower Textile Servs. Co., 253 F.R.D. 354, 364 (D. Md. 2008); The Hon. Paul W. Grimm, *Proportionality in the Post-Hoc Analysis of Pre-Litigation Preservation Decisions*, 37 U. BALT. L. REV. 381 (2008); The Sedona Conference, *Commentary on Proportionality*, 11 SEDONA CONF. J. 291 (2010); see chapter 9.

the construction of a court complex of buildings.[36] At the opposite end of the spectrum, in the recent case of *Capitol Records v. MP3 Records*, the court expressed seeming exasperation at counsel's argument that applying even a "one word" search term might be overly broad—especially after the judge had "directed counsel to confer further in an attempt to agree on search terms."[37] Counsel are advised to avoid such extreme positions in proposing search terms, and would be especially well advised to consider principles of proportionality when developing search protocols that might yield huge numbers of false-positive hits all out of proportion to the existing stakes in the case, with the effect of running up time and labor costs in document review costs on both sides.

As pointed out in chapter 20 of this book, Judges Facciola and Grimm have further challenged lawyers to think about other means and methods of search that were out there. While (as that chapter notes) the jury is out with respect to whether any one method has proven to be more efficacious than conducting keyword searches, that doesn't mean that lawyers should ignore an increasingly cacophonous world of more sophisticated techniques to think about employing in practice. Indeed, keyword and Boolean searches supplemented by the aforementioned clustering and concept technologies are already proving efficacious in speeding up document review, and also hold out the promise in the future for richer and more targeted searches than what are achievable by traditional keyword methods today.[38] In the meantime, the most recent findings of the TREC Legal Track and other research together strongly suggest that attorneys can improve what constitutes a reasonable search, without necessarily using "Star Wars"-like new technologies.[39] In short, attorneys can design a better search "process."

---

36. William A. Gross Constr. Assocs., Inc. v. Am. Mfrs. Mut. Ins. Co., 256 F.R.D. 134, 134 (S.D.N.Y. 2009).

37. Capitol Records v. MP3 Tunes, 261 F.R.D. 44, 47 (S.D.N.Y. 2009).

38. Patrick Oot, Anne Kershaw & Herbert L. Roitblat, *Mandating Reasonableness in a Reasonable Inquiry*, 87 DENVER U.L. REV. 533, 551 (2010) ("use of autocategorization systems can potentially reduce document response times from over four months to as little as thirty days for even the largest datasets").

39. *See* Douglas W. Oard, Jason R. Baron, *et al.*, *Evaluation of Information Retrieval in E-Discovery*, 18 ARTIFICIAL INTELLIGENCE & LAW J. 347 (2010); Bruce Hedin, Stephen Tomlinson, Jason R. Baron & Douglas W. Oard, TREC 2009 Overview paper, Eighteenth Text Retrieval Conference, http://trec.umiacs.umd.edu. The 2009 TREC Legal interactive task results show that some participating teams

4. Design of an effective search

There is no "one size fits all" way to effective search methodology. There may be times, and cases, that call for one, two, three, or more experts, and others that need no experts. In many cases, design of an effective search begins with a review of elements of the dispute, be it a demand or preservation letter, civil complaint, or discovery request. This review will help narrow the applicable time frame, issues, and concepts, and suggest some possible keywords.

After that, synonyms and terminology should be considered by, for example, interviewing people who created the ESI, considering terms of art, running a "vocabulary" search of words contained in the database, and consulting standard reference tools, such as a dictionary, thesaurus, or appropriate website.[40] At this stage, it would be advisable to review known, responsive documents to look for valuable keywords and their mirror image, "noise words"—words that, although they could be responsive, generate false hits. Project management is crucial and the goal is to develop a well-thought-out plan with substantial "human input" from all of the stakeholders. Just as "fuzzy searching" is technologically possible, "fuzzy thinking"—thinking outside the box—is the technique that is applicable at this early point.

The next step is to review an available range of search methods, tools, and technologies.[41] As stated above, simple or naïve keyword searching will seldom be adequate; however, Boolean-capable software may suffice. What is required is a review of available options and analysis of the cost in proportion to what is at stake in the case, with thought given to any shortcomings of the software, for example, inability to search certain types of files, or failure to generate "exceptions" reports. Consideration should also be given to handwritten documents and to password-protected or encrypted files. The two generic sources are in-house capabilities and forensic consultants. For example, one organization may

who conducted searches in the Enron database achieved between 70 and 90 percent recall and precision; in a number of cases, teams used automated methods supplemented through greater use of "expert" humans in the loop, the latter of whom served to train or tune the search systems utilizing their greater knowledge of the repository being searched. *See also* Oot, *supra* note 38, at 558; Krause, *Human-Assisted Computer Search in EDD*, Law Tech. News, Dec. 20, 2010, http://www.law.com/jsp/lawtechnologynews/PubArticleFriendlyLTN.jsp?id=1202476197639.

40. For example, http://www.synonym.com/.

41. See *Sedona Search Commentary*, *supra* note 6, app. at 217 *et seq.*

have an in-house, enterprise-wide search engine that is capable of forensic preservation, while another is unable to search across email custodians.

The selected software should then be applied to at least a representative sample of, if not the entire, database for a sample search of the chosen keywords and operators. This is to be followed with a manual review of a sample of hits and misses, looking for false positives and false negatives. The search, and perhaps the search tool, can then be refined and the test and manual review repeated in an iterative process.

Courts are beginning to recognize need for "iteration" and sampling as part of the overall e-discovery search equation. Judge Scheindlin, writing in *Pension Committee,* went so far as to say that "failure to assess the accuracy and validity of selected search terms" constitutes "negligence."[42] In another case, in Utah, where the court was willing to adjudicate a dispute on the use of certain Boolean operators, the court stated that the "search protocol is not the 'last word'" on e-discovery in the case.[43] The opinion went on to say that the "use of key word protocols is one step in the process which contemplates many more steps," including revisiting the search protocol, and "if documents are discovered which suggest that other documents exist which were not identified as potentially responsive, or if a surprisingly small or unreasonably large number of documents is identified as potentially responsive, refinement may be needed."[44] Indeed, the court recognized that "[m]uch of the argument is now speculative, since there is no actual experience with a search. This first protocol may suffice, or it may in effect be a sampling which reveals the need for more—or less—or different—key words."[45] In the same vein, in *In re Seroquel Products Liability Antitrust Litigation,*[46] the court wrote: "Common sense dictates that sampling and other quality assurance techniques must be employed to meet requirements of completeness. . . ."[47]

42. Pension Comm. of Univ. of Montreal Pension Plan v. Banc of Am. Sec. LLC, 685 F. Supp. 2d 456, 465 (S.D.N.Y. 2010).
43. ClearOne Commc'ns Inc. v. Chiang, 2008 WL 920336, at *2 (D. Utah Apr. 1, 2008).
44. *Id.*
45. *Id.*
46. *In Re Seroquel Prod. Liab. Antitrust Litig.,* 244 F.R.D. 650 (M.D. Fla. 2007).
47. *See also* Mt. Hawley Ins. Co. v. Felman Prod., Inc. 2010 WL 1990555 (S.D. W. Va. May 18, 2010) (criticizing quality of process employed in using search terms for privilege review, citing *Victor Stanley I*).

In fact, this is reinforced by Judge Peck's decision,[48] in which the court wrote of the "[n]eed for careful thought, quality control, testing, and cooperation with opposing counsel in designing keyword searches." There, the court criticized lawyers "designing keyword searches in the dark, by the seat of their pants, without adequate (indeed, here, apparently without any) discussion with those who wrote the emails." The court went on to opine:

> [W]here counsel are using keyword searches for retrieval of ESI, they at a minimum must carefully craft the appropriate keywords, with input from the ESI's custodians as to the words and abbreviations they use, and the proposed methodology must be quality control tested to assure accuracy in retrieval and elimination of "false positives." It is time that the Bar—even those lawyers who did not come of age in the computer era—understand this.[49]

The general subject of designing what constitutes a "quality e-discovery process" is dealt with in much greater depth in the Sedona *Achieving Quality Commentary*, to which the reader here is referred.[50]

5. Are experts required?

The court in *William Gross Construction* went on to find: "This Court need not now decide whether expert testimony is required; what is required is something other than lawyer's guesses, without client input, and without any quality control testing. . . ."

Thus, the most recent guidance on keyword searches—guidance that is consistent with *Seroquel*, *O'Keefe*, *Equity Analytics*, and *Victor Stanley I*—is: "[W]here counsel are using keyword searches for retrieval of ESI, they at a minimum must carefully craft appropriate keywords, with input from the ESI's custodians as to the words and abbreviations they use, and the proposed methodology must be quality control tested to assure accuracy in retrieval and elimination of 'false positives.'" In fact, the court in *Victor Stanley I* stated: "In neither case [*O'Keefe* nor *Equity Analytics*] did the court expressly hold that Fed.R.Evid. 702 and 104(a) were 'engrafted' into

48. William A. Gross Constr. Assocs., Inc. v. Am. Mfrs. Mut. Ins. Co., 256 F.R.D. 134, 136 (S.D.N.Y. 2009).

49. *Id.*

50. *See supra* note 7.

the rules of discovery in civil proceedings (indeed, neither opinion even mentions Rule 104(a))."

We suggest that the central considerations for keyword searching involve first proportionality, then proper design, followed by an iterative testing, sampling, and refining process, combined with transparent attempts to discuss, in a Rule 26(f) conference or elsewhere, appropriate keyword searches with the opposing litigants, after detailed consultation with the custodians who created the ESI. The *Seroquel* decision made clear: "[W]hile key word searching is a recognized method to winnow documents from large repositories, use of this technique must be a cooperative and informed process."

The choice of search technology, therefore, is not alone sufficient. "In addition to using alternative search methods and to understanding search and retrieval concepts, lawyers will wish to make much greater use of statistical sampling techniques for the purpose of best meeting discovery obligations, both on their own initiative and as part of requests made by opposing parties."[51] Sampling is followed by testing, that is, checking the hits as well as the "discard pile" (the universe not subject to whatever search was performed), so as to determine the efficacy of the search.[52]

It is difficult to imagine a single expert—a linguist, statistician, or information technology expert[53]—who could perform all of these tasks on a database. In light of proportionality principles, in all but the most sophisticated litigation, it is equally difficult to imagine that courts have mandated, or will routinely require, the retention of multiple experts, such as statisticians, linguists, forensic information technology personnel, and perhaps others, to design a defensible search in all cases.

What is clear is that both in *Victor Stanley I* and in an increasing number of cases, courts are expecting that counsel be prepared to be articulate in comprehensively explaining and providing

51. *Id.* at 30. In the words of *Victor Stanley I*: "The only prudent way to test the reliability of the keyword search is to perform some appropriate sampling of the documents determined to be privileged and those determined not to be in order to arrive at a comfort level that the categories are neither over-inclusive nor under-inclusive."

52. *Id.* at 32–36.

53. United States v. O'Keefe, 537 F. Supp. 2d 14, 24 (D.D.C. 2008) ("Whether search terms or 'keywords' will yield the information sought is a complicated question involving the interplay, at least, of the sciences of computer technology, statistics and linguistics. . . .").

documentation of the search process that has been employed. For example, in her recent decision in *Pension Committee*, Judge Scheindlin had "directed" each plaintiff "to submit a declaration documenting its search efforts for two periods—2003/2004 and 2007/2008, as well as any steps taken in between."[54] The judge went on to find:

> In the end, almost every plaintiff submitted a declaration that—at best—lacked attention to detail, or—at worst—was intentionally vague in an attempt to mislead the Citco Defendants and the Court. In addition, plaintiffs had a duty to adequately prepare knowledgeable witnesses with respect to these topics. Which files were searched, how the search was conducted, who was asked to search, what they were told, and the extent of any supervision are all topics reasonably within the scope of the inquiry. Several plaintiffs violated this duty.[55]

This is simply application of a broader principle that judges expect counsel to be comprehensive in their descriptions of whatever process has been employed.[56] Counsel should be aware of a practical, real-world expectation on the part of judges to be informed as to how he or she and of course, the client, has gone about choosing search terms, running samples, and performing whatever other quality controls might be appropriate.

In short, what courts have condemned is *ipse dixit* justifications of a search without adequate groundwork and a supportive predicate, as was seen in *Victor Stanley I*. It does not appear that there is either a present or emerging standard requiring experts in all search design. As Practice Point 7 of the Sedona Conference states: "Parties should expect that their choice of search methodology will need to be explained, either formally or informally, in

54. 685 F. Supp. 2d at 477.

55. *Id.*

56. *Cf.* Amobi v. D.C. Dep't of Corr., 262 F.R.D. 45, 54 (D.D.C. 2009) (in a related discovery context, Judge Facciola observed, "[D]efendants do not indicate how many total documents they produced, so the court cannot determine the magnitude of the error in producing this one document consisting of four pages. Indeed, one keeps searching for some statement somewhere in the defendants' papers that speaks to what they did when they got the documents, how they segregated them so that the privileged documents were kept separate from the non-privileged, and how, despite the care they took, the privileged document was inadvertently produced.").

subsequent legal contexts (including in depositions, evidentiary proceedings, and trials)."[57] Obviously, careful records of the entire process should be maintained, and, at all stages, to the greatest extent possible, transparency and cooperation are beneficial. There is, after all, no reported case sanctioning a party for using *agreed-upon* search terms and methodologies.[58]

6. Final words

Unfortunately for counsel, the area of search and information retrieval is necessarily one involving accelerated scientific and technological development over which educated counsel will need to keep abreast. Practice Point 8 of the *Sedona Search Commentary* states that "parties and the courts should be alert to new and evolving search and information retrieval methods." What may pass for a reasonable search at the time this chapter is written may be viewed a few years hence as insufficiently comprehensive or missing a key ingredient in terms of what constitutes a good "quality" process. Interested counsel would be well advised to keep up with the literature and of course at all times apply common sense. In the authors' view, the latter necessarily includes a sense of proportionality, as well as a willingness to cooperate with opposing counsel in the development of search protocols in a fashion that is both strategically beneficial to the client, and fair to the interests of the tribunal and justice, consistent with Rule 1.

57. *Sedona Search Commentary, supra* note 6, at 195.

58. Victor Stanley, Inc. v. Creative Pipe, Inc. (*Victor Stanley I*), 250 F.R.D. 251, 261 (D. Md. 2008) ("For those understandably concerned about keeping discovery costs within reasonable bounds, it is worth repeating that the cost-benefit balancing factors of Fed. R. Civ. P. 26(b)(2)(C) apply to all aspects of discovery, and parties worried about the cost of employing properly designed search and information retrieval methods have an incentive to keep the costs of this phase of discovery as low as possible, including attempting to confer with their opposing party in an effort to identify a mutually agreeable search and retrieval method. This minimizes cost because if the method is approved, there will be no dispute resolving its sufficiency, and doing it right the first time is always cheaper than doing it over if ordered to do so by the court.").

CHAPTER 22

RULE 30(B)(6) DEPOSITIONS DIRECTED TO ESI ISSUES

BY MICHAEL B. MACWILLIAMS

As e-discovery practice ascends to an increasingly significant role in civil litigation, depositions focusing on electronically stored information will become both more common and more important. This chapter provides a thorough briefing on considerations of whether, when, and how to undertake such depositions to the greatest effect. It also includes advice on defending depositions focused on electronically stored information (ESI).

Not every case calls for a level of focus on ESI sufficient to justify a deposition devoted primarily to the topic, particularly where less formal mechanisms succeed in securing the information required. Knowing how to take and defend such specialized depositions when justified by the circumstances of a given case, however, is a critical skill set counsel must be prepared to bring to bear.

1. Purposes of an ESI-focused Rule 30(b)(6) deposition

As it relates to the deposition of parties (and nonparties) that are not individual persons, Federal Rule of Civil Procedure 30, "Depositions by Oral Examination," provides as follows:

> *Notice or Subpoena Directed to an Organization.* In its notice or subpoena, a party may name as the deponent a public or private corporation, a partnership, an association, a governmental agency, or other entity and must describe with reasonable particularity the matters for examination. The named organization must then designate one or more officers, directors, or managing agents, or designate other persons who consent to testify on its behalf; and it may set out the matters on which each person designated will testify. A subpoena must advise a nonparty organization of its duty to make this designation. The persons designated must testify about information known or reasonably available to the organization. This paragraph (6) does not preclude a deposition by any other procedure allowed by these rules.[1]

A deposition noticed pursuant to this rule presents a flexible and potent mechanism for inquiry about an opposing party's (or nonparty's) ESI.[2] Depending upon the circumstances, an oral deposition can be an adjunct to an efficient and cooperative Rule 26(f) exchange (e.g., as a means to confirm or fine-tune under oath information regarding ESI otherwise received in the ordinary course of the litigation),[3] a traditional mechanism to undertake formal discovery into ESI issues when more cooperative efforts have come up short, or a means to explore (again, under oath) the extent to which an opposing party or nonparty has fulfilled its obligation to identify, locate, preserve, and produce discoverable ESI.

Broadly, there are three justifications for undertaking a deposition focused on ESI: (1) to identify and investigate the sources and accessibility of the ESI that might be germane to the case as appropriate objects of discovery; (2) to determine the particulars of the ESI and the manner in which it might be collected and produced so as to address considerations of usability, authenticity,

1. FED. R. CIV. P. 30(b)(6).

2. The reader is assumed to be familiar with civil practice respecting such depositions, which are sometimes referred to as "corporate designee depositions," or, in certain state court parlance, depositions of a "person most knowledgeable" (a "PMK" deposition).

3. Each party is required to "provide to the other parties: . . . (ii) a copy—or a description by category and location—of all documents, electronically stored information, and tangible things that the disclosing party has in its possession, custody, or control and may use to support its claims or defenses, unless the use would be solely for impeachment." FED. R. CIV. P. 26(a)(1)(A)(ii); *see also* chapters 1 and 18.

and admissibility; and (3) to determine the appropriateness and sufficiency of the efforts undertaken to identify, locate, collect, preserve, and produce discoverable (or potentially discoverable) ESI.

Within those broader outlines, the more specific reasons and justifications for undertaking a Rule 30(b)(6) deposition targeting ESI issues are many and varied, including at least the following:

A. To identify potential sources, locations, and storage and retrieval methodologies of ESI

Pursuant to Rule 26(b)(1):

> Unless otherwise limited by court order, the scope of discovery is as follows: Parties may obtain discovery regarding any nonprivileged matter that is relevant to any party's claim or defense—*including the existence, description, nature, custody, condition, and location of any documents or other tangible things* and the identity and location of persons who know of any discoverable matter.[4]

In accordance with this rule, courts have permitted depositions to explore, for example, the architecture of computer systems in which ESI is housed; where and in what form ESI is kept; and the manner and extent to which the information itself or the systems in which it is maintained may have changed over time.[5]

B. To determine the nature and volume of potentially responsive ESI

An effective ESI discovery strategy must consider the types and anticipated volume of ESI that will be germane to the litigation. A corporate litigant that routinely overwrites its email backups on a monthly basis can be expected to have proportionately less ESI

4. Fed. R. Civ. P. 26(b)(1) (emphasis added). Unlike the many other relevant Federal Rules revised by the e-discovery amendments of 2006, this provision of Rule 26 was not expressly modified to refer to "electronically stored information," in addition to "documents" and "tangible things." Nonetheless, the Advisory Committee Notes clearly provide that "documents" shall be interpreted to include ESI where appropriate. *See, e.g.*, Fed. R. Civ. P. 34 advisory committee note to 2006 Amendment ("[A] Rule 34 request should be understood to encompass, and the response should include, electronically stored information unless discovery in the action has clearly distinguished between electronically stored information and 'documents.'").

5. *See, e.g.*, Bray & Gillespie Mgmt. Co. v. Lexington Ins. Co., 2008 WL 3480321 (M.D. Fla. Aug. 12, 2008).

than a similarly situated corporation that maintains backed-up email for a much longer period. Likewise, in addition to identifying the geographic and network locations where ESI might be stored (point A, above), counsel will need to identify early in the litigation the types of ESI potentially at issue. Does the case involve large data stores, proprietary applications, audio/video/media files, or ephemeral data stored only in random access memory (RAM)? Each of these (and other types of ESI beyond the more familiar email, PDF, and word processing documents) presents unique challenges and considerations. Exploration of the extent to which ESI is housed in "inaccessible" formats or locations (e.g., obsolete, "legacy," or superseded backup systems) will likely prove critical in any cost-shifting controversy that arises.

C. As a mechanism in aid of the proper formulation of the forthcoming substantive discovery requests, including, for example, the extent to which discovery in excess of the specified default limits might be necessary or advisable

Federal Rule of Civil Procedure 34 reserves to the requesting party the option, at least in the first instance, to "specify the form or forms in which electronically stored information is to be produced."[6] As Rule 34 expressly provides, "the response [to a request for the production of ESI] "may state an objection to a requested form for producing electronically stored information."[7] In the event of such an objection, or where the requesting party has not specified a production format, "the [responding] party must state the form or forms it intends to use."[8] Not only will the ability to appropriately specify the most useful production format(s)—or, at the least, an appropriate production format[9]—be facilitated by a greater understanding of the available alternatives, but the question of whether the specified format ultimately prevails over the alternative format(s) that may be proffered by an objecting party is likely

6. FED. R. CIV. P. 34(b)(1)(C).

7. FED. R. CIV. P. 34(b)(2)(D).

8. *Id.*

9. *See* FED. R. CIV. P. 34(b) advisory committee note to 2006 Amendment ("If the responding party ordinarily maintains the information it is producing in a way that makes it searchable by electronic means, the information should not be produced in a form that removes or significantly degrades this feature."); *see also* chapter 2.

to be illuminated by the types of information that can be elicited in a deposition exploring those issues.[10]

Similarly, issues explored during the course of an ESI-focused deposition may suggest a need to alter the number of interrogatories, depositions, or requests for admission otherwise permissible under the federal or local rules.[11] A deposition also is well suited to the exploration of the relative merits of the available discovery mechanisms,[12] and the burdens of undertaking such discovery as compared with the likely outcomes of having done so.[13]

D. To determine the extent to which electronic documents might need to be produced in native format

Even in a case involving only "garden variety" ESI, there may be cause for some portion of that ESI to be produced in its native format(s). A deposition allows a party to explore, for example, the extent to which an adversary's heavy use of spreadsheets—notorious for the shambles that often results when they are produced in

10. Of course, a deposition that takes place sufficiently early in the process to aid in the preparation of document requests will likely occur too early in the discovery period to inquire into the propriety of the alternative production formats specified by a party responding to those requests. Nonetheless, an early deposition will afford an opportunity to inquire into the nature and particulars of the various alternatives, particularly where the topic has been broached to some degree in any exchange addressed to the issue of ESI sources that the responding party identifies as those the party intends to neither search nor produce. *See infra* section C.

11. *See* FED. R. CIV. P. 30(a)(2)(A)(i) (limiting depositions to 10 per side); FED. R. CIV. P. 30(d)(1) (limiting the default length of depositions to "1 day of 7 hours"); FED. R. CIV. P. 33(a)(1) (imposing a default limit of 25 interrogatories per party); FED. R. CIV. P. 26(b)(2)(A) (allowing for the alteration of such limits, and of any limit on the number of requests for admission a party may serve as prescribed by local rule).

12. *See* FED. R. CIV. P. 26(b)(2)(C)(i).

13. *See* FED. R. CIV. P. 26(b)(2)(C)(iii). A court might well look to the occurrence *vel non* of an ESI-focused deposition, and certainly would be expected to look to the information gained by way of any such deposition that took place, in an effort to determine whether and how the court might or must limit the frequency or extent of discovery otherwise permissible. *See* FED. R. CIV. P. 26(b)(2)(C)(ii) (directing the court to consider whether "the party seeking discovery has had ample opportunity to obtain the information by discovery in the action"); *see also, e.g.*, United States *ex rel.* Branch Consultants, LLC v. Allstate Ins. Co., 2010 WL 1254665 (E.D. La. Mar. 25, 2010) (ordering the parties to undertake an ESI-focused deposition "pursuant to Fed. R. Civ. P. 30(b)(6), so that the parties could present testimony and other evidence regarding defendants' record keeping and maintenance of ESI").

a static-image format—might suggest the need for productions in native format. Similar questions may arise in the context of proprietary databases and other applications (whether or not those applications might allow for export and production of ESI in a more familiar or user-friendly format), and in cases involving allegations that information may have been misappropriated, altered, lost, or destroyed.

At least one court has ordered a party seeking discovery of native-format ESI to "depose [its adversary's] representative to determine the impact that production of that information in native format would have upon the operations of [the resisting party, and] inviting [the resisting party] to file a Motion for a Protective Order if necessary following the gathering of that information."[14]

E. To explore issues concerning the accessibility of ESI, including, for example, whether and how the sampling of putatively inaccessible ESI might be appropriate, and the commensurate considerations of cost shifting

The taking of depositions as a means of exploring the accessibility of ESI—that is, the extent to which the discovery of ESI may be technically challenging, prohibitively expensive, or otherwise unduly burdensome—is expressly condoned by the advisory committee notes to Rule 26(b)(2):

> If the parties do not resolve the [accessibility] issue and the court must decide, the responding party must show that the identified sources of information are not reasonably accessible because of undue burden or cost. *The requesting party may need discovery to test this assertion.* Such discovery might take the form of requiring the responding party to conduct a sampling of information contained on the sources identified as not reasonably accessible; allowing some form of inspection of such sources; *or taking depositions of witnesses knowledgeable about the responding party's information systems.*[15]

14. *In re* Classicstar Mare Lease Litig., 2009 WL 260954, at *2 (E.D. Ky. Feb. 2, 2009).
15. FED. R. CIV. P. 26(b)(2) advisory committee note to 2006 Amendment (emphasis added).

F. To determine the extent to which, or the manner in which, discovery might be phased (i.e., undertaken in stages)

Not every aspect of a discovery plan must be once and finally resolved at the Rule 26(f) or Rule 16(b) conference(s). To the contrary, and particularly in light of the potentially outsized expense of undertaking full-scale electronic discovery, courts, counsel, and clients alike are increasingly receptive to the possibility of conditioning (or at least tailoring) more extensive discovery on the results of initially limited discovery. Similarly, the Sedona Principles expressly recognize the iterative nature of the discovery process, including particularly those aspects of the process related to the discovery of ESI.[16] Where the potential for phased discovery exists, a deposition exploring the possible alternatives to producing everything all at once—for example, whether the collection and production of emails might be limited initially to a subset of custodians most likely to have engaged in the relevant communications—holds the potential to foster substantial efficiencies in an area occasionally characterized by outsized and unproductive costs.

G. To facilitate the efficient identification, organization, and utilization of the most relevant information upon receipt of your adversary's ESI

An understanding of how ESI is stored, organized, recalled, and utilized as it is maintained by the custodians or other persons who collect or utilize that information in the ordinary course of business should be expected to improve the efficiency with which that information is evaluated and utilized by the requesting party in the litigation.

H. To confirm the propriety and sufficiency of a party's efforts to identify and collect ESI

If and when questions arise related to the extent to which a party (or nonparty) has collected and produced all of its responsive and discoverable ESI, a deposition is an appropriate means of exploring

16. *See* The Sedona Principles: Best Practices Recommendations & Principles for Addressing Electronic Document Discovery (2d ed. 2007), cmt. 11.a ("Parties should understand the use of search methods may involve an iterative approach with search terms and concepts subject to expansion or refinement as the case progresses.").

that issue.[17] Indeed, a deposition may be the preferred and most efficient available means of exploring such issues, in light of the fact that such questions generally arise in the wake of written discovery regarded as unsatisfactory.[18] Sedona Principle 11 expressly contemplates the deposition as a likely manifestation of a party's obligation to explain the methodologies employed in an effort to satisfy its ESI collection and production obligations.[19] Such a deposition would, quite obviously, fall much later in the discovery period than the deposition conducted for any of the purposes described above.

I. To address authenticity and admissibility issues

In a manner loosely analogous to the traditional "custodian of records" deposition, a late-stage ESI-related Rule 30(b)(6) deposition may well facilitate or be integral to the authentification and

---

17. *See, e.g.,* Alexander v. FBI, 192 F.R.D. 37, 40 (D.D.C. 2000) ("Accordingly, a deposition of a custodian of records may be taken in order to address these concerns about the adequacy of DoD's search and compliance with the subpoena."); *cf. In re* eBay Seller Antitrust Litig., 2007 WL 2852364 (N.D. Cal. 2007) (noting the parties' agreement to undertake a Rule 30(b)(6) deposition "regarding . . . ESI preservation and collection efforts"). As to privilege and work-product issues, see chapters 14–17.

18. See, for example, *Bray & Gillespie Management Co. v. Lexington Insurance Co.,* 2008 WL 2609719 (M.D. Fla. June 30, 2008), in which the district court concluded that a deposition was preferable to further exchanges of insufficient and apparently evasive written discovery:

> The history of discovery disputes in this case persuades me that ordering Ocean Waters to identify documents that were kept by or for it would likely further delay the discovery efforts without a likelihood of a better response from Ocean Waters. Accordingly, the motion to compel is GRANTED in part as follows: It is ORDERED that within eleven days from the date of this Order, at a time mutually agreed to or otherwise established by the Court or a special master, Ocean Waters shall produce for a Rule 30(b)(6) deposition one or more corporate representatives with the most knowledge of how Ocean Waters maintains its business records, both in paper and in electronic form. . . . If responsive to questions, Ocean Waters' corporate representatives shall allow Belfor's counsel and its IT expert or consultant to view Ocean Waters' computer(s) to determine how information is organized and stored therein.

Id. at *2.

19. *See* THE SEDONA PRINCIPLES, *supra* note 16, cmt. 11.a ("Absent an agreement on the search methods to be used, parties should expect that their choice of search methods will need to be explained, either formally or informally, in subsequent legal contexts, including in depositions, evidentiary proceedings, and possibly even at trial.").

admissibility of the ESI produced in the litigation. Of course, the particulars of such an undertaking are a book chapter (if not more) unto themselves, and any attorney contemplating the taking of a deposition as part of this critical trial-preparation effort would do well to consult the case law and leading authorities addressed specifically to the topic.[20]

2. Deciding whether to pursue an ESI-focused deposition

Having established that a Rule 30(b)(6) deposition is *an* appropriate method of conducting ESI-related discovery, the tactical question becomes: Is such a deposition *the most* appropriate method to obtain the desired ESI-related information under the circumstances of a particular case? More to the point, is an oral Rule 30(b)(6) deposition an efficient and practical means of accomplishing your client's e-discovery objectives? Can you improve the efficiency of any such deposition by undertaking other discovery in advance of or in conjunction with the deposition?

The level of cooperation exhibited between or among opposing counsel has much to say about how effectively a party might conduct a Rule 30(b)(6) deposition for electronic discovery purposes and, indeed, much to say about whether a deposition is necessary or useful. For example, if opposing counsel are knowledgeable and experienced in matters of electronic discovery (both generally and with respect to the types and sources of ESI germane to the litigation at hand), empowered by a client of similar sophistication and understanding, and motivated more toward cooperation than confrontation, less formalized and more fluid exchanges of information may prove so productive and efficient as to eliminate altogether the need for any deposition. The cooperative aims of the Rule 26(f) conference, certainly as they relate to ESI, carried to their logical and most helpful conclusion, favor such an outcome. Recognizing that oral depositions consume both time and money—and usually more of both than do alternative discovery mechanisms—counsel would do well to start the process by asking whether there is a better way than a deposition to obtain the necessary information.[21]

---

20. *See, e.g.*, chapter 27; Lorraine v. Markel Am. Ins. Co., 241 F.R.D. 534 (D. Md. 2007); *see generally* G. PAUL, FOUNDATIONS OF DIGITAL EVIDENCE (2008).

21. *See, e.g.*, Garcia v. Tyson Foods, Inc., 2010 WL 5392660, at *5–6 (D. Kan. Dec. 21, 2010) (noting the parties' apparent agreement to postpone a Rule 30(b)(6) ESI-focused deposition "while the parties engaged in an ongoing dialogue about ESI

The alternatives to an oral deposition are as varied as counsel's imagination (albeit constrained by the rules) will permit, including any of the following, alone or in combination:

ESI questionnaire. An advanced understanding of the parties' respective e-discovery particulars may be as simple as the exchange of written questions and answers among counsel.

Informal interviews. Assuming that a sufficiently cooperative environment has taken root, the informal (and off-the-record) interview of client information technology (IT) personnel (including those who might or might not otherwise be deposed) could prove to be a viable alternative. Counsel may wish to agree in advance of any such interviews that the party being informally "deposed" will remain at liberty to designate the ESI-related deponent(s) of that party's choosing, and that the party seeking the information through the interview will not seek to depose a particular individual, even though the option to identify topics to be covered pursuant to Rule 30(b)(6) does not ordinarily prevent an adverse party from targeting a specific individual as a deponent. Such an agreement could facilitate a productive interview by allowing access to more knowledgeable personnel who might otherwise be considered "unattractive" witnesses (from the deponent's perspective), for one reason or another unrelated to the witnesses' knowledge of the matters at hand.

Affidavit. If adequate information has been obtained through exchanges between or among counsel, or through informal interviews of party personnel, but concerns remain regarding the extent to which the parties can rely upon the information thus obtained, those concerns might be alleviated by an affidavit confirming that information and vouching for its accuracy.

Interrogatories, or (as directed to nonparties) deposition by written question. Although oral depositions are much more frequently undertaken, interrogatories served on an opposing party pursuant to Rule 33, or (because interrogatories are unavailable) a deposition by written question taken of a nonparty pursuant to Rule 31, should not be overlooked. Of course, these written

issues" and counsel discussed "whether a Rule 30(b)(6) deposition on ESI issues was necessary").

discovery mechanisms are substantially less flexible than the oral deposition, and devoid of opportunities for contemporaneous and dynamic follow-up, but they may well prove more efficient and cost-effective means of obtaining all of the information sought, or information sufficient to narrow the scope of a follow-up oral deposition. Moreover, as with an affidavit, the opportunity to obtain this information under oath serves as a means of importing the information obtained into the "evidentiary" record.

Consideration of these alternatives is not merely an academic exercise, or a matter of counsel's convenience or simple prerogative, because the Federal Rules of Civil Procedure reserve to the court the option, if not indeed the obligation, to intervene in the process and limit the discovery, "if [the court] determines that . . . the discovery sought is unreasonably duplicative, or can be obtained from some other source that is more convenient, less burdensome, or less expensive."[22]

Finally, as with all depositions, counsel is obliged to consider whether the information gained from an ESI-related deposition is worth the effort required to undertake the exercise.[23]

3. Timing of an ESI-focused deposition

Having determined that an ESI-related deposition is both necessary and appropriate, counsel will invariably confront considerations of timing. To the extent that the purpose underlying the deposition does not, by itself, settle the question,[24] counsel might consider the following in determining when in the process an

22. FED. R. CIV. P. 26(b)(2)(C)(i); *see, e.g.*, Newman v. Borders, Inc., 257 F.R.D. 1 (D.D.C. 2009) (granting motion for protective order in connection with requested Rule 30(b)(6) deposition, but ordering the resisting party to provide information concerning the party's ESI in the form of an affidavit addressing court-specified topics).

23. FED. R. CIV. P. 26(g).

24. Fairly obvious examples include a deposition targeting a nonparty's ESI (undertaken whenever in the discovery period substantive discovery from that nonparty merits the parties' attention); a deposition to explore the propriety of a party's collection, preservation, and production efforts (undertaken only after alternative efforts to explore this topic have proved unsatisfactory); or a deposition seeking to authenticate and lay the foundation for the admissibility of ESI obtained earlier in the discovery process (presumably employed as a means of "filling in" any knowledge gaps remaining after the "substantive" witnesses are examined about the provenance of the relevant evidence).

ESI-related deposition would most effectively enhance the overall discovery effort.

First, pressing too soon for an ESI-related deposition will, under most circumstances, prove both inefficient and counterproductive. Notwithstanding the numerous salutary attributes of a deposition, the fact remains that the Federal Rules of Civil Procedure, and increasingly so the federal district courts, regard the exchange of ESI-related information as a fundamentally cooperative endeavor, whereas the deposition is, by its nature, mechanics, and recent historical practice, decidedly adversarial. This conflict, viewed through the prism of the obligations imposed by Rule 26(f), should and likely will be resolved in favor of less formal mechanisms, or perhaps formal exchanges short of sworn witness testimony, and those alternatives should almost always be given an opportunity to prove inadequate before the prospect of a deposition takes center stage.[25] Moreover, a deposition taken too early in the process, before less formal exchanges might provide an appropriate roadmap of the subjects requiring further exploration, runs the risk of proceeding haphazardly, with predictably unsatisfactory results.

Second, whereas a deposition that proceeds before the parties have undertaken in good faith much of the exchange required by Rule 26(f), a deposition noticed well after those initial exchanges have run their course may occur too late in the process to make effective use of the information obtained in structuring the "substantive" discovery process. Moreover, the structure of Rules 16 and 26 contemplates that the types of questions likely to be the focus of a "prediscovery" ESI deposition will be addressed very early in the life of the litigation. Indeed, waiting months to undertake a "preliminary" deposition directed to the understanding of ESI-related issues is potentially oxymoronic, or at the least inefficient.[26]

With these two considerations in mind, the most productive "preliminary" ESI deposition is likely to proceed at the outset of

---

25. Rule 30(a)(2)(A)(iii) generally prohibits the taking of a deposition without leave of court before the parties have conferred pursuant to Rule 26(f), and the court from which a party would seek such leave almost certainly would insist that any such deposition first be a topic of discussion at the Rule 26(f) conference.

26. *Cf.* U.S. DIST. CT., DIST. OF MD., SUGGESTED PROTOCOL FOR DISCOVERY OF ELECTRONICALLY STORED INFORMATION, subpara. 8.L (bearing the heading "Preliminary depositions of information systems personnel, and limits on the scope of such depositions."), http://www.mdd.uscourts.gov/news/news/ESIProtocol.pdf.

fact discovery, when there remains sufficient flexibility and time to incorporate the results of the deposition into the bulk of the fact discovery process.

4. Mechanics of an ESI-focused deposition

The differing objectives underlying an ESI deposition and a more "substantive" corporate designee deposition should be factored into the parties' discussion of the manner in which the former should proceed. Perhaps most significantly, the parties should explore whether they can reach agreement in advance on the permissible scope of the deposition. Rule 30(c)(2) provides that counsel "may instruct a deponent not to answer [a question posed during a deposition] only when necessary to preserve a privilege, to enforce a limitation ordered by the court, or to present a motion under Rule 30(d)(3)."[27] Depending upon the circumstances, this limitation—often regarded as critical to the effectiveness of a "substantive" deposition—may be inappropriate, perhaps even counterproductive, in the context of an ESI-focused deposition. For this reason, the U.S. District Court for the District of Maryland's Suggested ESI Protocol encourages counsel to "specifically consider whether limitations on the scope of such depositions should be submitted to the Court with a proposed order that, if entered, would permit Counsel to instruct a witness not to answer questions beyond the scope of the limitation."[28] Indeed, parties are likely to be more receptive to the idea of an early "prediscovery" deposition undertaken pursuant to appropriate assurances that their counsel can prohibit forays into the substantive underpinnings of the case. Particularly in any instance in which a representative designated with respect to ESI issues may also harbor "substantive" information germane to the case (a circumstance not uncommon where the deponent is a small or medium-sized business), advance agreement on this issue, memorialized in a suitable writing or order, may prove essential. In crafting the language defining the permissible scope, counsel should consider the extent

27. *See, e.g.*, Am. Gen. Life Ins. Co. v. Billard, 2010 WL 4367052 (N.D. Iowa Oct. 28, 2010) (noting the majority rule that it is presumptively improper to instruct a deponent not to answer a question on the grounds that the subject matter lies beyond the scope of a Rule 30(b)(6) deposition as framed by the categories identified in the deposition notice).

28. Suggested Protocol, *supra* note 26, at subparagraph 8.L. ("TOPICS TO DISCUSS AT RULE 26(f) CONFERENCE—Preliminary depositions of information systems personnel, and limits on the scope of such depositions.").

to which it may be appropriate to explore with any such witness the terminology unique to the case that will inform the relevancy or privilege-related terms to be used in searching or sampling the potentially responsive ESI.[29]

In addition to limitations on the subject-matter scope of the deposition, the parties may also wish to agree to and specify appropriate time limits. Although Rule 30(d)(1) imposes a seven-hour default limit on the length of depositions of individuals, that same limitation does not typically apply to Rule 30(b)(6) depositions in which more than one witness is required in order to address the full range of topics specified by the notice of deposition. To the contrary, in the Rule 30(b)(6) context, the seven-hour limit generally applies on a per-witness basis, as opposed to forcing a party to explore all of the topics specified pursuant to the rule in a total of seven hours.[30] Thus, the time spent deposing Rule 30(b)(6) representatives regarding ESI issues would not generally cut into the time available to depose the party regarding more substantive matters.[31] Nonetheless, depending on the breadth and scope of the topics to be addressed, more or less than seven hours might be appropriate,[32] and counsel should attempt to memorialize in

29. Efforts to explore the lexicon of the case in question as a means of identifying "keywords" or search terms, as well as the use of suitable technology, or similarly diligent efforts to identify and capture potentially privileged ESI, will auger in favor of a conclusion that reasonable steps were undertaken by the party to prevent disclosure. *See* FED. R. EVID. 502(b)(2); *cf.* United States v. Sensient Colors, Inc., 2009 WL 2905474, at *4 (D.N.J. Sept. 9, 2009) ("Plaintiff's production was made in the midst of a commendable effort to employ a sophisticated computer program to conduct its privilege review. Unfortunately, mistakes occurred. Plaintiff should not be unduly punished for occasional mistakes that occurred while it started to use new software to organize and sort its documents."); *see also* chapters 19, 20, and 16.

30. *See* FED. R. CIV. P. 30(d) advisory committee note to 2000 Amendment ("For purposes of this durational limit, the deposition of each person designated under Rule 30(b)(6) should be considered a separate deposition.").

31. In an abundance of caution, the party noting the deposition might seek confirmation from the opposing party that the contemplated ESI-focused deposition would not comprise the single deposition of that party to which parties are limited without leave of court, *see* FED. R. CIV. P. 20(a)(2)(A)(ii), although that result would seem to be axiomatic.

32. *Cf.* Canal Barge Co. v. Commonwealth Edison Co., 2001 WL 817853, at *4 (N.D. Ill. July 19, 2001) (extending the time limit on a Rule 30(b)(6) deposition to three seven-hour days notwithstanding that only one individual witness was expected to appear).

advance of the deposition any planned deviation from the default limit.

Counsel may also wish to memorialize an agreement that the ESI deposition does not count against the permissible number of depositions.[33] The argument in favor of this position benefits from the fact that much of the information to be sought (for example, "a description by category and location [] of all documents, electronically stored information, and tangible things that the disclosing party has in its possession, custody, or control and may use to support its claims or defenses"[34]) is information to which a party is otherwise entitled, and as to which the ESI deposition may be viewed as an alternative means to accomplish that which the deponent/opposing party is obliged to provide in any event.

5. Content of the ESI-focused deposition notice

Having established the procedural and mechanical parameters of the deposition, the party noting the deposition is obliged by Rule 30(b)(6) to "describe with reasonable particularity the matters for examination." If anything, given the variability among the members of the Bar in terms of lawyers' knowledge of and familiarity with ESI issues, the requirement of particularity in identifying the topics to be covered in an ESI-focused deposition probably is somewhat heightened.[35] Because there is no limit (by rule) on the

33. *See, e.g.*, United States *ex rel.* Branch Consultants, LLC v. Allstate Ins. Co., 2010 WL 1254665 (E.D. La. Mar. 25, 2010) (reflecting objections to multiple ESI-focused depositions); Bray & Gillespie Mgmt. Co. v. Lexington Ins. Co., 2008 WL 2609719, at *2 (M.D. Fla. June 30, 2008) ("The deposition [ordered by the court in exploration of the nonparty deponent's efforts to collect and produce responsive ESI] shall not count against the number of depositions that Belfor is authorized to take."); *cf. In re* Medtronic, Inc. Implantable Defibrillator Prod. Liab. Litig., 2007 WL 846642, at *2 (D. Minn. Mar. 6, 2007) ("Each 7 hours of a [non-ESI] Rule 30(b)(6) deposition shall count as one of the allowed depositions."). The default number of permissible depositions under the Federal Rules is 10. Fed. R. Civ. P. 30(a)(2)(A)(i).

34. Fed. R. Civ. P. 26(a)(1)(A)(ii).

35. *Cf.* Newman v. Borders, Inc., 257 F.R.D. 1, 3 (D.D.C. 2009) ("There is . . . a . . . responsibility upon the party who had noticed the 30(b)(6) deposition to define *as clearly as possible* the topics for the deposition. While topic one speaks of '[g]eneral document and information retention policies' and topic nine of 'Defendants' search for records or documents or information responsive to Plaintiff's Request for Production of Documents, the words 'e-mail' or 'electronically stored information' do not appear in the description of the topics. . . . I cannot say that a reasonable lawyer reading that document would conclude that [the defendant's] e-mail retention policy and the search for e-mails pertaining to this

number of topics that can be specified, and in light of the fact that there is little to be gained by a notice that lacks sufficient specificity (except, perhaps, a modicum of leeway during the deposition), counsel would do well to err on the side of "too much" specificity. This is not an opportunity for subtlety or obfuscation: spend the time and energy necessary to assemble an appropriately particularized notice (which will redound to the client's benefit in any event when the suitably particularized list of topics serves as the foundation for an outline of the questions to be asked), and make every effort to alert the deponent to precisely what will be covered at the deposition. Greater specificity will (or, at least, should) lead to better-prepared, more-knowledgeable witnesses, and more efficient and productive depositions.

Although every case, and every organizational witness, is different, the following suggested topics should be considered for inclusion in the notice of deposition:

- the email and other software applications, databases, and operating systems utilized by the deponent's relevant employees (both currently, and during the relevant past)
- the structure, operation, and output/export alternatives of any relevant legacy or custom software applications
- the structure, operation, and output/export alternatives of any relevant databases
- the number, location, designation, function, and operation of the organization's email, file, and application servers
- the organization's utilization of "cloud computing" or other external storage or collaboration systems
- the particulars of the deponent's ESI backup and/or disaster recovery practices, including the media rotation schedules and the technical specifications of the software and storage media utilized to generate and retrieve data from the backup media
- the factual basis and underpinnings of any assertion by the deponent that any of its ESI is not reasonably accessible because of undue burden or cost
- the records information management (RIM), document control, document retention, and similar policies applicable to all sources of the deponent's potentially discov-

case were going to be topics of the deposition." (first and second alterations in original) (emphasis added)).

erable ESI (including employees' use of home computers or other computers or access points from outside of the company)
- the location and types of ESI storage media, whether fixed or portable
- the passwords or other protocols necessary to access and make use of the deponent's computer systems
- the organizational structure of the party's IT department/personnel
- the parameters of any applicable litigation hold, the modifications to standard protocols necessary to account for any such hold, and the particulars of other efforts undertaken to implement any such preservation directives

6. Taking an ESI-focused deposition

As suggested above, an ESI-focused preliminary deposition will function most effectively when it follows on the heels of other efforts to secure the targeted information. Counsel should thus seek to accomplish as much as possible in advance of the deposition itself, through cooperative exchanges undertaken as part of and in follow-up to the Rule 26(f) conference, or through targeted formal written discovery requests. The deposition should not necessarily be regarded as a "last resort," but it is, in most contexts, a relatively inefficient (in terms of lawyer time) alternative to a reasonably cooperative (or at least functional and less formalized) exchange that might well produce comparable, or even superior, results.

Counsel should consider presenting to the deponent the following requests or issues, whether formally[36] or informally, sufficiently in advance of the deposition to allow for a suitable response, including the likely back-and-forth on these matters:

---

36. The applicable Federal Rules expressly authorize the service of document requests in conjunction with a notice of deposition or a subpoena, whether the deponent is a party (*see* FED. R. CIV. P. 30(b)(2)) or a nonparty (*see* FED. R. CIV. P. 45(a)(1)(C), (D)). Note, however, that document requests appended to a notice of deposition (at least where the deponent is a party) are generally regarded as "a complement to a Rule 30 deposition, not a substitute for a Rule 34 document request." Carter v. United States, 164 F.R.D. 131, 133 (D. Mass. 1995) (citing FED. R. CIV. P. 30(b)(5) advisory committee note to 1970 Amendment). Accordingly, an overreaching document request served pursuant to Rule 30(b)(5) may be impermissible, particularly if served after a separate deadline applicable to written discovery has passed.

- *A request for documents concerning the deponent's relevant document management or control policies (sometimes referred to as "RIM policies"), including ESI backup procedures and storage media rotation schedules.* Understanding the information a deponent organization should or should not have retained according to its own policies can be as important as identifying the information the organization claims that it has or has not retained.[37]
- *A request for documents concerning the structure of the deponent's information management systems.* System architecture diagrams and the like can serve as useful roadmaps in exploring the various locations and formats in which relevant information is likely to be found.[38]
- *A request for historically relevant and current organizational charts for IT personnel.* Expecting any witness to recall accurately even his or her own employment history is a recipe for disappointment; all the more so when the subject turns to the employment and job function histories of other individuals or suborganizations.[39]
- *A request that the deponent identify the categories of information that it does not intend to collect or produce because of undue burden or cost.* The advisory committee notes to Rule 26(b)(2) provide that "[t]he responding party must also identify, by category or type, the sources containing potentially responsive information that it is neither searching nor producing. The identification should, to the extent possible, provide enough detail to enable the requesting party to evaluate the burdens and costs of providing the discovery and the likelihood of finding responsive information on the identified sources."[40] This information is the logical starting point for investigating a deponent's claims that it should not be required to produce "inaccessible" ESI because of undue burden or cost.
- *The suggestion of an informal interview of an adversary's IT manager or other appropriate technical person as a means of facilitating efficient use of the parties' deposition time.* As men-

37. *See* chapters 5 and 11.
38. *See* chapter 4.
39. *See* chapter 5.
40. Fed. R. Civ. P. 26(b)(2) advisory committee note to 2006 Amendment; *see* chapter 2.

tioned above, an appropriately circumscribed predeposition interview may allow for significant streamlining of the more formal efforts to follow.

In addition to seeking information from the deponent, counsel not otherwise thoroughly familiar with and fluent in the electronic discovery issues germane to the case should consult at length with client, law firm, or outside IT and/or e-discovery consultants, lest they find themselves tied in knots at the deposition by a witness with far superior technical competence. Of course, the witness is expected to be more familiar than counsel with the technical intricacies of many of the subjects to be covered in the deposition. Technical mastery is not necessarily the order of the day, but two hours into the deposition is neither the time nor the place for counsel to discover a gaping hole in their e-discovery knowledge that might have been filled by advance consultation with someone whose job it is to fill in, rather than exploit, those holes.

Likewise, and even though an ESI-focused deposition is likely to occur relatively early in the case, counsel should be certain to know enough about the underlying substance of the case to be in a position to ferret out the relevant sources of information, including the identities and roles of the key players. In all likelihood, such information will have been explored and collected to some extent as part of the earlier Rule 26 exchanges, and the preparation for the ESI deposition will present a further opportunity to explore these issues with the client.

7. Defending an ESI-focused deposition

Preparing to defend an ESI-focused deposition is potentially complicated by three factors not otherwise typically encountered: The witness may be entirely unfamiliar with *both* the litigation process *and* the substantive subject matter of the case; defense counsel *and/or* examining counsel may be operating in unfamiliar territory; and counsel and witness may speak very different "languages," leading to a greater-than-usual risk of miscommunication. Each of these considerations suggests that the ordinary tasks of selecting and preparing a Rule 30(b)(6) deponent must be undertaken with extraordinary diligence.

The deponent's obligation to present for deposition an appropriate witness is no different with regard to ESI than in the ordinary, "substantive" context. The rule requires that "the named organization must . . . designate one or more officers, directors, or managing agents, or designate other persons who consent to testify on its behalf; and it may set out the matters on which each person designated will testify. . . . The persons designated must testify about information known or reasonably available to the organization."[41] Because the witness candidates with the appropriate technical background and knowledge are unlikely to be "officers, directors, or managing agents" (except where the deponent is a small organization), the witness(es) will need to consent to testify on behalf of the organization. To the extent that a witness better suited to address one or more topics is unavailable or unwilling to be deposed (for example, if that individual has left the party's employ), the party responding to the deposition notice nonetheless may, and likely does, have an obligation to educate a witness sufficiently to provide competent testimony on the topics identified in the notice.[42]

A sufficiently particularized deposition notice will serve as both the touchstone in identifying one or more appropriate witnesses and the roadmap in preparing those witnesses for the deposition.[43] Having been presented with an outline of the ESI topics that the opposing party considers worthy of exploration, defending counsel would be remiss in failing to seize the opportunity to become as well versed as reasonably practicable in the particulars of the client's ESI situation.

Here, the area in which counsel most frequently encounters a confusing level of complexity and potential misinformation is the subject of electronic backup procedures, practices, and schedules. Not infrequently, even IT managers above a certain level (perhaps without realizing that it is the case) have an incorrect or superficial understanding of these procedures, and counsel must be prepared to dig into the subject with gusto for three reasons. First, the ways in which computerized backups are created, maintained, preserved, and recycled determine and define a significant aspect of the information potentially available to the organization, both offensively and defensively. Second, the intensive discussion of backup procedures (in preparation for the deposition or during the deposition itself) often reveals or suggests deficiencies in a party's

41. Fed. R. Civ. P. 30(b)(6).

42. *See, e.g., In re* Application of Michael Wilson & Partners, 2009 WL 1193874, at *3–5 (D. Colo. Apr. 30, 2009); Alexander v. FBI, 186 F.R.D. 137, 141 (D.D.C. 1998).

43. An insufficiently particularized notice should meet with objection on that basis.

document preservation (i.e., "litigation hold") practices in ways that may have far-reaching implications.[44] Third, what the deposition reveals about the difficulty and expense likely to be encountered in attempting to recover ESI from these sources may leave an indelible, case-long (or more lasting) imprint on the questions of whether and to what extent these potentially massive warehouses of data are "inaccessible" (and therefore undiscoverable), as well as who pays for any efforts undertaken to retrieve or sample such data.[45] All of these topics must be addressed with the witnesses in sufficient depth and detail that deposition-day surprises are kept to a minimum.

In the author's experience, there is an additional reason to be concerned about the potential for miscommunication on these subjects. Bluntly stated, and at the risk of painting with too broad a brush, most lawyers do not process information in the way that most IT professionals do. Whereas lawyers are trained to spot and explore issues, pull threads of ideas, and revel (or wallow) in the ambiguities of language, most IT professionals (particularly software engineers), no matter how creative, tend to process requests and respond to questions with very precise and literal responses. This tendency can be exacerbated by the standard battery of deposition preparation instructions imploring witnesses to "answer precisely the question that is asked—no more and no less." The literally and precisely correct answer can be a blessing (or a source of tedium) during the deposition, but it can also be an obstacle to clear and comprehensive communication in preparing for the deposition. Thus, counsel should recognize that, even more so than in the more traditional deposition (and deposition preparation) environment, exactly the right question (or series of questions) might be required to elicit a full and correct answer when it comes to technical matters within the purview of IT personnel.

8. Conclusion

In the ideal case, with technically competent and capable counsel on all sides, fully versed in all things ESI, suitably empowered by their

44. Of course, counsel will have initiated the litigation hold much earlier in the dispute. *See* chapters 8 and 9.

45. *See, e.g.*, *In re* CV Therapeutics, Inc. Sec. Litig., 2006 U.S. Dist. LEXIS 38909, at *29 n.5 (N.D. Cal. Apr. 4, 2006) (citing the testimony of a party's Rule 30(b)(6) designee taken earlier in the case as grounds for rejecting the party's effort to thwart discovery on the grounds that the discovery sought was unduly burdensome).

respective clients, and equally inspired by the e-discovery battle scars of cases past to proceed as perfect role models of cooperation, the e-discovery aspects of the Rule 26(f) conference unfurl without so much as a hiccup,[46] and an ESI-focused deposition never enters the calculus. In reality, however, an ESI-focused deposition is an effective response to any number of electronic discovery-related challenges, and an option that should, and will, be employed more frequently as these challenges grow in number and complexity. Armed with the tools presented above, counsel will be in a position to diligently press and adequately defend such depositions as the circumstances require.

46. *See* chapter 18.

CHAPTER 23

USE OF ESI IN DEPOSITIONS

BY MICHAEL D. BERMAN

Chapter 22 looked at depositions that focus on the topic of ESI to aid in acquiring it through e-discovery. This chapter talks about how best to use ESI—once it has been acquired—in the deposition of a party or witness. Included in the discussion are the forms of ESI that may be used, the application of rules including the "original document rule," some hypothetical examples, and practice tips.

1. Introduction

In *Lorraine v. Markel American Insurance Co.*,[1] the court noted the body of information discussing preservation and production of electronically stored information (ESI), and then stated:

> Very little has been written, however, about what is required to insure that ESI obtained during discovery is admissible into evidence at trial, or whether it constitutes "such facts as would be admissible in evidence" for use in summary judgment practice. Fed.R.Civ.P. 56(e). This is unfortunate, because considering the significant costs associated with discovery of ESI, *it makes little sense to go to all the bother and expense to get electronic information only to have it excluded from evidence or*

1. 241 F.R.D. 534 (D. Md. 2007); P. Grimm, et al., *Back to the Future:* Lorraine v. Markel American Insurance Co. *and New Findings on the Admissibility of Electronically Stored Information,*" 42 AKRON L.REV. 359 (2009).

rejected from consideration during summary judgment because the proponent cannot lay a sufficient foundation to get it admitted. The process is complicated by the fact that ESI comes in multiple evidentiary "flavors," including e-mail, website ESI, internet postings, digital photographs, and computer-generated documents and data files.[2]

Much the same could be written about use of ESI in depositions. This chapter discusses what form or forms of ESI may or should be used in a deposition. It is suggested that the "default" rule is that use of a paper printout of ESI is almost universally permissible for questioning a deponent. For example, in the overwhelming majority of circumstances, there is no requirement that an interrogating attorney show a deponent metadata while questioning the deponent about a document. There may, however, be unique instances in which a deponent may legitimately object to interrogation without being shown metadata or embedded data.

The initial decision, of course, is made by the party noting the deposition. The burden should be on the party that "wants more" to show the need by a preponderance of the evidence. A failure to comply with a legitimate request to show a deponent metadata would not, in the majority of instances, be a basis for instructing a deponent to refuse to answer a deposition question.

The chapter begins with an analogy to paper, that is, questioning a deponent using a multipage letter. It proceeds to a discussion of the various forms and "flavors" of ESI that might be presented to a deponent. It then examines the application of the rule of completeness and the original document rule, and applies these doctrines to several examples. Finally, the chapter concludes with a discussion of some practical suggestions to avoid unnecessary complication by preplanning and cooperation.

2. Use of part of a paper letter in deposition: A hypothetical

We begin by examining a paper analog to the use of ESI in a deposition. The deposing attorney, whom we will call the interrogator, seeks to use information produced by the opponent in the upcoming deposition of the opponent. If the produced information was a three-page letter on paper, the interrogator would have decades of decisional authority and dozens of treatises explaining how to

2. *Lorraine*, 241 F.R.D. at 537–38 (emphasis added).

use it in the deposition. The interrogator would make three copies of the letter[3] and state: "Mr./Ms. Court Reporter, I now hand you a three-page letter dated January 1, 2009, and ask that you mark it as Jones Deposition Exhibit No. 1. Let the record reflect that I am also handing counsel for the producing party a copy of the January 1, 2009, letter." When the letter was marked, the interrogator would hand Jones Deposition Exhibit No. 1 to the deponent and ask the deponent to review it. The interrogator would then ask the deponent if he or she had sufficient time to review the exhibit, and, upon receiving an affirmative reply, would ask the deponent if the deponent recognized the letter marked as Jones Deposition Exhibit No. 1. Receiving an affirmative response, the interrogator would commence asking substantive questions.

Now, however, assume that interrogator wishes to pursue a different course. In this alternative scenario, the interrogator makes three copies, but copies only the first page of the three-page letter. The interrogator then states: "Mr./Ms. Court Reporter, I now hand you the first page of a three-page letter dated January 1, 2009, and ask that you mark it as Jones Deposition Exhibit No. 1. Let the record reflect that I am handing counsel for the producing party a copy of the first page of the January 1, 2009, three-page letter." When the page is marked, the interrogator then hands Jones Deposition Exhibit No. 1 to the deponent and asks the deponent to review it. Next, the interrogator asks the deponent if he or she has had sufficient time to review the page, and, upon receiving an affirmative reply, asks the deponent if the deponent recognizes the page marked as Jones Deposition Exhibit No. 1.

It is likely that counsel for the deponent would object and that the objection would be that it was unfair to interrogate the deponent using only a partial document. The deponent's counsel would likely demand that the interrogator provide the deponent with the full and complete letter before the deponent could be questioned about it. This would likely be couched as an objection to the form of the question.[4]

3. Assuming a two-party case, the interrogator would make one copy for the court reporter to mark as an exhibit, one copy for the deponent, and one copy for the interrogator's use during the deposition.

4. Rule 30(c)(2) states: "An objection at the time of the examination—whether to evidence, to a party's conduct, to the officer's qualifications, to the manner of taking the deposition, or to any other aspect of the deposition—must be noted on the record, but the examination still proceeds; the testimony is taken subject to any objection. An objection must be stated concisely in a nonargumentative

3. Forms of ESI that may be used in a deposition

Before analyzing that objection, it is helpful to examine the mechanics of how ESI may be used in a deposition. During the FRCP 26(f) conference of parties,[5] or in connection with FRCP 34 requests for production,[6] the litigants may have agreed to the form or forms of production of ESI. Generally speaking, ESI may be produced in native, static, or paper form. If it is in native or static form, it is likely electronically residing on an attorney's litigation support software. In these circumstances, the interrogator has a number of choices:

- The interrogating party could print on paper a copy of static-image ESI that was produced electronically, without metadata.[7]

---

and nonsuggestive manner. A person may instruct a deponent not to answer only when necessary to preserve a privilege, to enforce a limitation ordered by the court, or to present a motion under Rule 30(d)(3)."

Rule 30(d)(3) provides:

> Motion to Terminate or Limit. (A) Grounds. At any time during a deposition, the deponent or a party may move to terminate or limit it on the ground that it is being conducted in bad faith or in a manner that unreasonably annoys, embarrasses, or oppresses the deponent or party. The motion may be filed in the court where the action is pending or the deposition is being taken. If the objecting deponent or party so demands, the deposition must be suspended for the time necessary to obtain an order.

Rule 32(d)(3) addresses objections to the taking of the deposition:

> "(A) Objection to Competence, Relevance, or Materiality. An objection to a deponent's competence—or to the competence, relevance, or materiality of testimony—is not waived by a failure to make the objection before or during the deposition, unless the ground for it might have been corrected at that time.
>
> (B) Objection to an Error or Irregularity. An objection to an error or irregularity at an oral examination is waived if:
>
> (i) it relates to the manner of taking the deposition, the form of a question or answer, the oath or affirmation, a party's conduct, or other matters that might have been corrected at that time; and
>
> (ii) it is not timely made during the deposition."

5. See chapter 19.
6. See chapter 2.
7. In this chapter, the word "metadata" is generally used to incorporate all forms of metadata, including embedded data, tracked changes, and "comments." For a discussion of metadata, see chapter 6.

- The interrogating party could use a native program, for example, Word or Outlook, and print a paper copy of the native copy using the native program, without metadata.
- The interrogating party could use a native (or other) program, for example, Word or Outlook, and print a paper copy of the native copy using the native program, with some, or all, metadata printed on the paper.
- The interrogating party could use a paper copy of ESI that was produced by agreement in paper format, likely without metadata.
- The interrogating party could bring a native-format copy of the ESI, copied from counsel's computer system, to the deposition on a CD-ROM.
- The interrogating party could bring a laptop computer with native programs and electronic copies of the ESI produced by the deponent, with metadata.
- The interrogating party could use "hi-tech" presentation hardware and software to show the ESI on a large monitor.[8]

These multiple options may raise a number of questions. If the interrogating party shows the deponent a paper representation of the ESI, without metadata, is that the functional equivalent of showing only page one of a three-page letter? Or, is it different because some metadata, although available, is not generally visible on the computer monitor? Should a deponent have the right to view the comments and other embedded information before answering questions about a "document" in a deposition? Consider the situation where a deponent is being asked questions regarding the negotiating history of a commercial document that was prepared using the "track changes" option. Is it fair to permit questioning based on a paper document that obscures those changes? Is each version of the document a single document? How would an "object linked and embedded" document be handled?[9]

8. *See World's First Paperless Video Deposition System*, http://www.flixya.com/video/998915/Worlds-First-Paperless-Video-Deposition-System; *see also* B. Parker, *et al.*, *The Paperless Deposition*, UTAH BAR J., http://webster.utahbar.org/barjournal/2007/04/the_paperless_deposition.html.

9. Object linking and embedding (OLE) "is a technology that enables an application to create compound documents that contain information from a number of different sources. For example, a document in an OLE-enabled word processor can accept an embedded spreadsheet object. Unlike traditional "cut and paste" methods where the receiving application changes the format of the

Assume, for example, that there is a genuine question regarding the authenticity of an electronic document that purports to be a contract, or there is a genuine question about whether a deponent actually saw a certain email message. Assume, further, that the hidden data that would be available on an electronic, but not a paper, version would answer that question. Should a deponent be required to answer under oath without having the opportunity to view the hidden data?

Is it fair to divide up an email "string" or thread[10] when questioning a deponent? Assume that an email was sent from Mr. A to the deponent, and the deponent replied to Mr. A. Assume further that the events occurred six years ago. Is it fair to show the deponent the email from Mr. A to the deponent, without also showing at the same time the deponent's reply to Mr. A? Or, using a paper analog, is that parallel to separately marking, and using, a letter and a reply letter?

How must attachments to email be handled? At the time the email was transmitted, the sender or recipient saw the email message with the unopened attachment on the screen. Nevertheless, is it fair to show the deponent an email that had attachments—regardless of whether it is shown on paper or some other way—without simultaneously showing the attachments to the deponent? If not, how is a chain of 10 emails with eight attachments to be handled in deposition? Is each component to be marked individually, breaking up the parent-child relationship? Are they to be marked as Exhibit 1-A, 1-B, 1-C, and so on? Must the metadata and tracked changes for each document be presented to the deponent for review before questioning? The many "flavors" of ESI present multiple options.

4. The rules

A. Examination during depositions proceeds as testimony would at trial

Rule 32(a) of the Federal Rules of Civil Procedure permits deposition testimony to be used at trial only if it is admissible under the Federal Rules of Evidence. FRCP 30(c)(1) provides: "The

---

pasted information, embedded documents retain all their original properties. If the user decides to edit the embedded data, Windows activates the originating application and loads the embedded document." *OLE Concepts and Requirements Overview*, http://support.microsoft.com/kb/86008.

10. See chapter 15 for a definition of these terms.

examination and cross-examination of a deponent *proceed as they would at trial under the Federal Rules of Evidence,* except Rules 103 and 615."[11] Thus, the questioning of a deponent using ESI must proceed as it would at trial. This brings several evidentiary rules into focus. Specifically, FRE 106 addresses the complete document requirement. The original document rule is set forth in FRE 1001 et seq.[12]

B. The rule of completeness

"Long before it became a staple of movie advertisements, trial lawyers discovered that by carefully trimming a quotation they could tell the truth but use it like a lie."[13] FRE 106 provides:

> When a writing or recorded statement or part thereof is introduced by a party, an adverse party may require the introduction at that time of any other part or any other writing or recorded statement which ought in fairness to be considered contemporaneously with it.

> The Advisory Committee Notes state:

> The rule is an expression of the rule of completeness. McCormick § 56. It is manifested as to depositions in Rule 32(a)(4) of the Federal Rules of Civil Procedure, of which the proposed rule is substantially a restatement.[14]
>
> The rule is based on two considerations. The first is the misleading impression created by taking matters out of context. The second is the inadequacy of repair work when delayed to a point later in the trial. See McCormick § 56; California Evidence Code § 356. The rule does not in any way circumscribe the right of the adversary to develop the matter on cross-examination or as part of his own case.
>
> For practical reasons, the rule is limited to writings and recorded statements and does not apply to conversations.

---

11. Fed. R. Civ. P. 30(c)(1) (emphasis added).
12. FRE 901 addresses authentication, a topic addressed in chapter 24.
13. C. Wright & K. Graham, Federal Practice and Procedure § 5072.
14. Rule 32(a)(1) states that deposition testimony may be used at trial provided:

> (B) it is used to the extent it would be admissible under the Federal Rules of Evidence if the deponent were present and testifying; and
> (C) the use is allowed by Rule 32(a)(2) through (8).

Application[15] of FRE 106 to the hypothetical involving the paper letter is straightforward. If presenting the deponent with only the first page of the letter would be unfair, due, for example, to the context or the passage of time, then the deponent should be presented with the entire letter.

Application of FRCP 32(a) and FRE 106 to email, a word processing document, or a spreadsheet used in a deposition may be less clear. Certainly, as to what the deponent would have seen on the computer monitor, FRE 106 is of similar applicability. Showing half of an email that appeared on the computer monitor would be no different than using a partial letter.

What about information that would not have been seen, for example, metadata or embedded data? What about a spreadsheet formula? How does FRE 106 apply to a received email with an attachment that was viewed on the monitor without the attachment being displayed on screen? Does "fairness" demand that the metadata or attachment be "considered contemporaneously" with the portion that was viewed on the monitor?[16] The answer seems to be "it depends."

If, for example, the deponent was "blind copied" on an email and does not have an independent recollection of it, and the metadata would show that the deponent received and opened the email, an argument can be presented that, in fairness, the metadata ought to be shown to the deponent simultaneously with the email. Similarly, it would could be unfair to ask a deponent questions about an email stating only "attached please find a letter," unless the

15. The nuances of FRE 106 are beyond the scope of this chapter. "Rule 106 arises from the common law completeness doctrine. Both the common law and Rule 106 presume two tenets of the adversary system. First, under the principle of party presentation of evidence, parties—not the court—bear the responsibility to produce evidence of their respective factual claims. An important corollary of party presentation holds that neither party has any obligation to produce evidence that favors the adversary. Second, the principal of sequential procedure, sometimes called 'stage preclusion,' provides that the trial of an issue of fact follows a sequence of proof and counterproof whereby at each stage the parties alternate roles in presenting and challenging evidence. Sequential procedure resembles the game of baseball in that each side alternates turns at bat and in the field; just as the team in field cannot swing a bat, so the defendant cannot try to prove her case while the plaintiff is 'at bat.' The two tenets that give rise to Rule 106 are also embodied in Rule 611." C. WRIGHT & K. GRAHAM, FEDERAL PRACTICE AND PROCEDURE § 5072.

16. One could ask whether unseen metadata is even part of the "document" for this purpose.

attached letter was simultaneously produced.[17] It could be equally unfair to question a deponent about a reply that is divorced from the underlying message that is part of the string. And an accountant being questioned about a spreadsheet that he or she prepared or used might reasonably demand access to embedded formulae prior to being questioned.

Other instances would lead to a different result. If a deponent received an email and replied to it in the relatively recent past, there is no issue as to authenticity or receipt, and the email contains sufficient descriptive detail to trigger an average person's recollection of it, it seems unnecessary to demand production of anything more than what was visible on the computer monitor in order to question the deponent. Similarly, with regard to a "run of the mine" word processing document, it would not appear that the rule of completeness would demand showing the deponent metadata that was not visible when the deponent saw the document on screen and printed it for signature.

In short, it seems fair to conclude that there are instances, likely infrequent, where FRE 106 would require, in fairness, the interrogator to show the producing party the "complete" document, including metadata or embedded data, in deposition. The default rule, however, would be that no such need exists as a general matter. It seems equally reasonable to permit the interrogating party to make the initial choice of form and to place the burden on the objecting party that is "seeking more" to demonstrate a particularized need for that additional data.

C. The original document rule

FRE 1002 states: "To prove the content of a writing, recording, or photograph, the original writing, recording, or photograph is required, except as otherwise provided in these rules or by Act of Congress." The application of this rule to ESI was extensively discussed in *Lorraine*,[18] and will not be repeated in detail in this chapter.

FRE 1001(3) defines an "original" of a writing or recording as "the writing or recording itself or any counterpart intended to have the same effect by a person executing or issuing it. . . . If data

17. A different conclusion might be reached if the cover email stated, "Attached please find a letter summarizing our discussion last week of the green widget transaction and the price, terms, insurance obligations, and delivery methods."
18. *See* sources cited *supra* note 1; chapter 24.

are stored in a computer or similar device, any printout or other output readable by sight, shown to reflect the data accurately, is an 'original.'" Thus, as noted in *Lorraine*, the paper printout of an email, word processing document, or spreadsheet is an "original."

Furthermore, FRE 1003 states: "A duplicate is admissible to the same extent as an original unless (1) a genuine question is raised as to the authenticity of the original or (2) in the circumstances it would be unfair to admit the duplicate in lieu of the original." Under FRE 1001(4): "A 'duplicate' is a counterpart produced by the same impression as the original, or from the same matrix, . . . or by mechanical or electronic re-recording, . . . or by other equivalent techniques which accurately reproduces the original." Thus, even if the proponent was unable to lay a foundation showing that a printout was an original, a printout from a computer would likely be a duplicate, admissible to the same extent as the original, absent a genuine question as to authenticity.[19]

In sum, under FRE 1002 and FRE 1003, the original document rule generally presents no impediment to using a paper printout during a deposition, even though that printout does not show the metadata or embedded data.

5. Examples

Assume that Mr. A is being questioned about a word processing document that he generated on his computer at work. Generally, neither the rule of completeness nor the original document rule would mandate that he be shown metadata related to the author, date created, date modified, or tracked changes. If, however, the document contained a complex history of tracked changes and comments entered over an extended period of negotiations, it might be necessary under the complete document rule, in fairness, to show Mr. A those data before questioning him.

Assume that Ms. B, an accountant, is to be questioned about a complex financial computation. Assume further that she generated a multipage, multicolumn, multirow, linked spreadsheet with complex formulae embedded in it. While a paper printout would not run afoul of the original document rule, fairness under the rule of completeness might compel the interrogator to show Ms. B at least a fair representation of embedded formulae, prior to asking questions.

19. See FRE 901 regarding authentication.

Assume that ABC corporation has, in its answer to the complaint, denied receiving an email on January 1, 2009. Assume that XYZ notes the FRCP 30(b)(6) deposition of ABC for the purpose of interrogating the designee about the email. While the original document rule would not prohibit use of a paper printout, if the native file header and footer information showed routing and opening of the email, it might be necessary under the rule of completeness to show that information to the deponent in some form.[20]

6. Conclusion and practice points

As with most ESI issues, there is often no hard-and-fast rule. It may be advisable to either reach an agreement in advance of a deposition or, if agreement is not possible, at least to give an opposing deponent advance notice of the interrogating party's intention to use less than what may arguably be a full document and not show metadata, tracked changes, spreadsheet formulae, and so on.[21]

Counsel planning to take a deposition may wish to be prepared to show data hidden in critically important ESI by, for example, marking a copy on a CD-ROM as an exhibit or printing it on paper, in order to address unforeseen objections under the rule of completeness or original documents rule. An interrogating party may, in appropriate circumstances where it would not be unduly burdensome, request that a deponent that unreasonably refuses agreement to the use of printed exhibits produce some native documents at the deposition.[22] Counsel defending a deposition should be alert to situations where presenting a paper printout or a partial representation of ESI may be unfair to the deponent.

As in any deposition, the deposing party should make the initial decision. Just as, at trial, the party seeking more complete presentation has the burden of making a timely objection, the deponent

20. Obviously, these generalized examples are illustrative and not exhaustive.

21. "Counsel intending to offer into evidence less than a complete document, deposition, or other recorded statement should consider the advisability of giving all other counsel sufficient notice of such intention prior to trial. One court ruled that, if such an incomplete document or statement was to be introduced, all counsel had to be provided with 1 week's notice of the intention to do so in order that counsel representing any other party could have an opportunity to invoke Rule 106." Alois V. Gross, Annotation, *Requirement, under Rule 106 of the Federal Rules of Evidence That When Writing or Recorded Statement or Part Thereof Is Introduced in Evidence, Another Part or Another Writing or Recorded Statement Must also be Introduced in Evidence*, 75 A.L.R. Fed. 892, § 2(b).

22. Fed. R. Civ. P. 30(b)(2) and 30(f)(2).

should have the burden of presenting a "completeness" objection during a deposition. Because it is likely that the objection would be viewed as an objection to the form of the question, and one that could be obviated by the interrogating party if timely made, it is likely that a failure to present the objection would waive it.[23] An objecting party should state an objection with sufficient particularity to present the issue,[24] recognizing that courts retain substantial discretion under FRE 106.

The interrogating party may, either because of a disagreement as to the applicability of the rule of completeness or lack of preparation, choose to proceed with the deposition, notwithstanding the objection. A perceived violation of FRE 106 should not support an instruction that the deponent refuse to answer the question during the deposition.[25] While the objecting party may choose to terminate the deposition in order to seek a court determination,[26] because of the disruption inherent in that process and the court's broad discretion under FRE 106, such a step should not be taken absent facts specifically demonstrating the substantial unfairness of an interrogation absent presentation of the metadata or other hidden data.

In short, the interrogating party may seek prior agreement, but should be prepared to address objections under FRE 106 and 1001 et seq. in deposition. In appropriate circumstances, albeit generally unlikely to occur in most instances, this preparation may include presentation of metadata and other hidden or embedded information to the deponent during the deposition. The party defending the deposition should be prepared to discuss predeposition agreements, to object when FRE 106 or 1001 et seq. supports such action, and to place that objection on the record in sufficient detail to permit success at trial. Absent exceptional circumstances, the deposition should continue, and the testimony should be taken over objection and presented for a ruling at the appropriate time.

---

23. *See* FED. R. CIV. P. 32(d)(3)(B).

24. *See* FED. R. CIV. P. 30(c)(2). For example, Discovery Guideline 6(e) of the U.S. District Court for the District of Maryland provides: "If requested to supply an explanation as to the basis for an objection, the objecting attorney should do so. . . ."

25. *See* FED. R. CIV. P. 30(c)(2) and 30(d)(3).

26. *Id.*

CHAPTER 24

ADMISSIBILITY OF ELECTRONICALLY STORED INFORMATION

By Kevin F. Brady and Bryant L. Young

Obtaining electronically stored information is one thing; getting it admitted in evidence is another. Chapter 23 examined some evidentiary rules in the specific context of depositions where electronically stored information (ESI) is used. This chapter looks more broadly at the evidentiary hurdles that ESI can encounter and how those hurdles may be overcome. The chapter ends with a useful multipage graphic.

Evidentiary rules and issues concerning the admissibility of electronically stored information continue to expand and contract as advancements in digital technology evolve at an accelerated pace. Specifically, in the entire process of ESI, evidentiary considerations are "complicated by the fact that ESI comes in multiple evidentiary 'flavors,' including e-mail, website ESI, internet postings, digital photographs, and computer-generated documents and data files."[1] Therefore, ensuring the admissibility of ESI remains a foreseeable challenge to courts and lawyers as trends in evidence law spring forth from a constant digital evolution.

1. Lorraine v. Markel Am. Ins. Co., 241 F.R.D. 534, 538 (D. Md. 2007).

While everyone should agree that the Federal Rules of Evidence apply to ESI, only a small fraction of practitioners know *how* they apply. The influx of ESI and the technology for managing electronic information has caused a paradigm shift in how lawyers and judges should approach the subject of evidence and ESI. Indeed, there are new hurdles for practitioners to overcome with respect to ESI that did not exist for paper records.

1. Evidentiary hurdles

"Evidentiary hurdles," the principle determiners of ESI admissibility under the Federal Rules of Evidence, provide a reliable means of an initial assessment of ESI evidence.[2] In fact, "[f]ailure to clear any of [the] evidentiary hurdles means that the evidence will not be admissible."[3] Therefore, "[w]henever ESI is offered as evidence, either at trial or in summary judgment, these evidentiary hurdles must be considered in their entirety."[4]

The first hurdle is whether "the ESI [is] *relevant* as determined by [Federal Rule of Evidence] 401 (does it have any tendency to make some fact that is of consequence to the litigation more or less probable than it otherwise would be)."[5] The second hurdle is determining "if relevant under 401, is [the ESI] *authentic* as required by Rule 901(a) (can the proponent show that the ESI is what it purports to be)."[6] The third hurdle is "if the ESI is offered for its substantive truth, is it *hearsay* as defined by Rule 801, and if so, is it covered by an applicable exception (Rules 803, 804 and 807)."[7] The fourth hurdle is whether "the form of the ESI that is being offered as evidence is an *original* or *duplicate* under the original writing rule, if not, is there admissible secondary evidence to prove the content of the ESI (Rules 1001–1008)."[8] The fifth hurdle is whether "the probative value of the ESI is substantially outweighed by the danger of *unfair prejudice* or one of the other factors identified by Rule 403,

---

2. *Id.; see also* P. Grimm, *et al., Back to the Future:* Lorraine v. Markel American Insurance Co. *and New Findings on the Admissibility of Electronically Stored Information*, 42 Akron L. Rev. 357, 362 (2009) (identifying hurdles that must be evaluated to assess the admissibility of ESI evidence).
3. *Lorraine, Id.* at 538.
4. *Id.* at 538.
5. *Id.* at 538 (emphasis in original).
6. *Id.* at 538 (emphasis in original).
7. *Id.* at 538 (emphasis in original).
8. *Id.* at 538 (emphasis in original).

such that it should be excluded despite its relevance."[9] The *Lorraine* opinion also indicated that "[p]reliminarily, the process by which the admissibility of ESI is determined is governed by Rule 104, which addresses the relationship between the judge and the jury with regard to preliminary fact finding associated with the admissibility of evidence."[10]

The *Lorraine* opinion highlighted one of the most overlooked stages of evidentiary proceedings when Judge Grimm explained the importance for practitioners to understand "Federal Rules of Evidence 104(a) and 104(b), which deal with preliminary rulings on admissibility of evidence, existence of a privilege, and qualifications of witnesses, and the related concept of conditional relevance," prior to evaluation of the evidentiary hurdles.[11]

2. FRE 104(a) and 104(b)—rules governing the initial admissibility of evidence

Generally, information that can be used in the determination of preliminary conditions, such as relevancy and authenticity, is governed by FRE 104(a) and 104(b).[12]

FRE 104(a) provides that before evidence goes to a jury, the judge must determine whether the proponent has offered a satisfactory foundation from which the jury could reasonably find that the evidence is authentic. The information the judge uses to base his or her decision is not bound by the Federal Rules of Evidence, except those with respect to privileges.[13]

Reasons further explaining why FRE 104(a) is significant for initial consideration are as follows:

> First, it establishes the role of the trial judge as the one who must determine whether evidence is admissible, which includes the familiar foundational rulings such as whether evidence is relevant, and if so, if it is excessively prejudicial; whether an expert witness is qualified to testify, and if so whether her opinions have a sufficient factual basis and are based on reliable methodology; whether out of court statements, whether written or oral, are hearsay, and if so, whether

9. *Id.* (emphasis in original).
10. *Id.*
11. *Id.*
12. *See* Grimm *et al.*, *supra* note 2, at 362 (explaining the significance of relevancy, and that FRE 104(a) is qualified by FRE 104(b)).
13. *Id.*

> they fall within the scope of a hearsay exception; whether an evidentiary privilege applies; and when the contents of a writing, recording or photograph are being proved, whether the proof constitutes an original, duplicate, or acceptable secondary evidence of its contents under the original writing rule.[14]

FRE 104(a) is also qualified by FRE 104(b), which states: "When the relevancy of evidence depends upon the fulfillment of a condition of fact, the court shall admit it upon, or subject to, the introduction of evidence sufficient to support a finding of the fulfillment of the condition."[15]

Under FRE 104(b), when a jury actually determines authenticity, the information that it can use in its decision must be admissible under the Federal Rules of Evidence. The *Lorraine* court specifically addressed the importance of the distinction of FRE 104(a) and 104(b) with respect to ESI:

> In short, there is a significant difference between the way that Rule 104(a) and 104(b) operate. Because under Rule 104(b), the jury, not the court, makes the factual findings that determine admissibility, the facts introduced must be admissible under the rules of evidence. It is important to understand this relationship when seeking to admit ESI. For example, if an e-mail is offered into evidence, the determination of whether it is authentic would be for the jury to decide under Rule 104(b), and the facts that they consider in making this determination must be admissible into evidence. In contrast, if the ruling on whether the e-mail is an admission by a party opponent or a business record turns on contested facts, the admissibility of those facts will be determined by the judge under 104(a), and the Federal Rules of Evidence, except for privilege, are inapplicable.[16]

The *Lorraine* case further pointed out that the "interplay" between FRE 104(a) and FRE 104(b) "can be a bit tricky," since "evi-

14. Grimm *et al.*, *supra* note 2, at 363–64 (citing CHRISTOPHER B. MUELLER & LAIRD C. KIRKPATRICK, EVIDENCE 31–37 (3d ed. 2003)).

15. *Id.* at 364 (explaining that "[t]his is the so-called 'conditional relevance' rule, [which] reserves for the jury the determination of disputed facts that must be established in order for certain proffered evidence to be relevant").

16. Lorraine v. Markel Am. Ins. Co., 241 F.R.D. 534, 540 (D. Md. 2007).

dence, whether ESI or 'hard copy,' must be authenticated under Rule 901(a)."[17]

3. Relevance

The first step a court should consider when determining the admissibility of ESI is whether the evidence is relevant. To determine relevancy under FRE 401, the court must ask if the evidence has a tendency to make some fact that is of consequence to the litigation more or less probable than it otherwise would be. To be relevant, "evidence does not have to carry any particular weight—it is sufficient if it has 'any tendency' to prove or disprove a consequential fact in the litigation."[18] If the evidence is not relevant, FRE 402 unambiguously states that the evidence is not admissible. If the threshold requirement of relevancy is met, it is "presumptively admissible unless the constitution, a statute, rule of evidence or procedure, or case law requires that it be excluded."[19]

There is a distinction between admissibility and the weight given to the evidence. As the court in *Lorraine* stated:

> In assessing whether evidence is relevant under Rule 401, it also is important to remember that there is a distinction between the admissibility of evidence, and the weight to which it is entitled in the eyes of the fact finder, as Rule 104(e) instructs. To be relevant, evidence does not have to carry any particular weight—it is sufficient if it has "any tendency" to prove or disprove a consequential fact in the litigation. Whether evidence tends to make a consequential fact more probable than it would be without the evidence is not a difficult showing to make. Fed. R. Evid. 401 advisory committee's note; Saltzburg at § 401.02[1] ("To be relevant it is enough that the evidence has a *tendency* to make a consequential fact even the least bit more probable or less probable than it would be without the evidence. The question of relevance is thus different from whether evidence is *sufficient* to prove a point.") *See also Weinstein* at § 401.05–06.[20]

Specifically, FRE 403 states that "although relevant, evidence may be excluded if its probative value is substantially outweighed

---

17. *Id.* at 540.
18. *Id.* at 541.
19. *Id.* at 541 (citing Fed. R. Evid. 402).
20. *Id.* at 542.

by the danger of unfair prejudice, confusion of the issues, or misleading the jury, or by considerations of undue delay, waste of time, or needless presentation of cumulative evidence." Thus if the probative value is high enough or the danger is low enough, the evidence will be admissible. The *Lorraine* court has warned counsel to carefully evaluate "each potential basis for admissibility" with respect to ESI because "evidence that might otherwise be admitted may be excluded because the proponent put all his or her eggs in a single evidentiary basket."[21]

4. Authentication

Once relevancy is determined, the next inquiry focuses on authenticity.[22] FRE 901 requires that information must be shown to be authentic in order for it to be admissible. For instance, FRE 901(a) states that "[t]he requirement of authentication or identification as a condition precedent to admissibility is satisfied by evidence sufficient to support a finding that the matter in question is what its proponent claims." Thus, "the court need not find that the evidence is necessarily what the proponent claims, but only that there is sufficient evidence that the *jury* ultimately might do so."[23] The purpose of the authentication requirement is to require a "threshold preliminary standard to test the reliability of evidence."[24]

In the context of ESI, the *Lorraine* court noted that while "authentication of ESI may require greater scrutiny" than hard copy documents, the analysis is the same.[25] For ESI, the factors that should be considered include "the error rate in data inputting, and the security of the systems. The degree of foundation required to authenticate computer-based evidence depends on the quality and completeness of the data input, the complexity of the computer

21. *Id.* at 541.
22. *See id.* at 557 (referencing FEDERAL JUDICIAL CENTER'S MANUAL FOR COMPLEX LITIGATION § 11.447 (4th ed. 2004) (noting that "'[c]omputerized data,' however, raise unique issues concerning accuracy and authenticity . . . The proponent of computerized evidence has the burden of laying a proper foundation by establishing its accuracy").
23. United States v. Safavian, 435 F. Supp. 2d 36, 38 (D.D.C. 2006).
24. *Id.* at 544 (quoting JACK B. WEINSTEIN & MARGARET A. BERGER, WEINSTEIN'S FEDERAL EVIDENCE § 900.06[3] (Joseph M. McLaughlin ed., Matthew Bender 2d ed. 1997) [hereinafter WEINSTEIN].
25. Lorraine v. Markel Am. Ins. Co., 241 F.R.D. 534, 542–43 (D. Md. 2007).

processing, the routineness of the computer operation and the ability to test and verify results."[26]

Illustrations of various pathways to determine authenticity are explained in FRE 901(b). A nonexclusive list of illustrations that have been applied to ESI include FRE 901(1), Testimony of witness with knowledge; FRE 901(b)(3), Comparison by trier or expert witness; FRE 901(b)(4), Distinctive characteristics and the like (email address, hash values, "reply" doctrine); FRE 901(b)(7), Public records or report; and FRE 901(b)(9), Process or system.

A witness with personal knowledge under FRE 901(b) (1) can authenticate ESI by testifying that an exhibit is what it is claimed to be.[27] The witness can be the drafter of the exhibit or someone who has "personal knowledge of how that type of exhibit is routinely made."[28] The latter witness must provide facts about the method that the ESI was "created, acquired, maintained, and preserved without alteration or change."[29]

FRE 901(b)(3) permits authentication of ESI by allowing the trier of fact to compare the exhibit to an exhibit that has already been authenticated.[30] Thus, an expert witness can provide testimony that compares the exhibits or the fact finder can compare the exhibits on its own.[31]

Under FRE 901(b)(4), ESI can be authenticated or identified by "[a]ppearance, contents, substance, internal patterns, or other distinctive characteristics, taken in conjunction with circumstances." This broad rule allows for authentication based solely on circumstantial evidence. For example, one particular method of authenticating ESI under this rule is by using "hash values" or "hash marks" when marking documents. A "hash mark" is basically the "digital equivalent of a bates stamp" at the time of document creation.[32] Metadata can also be examined to determine authenticity under FRE 901(b) (4).[33] Metadata can include the document's name,

---

26. *Id.*
27. *See Lorraine*, 241 F.R.D. at 545 (citing *Safavin*, 435 F. Supp. 2d at 40 n. 2).
28. *Lorraine*, 241 F.R.D. at 545.
29. *Id.*
30. *Id.* (quoting Weinstein, *supra* note 24, § 901.03[7][b]).
31. *Id.*
32. *Id.* (quoting Fed. Judicial Ctr., Managing Discovery of Electronic Information: A Pocket Guide for Judges 24 (2007); Williams v. Sprint/United Mgmt. Co., 230 F.R.D. 640, 655 (D. Kan. 2005)); R. Losey, *HASH: The New Bates Stamp*, 12 J. Tech. Law & Policy 1 (June 2007).
33. *Id.* at 547.

location, format, type, size, creation dates, permissions, modification dates, last access dates, and more.[34]

FRE 901(b)(7) permits authentication of computerized public records. The *Lorraine* court instructed that "[t]o use [FRE 901(b)(7)], the 'proponent of the evidence need only show that the office from which the records were taken is the legal custodian of the records,'" which can be shown by a certificate or a witness.[35] FRE 901(b)(9) recognizes a method of authentication by "[e]vidence describing a process or system used to produce a result and showing that the process or system produces an accurate result."

ESI has also been authenticated under FRE 902, which allows for authentication based solely on extrinsic evidence and does not require sponsoring testimony. Three specific sections of FRE 902 that are applicable to ESI are FRE 902(5), which deals with official publications; FRE 902(7), which deals with trade inscriptions; and FRE 902(11), which concerns certified domestic records of regularly conducted activity.

FRE 902(5) allows for authentication of "official publications, books, pamphlets or other publications purporting to be issued by public authority." Under FRE 902(5), an official record is presumed authenticated on its face, although the "proponent may also need to establish that the official record qualifies as a public record hearsay exception under FRE 803(8).[36] The *Lorraine* court also suggested that "official publications posted on government agency websites should be admitted into evidence easily."[37]

In the employment compensation case of *Williams v. Long*, the plaintiffs filed for conditional class action certification and submitted several affidavits and printed web pages, obtained from various state government websites.[38] The court determined whether these printed web pages could qualify as self-authenticating official publications under FRE 902(5).[39] The court stated that accepting ESI as evidence implicates a series of "evidentiary hurdles" that must be cleared, including relevancy and authenticity.[40]

---

34. *Id.*
35. *Lorraine*, 241 F.R.D. at 548 (quoting WEINSTEIN, *supra* note 24, § 901.10[2]).
36. *Id.* at 551 (quoting WEINSTEIN, *supra* note 24, § 902.02[2]).]).
37. *Id.*
38. 585 F. Supp. 2d 679 (D. Md. 2008).
39. *Id.* at 687.
40. *See Lorraine*, 241 F.R.D. at 538 (identifying evidentiary hurdles for the admissibility of ESI).

The court held that since the web pages were printed from government websites, they were self-authenticating, official publications, and thus cleared the authentication hurdle. The court also defined the applicability of FRE 902(5) to any information posted on the Internet.[41] This resulted in the court analyzing how a "public authority" was defined under the rule, as well as an "other publication."[42] The court also noted the following:

> [First,] "Rule 902(5) [was] silent on what level of government must authorize the publication"; however, "Rule 902(5) [was] most often construed to cover the governmental bodies listed in [Rule 902(1)], which provides for self-authentication of domestic publication documents under seal." As a result, the following entities would be regarded as public authorities: "(1) the United States, (2) any State, (3) any district, commonwealth, territory, or insular possession of the United States, (4) the Panama Canal Zone, (5) the Trust Territory of the Pacific Islands, [and] (6) a political subdivision, department, officer, or agency of any of the preceding bodies." The universe of public authorities, thus, is broad. Second, [ ] Rule 902(5) would cover the self-authentication of "statute books and case reports," as well as "legislative reports, published transcripts of hearings, maps and surveys, collected statistics, commissioned studies, manuals," and "other data compilation publications from public authorities."[43]

Another avenue for self-authentication is FRE 902(7), which uses "inscriptions, signs, tags, or labels purporting to have been affixed in the course of business and indicating ownership, control, or origin." Under FRE 902(7), business records could be self-authenticated if they contain an indicium of ownership. For example, many business emails, websites, and other ESI contain the company's trademark or logo, which may be enough to self-authenticate.

FRE 902(11) allows self-authentication of those documents that are admissible under the business records hearsay exception in FRE 803(6), which requires a written declaration by the ESI's custodian or other qualified person certifying the document was kept

41. *See id.* at 685–87.

42. *Id.* at 686–87.

43. *Id.* at 686 (quoting Weinstein, *supra* note 24, § 902.07[1], at 902–29; Christopher B. Mueller & Laird C. Kirkpatrick, Federal Evidence § 9:34, at 589 (3d ed. 2007)).

in regularly conducted activity and made as a regular practice.[44] Unlike the other authentication rules, FRE 902(11) contains a notification provision, which requires "the proponent to provide written notice of the intention to use the rule to all adverse parties and to make available to them the records sufficiently in advance of litigation to permit a fair opportunity to challenge them."[45]

Each illustration is explained in further detail with respect to the specific type of ESI in section 9, *infra*.

5. Determine whether the authenticated evidence is hearsay

After establishing the authenticity of the ESI, the court must determine whether the evidence constitutes hearsay. The hearsay rule bars from evidence out-of-court statements offered to prove the truth of the matter asserted under FRE 801.

The first question for analysis with respect to hearsay is whether the evidence is a statement under FRE 801(a), which has been a frequent point of analysis in the context of ESI. For a statement to be hearsay, it must make an assertion. Nonassertive writings or writings not made by a person have been held to not be "statements."[46]

The second question for analysis is whether the statement was made by a declarant. The court in *Lorraine* specified a logical approach to this question for ESI. "When an electronically generated record is entirely the product of the functioning of a computerized system or process, such as the 'report' generated when a fax is sent showing the number to which the fax was sent and the time it was received, there is no 'person' involved in the creation of the record, and no 'assertion' being made."[47] Such a document would not be hearsay and thus be admissible.

44. *See In re* Vee Vinhnee, 336 B.R. 437, 444 (9th Cir. BAP 2005) (stating that in deciding whether to admit business records, the authenticity analysis is merged into the business record analysis).

45. *See Lorraine*, 241 F.R.D. at 551–52 (citing Weinstein, *supra* note 24, § 902.13[2]).

46. *See* United States v. Khorozian, 33 F.3d 498, 506 (3d Cir. 2003) (header and footer of text of a fax was not hearsay); United States v. Safavian, 435 F. Supp. 2d 36, 44 (D.D.C. 2006) (portions of emails making "imperative statements" that instruct or ask questions are nonassertive and not hearsay); United States v. Rollins, 2004 WL 26780, at *9 (A.F. Ct. Crim. App. Dec. 24, 2003) (holding that computer generated records are not hearsay), *rev'd on other grounds*, 61 M.J. 338 (U.S. Armed For. Aug. 25, 2005).

47. *Lorraine*, 241 F.R.D. at 564.

The third question to ask is whether the statement is being offered to prove the truth of the matter asserted under FRE 801(c). If so, the statement is hearsay and the next question would be to determine if the evidence is excluded from the definition of hearsay under FRE 801(d). If not, the statement is not hearsay and is admissible. Various examples of instances in which the court found that the statement was not being offered to prove the truth of the matter asserted include statements offered to show the communication capacity of the declarant, the effect on the hearer, circumstantial evidence of the declarant's state of mind or motive, verbal acts or parts of acts or utterances of independent legal significance, and questions or imperative commands. In the context of ESI, courts have found certain computerized documents are not hearsay. For example, in *United States v. Siddiqui* an email between the defendant and his coworker was not hearsay because it was being offered to prove that a relationship existed.[48] In *Safavian*, an email from a lobbyist to a defendant was not hearsay because it was being offered to show the nature of the lobbyist's work.[49]

6. Determine any exceptions to hearsay rule

Statements that are determined to be hearsay can still be admissible if there is an applicable hearsay exception. The first question to ask in this analysis is whether the declarant is testifying at trial. If so, FRE 801(d)(1)(A) excludes from the definition of hearsay prior inconsistent testimonial statements made under oath at a trial, hearing, court proceeding, or deposition. In other words, statements made under oath that contradict current testimony by the same declarant are not hearsay. Furthermore, FRE 801(d)(1)(B) excludes from hearsay prior consistent statements offered to rebut an express or implied allegation of recent fabrication, or improper influence or motive. And still further, FRE 801(d)(1)(C) excludes from hearsay statements of identification of a person made after perceiving that person. These three types of statements are excluded from hearsay only because the declarant is testifying at trial and subject to cross-examination. If the declarant is not testifying at trial, then the court must determine if the declarant is unavailable under FRE 804(a). If the declarant is unavailable, the statement can still be admissible if it fits within one of the following exceptions: (1) when the statement is former testimony under FRE 804(b)(1);

48. 235 F.3d 1318, 1323 (11th Cir. 2000).

49. 435 F. Supp. 2d at 44.

(2) when the statement is a dying declaration under FRE 804(b)(2); (3) when it is a statement against the declarant's interest under FRE 804(b)(3); (4) when the statement concerns family history under FRE 804(b)(4); or (5) when the declarant has forfeited the protection of the hearsay rule because of his or her own wrongdoing under FRE 804(b)(5). If any of these exceptions apply, then the statement is admissible. If the declarant is available, the analysis turns to the exceptions under FRE 803, which will be discussed below.

FRE 801(d) also excludes from the hearsay rule statements by party-opponents under certain situations. FRE 801(d)(2)(A) excludes from hearsay protection the party's own statement, made in either an individual or representative capacity. FRE 801(d)(2)(B) excludes adoptive admissions, which are statements made by another that a party has adopted or manifested a belief in its truth. FRE 801(d)(2)(C) addresses when a statement by an authorized party of the declarant is excluded from hearsay. FRE 801(d)(2)(D) excludes admissions by agents or employees of a party. Finally, FRE 801(d)(2)(E) excludes from the hearsay rule a statement made by a coconspirator in the furtherance of the conspiracy. If none of the above exceptions apply or the statement was not made by a party-opponent, the next place to look are the exceptions under FRE 803 and 807.

Several hearsay exceptions in FRE 803 have been applied to ESI.[50] These exceptions apply because there is an indicia of reliability based on the circumstances of the statement being made. These exceptions have particular applicability to ESI are outlined as follows.

A. Present sense impression under FRE 803(1)

FRE 803(1) admits hearsay evidence if a statement was made "describing or explaining an event or condition made while the declarant was perceiving the event or condition, or immediately thereafter." Thus, there are three elements to satisfy: "(1) the declarant must have personally perceived the event that is described in the statement; (2) the statement must be a simple explanation or description of the event perceived; and (3) the declaration and the event described must be contemporaneous."[51] In the context of ESI, this rule can readily apply for text messages or emails that are sent after experiencing an event, the key being whether the electronic

50. *Lorraine*, 241 F.R.D. at 569.

51. *Id.* (citing WEINSTEIN, *supra* note 24, § 803.03[1]).

communication was sent contemporaneously with the perception of the event.[52]

B. Excited utterance under FRE 803(2)

FRE 803(2) allows "a statement relating to a startling event or condition made while the declarant was under the stress of excitement caused by the event or condition." This type of evidence carries with it an indicia of reliability because a declarant is unlikely to "blurt" out an untrue statement.[53] In *Lorraine*, the court also cited *New York v. Microsoft*,[54] in which it was determined that "an e-mail prepared several days after a telephone call that described the call did not qualify as a present sense impression under FRE 803(1) because the requirement of 'contemporaneity' was not met."[55]

C. State of mind exception under FRE 803(3)

FRE 803(3) allows hearsay statements into evidence if the statement concerns the declarant's state of mind, sensation, mental, emotional, or physical condition, as well as statements of motive, intent, plan, or design. This rule can be very useful in admitting ESI, especially emails.[56] In *Lorraine*, the court also pointed out the Advisory Committee Note to FRE 803(3), which states that "[t]he exclusion of 'statements of memory or belief to prove the fact remembered or believed' is necessary to avoid the virtual destruction of the hearsay rule which would otherwise result from allowing state of mind, provable by a hearsay statement, to serve as the basis for an inference of the happening of the event which produced the state of mind."[57]

---

52. *See, e.g.*, United States v. Ferber, 966 F. Supp. 90 (D. Mass. 1997) (holding that an employee's email to his boss after a telephone call concerning a wire fraud case satisfied FRE 803(1)).
53. *See Lorraine*, 241 F.R.D. at 569–70 (explaining that "[t]he prevalence of electronic communication devices, and the fact that many are portable and small, means that people always seem to have their laptops, PDA's, and cell phones with them, and available for use to send e-mails or text messages describing events as they are happening").
54. 2002 WL 649951 (D.D.C. Apr. 12, 2002).
55. *Lorraine*, 241 F.R.D. at 570.
56. *See id.* (indicating that FRE 803(3) "is particularly useful when trying to admit e-mail, a medium of communication that seems particularly prone to candid, perhaps too-candid, statements of the declarant's state of mind, feelings, emotions, and motives").
57. *Id.*

D. Business records under FRE 803(6)

FRE 803(6) allows admission of hearsay evidence for business records made during the normal course of business. The *Lorraine* court specified four specific foundational elements that must be met in order for the business records exception to apply, specifically "(1) [t]he document must have been prepared in the normal course of business; (2) it must have been made at or near the time of the events it records; (3) it must be based on the personal knowledge of the entrant or of an informant who had a business duty to transmit the information to the entrant; and (4) to have been made in the normal course of business means that the document was made in the regular course of a regularly conducted business activity, for which it was the regular practice of the business to maintain a memorandum."[58]

Furthermore, as discussed above, the requirements of FRE 803(6) are identical to the requirements to establish self-authentication of a record under FRE 902(11).[59] Because business records can be self-authenticated and overcome the hearsay bar using the same proof, FRE 803(6) is frequently applied to ESI. Also, the fact that most business records in the world today are kept by a computer database results in extensive review of the business records exception by the courts.

Courts holding that FRE 803(6) did not apply have predominantly done so when the business record was not kept as an ordinary course of business. For example, in *New York v. Microsoft*, the court analyzed the admissibility of a particular "email chain" and held that even though the emails were prepared by an employee during the course of business, the chain did not qualify as a business record because there had been no showing that it was the regular practice of the employer to require that the employee make and maintain such emails.[60]

E. Public records or reports under FRE 803(8)

FRE 803(8) allows for admission of public records or reports if it was the government's duty to report or they regularly reported the information during its ordinary activities. As indicated in the Advisory Committee Note to FRE 803(8), "[j]ustification for the

58. *Id.* at 572 (citing WEINSTEIN, *supra* note 24, § 803.08[1]).

59. *See* Rambus v. Infineon Tech. AG, 348 F. Supp. 2d 698, 701 (E.D. Va. 2004) (holding that analysis of FRE 803(6) and 902(11) go "hand in hand").

60. 2002 WL 649951, at *9 (D.D.C. Apr. 12, 2002).

exception is the assumption that a public official will perform his duty properly, and the unlikelihood that he will remember details independently of the record." In *Lorraine*, the court pointed out that "[s]ince the assurances of accuracy are generally greater for public records than for regular business records, the proponent is usually not required to establish their admissibility through foundation testimony," and that "courts have applied this deferential standard of admissibility for electronic public records."[61]

F. Market reports, commercial publications under FRE 803(17)

FRE 803(17) allows for the admission of hearsay evidence when such information is "generally used and relied upon by the public or by persons in particular occupations." For example, in *Elliott Assoc. L.P. v. Banco de la Nacion*, the plaintiff's expert report properly relied on prime rates of interest obtained from the Federal Reserve Board website because they were reliable under FRE 803(17).[62] In *Lorraine*, it was also noted by the court that the exception covers "lists, etc., prepared for the use of a trade or profession . . . newspaper market reports, telephone directories, and city directories. The basis of trustworthiness is general reliance by the public or by a particular segment of it, and the motivation of the compiler to foster reliance by being accurate."[63]

7. Considerations under the original writing rule

The fourth hurdle in determining whether ESI is admissible has to do with what is commonly referred to as the "Best Evidence Rule" or the original writing rule, which "requires an original or duplicate original to prove the contents of a writing, recording or photograph unless secondary evidence is deemed acceptable."[64] The substance of the original writing rule is stated in FRE 1002, which mandates that "[t]o prove the content of a writing, recording, or photograph, the original writing, recording, or photograph is required, except as otherwise provided in these rules or by Act of Congress."

Under FRE 1003, "[i]f data are stored in a computer or similar device, any printout or other output readable by sight, shown to

61. *Lorraine*, 241 F.R.D. at 570 (citing WEINSTEIN, *supra* note 24, § 803.10[2]).

62. 194 F.R.D. 116, 121 (S.D.N.Y. 2000).

63. *Id.* (quoting FED. R. EVID. 803(17) advisory committee's note; WEINSTEIN, *supra* note 24, § 803.10[2])).

64. *Id.* at 576 (quoting FED. R. EVID. 1001–1008).

reflect the data accurately, is an 'original.'" Thus, "the 'original' of information stored in a computer is the readable display of the information on the computer screen, the hard drive or other source where it is stored, as well as any printout or output that may be read so long as it accurately reflects the data."[65] Furthermore, duplicates are coextensively admissible as originals unless there is a genuine issue of authenticity of the original or circumstances indicate that it would be unfair to admit a duplicate in lieu of the original. Secondary evidence can be admissible under FRE 1004 if there was a non-bad-faith loss or destruction of the original or duplicate; there was an inability to subpoena the original or duplicate; the original or duplicate is in the possession, custody, or control of the opposing party; or it is a collateral record, which is a record that is not closely related to a controlling issue in the case.[66]

FRE 1006 allows the admission of a summary of voluminous books, records, or documents as long as notice and copies were given to the opposing party in a reasonable time. FRE 1007 "allows the proof of the contents of a writing, recording or photograph by the deposition or testimony of a party opponent, without having to account for the non-production of the original."[67]

Finally, under FRE 1008, if admissibility depends on the fulfillment of a condition or fact, the question of whether the condition has been fulfilled is for the court to determine under FRE 104(a). However, the issue is reserved for the trier of fact, if it is a question of (1) whether the asserted writing ever existed; (2) whether another writing, recording, or photograph produced at trial is the original; or (3) whether other evidence of contents correctly reflects the contents, the issue is for the trier of fact.

8. Practice tips

First, be well prepared. Preparation and forethought about the details and capabilities of both your records and your client's records is the first step to navigating the ESI minefield. Starting with a defensible and comprehensive records management program will put the right foot forward.[68]

65. *Lorraine*, 241 F.R.D. at 577–78 (citing WEINSTEIN, *supra* note 24, § 900.07[1][d][iv]).
66. See chapter 10.
67. *Lorraine*, 241 F.R.D. at 577–78.
68. See chapters 5 and 12.

Second, think strategically about the case and the evidence to be admitted from the beginning. Line up the prerequisites for authentication and ensure that arguments can be made about the relevancy and the reliability of the evidence. For a discussion of how to address admissibility in Rule 26(f) conferences, see chapter 19.

Third, memorialize each step of the collection and production process to bolster reliability. In other words, keep notes about how the ESI was obtained, who obtained it, and verify its accuracy.

Fourth, use every opportunity during discovery to authenticate potential evidence. For example, under Rule 26(a), a party has 14 days to file objections to pretrial disclosures or else there is a possible waiver. Furthermore, documents produced by an opposing party are presumed to be authentic.[69] In this scenario, the burden shifts "to the producing party to demonstrate that the evidence that they produced was not authentic."[70] Another example is Rule 36, which deals with requests for admissions. Lastly, the parties can request a stipulation of authenticity.

Fifth, be prepared to provide the court with enough information to understand the technology issues as they relate to the reliability of the evidence at hand.

Sixth, be creative and consider whether there are expert witnesses or case management tools that might assist the court and the other parties in addressing evidentiary problems concerning some of the more complex issues, such as "dynamic" data in a database[71] or what is a "true and accurate copy" of ESI.

Lastly, keep your audience in mind. In other words, be cognizant of whether the characterization of the ESI will be determined by the judge or the jury as provided for under FRE 104(a) and 104(b).

---

69. *See generally Lorraine,* 241 F.R.D. at 552 (explaining that courts have "held that documents provided to a party during discovery by an opposing party are presumed to be authentic"). At least one state court, however, has held that there is no presumption of authenticity. *See* Hollie v. State, 298 Ga. App. 1, 3, 679 S.E.2d 47, 50 (2009) (establishing that "[a]s a general rule, a writing will not be admitted into evidence unless the offering party tenders proof of the authenticity or genuineness of the writing. There is no presumption of authenticity, and the burden of [ ] proof rests upon the proffering party to establish a prima facie case of genuineness.").

70. *Id.*

71. See chapter 7.

9. Illustrations of the admissibility of electronic evidence

A. Emails

The court in *Lorraine* identified various ways that emails can be authenticated under FRE 901 and 902.

First, a witness with personal knowledge under FRE 901(b)(1) can authenticate the email communication by testifying that an exhibit is what it is claimed to be.[72] As such, certainly the drafter could authenticate the email, but the email also can be authenticated by a witness having personal knowledge of how that type of exhibit is routinely made.[73] With the latter approach, however, it is necessary that the authenticating witness provide factual specificity about the process by which the email is created, acquired, maintained, and preserved.[74]

Second, expert testimony or comparison with authenticated examples under FRE 901(b)(3) can be used to authenticate emails. Under this rule, email messages "that are not clearly identifiable on their own can be authenticated . . . by comparison by the trier of fact (the jury) with 'specimens which have been [otherwise] authenticated.'"[75] For example, the court in *Safavian* recognized that emails could be compared with other emails using nicknames and other information personal to the sender and recipient.[76]

The third and most frequently used rule to authenticate email messages is FRE 901(b)(4), which allows authentication by "appearance, contents, substance, internal patterns, or other distinctive characteristics, taken in conjunction with circumstances." The commentary to the rule states that "[t]he characteristics of the offered item itself, considered in the light of circumstances, afford authentication techniques in great variety," including authenticating an exhibit by showing that it came from a "particular person by virtue of its disclosing knowledge of facts known peculiarly to him," or authenticating "by content and circumstances indicating it was in reply to a duly authenticated" document. For example, in *United States v. Siddiqui*, the court allowed authentication of an email based on the defendant's work email address, content that

72. *See Lorraine*, 241 F.R.D. at 545 (citing United States v. Safavian, 435 F. Supp. 2d 36, 40 n.2 (D.D.C. 2006) (D.D.C. 2006)).

73. *Id.*

74. *Id.*

75. *Safavin*, 435 F. Supp. 2d at 40.

76. *Id.*

the defendant was familiar with, use of the defendant's nickname, and testimony by witnesses that the defendant spoke to them about the subjects contained in the email.[77]

FRE 902 also provides two particular instances in which emails can be authenticated without the use of extrinsic evidence, particularly FRE 902(7) and 902(11).

Under FRE 902(7), no extrinsic evidence is necessary to authenticate emails displaying "trade inscriptions and the like. Inscriptions, signs, tags, or labels purporting to have been affixed in the course of business and indicating ownership, control, or origin" can be sufficient on their own to authenticate an email. As such, business emails, which often contain information detailing "the origin of the transmission and identifying the employer-company . . . may alone be sufficient to authenticate an e-mail under Rule 902(7)."[78]

FRE 902(11) also allows for authentication of business emails under the business records hearsay exception, FRE 803(6). For example, in *Lorraine*, the court indicated that emails admissible under FRE 803(6) are self-authenticating under FRE 902(11). "Email that qualifies as business record may be self-authenticating under 902(11)" and "authenticated by direct or circumstantial evidence."[79]

B. Internet website postings

Internet website postings are very common and can encompass a wide variety of ESI. Courts have permitted authentication of Internet website postings using a wide range of evidence rules, including FRE 901(b)(1), 901(b)(3), 901(b)(4), 901(b)(7), 901(b)(9), and 902(5).

Under FRE 901(b)(1), Internet website postings can be authenticated by "proof by the proponent that the organization hosting the website actually posted the statements or authorized their posting." Expert testimony or comparison with authenticated examples under FRE 901(b)(3) can also be used to authenticate Internet web postings.

Internet website postings have also been authenticated under FRE 901(b)(4), which allows for authentication based on circumstantial evidence.[80] However, the court in *Lorraine* noted a concern

77. 235 F.3d at 1322–23.

78. *See Lorraine*, 241 F.R.D. at 551–52 (citing Weinstein, *supra* note 24, § 900.07[3][c]).

79. *Id.* at 554–55 (citing Rambus v. Infineon Tech. AG, 348 F. Supp. 2d 698, 705 (E.D. Va. 2004); *In re* F.P., 878 A.2d 91, 94 (Pa. Super. Ct. 2005)).

80. *See* Grimm *et al.*, *supra* note 2, at 366.

that websites might contain information that is not officially sanctioned by the owner of the website. That concern was addressed in *Whealen v. Hartford Life and Accident Ins. Co.*, decided after *Lorraine*, where the court found that although the documents bear the URL address and date stamp, the evidence was inadmissible because the plaintiff had failed to include a "declaration by the person who personally conducted the search, or by the company stating that the computer printouts are a true and correct copy of the information from its website."[81]

C. Text messages, instant messaging, and chat rooms

The challenge in identification and authentication of this type of ESI is that the parties are typically protecting their identity using "screen names" or anonymous names. Courts have applied two avenues for authentication of text messages and chat room conversations, FRE 901(b)(1) and 901(b)(4).[82] For example, in *Adams v. Disbennett*, the plaintiff's own testimony about the text message conversation between himself and the defendant was sufficient to satisfy FRE 901(b)(1).[83] In another case, *In re F.P.*, the use of the defendant's screen name in the text message, the use of the defendant's first name, and the subject matter of the messages together authenticated the electronic communication transcripts under FRE 901(b)(4).[84] Finally, in *United States v. Simpson*, the use of the defendant's email address and his correct home address in the chat room sessions that were verified by evidence obtained at the defendants house satisfied FRE 901(b)(4).[85]

D. Computer-stored records and data

Computer-stored records and data are a very broad category that encompasses almost a limitless type of ESI documents. Courts have applied FRE 901(b)(1), 901(b)(3), 901(b)(4), and 901(b)(9) to authenticate computer-stored records and data. For example, in *United States v. Baker*, the court pointed out that the only showing required to authenticate a tip and search from Yahoo concerning the defendant's

81. No. CV06-4948PSG (PLAX), 2007 WL 1891175 (C.D. Cal. June 28, 2007).
82. *Lorraine*, 241 F.R.D. at 555 (citing United States v. Jackson, 208 F.3d 633, 638 (7th Cir. 2000); St. Luke's Cataract & Laser Inst. PA v. Sanderson, No. 8:06-CV-223-T-MSS, 2006 WL 1320242 (M.D. Fla. May 12, 2006); Wady v. Provident Life and Accident Ins. Co. of Am., 216 F. Supp. 2d 1060 (C.D. Cal. 2002)).
83. 2008 WL 4615623 (Oct. 20, 2008).
84. *In re F.P.*, 878 A.2d at 93–94 (Pa.Super. 2005).
85. 152 F.3d 1241, 1249 (10th Cir. 1998).

uploading of child pornography was to call the record custodian under FRE 901(b)(7).[86]

In *Lorraine*, the court used an 11-step foundation for computer records from Professor Edward Imwinkelried, as follows:

1. The business uses a computer.
2. The computer is reliable.
3. The business has developed a procedure for inserting data into the computer.
4. The procedure has built-in safeguards to ensure accuracy and identify errors.
5. The business keeps the computer in a good state of repair.
6. The witness had the computer readout of certain data.
7. The witness used the proper procedures to obtain the readout.
8. The computer was in working order at the time the witness obtained the readout.
9. The witness recognizes the exhibit as the readout.
10. The witness explains how he or she recognizes the readout.
11. If the readout contains strange symbols or terms, the witness explains the meaning of the symbols or terms for the trier of fact.[87]

The *Lorraine* court further recognized that other courts emphasized the importance of the accuracy of computer records.[88]

When dealing with digital images of paper records, three additional steps have been proposed for further consideration, as follows:

- The business has established policies and procedures guiding the execution of specific activities and serving to enhance the quality with which those activities are performed.

86. *See* Grimm *et al.*, *supra* note 2, at 369 (citing United States v. Baker, 538 F.3d 324 (5th Cir. 2008)).

87. *Id.* at 558 (citing *In re* Vee Vinhnee, 336 B.R. 437, 446–47 (9th Cir. BAP 2005); EDWARD J. IMWINKELRIED, EVIDENTIARY FOUNDATIONS §4.03[2] (LexisNexis 6th ed. 2005) (perceiving "electronic records as a form of scientific evidence")).

88. *See id.* (citing, for example, State v. Dunn, 7 S.W.3d 427, 432 (Mo. Ct. App. 2000) (indicating that the "'[a]dmissibility of computer-generated records 'should be determined on the basis of the reliability and accuracy of the process involved.' ").

- The business demonstrates it has created and retained "management evidence" detailing (for future quality verification) who did what, where and when in the execution of the specific activities in the regular course of business—showing that degree to which the policies and procedures were followed.
- The business manifests that its "management evidence" was regularly audited for quality—and, as part of an ongoing continuous improvement process, deficiencies were addressed and improvements were made to achieve high quality.[89]

Regarding the importance of considering these proposed additional steps, it was noted that "[i]f, at trial, the process used by the proponent of digitized records is found faulty, 'the consequence of a ruling that some or all of that small percentage [of litigation relevant documents] is inadmissible could prove very costly.' "[90]

E. Computer animations and computer simulations

Courts have applied FRE 901(b)(1) and 901(b)(3) to authenticate computer animations and computer simulations. For example, in *State v. Foreman*, authentication of computer generated fingerprint evidence was satisfied by showing the technology was sound, the user was highly trained, and the results were verified independently.[91] In *State v. Sayles*, the court noted that the authentication of computer animations could occur under FRE 901(b)(1) or 901(b)(3) if a witness could fairly and adequately portray the facts and that it will help to illustrate the testimony.[92] Furthermore, in *Clark v. Cantrell*, the court held that a "party may authenticate a video animation by offering testimony from a witness familiar with the preparation of the animation and the data on which it is based . . . [including] the testimony of the expert who prepared the underlying data and the computer technician who used that data to create it."[93] The coalescence of these cases demonstrates

89. Grimm *et al.*, *supra* note 2, at 375–76 (citing Cohasset Assocs., Inc., The Legality of Digital Image Copies of Paper Records 15–16 (Oct. 2008), http://www.cohasset.com/retrievePDF.php?id=9)).

90. *Id.* at 376 (noting a comment by Judge Ronald J. Hedges).

91. 954 A.2d 135, 157 (Conn. 2008).

92. 662 N.W.2d 1, 10 (Iowa 2003).

93. 339 S.C. 369, 391 (2000).

that the key to authenticating computer animations or simulations is to demonstrate their reliability and accuracy.

F. Digital photographs

Traditional photographs have been authenticated under FRE 901(b)(1) for decades by a "witness familiar with the scene depicted in the photograph who testifies that the photograph fairly and accurately represents the scene."[94] However, digital photographs are much more susceptible to manipulation and thus present a unique authentication problem. The court in *Lorraine* stated different authentication measures for (1) original digital images, (2) digitally converted images, and (3) digitally enhanced images.[95]

An original digital photograph is treated the same as a traditional photograph and the authentication measures are identical. For digitally converted images, authentication requires a description of the method of conversion by a person of knowledge under FRE 901(b)(1).[96] Authentication for both digitally converted and enhanced images can be obtained under FRE 901(b)(9) by showing that the conversion or enhancement process produces reliable and accurate results, which is usually shown by expert testimony.[97] Under the FRE 901(b)(9) standard, "it is common for the proponent to provide evidence of the input procedures and their accuracy and evidence that the computer was regularly tested for programming error. At a minimum, the proponent should present evidence sufficient to warrant a finding that the information is trustworthy and provide the opponent with an opportunity to inquire into the accuracy of the computer and of the input procedures."[98]

G. Cloud computing

Cloud computing provides a vehicle for users to access many applications or storage through an Internet browser without the user owning those applications or having to deal with acquisition or maintenance costs associated with the software, hardware, and applications.[99] The end user's data is stored in the cloud on

94. Lorraine v. Markel Am. Ins. Co., 241 F.R.D. 534, 561 (D. Md. 2007).

95. *Id.*

96. *Id.*

97. *Id.*

98. *See* Grimm *et al.*, *supra* note 2, at 375 (citing WEINSTEIN, *supra* note 24, § 901.12[3], at 901–1001 (2d ed. Supp. 2002)).

99. *See* Kevin F. Brady, *Cloud Computing—Is It Safe For IP?*, LAW360, Aug. 27, 2009; *see also* PETER MELL & TIM GRANCE, NAT'L INST. OF STANDARDS & TECH.,

information systems owned and operated by third parties. End users or customers can access their data whenever and wherever they choose through the Internet (cloud). According to Brady, these "[c]ustomers [pay as they go] for what they need to perform the function at hand . . . [while] the third-party cloud service providers act as technology [monitors] regulating the utilization of their technology infrastructure based on their customers ever-changing demands for applications, infrastructure or storage."[100]

One of the critical issues with ESI and litigation involves the management or control of that information. Indeed, the fundamental premise for the entire litigation continuum from retention to production involves management and control of ESI. However, cloud computing services call into question every step of that continuum, based solely on the issue of where the data resides and how the data storage is managed by service providers.

For instance, the cloud presents complicated issues concerning the gathering of electronic evidence. In particular, a third-party cloud provider will be necessary in order to obtain the information relevant to the litigation. Depending on the platform and provider, data in the cloud may not be readily accessible and/or preserved by the cloud provider. In addition, due to the ease of continuous creation, modification, and destructions of data, determining what constitutes the electronic evidence and its authentication are difficult in the cloud environment.

In light of these intricacies and complications, as forecasted by Brady, "cloud computing services will be the panacea for all of the new challenges that technology has injected into the ways companies do business"[101] and a widening area for unintended pitfalls in litigation management. Thus, from a practical standpoint, an adoption or promulgation of standards for authenticating data preserved in and obtained from the cloud is necessary. For instance, courts may implement standards in the same manner as Internet website postings, in which the courts have applied FRE 901(b)(1), 901(b)(3), 901(b)(4), and 901(b)(9), discussed *supra*.

INFO. TECH. LAB., DRAFT NIST WORKING DEFINITION OF CLOUD COMPUTING (Aug. 2009), http://csrc.nist.gov/publications/drafts/800-145/Draft-SP-800-145_cloud-definition.pdf (outlining the essential characteristics, service models, and deployment models of the evolving paradigm of clouding computing).

100. Brady, *supra* note 99.

101. *Id.*

According to Brady, customers engaging in cloud computing may be able to avoid many of the pitfalls that may occur with storing data in a cloud by addressing several issues in their service agreement before any data is remotely stored.[102] The issues/questions for consideration include the following:

- How is the company's record retention policy going to be enforced and by whom?
- How will a litigation hold be implemented?
- How will potentially relevant information be preserved?
- Will information subject to a litigation hold be segregated so as to preserve the integrity of the data (and this includes metadata)?
- Are there redundancy or backup systems; will the data be preserved?
- How will privileged, confidential, or proprietary information like intellectual property be handled in the litigation?
- When it comes to production, how will that be handled?
- Will the customer be able to manage the review and production/inspection or will the third-party provider need to be involved?

However, even with addressing these issues head-on, the area of cloud computing remains an area for determination by the rules and courts.

10. Conclusion

ESI admissibility is and will continue to be a formidable challenge as technology-driven evidentiary hurdles become more complex and inescapable. From a practical view, practitioners should start thinking about evidentiary issues as early as the preservation stage. Early case assessment is critical when dealing with electronic information in litigation. Mistakes concerning evidentiary issues made early on can become very costly later in the litigation. Moreover, a thorough understanding of the applicability of the Federal Rules of Evidence and related case law regarding ESI admissibility is essential for successfully navigating this area. Thus far, in light of the rules, the *Lorraine* decision provides the most comprehensive framework of valuable considerations that other courts and practitioners should carefully consider.

102. *Id.*

ADMISSIBILITY OF ELECTRONIC EVIDENCE

Paul W. Grimm & Kevin F. Brady

Checklist of Potential Authentication Methods

E-MAIL

- Witness with personal knowledge (901(b)(1))
- Expert testimony or comparison with authenticated examples (901(b)(3))
- Distinctive characteristics including circumstantial evidence (901(b)(4))
- Trade inscriptions (902(7))
- Certified copies of business record (902(11))

INTERNET WEBSITE POSTINGS

- Witness with personal knowledge (901(b)(1))
- Expert testimony or comparison with authenticated examples (901(b)(3))
- Distinctive characteristics including circumstantial evidence (901(b)(4))
- Public records (901(b)(7))
- System or process capable of proving a reliable result (901(b)(9))
- Official publications (902(5))

TEXT MESSAGES, TWEETS, AND THE LIKE

- Witness with personal knowledge (901(b)(1))
- Circumstantial evidence of distinctive characteristics (901(b)(4))
- Expert testimony or comparison with authenticated examples (901(b)(3))

COMPUTED STORED RECORDS AND DATA

- Witness with personal knowledge (901(b)(1))
- Expert testimony or comparison with authenticated examples (901(b)(3))
- Distinctive characteristics including circumstantial evidence (901(b)(4)
- System or process capable of proving a reliable result (901(b)(9))

COMPUTER ANIMATIONS AND COMPUTER SIMULATIONS

- Witness with personal knowledge (901(b)(1))
- Expert testimony or comparison with authenticated examples (901(b)(3))
- System or process capable of proving a reliable result (901(b)(9)

DIGITAL PHOTOGRAPHS

- Witness with personal knowledge (901(b)(1))
- System or process capable of providing reliable result (901(b)(9)

1. Preliminary Rulings on Admissibility

- Before evidence goes to jury, judge must determine whether proponent has offered satisfactory foundation (preponderance of the evidence) from which jury could reasonably find that evidence is authentic (104(a)) (FRE, except for privilege, do not apply)
- When relevance of evidence depends on a disputed antecedent fact being established ("conditional relevance"), judge determines whether a reasonable jury could find that the fact has been proved, then submits the question to jury to decide. If jury finds that the antecedent fact has been proved, it considers the evidence. If not, it does not consider it. Example: dispute on authenticity.

2. Is Evidence Relevant? FRE 401

Does it have a tendency to make some fact that is of consequence to the litigation more or less probable than it otherwise would be?

YES

FRE 401

ADMISSIBLE - Go to FRE 402

FRE 402
Does Constitution, Statute or Rule Require Exclusion?
Yes - Inadmissible
No - Admissible - Go to FRE 403

FRE 403
Is probative value substantially outweighed by:
1) Danger of unfair prejudice?
2) Confusion of the issues?
3) Misleading the jury?
4) Undue delay?
5) Waste of time?
6) Needless presentation of cumulative evidence?

NO — ADMISSIBLE
YES — INADMISSIBLE

NO

FRE 401 INADMISSIBLE

3. If Relevant, Is It Authentic? FRE 901– 902

- **FRE 901(a)** Is the evidence sufficient to support a finding that the matter in question is what proponent claims?

  Determining the degree of foundation required to authenticate electronic evidence depends on the quality and completeness of the data input, the complexity of the computer processing, the routines of the computer operation and the ability to test and verify the results.

- **FRE 901(b)**
  Non-exclusive list of examples includes:
  (1) Testimony of witness with knowledge;
  (3) Comparison by trier or expert witness;
  (4) Distinctive characteristics and the like (e-mail address, hash values, "reply" doctrine);
  (7) Public records or report; and
  (9) Process or system capable of producing a reliable result.

- **FRE 902**
  Methods by which information may be authenticated WITHOUT EXTRINSIC EVIDENCE:

  Ways to authenticate e-records:
  - 902(1)-(4) Public Records/Documents
  - 902(5) Official publications
  - 902(6) Newspapers, Magazines, Similar Publications
  - 902(7) Trade inscriptions
  - 902(11) Certified domestic records of regularly conducted activity (authenticate business records under FRE 803(6)).

4. IS EVIDENCE HEARSAY? FRE 801 (a-c)

YES

1. Is it a statement (written/spoken assertion, non-verbal/non-assertive verbal conduct intended to be assertive)?
2. Is statement made by "Declarant" (person, not generated by machine)?
3. Is statement offered for proving truth of assertion?
   NOTE: Statement is not offered for substantive truth if offered to prove:
   a. Communicative/comprehension capacity of declarant;
   b. Effect on the hearer;
   c. Circumstantial evidence of state of mind of declarant;
   d. Verbal acts/parts of acts;
   e. Utterances of independent legal significance.
4. Is statement excluded from definition of hearsay by 801(d)(1) and (2)?

Prior witness statements – 801(d)(1)

- Prior testimonial statement 801(d)(1)(A)
- Prior consistent statement 801(d)(1)(B) to rebut allegations of recent fabrication
- Statement of identification 801(d)(1)(C)

Admission by party opponents – 801(d)(2)

- Individual admission 801(d)(2)(A)
- Adoptive admission 801(d)(2)(B)
- Admission by person with authority 802(d)(2)(C)
- Admission by agent/employees 802(d)(2)(D)
- Co-conspirator statements 801(d)(2)(E)

If HEARSAY, then it is INADMISSIBLE unless covered by a recognized exception:

NO

HEARSAY EXCEPTION

Availability of Declarant Irrelevant – 803

- Present Sense Impression 803(1)
- Excited Utterance 803(2)
- State of Mind Exception 803(3)
- Statements for Purposes of Medical Diagnosis or Treatment 803(4)
- Past Recollection Recorded 803(5)
- Business Records 803(6)
- Absence of an entry in records kept in the regular course of business 803(7)
- Public Records or Reports 803(8)
- Records of Vital Statistics 803(9)
- Absence of public record or entry 803(10)
- Records/ Documents affecting interest in property 803(14) & (15)
- Statements in Ancient Documents 803(16)
- Market Reports, Commercial Publications 803(17)
- Learned Treatises 803(18)
- Character Reputation Testimony 803(21)
- Record of Felony Convictions 803(22)

Declarant Unavailable – 804

- Unavailability – 804(a)(1-5) (privilege, refused to testify, lack of memory, death/illness beyond subpoena power)
- Unavailability Exceptions – 804(b)
  - – Former Testimony 804(b)(1)
  - – Dying Declaration 804(b)(2)
  - – Statement Against Interest 804(b)(3)
  - – Statement re family history 804(b)(4)
  - – Forfeiture by wrongdoing 804(b)(6)

Residual "Catchall" Exception -- 807

6 Original Writing Rule – FRE 1001 – 1008

- Is the evidence "original", "duplicate", "writing", "recording" (1001)
- Rule 1002 requires the original to prove the contents of a writing, recording or photograph unless "secondary evidence" (any evidence other than original or duplicative) is admissible. Rules 1004, 1005, 1006, 1007.
- Duplicates are co-extensively admissible as originals unless there is a genuine issue of authenticity of the original or circumstances indicate that it would be unfair to admit duplicate in lieu of original (1003)
- Permits proof of the contents of writing, recording or paragraph by use of "secondary evidence" – any proof of the contents of a writing, recording or photograph other than the original or duplicate (1004) if:
    i. Non-bad faith loss/destruction of original/duplicate
    ii. Inability to subpoena original/duplicate
    iii. Original/duplicate in possession, custody, control of opposing party
    iv. "Collateral record" (i.e., not closely related to controlling issue in case)
- Admission of summary of voluminous books, records or documents (1006)
- Testimony or deposition of party against whom offered or by that party's written admission (FRCP 30, 33, 36) (1007)
- If admissibility depends on the fulfillment of a condition or fact, question of whether condition has been fulfilled is for fact finder to determine under 104(b) (1008)
- But, the issue is for the trier of fact, if it is a question:
    (a) whether they asserted writing ever existed;
    (b) whether another writing, recording or photograph produced at trial is the original; or
    (c) whether other evidence of contents correctly reflects the contents, the issue is for the trier of fact.

7 Practice Tips

1 Be prepared. Start with a defensible and comprehensive records management program.

2 Think strategically about the case and the evidence from the beginning of the case.

3 Memorialize each step of the collection and production process to bolster reliability.

4 Use every opportunity during discovery to authenticate potential evidence.

Examples:

a) For pretrial disclosures under F.R.C.P. 26(a)(3), you have 14 days to file objections or possible waiver;

b) Documents produced by opposing party are presumed to be authentic – burden shifts

c) F.R.C.P. 36 Requests for Admissions

d) Request stipulation of authenticity from opposing counsel

5 Be prepared to provide the court with enough information to understand the technology issues as they relate to the reliability of the evidence at hand.

6 Be creative and consider whether there are case management tools that might assist the court and the other parties in addressing evidentiary problems concerning some of the more complex issues (such as "dynamic" data in a database or what is a "true and accurate copy" of ESI).

7 Keep your audience in mind... will this be an issue for the judge or the jury? (e.g., Rule 104(a) or (b).

PART SEVEN

COST, BURDENSOMENESS, AND RESOLVING DISPUTES REGARDING E-DISCOVERY REQUESTS

CHAPTER 25

RULE 26(B)(2)(B): NOT REASONABLY ACCESSIBLE BECAUSE OF UNDUE BURDEN OR COST

By Jared S. Hosid and
Courtney Ingraffia Barton

Chapter 2 of this book included an overview of Rule 26(b)(2)(B), under which a party may object to an e-discovery request on grounds of undue burden or cost. The current chapter delves into this vital rule at greater depth, in very practical terms. It includes a look at the rule's history, the two-step analysis employed by the courts, and the possibility of cost shifting. The chapter concludes with some practice tips.

1. Introduction

Your client calls. The company has been served with a lawsuit, a consumer class action. Although the company has seen tremendous change over the past few years, including moving its headquarters across the country and implementing a new email system, fortunately, it has not been involved in much litigation.

Your first thought is to get a handle on your clients' information systems so that you can fulfill the duty to preserve. You meet with the legal department, information technology (IT), and records management and ask (what you think are) all of the right questions to cast a broad preservation net. Several months later, you are preparing your initial disclosures and you reconvene your original team to ensure you understand where you need to start looking to collect sources of electronically stored information. During that meeting someone mentions—for the first time—an electronic claims system no longer in use. You inquire further, and as it turns out, your client has not just one, but dozens of legacy applications located all over the country. Some of these systems are still accessed; others are no longer used, but the company maintains dozens and dozens of backup tapes for the systems. What do you do?

Prior to the enactment of Federal Rule of Civil Procedure 26(b)(2)(B), a party's discovery requirements regarding these types of backup tapes was unclear. Did you have to search them and disclose them for purposes of Rule 26(a)? Did they need to be preserved? What if the cost of restoring the data was more than the value of the case? What if they were incapable of being searched? What then?

Under the Federal Rules of Civil Procedure as amended in 2006, parties now have a greater understanding of their obligations to preserve[1] and disclose[2] this type of information. Although Rule 26(b)(2)(B) does not provide all of the answers, it does provide much needed guidance. This chapter will look at the addition of Rule 26(b)(2)(B) and provide some practical guidance for its application.

2. Rule 26(b)(2)(b)

As always, the text of the Rule and Committee Note is a starting point.

1. Preservation of information that is not reasonably accessible is outside of the scope of this chapter. For more information on preservation, see chapters 8 and 9. In general, however, information that is not reasonably accessible is still subject to the duty of preservation.
2. If a party is unable to access the information, it does not have to be divulged for initial disclosures because at this point the party does not know if any of the information contained therein will be used for the party's claims and defenses. For more information on initial disclosures, see chapter 13.

Rule 26. Duty to Disclose;
General Provisions Governing Discovery

(b) Discovery Scope and Limits

. . . .

(2) *Limitations on Frequency and Extent*

. . . .

(B) *Specific Limitations on Electronically Stored Information.* A party need not provide discovery of electronically stored information from sources that the party identifies as not reasonably accessible because of undue burden or cost. On motion to compel discovery or for a protective order, the party from whom discovery is sought must show that the information is not reasonably accessible because of undue burden or cost. If that showing is made, the court may nonetheless order discovery from such sources if the requesting party shows good cause, considering the limitations of Rule 26(b)(2)(C). The court may specify conditions for the discovery.

Committee Notes:

Note to Subdivision (b)(2). The amendment to Rule 26(b)(2) is designed to address issues raised by difficulties in locating, retrieving, and providing discovery of some electronically stored information. Electronic storage systems often make it easier to locate and retrieve information. These advantages are properly taken into account in determining the reasonable scope of discovery in a particular case. But some sources of electronically stored information can be accessed only with substantial burden and cost. In a particular case, these burdens and costs may make the information on such sources not reasonably accessible.

It is not possible to define in a rule the different types of technological features that may affect the burdens and costs of accessing electronically stored information. Information systems are designed to provide ready access to information used in regular ongoing activities. They also may be designed so as to provide ready access to information that is not regularly used. But a system may retain information on sources that are accessible only by incurring substantial burdens or costs. Subparagraph (B) is added to regulate discovery from such sources.

Under this rule, a responding party should produce electronically stored information that is relevant, not privileged, and reasonably accessible, subject to the (b)(2)(C) limitations that apply to all discovery. The responding party must also identify, by category or type, the sources containing potentially responsive information that it is neither searching nor producing. The identification should, to the extent possible, provide enough detail to enable the requesting party to evaluate the burdens and costs of providing the discovery and the likelihood of finding responsive information on the identified sources.

A party's identification of sources of electronically stored information as not reasonably accessible does not relieve the party of its common-law or statutory duties to preserve evidence. Whether a responding party is required to preserve unsearched sources of potentially responsive information that it believes are not reasonably accessible depends on the circumstances of each case. It is often useful for the parties to discuss this issue early in discovery.

The volume of—and the ability to search—much electronically stored information means that in many cases the responding party will be able to produce information from reasonably accessible sources that will fully satisfy the parties' discovery needs. In many circumstances the requesting party should obtain and evaluate the information from such sources before insisting that the responding party search and produce information contained on sources that are not reasonably accessible. If the requesting party continues to seek discovery of information from sources identified as not reasonably accessible, the parties should discuss the burdens and costs of accessing and retrieving the information, the needs that may establish good cause for requiring all or part of the requested discovery even if the information sought is not reasonably accessible, and conditions on obtaining and producing the information that may be appropriate.

If the parties cannot agree whether, or on what terms, sources identified as not reasonably accessible should be searched and discoverable information produced, the issue may be raised either by a motion to compel discovery or by a motion for a protective order. The parties must confer before bringing either motion. If the parties do not resolve the issue and the court must decide, the responding party must show that the identified sources of information are not reasonably accessible because of undue burden or cost. The requesting party may need discovery to test this assertion. Such discovery might take the form of requiring the responding party to conduct a sampling of information contained on the sources identified as not reasonably accessible; allowing some form of inspection of such sources; or taking depositions of witnesses knowledgeable about the responding party's information systems.

Once it is shown that a source of electronically stored information is not reasonably accessible, the requesting party may still obtain discovery by showing good cause, considering the limitations of Rule 26(b)(2)(C) that balance the costs and potential benefits of discovery. The decision whether to require a responding party to search for and produce information that is not reasonably accessible depends not only on the burdens and costs of doing so, but also on whether those burdens and costs can be justified in the circumstances of the case. Appropriate considerations may include: (1) the specificity of the discovery request; (2) the quantity of information available from other and more easily accessed sources; (3) the failure to produce relevant information that seems likely to have existed but is no longer available on more easily accessed sources; (4) the likelihood of finding relevant, responsive information that cannot be obtained from other, more easily accessed sources; (5) predictions as to the importance and usefulness of the further information; (6) the importance of the issues at stake in the litigation; and (7) the parties' resources.

The responding party has the burden as to one aspect of the inquiry—whether the identified sources are not reasonably accessible in light of the burdens and costs required to search for, retrieve, and produce whatever responsive information may be found. The requesting party has the burden of showing that its need for the discovery outweighs the burdens and costs of locating, retrieving, and producing the information. In some cases, the court will be able to determine whether the identified sources are not reasonably accessible and whether the requesting party has shown good cause for some or all of the discovery, consistent with the limitations of Rule 26(b)(2)(C), through a single proceeding or presentation. The good-cause determination, however, may be complicated because the court and parties may know little about what information the sources identified as not reasonably accessible might contain, whether it is relevant, or how valuable it may be to the litigation. In such cases, the parties may need some focused discovery, which may include sampling of the sources, to learn more about what burdens and costs are involved in accessing the information, what the information consists of, and how valuable it is for the litigation in light of information that can be obtained by exhausting other opportunities for discovery.

The good-cause inquiry and consideration of the Rule 26(b)(2)(C) limitations are coupled with the authority to set conditions for discovery. The conditions may take the form of limits on the

> amount, type, or sources of information required to be accessed and produced. The conditions may also include payment by the requesting party of part or all of the reasonable costs of obtaining information from sources that are not reasonably accessible. A requesting party's willingness to share or bear the access costs may be weighed by the court in determining whether there is good cause. But the producing party's burdens in reviewing the information for relevance and privilege may weigh against permitting the requested discovery.

3. History of the rule

Rule 26(b)(2)(B) was quite controversial when it was initially proposed.[3] Parties had previously been able to obtain discovery regarding any nonprivileged matter that was relevant to any claim or defense.[4] Under the new rule, however, an exception to the notion of broad discovery was created for information deemed "not reasonably accessible due to undue burden or cost."

The genesis of Rule 26(b)(2)(B), indeed of all of the Federal Rules related to e-discovery, was in October of 1999 shortly after the Judicial Conference approved what were to be the 2000 amendments to the rules.[5] The Civil Rules Advisory Committee met to discuss issues related to the explosion of electronic information and the impact this volume was having on the cost of discovery and the burden to the courts. Included in that discussion was the issue of "inaccessible information."[6] Meanwhile, the Sedona Conference, a legal think tank, formed a working group to address the unique discovery issues posed by electronically stored information (ESI).[7]

---

3. *See* Shira A. Scheindlin, *E-Discovery: The Newly Amended Federal Rules of Civil Procedure, in* MOORE'S FEDERAL PRACTICE (2006).

4. FED. R. CIV. P. 26(b)(1) (Scope of Discovery). Upon good cause being shown, the scope may be expanded to include all information relevant to the subject matter of the action.

5. K. Withers, *Two Tiers and Safe Harbor: Federal Rulemakers Grapple with E-Discovery,* August 23, 2004, http://www.kenwithers.com/articles/tfl0904.pdf.

6. *Id.*

7. Sedona Conference, http://www.thesedonaconference.org. For the most current thinking from the Sedona Conference on Rule 26(b)(2)(B), see THE SEDONA CONFERENCE COMMENTARY ON PRESERVATION, MANAGEMENT, AND IDENTIFICATION OF SOURCES OF INFORMATION THAT ARE NOT REASONABLY ACCESSIBLE

Judge Shira Scheindlin, U.S. District Judge for the Southern District of New York and member of the Advisory Committee on Civil Rules, has noted that those in favor of the new rule were defense-oriented attorneys who took the position that just because sources of ESI might exist somewhere, they did not have to be restored and produced for litigation—particularly if the cost and burdens of retrieving that information were significant.[8] Those opposed to the rule felt that the limitations in then-Rule 26(c) (now Rule 26(b)(2)(C)) were sufficient to safeguard against onerous discovery such that the new rule would only serve to block access to discoverable information.[9] Another concern was the difficulty of identifying "information" that was not reasonably accessible because the information could not be accessed in order to be identified.[10] The rule specifies that the *sources* of information must be identified—with enough detail to determine what those sources might contain.[11] Others were concerned that parties would purposefully make information less accessible in an attempt to thwart discovery. However, the rule requires that information must be not reasonably accessible for *all* business purposes, not just for litigation; if a party can access information for business purposes, it does not fall under Rule 26(b)(2)(B).[12]

In the end, the rule was adopted, with a notation that it will be applied on a case-by-case basis, thereby eliminating most of the aforementioned controversies while still preserving the intent of the rule, which accounts for the fact that some types of ESI can be

(2008), http://www.thesedonaconference.org/dltForm?did=NRA.pdf. For more information on the Sedona Conference's impact on e-discovery, see chapter 1.

8. *See* Scheindlin, *supra* note 3, at 15.

9. *Id.* Rule 26(b)(2)(C) is considered the rule on proportionality and outlines three factors that can limit discovery, including whether the discovery sought is unreasonably cumulative or duplicative and whether the burden and expense of the discovery outweighs the benefits.

10. Report of Civil Rules Advisory Committee (May 27, 2005, rev. July 25, 2005), www.uscourts.gov/uscourts/RulesandPolicies/rules/Reports/CV5-2005.pdf (original report).

11. *Id.* at 42. The Report of the Civil Rules Advisory Committee makes clear that even though parties will look to accessible sources first, the rule—in an improvement over past practices where parties just did not produce information that is not reasonably accessible—now requires that parties identify those sources in order to clarify and focus the issue for the requesting party.

12. *Id.* at 43.

extremely difficult to search.[13] The Civil Rules Advisory Committee also noted that in many instances the rule—often regarded as a two-tiered system—will be applied via negotiation.[14]

Rule 26(b)(2)(B) is intentionally broad. The drafters recognized that to delineate specific types of information that would be considered "not reasonably accessible" would require that the rules be constantly updated to reflect changing technologies.[15] Nevertheless, a party needs to be prepared to show that the sources are indeed not reasonably accessible. Even if that showing is made, a court may still order the discovery for good cause and may specify conditions—such as cost shifting—for the discovery.

4. The court's two-step analysis

A party may withhold ESI from sources it identifies as "not reasonably accessible because of undue burden or cost."[16] The decision to withhold ESI on these grounds should be explained to the requesting party with detail sufficient to allow an evaluation of the burdens and costs of providing the discovery and the likelihood of responsive information being found.[17] Although this may play out in the context of Rule 34 discovery requests and responses, it is

---

13. *See* Withers, *supra* note 5, at 32. The Committee Note states: "The decision whether to require a responding party to search for and produce information that is not reasonably accessible depends not only on the burdens and costs of doing so, but also on whether those burdens and costs can be justified in the circumstances of the case." FED. R. CIV. P. 26(b)(2)(B) advisory committee's note.

14. *See id.* Withers describes Rule 26(b)(2)(B) as a "two tiered system of relevance and accessibility"; Report of Civil Rules Advisory Committee, *supra* note 11.

15. *Id.* In *Zubulake III,* Judge Scheindlin attempted to categorize types of data that were considered accessible, such as active or online data and "inaccessible" data, such as backup tapes. Zubulake v. UBS Warburg LLC (*Zubulake III*), 216 F.R.D. 280 (S.D.N.Y. 2003). Since 2003, technology has changed such that backup tapes are not as costly or burdensome to produce as they once were. See appendix F. Moreover, at least one court has used Rule 26(b)(2)(B) to preclude discovery of active data that was too costly or burdensome to produce. *See* Ameriwood Indus., Inc. v. Lieberman, No. 4:06 CV 524-DJS, 2006 WL 3825291, at *3, *6 (E.D. Mo. Dec. 27, 2006), *amended by* 2007 WL 685623 (E.D. Mo. Feb. 23, 2007). As more fully discussed in this chapter, parties should look to the costs and burdens of producing certain types of information, rather than the media in which it is contained, when invoking Rule 26(b)(2)(B).

16. FED. R. CIV. P. 26(b)(2)(B).

17. *See, e.g.,* Mikron Ind., Inc. v. Hurd Windows & Doors, Inc., No. C07-532RSL, 2008 WL 1805727, at *1 (W.D. Wash. Apr. 21, 2008) ("[T]the responding party should present details sufficient to allow the requesting party to evaluate the costs and benefits of searching and producing the identified sources.").

far preferable for the parties to begin this process at the Rule 26(f) conference.[18]

A decision to withhold ESI based on the accessibility of the source may come before the court if the withholding party seeks a protective order or if the requesting party moves to compel discovery.[19] In either case, it is the withholding party that bears the burden of establishing that the ESI sought is not reasonably accessible because of undue burden or cost.[20] If this burden is met, the requesting party is given an opportunity to persuade the court that "good cause" exists to proceed with discovery notwithstanding that the search will result in undue burden or cost.[21]

A. Step one: Is the source of ESI "not reasonably accessible because of undue burden or cost"?

The rapidly evolving nature of technology makes it impractical to label certain data sources as reasonably or unreasonably accessible.[22] Rule 26(b)(2)(B) calls instead for a case-by-case analysis of whether a source can be accessed without causing the responding party "undue burden or cost."

This analysis requires the responding party to present a fact-based explanation of what would be required if it were to be ordered to comply with the discovery request.[23] Courts often expect this information to be provided in the form of live or written testimony from in-house practice technology staff or independent technical specialists.[24] Critical details include the technical characteristics of

18. *See* Report of Civil Rules Advisory Committee, *supra* note 11 ("It is often useful for the parties to discuss this issue early in discovery."); chapter 19.

19. FED. R. CIV. P. 26(b)(2)(B).

20. *Id.*

21. *Id.*

22. For a list of common factors influencing accessibility, see THE SEDONA CONFERENCE COMMENTARY ON PRESERVATION, MANAGEMENT, AND IDENTIFICATION OF SOURCES OF INFORMATION THAT ARE NOT REASONABLY ACCESSIBLE, *supra* note 7, at 12.

23. *See, e.g.*, Rodriguez-Torres v. Gov't Dev. Bank of P.R., 265 F.R.D. 40, 44 (D.P.R. 2010) ("[T]he parties were ordered to provide information on the cost and time it would take to produce the ESI requested by Plaintiffs.").

24. *See, e.g.*, Radian Asset Assur., Inc. v. Coll. of Christian Bros. of New Mexico, No. CIV 09-0885, 2010 WL 4928866, at *5 n.2 (D.N.M. Oct. 22, 2010) (requiring defendant "to produce affidavits or declarations supporting its representations regarding the cost of restoring and searching the tape backups"); Barrera v. Boughton, No. 3:07cv1436, 2010 WL 3926070, at *2–3 (D. Conn. Sept. 30, 2010) (burden met by defendants where declarations offered from two "IT experts who

the data source, how and what information is stored and retrievable, search capabilities, economic costs, disruption to business operations, required labor, and the information that is likely to be retrieved.[25] The responding party has little chance of meeting its burden if it relies on unsupported and conclusory assertions of burden and cost.[26]

Advances in technology have made it increasingly difficult for responding parties to demonstrate undue burden. A search can often be done remotely on a forensic copy of a data source, for example, thereby minimizing the disruption to business operations and reducing the risk of wear on older media and hardware.[27] Searches can now be done faster and on a wider variety of data sources than ever before, and modern databases are significantly

opine[d] that" the requested search would cost $60,000); *In re* Zurn Pex Plumbing Prods. Liab. Litig., MDL No. 08-1958, 2009 WL 1606653, at *2–3 (D. Minn. June 5, 2009) ("The affidavit of Ms. Freestone, an attorney and not an expert on document search and retrieval, is not compelling evidence that the search will be as burdensome as Zurn avers."). *But see* Bonn v. City of Omaha, No. 08-493, 2009 WL 1740783, at *2 (D. Neb. June 18, 2009) ("Upon the representations made by counsel in the defendant's brief as to cost and burden, the defendants' objections to providing further electronic discovery are sustained.").

25. *See, e.g.*, Cartel Asset Mgmt. v. Ocwen Fin. Corp., No. 01-cv-01644-REB-CBS, 2010 WL 502721, at *15 (D. Colo. Feb. 8, 2010) (proffer insufficient insofar as it lacked "specific information indicating how the [responding party] store[s] electronic information, the number of back-up or archival systems that would have to be searched . . . or Defendants' capability to retrieve information stored in those back-up or archival systems"); Yingling v. eBay, Inc., No. 09-01733, 2010 WL 373868, at *5 (N.D. Cal. Jan. 29, 2010) (responding party failed to meet its burden where it established that "potential cache of responsive documents may be significant" but did not address whether it could "formulate search queries to search its multiple proprietary systems, thus narrowing the scope of responsive documents"); Mikron Ind., Inc. v. Hurd Windows & Doors, Inc., No. C07-532RSL, 2008 WL 1805727, at *2 (W.D. Wash. Apr. 21, 2008).

26. *Cartel Asset Mgmt.*, 2010 WL 502721, at *16 ("The benefits of Rule 26(b)(2)(B) cannot be invoked on mere speculation or unsubstantiated assumptions."); Flying J Inc. v. Pilot Travel Ctrs. LLC, No. 06-0003, 2009 WL 1834998, at *2 (D. Utah. June 25, 2009) ("Plaintiffs argue that accessing the information on Plaintiffs transaction database is unreasonably burdensome, but provide no proof to support a claim of unreasonable expense."); *Mikron Ind.*, 2008 WL 1805727, at *2 (permitting discovery where responding party "offer[ed] little evidence beyond a cost estimate and conclusory characterizations of their ESI as 'inaccessible' "); City of Seattle v. Prof'l Basketball Club, LLC, No. C07-1620MJP, 2008 WL 539809, at *3 (W.D. Wash. Feb. 25, 2008) ("[A] bald assertion that discovery will be burdensome is insufficient.").

27. *See, e.g.*, Covad Commc'ns Co. v. Revonet, Inc., 258 F.R.D. 5, 12 (D.D.C. 2009).

more search-friendly than their predecessors.[28] Nevertheless, there remain circumstances where technology cannot sufficiently reduce the responding party's burden.[29]

As stated above, the case-by-case nature of Rule 26(b)(2)(B) precludes a formula for determining whether a data source is not reasonably accessible because of undue cost, and courts often blend this analysis with the contextual "good cause" analysis of Step Two (described in greater detail below).[30] As a rule, however, the responding party should not expect the court to blindly accept a high estimate; that estimate is likely to be scrutinized and, if based on an inefficient methodology, altered by the court.[31] The court may also, sua sponte, make changes to the scope of the requested

28. *See, e.g.*, Capitol Records, Inc. v. MP3TUNES, LLC, No. 07-cv-9931, 2009 WL 2568431, at *7 (S.D.N.Y. Aug. 13, 2009) ("The day undoubtedly will come when burden arguments based on a large organization's lack of internal ediscovery software will be received about as well as the contention that a party should be spared from retrieving paper documents because it had filed them sequentially, but in no apparent groupings, in an effort to avoid the added expense of file folders or indices."); W.E. Aubuchon Co., Inc. v. BeneFirst, LLC, 245 F.R.D. 38, 43 (D. Mass. 2007) (organization of ESI seemed to serve no purpose other than to "to discourage audits and the types of inquiries" at issue).

29. *See, e.g.*, Helmert v. Butterball, LLC, No. 4:08CV00342, 2010 WL 2179180, at *8 (E.D. Ark. May 27, 2010) (backup tapes inaccessible because not searchable without burdensome and costly restoration); Dilley v. Metro. Life Ins. Co., 256 F.R.D. 643, 645 (N.D. Cal. 2009) (electronic database not reasonably accessible because responding party had "no ability to query [it] in a manner that would capture" the information sought); Aguilar v. Immigration & Customs Enforcement Div. of U.S. Dep't of Homeland Sec., 255 F.R.D. 350, 360 (S.D.N.Y. 2008) (backup tapes of decentralized email system not searchable without burdensome restoration); Best Buy Stores, L.P. v. Developers Diversified Realty Corp., 247 F.R.D 567 (D. Minn. 2007) (archived database from prior litigation not reasonably accessible because of inability to conduct effective searches). *Cf.* Overlap, Inc. v. Alliance Bernstein Invs., Inc., No. 07-0161, 2008 WL 5780994, at *2 (W.D. Mo. Dec. 29, 2008) (email database reasonably accessible based on testimony that the database can be searched in-house with minimal labor); Parkdale Am., LLC v. Travelers Cas. & Sur. Co. of Am., Inc., No. 3:06CV78-R, 2007 WL 4165247, at *13 (W.D. N.C. Nov. 19, 2007) (email in LotusNotes format was reasonably accessible).

30. Peskoff v. Faber, 244 F.R.D. 54, 59 (D.D.C. 2007) (cost of discovery should not dwarf potential recovery).

31. *See, e.g.*, *In re* Zurn Pex Plumbing Prods. Liab. Litig., MDL No. 08-1958, 2009 WL 1606653, at *2–3 (D. Minn. June 5, 2009) (directing the parties to use modified search terms to more efficiently search the data source); Spieker v. Quest Cherokee, LLC, No. 07-1225, 2009 WL 2168892, at *3 (D. Kan. July 21, 2009) ("[T]here are multiple approaches to electronic discovery and alternatives for reducing costs and it appears that defendant asserts the highest estimates possible merely to support its argument that electronic discovery is unduly burdensome.").

discovery in order to reduce costs.[32] The requesting party may also influence the analysis by offering to pay for some or all of the disputed discovery, which significantly weakens the responding party's argument that the discovery is unduly costly,[33] or by presenting contrary evidence disputing the responding party's cost estimates.[34]

Although the discovery at issue will be compelled if the responding party fails to meet its burden, the converse is not necessarily true: if the producing party establishes that the source is not reasonably accessible as a result of undue burden or cost, the requesting party will have an opportunity to persuade the court that good cause nevertheless exists for the discovery to proceed.[35]

B. Step two: Has the requesting party shown "good cause," considering the limitations of Rule 26(b)(2)(c), for the discovery to be ordered?

If it is determined that the requested discovery is sought from a source that is not reasonably accessible, the requesting party is given the opportunity to demonstrate that, notwithstanding undue burden or cost, "good cause" exists for the production to be ordered.[36] This necessarily entails a closer look at "the circumstances of the case."[37]

The Advisory Committee Notes set forth seven relevant considerations:[38]

---

32. *See, e.g.*, Petcou v. C.H. Robinson Worldwide, Inc., 2008 WL 542684, at *2 (N.D. Ga. Feb. 25, 2008) (holding that a subset of the disputed discovery did not impose an undue burden on the responding party, and compelling a response to that subset).

33. *See* Conrad Jacoby, *Deconstructing the "Not Reasonably Accessible" Standard for Production of Electronically Stored Information*, LLRX.COM, Nov. 24, 2007, http://www.llrx.com/columns/fios23.htm.

34. *Cf.* Major Tours, Inc. v. Colorel, No. 05-3091, 2009 WL 3446761, at *3 (D.N.J. Oct. 20, 2009) ("It is not sufficient for plaintiffs to merely claim that defendants' estimates are exaggerated or inaccurate. Plaintiffs should have presented contrary estimates or affidavits.").

35. *See, e.g.*, W.E. Aubuchon Co., Inc. v. BeneFirst, LLC, 245 F.R.D. 38, 47 (D. Mass. 2007) (compelling production of claim forms held not to be reasonably accessible based on good cause).

36. FED. R. CIV. P. 26(b)(2)(B).

37. *See* Report of Civil Rules Advisory Committee, *supra* note 11.

38. *Cf.* Helmert v. Butterball, LLC, No. 4:08CV00342, 2010 WL 2179180, at *9 (E.D. Ark. May 27, 2010) ("A court should not treat the 'good cause' factors as a checklist; rather, the factors should be weighed by importance."); Johnson v. Neiman,

(1) the specificity of the discovery request;
(2) the quantity of information available from other and more easily accessed sources;
(3) the failure to produce relevant information that seems likely to have existed but is no longer available on more easily accessed sources;[39]
(4) the likelihood of finding relevant, responsive information that cannot be obtained from other, more easily accessed sources;
(5) predictions as to the importance and usefulness of the further information;[40]
(6) the importance of the issues at stake in the litigation; and
(7) the parties' resources.[41]

As in any discovery dispute, the court must consider the limitations of Rule 26(b)(2)(C) when analyzing whether good cause exists to order the requested discovery.[42] This involves an analysis of the "technological feasibility and realistic costs of preserving, retrieving, reviewing, and producing electronically stored information, as well as the nature of the litigation and the amount in controversy."[43]

More specifically, the court is to consider whether:

No. 4:09CV00689, 2010 WL 4065368, at *2 (E.D. Mo, Oct. 18, 2010) (finding the fifth consideration the "most significant").

39. *Cf.* Major Tours, Inc. v. Colorel, 720 F. Supp. 2d 587, 619–20 (D.N.J. 2010) (holding that "there is no bright line rule preventing a party from invoking Rule 26(b)(2)(B) when that party's negligence is responsible for the inaccessibility of the data," and affirming magistrate judge's ruling that good cause did not exist to order the disputed discovery even where the defendant failed to institute a timely and effective litigation hold).

40. Case-specific facts are generally required. *See, e.g.*, Rodriguez-Torres v. Gov't Dev. Bank of P.R., 265 F.R.D. 40, 44 (D.P.R. 2010) (journal articles "suggest[ing] that e-mail encourages senders to write unguarded, unwise and often inappropriate comments . . . not a sufficient basis to believe that" the requested email will contain such comments).

41. FED. R. CIV. P. 26(b)(2)(C) advisory committee's note.

42. FED. R. CIV. P. 26(b)(2)(B).

43. THE SEDONA CONFERENCE, THE SEDONA PRINCIPLES: BEST PRACTICES RECOMMENDATIONS & PRINCIPLES FOR ADDRESSING ELECTRONIC DOCUMENT DISCOVERY (2d ed. 2007).

(1) the discovery sought is unreasonably cumulative or duplicative, or can be obtained from some other source that is more convenient, less burdensome, or less expensive;[44]
(2) the party seeking discovery has had ample opportunity to obtain the information by discovery in the action; or
(3) the burden or expense of the proposed discovery outweighs its likely benefit, considering the needs of the case, the amount in controversy, the parties' resources, the importance of the issues at stake in the action, and the importance of the discovery in resolving the issues.[45]

It is not unusual for courts to seek additional information prior to making a final determination on good cause, usually to better understand the costs of the requested discovery and its likely results. The responding party may be ordered to conduct a sampling of the source, for example, or the parties may be ordered to obtain cost proposals from vendors.[46] The court may also seek testimony concerning what discovery has already occurred in order to assess whether further discovery is necessary.[47]

5. Cost shifting

As described above, it is possible under Rule 26(b)(2)(B) for a party to be ordered to search a source that is not reasonably accessible. Although there is a long-standing presumption that the party responding to a discovery request is responsible for the costs of complying with that request,[48] responding parties often seek to

44. *See, e.g.*, Radian Asset Assur., Inc. v. Coll. of Christian Bros. of New Mexico, No. CIV 09-0885, 2010 WL 4928866, at *5 (D.N.M. Oct. 22, 2010) (noting that backup tapes may contain nothing more than copies of the 125,000 pages of materials already produced by defendant); Calixto v. Watson Bowman Acme Corp., No. 07-60077-CIV, 2009 WL 3823390, at *12 (S.D. Fla. Nov. 16, 2009) (requesting party failed to provide good cause as to why search of backup tapes would "generate [any]thing more than [what producing party] has already produced or identified on a privilege log").

45. FED. R. CIV. P. 26(b)(2)(C)(i)–(iii).

46. *See, e.g.*, Hagemeyer N. Am., Inc. v. Gateway Data Sci. Corp., 222 F.R.D. 594, 603 (E.D. Wis. 2004) (ordering sampling); Peskoff v. Faber, 251 F.R.D. 51 (D. DC. 2008) at 60 (ordering vendor proposals).

47. *See, e.g.*, Baker v. Gerould, No. 03-CV-6558L, 2008 WL 850236 (W.D.N.Y. Mar. 27, 2008) (insufficient information in record to determine adequacy of defendants' search for responsive mails from accessible sources).

48. Oppenheimer Fund, Inc. v. Sanders, 437 U.S. 340, 358 (1978). This presumption continues to operate where the discovery sought is electronically stored information. Zubulake v. UBS Warburg LLC (*Zubulake I*), 217 F.R.D. 309, 317

shift those costs to the requesting party when required to search a source that is not reasonably accessible.[49] Courts possess the power to grant such a request,[50] but will do so only in "exceptional" circumstances.[51] (For a more in-depth look at cost shifting, see chapter 27.)

6. Conclusion and practice tips

Rule 26(b)(2)(B) is an important tool for any party concerned about the potential for runaway electronic discovery costs, as it permits a responding party to exclude from its search a source of ESI it deems to be "not reasonably accessible because of undue burden or cost." That decision, when challenged by the requesting party, triggers a two-step analysis in which the court determines (1) whether the source of ESI is, in fact, "not reasonably accessible because of undue burden or cost," and (2) if so, whether there nevertheless exists "good cause" for the discovery to proceed.

As described in greater detail above, several trends have emerged from cases that have interpreted this intentionally broad rule:

- *Courts want details.* It is no longer enough to describe cost and burden in generalities; courts now want to know precisely what will be required to comply with the discovery request, what is likely to be discovered, and how much it will cost.
- *Courts want to hear from professionals.* It is essential that cost and burden be described by in-house practice technology staff or independent technical specialists in live or written testimony.
- *Courts are increasingly skeptical of claims of undue burden.* Searches can often be swiftly completed off-site with minimal disruption or risk of data loss.

(S.D.N.Y. 2003) ("Any principled approach to electronic evidence must respect this presumption.").

49. Such a request should be made before the costs are incurred. Cason-Merenda v. Detroit Med. Ctr., No. 06-15601, 2008 WL 2714239, at *1 (E.D. Mich. Jul. 7, 2008).

50. FED. R. CIV. P. 26 advisory committee's note (2006) (court may order "payment by the requesting party of part or all of the reasonable costs of obtaining information from sources that are not reasonably accessible"); *Oppenheimer*, 437 U.S. at 358 (court may "condition[ ] discovery on the requesting party's payments of the costs of discovery").

51. Dahl v. Bain Capital Partners, LLC, No. 07-12388, 2009 WL 1748526, at *1 (D. Mass. June 22, 2009). See chapter 19 for examples.

- *Courts are increasingly hands-on.* Courts may alter or amend discovery requests, order sampling, impose search terms or protocols, shift costs, or craft other remedies to reduce the cost and burden on the responding party.

Below are some practice tips for working with Rule 26(b)(2)(B):

- Meet with your clients to discuss litigation planning, including sources of information that might not be reasonably accessible.[52]
- If possible, attempt to identify accessible sources that may be duplicative of more difficult-to-access sources.
- Address the issue of accessibility at the Rule 26(f) conference[53] or shortly after receiving the problematic discovery request. Attempt to amicably resolve the issue—perhaps by limiting the scope of the request, sharing costs, or agreeing to search terms or sampling—prior to seeking assistance from the court.
- To the extent information is no longer accessed for business purposes—and not subject to a legal hold or regulatory requirement for retention—consider deleting and discarding it.[54]
- Be prepared to show the costs and burdens of restoring any information that is not reasonably accessible through affidavits of your clients' IT specialists or independent experts.

52. For more on litigation preparedness, see chapter 12.

53. See chapter 19.

54. For further information in how to justify discarding data no longer accessed for business purposes, see THE SEDONA CONFERENCE, COMMENTARY ON INACTIVE INFORMATION SOURCES (Public Comment Version, July 2009), http://www.thesedonaconference.org; *see also* chapter 5 and chapter 11.

CHAPTER 26

CRAWLING AND INDEXING: HAVE TECHNOLOGICAL INNOVATIONS MADE DATA MORE ACCESSIBLE AND BYPASSED PORTIONS OF *ZUBULAKE*?

By Michael D. Berman, Scott Fischer, and Richard E. Davis

Some other chapters of this book have discussed possible objections to e-discovery requests on grounds of undue burden or cost—a concept introduced in the influential Zubulake *decisions and subsequently incorporated into the Federal Rules of Civil Procedure. This chapter considers the impact on such objections of newer electronic search methods that make vast searches more affordable.*

1. Introduction

Prior to the December 2006 amendments to the Federal Rules of Civil Procedure, the comprehensive *Zubulake* decisions addressed

---

This chapter is based on an article that first appeared in ABA Technology for the Litigator.

the production of electronically stored information (ESI) that was not reasonably accessible, specifically, backup tapes, using cost-shifting concepts. The December 2006 amendment to Rule 26(b)(5)(B) subsequently introduced the concept of "not reasonably accessible because of undue burden or cost." As commentator Paul Rice has noted, "[a]s hardware and software change, the currently inaccessible (or the 'difficult to access'), may become accessible. As a result, the cost-shifting precedent of the past may not be a reliable guide to how courts will rule in the future."[1]

Currently, at least five procedural devices address the proportionality requirement of the rules: (1) Rule26(b)(2)(C) (cost-benefit analysis); (2) Rule 26(b)(5)(B) (not reasonably accessible because of undue burden or cost); (3) Rule 26(g)(1)(B)(iii) (certification that discovery is "neither unreasonable nor unduly burdensome or expensive"); (4) Rule 26(c) (protective order against "oppression, or undue burden or expense"); and (5) Rule 1 (just, speedy, and inexpensive resolution of every action). Stated simply, proportionality means that a litigant need not spend $750,000 preserving and producing information in a case where the damages claimed are $75,000. Application of the principle is, however, often complex and fact-sensitive.

New high-capacity computer and network data-searching technologies have changed the cost-benefit landscape. The *Zubulake* decisions were issued between 2003 and 2005. While the December 2006 amendments did nothing to undermine the legal analysis of *Zubulake,* technological improvements have occurred that suggest rethinking the information technology aspect of those decisions, especially as they relate to disaster-recovery backup tapes. In short, if the computerization of industry has created an information overflow problem that was addressed in *Zubulake,* innovations in information technology have begun to solve it.

Zubulake was employed by UBS Warburg. She contended that she was discriminated against in employment decisions and filed suit. During discovery, UBS produced ESI. Zubulake, however, had kept copies of certain responsive email and demonstrated that UBS's production was incomplete. This led to an analysis of UBS's backup tapes. By directing restoration of a sample of backup tapes, the court quantified the value of the unreviewed data residing on

1. P. RICE, ELECTRONIC EVIDENCE: LAW AND PRACTICE 34 (ABA 2d ed. 2008) (citations omitted).

the remainder of the tapes, and determined who should bear the substantial costs of restoring, reviewing, and producing data contained on those tapes.

Much of the *Zubulake* court's factual analysis addresses the problems inherent in reviewing backup tapes. Tapes store data in a linear fashion, which effectively means that entire tapes need to be scanned before responsive data at or near the end of a backup tape can be identified and then restored. In order to verify and extract data from backup tapes, the information must first be restored to the form that it was in prior to being stored on the tape. Once the data is restored to its original native state, the data can be searched for potentially responsive information.

Indexing software has changed the technological underpinnings of *Zubulake*, while leaving its legal analysis untouched. This type of software creates an index of all of the words in a database so that a searcher may rapidly find any information in that database. For example, Windows Search, installed on many computers running Windows software, automatically indexes the computer, permitting instantaneous searches. Indexing software performs the same function on a series of backup tapes, permitting searches and retrieval without the costly restoration process described in *Zubulake*. And there are products that perform similar tasks on active data, by "crawling" through all of the data to create an index that permits rapid searches. As a result, contemporary litigants should exercise caution before assuming that *Zubulake*'s information technology analysis remains applicable in the current environment.

In short, *Zubulake* properly addressed the factual, technological, and legal issues as they existed at that time. In the years following, however, technology has advanced to suggest solutions to at least some of the problems presented to the litigants in that case. Six years is a very long time in terms of twenty-first-century computer technology, and tasks that placed significant operational pressures on corporate organizations in terms of cost and time in 2003 may be relatively simple and inexpensive in 2009.

2. Backup-tape technology at the time of *Zubulake* and today

In *Zubulake III*, the court examined the costs claimed by UBS for restoring and searching five 60-gigabyte backup tapes. The projected costs, without including infrastructure requirements, were as follows:

Task	Item	Item Cost	Total
Restoration services	Consultant time	31.5 hours @ $245	$ 7,717.50
Script creation services	Consultant time	6 hours @ $245	1,470.00
Computer use	Machine time	101.5 hours @ $18.50	1,877.75
Administration fee	Percentage	5% of services cost	459.38
Restoration cost for five tapes			$ 11,524.63

UBS then extrapolated the cost to the entire 77-tape production, which would result in tape restoration and searching costs of approximately $166,000. The court held that the data were not reasonably accessible because of undue burden or cost, and ordered partial cost shifting.

Had the same tapes been presented in 2009, the result may have differed. Newer technology can index, search, extract, and forensically copy selected files from backup tapes. One limitation of that approach is that indexing technology cannot index every conceivable tape format and backup system available on the market. However, most of today's standard backup systems can be indexed.

The indexing process avoids many of the costs attendant to prior tape-review techniques. For example, if an indexing platform is applied by a consultant, that "vendor" generally performs many or all of the services previously imposed as separate line items. An attorney could retain the consultant, who would either use an existing tape silo[2] or, if none is available, for an additional fee, place the tapes in the vendor's tape library. At that point, the tapes would be indexed and searched by the software and "hits" would be forensically preserved. Actual searching can be performed by the client or counsel and, because the software is capable of forensic preservation of the desired hits, additional consulting fees may be unnecessary. The following table provides the cost structure in an illustrative Index Engines[3] project. In this scenario, the data is stored on the vendor's site and the client may run unlimited

2. A "tape silo" is a hardware system that stores and retrieves multiple tapes.
3. Index Engines is a commercial provider of a system that indexes backup tapes.

searches for 30 days. Unlike the tape restoration option, in which the vendor is given the search terms to run, the indexing option allows attorneys to log on to the system as often as required and run as many searches as are deemed necessary. There is a one-time charge of $1,500 for setup and a monthly charge of $1,500 for five users. This charge is the same regardless of the number of tapes involved. The costs are as follows:

Task	Item	Item Cost	Total
Index, search, and extract files from tapes	Tape charge	5 tapes @ $400	$ 2,000.00
Set up data for searching	One-time charge	$1,500.00	1,500.00
Hosting—unlimited searching	Monthly hosting	$1,500.00 for 5 users	1,500.00
File extraction cost for five tapes			$ 5,000.00

Using modern indexing technology, with the stated assumptions, for 77 tapes, the cost of making the tapes instantly searchable would be $38,500 instead of $166,000. There would be additional costs, if, for example, the client lacked a tape silo and wanted the tapes to be continuously searchable, because it would then be necessary to lease a long-term storage device; however, if continued accessibility is not required, absent a client-owned silo, there would be a one-time charge for loading the tapes into a library, the cost of which would be dependent on the number of tapes and duration of the lease.

The cost disparity between restoration and indexing, however, remains substantial and it is even more pronounced because another cost that was required in 2003—the infrastructure to hold restored backup data—has been rendered insignificant due to indexing. In 2003, tape restoration required a major investment in additional storage space in order to hold the restored data. For example, restoring the 77 tapes of 60 gigabytes each involved in *Zubulake* and keeping them readily accessible would require storing 4.6 terabytes of data. Such an environment would have cost in excess of $30,000 for the hardware alone. In contrast, with tape-indexing technology, only the index needs to be stored, and that is roughly 8 percent of the data size. Applying this to the *Zubulake* tapes, only 368 gigabytes of storage, rather than 4.6 terabytes, would be needed. That difference would again significantly reduce the cost of tape review because, instead of requiring the implementation of a server environment to restore the original tapes, the index could be stored on a workstation or a $250 external USB hard drive.

In *Zubulake,* the plaintiff sought substantial damages. The $38,500 cost of an indexed tape review, even considering the added cost of an indexing platform, would most likely not result in a conclusion that the ESI was not reasonably accessible "because of undue burden or cost."

In fact, the availability of indexing also raises the question of whether data on tape will, in the future, be considered "not reasonably accessible." Judge Scheindlin provided the classic delineation between accessible and inaccessible data in *Zubulake I,* where the court wrote: "The difference between the two classes is easy to appreciate. Information deemed 'accessible' is stored in a readily usable format. Although the time it takes to actually access the data ranges from milliseconds to days, the data does not need to be restored or otherwise manipulated to be usable. 'Inaccessible' data, on the other hand, is not readily usable. Backup tapes must be restored using a process similar to that previously described . . . before the data is usable. That makes such data inaccessible." Indexing technology, however, makes data on backup tapes usable without restoration. Tapes can be indexed and searched in a tape library, without additional demands on infrastructure resources. Therefore, in some circumstances, they may no longer be viewed as inaccessible.

3. Identification, collection, and preservation

Just as the concept of "undue burden or cost" limits production of data that is not reasonably accessible, "proportionality" limits a litigant's duty vis-à-vis active ESI.[4] Imposing and monitoring a litigation hold, including locating, gathering, preserving, and culling information for responsive data, as well as production of the data to the opposing side, can be very costly. Thorough efforts in a complex case could involve identifying the data in its various locations throughout the network infrastructure; forensically collecting the data; safely copying it to a clean, "read only" location;

4. *See* P. Grimm, *et al., Proportionality in the Post-Hoc Analysis of Pre-Litigation Preservation Decisions,* 37 U. BALT. L. REV. 413 (2008), reprinted in chapter 9.

culling the data by properly designed and tested keyword searches and date range; determining which fields of metadata to export into a review platform; and providing the resulting set of information to the attorneys for privilege and responsiveness review in an appropriate format. Because employees should not review any of the potentially relevant data, let alone modify or delete it, before preservation efforts are implemented, there may be a loss of business during the preparatory period before the litigation hold is implemented, and that may require costly, expedited preservation efforts. The chart below illustrates the "hard costs" for a hypothetical 100-gigabyte set of data:

Costs of Collecting, Preserving, Culling, and Processing for Review			
Task	**Item**	**Item Cost**	**Total Cost**
Microsoft Exchange Server—data retrieval	Technician time to perform action	7 hours @ $300/hour	$ 2,100
Windows File Server—data retrieval	Technician time to perform action	7 hours @ $300/hour	2,100
30 workstations—data retrieval	Technician time to perform action	30 hours@ $300 for 30 computers	9,000
Keyword searching of 100GB of data	Vendor searching by keyword and date range of the acquired data for responsive text and/or metadata	100GB @ $50/GB	5,000
Processing of resulting data for responsiveness and privilege review	Vendor processing and online hosting for attorneys	40GB @ $450/GB	18,000
File collection and processing cost (before review)			$36,200

This example presents a relatively small case. A typical midsize corporation may deal with many similarly sized cases every year. For companies in litigious arenas, there can be many more potential litigation matters each year, and each one may require a process similar to the one described above. Obviously, the cumulative costs can become quite significant.

In the hypothetical described above, the potential litigant will expend $36,000 simply to prepare the information that needs to be reviewed for a single, anticipated lawsuit. These costs do not include attorney review or production costs and are not transferable to another, separate anticipated lawsuit. In short, they are "project-based" charges. While the volume of data is well-recognized as a key cost factor, other factors that need to be considered include the increasing complexity of the data types that comprise the growing data volume, and those factors may increase the hypothetical's cost.

There is an alternative. "Enterprise solutions" employ search and indexing technology to change the landscape of preservation and collection. Imagine a program that "crawls" the data residing on a network, including all the mail servers, file servers, Internet and intranet locations, workstations and ancillary storage devices, such as external hard drives and thumb drives. The program would function the way Google, Yahoo, Bing, and other similar search engines crawl and search the Internet. And imagine that the program indexes not only the text of every document, but its metadata as well.

This concept is now a reality, and is used by an increasing number of firms to prepare for litigation, long before it becomes "reasonably anticipated." This proactive approach means that once the "crawl" is completed, and an index is built, counsel can access a search screen and simply run queries across every indexed file on the network. Because of the high-speed nature of the indexes, a query for a series of keywords and date ranges will return search results in a matter of seconds. Once the results are displayed, they may be tagged and frozen in place—thereby instantly implementing a litigation hold. The tagging and preserving process takes a few seconds to complete. The documents are then forensically copied to a safe location, where they may be reviewed for privilege and responsiveness.

The key concept of an enterprise solution is that it is "proactive" and deploys a reusable search engine. Once the crawl is complete, the firm's data is indexed and repeatedly searchable without a new project-based expenditure. Incremental and differential crawls are conducted periodically to ensure that the index is kept up to date and new data is included in each search. Once ESI is indexed, a search can be rapidly run whenever litigation becomes reasonably anticipated. Additionally, organizations may choose to use the technology for safeguarding confidential information and for preventive searches to avoid future problems. All of this may be accomplished without the need for project-based consultants, thereby reducing the cost of collection and preservation.

Unfortunately, the initial cost of deployment of enterprise solutions currently remains high. A typical six-terabyte implementation costs approximately $250,000 to install; however, for firms faced with multiple annual preservations, or litigation involving substantial sums, the initial investment may be justified. For example, if a corporation had to impose 50 litigation holds similar to the size of the hypothetical case described above, the cost would be $1,800,000 (50 cases at $36,000 per case). If, however, an enterprise approach was implemented, the cost would drop to approximately $5,000 per case (the $250,000 spent on the software divided by 50 cases), plus some costs for in-house personnel and storage.

4. Conclusion

As predicted by Paul Rice's treatise, because of technological improvements, "the currently inaccessible (or the 'difficult to access'), may become accessible," and crawling and indexing technologies may change the technological analysis related to "proportionality" and when ESI is "not reasonably accessible because of undue burden or cost."

CHAPTER 27

COST SHIFTING IN E-DISCOVERY

BY THE HON. JAMES C. FRANCIS IV

Requests for electronically stored information in discovery sometimes give rise to applications for cost shifting. In this chapter, Judge Francis looks closely at (1) the courts' established methods of analysis for adjudicating such requests and (2) the questions that remain open on this front.

1. Overview

The costs associated with preserving, collecting, reviewing, and producing documents have traditionally been borne by the party responding to discovery requests. The explosion of electronically stored information (ESI), however, has magnified discovery costs and caused courts to consider shifting costs to the requesting party on a more frequent basis.

The Federal Rules of Civil Procedure provide little specific guidance in identifying the circumstances under which cost shifting might be appropriate. The rules do generally authorize the courts to place conditions on discovery, and the advisory committee notes indicate that these conditions may include the transfer of costs. Yet the rules do not set out criteria for determining when and how to shift discovery costs. Instead, a common law of cost shifting has developed. As courts have confronted the costs generated by e-discovery, they have fashioned a new body of law for dealing with cost allocation.

Because the jurisprudence of cost shifting has developed through case law, it is fluid. As courts encounter different factual circumstances, they add to or modify the standards that previous courts have established. At the same time, important questions remain unanswered or are the subject of disagreement among the courts. For example, even if there is a consensus about the factors to be considered in evaluating cost shifting, how are those factors to be weighed one against another? Are some factors more important than others? What is the relationship of cost shifting to the courts' well-established power to limit discovery that appears unduly costly or burdensome? Are the criteria for cost shifting the same for parties as for nonparties who are subject to subpoena? Is cost shifting limited to situations in which the information sought can be categorized as "inaccessible?"

The possibility of cost shifting also generates a variety of intensely practical issues. When, for instance, must a cost-shifting motion be made? What proof of extraordinary cost must be proffered? Must the parties' arguments be supported by expert testimony? What types of costs may be shifted? Can and should the parties consider entering into a cost-sharing agreement that obviates the need for motion practice?

This chapter addresses—but does not necessarily answer—each of these questions. It is intended to be a descriptive rather than a normative analysis, an inquiry into what the law is rather than what it ought to be.

2. Traditional cost allocation

In *Oppenheimer Fund, Inc. v. Sanders*,[1] the Supreme Court observed that the Federal Rules of Civil Procedure presume that "the responding party must bear the expense of complying with discovery requests."[2] With the exception of the cost of copying documents designated by the requesting party,[3] then, all discovery expenses are generally borne by the responding party. These may

1. 437 U.S. 340 (1978).

2. *Id.* at 358.

3. *See* Clever View Invs., Ltd. v. Oshatz, 233 F.R.D. 393, 394 (S.D.N.Y. 2006); Brassco, Inc. v. Klipo, No. 99 Civ. 3014, 2004 WL 1385816, at *5 (S.D.N.Y. June 21, 2004) ("[A] party need only make requested documents available for inspection and copying; it need not pay copying costs."); 7 MOORE'S FEDERAL PRACTICE 34.13[5], at 34-92 (2008) ("A party producing documents will ordinarily not be put to the expense of making copies for the requesting party.").

include the costs of identifying responsive information; collecting it; reviewing it for relevance, privilege, or confidentiality; and making it available to the requesting party. Courts have consistently alluded to and relied upon this presumption.[4]

The Federal Rules of Civil Procedure do not explicitly address cost shifting in discovery. Nevertheless, there is ample authority for a court to deviate from the presumption that the responding party pays. Rule 26(c) has long empowered courts to issue protective orders to shield parties from the undue burden or expense of discovery. The Supreme Court held in *Oppenheimer Fund* that remedies under this rule may include "orders conditioning discovery on the requesting party's payment of the costs of discovery."[5] Since the party opposing discovery must show good cause for the issuance of a protective order, it therefore bears the burden of proof for any shifting of discovery costs.[6]

3. The electronic environment

When technological constraints limited the volume of information that could be stored, the costs of responding to discovery requests usually remained modest in relation to the amount at stake in litigation. As a practical matter, there was simply a ceiling on the number of file cabinets filled with papers that a business was willing to maintain for an extended period. Consequently, cost shifting was rarely an issue in discovery, and the presumption that the responding party would pay its own costs for producing documents in discovery was seldom challenged.

With the advent of ESI, everything changed. "As data storage manufacturers increase storage capacities and cut costs, our electronic file cabinets are fast approaching a capacity that is effectively

4. *See, e.g.*, *In re* P.R. Elec. Power Auth., 687 F.2d 501, 507–08 (1st Cir. 1982); Peskoff v. Faber, 251 F.R.D. 59, 61 (D.D.C. 2008); Quinby v. WestLB AG, 245 F.R.D. 94, 101 (S.D.N.Y. 2006); Guy Chem. Co. v. Romaco AG, 243 F.R.D. 310, 312 (N.D. Ind. 2007); Semsroth v. City of Wichita, 239 F.R.D. 630, 633 (D. Kan. 2006); Wiginton v. CB Richard Ellis, Inc., 229 F.R.D. 568, 572 (N.D. Ill. 2004); Medtronic Sofamor Danek, Inc. v. Michelson, 229 F.R.D. 550, 553 (W.D. Tenn. 2003); Zubulake v. UBS Warburg LLC (*Zubulake I*), 217 F.R.D. 309, 316 (S.D.N.Y. 2003); Rowe Ent., Inc. v. William Morris Agency, Inc., 205 F.R.D. 421, 428 (S.D.N.Y. 2002).

5. *Oppenheimer Fund*, 437 U.S. at 358.

6. *See id.*; Hagemeyer N. Am., Inc. v. Gateway Data Scis. Corp., 222 F.R.D. 594, 600 (E.D. Wis. 2004).

infinite."[7] One court provided an illustration: "a CD-ROM's storage capacity is 650 megabytes, the equivalent of 325,000 typewritten pages; computer networks create backup data measured in terabytes—1,000,000 megabytes—which is the equivalent of 500 [m]illion typewritten pages."[8] Furthermore, companies actually use this ever-expanding capacity. Exxon Mobil has estimated that it stores 800 terabytes of information, which equates to approximately 400 billion hard-copy pages.[9]

At the same time that more information is being generated and stored, it is in some ways becoming harder to collect for purposes of discovery. It is no longer a matter simply of ascertaining who the key players are and culling their file cabinets. A party responding to discovery demands must now determine where relevant ESI might be located: in servers, desktop computers, laptops, home computers, flash drives, backup tapes, PDAs, smartphones, and any other device that stores information electronically.

ESI is also more difficult to obtain because it may not exist in an easily accessible form. "[I]n the modern computer environment, data tends to persist, often well beyond its intended useful life."[10] In part, this is because when a user deletes information from a computer file, that information generally remains in the computer's memory even if it is thereafter less accessible. "So-called 'deleted data' can continue to exist nearly forever in forms that range from immediately available to quite costly to recover, but the data is often recoverable nonetheless."[11] Similarly, information will be retained for disaster recovery purposes on backup tapes and other media, often in a form that is difficult and expensive to review.

> The data on a backup tape are not organized for retrieval of individual documents or files, but for wholesale, emergency uploading onto a computer system. Therefore, the

7. Steven C. Bennett & Thomas M. Niccum, *Two Views from the Data Mountain*, 36 CREIGHTON L. REV. 607, 609 (2003) (footnote omitted).

8. *Hagemeyer N. Am.*, 222 F.R.D. at 601 (citing MANUAL FOR COMPLEX LITIGATION, FOURTH § 11.446). Both the *Hagemeyer* case and the section of the *Manual for Complex Litigation* that it cites mistakenly equate one terabyte of information with 500 billion typewritten pages; in fact, one terabyte is equivalent to 500 million pages.

9. Ameet Sachdev, *E-Mails Become Trials for Courts: Costly Electronic Discovery "Part of Potentially Every Case in the 21st Century,"* CHI. TRIBUNE (online ed.), Apr. 10, 2005.

10. Bennett & Niccum, *supra* note 7, at 611.

11. *Id.*

organization of the data mirrors the computer's structure, not the human records management structure, if there is one.[12]

Furthermore, "[b]ackup tapes also typically employ some sort of data compression, permitting more data to be stored on each tape, but also making restoration more time-consuming and expensive, especially given the lack of uniform standard governing data compression."[13]

Increased volume and greater difficulty in collecting responsive information necessarily result in increased discovery costs. In 2004, it was estimated that over $700 million was spent annually on e-discovery, with that figure expected to rise to more than $1.8 billion within two years.[14] A recent survey of trial lawyers indicates that 87 percent of the respondents believed that electronic discovery increases the costs of litigation, while over 75 percent agreed that discovery costs, as a share of all litigation costs, had increased disproportionately as a consequence of electronic discovery.[15]

The extraordinary costs that electronic discovery can impose on a single entity are illustrated by *In re Fannie Mae Securities Litigation*.[16] There, the Office of Federal Housing Enterprise Oversight (OFHEO), a nonparty, hired 50 contract attorneys in an effort to process ESI in response to subpoenas issued by the parties to the litigation;[17] it ultimately cost OFHEO over $6 million—more than 9 percent of its entire annual budget—to comply.[18]

4. The courts' response

A. Early cases

Initially, courts took disparate approaches to the possibility of cost shifting for electronic discovery. One line of cases adhered to the

12. Kenneth J. Withers, *Computer-Based Discovery in Federal Civil Litigation*, SF97 ALI-ABA 1079, 1085 (2001).

13. Zubulake v. UBS Warburg LLC (*Zubulake I*), 217 F.R.D. 309, 319 (S.D.N.Y. 2003) (footnote omitted).

14. 80 FLA. B.J. 34, 35 (2006) (citing Lloyd S. Van Osstenrijk, *Paper or Plastic?: Electronic Discovery and Spoliation in the Digital Age*, 42 HOUS. L REV. 1163, 1186 (2005)).

15. Interim Report on the Joint Project of the American College of Trial Lawyers Task Force on Discovery and the Institute for the Advancement of the American Legal System (2008), at A-4.

16. 552 F.3d 814 (D.C. Cir. 2009).

17. *Id.* at 816.

18. *Id.* at 817. Indeed, because the OFHEO was unable to meet agreed-upon deadlines incorporated in a court order, it was held in contempt, a determination upheld on appeal. *Id.* at 818, 824.

traditional presumption that the responding party pay all costs of answering discovery demands. These cases reasoned that a party is in a position to exercise choice concerning its information system and should not be excused if its choice is accompanied by added litigation costs. This viewpoint is illustrated by *In re Brand Name Prescription Drugs Antitrust Litigation*,[19] where the court observed that "if a party chooses an electronic storage method, the necessity for a retrieval program or method is an ordinary and foreseeable risk."[20]

Other cases rejected the logic that responding to all electronic discovery requests is simply the cost of doing business in the digital age. In *McPeek v. Ashcroft*,[21] the court reasoned that there is really no option of doing without computers:

> It is impossible to walk ten feet into the office of a private business or government agency without seeing a network computer, which is on a server, which, in turn, is being backed up on tape (or some other media) on a daily, weekly or monthly basis. What alternative is there? Quill pens?[22]

Commentators, too, challenged that view that the traditional presumption should apply with full force to electronic discovery. One noted that the court in *In re Brand Name Prescription Drugs* "demonstrated its lack of a true understanding of today's technological world . . . [by] effectively punishing the defendants simply for using technology consistent with normal practices of the time."[23]

Some cases evinced a greater willingness to consider cost shifting. For example, in *Bills v. Kennecott Corp.*,[24] the court identified a series of factors that might be considered in determining that a responding party would be subject to an undue burden unless some of the costs associated with electronic discovery were transferred to the requesting party. Nevertheless, in that case the court declined to shift costs because:

---

19. Nos. 94 C 897, MDL 997, 1995 WL 360526 (N.D. Ill. June 15, 1995).
20. *Id.* at *2.
21. 202 F.R.D. 31 (D.D.C. 2001).
22. *Id.* at 33.
23. Corrine L. Giacobbe, *Allocating Discovery Costs in the Computer Age: Deciding Who Should Bear the Costs of Discovery of Electronically Stored Data*, 57 WASH. & LEE L. REV. 257, 285 (2000).
24. 108 F.R.D. 459 (D. Utah 1985).

> (1) The amount of money involved is not excessive or inordinate; (2) The relative expense and burden in obtaining the data would be substantially greater to the requesting party as compared with the responding party; (3) The amount of money required to obtain the data as set forth by the defendant would be a substantial burden to plaintiffs; [and] (4) The responding party is benefitted in its case to some degree by producing the data in question.[25]

Indeed, given that the costs involved were only $5,411.25,[26] it is hardly surprising that the court did not feel compelled to depart from the traditional presumption.

B. *McPeek*—the marginal utility test

One of the first cases to attempt a comprehensive approach to cost shifting in e-discovery was *McPeek*. There the court was confronted with a dispute over which party should bear the expense of restoring from backup tapes email that was no longer available in the responding party's active computer files.[27] Initially, the court recognized that it was presented with a problem unique to ESI. "In a traditional 'paper case,' the producing party searches . . . files [that] are traditionally organized by subject or chronology ('chron' files), such as all files of a particular person, independent of subject."[28] Such a straightforward approach was not possible with backup tapes: "Backup tapes are by their nature indiscriminate. They capture all information at a given time and from a given server but do not catalogue it by subject matter."[29]

The court then considered the two possible bright line rules: the traditional presumption that the responding party bear the burden and the alternative principle that a requesting party be required to pay for the discovery it seeks. The court rejected the first alternative on the ground that "making the producing party pay for all costs of restoration as a cost of its 'choice' to use computers creates a disincentive for the requesting party to demand anything less than all of the tapes."[30] The court then spurned the "market approach" as well, pointing out that if backup tapes contain relevant

25. *Id.* at 464.
26. *Id.* at 460.
27. 202 F.R.D. at 32.
28. *Id.* at 32–33.
29. *Id.* at 33.
30. *Id.*

information, "shifting all costs to the requesting party means that the requesting party will have to pay for the [responding party] to search the backup tapes even though the requesting party would not have to pay for such a search of a 'paper' depository."[31]

Instead of selecting either bright line rule, the court adopted an approach based on the economic concept of marginal utility:

> The more likely it is that the backup tape contains information that is relevant to a claim or defense, the fairer it is that the [responding party] search at its own expense. The less likely it is, the more unjust it would be to make the [responding party] search at its own expense. The difference is "at the margin."[32]

The court concluded by requiring the responding party to search a discrete sample of the backup tapes to ascertain the likelihood that a more comprehensive analysis would unearth relevant information.[33]

C. *Rowe*—the multifactor analysis

The next major case to address cost shifting was *Rowe Entertainment, Inc. v. William Morris Agency, Inc.*[34] As in *McPeek*, the central issue was which party would assume the expenses for restoring and searching backup tapes. And, like in the *McPeek* case, the court began by considering allocation schemes that would impose costs on either the requesting party or the responding party uniformly in every case. First, the court questioned the force of the traditional presumption in a world of computers where information was retained not necessarily because it was essential to ongoing business needs but merely because costs of storage had become so low that there was no compelling reason to discard data.[35] Moreover, much of the information that is retained is not readily accessible,

31. *Id.*
32. *Id.*
33. *Id.* at 34–35. Following completion of this sampling procedure, the parties disagreed as to the significance of the information obtained. However, the court found that tapes were available only for certain limited periods, only one of which was likely to yield relevant information. Accordingly, the court required restoration of a single tape, apparently at the cost of the producing party. McPeek v. Ashcroft, 212 F.R.D. 33, 34, 36 (D.D.C. 2003).
34. 205 F.R.D. 421 (S.D.N.Y. 2002). The author of this chapter wrote the *Rowe* opinion.
35. *Id.* at 429.

as it is stored on media such as the backup tapes at issue.[36] But the court likewise rejected the "market approach" that would impose the costs of production on the requesting party, which could perform a cost-benefit analysis to determine whether the discovery was worthwhile.

> First, [the market approach] flies in the face of the well-established principle . . . that the responding party will pay the expenses of production. Second, it places a price on justice that will not always be acceptable: it would result in the abandonment of meritorious claims by litigants too poor to pay for necessary discovery.[37]

The court then went on to identify eight factors to be considered in determining when costs should be shifted to the requesting party.

(1) Specificity of requests

First, the court found that the broader the discovery demands, the greater the justification for shifting costs to the discovering party. "Where a party multiplies litigation costs by seeking expansive rather than targeted discovery, that party should bear the expense."[38]

(2) Likelihood of a successful search

Drawing on *McPeek*, the next factor the court identified was the marginal value of the suggested discovery: the likelihood that a search would turn up at least relevant, and perhaps critical, information.[39]

(3) Availability from other sources

The third factor considered by the court was whether the requested information might be available from another source. If so, the court would be more justified in relieving the responding party of the costs associated with production and imposing them on the requesting party.[40]

36. *Id.*
37. *Id.*
38. *Id.* at 430.
39. *Id.*
40. *Id.*

(4) Purposes of retention

Next, the court reasoned that if a party maintains ESI in connection with its current activities, it should be expected to respond to discovery requests at its own expense. Conversely, if it retained data for disaster recovery or merely because it neglected to discard it, there would be more justification for shifting the costs of production to the requesting party. Backup tapes and deleted emails would generally fall into the latter category.[41]

(5) Benefit to the parties

The production of some information may benefit the responding party as much as the requesting party, either because it serves a business interest for that party or is useful to it in the pending litigation. The court found that in such circumstances, the responding party should continue to bear the costs. On the other hand, where only the requesting party would benefit from the production, cost shifting is more likely warranted.[42]

(6) Total costs

The court found the total cost of the requested discovery to be a relevant consideration. Where the cost is expected to be insubstantial, there would be no reason to deviate from the traditional presumption and consider cost shifting at all.[43]

(7) Ability to control costs

Imposing the costs of production on the party best able to control them creates an incentive for that party to utilize the most efficient methods. Consequently, the *Rowe* court considered this to be another significant factor.[44]

(8) The parties' resources

Finally, the court found the ability of each party to bear the costs of discovery to be an important consideration. It noted that "[i]n some cases, the cost, even if modest in absolute terms, might outstrip the resources of one of the parties, justifying an allocation of those expenses to the other."[45]

41. *Id.* at 430–31.
42. *Id.* at 431.
43. *Id.*
44. *Id.* at 431–32.
45. *Id.* at 432.

The court weighed each of these factors to determine whether cost shifting was warranted. It found, first, that the plaintiffs' "extremely broad" and "nebulous" discovery requests favored shifting the costs to them. Next, the court observed that although some relevant information was likely to be obtained, the marginal value of searching the backup tapes would be modest at best, a factor that also supported cost shifting. On the other hand, the requested information was not available from other sources, and this consideration tilted in favor of requiring the defendants to bear their own costs of production. The fact that the requested information had been maintained for disaster relief purposes and was not used in routine business activities was a further factor militating in favor of cost shifting. So, too, was the fact that the defendants would derive no benefit from collecting the information, which was irrelevant both to their business needs and to any burden of proof they might have in the litigation. The substantial costs involved in restoring the backup tapes as well as the plaintiffs' ability to control those costs by sampling and staging discovery also supported shifting the costs to them. The last factor—the resources of the parties—was neutral, since both sides were capable of devoting substantial resources to discovery. On balance, the court found that the relevant factors tipped heavily in favor of the defendants and ordered that the plaintiffs bear the costs of restoring and searching the backup tapes.[46]

D. *Zubulake*—the multifactor analysis refined

(1) Prerequisites for considering cost shifting

In *Zubulake v. UBS Warburg LLC*,[47] the court confronted yet another request to shift the costs of discovery relating to backup tapes, this time in the context of a claim of employment discrimination. As a threshold matter, the court rejected the proposition that cost shifting should be available in every case involving electronic discovery. First, the presumption that the responding party bears the cost of complying with discovery requests—a principle endorsed by the Supreme Court—demanded respect.[48] Second, since cost shifting could effectively end discovery, particularly in cases where one party had vastly more resources than the other, its overuse

46. *Id.* at 430–32.

47. 217 F.R.D. 309 (S.D.N.Y. 2003).

48. *Id.* at 317.

could jeopardize meritorious litigation.[49] Accordingly, the court determined that "cost-shifting should be considered *only* when electronic discovery imposes an 'undue burden or expense' on the responding party."[50]

Next, the court rejected any assumption that electronic evidence necessarily engenders undue burden and expense. Rather, the court linked burden and expense to the accessibility or inaccessibility of the data at issue. As the court pointed out, even paper documents may be considered inaccessible under some circumstances. Such documents include "(a) documents in storage in a difficult to reach place; (b) documents converted to microfiche and not easily readable; or (c) documents kept haphazardly, with no indexing system, in quantities that make page-by-page searches impracticable."[51] With respect to ESI, the court suggested that active, online data; near-line data stored, for example, on optical disks; and information stored offline as in archives would generally be considered accessible.[52] By contrast, information contained in backup tapes or data that had been erased, damaged, or fragmented would be presumed inaccessible.[53]

(2) Modifications to **Rowe**

The court then proceeded to consider the appropriate standard for cost shifting. Because the court believed that the *Rowe* factors generally favored cost shifting,[54] it modified that test by eliminating some considerations, adding others, and suggesting that some factors should be weighed more heavily than others. First, the court found the cost of production to be less relevant in absolute terms than in relation to the amount in controversy in the litigation.[55] Similarly, any test should consider the relative ability of the parties to pay for discovery, though the court noted that this may have been implicit in *Rowe*.[56] Furthermore, the court found that "the importance of the issues at stake in the litigation" is a key issue,

49. *Id.* at 317–18.

50. *Id.* at 318 (quoting Fed. R. Civ. P. 26(c)).

51. *Id.*

52. *Id.* at 318–19.

53. *Id.* at 319–20.

54. *Id.* at 320. For a contrary view, see Jessica Lynn Repa, *Adjudicating Beyond the Scope of Ordinary Business: Why the Inaccessibility Test in Zubulake Unduly Stifles Cost-Shifting During Electronic Discovery*, 54 Am. U. L. Rev. 257 (2004).

55. *Zubulake I*, 217 F.R.D. at 321.

56. *Id.*

as in environmental cases, law reform litigation, and cases raising constitutional issues.[57] The court then combined the first and second *Rowe* factors—the specificity of the discovery request and the likelihood of a successful search—into a single consideration: "the extent to which the request is specifically tailored to discover relevant information."[58] Finally, the court reasoned that although the purpose for which a party maintained data was related to the accessibility of the information, these concepts were not identical, and it therefore declined to consider the former factor.[59]

(3) The reformulated test

On the basis of these modifications, the *Zubulake* court crafted a new test that analyzed seven factors:

1. The extent to which the request is specifically tailored to discover relevant information;
2. The availability of such information from other sources;
3. The total cost of production, compared to the amount in controversy;
4. The total cost of production, compared to the resources available to each party;
5. The relative ability of each party to control costs and its incentive to do so;
6. The importance of the issues at stake in the litigation; and
7. The relative benefits to the parties of obtaining the information.[60]

The court, however, made it clear that these factors should not simply be "added up" as if each were equally significant. Rather, the factors should be weighted in descending order of importance. The court considered the first two factors, which it characterized as comprising the marginal utility test, as the most important.[61] It noted that the sixth factor—the importance of the litigation—would rarely come into play but could potentially predominate over all other factors.[62] Finally, the court considered the seventh factor—the relative benefit of the production to each party—to be

57. *Id.*
58. *Id.*
59. *Id.* at 321–22.
60. *Id.* at 322.
61. *Id.* at 323.
62. *Id.*

shifting but did not rule it out.[70] The court found the relative ability of each party to control costs to be neutral since neither party was in a position to further refine the discovery requests or control the vendor's methods of restoring the backup tapes.[71]

The court determined that the question of the importance of the issues in the litigation was also a neutral consideration. While discrimination in the work place is a "weighty issue," the court found nothing unique about the issues in that litigation.[72]

Lastly, the court concluded that the defendant would not have voluntarily restored the tapes because it would not likely benefit from obtaining the evidence they contained. Therefore, the relative benefit to the parties favored cost shifting.[73]

The court then translated its analysis of the factors into an allocation of costs. First, it found that the costs should be split between the parties:

> Because some of the factors cut against cost shifting, but only *slightly so*—in particular, the possibility that the continued production will produce valuable new information—some cost-shifting is appropriate in this case, although [the defendant] should pay the majority of the costs. There is plainly relevant evidence that is only available on [the defendant's] backup tapes. At the same time, [the plaintiff] has not been able to show that there is indispensable evidence on those backup tapes[.][74]

The court then observed that since the seven-factor test implied that the defendant should shoulder the majority of the costs, the plaintiff should necessarily pay less than 50 percent. Moreover, imposing too great a share on a plaintiff could chill litigants from exercising their right to bring meritorious claims. On the other hand, because the success of the search would be somewhat speculative, it was necessary to protect the defendant from undue costs. In light of all of these considerations, the court assigned the costs of restoring and searching the backup tapes 75 percent to the defendant and 25 percent to the plaintiff.[75]

---

70. *Id.* at 288.
71. *Id.*
72. *Id.* at 289.
73. *Id.*
74. *Id.*
75. *Id.*

5. Open questions

The multifactor analysis is now widely utilized as the standard for determining when and to what extent discovery costs associated with ESI should be shifted.[76] Questions remain, however, with respect to the details of its application.

A. Threshold determinations

One issue that has continued to befuddle the courts is whether there should be an initial hurdle of some sort that must be overcome before cost shifting will even be considered. *Zubulake* was ambiguous on this point. First, as noted above, the court announced that cost shifting should not even be considered unless the requested discovery would impose "undue burden or expense" on the responding party.[77] The court then reasoned that "[t]he burden or expense of discovery is, in turn, 'undue' when it 'outweighs its likely benefit, taking into account the needs of the case, the amount in controversy, the parties' resources, the importance of the issues in the litigation, and the importance of the proposed discovery in resolving the issues.' "[78] Yet the court went on to suggest that "whether production of documents is unduly burdensome or expensive turns primarily on whether it is kept in an *accessible or inaccessible* format (a distinction that corresponds closely to the expense of production)."[79] This formulation, however, focused solely on costs and did not account for the other factors—the resources of the parties, the importance of the litigation, and the like—that the court had previously identified as relevant to the threshold determination of whether the requested discovery threatened to create an undue burden.

This ambiguity has been reflected in subsequent cases. For example, in *Mikron Industries, Inc. v. Hurd Windows & Doors, Inc.*,[80] the court adopted the accessibility/inaccessibility standard as the threshold test for whether to consider cost shifting. Citing *Zubulake*,

76. *See, e.g.*, Major Tours, Inc. v. Colorel, No. 05-3091, 2009 WL 3446761, at *5 (D.N.J. Oct. 20, 2009); Sue v. Milyard, No. 07-cv-1711, 2009 WL 1504747, at *1 (D. Colo. May 26, 2009).

77. Zubulake v. UBS Warburg LLC (*Zubulake I*), 217 F.R.D. 309, 318 (S.D.N.Y. 2003) (quoting FED. R. CIV. P. 26(c)); *accord* Cronas v. Willis Group Holdings, Ltd., No. 06 Civ. 15295, at *4 (S.D.N.Y. Oct. 8, 2008).

78. *Zubulake I*, 217 F.R.D. at 318 (quoting FED. R. CIV. P. 26(b)(2)(iii), since redesignated as 26(b)(2)(C)).

79. *Id.*

80. No. C 07-532, 2008 WL 1805727 (W.D. Wash. Apr. 21, 2008).

the court stated that "[c]ost-shifting would not be appropriate in the context of [searching employee hard drives], as this ESI is considered reasonably accessible within the meaning of Fed. R. Civ. P. 26(b)(2)(C)."[81] By contrast, in *Parkdale America LLC v. Travelers Casualty & Surety Co. of America*,[82] although the court found that the requested information was stored in accessible media, it did not automatically reject cost shifting but instead took into account additional factors including the parties' resources and the importance of the discovery in resolving critical issues.[83]

To the extent that accessibility is an important factor in the cost-shifting analysis, a related question is whether cost shifting is ever available with respect to information that is reasonably accessible. A number of courts have stated unequivocally that cost shifting is simply not appropriate unless the data at issue are inaccessible.[84] Others have entertained the possibility of cost allocation even where the information is apparently readily accessible.[85] A possible explanation for this seeming disagreement may lie in the definition of accessibility. Although the court in *Zubulake* referred to categories of media as typically accessible or inaccessible, it also suggested that its categorization was directly related to the normal costs of obtaining information from each medium.[86] The subsequent amendments to the Federal Rules of Civil Procedure make explicit this linkage between accessibility and cost. They refer to information that "is not reasonably accessible *because of undue*

81. *Id.* at *2.

82. No. 3:06 CV 78, 2007 WL 4165247 (W.D.N.C. Nov. 19, 2007).

83. *Id.* at *12–13.

84. *See* Peskoff v. Faber, 251 F.R.D. 59, 61 (D.D.C. 2008); Cason-Merenda v. Detroit Med. Ctr., No. 06-15601, 2008 WL 2714239, at *3 (E.D. Mich. July 7, 2008); Quinby v. WestLB AG, 245 F.R.D. 94, 101–02 (S.D.N.Y. 2006); OpenTV v. Liberate Techs., 219 F.R.D. 474, 476 (N.D. Cal. 2003).

85. *See* W.E. Aubuchon Co. v. Benefirst, LLC, 245 F.R.D. 38, 42–43 (D. Mass. 2007) (finding data accessible under *Zubulake* "media based analytical approach" but nevertheless considering cost shifting because of high cost of retrieval); Morgenstern v. Int'l Alliance of Theatrical Stage Employees, Local 16, No. C 05-03156, 2006 WL 2385233, at *5 (N.D. Cal. Aug. 17, 2006) (considering but ultimately rejecting cost-shifting application in connection with paper documents); Multitechnology Servs., L.P. v. Verizon Sw. F/K/A GTE Sw. Inc., No. 4:02-CV-702, 2004 WL 1553480, at *1 (N.D. Tex. July 12, 2004) (splitting costs of production of accessible information).

86. Zubulake v. UBS Warburg LLC (*Zubulake I*), 217 F.R.D. 309, 318–20 (S.D.N.Y. 2003).

burden or cost."[87] Thus, while some backup media may be inaccessible due to the expense involved in restoring data to an active form, other backup media will be reasonably accessible because technology permits restoration at minimal cost. As long as accessibility is defined in terms of cost, then it is correct that cost shifting should not be considered unless the information sought is abnormally expensive to access.[88] Conversely, if accessibility refers to different forms of media by category, then it is equally correct that cost shifting may occasionally be available even for data from sources usually recognized as readily accessible.

An alternative (or supplemental) threshold is the absolute cost of the requested discovery. In *Oppenheimer Fund*, the Supreme Court pointed out that in some cases there is no need to consider cost shifting because the expense involved is likely "so insubstantial as not to warrant the effort required to calculate it and shift it to the [requesting party]."[89] Other courts, however, have engaged in a cost-shifting analysis even where the costs at issue are quite modest. For example, in *Semsroth v. City of Wichita*,[90] the court engaged in a full-blown cost-shifting exercise even though the cost of compliance with the discovery requests was anticipated to be approximately $2,624.95.[91] The court reasoned that "even a very slight inconvenience may be unreasonable if there is no occasion for the inquiry and it cannot benefit the party making it."[92]

B. The meaning of hierarchy

Courts continue to tinker with the list of factors considered in determining whether to shift costs. In *Semsroth*, for example, the

87. FED. R. CIV. P. 26(b)(2)(B) (emphasis added).

88. Indeed, by these terms, traditional paper discovery could be subject to cost shifting in the unusual circumstance that the cost or burden of production would render the information "inaccessible." *See Zubulake I*, 217 F.R.D. at 318 ("Examples of inaccessible paper documents could include (a) documents in storage in a difficult to reach place; (b) documents converted to microfiche and not easily readable; or (c) documents kept haphazardly, with no indexing system, in quantities that make page-by-page searches impracticable."). *But cf.* Tierno v. Rite Aid Corp., No. C 05-2520, 2008 WL 3287035, at *4–5 (N.D. Cal. July 31, 2008) (finding *Zubulake* factors inapplicable to paper document production, at least with respect to copying costs).

89. 437 U.S. at 539.

90. 239 F.R.D. 630 (D. Kan. 2006).

91. *Id.* at 635.

92. *Id.* at 636. (quoting 8 CHARLES ALAN WRIGHT, ARTHUR R. MILLER & RICHARD L. MARCUS, FEDERAL PRACTICE AND PROCEDURE § 2036 (2d ed. 1994)).

court took into account the purposes for which the responding party retained information, a factor that had been introduced in *Rowe* but rejected in *Zubulake*.[93] More significant, however, is how the courts have responded to the suggestion in *Zubulake* that the relevant factors should be considered as a hierarchy, with some more heavily weighted than others. There, the court pointed out that it did not make sense simply to "add up" the factors favoring cost shifting and compare that sum to the number of factors militating against a transfer of costs.[94] The court left open, however, how the factors might be weighted. This is a thorny issue since factors may be measured on different scales. For example, while cost factors are measurable in dollars, the likelihood of obtaining relevant information and the broader societal significance of the litigation are not. Since the weighing of these factors is necessarily impressionistic, the value of establishing a hierarchy is not readily apparent.

Some courts, as in *Hagemeyer North America, Inc. v. Gateway Data Sciences Corp.*, have adopted the hierarchical approach without articulating how it might be applied.[95] Others, as in *Semsroth*, have focused on the factors relating to the benefits likely to be derived from the proposed discovery but have also acknowledged that other factors, such as the importance of the issues at stake in the litigation, "may be vital to the analysis under [] certain circumstances."[96] It appears, then, that the weight accorded to any factor within a hierarchical scheme will be highly subjective and dependent on the context of the individual case.

C. Absolute limits on discovery

The case law has also left unclear the relationship between the authority to shift discovery costs and the well-established power of the courts to deny discovery requests altogether. In *Cognex Corp. v. Electro Scientific Industries, Inc.*,[97] the responding party objected to certain electronic discovery notwithstanding the requesting party's professed willingness to pay the costs of production.[98] The court found the objection to be well-founded.

93. *Id.* at 634–35.

94. Zubulake v. UBS Warburg LLC (*Zubulake I*), 217 F.R.D. 309, 323 (S.D.N.Y. 2003).

95. 222 F.R.D. 594, 602 (E.D. Wis. 2004).

96. 239 F.R.D. at 639.

97. No. 01 CV 10287, 2002 WL 32309413 (D. Mass. July 2, 2002).

98. *Id.* at *3.

> There is something inconsistent with our notions of fairness to allow one party to obtain a heightened level of discovery because it is willing to pay for it. There are limits on the number of depositions and interrogatories even though more might well provide relevant information. There is no exception to those limitations based upon one party's willingness to pay. The sense of fairness underpinning our system of justice will not be enhanced by the courts participating in giving strategic advantage to those with deeper pockets.[99]

To be sure, the availability of cost shifting as a judicial tool does not displace the courts' responsibility to disallow discovery where its value in the litigation is plainly exceeded by the cost and burden of production, whoever might bear that burden. What remains uncertain, however, is where the line should be drawn between denying a discovery request altogether and granting discovery on the condition that the requesting party bear the costs.

D. Evaluating party resources

One consideration common to all versions of the multifactor analysis is the resources of the parties.[100] How those resources are evaluated, however, is a matter of potential dispute. Some cases look only to the wherewithal of the parties themselves. In *Quinby*, for instance, the court observed that "Defendant is a large European commercial bank with assets in excess of Q265[101] billion," while, by contrast, "Plaintiff's resources are undoubtedly more limited, though she may be able to pay part of the costs of electronic discovery considering how much she earned while employed by [Defendant]."[102] Other courts, however, take into account the resources of counsel, at least insofar as the attorneys have initially assumed some of the costs of litigation. Thus, in *Wiginton v. CB Richard Ellis, Inc.*,[103] a putative class action challenging alleged sexual harassment in the workplace, the court acknowledged that "Plaintiffs, who include former employees of [Defendant], are clearly at a serious financial disadvantage" compared to the defendant corporation that had

99. *Id.* at *5.

100. *See, e.g., Zubulake I*, 217 F.R.D. at 324; Rowe Ent., Inc. v. William Morris Agency, Inc., 205 F.R.D. 421, 431 (S.D.N.Y. 2002).

101. The abbreviation "Q" refers to Euros.

102. 245 F.R.D. at 110.

103. 229 F.R.D. 568 (N.D. Ill. 2004).

least significant, since it is generally the requesting party that is benefited.[63]

(4) Application

Having created this modified multifactor test, the *Zubulake* court did not immediately apply it. Rather, the court expressed concern about the ability to evaluate the likelihood of discovering relevant information without a "test run." It therefore directed the defendant, at its own expense, to sample five backup tapes so that those results could be used to conduct a more informed cost-shifting analysis.[64]

After the sampling process was completed, the court issued a further opinion.[65] The sampling had located relevant emails that had been available only on the backup tapes. Addressing the first two factors of the cost-shifting test, the court inferred that "direct evidence of discrimination may only be available through restoration. As a result, the marginal utility of this additional discovery may be quite high."[66] However, because the emails that had been recovered did not themselves demonstrate bias,[67] the ultimate value of reviewing further backup tapes remained a matter of speculation. The court concluded that "[a]ll-in-all, because UBS bears the burden of proving that cost-shifting is warranted, the marginal utility test tips slightly against cost-shifting."[68]

Next the court reviewed the third, fourth, and fifth factors, which it characterized as the "cost issues." It found the total cost of additional discovery to be approximately $170,000 and the amount in controversy to be in the millions of dollars. The court concluded that because "the cost of restoration is surely not 'significantly disproportionate' to the projected value of this case," this factor weighed against cost shifting.[69] Finding that the defendant had "exponentially more" resources than the plaintiff but that the plaintiff could probably bear some of the cost of the requested discovery, the court determined that this factor weighed against cost

63. *Id.*

64. *Id.* at 323–24. Subsequent cases have adopted this approach and required sampling as a predicate to a determination about cost shifting. *See, e.g.*, AAB Joint Venture v. United States, 75 Fed. Cl. 432, 442–44 (Fed. Cl. 2007).

65. Zubulake v. UBS Warburg LLC (*Zubulake III*), 216 F.R.D. 280 (S.D.N.Y. 2003).

66. *Id.* at 287.

67. *Id.* at 286.

68. *Id.* at 287.

69. *Id.* at 287–88 & n.65.

net revenues in excess of $1.6 billion in the previous year.[104] Yet the court also observed that "Plaintiff's counsel . . . obviously has been willing to front substantial amounts of money, and probably could contribute to these discovery costs."[105] This approach originated in *Zubulake*, where the court noted that "it is not unheard of for plaintiffs' firms to front huge expenses when multi-million dollar recoveries are on the horizon."[106] This is somewhat surprising, as the court in *Zubulake* had expressed concern that frequent cost shifting might deter potentially valid claims,[107] yet including the assets of counsel when evaluating the plaintiff's resources makes a decision in favor of cost shifting more likely.

E. Data downgrading

It is an open question whether a party that permits ESI to migrate to a less accessible form while under an obligation to preserve the data has committed an act of spoliation.[108] What does seem clear, however, is that a party that downgrades data to a less accessible format is likely to be estopped from subsequently seeking to shift the costs necessary to collect and produce that data in response to a discovery demand. As the court said in *Quinby*,

> if a party creates its own burden or expense by converting into an inaccessible format data that it should have reasonably foreseen would be discoverable material at a time when it should have anticipated litigation, then it should not be entitled to shift the costs of restoring and searching the data.[109]

Similarly, in *Peskoff*, the court rejected a suggestion that it shift costs for a forensic examination of a party's computer where that

104. *Id.* at 575–76.
105. *Id.* at 576.
106. 216 F.R.D. at 288.
107. 217 F.R.D. at 317–18.
108. *Compare* Treppel v. Biovail Corp., 233 F.R.D. 363, 372 n.4 (S.D.N.Y. 2006) ("permitting the downgrading of data to a less accessible form—which systematically hinders future discovery by making the recovery of the information more costly and burdensome—is a violation of the preservation obligation"), *with* Quinby v. WestLB AG, No. 04 Civ. 7406, 2005 WL 3453908, at *8 n.10 (S.D.N.Y. Dec. 15, 2006) (declining to sanction party for converting data from accessible to inaccessible format, even assuming preservation obligation).
109. 245 F.R.D. at 104.

examination was required due to that party's failure to preserve its data in a more accessible format.[110]

F. Costs to be shifted

It is generally accepted that the costs that may be shifted in connection with electronic discovery include the expenses involved in restoring data to an accessible format and searching for responsive information.[111] Whether other types of costs may be shifted is more controversial.

Some courts have suggested that expenses attributable to the preservation of ESI may be shifted under appropriate circumstances. For instance, in *Treppel v. Biovail Corp.*,[112] the court explained the rationale for cost shifting in that context:

> Certainly, the presumption is that the party possessing information must bear the expense of preserving it for litigation. However, especially with respect to electronic data, that cost can become prohibitive. If the demanding party seeks the preservation of information that is likely to be of only marginal relevance but is costly to retain, then rather than deny a preservation order altogether, a court may condition it upon the requesting party assuming responsibility for part or all of the expense.[113]

On the other hand, another court questioned the authority to transfer the costs of preservation, stating:

> Computers have become a standard tool of doing business, with many associated benefits and costs. . . . One of the unexpected costs of using the electronic tool is that it may become costly to abide by one's duty to preserve evidence,

110. 2008 WL 2649506, at *3.

111. *See* Peskoff, v. Faber, 251 F.R.D. 59, 63 (D.D.C. 2008). 251 F.R.D. at 63 (cost of forensic examination of computer); *Quinby*, 245 F.R.D. at 111 (costs of restoring and searching backup tapes); Medtronic Sofamor Danek, Inc. v. Michelson, 229 F.R.D. 550, 558 (W.D. Tenn. 2003) (cost of restoring, de-duplicating, and searching backup tapes); *Wiginton*, 229 F.R.D. at 577 (cost of restoring backup tapes, searching data, and transferring data to electronic data viewer); *Zubulake III*, 216 F.R.D. at 290 (costs of restoring and searching backup tapes); Rowe Ent., Inc. v. William Morris Agency, Inc., 205 F.R.D. 421, 433 (S.D.N.Y. 2002) (same).

112. 233 F.R.D. 363 (S.D.N.Y. 2006).

113. *Id.* at 373 (citations omitted); *see also* Columbia Pictures Indus. v. Bunnell, No. CV 06-1093, 2007 WL 2080419, at *14 n.32 (C.D. Cal. May 29, 2007) (granting preservation order without prejudice to application to shift costs).

but that is not a cost which can be shifted to the opposing party, at least in the absence of a demand for a litigation hold which seeks court enforcement and/or requests for discovery which can limit the amount of information which needs to be preserved.[114]

Generally, the costs of providing the information culled to the responding party are borne by the producing party and are not subject to being shifted.[115] This is consistent with the traditional presumption, reinforced by the fact that undue cost or burden is rarely associated with the act of reducing information to a computer disk or to printed form for purposes of conveying it to the requesting party.[116] However, there are instances in which, for instance, the conduct of the producing party necessitates multiple productions, and the courts have not hesitated to shift the costs to that party. For example, in *PSEG Power New York, Inc. v. Alberici Constructors, Inc.*,[117] the vendor retained by the producing party to collect and produce responsive data produced emails separated from their corresponding attachments.[118] When the requesting party objected, the court ordered the emails to be produced again, properly organized, at the expense of the producing party.[119]

Courts appear to be relatively uniform in the view that the costs of reviewing ESI for privilege and confidentiality should remain with the producing party and not be shifted.[120] They have advanced at least three rationales for this principle. First, placing the responsibility for the costs of review on the responding party creates an incentive for entities to maintain their privileged or confidential

114. Kemper Mortgage, Inc. v. Russell, No. 3:06-cv-042, 2006 WL 2319858, at *2 (S.D. Ohio Apr. 18, 2006).

115. *See, e.g.*, *Wiginton*, 229 F.R.D. at 577 (shifting other costs, but requiring each party to bear own expenses for printing documents).

116. In one recent case, the court noted that the process of performing optical character recognition (OCR) on documents produced in tagged image file format (TIFF) could be quite expensive. Nevertheless, the court declined to shift costs to the requesting party, in part because OCR would facilitate review of the documents and expedite the litigation. Procter & Gamble Co. v. S.C. Johnson & Son, Inc., No. 9:08-CV-143, 2009 WL 440543, at *1–2 (E.D. Tex. Feb. 19, 2009).

117. No. 1:05-CV-657, 2007 WL 2687670 (N.D.N.Y. Sept. 7, 2007).

118. *Id.* at *2.

119. *Id.* at *9–12.

120. *See, e.g.*, Semsroth v. City of Wichita, 239 F.R.D. 630, 637 n.12 (D. Kan. 2006); *Wiginton*, 229 F.R.D. at 577; Medtronic Sofamor Danek, Inc. v. Michelson, 229 F.R.D. 550, 558 (W.D. Tenn. 2003).

documents in a manner that makes them easier to identify and protect.[121] Second, it creates a further incentive for the responding party to choose the most cost-efficient means of review. This may include using junior associates or paralegals rather than law firm partners or senior associates to conduct the actual review;[122] outsourcing that function; utilizing word searches or other computerized techniques to identify privileged documents in lieu of engaging in a document-by-document review;[123] and entering into stipulations that the privileges will not be waived if documents are inadvertently produced, such as clawback and quick-peek agreements.[124] Third, once previously inaccessible data has been rendered accessible, the further costs of responding to discovery are no longer "undue," and the traditional presumption that the responding party bears its own costs is resurrected.[125] At first glance, *Covad Communications Co. v. Revonet, Inc.*[126] appears to be an exception to this trend, since the court there required the parties to split the costs of a privilege review of electronic documents. However, that case is unique because a second privilege review was necessitated by the parties' failure to agree on the appropriate form of production of ESI; the responding party initially reviewed, redacted, and produced documents in paper form, but the court required documents to be produced again in native electronic format. Costs were shifted only in connection with the privilege review for this second production.[127]

Finally, the cost of conducting a forensic examination is generally borne by the party whose computer is being searched, even though that party is, in a sense, responding to discovery requests. This is because a forensic analysis is usually a form of sanction, imposed when the responding party has been found to have

121. *See* Rowe Ent., Inc. v. William Morris Agency, Inc., 205 F.R.D. 421, 432 (S.D.N.Y. 2002).

122. *See Zubulake III*, 216 F.R.D. at 290.

123. *See* Victor Stanley, Inc. v. Creative Pipe, Inc., 250 F.R.D. 251. 254–55 (D. Md. 2008).

124. *See Zubulake III*, 216 F.R.D. at 290.

125. *See id.* at 291. This last argument seems to equate accessibility with particular categories of ESI storage rather than defining it in terms of cost and burden, since there may well be undue cost and burden associated with privilege review even for information obtained from accessible sources.

126. 254 F.R.D. 147 (D.D.C. 2008).

127. *Id.* at 150–51.

withheld or destroyed evidence.[128] In that situation, requiring the responding party to pay the costs of the examination is consistent with a determination of blameworthiness. In at least one case, however, a court has ordered a forensic examination without a finding of culpable conduct where the requesting party voluntarily offered to bear the costs.[129]

G. Nonparties

One final matter that remains undecided is how nonparties should be treated for purposes of shifting the costs of electronic discovery. In *Capricorn Power Co. v. Siemens Westinghouse Power Corp.*,[130] the court suggested that the costs of preserving ESI should not always be borne by a nonparty responding to discovery:

> Certain circumstances may impose burdens upon . . . non-parties possessing evidence which may be unfair or oppressive to the point that a judicially imposed allocation of the burdens between the parties to the civil action may be required. Preservation of evidence may be particularly burdensome for non-parties, considering that their interest in the pending civil action is minuscule while the restrictions that can be imposed in a motion for preservation may be expensive and voluminous. In such instances, the party seeking preservation, and possibly the opposing party, may be required to ensure the preservation of the evidence, rather than placing that burden upon uninvolved third party possessors of the evidence.[131]

In another case, the court found the nonparty status of the entity responding to a subpoena to be "the most important factor" in determining how the costs of production should be allocated.[132] Indeed, the 2006 amendments to Rule 45 of the Federal Rules of Civil Procedure governing discovery of nonparties incorporated

128. *See* Canon U.S.A., Inc. v. S.A.M., Inc., Civ. A. No. 07-01201, 2008 WL 2522087, at *2, *5 (E.D. La. June 20, 2008) (requiring forensic analysis of server that responding party "forgot about" when answering discovery requests); Treppel v. Biovail Corp., 249 F.R.D. 111, 123–24 (S.D.N.Y. 2008) (ordering forensic examination of chief executive's laptop at company's expense where company failed to institute timely litigation hold).

129. *See* Coburn v. PN II, Inc., No. 2:07-cv-00662, 2008 WL 879746, at *2 (D. Nev. Mar. 28, 2008).

130. 220 F.R.D. 429 (W.D. Pa. 2004).

131. *Id.* at 436.

132. Guy Chem. Co. v. Romaco AG, 243 F.R.D. 310, 313 (N.D. Ind. 2007).

the same distinction between accessible and inaccessible ESI that exists in Rule 26.[133] It is also clear that courts may continue to establish conditions for enforcing a subpoena on a nonparty,[134] conditions that have long included requiring the requesting party to bear the costs.[135] Indeed, Rule 45(c)(2)(B)(ii) mandates that a court "protect a person who is neither a party nor a party's officer from significant expense resulting from compliance" with a subpoena, and some courts have interpreted this provision as requiring cost shifting.[136] Where the nonparty is not entirely disinterested in the litigation, however, a court is less likely to relieve it altogether of the costs of compliance.[137] At any rate, the fact that the entity from whom ESI is sought is a nonparty is a factor weighing in favor of shifting the costs of production to the requesting party.

6. Practicalities

A number of practical issues should be kept in mind in connection with cost shifting. Foremost among these is that litigation of a motion to shift costs is likely to be costly in itself. In *Rowe*, the plaintiffs and four separate defendants each engaged experts to estimate the expenses involved in responding to the discovery requested.[138] To some extent, such costs can be reduced by conducting sampling to determine with greater certainty not only the likelihood of obtaining responsive information, but also the actual costs involved in doing so.[139] And, of course, the costs of litigating a

133. *Compare* FED. R. CIV. P. 45(d)(1)(D) *with* FED. R. CIV. P. 26(b)(2)(B).

134. FED. R. CIV. P. 26(b)(2)(B).

135. *See, e.g.*, MDK, Inc. v. Mike's Train House, Inc., 27 F.3d 116, 119 (4th Cir. 1994) (referencing district court's enforcement of subpoena on condition that requesting party bear costs of compliance); Broussard v. Lemons, 186 F.R.D. 396, 398 (W.D. La. 1999); *In re* First Am. Corp., 184 F.R.D. 234, 240 (S.D.N.Y. 1998).

136. *See* Kwong v. Battery Tai-Shing Corp., No. C 08-80142, 2009 WL 290459, at *3 (N.D. Cal. Feb. 5, 2009).

137. *See* Dow Chem. Co. v. Reinhard, No. M8-85, 2008 WL 1968302, at *2 (S.D.N.Y. Apr. 29, 2008) (splitting costs of production of ESI evenly between requesting party and nonparty). *But cf.* Universal Del., Inc. v. Comdata Corp., No 07-1078, 2010 WL 1381225, at *6–8 (E.D. Pa. Mar. 31, 2010) (shifting costs incurred by nonparty responding to subpoena even where that entity likely to be added as party; decision based in part on fact that requested ESI on backup tapes determined not to be reasonably accessible).

138. Rowe Ent., Inc. v. William Morris Agency, Inc., 205 F.R.D. 421, 424–28 (S.D.N.Y. 2002).

139. *See Zubulake III*, 216 F.R.D. at 287 (relying on costs required for sampling to project expense of broader discovery).

fee-shifting motion can be obviated altogether if the parties agree at the outset how to share the expenses of electronic discovery.

It is also important for the party seeking to shift costs to make its application in a timely manner. Some courts will consider expenses already incurred when determining whether to shift costs.[140] Indeed, one court directed the parties to proceed with discovery while holding a fee-shifting application in abeyance.[141] However, other courts have found a fee-shifting motion made after the discovery requests had been complied with to be untimely. After quoting the provisions of Rule 26(c) authorizing the issuance of a protective order, one court stated:

> The clear import of the language employed is that the court has wide discretion to *prevent* undue burden or expense. But for [the responding party's] delay [in seeking to shift costs], the court would have been in a position to select from a range of alternative actions. In addition, had the court determined to impose conditions upon [the responding party's] production, [the requesting party] presumably would have been in a position to elect either (a) to accept the conditions or (b) to [forgo] the discovery and save [the responding party] the burden and expense of producing it. Unfortunately, [the responding party's] tardy filing has deprived this court of its most valuable prerogatives. Having elected to martyr itself rather than to seek relief in a timely fashion, [the responding party] seeks an order imposing the cost of its choice upon its opponents. I find neither substantive merit nor equity in its request.[142]

Counsel are well-advised, then, to make any fee-shifting application before the costs of responding to the discovery requests are actually incurred. This will ensure that the motion is timely, and if the court then chooses to defer a determination, no harm is done.

7. Conclusion

There is ample authority for a court to shift to the requesting party the cost of electronic discovery. However, in light of the traditional presumption that the responding party bears its own costs

140. *See* Semsroth v. City of Wichita, 239 F.R.D. 630, 637 (D. Kan. 2006).

141. *In re* Veeco Instruments, Inc. Sec. Litig., No. 05 MD 1695, 2007 WL 983987, at *2 (S.D.N.Y. Apr. 2, 2007).

142. Cason-Merenda v. Detroit Med. Ctr., No. 06-15601, 2008 WL 2714239, at *4 (E.D. Mich. July 7, 2008).

of production, it is not likely that fee-shifting applications will be lightly granted. Although the courts are developing a body of common law governing how any determination about fee-shifting should be made, there are many issues as to which no clear consensus has yet been reached.

CHAPTER 28

ALTERNATIVE DISPUTE RESOLUTION OF E-DISCOVERY ISSUES

By Michael D. Berman

The value of alternative dispute resolution (ADR), such as the use of court-appointed masters or private mediators, has long been recognized in connection with specialized discovery issues. Even so, "[l]awyers who recognize the value of resources such as ADR and special masters may nevertheless overlook their application to discovery."[1] *This chapter explains why ADR has great potential in helping to resolve disputes in the electronically stored information (ESI) arena and will likely play a key role in the future of e-discovery.*

1. The Sedona Conference Cooperation Proclamation, http://www.thesedonaconference.org/content/tsc_cooperation_proclamation/proclamation.pdf.

1. Introduction

The applicability of alternative dispute resolution to electronically stored information is clear. In 2004, the Sedona Conference[2] noted:

> In certain circumstances, a court may find it beneficial to appoint a "neutral" person (e.g., a special master or court-appointed expert) who can help mediate or manage electronic discovery issues. *See Antioch Co. v. Scrapbook Borders, Inc.*, 210 F.R.D. 645, 652–54 (D. Minn. 2002) (granting motion to appoint "neutral expert in computer forensics"); *Simon Prop. Group L.P. v. mySimon, Inc.*, 194 F.R.D. 639, 641–42 (S.D. Ind. 2000) (using appointed expert operating under constraints of protective order); *Dodge, Warren & Peters Ins. Servs., Inc.*, 105 Cal. App. 4th 1414, 1417, 130 Cal. Rptr. 385 (4 Dist. 2003) (affirming order that allowed inspection by court-appointed expert).
>
> The December 1, 2003, amendment to Rule 53 (Special Masters) should help clarify the availability of special masters to federal courts for addressing electronic discovery issues in appropriate cases where the matters cannot be addressed effectively and timely by an available district judge or magistrate judge of the district. See Fed. R. Civ. P. 53(a)(1)(C).
>
> One immediate benefit of using such a court-appointed "neutral" third party is the probable elimination of privilege waiver[3] concerns with respect to the review of information by that person. In addition, the "neutral" may be able to speed the resolution of disputes by fashioning fair and reasonable discovery plans based upon specialized knowledge of electronic discovery and/or technical issues with access to specific facts in the case. See id.
>
> Special care should be used in crafting the order of appointment (and any protective order) to precisely tailor the scope of appointment and protections against the disclosure

2. For a discussion of the Sedona Conference's history and significance, see chapter 1 of this book.

3. Masters have frequently been used in connection with privilege review. *In re* Intel Corp. Microprocessor Antitrust Litig., 2008 WL 2310288 (D. Del. 2008); *In re* Vioxx Prods. Liab. Litig., 501 F. Supp. 2d 789 (E.D. La. 2007) (citations to subsequent decisions omitted) ("Before the Court are Special Master Paul R. Rice's Report and Recommendations . . . on a representative sampling of documents as to which Merck & Co., Inc. has asserted privilege in this multidistrict litigation. . . .").

or loss of any privileges or protections. It should also be noted such appointments likely will remain the exception and not the rule as most parties, through the disclosure and discovery process should be able to address electronic discovery issues and remaining disputes often can be decided by an available district court or magistrate judge of the district.[4]

Thus, "[a] special master, referred to serve as an impartial officer of the court pursuant to Rule 53 of the Federal Rules of Civil Procedure, can bring a greater level of specialized knowledge, flexibility, involvement, and efficiency to pretrial discovery of electronically generated and stored data ('electronic data') than can most trial court judges burdened with managing a full docket."[5] "The key to successful electronic data discovery management, then, is to enlist the services of an individual with the requisite time, legal knowledge, and business skills to determine the appropriate boundaries of discovery requests, the feasibility of producing the requested data, and the apportionment of costs among the parties."[6] The "mere introduction [of a master] into the discovery process may induce the parties to be more cooperative because they are compelled to deal with an unbiased individual focused exclusively on the discovery process, rather than with a beleaguered judge who is too busy to take note of their dilatory maneuvering."[7]

2. Use of masters

Appointment of Masters is governed by Rule 53(b) of the Federal Rules of Civil Procedure, which provides:

4. *The (2004) Sedona Principles: Best Practices, Recommendations & Principles for Addressing Electronic Document Production*, 5 Sedona Conf. J. 151, 188, cmt. 10.c (2004); *The Sedona Principles: Best Practices, Recommendations and Principles for Addressing Electronic Document Production* (June 2007 2d ed.), 53, http://www.thesedonaconference.org/content/miscFiles/publications_html?gp=wgpus110.
5. R. Agins, *An Argument for Expanding the Application of Rule 54(b) to Facilitate Reference of the Special Master in Electronic Data Discovery*, 23 Pace L. Rev. 689, 690 (2003).
6. *Id.* at 697. For a discussion of the distinctions between a United States Magistrate Judge, who may also be a special master, a special master, and a court-appointed expert, *see id.* at 600–700. For a description of the arguments against use of special masters, *see id.* at 724–25.
7. *Id.* at 720.

Rule 53. Masters

(a) Appointment.
- (1) Scope. Unless a statute provides otherwise, a court may appoint a master only to:
  - (A) perform duties consented to by the parties;
  - (B) hold trial proceedings and make or recommend findings of fact on issues to be decided without a jury if appointment is warranted by:
    - (i) some exceptional condition; or
    - (ii) the need to perform an accounting or resolve a difficult computation of damages; or
  - (C) address pretrial and posttrial matters that cannot be effectively and timely addressed by an available district judge or magistrate judge of the district.
- (2) Disqualification. A master must not have a relationship to the parties, attorneys, action, or court that would require disqualification of a judge under 28 U.S.C. § 455, unless the parties, with the court's approval, consent to the appointment after the master discloses any potential grounds for disqualification.
- (3) Possible Expense or Delay. In appointing a master, the court must consider the fairness of imposing the likely expenses on the parties and must protect against unreasonable expense or delay.

(b) Order Appointing a Master.
- (1) Notice. Before appointing a master, the court must give the parties notice and an opportunity to be heard. Any party may suggest candidates for appointment.
- (2) Contents. The appointing order must direct the master to proceed with all reasonable diligence and must state:
  - (A) the master's duties, including any investigation or enforcement duties, and any limits on the master's authority under Rule 53(c);
  - (B) the circumstances, if any, in which the master may communicate ex parte with the court or a party;

(C) the nature of the materials to be preserved and filed as the record of the master's activities;
(D) the time limits, method of filing the record, other procedures, and standards for reviewing the master's orders, findings, and recommendations; and
(E) the basis, terms, and procedure for fixing the master's compensation under Rule 53(g).

(3) Issuing. The court may issue the order only after:
(A) the master files an affidavit disclosing whether there is any ground for disqualification under 28 U.S.C. § 455; and
(B) if a ground is disclosed, the parties, with the court's approval, waive the disqualification.

(4) Amending. The order may be amended at any time after notice to the parties and an opportunity to be heard.

(c) Master's Authority.

(1) In General. Unless the appointing order directs otherwise, a master may:
(A) regulate all proceedings;
(B) take all appropriate measures to perform the assigned duties fairly and efficiently; and
(C) if conducting an evidentiary hearing, exercise the appointing court's power to compel, take, and record evidence.

(2) Sanctions. The master may by order impose on a party any noncontempt sanction provided by Rule 37 or 45, and may recommend a contempt sanction against a party and sanctions against a nonparty.

(d) Master's Orders. A master who issues an order must file it and promptly serve a copy on each party. The clerk must enter the order on the docket.

(e) Master's Reports. A master must report to the court as required by the appointing order. The master must file the report and promptly serve a copy on each party, unless the court orders otherwise.

(f) Action on the Master's Order, Report, or Recommendations.

(1) Opportunity for a Hearing; Action in General. In acting on a master's order, report, or recommendations, the court must give the parties notice and an opportunity to be heard; may receive evidence; and may adopt or affirm, modify, wholly or partly reject or reverse, or resubmit to the master with instructions.

(2) Time to Object or Move to Adopt or Modify. A party may file objections to—or a motion to adopt or modify—the master's order, report, or recommendations no later than 21 days after a copy is served, unless the court sets a different time.

(3) Reviewing Factual Findings. The court must decide de novo all objections to findings of fact made or recommended by a master, unless the parties, with the court's approval, stipulate that:

(A) the findings will be reviewed for clear error; or

(B) the findings of a master appointed under Rule 53(a)(1)(A) or (C) will be final.

(4) Reviewing Legal Conclusions. The court must decide de novo all objections to conclusions of law made or recommended by a master.

(5) Reviewing Procedural Matters. Unless the appointing order establishes a different standard of review, the court may set aside a master's ruling on a procedural matter only for an abuse of discretion.

(g) Compensation.

(1) Fixing Compensation. Before or after judgment, the court must fix the master's compensation on the basis and terms stated in the appointing order, but the court may set a new basis and terms after giving notice and an opportunity to be heard.

(2) Payment. The compensation must be paid either:

(A) by a party or parties; or

(B) from a fund or subject matter of the action within the court's control.

(3) Allocating Payment. The court must allocate payment among the parties after considering the nature and amount of the controversy, the parties' means, and the extent to which any party is more responsible

than other parties for the reference to a master. An interim allocation may be amended to reflect a decision on the merits.

(h) Appointing a Magistrate Judge. A magistrate judge is subject to this rule only when the order referring a matter to the magistrate judge states that the reference is made under this rule.

Rule 53 was amended prior to the "ESI amendments" of December 2006, and "[t]his rule revision was undoubtedly intended to expand the use of masters in new directions in order to assist courts in coping with ever-increasing caseloads and in addressing difficult issues that require disproportionate judicial attention and expertise not otherwise available to the court."[8] In short:

8. S. Scheindlin & J. Redgrave, *Special Masters and E-Discovery: The Intersection of Two Recent Revisions to the Federal Rules of Civil Procedure*, 30 Cardozo L.Rev. 347, 347 (2008); S. Scheindlin, *The Evolution and Impact of the New Federal Rule Governing Special Masters*, 51-Feb Fed. Law 34 (2004); K. Withers, *Computer-Based Discovery in Federal Civil Litigation*, 2000 Fed. Cts. L. Rev. 2 (2000), § F ("The use of court-appointed neutral experts in these may represent the 'state of the art' in discovery management. But it also represents a major step in the ongoing evolution of the role of the judge in discovery, from bystander and occasional referee to active manager."); D. Isom, *Electronic Discovery Primer for Judges*, 2005 Fed. Cts. L. Rev. 1 (2005); E. M. Lange & K. Minsger, Electronic Evidence and Discovery: What Every Lawyer Should Know 91 (ABA 2009), app. G & H; R. Hedges, *Discovery of Digital Information*, 747 PLI/Lit 41, 52 (2006) ("'The complexity and rapidly changing character of technology for the management of computerized materials may make it appropriate for the judge to seek the assistance of a special master or neutral expert, or call on the parties to provide the judge with expert assistance, in the form of briefings on the relevant technological issues.'") (citations omitted).

Retired Magistrate Judge Hedges notes that "courts must be willing to immediately inject themselves into the middle of a discovery dispute involving electronic materials. Avoiding a dispute over electronic materials is a disservice to the litigants, their lawyers and the cause of justice. If the dispute arises in a case assigned to a district judge who cannot immediately intervene, then the district judge should consider the immediate reference of that matter to a magistrate judge or a discovery master." *Id.* at 439; *accord* Gipson v. Sw. Bell Tel. Co., Case 08-217 (D. Kan. Dec. 23, 2008) ("During the discovery conference, the Court discussed the possibility of appointing, pursuant to Federal Rule of Civil Procedure 53(a)(1)(C), a special master to assist counsel and address pretrial discovery matters that the Court is unable to timely and effectively address. The special master would handle and resolve all discovery disputes of an administrative nature raised by the parties, as well as scheduling matters. The special master would first proceed to obtain agreed resolutions of any disputed matters;

> The revised Rule 53 . . . permits the use of special masters on an as-needed basis, with the parties' consent, or, when exceptional conditions require, by court order. In addition, the Rule encourages, if not requires, a new level of participation by the litigants. Finally, the Rule requires that an order of appointment explicitly address the duties of the special master, the cost of this service to the parties, communications between the court and the special master, and between the parties and the special master, and the standard of review for a special master's decisions.[9]

Rule 53 has seen increased prominence in e-discovery: "Courts are appointing special masters to address electronic discovery issues with increasing frequency, although the number of reported appointments is still relatively small. Examination of reported and unreported cases regarding the appointment of special masters for such matters (including cases reflecting a decision declining to appoint a Rule 53 master) illuminates the considerations governing such appointments."[10]

3. Private mediation

While court-appointed special masters and magistrate judges can engage in mediation of ESI disputes,[11] another option, separate from a court-appointed master or mediator, is private mediation. "The types of facilitation include: (1) assisting with the Rule 26(f) conference discussions; (2) developing preservation protocols; (3) developing processes to identify locations and sources of potentially relevant documents and ESI; (4) assisting the parties to develop protocols for the identification and depositions of knowledgeable witnesses regarding ESI issues (including guidelines for the scope

---

however, if agreements could not be reached, the special master would have the authority to enter orders on these types of discovery disputes and matters. The Court recognizes that the parties may be able to agree upon a method other than using a special master to accomplish these same goals. Accordingly, the Court issues the following order. The parties are directed to confer and attempt to reach an agreement as to how the parties might better handle discovery and other pretrial disputes in this case. If the parties are unable to reach such an agreement, the parties shall further confer and attempt to agree on the selection of a person to be appointed as special master."), http://www.thesedonaconference.org/content/miscFiles/gipson.pdf.

9. Scheindlin & Redgrave, *supra* note 8, at 352.

10. *Id.* at 369–70 (discussing cases).

11. *Id.* at 374–75.

of pre-trial examinations); (5) developing protective orders to address privilege and privacy protection concerns; (6) addressing search and retrieval issues (such as negotiating search terms); and (7) agreeing upon form of production issues."[12]

One advantage of privately contracted mediation is that it is party-controlled. "Despite the increase in the appointments of special masters to address e-discovery issues, a number of courts have declined to make such appointments concluding that the matters can be handled by the parties' experts or by the court itself."[13] "When disputes arise in discovery, a master with substantial prior technical and business experience will be more likely to reach a rapid resolution than will a judge who, lacking this experience, will tend to impose a resolution by fiat."[14] As recently noted, despite the best efforts of conscientious members of the judiciary, "[t]he Court acknowledges that this [court-imposed] result is less than perfect."[15] A mediated approach may also be less costly.[16]

4. Conclusion

Contemporary litigation demands that attorneys and courts have many tools in their tool kit. "Generalist judges are not and cannot be experts on electronic hardware and software that enable people to create, store, retrieve, and search ESI. In order to manage discovery in cases involving a substantial amount of ESI, and assuming the stakes at risk warrant the cost, court adjuncts with specialized knowledge may become more the rule than the

12. *Id.* at 375.

13. *Id.* at 382. After discussion of cases in which courts declined to appoint special masters, Judge Scheindlin and Mr. Redgrave noted: "These cases demonstrate that the appointment of a master lies within the sound discretion of the district court. Thus, if the parties believe it is advantageous to seek appointment of a special master, they may need to provide some justification for that appointment. Our review indicates that the appointment of a special master is more likely where: (1) the proposed special master's tasks are clearly identified and (2) a good case has been made that the special master's role will reduce the burden on the judicial officer and expedite the proceedings for the parties." *Id.* at 383.

14. Agins, *supra* note 5, at 720.

15. Wm. A. Gross Constr. Assocs., Inc. v. Am. Mfrs. Mut. Ins. Co., 2009 U.S. Dist. Lexis 22903 n.2 (S.D.N.Y. Mar. 19, 2009).

16. LANGE & MINSGER, *supra* note 8, at 91. For a discussion of the appropriate qualifications of a special master, see Agins, *supra* note 5, at 718–19.

exception."[17] Attorneys approaching ESI issues should be aware of the potential benefits of masters and private mediation.[18]

17. Scheindlin & Redgrave, *supra* note 8, at 388; Carnegie Int'l Corp. v. Grant Thornton, LLP, 2005 WL 851064 (Md. Cir. Ct. Apr. 6, 2005); DeVetter v. Alex Brown Mgt. Servs., Inc., 2006 WL 1314014 (Md. Cir. Ct. Mar. 22, 2006).

18. In the interest of disclosure, the author offers private ESI mediation services.

PART EIGHT

PROFESSIONAL CONDUCT AND THE DUTY TO COOPERATE IN E-DISCOVERY

CHAPTER 29

ETHICS IN E-DISCOVERY

BY DENNIS P. DUFFY AND COURTNEY INGRAFFIA BARTON

This chapter covers a range of areas in e-discovery where ethics rules may govern a litigator's conduct, including the mining of metadata, vendor oversight and outsourcing, ownership of electronic files—and even a possible duty to understand technology! As the authors write, the ethics opinions discussed here "highlight how evolving technologies have changed the practice of law."

1. Introduction

Although the e-discovery news of the past few years has focused on the adoption and application of the Federal Rules of Civil Procedure, as well as the corresponding state rules and their application by the courts, state and local bar associations have been quietly issuing ethics opinions that will no doubt have a tremendous impact on pretrial practice. These opinions have already generated a great deal of interest among practitioners as many are

---

Portions of this chapter previously appeared in *Digital Discovery and E-Evidence*, BNA, Inc., Vol. 7, No. 12 (Dec. 1, 2007). The authors wish to thank Shane Pennington (University of Texas, J.D. 2010) for his research and editorial assistance with respect to this chapter.

grappling with the legal and ethical implications discussed: sending and receiving electronic files containing potentially privileged embedded data, overseas document review, and ownership and control of client data as well as access to it.

Beyond some of these very specific e-discovery ethics opinions, state bar associations have been relatively slow to address how advances in technology change or affect our ethical obligations as lawyers.[1] Yet some of the more traditional ethical issues such as competency of counsel, protecting client confidences, the duty to preserve evidence, and even candor to the Bar have come up in the context of e-discovery with little or no guidance and, in instances such as in the case of *Qualcomm Inc. v. Broadcom Corp.*,[2] with devastating consequences. Although this chapter is not able to address every ethical issue related to e-discovery, it provides an overview of some of the common ethical challenges that practitioners may face as they work through the e-discovery's complexities.[3]

---

1. In August 2009, incoming ABA President Carol Lamm established a new commission to study ethics and technology. Lamm was quoted as saying: "Technological advances and globalization have changed our profession in ways not yet reflected in our ethics codes and regulatory structure. Technologies such as e-mail, the Internet and smart phones are transforming the way we practice law and our relationships with clients, just as they have compressed our world and expanded international business opportunities for our clients." News Release, ABA, ABA President Carolyn B. Lamm Creates Ethics Commission to Address Technology and Global Practice Challenges Facing U.S. Lawyers, Aug. 4, 2009, http://www.abanet.org/abanet/media/release/news_release.cfm?releaseid=730. For an example of a novel ethical challenge involving search terms, see Jason R. Baron, E-Discovery and the Problem of Asymmetric Knowledge, Presentation at the Mercer Law School Ethics in the Digital Age Symposium, *in* 60 Mercer L. Rev. (2009), discussed in chapter 21. The ethics commission will review lawyer ethics rules and regulation across the United States in the context of a global legal services marketplace.
2. 2008 WL 66932 (S.D. Cal. Jan. 7, 2008) (sanctioning several lawyers severely for failure to comply with e-discovery rules), *vacated in part and remanded*, 2008 WL 638108 (S.D. Cal. Mar. 5, 2008) (vacating the order of sanctions *only* as ordered against certain outside counsel), *subsequent opinion*, 2010 WL 1336937 (S.D. Cal. Apr. 2, 2010).
3. Additional works are devoted to ethical issues in e-discovery. *See, e.g.*, J. Barkett, The Ethics of E-Discovery (ABA 2009).

2. Competent representation

Probably one of the most important of the ethical rules for e-discovery is the very first one—the one attorneys often take for granted: the rule requiring competent representation. We all assume that because we are experienced attorneys, we know what we are doing. But e-discovery—a complex process that can easily go wrong—underscores the need to pay close attention to this first principle. ABA Model Rule 1.1 states that "a lawyer shall provide competent representation to a client. Competent representation requires the legal knowledge, skill, thoroughness, and preparation reasonably necessary for the representation."[4] As more fully explored below, competent representation is a broad requirement that necessitates a thorough understanding of both the legal and technological processes involved in e-discovery.

A. Understanding technology

The American Bar Association has stated that "[c]ompetence in using technology can be a requirement of practicing law."[5] Although there is no *specific* ABA standard for technological competence, nor have the state bar associations explicitly opined on the topic, the ABA has referenced a statement by the Law Society of Alberta opining that ethics rules require " 'maintenance and improvement of knowledge and skills' . . . includ[ing] technological proficiency, especially in areas directly connected to an attorney's area of practice."[6] Moreover, several recent court opinions have been quick to point out the need for technological expertise, particularly in the context of e-discovery. In *In re Seroquel*,[7] for example, the plaintiffs moved for sanctions based on the defendant's discovery deficiencies.[8] Many of the disputes involved technical issues.[9] And while the law firm representing the plaintiffs had internal information technology (IT) expertise, the plaintiffs requested that they be allowed to speak to technical people

4. MODEL RULES OF PROF'L CONDUCT R. 1.1.
5. ABA, Legal Technology Research Center, http://www.abanet.org/tech/ltrc/research/ethics/competence.html (last visited June 29, 2009).
6. *Id.*
7. 244 F.R.D. 650 (M.D. Fla. 2007).
8. *Id.* at 651.
9. *Id.*

but were told there was no IT person with whom the plaintiffs could confer.[10] In noting that the parties' "uncooperative effort to resolve technical issues are a violation of e-discovery rules and principles,"[11] the court took the parties to task for their failure to engage appropriate technical expertise: "[The defendant's] refusal to allow contact between individuals with appropriate technical backgrounds as part of the effort to resolve technical issues is an inexplicable departure from the requirements of Rule 26, the Sedona Principles and this Court's expressed expectations."[12] The court also admonished that the need for technical understanding should not just fall to the most junior attorneys:

> [The defendant's] decision to offer only the testimony [at the hearing on the discovery issues] of a junior level attorney, only somewhat versed in technical issues and one who came late to the process is puzzling. . . . Its efforts at finding solutions to technical problems are likewise unilluminated.[13]

In re Seroquel is just one in a number of cases that showcase the need for lawyers involved in handling electronically stored information (ESI) to understand not just technology, but the entire e-discovery process, from preservation to collection and through to production, as each of these steps has a technological component in today's digital world.[14] Moreover, fulfilling their ethical duty of competent representation also requires lawyers to be aware of

10. *Id.* at 658.

11. *Id.* at 652.

12. *Id.* at 658 n.4. The Committee Notes to Rule 26(f) also encourage this notion of technological expertise: "In appropriate cases identification of, and early discovery from, individuals with special knowledge of a party's computer systems may be helpful." FED. R. CIV. P. 26(f) advisory committee's note. Some courts have even gone so far as to recommend experts that meet the requirements of Federal Rule of Evidence 702. *See* United States v. O'Keefe, 537 F. Supp. 2d 14, 20 (D.D.C. 2008). "The Sedona Principles for Electronic Document Production" is a set of best practices in electronic discovery developed by the Sedona Conference Working Group on Electronic Document Production.

13. *In re Seroquel,* 244 F.R.D. at 660 n.6.

14. *See, e.g.,* Bray & Gillespie Mgmt. LLC v. Lexington Ins. Co., 2009 WL 546429 (M.D. Fla. Mar. 4, 2009) (ordering sanctions against several attorneys, including attorneys who claimed to have only a supervisory role in the discovery process, for failure to produce electronically stored information in the form specified by the requestor).

their own technological knowledge deficiencies so that they can procure assistance if necessary.[15]

B. Duty to make reasonable inquiry

Although an entire chapter in this book is solely dedicated to the topic,[16] it is worth mentioning the ethical considerations surrounding the duty of reasonable inquiry under Federal Rule of Civil Procedure 26(g).[17] And in no case has the intersection between Rule 26(g) and ethics been clearer than in *Qualcomm v. Broadcom*.[18] In that case, the court reprimanded the plaintiff, Qualcomm, and its counsel for their failure to make reasonable inquiry:

> [O]ne or more of the retained lawyers chose not to look in the correct locations for the correct documents, to accept the unsubstantiated assurances of an important client that its search was sufficient, to ignore the warning signs that the document search and production were inadequate, not to press Qualcomm employees for the truth, and/or to encourage employees to provide the information (or lack of information) that Qualcomm needed to assert its non-participation argument and to succeed in this lawsuit. These choices enabled Qualcomm to withhold hundreds of thousands of pages of relevant discovery and to assert numerous false and misleading arguments to the court and jury. This conduct warrants the imposition of sanctions.[19]

---

15. *See, e.g.*, Malletier v. Dooney & Bourke, Inc., 2006 WL 3476735, at *8 (S.D.N.Y. Nov. 30, 2006) (chastising plaintiff for attempting to provide in-house technical services for discovery beyond its expertise). In addition to scolding parties for their lack of technological competence, courts have also ordered parties to engage technological assistance. *See, e.g.*, Peskoff v. Faber, 244 F.R.D. 54, 66 (D.D.C. 2007) (ordering counsel to collaborate with the court on a request for proposals seeking bids from qualified forensic computer technicians to perform a forensic exam of computers in question); Coleman (Parent) Holdings, Inc. v. Morgan Stanley & Co., 2005 WL 674885 (Fla. Cir. Ct. Mar. 23, 2005) (ordering Morgan Stanley to pay for a third-party vendor to check its compliance with an agreed order).

16. *See* chapter 31.

17. FED. R. CIV. P. 26(g). Rule 26(g) is discussed at length in chapter 31.

18. Qualcomm v. Broadcom, 2008 U.S. Dist. LEXIS 911 (S.D. Cal. Jan 7, 2008). Ultimately, the sanctions in the case were lifted; nevertheless, Qualcomm remains a cautionary tale. Qualcomm Inc. v. Broadcom Corp., No. 05cv1958-B, 2010 U.S. Dist. LEXIS 33889 (S.D. Cal. April 2, 2010).

19. *Id.* at *45.

The court awarded Broadcom all of its attorney's fees and costs incurred in the litigation in the amount of $8,568,633.24 for Qualcomm's "monumental and intentional" discovery violation.[20] In addition, the court referred six of the outside counsel to the California Bar.[21] The opinion shows not only the interplay between the ethics rules and Rule 26(g), but also that the ethics rules give courts another way to sanction parties for discovery violations—one that may cut at the heart and soul of a lawyer's livelihood.[22]

C. Duty to preserve

Judges take the duty to preserve potentially relevant electronic information very seriously.[23] Failure to comply with that duty often results in spoliation, which is defined as "'the destruction or significant alteration of evidence, or the failure to preserve

20. *Id.* at *56.

21. *Id.* at *64. The court also ordered both in-house and outside counsel to undergo a CREDO (Case Review and Enforcement of Discovery Obligations) process. *Id.* at *18–20.

22. For an in-depth examination of the ethical considerations from *Qualcomm*, see David Cross & Ty Carson, *Ethics and E-Discovery—"Reasonable Inquiry" in the Wake of* Qualcomm v. Broadcom, 9(1) DIGITAL DISCOVERY & E-EVIDENCE (BNA), Jan. 1, 2009. *See also* Mancia v. Mayflower Textile Servs. Co., 253 F.R.D. 354, 357–58 (D. Md. 2008) (the "spirit and purposes" of the reasonable inquiry and other discovery rules in Rule 26 "requires cooperation by counsel to identify and fulfill legitimate discovery needs, yet avoid seeking discovery the cost and burden of which is disproportionately large to what is at stake in the litigation Counsel cannot 'behave responsively' during discovery unless they do both, which requires cooperation rather than contrariety, communication rather than confrontation.").

23. The discoverability of electronically stored information, including the duty to preserve, is now expressly recognized by the Federal Rules of Civil Procedure. FED. R. CIV. P. 26(f) (creating a Rule 26(f) planning meeting to "discuss any issues about preserving discoverable information," and to address "any issues about disclosure or discovery of electronically stored information"); FED. R. CIV. P. 34 (making electronically stored information "in any medium from which information can be obtained," subject to production). *See also* United Med. Supply Co. v. United States, 77 Fed. Cl. 257 (Ct. Claims 2007): "Aside perhaps from perjury, no act serves to threaten the integrity of the judicial process more than the spoliation of evidence. Our adversarial process is designed to tolerate human failings—erring judges can be reversed, uncooperative counsel can be shepherded, and recalcitrant witnesses compelled to testify. But when critical documents go missing, judges and litigants alike descend into a world of *ad hocery* and half measures—and our civil justice system suffers."

property for another's use as evidence in pending or reasonably foreseeable litigation.'"[24] The moment that an actual or potential legal conflict evolves to the point that litigation is "reasonably anticipated," there arises a "duty to suspend any routine document purging system . . . and to put in place a litigation hold to ensure the preservation of relevant documents—failure to do so constitutes spoliation."[25]

Once this preservation duty arises, the "destruction of evidence raises [a] presumption that disclosure of the materials would be damaging."[26] The possible litigation consequences for spoliation include monetary penalties (such as pay-for-proof sanctions),[27] exclusion of evidence, delay of the start of trial, mistrial, adverse-inference jury instructions,[28] and, in an extreme case, a dismissal

24. Zubulake v. UBS Warburg, LLC (*Zubulake V*), 229 F.R.D. 422, 430 (S.D.N.Y. 2004) (quoting West v. Goodyear Tire & Rubber Co., 167 F.3d 776, 779 (2d Cir. 1999); *see* chapter 8.

25. *See* Rambus, Inc. v. Infineon Techs. AG, Inc., 222 F.R.D. 280, 288 (E.D. Va. 2004) (enforcing a "litigation hold" by granting a motion to compel production of documents and testimony relating to Rambus's document retention, collection, production, and "Shred Days").

26 Arista Records, Inc. v. Sakfield Holding Co., 314 F. Supp. 2d 27, 34 (D.D.C. 2004) (finding that the defendant's destruction of electronic information precluded the defendant from attacking the plaintiff's analysis of existing electronic information, while denying the defendant's motion to dismiss on jurisdictional grounds).

27. *See, e.g.*, Network Computing Servs. Corp. v. Cisco Sys., Inc., 223 F.R.D. 392 (D.S.C. 2004) (awarding monetary sanctions supplemented by adverse instruction); Mosaid Techs. Inc. v. Samsung Elecs. Co., 224 F.R.D. 595, (D.N.J. 2004), *aff'd*, 348 F. Supp. 2d 332 (D.N.J. 2004) (awarding $566,838 for destruction of emails in a patent infringement case); Advantacare Health Partners, LP v. Access IV, 2004 WL 1837997 (N.D. Cal. Aug. 17, 2004) (awarding evidentiary and monetary sanctions against former employees who participated in the establishment of a competing company and intentionally destroyed electronic information in contravention of a temporary restraining order); United States v. Philip Morris USA, Inc., 2004 U.S. Dist. LEXIS 13580 (D.D.C. July 21, 2004) (awarding a $2.75 million spoliation fine plus costs associated with the discovery dispute).

28. *See, e.g.*, Flury v. Daimler Chrysler Corp., 427 F.3d 939 (11th Cir. 2005) ($250,000 personal injury award reversed and case dismissed due to plaintiff's bad faith spoliation of evidence: "Plaintiff failed to preserve an allegedly defective vehicle in a crash worthiness case. The vehicle was, in effect, the most crucial and reliable evidence available to the parties at the time plaintiff secured representation and notified defendant of the accident. By the time plaintiff filed suit, years after the accident had taken place, plaintiff had allowed the vehicle to be sold for salvage despite a request from defendant for the vehicle's location. For these reasons, we

on the merits.[29] "'The determination of an appropriate sanction for spoliation, if any, is confined to the sound discretion of the trial

believe the resulting prejudice to the defendant incurable, and dismissal necessary."); Pension Comm. of the Univ. of Montreal Pension Plan v. Banc of Am. Sec., LLC, 685 F. Supp.2d 456 (S.D.N.Y. 2010) (opinion by Scheindlin, J. entitled "*Zubulake*, Revisited: Six Years Later.") (sanctions in form of adverse inference instructions for spoliation of evidence and attorney's fees and costs assessed against plaintiffs where most of them conducted discovery in "an ignorant and indifferent fashion" and several were grossly negligent: "While litigants are not required to execute document productions with absolute precision, at a minimum they must act diligently and search thoroughly at the time they reasonably anticipate litigation."); Coleman (Parent) Holdings, Inc. v. Morgan Stanley & Co., 2005 WL 679071 (Fla. 15th Cir. Mar. 1, 2005) (granting instruction request based on the defendant's repeated knowing failures to produce emails and pattern of deliberate misrepresentations to court); United States v. Philip Morris USA, Inc., 2004 U.S. Dist. LEXIS 13580 (D.D.C. July 21, 2004) (granting instruction based on the defendant's "reckless disregard and gross indifference" to email preservation obligations); Network Computing Servs. Corp. v. Cisco Sys., Inc., 223 F.R.D. 392, 401 (D.S.C. 2004) (instructing the jury that it could consider the plaintiff's disingenuous repeated representations to the court that it was certain that some ultimately produced and "garden variety" electronic files did not exist).

29. *See, e.g.*, Leon v. IDX Sys. Corp., 464 F.3d 951 (9th Cir. 2006) (employee's destruction of data on his employer-owned laptop amounted to willful spoliation of evidence, as would support dismissal with prejudice and award of $65,000 as sanction in his action against employer; employee knew he was under a duty to preserve all data on the laptop, and employee not only destroyed private files but intentionally deleted employment-related files and then wrote a program to write over deleted documents, after he filed his lawsuit; some of the deleted files were likely at the heart of employer's defense); Krumwiede v. Brighton Assocs., 2006 WL 1308629, at *4 (N.D. Ill. May 8, 2006) (entering default judgment for breach of noncompete agreement against ex-employee who deleted and altered thousands of files while delaying producing laptop); Metro. Opera Ass'n v. Local 100 Hotel Empl. & Rest. Empl. Int'l Union, 212 F.R.D. 178 (S.D.N.Y. 2003), *aff'd*, 175 L.R.R.M. 2870 (S.D.N.Y. Aug. 27, 2004) (granting the plaintiff's motion for judgment against the labor union); Kucala Enters., Ltd. v. Auto Wax Co., Inc., 2003 WL 22433095 (N.D. Ill Oct. 27, 2003) (adopting magistrate judge's recommended dismissal of most of plaintiff's case where plaintiff used computer program called "Evidence Eliminator" to delete documents from computer and "clean" the hard drive); Computer Assocs. Int'l, Inc. v. Am. Fundware, Inc., 133 F.R.D. 166 (D. Colo. 1990) (sanctioning with default judgment on liability entered against developer of computer program that destroyed source code after service of complaint, request for production, and motion to compel discovery of source code); *In re* Krause, 367 B.R. 740 (Bankr. D. Kan. 2007) (holding that debtor's spoliation warranted severe sanction of entry of partial default judgment).

judge, and is assessed on a case-by-case basis.' "[30] "The spoliation of evidence germane 'to proof of an issue at trial can support an inference that the evidence would have been unfavorable to the party responsible for its destruction.' "[31] This common law duty dovetails with the applicable ABA Model Rules, particularly Rule 3.4, which states that "a lawyer shall not unlawfully obstruct another party's access to evidence or unlawfully alter, destroy, or conceal a document or other material having potential evidentiary value."[32] Hence, practitioners must advise their clients of what plans should be in place to comply with the duty to preserve and companies and the counsel who advise them must take the duty to preserve more seriously than ever. It is not enough to follow a retention policy by rote.[33] Affirmative steps must be taken well in advance to comply with the rules laid out in the recent cases.[34]

3. Ethical rules regarding metadata

A. Introduction

Simply put, metadata is "data about data." Metadata is not typically apparent on the face of a document but can be discovered using the right tools when a document is accessed in its native file or when that information is processed. Examples of metadata can include file name, file location, file format or file type, file size, and file dates such as creation date, date of last data modification, date of last data access, and date of last metadata modification. Other examples of metadata include track changes in Microsoft Word and blind copies on emails.[35]

30. *Zubulake V*, 229 F.R.D. 430 (quoting Fujitsu v. Fed. Express Corp., 247 F.3d 423, 436 (2d Cir. 2001). "The authority to sanction litigants for spoliation arises jointly under the Federal Rules of Civil Procedure and the court's inherent power." *See* Turner v. Hudson Transit Lines, Inc., 142 F.R.D. 68, 72 (S.D.N.Y. 1991) (citing FED. R. CIV. P. 37); *see also* Shepherd v. Am. Broad. Cos., 62 F.3d 1469, 1474 (D.C. Cir. 1995) ("When rules alone do not provide courts with sufficient authority to protect their integrity and prevent abuses of the judicial process, the inherent power fills the gap.").

31. *Zubulake V*, 229 F.R.D. at 430 (quoting Kronisch v. United States, 150 F.3d 112, 126 (2d Cir. 1998)).

32. *See also* MODEL RULES OF PROF'L CONDUCT R. 3.3, Candor Toward the Tribunal, & R. 4.1, Truthfulness in Statements to Others.

33. Broccoli v. Echostar Commc'ns Corp., 229 F.R.D. 506 (D. Md. 2005).

34. For an in-depth discussion of the duty to preserve, see chapter 8.

35. For an in-depth discussion of metadata, see chapter 6.

Although metadata is often irrelevant to the litigation, in some cases uncovering key metadata can give an opposing party an advantage. For example, in a contract dispute case, metadata may reveal prior iterations of pertinent provisions; in a products liability case, metadata may reveal prior knowledge or a key element of the case. However, an ethical issue is presented when a document containing privileged metadata is transmitted to an opponent.

All electronic documents have metadata. Thus, in the attorney-client privilege context, metadata attaches both to the electronic documents passed between counsel on a particular matter and to documents produced in litigation. But is it ethical for an attorney to go looking for metadata in either context? Several states have weighed in on the issue, and the opinions are summarized here and in the tables at the end of this chapter.

B. District of Columbia

The most comprehensive opinion discussing metadata is the District of Columbia Bar Association Opinion 341, issued September 2007.[36] The D.C. Bar approach stands out because it distinguishes between the two types of documents at issue: those voluntarily sent by opposing counsel in the normal course of business and those produced in discovery or as the result of a subpoena.[37] While some other states have made this distinction,[38] none has specifically addressed how to handle the two types of information.

As for the first set of documents—those voluntarily sent—the D.C. Bar opined that the sending lawyer has an obligation under D.C. Rules of Professional Conduct Rule 1.6 to take reasonable steps to maintain the confidentiality of documents in their possession.[39] To that end, lawyers must remove metadata before sending

36. D.C. Bar, Op. 341 (2007).

37. *Id.*

38. *See* Ala. Ethics Comm'n, Op. R0-2007-02 (2007) (recognizing a distinction similar to the one recognized by D.C. Bar Op. 341); Fla. State Bar Ass'n Comm. on Prof'l Ethics, Op. 06-2 (2006) (recognizing a distinction similar to the one recognized by the D.C. Bar). *But see* ABA Comm. on Ethics & Prof'l Responsibility, Formal Op. 06-442 (2006) (declining to recognize a distinction between documents sent by opposing counsel voluntarily in the normal course of business and those produced in discovery or as the result of a subpoena); Md. Bar Ass'n Ethics Docket, Op. No. 2007-09 (2007) (same).

39. D.C. Bar, Op. 341 (2007) (citing D.C. BAR RULES OF PROF'L CONDUCT R. 1.6 (2007)). Recently, a Vermont ethics opinion described this principle as

a document.[40] To the extent the receiving lawyer in this situation has actual knowledge that any metadata was sent with the document inadvertently, he or she must refrain from using the document.[41] But a situation where the privileged nature of the material is uncertain does not trigger a duty to refrain from use.[42]

As for documents received in discovery, the D.C. Bar recognizes that the Federal Rules of Civil Procedure address inadvertent production of privileged material.[43] Rule 26(b)(5) sets up a mechanism for a party to request that inadvertently produced information be returned until a ruling can be made on any claim of waiver of privilege.[44] In addition, a party producing discovery documents must be careful not to alter the metadata and may have an obligation to preserve and produce it.[45] As such, the receiving party can assume that metadata was provided intentionally and can therefore review and use that information.[46] On the other hand, if the receiving lawyer has actual knowledge that the material was produced

"universally" accepted. Vt. Ethics Op. 2009-01 ("The Bar Associations that have examined the duty of the sending lawyer with respect to metadata have been virtually unanimous in concluding that lawyers who send documents in electronic form to opposing counsel have a duty to exercise reasonable care to ensure that metadata containing confidential information protected by the attorney client privilege and the work product doctrine is not disclosed during the transmission process.").

40. D.C. Bar, Op. 341 (2007) (citing N.Y. State Bar Ass'n Comm. on Prof'l Ethics, Op. 782).

41. *Id. See also* D.C. Bar, Op. 318 (2003) (holding that where a lawyer knows that a privileged document was inadvertently sent by a third party, it is a dishonest act for the lawyer to review and use it without consulting the sender); D.C. Bar, Op. 256 (1995) (holding that where a lawyer knows that a privileged document was inadvertently sent by opposing counsel, it is a dishonest act, under D.C. BAR RULES OF PROF'L CONDUCT R. 8.4(c) (1995), for the lawyer to review and use it without consulting the sender).

42. D.C. Bar, Op. 341 (2007). *See also* D.C. Bar, Op. 318 (2003) (noting that where the privileged nature of the document is not apparent on its face, there is no obligation to refrain from reviewing it, and the duty of diligent representation under D.C. Rule 1.3, D.C. BAR RULES OF PROF'L CONDUCT R. 1.3 (2003), may trump confidentiality concerns).

43. D.C. Bar, Op. 341 (2007) at n.10 (referring to FED. R. CIV. P. 26(b)(5)(B) and to D.C. BAR RULES OF PROF'L CONDUCT R. 3.4(c)).

44. FED. R. CIV. P. 26(b)(5).

45. D.C. Bar, Op. 341 (2007). *See also* D.C. BAR RULES OF PROF'L CONDUCT R. 3.4, cmt. 4 (2007) (making it a crime, under some circumstances, to alter or destroy evidence).

46. D.C. Bar, Op. 341 (2007).

inadvertently, he or she must notify and follow the directives of the sending attorney.[47]

In sum, according to the D.C. Bar, when a receiving lawyer has *actual knowledge* that an adversary has inadvertently provided metadata in an electronic document, the lawyer should not review the metadata without notifying the sender and then abiding by the sender's instructions. In all other circumstances, a receiving lawyer may review metadata contained within the electronic files provided by the adversary.

C. The ABA approach

Although the ABA does not distinguish between information voluntarily sent and that produced as a result of a document request or subpoena, its view on metadata is similar to that of the D.C. Bar. ABA Formal Opinion 06-442 makes clear that the ABA Model Rules do not contain any specific prohibition against lawyers receiving and using metadata in electronic documents sent by opposing counsel or an adverse party.[48] Like the D.C. Bar, the ABA opinion places the burden on the sending lawyer to scrub or send a different version of the document to limit the likelihood of transmitting potentially protected metadata.[49]

Again, the reasoning underlying the ABA approach is that under the Model Rules, a lawyer must act competently to safeguard information related to the representation of the client against inadvertent or unauthorized disclosure.[50] Because metadata is "ubiquitous" and often automatic, the burden to remove it falls on the sender.[51] Moreover, because the ABA's Model Code does not pro-

47. *Id. See also* D.C. BAR RULES OF PROF'L CONDUCT R. 8.4(c) (2007) (mandating that the lawyer receiving documents with metadata that contains protected information, when the lawyer knows the documents were sent inadvertently, should advise the sending lawyer and determine whether such protected information was disclosed inadvertently); D.C. Bar, Op. 256 (1995) ("The line we have drawn between an ethical and an unethical use of inadvertently disclosed information is based on the receiving lawyer's knowledge of the inadvertence of the disclosure.").

48. ABA Comm. on Ethics & Prof'l Responsibility, Formal Op. 06-442 (2006).

49. *Id.*

50. MODEL RULES OF PROF'L CONDUCT R. 1.1 & R. 1.6 (2007). *See also* ABA Comm. on Ethics & Prof'l Responsibility, Formal Op. 06-442 (2006).

51. ABA Comm. on Ethics & Prof'l Responsibility, Formal Op. 06-442 (2006).

hibit the use of inadvertently produced materials—electronic or not—the same standards apply to metadata.[52]

As for the receiving attorney, metadata can be reviewed and even mined, but if the party "'knows or reasonably should know that the [information] was inadvertently sent, [the party] shall promptly notify the sender.'"[53]

Like the D.C. Bar opinion, the ABA opinion cites the amendments to the Federal Rules of Civil Procedure that offer safeguards parties can put into place if they are concerned about the inadvertent production of information and metadata, such as "quick peek" and "clawback" agreements[54] under Rule 26(b)(5).[55]

D. Other state bar associations

At least nine other state bar associations have issued opinions on the use and mining of metadata.[56] Notably, unlike the ABA, the Florida Bar opinion states that lawyers should refrain from "harvesting" or "mining" metadata and, also unlike the ABA opinion,

52. *Id.*

53. *Id.* (quoting Model Rules of Prof'l Conduct R. 4.4(b), (2007) and further noting that "[c]omment 3 to the same Model Rule indicates that, unless other law requires otherwise, a lawyer who receives an inadvertently sent document ordinarily may, but is not required to, return it unread, as a matter of professional judgment" (citations omitted)).

54. A "quick peek" agreement is one where the producing party provides requested responses without waiving any privileges. *See generally* Kroll Ontrack, *Rowe v. Zubulake*: A Perspective from the Bench (E-Evidence Thought Leadership Luncheon, New York City, Sept. 23, 2003), http://krollontrack.com/upcoming events/documents/zubulake.pdf. The requesting party then requests certain designated documents it wants produced. A "clawback" agreement provides that documents inadvertently produced must be returned, without a privilege waiver, when the producing party identifies the documents as inadvertently produced. Dennis P. Duffy, Ethics and Professionalism Handbook for Labor and Employment Lawyers 137 (Nat'l Law Inst. 5th ed. 2010).

55. ABA Comm. on Ethics & Prof'l Responsibility, Formal Op. 06-442 (2006) (citing Fed. R. Civ. P. 26(b)(5)). The ABA opinion predates the enactment of Federal Rule of Evidence 502, which offers additional safeguards to parties concerned about inadvertent disclosure. For an in-depth look at Federal Rule 502, see Courtney Barton & David D. Cross, *Protecting the Privilege: New Federal Rule of Evidence 502*, 23(2) ABA In-House Litigator, Winter 2009, and chapters 17 and 18.

56. See the tables at the end of this chapter for additional detail. Although the North Carolina Bar proposed an opinion on the topic in early 2010, in October the Ethics Committee voted to withdraw the opinion and sent it to a subcommittees for further study.

suggests that metadata is almost always produced inadvertently, recognizing that metadata may "reveal confidential and privileged client information that the sender of the document or electronic communication does not wish to be revealed."[57] Like the ABA approach, however, the Florida Bar opinion requires a party that receives inadvertently sent metadata to promptly notify the sender.[58] The Florida Bar opinion specifically states that it is not intended to address the production or viewing of metadata in the discovery context.[59]

The Maryland State Bar likewise ruled that the sending party has an ethical obligation to take reasonable measures to avoid the disclosure of confidential or work-product materials embedded in electronic discovery.[60] But unlike the approach taken by the Florida Bar and similar to the approach taken by the ABA, the Maryland Bar opined that there is no ethical violation if a party reviews or makes use of the metadata without first deciding if it was inadvertently produced.[61] Unlike the ABA, however, the Maryland Bar opinion states that even if the party knows the information was inadvertently produced, there is no obligation to notify the producing party.[62] Although not explicit, it appears that the Maryland opinion applies to both electronic discovery and client confidences, as both are discussed in the opinion; on the other hand, the opinion specifically addresses the use of metadata in the context of litigation.[63]

In the nonlitigation context, attorneys are ethically required to ensure that they are properly managing metadata to prevent disclosing confidential information. This can include routine practices such as forwarding only hard copies, converting documents to static, nonsearchable images, or employing metadata scrubbers. In the litigation context, lawyers should understand their client's practices with respect to metadata, and to the extent metadata is produced, ensure that any and all privileged metadata is redacted and logged as privileged.

57. Fla. State Bar Ass'n Comm. on Prof'l Ethics, Op. 06-2 (2006).

58. *Id.*

59. *Id.*

60. Md. State Bar Ass'n Comm. on Ethics, Op. No. 2007-09 (2006).

61. *Id.*

62. *Id.* Maryland has not adopted ABA Rule 4.4(b), which includes the notice requirement.

63. *Id.*

4. The ethics of vendor oversight and outsourcing

As e-discovery becomes more and more expensive, clients and their attorneys look for creative ways to reduce costs. Outsourcing has become a commonplace vehicle for budget-certainty and to provide data processing and hosting services that are not part of traditional legal assistance.[64] But outsourcing raises some very important ethical considerations that cannot be overlooked.[65] And compliance with ethics rules can add to the costs of using such processes.[66] Parties must consider the all of the costs—including those associated with complying with ethical requirements—in their overall assessment of whether outsourcing is the right avenue in any particular case.

A. Vendor oversight

ABA Model Rule 5.3 governs nonlawyer assistance responsibilities. It states in relevant part:

> With respect to a non-lawyer employed or retained by or associated with a lawyer:

64. *See* DAVID R. ALMOND, JOHN M. MEE & MYRNA SCHACK LATHAM, SUCCESSFUL PARTNERING BETWEEN INSIDE AND OUTSIDE COUNSEL § 26:15, Choosing an Outsourcing Strategy Using Temporary or Contract Lawyers (2009) ("For many corporate legal departments, the use of temporary attorneys is simply an extension of the outsourcing common both in the legal department and in other divisions throughout large companies."); Laurel S. Terry et al., *Transnational Legal Practice*, 43 INT'L LAW. 943, 964 (2009) (noting that the rise in outsourcing particular legal services has made offshore legal outsourcing "another hot topic" in transnational legal practice).

65. *See* ALMOND ET AL., *supra* note 65, §§ 24:46, 24:53, 26:27 (2009) (discussing ethical issues associated with outsourcing legal services). *See also* ABA Comm. on Ethics & Prof'l Responsibility, Formal Op. 08-451 (2008); Fla. Bar, Op. 07-2 (2008), http://www.floridabar.org/tfb/tfbetopin.nsf/SearchView/ETHICS,+OPINION+07-2?opendocument; N.C. State Bar, Formal Ethics Opinion 12 (2007), http://www.ncbar.com/ethics/ethics.asp?page=300 ; San Diego Cnty. Bar Ass'n, Legal Ethics Opinion 2007-1 (2007), https://www.sdcba.org/index.cfm?Pg=ethicsopinion07-1; L.A. Cnty. Bar Ass'n, Formal Op. No. 518 (2006), http:// www.lacba.org/Files/LAL/Vol29No9/2317.pdf; Ass'n of the Bar of the City of N.Y. Comm. on Prof'l & Judicial Ethics [ABCNY], Formal Op. 2006-3 (2006), http://www.abcny.org/index.php/ethics/ethics-opinions-local/2006-opinions.

66. ALMOND ET AL., *supra* note 65 (2009) (discussing additional costs associated with outsourcing legal services). *See also* L.A. Cnty. Bar Ass'n, Formal Op. No. 518 (2006), http://www.lacba.org/Files/LAL/Vol29No9/2317.pdf (discussing costs associated with outsourcing legal services and several methods of distributing those costs between the lawyers and clients).

> * * *
>
> (b) a lawyer having direct supervisory authority over the non-lawyer shall make reasonable efforts to ensure that the person's conduct is compatible with the professional obligations of the lawyer.[67]

The Sedona Conference has also weighed in on this issue. Sedona Principle 6(d) states that "ultimate responsibility for ensuring the preservation, collection, processing, and production of electronically stored information rests with the party and its counsel, not with the non-party consultant or vendor."[68]

Thus, lawyers must adequately supervise the vendors they and/or their client hire to perform e-discovery services. The duties imposed by Rule 26(g) are similar or identical to, and bolster, this ethical requirement.[69] As stated above, Rule 26(g) requires that at least one attorney of record sign every discovery response to certify that the response has been made after reasonable inquiry.[70] If discovery is delegated to vendors without proper oversight, attorneys will not be able to fulfill their duty under Rule 26(g). Sanctions under Rule 26(g) are mandatory.[71]

B. Outsourcing document review and legal work

California, New York, and the ABA each have addressed the ethics of outsourcing legal work. This issue is of particular interest in electronic discovery as much of the review that takes place is outsourced to contract attorneys, sometimes even in other states or abroad.

ABA Formal Opinion 08-451, issued on July 9, 2008, condones outsourcing both legal and nonlegal services—even abroad.[72] The

---

67. MODEL RULES OF PROF'L CONDUCT R. 5.3(b) (2007).
68. THE SEDONA PRINCIPLES: BEST PRACTICES RECOMMENDATIONS & PRINCIPLES FOR ADDRESSING ELECTRONIC DOCUMENT DISCOVERY, Principle 6(d) (2d ed. 2007), http://www.thesedonaconference.org/content/miscFiles/TSC_PRINCP_2nd_ed_607.pdf.
69. FED. R. CIV. P. 26(g). For more on Rule 26(g), see chapter 31.
70. FED R. CIV. P. 26(g). *See also* Mancia v. Mayflower Textile Servs., Co., 253 F.R.D. 354, 257 (D. Md. 2008) (discussing Rule 26(g)'s requirement that every discovery response must be signed by at least one attorney of record certifying that the response has been made after reasonable inquiry).
71. FED. R. CIV. P. 26(g).
72. ABA Comm. on Ethics & Prof'l Responsibility, Formal Op. 08-451 (2008). For a general discussion of outsourcing, see J. BARKETT, *supra* note 3, 81–98.

lawyer must disclose these arrangements to the client, and Rules 1.1,[73] 5.3(b),[74] and 5.1(b) apply.[75] Rule 5.1(b) states that "[a] lawyer having direct supervisory authority over another lawyer shall make reasonable efforts to ensure that the other lawyer conforms to the Rules of Professional Conduct."[76] Moreover, lawyers who outsource abroad must assess whether the system of legal education in the country where they plan to outsource is comparable to that in the United States, whether the legal profession has core ethical principles similar to the United States, and whether its disciplinary system is effective for enforcement.[77] If the country does not have comparable systems, the level of scrutiny and oversight over the outsourced work is heightened.[78] The opinion also requires that fees for outsourced work must be reasonable, and it holds that firms can mark up the actual costs of outsourcing only for reasonable overhead.[79]

Los Angeles Bar Opinion 518 addresses whether it is ethically permissible for a California attorney in a civil case to hire an out-of state legal research and brief-writing company to perform legal research and draft briefs for the attorney to use in connection with the attorney's representation of the client.[80] The Los Angeles County Bar Association Professional Responsibility and Ethics Committee opined that such arrangements are ethically permissible, provided the attorney complies with certain ethical requirements, including that the attorney at all times retains independent professional judgment, that the attorney signs the brief and remains ultimately responsible for its accuracy and content, and the attorney may have a duty to disclose the arrangement to the client.[81] In addition, the attorney must ensure that there is no conflict of interest and no

73. MODEL RULES OF PROF'L CONDUCT R. 1.1 (2007).
74. *Id.* R. 5.3(b) (2007). *See supra* note 67 and accompanying text.
75. MODEL RULES OF PROF'L CONDUCT R. 5.1(b) (2007).
76. *Id.*
77. ABA Comm. on Ethics & Prof'l Responsibility, Formal Op. 08-451 (2008).
78. *Id.*
79. *Id.*
80. L.A. Cnty. Bar Ass'n, Formal Op. No. 518 (2006), http://www.lacba.org/Files/LAL/Vol29No9/2317.pdf.
81. *Id.*

violation of client confidences or secrets.[82] The attorney may pass on the costs of the outsourcing to the client.[83]

New York Formal Opinion 2006-3 addresses the outsourcing of legal support services generally in much the same was as the ABA does. But it also addresses whether it is ethically permissible to outsource these services to a nonlawyer overseas.[84] Like Los Angeles, New York also found outsourcing ethically permissible as long as safeguards similar to those required by the ABA are in place: the lawyer must rigorously supervise the nonlawyer, preserve the client's confidences and secrets, avoid conflicts of interest, and when necessary, obtain advance client consent to outsourcing.[85] The lawyer may pass on only the direct costs associated with outsourcing plus a reasonable allocation of overhead expenses.[86]

5. Electronic files: Who owns them?

Another ethics issue arising from the intersection of law and technology is whether an attorney is ethically obligated, upon termination of employment, to promptly release to a client electronic versions of all correspondence, pleadings, discovery requests and responses, depositions, and/or transactional documents.[87] The State Bar of California, in Formal Opinion 2007-174, answered that an attorney is ethically obligated to release such information to a former client.[88] But this ethical obligation does not require an attorney to create electronic files if they do not exist or to change

82. *Id.*

83. *Id.*

84. N.Y. City Bar Ass'n, Formal Op. No. 2006-3, http://www.abcny.org/Ethics/eth2006.htm.

85. *Id.* (agreeing with L.A. Cnty. Bar Ass'n, Formal Op. No. 518 (2006), http://www.lacba.org/Files/LAL/Vol29No9/2317.pdf).

86. N.Y. City Bar Ass'n, Formal Op. No. 2006-3, http://www.abcny.org/Ethics/eth2006.htm (citing ABA Comm. on Ethics & Prof'l Responsibility, Formal Opinion 93-379 (1993)).

87. *See* Cal. State Bar Standing Comm. on Prof'l Responsibility & Conduct, Formal Op. 2007-174 (2007) (addressing the issue of whether "[a]n attorney [is] ethically obligated, upon termination of employment, promptly to release to a client, at the client's request, (1) an electronic version of e-mail correspondence, (2) an electronic version of the pleadings, (3) an electronic version of discovery requests and responses, (4) an electronic deposition and exhibit database, and/or (5) an electronic version of transactional documents"). For a general discussion, see J. BARKETT, *supra* note 3, 52–58.

88. *Id.*

the application in which the documents were created.[89] Prior to releasing the information, the attorney must take reasonable steps to strip the documents of any confidential metadata.[90]

6. Conclusion

These ethics opinions highlight how evolving technologies have changed the practice of law. They should remind lawyers that the duty of competency affects all aspects of legal practice—even topics like metadata, outsourcing, and the return of electronic files, which may appear unrelated. More importantly, they underscore the need for lawyers practicing in the twenty-first century to grasp the fundamentals of technology in order to meet their obligation of ethical client representation.

89. *Id.* For a discussion of the "mirror image" issue, that is, whether an attorney is permitted to digitize clients' paper documents, in an attempt to create a "paperless" office, see J. BARKETT, supra note 3, 46–49.
90. *Id.*

Comparison of Metadata Ethics Opinions

A summary of ethics opinions from the ABA and selected states as of December 2010.

Jurisdiction	Ethics Opinion/ Rules	Duty upon Sender to Exercise Reasonable Care?
ABA	Formal Op. 06-442 (Aug. 5, 2006) Formal. Op. 05-437 (2005) ABA Model Rule 4.4(b) (2002)	**YES.** "A lawyer who is concerned about the possibility of sending, producing, or providing to opposing counsel a document that contains or might contain metadata, or who wishes to take some action to reduce or remove the potentially harmful consequences of its dissemination, may be able to limit the likelihood of its transmission by "scrubbing" metadata from documents or by sending a different version of the document without the embedded information." (06-0442)

Mining Metadata Prohibited?	Notification Required for Metadata?	Discovery/FRCP
NO. "Some authorities have addressed questions related to a lawyer's search for, or use of, metadata under the rubric of a lawyer's honesty, and have found such conduct ethically impermissible. The Committee does not share such a view, but instead reads the recent addition of Rule 4.4(b) identifying the sole requirement of providing notice to the sender of the receipt of inadvertently sent information, as evidence of the intention to set no other specific restrictions on the receiving lawyer's conduct found in other Rules." (06-0442)	**YES, if inadvertent.** "Whether the receiving lawyer knows or reasonably should know that opposing counsel's sending, producing, or otherwise making available an electronic document that contains metadata was "inadvertent" within the meaning of Rule 4.4(b), and is thereby obligated to provide notice of its receipt to the sender, is a subject that is outside the scope of this opinion." (06-442) "A lawyer who receives a document from opposing parties or their lawyers and knows or reasonably should know that the document was inadvertently sent should promptly notify the sender in order to permit the sender to take protective measures." (05-437)	06-442 would seem to apply in the discovery context as the commentators discuss discovery and the applicability of nonwaiver agreements under the Federal Rules of Civil Procedure in footnotes 13 and 15.

State Opinions

Jurisdiction	Ethics Opinion	Duty upon Sender to Exercise Reasonable Care?
Alabama	R0-2007-02	**YES.** "An attorney has an ethical duty to exercise reasonable care when transmitting electronic documents to ensure that he or she does not disclose his or her client's secrets and confidences . . . an attorney would need to exercise greater care in submitting an electronic document to an opposing party"

Mining Metadata Prohibited?	Notification Required for Metadata?	Discovery/FRCP
YES. "Absent express authorization from a court, it is ethically impermissible for an attorney to mine metadata from an electronic document he or she inadvertently or improperly receives from another party."	**YES.** The opinion does not address the notification requirement and the Alabama Model Rules of Professional Responsibility have not been amended to include ABA Model Rule 4.4(b). However, Alabama adopted ABA Formal Op. 92-368, which requires notification.	"One possible exception to the prohibition . . . involves electronic discovery . . . metadata may be relevant and material to the issues at hand."

Jurisdiction	Ethics Opinion	Duty upon Sender to Exercise Reasonable Care?
Arizona	Arizona Ethics Opinion 07-03 (Nov. 2007)	**YES.** "The lawyer must take reasonable care not to violate any duty of disclosure to which the lawyer or the lawyer's client is subject."

Mining Metadata Prohibited?	Notification Required for Metadata?	Discovery/FRCP
YES. "The recipient lawyer has a corresponding duty not to 'mine' the document for metadata that may be embedded therein or otherwise engage in conduct which amounts to an unjustified intrusion into the client-lawyer relationship that exists between the opposing party and his or her counsel."	**YES.** "A lawyer who received an electronic document from another party, and who discovers metadata embedded in the document that the lawyer knows or reasonably should know is revealing confidential or privileged information, has a duty to notify the sender and to preserve the status quo for a reasonable period of time in order to permit the sender to take protective measures."	It is unclear whether this opinion applies in the discovery context. However, the opinion states that "a lawyer who receives an electronic communication may attempt to discovery the metadata that is embedded therein if he or she has the consent of the sender, or if such conduct is allowed by rule, order, or procedure of a court or other applicable provision of law. Even so, if the lawyer comes across information that the lawyer knows or reasonably should know was not intended to be transmitted by the sender, the recipient has a duty to follow the procedures set forth in ER 4.4(b).

Jurisdiction	Ethics Opinion	Duty upon Sender to Exercise Reasonable Care?
Colorado	Ethics Opinion 119 (May 17, 2008)	**YES.** "A Sending Lawyer who transmits electronic documents or files has a duty to use reasonable care to guard against the disclosure of metadata containing Confidential Information."

Mining Metadata Prohibited?	Notification Required for Metadata?	Discovery/FRCP
NO (unless receiving lawyer reasonably should know that metadata contain or constitute Confidential Information, or if a Sending Lawyer notifies the Receiving Lawyer that Confidential Information was inadvertently sent). "A Receiving Lawyer who receives electronic documents or files general may search for and review metadata." Note: Colorado disagrees with the term "mining": "referring to searching for metadata as 'mining' . . . is misleading."	**YES.** "If a Receiving Lawyer knows or reasonably should know that the metadata contain or constitute Confidential Information, the Receiving Lawyer should assume that the Confidential Information was transmitted inadvertently, unless the Receiving Lawyer knows that confidentiality has been waived. The Receiving Lawyer must promptly notify the sender."	Although not explicitly addressing the issue, the opinion alludes to FRCP 34 as an example of how in some circumstances metadata are intended to be searched for, reviewed, and used.

Jurisdiction	Ethics Opinion	Duty upon Sender to Exercise Reasonable Care?
District of Columbia	D.C. Bar Opinion 341 (Sept. 2007)	**YES.** "Lawyers sending electronic documents outside of the context of responding to discovery or subpoenas have an obligation under Rule 1.6 to take reasonable steps to maintain confidentiality of documents in their possession."
Florida	06-02 (Sept. 15, 2006)	**YES.** "A lawyer who is sending an electronic document should take care to ensure the confidentiality of all information contained in the document, including metadata."

Mining Metadata Prohibited?	Notification Required for Metadata?	Discovery/FRCP
NO (unless actual knowledge). "Where the privileged nature of the documents it not apparent on it's [sic] face, there is no obligation to refrain from reviewing it, and the duty of diligent representation under D.C. Rule 1.3 may trump confidentiality concerns." If, on the other hand, a party has actual knowledge that the sender inadvertently included metadata in an electronic document, it is a dishonest act for the lawyer to review and use it without consulting with the sender.	**YES, if actual knowledge.** But also, "a prudent receiving lawyer who is uncertain whether the sender intended to include particular information should contact the sending lawyer to inquire."	The opinion applies to and distinguishes between information produced as a result of a document request or subpoena and that voluntarily sent (e.g., letter to opposing counsel).
YES. "A lawyer receiving an electronic document should not try to obtain information from metadata that the lawyer knows or should know is not intended for the receiving lawyer."	**YES.** "A lawyer who inadvertently receives information via metadata in an electronic document should notify the sender of the information's receipt."	"The opinion is not intended to address metadata in the context of discovery documents."

Jurisdiction	Ethics Opinion	Duty upon Sender to Exercise Reasonable Care?
Maine	Ethics Opinion No. 196 (Oct. 16, 2008)	**YES.** "Attorneys are ethically required to take reasonable measures to avoid the communication of confidential information, regardless of the mode of transmission."
Maryland (context of litigation)	2007-09	**YES.** "The Committee believes that, absent an agreement with the other parties (such as is contemplated in proposed Federal Rules 16(b)(5) and (6), the sending attorney has an ethical obligation to take reasonable measures to avoid the disclosure of confidential or work product materials imbedded in the electronic discovery."

Mining Metadata Prohibited?	Notification Required for Metadata?	Discovery/FRCP
YES. "An attorney may not ethically take steps to uncover metadata, embedded in an electronic document sent by counsel for another party, in an effort to detect information that is legally confidential and is or should be reasonably known not to have be intentionally communicated."	The opinion is silent on notice.	The opinion "is not intended to deal with the extent to which relevant information may be sought in litigation through proper discovery under the guidance of the court."
NO. "Subject to any legal standards or requirements (case law, statutes, rules of procedure, administrative rules, etc.), this Committee believes that there is no ethical violation if the recipient attorney (or those working under the attorney's direction) reviews or makes use of the metadata without first ascertaining whether the sender intended to include such metadata."	**NO.** "The Maryland R. of Prof. Cond. . . . have not been mended to include ABA M.R. 4.4(b). Accordingly, the Md. R. Prof. Cond. do not require the receiving attorney to notify the sending attorney that there may have been an inadvertent transmittal of privileged . . . materials. Of course, the receiving lawyer can, and probably should, communicate with his or her client concerning the pros and cons of whether to notify the sending attorney . . ."	"The Committee believes that, absent an agreement with the other parties (such as is contemplated in proposed Federal Rules 16(b)(5) and (6), the sending attorney has an ethical obligation to take reasonable measures to avoid the disclosure of confidential or work product materials imbedded in the electronic discovery."

Jurisdiction	Ethics Opinion	Duty upon Sender to Exercise Reasonable Care?
Minnesota	No. 22 (Mar. 26, 2010)	**YES.** Senders have a duty to remove confidential information from metadata before sending electronic information to opposing parties.
New Hampshire	No. 2008-2009/4 (Apr. 16, 2009)	**YES.** Lawyers sending electronic materials to opposing counsel are ethically required to take reasonable care to avoid improper disclosure of confidential information in metadata, including appropriate training and education on reasonable measures that can be taken to reduce the likelihood of improper disclosure of confidential information through transmission of metadata.

Mining Metadata Prohibited?	Notification Required for Metadata?	Discovery/FRCP
"Whether and when a [receiving] lawyer may be advised to look or not look for such metadata is a fact specific question beyond the scope of this Opinion."	**YES.** If a lawyer receives a document which the lawyer knows or reasonably should know inadvertently contains confidential or privileged metadata, the lawyer shall promptly notify the sender as required by Rule 4.4(b), MRPC.	Opinion 22 addresses only a lawyer's ethical obligations regarding metadata under the MRPR and not in the context of litigation or other circumstances.
YES. Receiving lawyers have an obligation not to search for, review, or use metadata containing confidential information that is associated with transmission of electronic materials from opposing counsel.	**YES.** Receiving lawyers necessarily know that any confidential information contained in electronic materials is inadvertently sent, triggering the obligation under Rule 4.4(b). To the extent that metadata is mistakenly reviewed, receiving lawyers should abide by the directives in Rule 4.4(b).	"This opinion does not address electronic materials subject to discovery or subpoena under applicable rules of court or law."

Jurisdiction	Ethics Opinion	Duty upon Sender to Exercise Reasonable Care?
New York	NY Comm. on Prof'l Ethics Op. 749 (2001) Op. 782 (2004) State Bar Op. 2003-04 (2003)	**YES.** "Lawyers have a duty to use reasonable care when transmitting documents by e-mail to prevent the disclosure of metadata containing client confidences or secrets." (782) Attorneys who use technology to communicate with clients must exercise reasonable care by familiarizing themselves with the attendant risks associated with metadata and taking affirmative steps to eliminate those risks. (782)

Mining Metadata Prohibited?	Notification Required for Metadata?	Discovery/FRCP
YES. "[U]se of computer technology to access client confidences and secrets revealed in metadata constitutes an impermissible intrusion on the attorney-client privilege in violation of the Code." (749)	**YES, if inadvertent.** "A lawyer who receives a misdirected communication containing confidences or secrets should promptly notify the sender and refrain from further reading or listening to the communication, and should follow the sender's directions regarding destruction or return of the communication. However, if there is a legal dispute before a tribunal and the receiving attorney believes in good faith that the communication appropriately may be retained and used, the receiving attorney may submit the communication for in camera consideration by the tribunal as to its disposition. Additionally, the receiving attorney is not prohibited as an ethical matter from using the information to which the attorney was exposed before knowing or having reason to know the communication was inadvertently sent . . ." (2003–04)	These opinions predate the December 2006 amendments to the Federal Rules of Civil Procedure.

Jurisdiction	Ethics Opinion	Duty upon Sender to Exercise Reasonable Care?
North Carolina	1009 Formal Ethics Op. No. 1 (Jan. 15, 2010)	**YES.** Lawyer must use reasonable care to prevent disclosure of confidential information hidden in metadata when transmitting an electronic document.
Pennsylvania	Formal Opinion 2009-100 (2009)	**YES.** Sender has an obligation to avoid sending electronic materials containing metadata where the disclosure of such metadata would harm the client's interests.

Mining Metadata Prohibited?	Notification Required for Metadata?	Discovery/FRCP
YES. A lawyer may not search for confidential information embedded in metadata of an electronic communication from another party or a lawyer for another party.	**YES.** If the lawyer unintentionally views metadata, the lawyer must notify the sender and may not subsequently use the information revealed without the consent of the other lawyer or party.	Although not explicitly addressed, the opinion appears to apply in the context of judicial proceedings, including discovery.
NO. An attorney who receives inadvertently transmitted information from opposing counsel may generally examine and use the metadata for the client's benefit.	**YES.** If the receiving lawyer knows or reasonably should know that the document was inadvertently sent, the lawyer must treat such metadata as an inadvertent communication under Rule 4.4(b) and promptly notify the sender of the receipt of the materials.	"The substantive law governing whether the recipient may use the metadata received in legal proceedings or negotiations is outside the scope of this Opinion."

Jurisdiction	Ethics Opinion	Duty upon Sender to Exercise Reasonable Care?
Vermont	Ethics Opinion 2009-1	**YES.** "Based on the language of the VRPC, a lawyer has a duty to exercise reasonable care to ensure that confidential information protected by the attorney client privilege and the work product doctrine is not disclosed."

Mining Metadata Prohibited?	Notification Required for Metadata?	Discovery/FRCP
NO. "The Vermont Bar Association Professional Responsibility Section finds nothing to compel the conclusion that a lawyer who receives an electronic file from opposing counsel would be ethically prohibited from reviewing that file using any available tools to expose the file's content, including metadata."	**YES.** "With the adoption of Rule 4.4(b), Vermont lawyers are subject to the obligation to notify opposing counsel if they receive documents that they know or reasonably should know were inadvertently disclosed."	The opinion discusses metadata in the litigation context and states, "[T]he Professional Responsibility Section is aware of no authority or support for the proposition that a lawyer can redact, remove, or withhold metadata from electronic client documents that are being disclosed during discovery." All other provisions of the opinion apply in the litigation context.

Jurisdiction	Ethics Opinion	Duty upon Sender to Exercise Reasonable Care?
West Virginia	Ethics Opinion 2009-1	**YES.** "It is the duty of the lawyer sending electronic documents to protect sensitive metadata, and protecting metadata is not difficult."

Mining Metadata Prohibited?	Notification Required for Metadata?	Discovery/FRCP
YES. "[I]f a lawyer has received electronic documents and has actual knowledge that metadata was inadvertently sent, the receiving lawyer should not review the metadata before consulting with the sending lawyer to determine whether the metadata includes work-product or confidences."	**YES.** Receiving lawyer must consult with the sending lawyer.	"In a discovery or subpoena context, however, a lawyer must be careful in situations where electronic documents constitute tangible evidence. Rule 3.4(a) prohibits altering, destroying, or concealing material having potential evidentiary value. Therefore, in certain instances involving discovery responses or subpoena compliance, removal of metadata may be prohibited and must be produced when requested and not objected to. However, any metadata that is privileged can still be protected and exempt from discovery, upon proper assertion of a privilege."

CHAPTER 30

THE SEDONA CONFERENCE COOPERATION PROCLAMATION

BY MICHAEL D. BERMAN

Many chapters of this book contain references to the Sedona Conference, which has been highly influential in the e-discovery arena. In 2008, the Conference issued a Cooperation Proclamation—described by Judge Facciola (in chapter 1) as "nothing less than an attempt to replace the adversarial nature of discovery, particularly as it pertains to electronic discovery, with a cooperation model in which the parties and their counsel use every means at their disposal to resolve their controversies amicably." This chapter talks further about the Proclamation.

Discourage litigation. Persuade your neighbours to compromise whenever you can. Point out to them how the nominal

---

This chapter is based on an article that first appeared in the 2009 publication of the ABA Technology for the Litigator newsletter. A comprehensive discussion of the Cooperation Proclamation can be found in Volume 10 of The Sedona Conference Journal (Fall 2009).

winner is often a real loser—in fees, expenses, and waste of time. As a peace-maker the lawyer has a superior opportunity of being a good man. There will still be business enough.

—Abraham Lincoln, Note for a Law Lecture Written about July 1, 1850

Several years ago, many courts and bar associations, interested in increasing professionalism, promulgated civility codes aimed at preventing abrasive and inappropriate litigation behavior.[1] The 1997 Maryland code states: "Civility is the cornerstone of the legal profession." The need for such codes, although based on egregious and perhaps idiosyncratic instances, was clear.

In a famous example, during a deposition one attorney called the other a profane name and remarked that the opposing counsel "could gag a maggot off a meat wagon."[2] In another deposition, one attorney said to another attorney: "I don't have to talk to you, little lady." He then said: "Tell that little mouse over there to pipe down," and asked, "What do you know, young girl?"[3] Similarly, in *Freeman v. Schointuck*,[4] defendant's counsel was sarcastic, threatening, and "repeatedly and flagrantly" insulting.

The impact of such conduct is clear. The *Freeman* opinion noted that the "cooperative exchange of information without the need for constant court intervention" is the "very fabric which holds together the process of pretrial discovery" and ordered a written apology and professionalism training. In *Cache La Poudre Feeds LLC v. Land O'Lakes, Inc.*,[5] the court described an acrimonious discovery dispute and stated: "Both sides have engaged in discovery conduct that unnecessarily protracted the litigation and increased its attendant costs for all parties. The unnecessarily rancorous tone of counsels' rhetoric, both in writing and during court hearings, has only exacerbated the situation and hindered the parties' ability to find a reasonable solution to their discovery disputes."

1. For a collection of professionalism codes, see ABA, Professionalism Codes, http://www.abanet.org/cpr/professionalism/profcodes.html.
2. Paramount Commc'ns, Inc. v. QVC Network, Inc., 637 A.2d 34, 54 (Del. 1994).
3. Principe v. Assay Partners, 586 N.Y.S.2d 182 (Sup. Ct. 1992).
4. 192 F.R.D. 187 (D. Md. 2000).
5. 244 F.R.D. 614, 618 n. 3 (D. Colo. 2007).

Mullaney v. Aude[6] presented a situation where an attorney called opposing counsel "babe." When counsel replied, "Babe? What generation are you from?" the response was: "At least I didn't call you a bimbo." On review, the appellate court noted that "[t]he absence of civility and respect exhibited by lawyers towards one another has been for years the subject of significant concern for bar and bench leaders." Similarly, the New York court in *Principe* noted: "An attorney who exhibits a lack of civility, good manners and common courtesy tarnishes the image of the legal profession."[7] The *Freeman* court wrote: "No one expects the deposition of a key witness in a hotly contested case to be a non-stop exchange of pleasantries. However, it must not be allowed to become an excuse for counsel to engage in acts of rhetorical road rage against a deponent and opposing counsel. . . ."[8]

The emergence of broad discovery, often conducted in deposition rooms outside of the presence of judicial officers, and the implosion of trial practice provided a forum in which antagonistic conduct could occur, often "under the radar."[9] Professionalism programs, and state and local civility codes, took aim at this conduct. But, obviously, more was needed.[10]

A series of procedural developments, while aimed at redressing problems such as these as well as others, also occasionally operated to increase antagonistic conduct. The attorney certification

6. 126 Md. App. 639, *cert. denied*, 356 Md. 18 (1999).

7. *Principe*, 586 N.Y.S.2d at 184 (citation omitted).

8. 192 F.R.D. at 189.

9. *See Mullaney*, 126 Md. App. at 654; P. Grimm, *et al.*, MARYLAND DISCOVERY PROBLEMS AND SOLUTIONS at xiii (MICPEL 2008).

10. In a dissenting opinion, Justice Powell wrote that "the widespread abuse of discovery . . . is a prime cause of delay and expense in civil litigation. The extent of this abuse has been of increasing concern. It was the subject of close attention at the Pound Conference held in St. Paul, Minn., in April 1976, and it was scrutinized further by the Pound Conference Follow-Up Task Force. The Task Force, chaired by then Judge Griffin B. Bell, recommended that the appropriate organizations of the bench and bar should 'accord a high priority to the problem of abuses in the use of pretrial procedures . . . with a view to appropriate action by state and federal courts.' Following the studies that ensued, the Section of Litigation of the American Bar Association submitted recommendations for substantial changes in the provisions of the Rules of Civil Procedure respecting pretrial discovery. The Committee on Rules of Practice and Procedure of the Judicial Conference, after considering these and other recommendations, has circulated for comment a number of proposed amendments to the Rules." ACF Indus., Carter Carburetor Div. v. EEOC, 439 U.S. 1081, 1086–87 (1979).

requirement of Rule 11 of the Federal Rules of Civil Procedure, a mechanism for discouraging unjustified pleadings, frequently led to knee-jerk filing of sanctions motions. In fact, the U.S. District Court for the District of Maryland promulgated Local Rule 105.8, stating that sanctions motions should not be filed "as a matter of course," and providing that a party targeted in such a motion need not respond, unless the court, after review of the motion, directed a response.

Similarly, Federal Rule of Civil Procedure 26(g),[11] adding a certification requirement in connection with the filing of disclosures and discovery pleadings, has placed attorneys in the position of challenging the conduct of other attorneys.[12] And, of course, rules imposing sanctions for discovery lapses, such as Rule 37, often had the same effect.

This is not to say that the Federal Rules are misplaced or poorly drafted; however, one could assert that the sanctions components of Rules 11, 26(g), and 37, as well as motions directed at the courts' inherent powers, developed a civil procedure analog to a *Brady* attack on alleged prosecutorial misconduct.[13] In short, under the sanctions rules, civil litigators could obtain a tactical advantage by alleging deficiencies in the performance of opposing counsel. The opposing attorney, countering such allegations, was often tempted to respond in kind. Civility suffered.

While electronic discovery has been percolating through the courts for decades[14]—and became well recognized with the 18-minute gap in the Watergate tapes[15]—the December 2006 amend-

11. Rule 26(g) is discussed more fully in chapter 31.

12. *See* Qualcomm Inc. v. Broadcom Corp., 2008 U.S. Dist. LEXIS 911 (S.D. Cal. 2008), *vacated in part and remanded*, 2008 U.S. Dist. LEXIS 16897 (S.D. Cal. 2008), *appeal dismissed*, 2008 U.S. App. LEXIS 9103, 18934 (Fed. Cir. 2008) ("The Court finds that each of the following attorneys contributed to Qualcomm's monumental discovery violation and is personally responsible. . . ."), *on remand*, 2010 WL 1336937 (S.D. Cal. Apr. 2, 2010); *Land O'Lakes*, 244 F.R.D. at 626, 636 (deposition of general counsel).

13. Brady v. Maryland, 373 U.S. 83 (1963).

14. R. Marcus, *E-Discovery and Beyond: Toward a Brave New World or 1984?*, 25 REV. LITIG. 633 (2006), *reprinted in* 236 F.R.D. 598, 614, 618 (2006); J. Facciola & J. Redgrave, *Asserting and Challenging Privilege Claims in Modern Litigation: The Facciola-Redgrave Framework*, 4 FED. CTS. L. REV. 19, 36 (2009) ("Nearly twenty-five years ago, in a Utah district court Judge Greene saw this as a coming problem, noting that 'most court battles now involve discovery of some type of computer-stored information. . . .' ") (citation omitted).

15. Marcus, *supra* note 14.

ments to the Federal Rules of Civil Procedure, coupled with the emergence of the personal computer, the initial Sedona Conference "best practices" guidelines,[16] and *Zubulake v. UBS Warburg*,[17] introduced a new dimension to civil litigation. For example, *Intel Microprocessor* involved electronically stored information that would reach approximately 137 miles high, if it had been printed on paper.[18] Discovery cost $6 million in a recent case.[19] Concepts like "terabytes" of information began to creep into legal jargon. Electronically stored information, with its unique characteristics, such as large volume, fragility and persistence, metadata, variety of storage media, differences in form ("native" versus "static"), and potential high costs, presented new and different issues. The "information explosion" provided additional impetus to change the litigation system toward a more cooperative model.[20] Courts imposed significant sanctions for e-discovery lapses,[21] and delved deeply into attorney-client communications.[22] Decisions created situations in which the interests of in-house and retained counsel might be at odds with each other.[23] Again, there was a need for guidance.

16. THE SEDONA PRINCIPLES: BEST PRACTICES RECOMMENDATIONS & PRINCIPLES FOR ADDRESSING ELECTRONIC DOCUMENT PRODUCTION (Mar. 2003), http://www.thesedonaconference.org/content/miscFiles/SedonaPrinciples200303.pdf.

17. 229 F.R.D. 422 (S.D.N.Y. 2004) (one in a series of decisions).

18. *In re* Intel Microprocessor Antitrust Litig., 2008 WL 2310288, at * 2 (D. Del. 2008) (related decisions omitted).

19. *In re* Fannie Mae Sec. Litig., 552 F.3d 814 (D.C. Cir. 2009) ("OFHEO undertook extensive efforts to comply with the stipulated order, hiring 50 contract attorneys solely for that purpose. The total amount OFHEO spent on the individual defendants' discovery requests eventually reached over $6 million, more than 9 percent of the agency's entire annual budget.").

20. G. Paul & J. Baron, *Information Inflation: Can the Legal System Adapt?*, 13 RICH. J.L. & TECH. 10, 16–17 (2007) ("Without greater cooperation among adversaries, parties are doomed to any number of defeating consequences . . ."); *see* chapters 20 and 21.

21. *E.g.*, *Zubulake*, 229 F.R.D. at 422; Thompson v. U.S. Dep't of HUD, 219 F.R.D. 93 (D. Md. 2003).

22. See chapter 16.

23. Qualcomm Inc. v. Broadcom Corp., 2008 U.S. Dist. LEXIS 51748, at *11 n.6 (S.D. Cal. 2008) ("Qualcomm's self-serving statements that 'outside counsel selects . . . the custodians whose documents should be searched' . . . does not relieve Qualcomm of its obligations. . . . Qualcomm is a large corporation with an extensive [in-house] legal staff; it clearly had the ability to identify the correct witnesses and determine the correct computers to search and search terms to

Many courts promulgated local rules to provide that guidance.[24] For example, in the winter of 2006, the U.S. District Court for the District of Maryland, in conjunction with the Bar, formed a committee to draft a suggested protocol for the discovery of electronically stored information (ESI).[25] The Protocol was the product of over 20 attorneys and forensic experts who labored for months, and was posted on the court website to provide voluntary, nonbinding guidance. The goal of the Protocol is to provide "a comprehensive framework to address and resolve a wide range of ESI issues" and to "facilitate the just, speedy, and inexpensive conduct of discovery involving ESI in civil cases, and to promote, whenever possible, the resolution of disputes regarding the discovery of ESI without court intervention." In short, the Protocol is a road map to cooperative handling of ESI issues.

The Sedona Conference has, for years, written about the need for reason and dialogue in the ESI context.[26] In July 2008, it issued its Cooperation Proclamation.[27] The Proclamation notes that "courts have seen escalating motion practice, overreaching, obstruction, and extensive, but unproductive discovery disputes—in some cases precluding adjudication on the merits altogether—when parties treat the discovery process in an adversarial manner. Neither law nor logic compels these outcomes." The Proclamation "launches a national drive to promote open and forthright information sharing, dialogue (internal and external), training, and the development of practical tools to facilitate cooperative, collaborative, transparent discovery. This Proclamation challenges the bar to achieve these goals and refocus litigation toward the substantive resolution of legal disputes."

---

use. Qualcomm just lacked the desire to do so."); *see* Swofford v. Eslinger, 2009 WL 3818593, at *4, 11 n.10 (M.D. Fla. Sept. 28, 2009).

24. For a collection of local rules governing ESI practice, see LexisNexis, Online Law Library: Local Rules of Federal Circuit Courts and District Courts, http://www.applieddiscovery.com/ws_display.asp?filter=Federal%20District%20 Courts.

25. U.S. DIST. CT., DIST. OF MD., SUGGESTED PROTOCOL FOR DISCOVERY OF ELECTRONICALLY STORED INFORMATION (2007), http://www.mdd.uscourts.gov/news/news/ESIProtocol.pdf.

26. *See* THE SEDONA PRINCIPLES: BEST PRACTICES, *supra* note 16, at 2 (stating that a "rule of reasonableness" is a useful guide).

27. THE SEDONA CONFERENCE COOPERATION PROCLAMATION (2008), http://www.thesedonaconference.org/content/miscFiles/Cooperation_Proclamation.pdf.

The Cooperation Proclamation notes: "Lawyers have twin duties of loyalty: While they are retained to be zealous advocates for their clients, they bear a professional obligation to conduct discovery in a diligent and candid manner. Their combined duty is to strive in the best interests of their clients to achieve the best results at a reasonable cost, with integrity and candor as officers of the court. Cooperation does not conflict with the advancement of their clients' interests—it enhances it. Only when lawyers confuse advocacy with adversarial conduct are these twin duties in conflict." The Proclamation states: "Over-contentious discovery is a cost that has outstripped any advantage in the face of ESI and the data deluge. It is not in anyone's interest to waste resources on unnecessary disputes, and the legal system is strained by 'gamesmanship' or 'hiding the ball,' to no practical effect."[28] In the words of the Sedona Conference: "This 'Cooperation Proclamation' calls for a paradigm shift for the discovery process. . . ." The Proclamation concludes: "It is time to build upon modern Rules amendments, state and federal, which address e-discovery. Using this springboard, the legal profession can engage in a comprehensive effort to promote pre-trial discovery cooperation. Our 'officer of the court' duties demand no less."[29]

As the Sedona Conference notes: "This [Cooperation Proclamation] project is not utopian; rather, it is a tailored effort to effectuate the mandate of court rules calling for a 'just, speedy, and inexpensive determination of every action' and the fundamental ethical principles governing our profession."[30] In fact, more than 100 trial and appellate judges across the nation have endorsed the Cooperation Proclamation, and it has been repeatedly cited by the courts and commentators.[31]

---

28. *Accord* Hopson v. Mayor and C.C. of Balt., 232 F.R.D. 228 (D. Md. 2005) ("The days when the requesting party can expect to 'get it all' and the producing party to produce whatever they feel like producing are long gone.").

29. For a discussion of how Rule 26(g) imposes a duty to cooperate, see chapter 31.

30. *Id.*

31. The Sedona Conference, Judicial Endorsements (updated Sept. 30, 2010), http://www.thesedonaconference.org/content/tsc_cooperation_proclamation/endorsements.pdf. For example, the Cooperation Proclamation was endorsed, and supported the holding of the court in, *Mancia v. Mayflower Textile Services Co.*, 2008 U.S. Dist. LEXIS 83740 (D. Md. 2008). In that decision, battling litigants were directed to meet, confer, develop a "discovery budget," and attempt to resolve their differences in light of that budget.

Courts have not hesitated to negatively comment on a refusal to cooperate. In *In Re Seroquel Products Liability Litigation,*[32] for example, the court stated that a party's "failure to cooperate in the production of the databases and its failure to timely and systematically produce electronic discovery associated with eighty [of the party's] 'custodians' in any manageable, searchable form are sanctionable conduct." And in *Kay Beer Distributing, Inc. v. Energy Brands, Inc.,*[33] the court described "three separate emails from counsel for Energy Brands offering to work with Kay Beer's counsel in formulating search terms to locate emails that might be relevant." It then wrote: "Instead of working with Energy Brands' counsel, Kay Beer seems to have persisted in its demand that Energy Brands turn over all ESI that even mentions its name or some variant thereof." In *Mancia,*[34] after describing a lack of cooperation, the court ordered the parties to confer and summed up the dispute as follows:

> [H]ad these steps been taken by counsel at the start of discovery, most, if not all, of the disputes could have been resolved without involving the court. It also is apparent that there is nothing at all about the cooperation needed to evaluate the discovery outlined above that requires the parties to abandon meritorious arguments they may have, or even to commit to resolving all disagreements on their own. Further, it is in the interests of each of the parties to engage in this process cooperatively. For the Defendants, doing so will almost certainly result in having to produce less discovery, at lower cost. For the Plaintiffs, cooperation will almost certainly result in getting helpful information more quickly, and both Plaintiffs and Defendants are better off if they can avoid the costs associated with the voluminous filings submitted to the court in connection with this dispute. Finally, it is obvious that if undertaken in the spirit required by the discovery rules, particularly Rules 26(b)(2)(C) and 26(g), the adversary system will be fully engaged, as counsel will be able to advocate their clients' positions as relevant to the factors the rules establish, and if unable to reach a full agreement, will be able to bring their dispute back to the court for a prompt resolution. In

32. 244 F.R.D. 650, 652 (M.D. Fla. 2007).
33. 2009 WL 1649592, at * 6 (E.D. Wisc. June 10, 2009).
34. *Mancia*, 2008 U.S. Dist. LEXIS 83740.

> fact, the cooperation that is necessary for this process to take place enhances the legitimate goals of the adversary system, by facilitating discovery of the facts needed to support the claims and defenses that have been raised, at a lesser cost, and expediting the time when the case may be resolved on its merits, or settled. This clearly is advantageous to both Plaintiffs and Defendants.[35]

There is a clear and steady march of professionalism codes, procedural rules, and discovery decisions away from an adversarial model of, and toward a cooperative approach to, handling ESI in litigation.[36]

35. *Id.* at *41–42.

36. *See* Facciola & Redgrave, *supra* note 14, at 52.

CHAPTER 31

RULE 26(g): THE "STOP AND THINK," OR "PAUSE AND CONSIDER," RULE IN THE ESI ENVIRONMENT

BY THE HON. PAUL W. GRIMM AND MICHAEL D. BERMAN

As characterized by the rules committee's notes, Rule 26(g) of the Federal Rules of Civil Procedure imposes "a certification requirement that obliges each attorney to stop and think about the legitimacy of a discovery request, a response thereto, or an objection." In this chapter, a federal magistrate judge and a practicing litigator discuss the implications of this rule for the practice of e-discovery, including "its interrelationship with specific ethical obligations." Included is an unusually detailed account of the facts and rulings in the famous Qualcomm *series of judicial decisions on e-discovery violations.*

1. Introduction

"One of the most important, but apparently least understood or followed, of the discovery rules is Fed. R. Civ. P. 26(g), enacted in 1983."[1] Rule 26(g) is not specifically directed toward electronically stored information (ESI). In fact, the provision was added 23 years before the December 2006 amendments specifically addressing ESI. Nevertheless, in part because of recent, well-publicized decisions imposing substantial sanctions in the ESI context,[2] Rule 26(g) has achieved increased prominence. The overarching theme of Rule 26(g) in the ESI environment is that it, like other rules, including Rules 1, 26(a), 26(b)(2)(C), and 26(c), imposes a "proportionality" requirement on all aspects of e-discovery and that one key aspect of the Rule 26(g) duty is its interrelationship with specific ethical obligations.[3]

As with any rule-based matter, it is important to begin with the text of the rule and the Advisory Committee Note. Rule 26(g) provides:

(g) Signing Disclosures and Discovery Requests, Responses, and Objections.

(1) *Signature Required; Effect of Signature.* Every disclosure under Rule 26(a)(1) or (a)(3) and every discovery request, response, or objection must be signed by at least one attorney of record in the attorney's own name—or by the party personally, if unrepresented—and must state the signer's address, e-mail address, and telephone number. By signing, an attorney or party certifies that to the best of the person's knowledge, information, and belief formed after a reasonable inquiry:

1. Mancia v. Mayflower Textiles Servs., Co., 253 F.R.D. 354 (D. Md. 2008).

2. *E.g.*, Qualcomm, Inc. v. Broadcom Corp., 2008 WL 66932 (S.D. Cal. Jan. 7, 2008), *vacated and remanded in part*, 2008 WL 63810 (S.D. Cal. Mar. 5, 2008), *appeals dismissed*, 327 Fed. Appx. 877, 2008 WL 6400775 (Fed. Cir. Aug. 18, 2008), *on remand*, 2010 WL 1336937 (S.D. Cal. Apr. 2, 2010).

3. *See, e.g.*, *Mancia*, 253 F.R.D. at 362–63 ("Thus, rules of procedure, ethics and even statutes make clear that there are limits to how the adversary system may operate during discovery."); Victor Stanley, Inc. v. Creative Pipe, Inc. (*Victor Stanley II*), 269 F.R.D. 497 (D. Md. 2010), *affirmed in part and modified in part on unrelated grounds*, No.MJG-06-2662 (D.Md. Nov. 1, 2010), *subsequent opinion*, No. MJG-06-2662 (D.Md. Jan. 24, 2011); P. Grimm, *et al.*, *Proportionality in the Post-Hoc Analysis of Pre-Litigation Preservation Decisions*, 37 U. Balt. L. Rev. 381 (2008) (see chapter 9). The Sedona Conference has prepared a "Commentary on Proportionality in Electronic Discovery" and there are numerous authorities supporting the textual proposition.

(A) with respect to a disclosure, it is complete and correct as of the time it is made; and
(B) with respect to a discovery request, response, or objection, it is:
  (i) consistent with these rules and warranted by existing law or by a nonfrivolous argument for extending, modifying, or reversing existing law, or for establishing new law;
  (ii) not interposed for any improper purpose, such as to harass, cause unnecessary delay, or needlessly increase the cost of litigation; and
  (iii) neither unreasonable nor unduly burdensome or expensive, considering the needs of the case, prior discovery in the case, the amount in controversy, and the importance of the issues at stake in the action.

(2) *Failure to Sign.* Other parties have no duty to act on an unsigned disclosure, request, response, or objection until it is signed, and the court must strike it unless a signature is promptly supplied after the omission is called to the attorney's or party's attention.

(3) *Sanction for Improper Certification.* If a certification violates this rule without substantial justification, the court, on motion or on its own, must impose an appropriate sanction on the signer, the party on whose behalf the signer was acting, or both. The sanction may include an order to pay the reasonable expenses, including attorney's fees, caused by the violation.

It is immediately apparent that the rule applies to initial disclosures, and to discovery requests, responses, and objections, and that it contains different certification implications for different types of disclosures. Under Rule 26(g)(1)(A), for example, the certification is that the Rule 26(a)(1) initial disclosure "is complete and correct as of the time it is made." Under Rule 26(g)(1)(B), the certification is that Rule 27, 30, 31, 33, 34, 35, and 36 discovery requests, responses, and objections are not frivolous, not interposed for improper purposes, and that they are proportionate to the needs of the case. For both initial disclosures and discovery, however, the certification is "to the best of the person's knowledge, information, and belief formed after a reasonable inquiry."

The Advisory Committee Notes to the 1983 amendments to the Federal Rules of Civil Procedure point out:

> Excessive discovery and evasion or resistance to reasonable discovery requests pose significant problems. Recent studies have made some attempt to determine the sources and extent of the difficulties. . . . The purpose of discovery is to provide a mechanism for making relevant information available to the litigants. "Mutual knowledge of all the relevant facts gathered by both parties is essential to proper litigation." *Hickman v. Taylor,* 329 U.S. 495, 507 (1947). Thus the spirit of the rules is violated when advocates attempt to use discovery tools as tactical weapons rather than to expose the facts and illuminate the issues by overuse of discovery or unnecessary use of defensive weapons or evasive responses. All of this results in excessively costly and time-consuming activities that are disproportionate to the nature of the case, the amount involved, or the issues or values at stake.
>
> Given our adversary tradition and the current discovery rules, it is not surprising that there are many opportunities, if not incentives, for attorneys to engage in discovery that, although authorized by the broad, permissive terms of the rules, nevertheless results in delay. See Brazil, The Adversary Character of Civil Discovery: A Critique and Proposals for Change, 31 Vand.L.Rev. 1259 (1978). As a result, it has been said that the rules have "not infrequently [been] exploited to the disadvantage of justice." *Herbert v. Lando,* 441 U.S. 153, 179 (1979) (Powell, J., concurring). These practices impose costs on an already overburdened system and impede the fundamental goal of the "just, speedy, and inexpensive determination of every action." Fed.R.Civ.P. 1.

Turning specifically to Rule 26(g), the 1983 Committee Notes continue:

> *Note to Subdivision (g); Signing of Discovery Requests, Responses, and Objections.* Rule 26(g) imposes an affirmative duty to engage in pretrial discovery in a responsible manner[4] that is consistent with the spirit and purposes of Rules 26 through 37. In addition, Rule 26(g) is designed to curb discovery abuse

4. Poole v. Textron, Inc., 192 F.R.D. 494, 503 (D. Md. 2000).

by explicitly encouraging the imposition of sanctions. The subdivision provides a deterrent to both excessive discovery and evasion by imposing a certification requirement that *obliges each attorney to stop and think* about the legitimacy of a discovery request, a response thereto, or an objection. The term "response" includes answers to interrogatories and to requests to admit as well as responses to production requests. [emphasis added].

If primary responsibility for conducting discovery is to continue to rest with the litigants, they must be obliged to act responsibly and avoid abuse. With this in mind, Rule 26(g), which parallels the amendments to Rule 11, requires an attorney or unrepresented party to sign each discovery request, response, or objection. Motions relating to discovery are governed by Rule 11. However, since a discovery request, response, or objection usually deals with more specific subject matter than motions or papers, the elements that must be certified in connection with the former are spelled out more completely. The signature is a certification of the elements set forth in Rule 26(g).

Although the certification duty requires the lawyer to *pause and consider* the reasonableness of his request, response, or objection, it is not meant to discourage or restrict necessary and legitimate discovery. The rule simply requires that the attorney *make a reasonable inquiry* into the factual basis of his response, request, or objection. [emphasis added].

The duty to make a "reasonable inquiry" is satisfied if the investigation undertaken by the attorney and the conclusions drawn therefrom are reasonable under the circumstances. It is an objective standard similar to the one imposed by Rule 11. See the Advisory Committee Note to Rule 11. *See also Kinee v. Abraham Lincoln Fed. Sav. & Loan Ass'n*, 365 F.Supp. 975 (E.D. Pa. 1973). In making the inquiry, the attorney may rely on assertions by the client and on communications with other counsel in the case as long as that reliance is appropriate under the circumstances. Ultimately, what is reasonable is a matter for the court to decide on the totality of the circumstances.

Rule 26(g) does not require the signing attorney to certify the truthfulness of the client's factual responses to a discovery request. Rather, the signature certifies that the lawyer has made a reasonable effort to assure that the client has provided all the information and documents available to him that are responsive to the discovery demand. Thus, the lawyer's certification under Rule 26(g) should be distinguished from other signature requirements in the rules, such as those in Rules 30(e) and 33.

Nor does the rule require a party or an attorney to disclose privileged communications or work product in order to show that a discovery request, response, or objection is substantially justified. The provisions of Rule 26(c), including appropriate orders after in camera inspection by the court, remain available to protect a party claiming privilege or work product protection.

The signing requirement means that every discovery request, response, or objection should be grounded on a theory that is reasonable under the precedents or a good faith belief as to what should be the law. This standard is heavily dependent on the circumstances of each case. The certification speaks as of the time it is made. The duty to supplement discovery responses continues to be governed by Rule 26(e).

Concern about discovery abuse has led to widespread recognition that there is a need for more aggressive judicial control and supervision. *ACF Industries, Inc. v. EEOC*, 439 U.S. 1081 (1979) (certiorari denied) (Powell, J., dissenting). Sanctions to deter discovery abuse would be more effective if they were diligently applied "not merely to penalize those whose conduct may be deemed to warrant such a sanction, but to deter those who might be tempted to such conduct in the absence of such a deterrent." *National Hockey League v. Metropolitan Hockey Club*, 427 U.S. 639, 643 (1976). See also Note, The Emerging Deterrence Orientation in the Imposition of Discovery Sanctions, 91 Harv. L. Rev. 1033 (1978). Thus the premise of Rule 26(g) is that imposing sanctions on attorneys who fail to meet the rule's standards will significantly reduce abuse by imposing disadvantages therefor.

Because of the asserted reluctance to impose sanctions on attorneys who abuse the discovery rules, see Brazil, *Civil Discovery: Lawyers' Views of its Effectiveness, Principal Problems and Abuses, American Bar Foundation (1980); Ellington, A Study of Sanctions for Discovery Abuse,* Department of Justice (1979), Rule 26(g) makes explicit the authority judges now have to

> impose appropriate sanctions and requires them to use it. This authority derives from Rule 37, 28 U.S.C. § 1927, and the court's inherent power. *See Roadway Express, Inc., v. Piper*, 447 U.S. 752 (1980); *Martin v. Bell Helicopter Co.*, 85 F.R.D. 654, 661–62 (D. Col. 1980); Note, Sanctions Imposed by Courts on Attorneys Who Abuse the Judicial Process, 44 U.Chi.L.Rev. 619 (1977). The new rule mandates that sanctions be imposed on attorneys who fail to meet the standards established in the first portion of Rule 26(g). The nature of the sanction is a matter of judicial discretion to be exercised in light of the particular circumstances. The court may take into account any failure by the party seeking sanctions to invoke protection under Rule 26(c) at an early stage in the litigation.
>
> The sanctioning process must comport with due process requirements. The kind of notice and hearing required will depend on the facts of the case and the severity of the sanction being considered. To prevent the proliferation of the sanction procedure and to avoid multiple hearings, discovery in any sanction proceeding normally should be permitted only when it is clearly required by the interests of justice. In most cases the court will be aware of the circumstances and only a brief hearing should be necessary.

Thus, Rule 26(g) was designed to render sanctions mandatory[5] in an effort to control and discourage discovery abuse. It was amended in 1993 to reach initial disclosures. In pertinent part, the 1993 Committee Notes state:

> Note to Subdivision (g). Paragraph (1) is added to require signatures on disclosures, a requirement that parallels the provisions of paragraph (2) with respect to discovery requests, responses, and objections. The provisions of paragraph (3) have been modified to be consistent with Rules 37(a)(4) and 37(c)(1); in combination, these rules establish sanctions for violation of the rules regarding disclosures and discovery matters. Amended Rule 11 no longer applies to such violations.

5. As noted in *Mancia*: "If a lawyer or party makes a Rule 26(g) certification that violates the rule, without substantial justification, the court (on motion, or sua sponte) must impose an appropriate sanction, which may include an order to pay reasonable expenses and attorney's fees, caused by the violation. Fed. R. Civ. P. 26(g)(3)." 253 F.R.D. at 357.

Rule 26(g) reached its present form in 2007, when the Advisory Committee stated: "Former Rule 26(g)(1) did not call for striking an unsigned disclosure. The omission was an obvious drafting oversight. Amended Rule 26(g)(2) includes disclosures in the list of matters that the court must strike unless a signature is provided 'promptly * * * after being called to the attorney's or party's attention.' "

2. Rule 26(g), the Model Rules of Professional Conduct, and the duty to cooperate

Rule 26(g) is revolutionary because, in addition to being a rule of procedure, it is the embodiment of an ethical obligation that includes a duty to cooperate in civil litigation. The ethical underpinning of the Rule 26(g) was described in *Mancia*:

> Model Rules of Prof'l Conduct R. 3.4(d) (2007) ("[A lawyer shall not,] in pretrial procedure, make a frivolous discovery request or fail to make reasonably diligent effort to comply with a legally proper discovery request by an opposing party[.]"); Model Rules of Prof'l Conduct R. 3.4 cmt. [1] (2007) ("The procedure of the adversary system contemplates that the evidence in a case is to be marshaled competitively by the contending parties. Fair competition in the adversary system is secured by prohibitions against destruction or concealment of evidence, improperly influencing witnesses, *obstructive tactics in discovery procedure,* and the like.") (emphasis added). See also Restatement (Third) of the Law Governing Lawyers: Frivolous Advocacy § 110(3) (2000) ("A lawyer may not make a frivolous discovery request, fail to make a reasonably diligent effort to comply with a proper discovery request of another party, or intentionally fail otherwise to comply with applicable procedural requirements concerning discovery."); Restatement (Third) of the Law Governing Lawyers ch. 7, topic 2, introductory n. (2000) ("Advocates are guided primarily by the goal of advancing their individual clients' interests. They are expected to marshal evidence and legal arguments in support of the positions of their respective clients and to cross-examine and otherwise test the evidence and positions of opposing parties, without personal responsibility for the outcome of the proceeding. However, there are limitations on an advocate's forensic freedom. In addition to the general requirement of complying with legal requirements and

> rulings of tribunals, a lawyer is subject to the constraints described in this Topic concerning frivolous litigation [which includes prohibitions against frivolous advocacy and conduct during discovery].") (internal citations omitted).[6]

Thus, the ethical overtones of Rule 26(g) ring clearly. The combined impact of the Model Code of Professional Responsibility and Rule 26(g)[7] is to impose a duty to cooperate:

> Rule 26(g) and its commentary provide many important "take away points" that ought to, but unfortunately do not, regulate the way discovery is conducted. First, the rule is intended to impose an "affirmative duty" on counsel to behave responsibly during discovery, and to ensure that it is conducted in a way that is consistent "with the spirit and purposes" of the discovery rules, which are contained in Rules 26 through 37. . . . It cannot seriously be disputed that compliance with the "spirit and purposes" of these discovery rules requires cooperation by counsel to identify and fulfill legitimate discovery needs, yet avoid seeking discovery the cost and burden of which is disproportionally large to what is at stake in the litigation. *Counsel cannot "behave responsively" during discovery unless they do both, which requires cooperation rather than contrariety, communication rather than confrontation.*[8]

---

6. *Id.* at 362 n. 6.

7. Rule 26(g)(1)(B) states that the signer certifies that the response is "consistent with these rules and warranted by existing law or by a nonfrivolous argument for extending, modifying, or reversing existing law, or for establishing new law. . . ." And, under Rule 26(g)(1)(B)b(iii), a signer certifies that the discovery response is "neither unreasonable nor unduly burdensome or expensive, considering the needs of the case, prior discovery in the case, the amount in controversy, and the importance of the issues at stake in the action."

8. *Mancia,* 253 F.R.D. at 357–58 (emphasis added). "The extensive discovery clashes and vituperation that have characterized this case so far, it should be noted, give cause for concern in and of themselves. But that perhaps is best left for another sermon on another day." MMI Prods. v. Long, 231 F.R.D. 215, 220 (D. Md. 2005); *see generally* Nycomed U.S. Inc. v. Glenmark Generics Ltd., 2010 WL 3173785, at *1 n.3 (E.D.N.Y. Aug. 11, 2010) ("As detailed above, the dispute over the adequacy of Glenmark's ESI disclosures has lasted about a year and has generated thousands of pages of filings. The volume of documentation has required the Court to expend tremendous time not only poring over dense addenda and appendices, but also refereeing arguments between counsel that have, in many instances, devolved into vindictive bickering.").

Most recently, this duty has been emphasized by the Sedona Conference Cooperation Proclamation, addressed in more detail elsewhere in this book.[9] The impact of Rule 26(g) was described in *Mancia* as follows:

> However central the adversary system is to our way of formal dispute resolution, there is nothing inherent in it that precludes cooperation between the parties and their attorneys during the litigation process to achieve orderly and cost effective discovery of the competing facts on which the system depends. In fact, no less a proponent of the adversary system than Professor Lon L. Fuller observed:
>
> > Thus, partisan advocacy is a form of public service so long as it aids the process of adjudication; it ceases to be when it hinders that process, when it misleads, distorts and obfuscates, when it renders the task of the deciding tribunal not easier, but more difficult.
> >
> > . . . .
> >
> > The lawyer's highest loyalty is at the same time the most tangible. It is loyalty that runs, not to persons, but to procedures and institutions. The lawyer's role imposes on him a trusteeship for the integrity of those fundamental processes of government and self-government upon which the successful functioning of our society depends.
> >
> > . . . A lawyer recreant to his responsibilities can so disrupt the hearing of a cause as to undermine those rational foundations without which an adversary proceeding loses its meaning and its justification. Everywhere democratic and constitutional government is tragically dependant on voluntary and understanding co-operation in the maintenance of its fundamental processes and forms.
> >
> > It is the lawyer's duty to preserve and advance this indispensable co-operation by keeping alive the willingness to engage in it and by imparting the understanding necessary to give it direction and effectiveness. . . .

9. For a discussion of the Cooperation Proclamation, see chapter 30 and Ralph C. Losey, Mancia v. Mayflower *Begins a Pilgrimage to the New World of Cooperation*, 10 (Supp.) SEDONA CONF. J. 377 (2009).

> . . . It is chiefly for the lawyer that the term "due process" takes on tangible meaning, for whom it indicates what is allowable and what is not, who realizes what a ruinous cost is incurred when its demands are disregarded. For the lawyer the insidious dangers contained in the notion that "the end justifies the means" is not a matter of abstract philosophic conviction, but of direct professional experience.

> Lon L. Fuller & John D. Randall, *Professional Responsibility: Report of the Joint Conference*, 44 A.B.A. J. 1159, 1162, 1216 (1958). A lawyer who seeks excessive discovery given what is at stake in the litigation, or who makes boilerplate objections to discovery requests without particularizing their basis, or who is evasive or incomplete in responding to discovery, or pursues discovery in order to make the cost for his or her adversary so great that the case settles to avoid the transaction costs, or who delays the completion of discovery to prolong the litigation in order to achieve a tactical advantage, or who engages in any of the myriad forms of discovery abuse that are so commonplace is, as Professor Fuller observes, hindering the adjudication process, and making the task of the "deciding tribunal not easier, but more difficult," and violating his or her duty of loyalty to the "procedures and institutions" the adversary system is intended to serve. Thus, rules of procedure, ethics and even statutes make clear that there are limits to how the adversary system may operate during discovery.[10]

Courts increasingly expect parties and counsel to cooperate during the discovery process, and those who persist in engaging in obstructionist tactics can expect little sympathy or patience when their conduct is brought before the court.[11] It is in this context that we look at recent studies regarding the impact of unrestrained discovery on the judicial system, the specific application of Rule 26(g), and future directions.

10. *Mancia*, 253 F.R.D. at 362 (footnotes omitted).

11. Losey, *supra* note 9 (collecting cases that have discussed the obligation of counsel and the parties to cooperate during discovery).

3. Recent studies regarding discovery

A. The need for dialogue

Rule 26(g) is central to the civil justice process: "The failure to engage in discovery as required by Rule 26(g) is one reason why the cost of discovery is so widely criticized as being excessive—to the point of pricing litigants out of court."[12]

Until recently, it was accurate to state in *Mancia*: "Although judges, scholars, commentators and lawyers themselves long have recognized the problems associated with abusive discovery, what has been missing is a thoughtful means to engage all the stakeholders in the litigation process—lawyers, judges and the public at large—and provide them with the encouragement, means and incentive to approach discovery in a different way." That dialogue, however, has commenced with the Sedona Conference Cooperation Proclamation; been furthered by the American College of Trial Lawyers, the Federal Judicial Center, and an American Bar Association survey, as well as academic and practitioner articles; and is now the focus of the Committee on Rules of the Federal Judicial Center.[13]

B. The American College of Trial Lawyers survey

The American College of Trial Lawyers and the Institute for the Advancement of the American Legal System (collectively "the College") surveyed College members in 2007, and reported in 2008: "Although the civil justice system is not broken, it is in serious need of repair. The survey shows that the system is not working; it takes too long and costs too much. Deserving cases are not brought because the cost of pursuing them fails a rational cost-benefit test, while meritless cases, especially smaller cases, are being settled rather than being tried because it costs too much to litigate them."[14] The College issued its final report[15] last year, reit-

12. *Mancia*, 253 F.R.D. at 359.

13. The brief summaries in this chapter cannot do full justice to the comprehensive analysis provided by those organizations.

14. Am. Coll. of Trial Lawyers & Inst. for the Advancement of the Am. Legal Sys., Interim Report on the Joint Project of the American College of Trial Lawyers Task Force on Discovery and the Institute for the Advancement of the American Legal System 3 (2008).

15. Am. Coll. of Trial Lawyers & Inst. for the Advancement of the Am. Legal Sys., Final Report on the Joint Project of the American College of Trial Lawyers

erating that theme, and noting that "discovery can cost too much and become an end in itself."[16]

Part of the reported need for repair was in the area of ESI. One major, ESI-related theme[17] of survey respondents was the following:

> Electronic discovery, in particular, needs a serious overhaul. It was described by one respondent as a "morass." Another respondent stated: "The new rules are a nightmare. The bigger the case the more the abuse and the bigger the nightmare."[18]

The College wrote: "Recall that our current rules were created in an era before copying machines, computers and e-mail. Advances in technology are overtaking our rules, to the point that the Advisory Committee Notes to Rule 26(b)(2)(B) of the Federal Rules of Civil Procedure state that 'It is not possible to define in a rule the different types of technological features that may affect the burdens and costs of accessing electronically stored information.' "[19] It stated: "Electronic information is fundamentally different from other types of discovery in the following respects: it is everywhere, it is often hard to gain access to and it is typically and routinely erased."[20] It then explained:

> The issue here is not the scope of electronic discovery; rather the issue is what must be preserved before the scope of permissible electronic discovery can be determined. It is the preservation of electronic materials at the outset of litigation that engenders expensive retention efforts, made largely to avoid collateral litigation about evidence spoliation. Litigating electronic evidence spoliation issues that bloom after discovery is well underway can impose enormous expense on the parties and can be used tactically to derail a case, drawing the court's attention away from the merits of the underlying dispute. Current rules do not adequately address this issue.[21]

Task Force on Discovery and the Institute for the Advancement of the American Legal System (Mar. 11, 2009).

16. *Id.* at 2.

17. Because this book focuses on ESI, this chapter will not address the broad contours of the report that go beyond ESI.

18. *Id.*

19. *Id.* at 11.

20. *Id.* at 12.

21. *Id.* at 13. Note that the Federal Rules of Civil Procedure do not directly apply before a lawsuit is commenced. *See, e.g.*, Grimm, *et al.*, *supra* note 3.

The College issued a number of proposed principles and recommended actions. As it relates to ESI, one proposed principle is:

> Proportionality should be the most important principle applied to all discovery. Discovery is not the purpose of litigation. It is merely a means to an end. If discovery does not promote the just, speedy and inexpensive determination of actions, then it is not fulfilling its purpose. Unfortunately, many lawyers believe that they should—or must—take advantage of the full range of discovery options offered by the rules. They believe that zealous advocacy (or fear of malpractice claims) demands no less and the current rules certainly do not dissuade them from that view. Such a view, however, is at best a symptom of the problems caused by the current discovery rules and at worst a cause of the problems we face. In either case, we must eliminate that view. It is crippling our civil justice system. The parties and counsel should attempt in good faith to agree on proportional discovery at the outset of a case but failing agreement, courts should become involved. There simply is no justification for the parties to spend more on discovery than a case requires. Courts should be encouraged, with the help of the parties, to specify what forms of discovery will be permitted in a particular case. Courts should be encouraged to stage discovery to insure that discovery related to potentially dispositive issues is taken first so that those issues can be isolated and timely adjudicated.[22]

Because "[o]ur respondents told us that electronic discovery is a nightmare and a morass,"[23] in addition to the overriding goal of proportionality, the College suggested early discussion between counsel, prompt judicial attention to resolve disputes, and rules amendments that, in large part, followed the Sedona Guidelines.[24]

---

22. *Id.* at 7 (formatting omitted).

23. *Id.* at 14.

24. *Id.* at 15. The College wrote: "Although electronic discovery is becoming extraordinarily important in civil litigation, it is proving to be enormously expensive and burdensome. The vast majority (75 percent) of our respondents confirmed the fact that electronic discovery has resulted in a disproportionate increase in the expense of discovery and thus an increase in total litigation expense. Electronic discovery, however, is a fact of life that is here to stay. We favor an intensive study to determine how best to cope with discovery of this information in an efficient, cost-effective way to ensure expenses that are

C. The Federal Judicial Center survey

In October 2009, the Federal Judicial Center issued a "Preliminary Report to the Judicial Conference Advisory Committee on Civil Rules," following a "National, Case-Based Civil Rules Survey" of attorneys in recently closed cases.[25] In contrast to the results of the College survey, the FJC reported that more than 60 percent of the respondents said that disclosure and discovery provided the "right amount" of information at the "right amount" of cost for the case.[26] Significantly, "[a] majority of respondents reported that the parties were able to reduce the cost and burden of discovery by cooperating."[27] The FJC reported:

> When asked whether the Rules should be revised to limit electronic discovery specifically, respondents representing plaintiffs tended to disagree and those representing primarily defendants tended to agree. On the other hand, those representing plaintiffs and defendants about equally were opposed to limiting discovery in general but divided about evenly on the specific question of limiting electronic discovery.[28]

Interestingly, only approximately one-third of the surveyed attorneys reported that the conference to plan discovery addressed ESI.[29] And only approximately 20 percent of court-adopted

proportional to the value of the case." *Id.* at 15–16. The College continued: "Moreover, 76 percent of the respondents said that courts do not understand the difficultics parties face in providing electronic discovery. Likewise, trial counsel are often uninformed about the technical facets of electronic discovery and are ill-equipped to assist trial courts in dealing with the issues that arise." *Id.* at 16.

25. The report is available on the Federal Judicial Center website. The FJC stresses that the report is preliminary.

26. Fed. Judicial Ctr., National, Case-Based Civil Rules Survey: Preliminary Report to the Judicial Conference Advisory Committee on Civil Rules, at 2 [hereinafter FJC Report].

27. *Id.* "Question 70 asked respondents whether attorneys can cooperate in discovery while still being zealous advocates for their clients. . . . There was little disagreement with this statement, and no substantive difference among the groups of respondents. Fully 93.1 percent of those representing primarily plaintiffs, 94.5 percent of those representing plaintiffs and defendants about equally, and 95.1 percent of those representing primarily defendants agreed or strongly agreed." *Id.* at 62.

28. *Id.* at 3.

29. *Id.* at 15. For a discussion of topics that should be addressed during a Rule 26(f) conference, see chapter 19.

discovery plans related to ESI.[30] The FJC summarized the discussions as follows:

> For both plaintiff and defendant attorneys, the most common reported issue related to collection was the parties' practices with respect to retention of ESI, reported by 46.5 percent of plaintiff attorneys and 55.5 percent of defendant attorneys. For plaintiff attorneys, the next most common topics were the scope, cost, method, or duration of preserving ESI (36.1 percent); the potential cost or burden of collecting, reviewing, and producing ESI (34.4 percent); restricting the scope or avoiding altogether the discovery of ESI (32.8 percent); and whether potentially responsive information was stored on a device or in a format that a party considered "not reasonably accessible" (22.0 percent). For defendant attorneys, the next most common responses were restricting the scope or avoiding altogether the discovery of ESI (41.9 percent); the scope, cost, method, or duration of preserving ESI (37.5 percent); and the potential cost or burden of collecting, reviewing, and producing ESI (36 percent).[31]

Phased discovery was addressed in less than 15 percent of the cases.[32]

The FJC report also addressed litigation holds, the topic that the College had described (see section B, above) as engendering extensive efforts to preclude spoliation issues. The FJC found that "18.7 percent of plaintiff attorneys and 40.6 percent of defendant attorneys reported that their client in the closed case had initiated such a hold; 63 and 37 percent, respectively, reported no such hold; and 18.3 and 22.4 percent, respectively, declined to answer."[33]

This may, perhaps, indicate that many attorneys and many cases are not addressing ESI at all. The FJC reported that "requests for production of ESI were reported by 36.1 percent of respondents—38.9 percent of plaintiff attorneys and 33.4 percent of defendant attorneys. Again, a majority of respondents—54.1 percent of plain-

30. FJC Report, *supra* note 26, at 16.

31. *Id.* at 17.

32. *Id.* Rule 26(f)(3) provides: "A discovery plan *must* state the parties' views and proposals on: . . . (B) the subjects on which discovery may be needed, when discovery should be completed, and *whether discovery should be conducted in phases* or be limited to or focused on particular issues. . . ." [emphasis added].

33. FJC Report, *supra* note 26, at 18.

tiff attorneys and 59.1 percent of defendant attorneys—reported that no party requested production of ESI in discovery. . . ."[34]

In fact, notwithstanding the many highly publicized sanctions cases, the FJC found that "ESI disputes were not very common in the sampled electronic discovery cases."[35] This may be because

> Fully 17.4 percent of plaintiff attorneys and 18.8 percent of defendant attorneys responded that the ESI produced in discovery was not used at all in the closed case. The most common use of ESI was in preparing or deposing a witness—reported by 47.6 percent of plaintiff attorneys and 48.3 percent of defendant attorneys—followed by facilitating a settlement—44.2 and 40.1 percent, respectively—and in interviews with clients or clients' employees, 29.9 and 40.9 percent, respectively. Other relatively common responses included use in an additional discovery request—reported by 32.9 percent of plaintiff attorneys and 26.7 percent of defendant attorneys—and in a motion for summary judgment—reported by 25.3 and 24.4 percent, respectively.[36]

The FJC survey concludes that ESI has not reached a majority of civil cases: "In sum, a party requested production of ESI in 30 to 40 percent of the sampled cases with one or more reported type of discovery—in other words, in less than a majority of cases with discovery. Moreover, no disputes over electronic discovery occurred in a large percentage of those cases. Half of attorneys in the closed cases with some discovery activity reported that they spend no more than 5 percent of their overall practice in electronic discovery-related activities."[37]

The FJC asked respondents whether the Federal Rules needed amendment:

> Question 69 asked respondents whether the Rules should be revised to limit electronic discovery. . . . The responses to this question were highly polarized. A majority of those primarily representing defendants agreed or strongly agreed that the Rules should be revised to limit electronic discovery—57.6 percent. A majority of those primarily representing

34. *Id.* at 19.
35. *Id.* at 24.
36. *Id.* at 25.
37. *Id.* at 26.

plaintiffs disagreed—61.2 percent. Only 12.6 percent of those primarily representing plaintiffs agreed or strongly agreed, and 34.8 percent of those primarily representing defendants disagreed or strongly disagreed. Those representing plaintiffs and defendants about equally were about evenly split on this question—35.5 percent of this group agreed or strongly agreed that the Rules should be revised to limit electronic discovery, 39 percent disagreed or strongly disagreed, and 22.6 percent neither agreed nor disagreed.[38]

While the College surveyed members of the American College of Trial Lawyers, the FJC surveyed attorneys who had recently closed a case in a federal court. This may, or may not, account for differing responses; however, the FJC survey does not appear to describe a system that is in serious need of repair.

D. The American Bar Association survey

A recent American Bar Association survey[39] found that 63 percent of respondents felt that the Federal Rules led to a "just, speedy, and inexpensive determination"[40] of cases, while 37 percent disagreed. While 54 percent said that the rules required minor amendments, 25 percent called for a complete rewriting of them. And 66 percent reported that electronic discovery was abused.[41]

Not surprisingly, the ABA reported: "Electronic discovery is an area in which plaintiffs' lawyers and defense lawyers diverge in their opinions. While plaintiffs' lawyers are more likely to see benefits rather than burdens, to a large extent, defense and mixed practice lawyers appear to see the costs of e-discovery outweighing the benefits."[42]

The ABA survey, however, also found that e-discovery is much more prevalent than reported in the FJC study: "As a threshold

38. *Id.* at 61.

39. ABA Section of Litig., Member Survey on Civil Practice: Detailed Report (Dec. 11, 2009) [hereinafter ABA Report].

40. Fed. R. Civ. P. 1.

41. ABA Report, *supra* note 39, at 1. "Respondents, especially plaintiffs' lawyers, agree that e-discovery has enhanced their ability to discover all relevant information. But respondents, especially defense lawyers, believe that e-discovery increases the costs of litigation, has contributed disproportionately to the increased cost of discovery, and is overly burdensome. Defense lawyers also strongly agree that the burdens of e-discovery are misunderstood by courts and allowed to go unchecked." *Id.* at 7.

42. *Id.* at 12.

matter, 72% of all respondents reported having been involved in cases that involve e-discovery, which includes 63.8% of plaintiffs' lawyers, 74.9% of defense lawyers, and 75.3% of mixed practice lawyers."[43]

The ABA litigators reported that electronic discovery was valuable to their case: "Respondents were in general agreement that e-discovery has enhanced the ability to obtain all relevant information, although plaintiffs' lawyers were more likely to agree and much more likely to strongly agree than other groups. Of plaintiffs' lawyers, 89.4% agree with the statement, and of those, 43% strongly agree. Although 73.2% of defense lawyers agree, only 15.1% of them strongly agree. Of the 76.7% of mixed practice lawyers who agree, only 20.2% agree strongly. Very few respondents had no opinion on the subject."[44]

Many respondents reported that properly managed electronic discovery can *reduce* the costs of litigation.[45] However, "[o]ver 90% of defense and mixed practice lawyers agree that e-discovery increases the cost of litigation. Only 59.2% of plaintiffs' lawyers agree."[46]

E. Conclusion

These College, FJC, and ABA surveys demonstrate that the dialogue necessary to adopt the discovery process created in 1938 to the demands of litigation in the twenty-first century has begun in earnest. The last contemporary chapter, however, has not been written, and the upcoming developments will be discussed in section 7, below. One thing that should, however, be clear, is that the reasonable inquiry and proportionality provisions of Rule 26(g), which incorporate a number of ethical requirements, are likely to be in forefront of the debate.

4. The impact of Rule 26(g) on specific discovery issues: A road map to Rule 26(g) compliance through a "discovery budget"

"Rule 26(g) of the Federal Rules of Procedure defines the duty of counsel in responding to discovery requests."[47] Many publications

43. *Id.*
44. *Id.* at 101.
45. *Id.* at 102.
46. *Id.* at 103.
47. Poole v. Textron, Inc., 192 F.R.D. 494, 503 (D. Md. 2000).

provide a comprehensive collection of Rule 26(g) decisions[48] and there will be no attempt to replicate that effort in this chapter.

It is the "stop and think," or "pause and consider," aspect of the rule that will be the current focus. Among the improper tactics deployed in *Mancia* were overly broad, shotgun discovery requests and boilerplate objections. Each reflected a failure to "stop and think."

Overly broad discovery constitutes a Rule 26(g) violation: "[T]he rule aspires to eliminate one of the most prevalent of all discovery abuses: kneejerk discovery requests served without consideration of cost or burden to the responding party."[49] Although, as noted in *Mancia*, "lawyers customarily serve requests that are far broader, more redundant and burdensome than necessary to obtain sufficient facts to enable them to resolve the case through motion, settlement or trial," "this would not be so if lawyers approached discovery responsibly, as the rule mandates, and met and conferred[50] before initiating discovery, and simply discussed what the amount in controversy is, and how much, what type, and in what sequence, discovery should be conducted so that its cost to all parties is proportional to what is at stake in the litigation."

While the discovery requests were overly broad, *Mancia* was also characterized by an equally improper vice, boilerplate objections: "Rule 26(g) also was enacted over twenty-five years ago to bring an end to the equally abusive practice of objecting to discovery requests reflexively—but not reflectively—and without a factual basis." Conclusory, unsupported objections that "a request for discovery is 'overboard and unduly burdensome, and not reasonably calculated to lead to the discovery of material admissible in evidence,'" are violative of the rule. In short: "It would be difficult to dispute the notion that the very act of making such boilerplate objections is prima facie evidence of a Rule 26(g) violation, because if the lawyer had paused, made a reasonable inquiry, and discovered facts that demonstrated the burdensomeness or excessive cost of the discovery request, he or she should have disclosed them in the objection, as both Rule 33 and 34 responses must state objections with particularity, on pain of waiver." In short, as to objections, *Mancia* held:

---

48. *See, e.g.*, M. ARKFELD, ELECTRONIC DISCOVERY AND EVIDENCE § 7.4(L)(3) (LexisNexis 2d ed. 2009).

49. Mancia v. Mayflower Textiles Servs., Co., 253 F.R.D. 354, 358 (D. Md. 2008).

50. See chapter 19 for a more detailed discussion of Rule 26(f) conferences.

> The failure to particularize these objections as required leads to one of two conclusions: either the [objecting] Defendants lacked a factual basis to make the objections that they did, which would violate Rule 26(g), or they complied with Rule 26(g), made a reasonable inquiry before answering and discovered facts that would support a legitimate objection, but they were waived for failure to specify them as required. Neither alternative helps the [objecting] Defendants' position, and either would justify a ruling requiring that the Defendants provide the requested discovery regardless of cost or burden, because proper grounds for objecting have not been established.[51]

In order to effectuate the overarching goal that discovery be reasonable and proportionate to the needs of the case, *Mancia* suggested the following solution, known as a "discovery budget":

> I ordered counsel to meet and confer in good faith and do the following. First, I asked Plaintiffs and Defendants each to estimate the likely range of provable damages that foreseeably could be awarded if Plaintiffs prevail at trial. In doing so, I suggested that the Plaintiffs assume for purposes of this analysis that their pending motion to certify a FLSA collective action would be granted, because doing so would allow the parties to gauge the "worst case" outcome Defendants could face. I then ordered that counsel for Plaintiffs and Defendants compare these estimates and attempt to identify a foreseeable range of damages, from zero if Plaintiffs do not prevail, to the largest award they likely could prove if they succeed. I also asked Plaintiffs' counsel to estimate their attorneys' fees. While admittedly a rough estimate, this range is useful for determining what the "amount in controversy" is in the case, and what is "at stake" for purposes of Rule 26(b)(2)(C)'s proportionality analysis. The goal is to attempt to quantify a workable "discovery budget" that is proportional to what is at issue in the case.
>
> Second, I ordered Plaintiffs' counsel and Defendants' counsel to discuss the amount and type of discovery already provided, and then discuss the additional discovery still sought by Plaintiffs, in order to evaluate the Rule 26(b)(2)(C)

51. *Mancia*, 253 F.R.D. at 364.

factors, to determine whether Plaintiffs' legitimate additional discovery needs could be fulfilled from non-duplicative, more convenient, less burdensome, or less expensive sources than those currently sought by the Plaintiffs. I further instructed Defendants' counsel that during this portion of the discussion, the burden was on the Defendants to provide a particularized factual basis to support any claims of excessive burden or expense.

I then advised counsel that in their discussion they should attempt to reach an agreement, in full or at least partially, about what additional discovery (and from what sources) should be provided by Defendants to Plaintiffs. In doing so, I suggested that they consider "phased discovery," so that the most promising, but least burdensome or expensive sources of information could be produced initially, which would enable Plaintiffs to reevaluate their needs depending on the information already provided.

Finally, I advised counsel that when they had completed their discussion, they were to provide me with a status report identifying any unresolved issues, and if there were any, I gave them a format to use to present them to me in a fashion that would enable me to rule on them expeditiously.

It is apparent that the process outlined above requires that counsel cooperate and communicate, and I note that had these steps been taken by counsel at the start of discovery, most, if not all, of the disputes could have been resolved without involving the court. It also is apparent that there is nothing at all about the cooperation needed to evaluate the discovery outlined above that requires the parties to abandon meritorious arguments they may have, or even to commit to resolving all disagreements on their own. Further, it is in the interests of each of the parties to engage in this process cooperatively. For the Defendants, doing so will almost certainly result in having to produce less discovery, at lower cost. For the Plaintiffs, cooperation will almost certainly result in getting helpful information more quickly, and both Plaintiffs and Defendants are better off if they can avoid the costs associated with the voluminous filings submitted to the court in connection with this dispute. Finally, it is obvious that if undertaken in the spirit required by the discovery rules, particularly Rules 26(b)(2)(C) and 26(g), the adversary system will be fully engaged, as counsel will be able to advocate their clients' positions as relevant to the factors the rules establish, and if unable to reach a full agreement, will be able to bring their dispute back to the court for a prompt resolution. In fact, the cooperation that is necessary for this process to take place enhances the legitimate goals of the adversary system, by facilitating discovery of the facts needed to support the claims and defenses that have been raised, at a lesser cost, and expediting the time when the case may be resolved on its merits, or settled. This clearly is advantageous to both Plaintiffs and Defendants.[52]

The notion of a discovery budget flows from the requirements of Rule 26(b)(2)(C) that the discovery be proportional[53] to what is at issue in the litigation, and that it be tailored to address what is appropriate based on the facts of a particular case—which includes an assessment of what the anticipated cost of discovery will be, and the methods of discovery that are likely to be most effective and least burdensome or expensive, when considered in light of the likely outcome of the case. In brief, Rule 26(g) and 26(b)(2)(C) stand for the obvious proposition that it makes no sense at all to spend more on the discovery process than is warranted given the likely outcome of the case if the party initiating the action is likely to recover, or to spend more on what the defending party is likely to have to pay if an adverse judgment is rendered against it.

While Rule 26(f) contemplates that when they confer, counsel will "develop a proposed discovery plan" that will be submitted to the court in writing within 14 days of the conference, the Rule 16(f) conference with the court presents the perfect opportunity

52. *Id.* at 365.

53. The overarching proportionality standard was reemphasized in a recent decision stating: "Whether preservation or discovery conduct is acceptable in a case depends on what is *reasonable,* and that in turn depends on whether what was done—or not done—was *proportional* to that case and consistent with clearly established applicable standards." Rimkus Consulting Group, Inc. v. Cammarata, 688 F. Supp. 2d 598, 613 (S.D. Tex. 2010) (citing THE SEDONA PRINCIPLES: BEST PRACTICES RECOMMENDATIONS & PRINCIPLES FOR ADDRESSING ELECTRONIC DOCUMENT DISCOVERY 17 cmt. 2.b. (2d ed. 2007) ("Electronic discovery burdens should be proportional to the amount in controversy and the nature of the case. Otherwise, transaction costs due to electronic discovery will overwhelm the ability to resolve disputes fairly in litigation.")). This was reinforced by the Sedona Conference Commentary on Proportionality in Electronic Discovery.

for counsel to develop a realistic discovery budget. The starting point is to candidly discuss what the value of the case is, which involves a discussion of the causes of action, defenses, likely range of damages if a recovery is obtained, the scope and likely cost of any nonmonetary relief that may be granted, and an estimate of the attorney's fees that will be incurred during the litigation.

Skeptics will say that it is impossible to know all this information so early in the litigation. While it may not be possible to know this information with precision at this early stage of the litigation, that should not stop an experienced plaintiff's lawyer from having a fairly helpful estimate of what he or she is likely to recover if successful, because those who lack this skill are not likely to be in practice for very long. The truth is that good plaintiffs' lawyers have to have the ability to assess the likely outcome of the case before they bring suit, because they typically do not recover unless successful. If working on an hourly fee, economic exigencies also require that the lawyer be a good forecaster of the likely outcome, otherwise the client who is paying the costs and fees during discovery is likely to become disenchanted fairly quickly. The same applies for defense counsel, if they expect repeat business from their clients. Further, the discovery budget need not be set in stone; it readily can be modified by agreement or court order if during the case the existing budget no longer seems reasonable, and if counsel and the parties are behaving properly.

Part of the preparation of a realistic discovery budget entails a consideration of each method of discovery, as well as the possibility of informal discovery. In considering the phasing of discovery, for example, it is appropriate to focus first on the type and quantity of discovery that has the most promise for disclosing the information most likely to enable the parties, their counsel, and the court to evaluate the case to assess its likelihood of settlement, resolution by pretrial motion, or ultimate trial. As part of this process counsel should consider agreeing to limits to the discovery initially undertaken (reserving the ability to expand the scope if justified based on the initial phase of discovery). Examples including limiting the number of interrogatories or the type of interrogatories (for example, postponing use of contention interrogatories until later in the case), advancing the depositions of key players in the underlying events to the early stages of discovery, and phasing expert disclosures and depositions to occur after essential fact discovery has been completed.

If one party experiences unreasonable resistance to the development of a realistic discovery plan that is proportional to what is at issue in the case, then it is time to seek an expedited meeting with the court to resolve the disagreement. As a final note on this subject, it is manifestly obvious that counsel must cooperate to develop a discovery plan. As previously noted in this chapter, there is a duty to cooperate that is firmly rooted in the adversary system,[54] and courts increasingly are demanding that counsel do so.[55] Further, the three recent litigation surveys discussed above demonstrate the widely held views of the Bar that lawyers who cooperate during discovery reduce the costs and burdens to their clients, and enjoy smoother sailing before the court, all of which advances their clients' interests.

5. *Qualcomm, Inc. v. Broadcom, Inc.*

Rule 26(g) was promulgated decades ago (in 1983), and many publications have provided a comprehensive collection of authorities[56] interpreting the rule (which is not attempted here). Nevertheless, no overview of Rule 26(g) would be complete without discussion of *Qualcomm v. Broadcom*, a recent decision imposing sanctions under, inter alia, Rule 26(g).

Although perhaps (and hopefully) sui generis, *Qualcomm* blazed across the ESI landscape with intensity. One group of Qualcomm's attorneys admitted in posttrial pleadings: "The Court and Broadcom are properly incensed by what happened in this case."[57] Combining all of the drama of $8.5 million in sanctions, the specter of a subsequent malpractice claim, referral of six attorneys to Bar Counsel for possible disciplinary action, and pitting in-house counsel, outside counsel, and the former client against each other, thereby waiving the attorney-client privilege, the case has major ramifications, although it was decided on a factual predicate that is unlikely to be repeated and ended without sanctions being imposed on the attorneys.

54. *Mancia*, 253 F.R.D. at 360–61 n.3.

55. *See, e.g.*, Losey, *supra* note 9.

56. *E.g.*, Cache La Poudre Feeds, LLC v. Land O'Lakes, Inc., 244 F.R.D. 614, 636–37 (D. Colo. 2007); Books Are Fun, Ltd. v. Rosebrough, 239 F.R.D. 532, 550 (S.D. Iowa 2007).

57. Memorandum of Points and Authorities of Kyle Robertson, Jaideep Venkatesan, and Stanley Young in Response to the Order to Show Cause, 2007 WL 3005535.

Qualcomm presented a patent dispute. At the risk of oversimplification, the elements of the case pertinent to Rule 26(g) were (1) Qualcomm sued Broadcom for alleged infringement; (2) Qualcomm denied early participation[58] on the Joint Video Team (JVT);[59] (3) if Qualcomm had participated in the JVT at the relevant time, its claims would be defeated; (4) Broadcom propounded discovery and Qualcomm did not produce responses showing early participation in the JVT; (5) Qualcomm denied early participation in the JVT; (6) the case went to trial and a Qualcomm witness admitted to early participation in the JVT; (7) Qualcomm and its attorneys were, or should have been, aware of evidence showing this early participation, while they were denying early participation; and, (8) sanctions were imposed.

Qualcomm I was the unpublished[60] decision of the magistrate judge, while *Qualcomm II* was the district judge's decision affirming that decision in part and vacating it in part.[61] *Qualcomm III*[62] was the last chapter, in which the court declined to sanction outside counsel. The disclosure of Qualcomm's JVT participation came about through testimony about ESI, and the magnitude of Qualcomm's misconduct was demonstrated by posttrial searches of ESI. Because of the egregious actions, the magnitude of the sanctions, the involvement of respected law firms, the sanctions on experienced and inexperienced lawyers, and the role of Rule 26(g), as well as the court's inherent powers, the case deserves attention.

Qualcomm I begins after the trial. Broadcom had "made an oral motion [at trial] for sanctions after Qualcomm . . . witness Viji Raveendran testified about emails that were not produced

58. The summary in the text is accurate, but an oversimplification. Qualcomm's denial of JVT participation was limited to a denial during an early, particular, relevant time frame (2002 and early 2003). Qualcomm admitted to later participation in the JVT.

59. According to the court, the JVT "is the standards-setting body that created the H.264 standard" governing video coding. Qualcomm I, 2008 WL 66932 *1. Broadcomm offered H.264-compliant products for sale. *Id.* Qualcomm sued to enjoin the sale of those products and Broadcomm counterclaimed asserting, inter alia, unenforceability and waiver. *Id.* Broadcomm sought discovery concerning Qualcomm's participation in the JVT. *Id.* at *2. Qualcomm inaccurately denied participation during the relevant time frame.

60. 2008 WL 66932 (S.D. Cal. Jan. 7, 2008).

61. The district judge vacated the holding regarding privilege waiver. 2008 WL 638108 (S.D. Cal. Mar. 5, 2008). An appeal followed, but was dismissed. 327 Fed. Appx. 877, 2008 WL 6400775 (Fed. Cir. Aug. 18, 2008).

62. 2010 WL 1336937 (S.D. Cal. Apr. 2, 2010).

to Broadcom during discovery." Broadcom contended that Qualcomm had failed to produce tens of thousands of documents that had been requested in discovery. The court ordered 14 named attorneys, and all those who had signed discovery pleadings, to show cause why they should not be sanctioned. Nineteen attorneys responded. The magistrate judge granted in part, and denied in part, Broadcom's sanctions motion, and referred six attorneys to Bar Counsel.

The court held that Broadcom had requested information about early JVT participation during discovery. Describing the dispute, the *Qualcomm I* court noted: "Over the course of discovery, Broadcom sought information concerning Qualcomm's participation in and communications with the JVT through a variety of discovery devices."

Qualcomm stated that it *would* produce the requested discovery. For example, the court noted: "In response to Broadcom's request for JVT documents, Qualcomm, in a discovery response signed by attorney Kevin Leung, stated 'Qualcomm will produce non-privileged relevant and responsive documents describing QUALCOMM's participation in the JVT, if any, which can be located after a reasonable search.'" Thus, in part, the court was faced with a situation where discovery responses, signed pursuant to Rule 26(g), were at issue.

The court then looked at Qualcomm's answers, stating: "Qualcomm responded that it first attended a JVT meeting in December 2003 and that it first submitted a JVT proposal in January 2006. . . . In response to Interrogatory No. 13, Qualcomm stated that it submitted four proposals to the JVT in 2006 but had no earlier involvement." It is, of course, undisputed that counsel's signature on these responses constituted a Rule 26(g) certification.

Asked to produce a Rule 30(b)(6) deponent, Qualcomm designated Irvine, and "[a]lthough attorney Leung prepared Irvine for her deposition, Qualcomm did not search her computer for any relevant documents or emails or provide her with any information to review. Irvine testified falsely that Qualcomm had never been involved in the JVT. Broadcom impeached Irvine with documents showing that Qualcomm had participated in the JVT in late 2003. Qualcomm ultimately agreed to provide another Rule 30(b)(6) witness."[63]

63. The Qualcomm court's internal citations to the record, e.g., transcripts, declarations, and exhibits, and rules has been omitted from the discussion in the text for ease of reading.

The court notes: "Qualcomm [subsequently] designated Scott Ludwin as the new representative to testify about Qualcomm's knowledge of and involvement in the JVT. Leung prepared and defended Ludwin at his deposition. Qualcomm did not search Ludwin's computer for any relevant documents nor take any other action to prepare him. Ludwin testified falsely that Qualcomm only began participating in the JVT in late 2003. . . ."

Magistrate Judge Major then wrote: "As the case progressed, Qualcomm became increasingly aggressive in its argument that it did not participate in the JVT during the time the JVT was creating the H.264 standard. This argument was vital to Qualcomm's success in this litigation. . . . [P]articipation in the JVT in 2002 or early 2003 during the creation of the H.264 standard would have prohibited Qualcomm from suing companies, including Broadcom, that utilized the H.264 standard. In a nutshell, the issue of whether Qualcomm participated in the JVT in 2002 and early 2003 became crucial to the instant litigation."

The court continued: "[O]n September 1, 2006, Qualcomm submitted an expert declaration confirming the absence of any corporate records indicating Qualcomm's participation in the JVT. The declaration was prepared by the Heller Ehrman lawyers and reviewed by numerous Day Casebeer and Qualcomm in-house attorneys. . . . Numerous in-house and outside counsel reviewed the pleadings and attorneys. . . ." Qualcomm specifically denied that Raveendran had received email relating to JVT participation.

The court then explained: "Trial commenced on January 9, 2007, and throughout trial, Qualcomm argued that it had not participated in the JVT in 2002 and early 2003 when the H.264 standard was being created." It is at this point that, as the court notes, Qualcomm's defense began to unravel:

> While preparing Qualcomm witness Viji Raveendran to testify at trial, attorney Adam Bier discovered an August 6, 2002 email to viji@qualcomm.com welcoming her to the avc_ce mailing list. Several days later, on January 14, 2007, Bier and Raveendran searched her laptop computer using the search term "avc_ce" and discovered 21 separate emails, none of which Qualcomm had produced in discovery. The email chains bore several dates in November 2002 and the authors discussed various issues relating to the H.264 standard. While Raveendran was not a named author or recipient, the emails were sent to all members of two JVT email groups

> (jvt-experts and avc_ce) and Raveendran maintained them on her [Qualcomm] computer for more than four years.

The court, in stark terms, continued:

> The Qualcomm trial team decided not to produce these newly discovered emails to Broadcom, claiming they were not responsive to Broadcom's discovery requests. The attorneys ignored the fact that the presence of the emails on Raveendran's computer undercut Qualcomm's premier argument that it had not participated in the JVT in 2002. The Qualcomm trial team failed to conduct any investigation to determine whether there were more emails that also had not been produced.
>
> Four days later, during a sidebar discussion, [Qualcomm attorney] Stanley Young argued against the admission of the December 2002 avc_ce email reflector list, declaring: "Actually, there are no emails—there are no emails . . . there's no evidence that any email was actually sent to this list. This is just a list of email . . . addresses. There's no evidence of anything being sent." None of the Qualcomm attorneys who were present during the sidebar mentioned the 21 avc_ce emails found on Raveendran's computer a few days earlier.

On direct examination of Raveendran, Qualcomm's counsel avoided posing direct questions to her on the critical JVT issue. "But on cross-examination, Broadcom asked the right question and Raveendran was forced to admit that she had received emails from the avc_ce mailing list. Immediately following this admission, in response to Broadcom's request for the emails, and despite the fact that he had participated in the decision three days earlier not to produce them," Qualcomm's attorney argued that the email—which went to the central issue in the patent dispute—was not responsive to Broadcom's requests. During the lunch break, however, Qualcomm produced the 21 emails from Raveendran's archive. The jury then ruled, at least in part, in Broadcom's favor.

The district judge concluded that "Qualcomm's counsel participated in an organized program of litigation misconduct and concealment throughout discovery, trial, and post-trial before new counsel took over lead role in the case on April 27, 2007." The district judge ordered that Qualcomm pay Broadcom's defense costs. Magistrate Judge Major noted: "On December 11, 2007, [District] Judge Brewster adopted this court's recommendation and ordered

Qualcomm to pay Broadcom $9,259,985.09 in attorneys' fees and related costs, as well as post-judgment interest on the final fee award of $8,568,633.24 at 4.91 percent accruing from August 6, 2007."

Nevertheless, Judge Major continued, "Following trial, Qualcomm continued to dispute the relevancy and responsiveness of the 21 Raveendran emails. . . . In response to Broadcom's request that Qualcomm conduct additional searches to determine the scope of Qualcomm's discovery violation, Bier stated in a March 7, 2007 letter, we 'believe your negative characterization of Qualcomm's compliance with its discovery obligation to be wholly without merit' but he advised that Qualcomm agreed to search the current and archived emails of five trial witnesses using the requested JVT, avc_ce and H.264 terms."

After conducting that search, Qualcomm "admitted Qualcomm had thousands of relevant unproduced documents and that their review of these documents 'revealed facts that appear to be inconsistent with certain arguments that [counsel] made on Qualcomm's behalf at trial and in the equitable hearing following trial.'" Qualcomm "searched the email archives of twenty-one employees and located more than forty-six thousand documents (totaling more than three hundred thousand pages), which had been requested but not produced in discovery."

Not surprisingly, the magistrate judge found "clear and convincing evidence that Qualcomm intentionally engaged in conduct designed to prevent Broadcom from learning that Qualcomm had participated in the JVT during the time period when the H.264 standard was being developed. To this end, Qualcomm withheld tens of thousands of emails showing that it actively participated in the JVT in 2002 and 2003 and then utilized Broadcom's lack of access to the suppressed evidence to repeatedly and falsely aver that there was 'no evidence' that it had participated in the JVT prior to September 2003. Qualcomm's misconduct in hiding the emails and electronic documents prevented Broadcom from correcting the false statements and countering the misleading arguments."

The magistrate judge then analyzed sanctions under Rule 37, Rule 26(g), and the court's inherent powers. Rule 37, however, presented a conundrum. Because Qualcomm had said that it would produce JVT documents, Broadcom never filed a motion to compel production and Qualcomm had not violated any discovery order.[64]

64. Rule 37(a) provides for motions to compel disclosure or discovery. Rule 37(b) addresses sanctions for failing to comply with a court order. Rule 37(c) is

Therefore, Rule 37 was generally[65] inapposite. The court noted the obligations imposed by Rule 26(g), as well as its inherent powers, and explained that

> [T]he concerns are heightened in this age of electronic discovery when attorneys may not physically touch and read every document within the client's custody and control. For the current "good faith" discovery system to function in the electronic age, attorneys and clients must work together to ensure that both understand how and where electronic documents, records and emails are maintained and to determine how best to locate, review, and produce responsive documents. Attorneys must take responsibility for ensuring that their clients conduct a comprehensive and appropriate document search. Producing 1.2 million pages of marginally relevant documents while hiding 46,000 critically important ones does not constitute good faith and does not satisfy either the client's or attorney's discovery obligations. Similarly, agreeing to produce certain categories of documents and then not producing all of the documents that fit within such a category is unacceptable. Qualcomm's conduct warrants sanctions.

The magistrate judge explained the decision to sanction the attorneys: "The Court's review of Qualcomm's declarations, the attorneys' declarations, and Judge Brewster's orders leads this Court to the inevitable conclusion that Qualcomm intentionally withheld tens of thousands of decisive documents from its opponent in an effort to win this case and gain a strategic business advantage over Broadcom. Qualcomm could not have achieved this goal without some type of assistance or deliberate ignorance from its retained attorneys. Accordingly, the Court concludes it must sanction both Qualcomm and some of its retained attorneys."[66]

---

applicable where a party fails to disclose, supplement, or admit. No other provision of Rule 37 was apposite.

65. The court noted that Rule 37(c) was applicable.

66. The court wrote: "Qualcomm did not fail to produce a document or two; it withheld over 46,000 critical documents that extinguished Qualcomm's primary argument of nonparticipation in the JVT. In addition, the suppressed documents did not belong to one employee, or a couple of employees who had since left the company; they belonged to (or were shared with) numerous, current Qualcomm employees, several of whom testified (falsely) at trial and in depositions. Given the volume and importance of the withheld documents, the number of involved Qualcomm employees, and the numerous warning flags, the Court

The magistrate judge then turned to Qualcomm:

Qualcomm violated its discovery obligations by failing to produce more than 46,000 emails and documents that were requested in discovery and that Qualcomm agreed to produce. *See* Fed.R.Civ.P. 26(g) Advisory Committee Notes (1983 Amendment) ("Rule 26(g) imposes an affirmative duty to engage in pretrial discovery in a responsible manner that is consistent with the spirit and purposes of Rules 26 through 37). . . .

Qualcomm has not presented any evidence establishing that it searched for pre-September 2003 JVT, avc_ce, or H.264 records or emails on its computer system or email databases. Qualcomm also has not established that it searched the computers or email databases of the individuals who testified on Qualcomm's behalf at trial or in depositions as Qualcomm's most knowledgeable corporate witnesses; in fact, it indicates that it did not conduct any such search. The fact that Qualcomm did not perform these basic searches at any time before the completion of trial indicates that Qualcomm intentionally withheld the documents. This conclusion is bolstered by the fact that when Qualcomm "discovered" the 21 Raveendran emails, it did not produce them and did not engage in any type of review to determine whether there were additional relevant, responsive, and unproduced documents. . . .

Qualcomm's claim that it inadvertently failed to find and produce these documents also is negated by the massive volume and direct relevance of the hidden documents. As Judge Brewster noted, it is inexplicable that Qualcomm was able to locate the post-September 2003 JVT documents that either supported, or did not harm, Qualcomm's arguments but were unable to locate the pre-September 2003 JVT documents that hurt its arguments. Similarly, the inadvertence argument is undercut by Qualcomm's ability to easily locate the suppressed documents using fundamental JVT and avc search terms when forced to do so by Broadcom's threat to return to court. . . . Finally, the inadvertence argument also is belied by the number of Qualcomm employees and

finds it unbelievable that the retained attorneys did not know or suspect that Qualcomm had not conducted an adequate search for documents." Qualcomm I, 2008 WL 66932 *12.

> consultants who received the emails, attended the JVT meetings, and otherwise knew about the information set forth in the undisclosed emails.

The court strongly criticized Qualcomm's failure to produce knowledgeable Rule 30(b)(6) deponents, concluding that the company ignored a number of itemized warning flags.

Applying Rule 26(g), the magistrate judge wrote:

> Attorneys Leung, Mammen and Batchelder are responsible for the initial discovery failure because they handled or supervised Qualcomm's discovery responses and production of documents. The Federal Rules impose an affirmative duty upon lawyers to engage in discovery in a responsible manner and to conduct a "reasonable inquiry" to determine whether discovery responses are sufficient and proper. Fed.R.Civ.P. 26(g); Fed.R.Civ.P. 26 Advisory Committee Notes (1983 Amendment). In the instant case, a reasonable inquiry should have included searches using fundamental terms such as JVT, avc_ce or H.264, on the computers belonging to knowledgeable people such as Raveendran, Irvine and Ludwin. As the post-trial investigation confirmed, such a reasonable search would have revealed the suppressed documents. Had [Qualcomm attorneys] Leung, Mammen, Batchelder, or any of the other attorneys insisted on reviewing Qualcomm's records regarding the locations searched and terms utilized, they would have discovered the inadequacy of the search and the suppressed documents. Similarly, Leung's difficulties with the Rule 30(b)(6) witnesses, Irvine and Ludwin, should have alerted him (and the supervising or senior attorneys) to the inadequacy of Qualcomm's document production and to the fact that they needed to review whose computers and databases had been searched and for what. Accordingly, the Court finds that the totality of the circumstances establish that [Qualcomm attorneys] Leung, Mammen and Batchelder did not make a reasonable inquiry into Qualcomm's discovery search and production and their conduct contributed to the discovery violation.

Magistrate Judge Major wrote:

> Similarly, when Bier found the 21 emails on Raveendran's computer that had not been produced in discovery, he took

> the appropriate action and informed his supervisors, Mammen and Patch. Patch discussed the discovery and production issue with Young and Batchelder. While all of these attorneys assert that there was a plausible argument that Broadcom did not request these documents, only Bier and Mammen actually read the emails. Moreover, all of the attorneys missed the critical inquiry: was Qualcomm's document search adequate? If these 21 emails were not discovered during Qualcomm's document search, how many more might exist? The answer, obviously, was tens of thousands. If Bier, Mammen, Patch, Young or Batchelder had conducted a reasonable inquiry after the discovery of the 21 Raveendran emails, they would have discovered the inadequacy of Qualcomm's search and the suppressed documents. And, these experienced attorneys should have realized that the presence on Raveendran's computer of 21 JVT/avc_ce emails from 2002 contradicted Qualcomm's numerous arguments that it had not participated in the JVT during that same time period. This fact, alone, should have prompted the attorneys to immediately produce the emails and to conduct a comprehensive document search.

The court wrote that "[Qualcomm] attorneys Young, Patch, and Batchelder bear responsibility for the discovery failure because they did not conduct a reasonable inquiry into Qualcomm's discovery production before making specific factual and legal arguments to the court."

The court's Rule 26(g) conclusions were directly linked to the attorneys' ethical obligations: "Attorneys' ethical obligations do not permit them to participate in an inadequate document search and then provide misleading and incomplete information to their opponents and false arguments to the court." The court then referred the attorneys to Bar Counsel, stating:

> As set forth above, the Sanctioned Attorneys assisted Qualcomm in committing this incredible discovery violation by intentionally hiding or recklessly ignoring relevant documents, ignoring or rejecting numerous warning signs that Qualcomm's document search was inadequate, and blindly accepting Qualcomm's unsupported assurances that its document search was adequate. The Sanctioned Attorneys then used the lack of evidence to repeatedly and forcefully make false statements and arguments to the court and jury. As such,

> the Sanctioned Attorneys violated their discovery obligations *and also may have violated their ethical duties.* [emphasis added].

In determining the sanctions, the magistrate judge noted: "Qualcomm's failure to produce the massive number of critical documents at issue in this case significantly increased the scope, complexity and length of the litigation and justifies a significant monetary award. See, Fed.R.Civ.P. 26(g)(3) & 37(c). . . . Accordingly, for its monumental and intentional discovery violation, Qualcomm is ordered to pay $8,568,633.24 to Broadcom. . . ." The court did not impose monetary sanctions on counsel; however, it wrote:

> Monetary sanctions would be appropriate to address the discovery violations. However, the Court declines to impose monetary sanctions against the Sanctioned Attorneys for several reasons. First, if the imposed sanctions do not convince the attorneys to behave in a more ethical and professional manner in the future, monetary sanctions are unlikely to do so. Second, it is possible that Qualcomm will seek contribution from its retained attorneys after it pays Broadcom's attorneys' fees and costs and, in light of that significant monetary sanction, an additional fine is unlikely to affect counsel's future behavior.

Although Qualcomm paid the monetary fine,[67] *Qualcomm I* did not end the dispute. Central to its imposition of sanctions on counsel was the information-limitation imposed by the preservation of the attorney-client privilege between Qualcomm and its counsel: "While knowledge may be inferred from the attorney's conduct, evidence on this issue is limited due to Qualcomm's assertion of the attorney-client privilege."[68] In short: "Qualcomm asserted the attorney-client privilege and decreed that its retained attorneys could not reveal any communications protected by the privilege."[69] As a result, the magistrate judge noted that the court "does not have access to all of the information necessary to reach an informed decision regarding the actual knowledge of the attorneys."[70]

Qualcomm II vacated the privilege decision based on the "introduction of accusatory adversity between Qualcomm and its

67. 2008 WL 638108, at *1 (order "is nearly fully satisfied").

68. 2008 WL 66932, at *13.

69. *Id.* at n.8.

70. *Id.*

retained counsel."[71] After dismissal of the appeal,[72] the stage was set for resolution of the Rule 26(g) questions on a full record. The district court held that the attorneys "have a due process right to defend themselves" and that "the communications and conduct relevant to the topic area of records (electronic or other) discovery pertaining to JVT and its parents, its ad-hoc committees, and any other topic regarding the standards-setting process for video compression technology *is not privileged information*."[73]

Qualcomm III picks up after "an almost unlimited opportunity to conduct discovery" over a 15-month period.[74] The sanctioned lawyers deposed seven Qualcomm engineers, three in-house attorneys, two in-house paralegals, and one fellow attorney. After a three-day evidentiary hearing, the magistrate judge found that "this massive discovery failure resulted from significant mistakes, oversights, and miscommunication on the part of both outside counsel and Qualcomm employees." Based on new evidence, showing "ineffective and problematic" interactions between Qualcomm employees and outside counsel, however, the court concluded that the attorneys had made "significant efforts to comply with their discovery obligations" and declined to sanction them.[75] The *Qualcomm* court concluded: "The fundamental problem in this case was an incredible breakdown in communication."[76]

71. 2008 WL 638108, at *3. For a discussion of an alternative basis to challenge Qualcomm's assertion of the privilege, see P. Grimm, *et al.*, *Discovery About Discovery: Does the Attorney-Client Privilege Protect All Attorney-Client Communications Relating to the Preservation of Potentially Relevant Information?*, 37 U. Balt. L. Rev. 413 (2008) (see chapter 9).

72. 377 Fed. Appx. 877, 2008 WL 6400775 (Fed. Cir. Aug. 18, 2008).

73. 2008 WL 638108, at *3 (emphasis added) (citing Weil v. Inv./Indicators, Research & Mgmt., Inc., 647 F.2d 18, 24 (9th Cir. 1981)).

74. 2010 WL 1336937, at *1.

75. No mention is made of the referral to the California State Bar.

76. 2008 WL 1336937, at *2. In so doing, the court echoed *Zubulake*: "Lawyers and their clients need to communicate clearly and effectively with one another to ensure that litigation proceeds efficiently. When communication between counsel and client breaks down, conversation becomes 'just crossfire,' and there are usually casualties." Zubulake v. UBS Warburg, LLC, 229 F.R.D. 422, 424 (S.D.N.Y. 2004) (quotation and citation omitted). "Proper communication between a party and her lawyer will ensure (1) that all relevant information (or at least all sources of relevant information) is discovered, (2) that relevant information is retained on a continuing basis; and (3) that relevant non-privileged material is produced to the opposing party." *Id.* at 432. As the *Zubulake* court noted: "This case represents a failure of communication, and that failure falls on counsel and client alike." *Id.* at 436.

Qualcomm III did not clear the attorneys of error; it held that they did not act in bad faith and should not be sanctioned. The court pointed to errors aplenty. It was critical of the failure of in-house and outside counsel to meet in person with appropriate Qualcomm engineers.[77] It pointedly stated that outside counsel failed to obtain an understanding of Qualcomm's computer system, where emails were stored and portable computers were backed up, and noted: "Finally, no attorney took supervisory responsibility for verifying that the necessary discovery had been conducted (including ensuring that all of the correct locations, servers, databases, repositories, and computers were correctly searched for potentially relevant documents). . . ." It pointed to "a lack of agreement amongst the participants regarding responsibility for document collection and production."

Nevertheless, the court also described "an incredible lack of candor on the part of the principal Qualcomm employees. For example, Viji Raveendran repeatedly told Responding Attorneys, other outside counsel, and Qualcomm employees that she had not participated in, and had no involvement with, the JVT during development of the H.264 standard and she testified to those facts under oath. . . . Raveendran made these statements despite the fact that she personally had attended some of the JVT meetings." In fact, although "a number of" Qualcomm employees knew of Qualcomm's participation, none of them informed outside counsel, who "received confirmation by fifteen Qualcomm employees, including lawyers, on thirty-one occasions that Qualcomm did not participate in JVT or that the same was probably or almost certainly correct."[78]

In short, the court was forced to apply Rule 26 in the context of obfuscation by Qualcomm, inadequate efforts by counsel, contradictory or potentially contradictory evidence, and actual discovery of emails that undercut the arguments at trial. It noted that "Rule 26 provides for sanctions against individual attorneys who are remiss in complying with their discovery obligations. . . ."[79]

Because, for example, attorney Leung made inquiry but was misled by Qualcomm employees, he was not sanctioned. "The evidence presented during these proceedings clarified that, although a number of poor decisions were made, the involved attorneys did

77. 2010 WL 1336937, at *2.
78. *Id.* at *4.
79. *Id.* at *5.

not act in bad faith."[80] Thus, while the court concluded that it was "undisputed that Qualcomm improperly held back from Broadcom tens of thousands of documents that contradicted one of its key legal arguments,"[81] it also concluded that "while significant errors were made by" some of the attorneys, there was "insufficient evidence" to find bad faith or failure to make a reasonable inquiry before certifying Qualcomm's discovery responses.

Qualcomm may have ended, at least for the attorneys, with a whimper, not a bang.[82] Regardless of the outcome for counsel, however, the dispute itself demonstrates the vital importance of Rule 26(g) and the possible consequences of noncompliance. At a minimum, the rule imposes a duty of "reasonable inquiry" that is not met by finger-pointing[83] and ignoring warning flags in the hope that someone else will act.[84]

80. *Id.* at *6.

81. *Id.* at *7.

82. T. S. Eliot, "The Hollow Men" (1925). Several of the Qualcomm attorneys described their experience on video. Cal Law, *Surviving the Qualcomm Sanctions* (Apr. 9, 2010), http://vimeo.com/10815873. "[T]he sanctions had a devastating effect on their careers and their personal lives." *Id.* One attorney described the other attorneys as "top notch" and "quality individuals with integrity," stating: "[T]he takeaway is that this kind of thing could happen to anybody." *Id.* He describes a "bunch of Eagle scouts" who were too willing to believe others and who did not have sufficient cynicism. *Id.* In describing *Qualcomm III*, the *ABA Journal* wrote that the magistrate judge had "changed her mind after the lawyers were allowed to break attorney-client privilege to defend their actions." D. Weiss, *After Sanctions Are Lifted, Qualcomm Lawyers React: This "Can Happen to Anybody,"* ABA J., Apr. 15, 2010. Attorneys "Leung, Mammen, and two other lawyers, Lee Patch and Adam Bier, later left Day Casebeer 'under strained circumstances' and never landed a job with a new firm." *Id.* (quoting Z. Elinson, *Lawyers in Discovery Scandal Say Qualcomm Lied*, RECORDER (Nov. 3, 2009), http://www.law.com/jsp/article.jsp?id=1202435137932). Qualcomm's general counsel resigned shortly after *Qualcomm I*. Elinson, *supra*.

83. "[T]he Court's patience for the parties' incessant finger-pointing is at an end." Nycomed U.S. Inc. v. Glenmark Generics Ltd., 2010 WL 3173785, at *1 (E.D.N.Y. Aug. 11, 2010).

84. The appeal on the merits was also infected by the nondisclosure. 548 F.3d 1004, 1022 (Fed. Cir. 2008), *cert. dismissed*, 129 S. Ct. 2182 (2009) ("We agree with Broadcom that Qualcomm cannot withhold evidence of its JVT participation, make false factual assertions about this participation to the district court in opposition to Broadcom's equitable estoppel defense, and then argue on appeal that Broadcom failed to sufficiently plead equitable estoppel. Surely Qualcomm cannot expect to benefit by concealing documents, misrepresenting facts throughout trial, and then claiming ex post that Broadcom should have raised a similar equitable doctrine earlier.").

6. Reliance on the client, cocounsel, or an expert

Qualcomm illustrates that reliance on a client or cocounsel may be insufficient inquiry under Rule 26(g), at least when there are warning flags. It is not the purpose of this chapter to provide encyclopedic guidance. Suffice it to say that *Qualcomm* is not the only reported decision that demands more.[85]

The Advisory Committee Note bears repeating:

> In making the inquiry, the attorney may rely on assertions by the client and on communications with other counsel in the case as long as that reliance is appropriate under the circumstances. Ultimately, what is reasonable is a matter for the court to decide on the totality of the circumstances.
>
> Rule 26(g) does not require the signing attorney to certify the truthfulness of the client's factual responses to a discovery request. Rather, the signature certifies that the lawyer has made a reasonable effort to assure that the client has provided all the information and documents available to him that are

85. *See generally* R & R Sails, Inc. v. Ins. Co., 251 F.R.D. 520, 525 (S.D. Cal. 2008) ("Lombardo has been an insurance adjuster for twenty-six years and explains that he did not associate the AEGIS database with the claim file that he maintains because '[t]he AEGIS computer system records are kept on a computer system that is separate from my file materials and I do not have a practice of printing them out to put in my file.' (Dkt. No. 29-3 at PP 6-8) Defendant argues that this 'honest mistake' substantially justifies the incorrect certifications made to Plaintiff, as well as the false declaration provided to Plaintiff in response to this Court's Order of November 29, 2007. However, to give meaning to the certifications provided on discovery responses, Rule 26(g) requires attorneys or parties to sign their responses 'after a reasonable inquiry.' Evidence of such an inquiry prior to January 2007 may provide this Court with justification for the incorrect certifications provided to Plaintiff. Instead, this Court is presented with evidence that Lombardo was maintaining a claim log on his own computer using the AEGIS system while failing to recognize that this log was the same 'record/log' being requested by Plaintiff. Lombardo entered notes of a communication with counsel into the AEGIS system on November 16, 2007, immediately prior to counsel's representation to this Court that such a system was not possessed by Defendant and close in time to his signing a declaration that no such notes are maintained. (Dkt. No. 29-2 at P 5; Dkt. No. 29-3 at P 18) The Court cannot find that a reasonable inquiry was made into whether Defendant possessed discovery responsive to Plaintiff's requests, and therefore the Court does not find Defendant's incorrect certifications to be substantially justified. Defendant is liable for sanctions, pursuant to Federal Rule of Civil Procedure 26(g), for making incorrect certifications to Plaintiff regarding discovery responses.") (subsequent history omitted).

responsive to the discovery demand.

The 1983 Advisory Committee Notes state: "It is an objective standard similar to the one imposed by Rule 11."

Again, while it is not the purpose of this chapter to gather all cases and cover all issues, it is important to note that reliance on an expert may, or may not, be a reasonable Rule 26(g) inquiry, depending on the facts and circumstances. It has been held that the rule does not apply to submittal of false expert reports.[86] Generally, Rule 26(g) sanctions would not be appropriate where counsel relied on an expert in signing a discovery response,[87] but this is not without exception: "[I]t may be possible to imagine a scenario where such a sanction would be appropriate. . . ."[88] Nevertheless, that scenario is unlikely: "The Court has found no case in which an attorney or even the client has been sanctioned monetarily because of deficiencies or errors—however gross they may have been—in an expert's report produced pursuant to Rule 26, whether or not referred to in answers to interrogatories."[89] In short, "[t]ransporting the battle of experts to the pre-trial stage—holding out the possibility of a financial reward to the party with the more persuasive solon and corresponding punishment to the party with the less persuasive one—would open up an entirely new arena."[90] These words may be especially applicable in the context of expert opinions with regard to ESI.

---

86. Johnson v. Bon-Ton Dep't Stores, Inc., 2008 WL 2120547 (2d Cir. May 21, 2008) ("We agree with the district court that the mandatory sanction provision of Rule 26(g)(3) does not apply to expert disclosures under Rule 26(a)(2).").

87. MMI Prods., Inc. v. Long, 231 F.R.D. 215, 218–19 (D. Md. 2005) (reliance on expert's report that computer was tampered with in answers to interrogatories). "Indeed, the typical sanctions imposed in connection with expert reports because of the untimeliness or incompleteness of production have been exclusion of the reports in whole or part or, infrequently, dismissal of the case." *Id.* at 218.

88. *Id.*

89. *Id.* at 219.

90. *Id.* at 219. "MMI and its counsel's actions regarding the Velasco report were not, in the Court's view, part of a nefarious plot to play unfairly in this litigation. The extensive discovery clashes and vituperation that have characterized this case so far, it should be noted, give cause for concern in and of themselves. But that perhaps is best left for another sermon on another day." *Id.* at 220.

7. The future direction[91]

In section 3, we note the three major studies that have recently been completed. There are many ongoing efforts to ensure that the civil litigation system provides the just, speedy, and inexpensive determination of every action.[92] The Honorable Lee H. Rosenthal has said that "one of the promises of e-discovery that is about to be fulfilled is the opportunity to 'reexamine civil litigation' with an eye towards 'improving the system.'"[93] The Sedona Conference program "The Future of Civil Litigation: Legislative and Behavioral Changes, " held in April 2010, noted: "For more than 25 years, litigants, judges, rulemakers, and legislators have grappled with questions surrounding complex civil litigation: pleading requirements, the scope of discovery, the appropriate role for the judge, the 'disappearing trial,' and other issues. Attempts have been made to objectively define these issues, measure the level of attorney dissatisfaction with the current system, and propose rule-based or statutory solutions. But many observers point out that the current rules are not used to full advantage by lawyers or judges to avoid disputes and delays, or to reduce costs in litigation. Behavioral changes may be needed address the problems that the litigation cost studies articulate."[94]

Additionally, as a follow-up on the FJC and ABA surveys: "The American Bar Association Section of Litigation, in conjunction with the Advisory Committee for Civil Rules, the committee of the Federal Judicial Conference charged with initiating changes to the Federal Rules of Civil Procedure, is taking a comprehensive

91. The type of sanctions that may or should be imposed under Rule 26(g) are beyond the scope of this chapter. Rule 26(g)(3) is not limiting and provides discretion to impose an "appropriate sanction." Poole v. Textron, Inc., 192 F.R.D. 494, 498 (D. Md. 2000). The Advisory Committee Note states: "The nature of the sanction is a matter of judicial discretion to be exercised in light of the particular circumstances." For a discussion of sanctions, see chapter 8 and Victor Stanley, Inc. v. Creative Pipe, Inc. (*Victor Stanley II*), 269 F.R.D. 497 (D. Md. 2010), *affirmed in part and modified in part on unrelated grounds*, No.MJG-06-2662 (D.Md. Nov. 1, 2010), *subsequent opinion*, No. MJG-06-2662 (D.Md. Jan. 24, 2011).

92. FED. R. CIV. P. 1.

93. *Trends: 2010 Might Hold Significant Changes for E-Discovery Practice, Civil Litigation Overall*, DIGITAL DISCOVERY & E-EVIDENCE (BNA), Jan. 7, 2010, describing Judge Rosenthal's November 12 keynote address at the Georgetown University Law Center's Advanced E-Discovery Institute. Judge Rosenthal stated: "E-discovery is the inspiration for debate. . . ." *Id.*

94. The Sedona Conference, Complex Litigation XII-The Future of Civil Litigation: Legislative and Behavioral Changes (Apr. 2010), http://www.thesedona conference.org/conferences/20100408.

look at the federal civil litigation system to determine what, if any, changes need to be made to the current federal system, including changes to the rules. The survey results have just been made available to the public."[95] The ABA Litigation Section "organized the Future of Civil Litigation Special Committee to review the results and develop the recommendations, which [were] presented at the 2010 Conference on Civil Litigation on May 10–11, 2010 at the Duke University School of Law."[96] The Honorable John G. Koeltl, who is a member of the Advisory Committee and was chair of the planning committee for the 2010 conference, said: "The expectation is that the conference will provide suggestions for possible changes in the federal rules as well as for best practices for lawyers and judges to accomplish the purpose of the rules to secure the just, speedy, and inexpensive determination of every action. . . ."[97]

The Duke Conference concluded: "It is hoped that the papers and discussion at the Conference will frame an agenda for possible amendments to the Federal Rules of Civil Procedure, and that they will be a basis for judicial education through the Federal Judicial Center and for further action by the Bar."[98] The Conference included a discussion on the cost-benefit analysis of e-discovery and the degree to which the new rules are working.[99] The panel members agreed that "the rules in general, and a preservation rule in particular, should treat differently huge cases, with enormous discovery, and all others." The conference summary of the Institute for the Advancement of the American Legal System states the theme that "procedure should be tailored to the needs of each case early in the pretrial process, through a combination of attorney

95. J. Tracy, *ABA Section of Litigation to Recommend Changes to Federal Rules*, ABA LITIG. NEWS, Dec. 8, 2009, http://www.abanet.org/litigation/litigationnews/top_stories/federal-rules-civil-procedure-changes.html.

96. *Id.*

97. *Id.*

98. 2010 Conference on Civil Litigation, Duke Law School, Durham, N.C., May 10–11, 2010, http://civilconference.uscourts.gov/LotusQuickr/dcc/Main.nsf/h_RoomHome/4df38292d748069d0525670800167212/?OpenDocument.

99. 2010 Conference on Civil Litigation, E-Discovery Panel, http://civilconference.uscourts.gov/LotusQuickr/dcc/Main.nsf/h_Library/9E884B4174EE27B6852576E900738E7B/?OpenDocument. See Milberg LLP and Hausfeld LLP, "E-Discovery Today: The Fault Lies Not in Our Rules. . . ," 4 Fed.Cts.L.Rev. 1, 2-3 (2011) (rules "are blamed for things they were never intended to address. . . .").

cooperation, judicial management, and case type-specific rules and protocols."[100]

Rule 26(g), incorporating concepts of proportionality, reasonable inquiry, and ethics, may have a major role in that discussion.[101] Even in the absence of a federal preservation rule,[102] Rule 26(g) may be deemed to impose, directly or by analogy, a duty to negotiate a reasonable, proportionate preservation regime prior to the commencement of litigation. Because it incorporates ethical principles that are applicable regardless of whether a lawsuit has been commenced, Rule 26(g)'s mandate that discovery requests be reasonable and responses be formed upon reasonable inquiry would seem especially applicable to prelitigation preservation issues. If counsel are obligated by the rule to "stop and think" about discovery requests and responses during litigation, it seems equally appropriate to impose that obligation on a prelitigation process that is designed to ensure that discoverable information is preserved.[103]

What remains certain is that Rule 26(g) imposes a legal and ethical duty of reasonable requests and inquiry, and that courts will not hesitate to enquire into compliance, unburdened by attorney-client privilege,[104] into the details of that inquiry when there is a breach of the rule. Reliance on cocounsel, clients, or experts may or may not be "reasonable," depending on the unique facts presented.

---

100. Univ. of Denver, Summary of 2010 Conference on Civil Litigation at Duke Law School, http://www.du.edu/legalinstitute/pdf/DukeConference.pdf.

101. *See* Grimm, *et al.*, *supra* note 3 (arguing for application of proportionality rules by analogy prior to the commencement of litigation).

102. *See* K. Lambert, *Is It Time for a Federal Rule on Preservation?*, ABA LITIG. NEWS, Aug. 2, 2010, http://www.abanet.org/litigation/litigationnews/top_stories/080210-e-discovery-preservation-new-rule.html ("Judge Rosenthal echoed Judge Scheindlin's observations about the importance of establishing symmetry across the circuits on a number of critical points related to preservation, including a uniform federal standard for determining when—and what—sanctions are appropriate for spoliation.")

103. See chapter 9.

104. *Id.*

APPENDIX A

TIPS TO AVOID MISTAKES WITH ESI VENDORS

BY MICHAEL D. BERMAN

The first step in addressing the use of electronic discovery vendors is deciding whether to retain one. Authors have differed on whether to perform electronically stored information (ESI) services in-house or through outside vendors. The decision should be a reasoned one, considering the size and needs of the project, as well as the skill, training, and experience level of all involved persons. Just as a litigator may not be well suited to drafting a will, some in-house IT professionals lack forensic skills. The *Intel Microprocessor Antitrust Litigation*[1] exemplifies the dangers of an in-house solution.

Next, it is critical to define the roles of counsel, IT professionals, other forensic experts if any, and client substantive representatives. Georges Clemenceau said that war is too important to be left to generals. Complex e-discovery cannot be successfully handled by a single profession or person. Assemble a team and agree on areas of responsibility. Client representatives can assist in describing

This appendix item is based on an article that first appeared in an ABA periodical, TECHNOLOGY FOR THE LITIGATOR.

1. In re Intel Corp. Microprocessor Antitrust Litig., 2008 WL 2310288 (D. Del. June 4, 2008); see appendix B.

what has been created, saved, and purged, and by whom. IT professionals and experts can determine where the data was likely stored and how it can be preserved and harvested. Attorneys can act as guides and interpreters, applying legal principles to direct and assist the other disciplines.

An ESI vendor is like any other expert in one way: the vendor may have a conflict of interest. Just as you would with any expert, address conflicts and confidentiality up front.

Preplanning is better than reactive crisis management. The Sedona Conference *Best Practices for the Selection of Electronic Discovery Vendors: Navigating the Discovery Process*[2] sets out a detailed plan for selecting an ESI vendor. The "best practices," however, cannot be followed in a day, and prior planning is essential.

Define the scope of work in collaboration with the team. Identify key persons, central issues, a methodology for developing keyword searches, and hardware/software issues, in light of the size, importance, and complexity of the case and the data. Although every case is important to the litigants, not every case can support unlimited e-discovery.

Consider the full life cycle of the project. Sandy Ringer wrote the aptly titled *If You Don't Know Where You're Going, How Will You Know When You Get There?*[3] It does little good to preserve data in a manner that makes subsequent processing and review more costly. The goal is speedy and inexpensive production of admissible evidence, and all steps must be planned with that in mind. Will the preservation and processing vendor be able to provide load files that match the desired litigation support solution? Is metadata necessary for authentication? If a vendor uses proprietary software, does it fit your needs?

Understand the vendor pricing policy. ESI pricing can be trickier than the Rule Against Perpetuities. The Sedona Conference suggests reviewing a sample bill that contains every possible billable line item.

Enter into a written contract with the vendor. Address chain of custody and vendor security for sensitive ESI. Do you want the vendor to designate a key person? Is vendor size important, and does subcontracting present any problems? Recent substantive

2. THE SEDONA CONFERENCE, BEST PRACTICES FOR THE SELECTION OF ELECTRONIC DISCOVERY VENDORS: NAVIGATING THE DISCOVERY PROCESS (June 2007), http://www.thesedonaconference.org/content/miscFiles/RFP_Paper.pdf.
3. Transformata Publ'g LLC (Aug. 26, 2002).

decisions raise questions about reliance on Boolean searches—can the vendor provide "concept" searching?

The sanctions landscape is littered with instances in which a litigant had to present evidence through forensic ESI consultants. Consider whether, in addition to being technically qualified, the vendor will make a persuasive witness. Also consider whether any disclosures made to the vendor are privileged or protected work product. They likely are not.[4]

As the Sedona Conference noted: "The goal is to find the best fit—a vendor suited to both the organization and the particular project."[5] When the work begins and the money starts to flow, be sure you know what was purchased and sold.

4. P. Grimm, et al., *Discovery About Discovery: Does the Attorney-Client Privilege Protect All Attorney-Client Communications Relating to the Preservation of Potentially Relevant Information?* 37 U. BALT. L. REV. 413 (2008) (reprinted in chapter 16).
5. SEDONA CONFERENCE, supra note 2.

APPENDIX B

DISCOVERY LAPSE COULD RESULT IN LOSS OF PRIVILEGE: *IN RE INTEL CORP. MICROPROCESSOR ANTITRUST LITIGATION*

BY MICHAEL D. BERMAN

Six months into defending a complex case, your client informs you that its plan for the preservation of electronically stored information (ESI) failed, resulting in thousands of responsive emails being inadvertently destroyed. What are the risks faced if you conduct an investigation prior to disclosing your client's situation to opposing counsel and the court?

This appendix item is based on an article that first appeared in an ABA periodical, TECHNOLOGY FOR THE LITIGATOR.

In one recent decision, a party's voluntary actions taken to explain its own discovery lapses resulted in a partial waiver of privilege. In *In re Intel Corp. Microprocessor Antitrust Litig.*[1] Intel's admitted failure to preserve certain ESI in an antitrust case led a federal district court to order the production of redacted notes taken by its attorneys during interviews of 1,023 Intel employees regarding their document preservation efforts.

In the fall of 2006, during what may have been the "largest electronic production in history" of documents "somewhere in the neighborhood of a pile 137 miles high," Intel discovered some lapses in its preservation of ESI. Intel had imposed a litigation hold. However, it did not turn off the "auto delete" function that eliminated older email, believing that its hold instructions and other fail-safe processes were sufficient. This proved to be an error. It subsequently hired outside attorneys to begin an undisclosed process of interviewing 1,023 custodians "for the purpose of determining their e-mail preservation habits and their level of compliance with Intel's litigation hold notices/instructions." Then, in early February 2007, it notified the court and the opposing litigant of the discovery lapses. Intel contended that the problems were "inadvertent mistakes" and that its "investigation revealed no instance of deliberate deception."

In addition to other criticisms, the requesting party asserted that Intel failed to give clear litigation hold instructions and failed to adequately monitor compliance of its in-house preservation efforts. During "culpability discovery,"[2] Intel agreed to provide the "best information gathered after reasonable investigation," without referring to privilege. Intel disclosed 400 pages of summaries, "which drew upon thousands of pages of attorney notes." However, Intel asserted that this disclosure was not a work-product waiver, relying in part on its "general objection" to the document request to preserve its assertion of privilege.

Nevertheless, the court held that providing the summaries of those interviews, coupled with an assertion that its investigation revealed no deliberate deception, waived Intel's protection of all but core work product. The court ordered production of Intel's attorneys' notes to the extent that those notes revealed the substance of custodian statements that were already voluntarily disclosed through summaries by Intel's counsel. The court held that

1. 2008 WL 2310288 (D. Del. June 4, 2008).

2. See chapter 16.

Intel's opponent was not compelled to rely on Intel's description of what those custodians reported, but instead could review the actual attorneys' interview notes.

Balancing the need to make appropriate disclosure to the court and opposing counsel in these situations with the need to maintain confidentiality is not easy to do. Parties should be allowed a mechanism for critical self-study, free of the specter of privilege waiver and disclosure, says Andrew S. Pollis, Cleveland, Co-Chair of the ABA Section of Litigation's Ethics and Professionalism Committee.

Given the complexity of ESI, a litigant discovering a lapse such as Intel's is faced with the dilemma of a potential waiver versus responding without knowing the facts, Pollis says. "If there is reason to pursue discovery to unearth the facts, work product and attorney-client privilege should still be protected except in unusual circumstances," he adds.

"It is conceivable that a broad interpretation of this decision could have a real impact on the attorney-client relationship," says Robert J. Scheffel, Washington, D.C., Chair of the Attorney-Client Privilege Subcommittee of the Section's Pretrial Practice and Discovery Committee. "If a party believes that any investigation is discoverable, that party is unlikely to undertake such an investigation, or discuss the details with its counsel. This would seem to be at odds with one of the key purposes of the attorney-client privilege—encouraging frank communications between attorneys and their clients," Scheffel notes.

While sharing summaries of an internal investigation with the court and opposing counsel may be necessary during what some have called "discovery about discovery,"[3] it may result in a waiver of privilege—even when a party is simply trying to explain its own mistakes. The impact of *Intel* may extend beyond the ESI context. Litigators are cautioned to recognize that any selective disclosure of privileged materials could be considered a waiver of work-product, or other, protection.[4]

---

3. *Id.*
4. *Cf.* Fed. R. Evid. 502(a), (c), (d).

APPENDIX C

TIMING OF SPOLIATION MOTIONS: GOODMAN V. PRAXAIR SERVICES, INC.

By Michael D. Berman

The following article is reproduced here because the case it discusses, Goodman v. Praxair Services, Inc.,[1] *addressed a number of important issues and, specifically, the time at which a spoliation motion should or must be filed. Goodman holds that a spoliation motion should generally be filed promptly after the spoliation is discovered, during or soon after the close of the discovery period. In a subsequent case,* Davis v. Grant Park Nursing Home, LP,[2] *the court wrote: "Upon reviewing the record and briefing before me at this time, I have decided, sua sponte, to strike the plaintiff's motion for sanctions without prejudice, and to require*

This appendix item is based on an article that first appeared as "Magistrate Judge Recommends General Adverse Inference Instruction for Intentional Breach of Duty to Preserve." Reproduced with permission from 9(8) Digital Discovery & E-Evidence Rep. 240–42 (Aug.1, 2009).

1. 632 F. Supp. 2d 494 (D. Md. 2009).

2. 2010 U.S. Dist. Lexis 118853 (D.D.C. Nov. 9, 2010).

supplemental briefing at the conclusion of the limited discovery permitted by Judge Friedman." The Davis *court concluded that prejudice could not be determined until after discovery closed: "Accordingly, it is premature to consider the question of sanctions until discovery ends and the Court can assess accurately what prejudice, if any, the loss of the electronically stored information has caused. I will therefore strike the plaintiff's motion for sanctions without prejudice."[3] Procedural decisions on electronically stored information (ESI) issues are fact-sensitive.*

Prior to concluding that a pro se plaintiff was entitled to an adverse inference instruction, the court in *Goodman v. Praxair Services, Inc.*[4] comprehensively reviewed many of the central issues involved in electronically stored information (ESI) litigation, including

- the facts required to trigger the duty to preserve and a "litigation hold" in the context of escalating tension in a commercial dispute;
- when information in possession of a nonparty, third person is within the "control" of a preserving entity for preservation purposes;
- the distinction between the duty to preserve and the duty to produce, including whether backup tapes must be searched;
- the timing, necessary factual predicates, and resolution of a spoliation motion; and
- recovery of expenses for a partially successful spoliation motion.

Chief Magistrate Judge Paul W. Grimm issued the memorandum opinion.

The Facts

The underlying dispute involved a claim for breach of a contract providing for additional payment upon plaintiff's "success" in negotiations with the federal government. Essentially, the defendant retained plaintiff to assist in circumnavigating a costly regulatory requirement. The plaintiff was contractually entitled to additional funds if he obtained certain, specified results.

3. *Id.* at *4.
4. 632 F. Supp. 2d 494 (D. Md. 2009).

When the defendant retained other consultants to assist in obtaining the regulatory exemption, assertedly froze plaintiff out of the discussions, and later alleged that plaintiff was not the proximate cause of the positive outcome, the parties commenced negotiations.

When the discussions failed, plaintiff became dissatisfied, and, approximately three years later, filed suit.

Time Line. The commercial marriage unraveled slowly over the course of time. In 1998, the plaintiff began submitting work to the government on defendant's behalf. In April 1999, after some contacts with the government, the defendant told plaintiff to have no further discussions until there was a "complete strategy."

Due to the delay, in late 1999 plaintiff requested an advance of funds, and defendant noted it was "amenable to modifying" the contract. Because the defendant had brought in a second consultant, defendant also suggested, in a November 19, 1999, email, that there was a need to rework the contract if the second consultant was primarily responsible for success in negotiations with the government.

Plaintiff responded that the second consultant was merely an "additional asset." Defendant subsequently advanced funds to the plaintiff, and, in a November 24 email, noted a need to modify the contract; however, no modification was ever realized.

In January 2000, at the second consultant's request, the defendant retained another consulting firm (the "third consultant"). Then, in a March 6, 2000, email, the defendant told plaintiff that it and the third consultant had met with the government. When plaintiff asked why he was not included, the defendant responded that plaintiff's knowledge would be critical at a later point.

Plaintiff replied in a March email that he assumed there would be no contractual problem in the event of a success; however, a failure to succeed while he was "on the sidelines" would "create some real problems for us to resolve."

After additional meetings with the government were conducted without plaintiff's participation, the government approved the regulatory exemption, and defendant told plaintiff that he was not ultimately responsible for the project's success, and would not be paid the "success" fee. Although factually disputed, during a December 2000 telephone call defendant allegedly offered a release in return for permitting plaintiff to retain the advanced funds.

On January 5, 2001, plaintiff sent an email to the defendant stating that he had consulted counsel, and that if he were "forced to litigate" he was likely to recover a substantial sum.

On February 19, 2001, plaintiff increased his demand and noted that he might be forced to turn the matter over to attorneys. Because of plaintiff's "escalating letters," defendant sought counsel and, after February 19, instituted a "litigation hold." On February 27, 2001, defense counsel wrote to plaintiff asserting that plaintiff had no valid claim. Plaintiff did nothing until filling suit nearly three years later, on February 13, 2004.

System Upgrade. Sometime between the February 2001 exchange and the February 2004 lawsuit, probably in early 2003, the defendant migrated to a new computer system. Older computers were replaced and some were reimaged. Absent specific request by a user, data were not transferred from the old system to the replacement, and the company converted from Outlook to Lotus Notes.

Spoliation Motion

After plaintiff served a request for production of documents and ESI, defendant found one electronic document and 2,530 pages of other documents that were responsive to plaintiff's requests. Five months after the close of discovery and two months after filing of dispositive motions, plaintiff filed a spoliation motion.

Timeliness. Defendant contended, inter alia, that the spoliation motion was untimely. After a comprehensive review of the governing authorities, the court wrote that although the rules do not specify a time for filing a spoliation motion, one "lesson to be learned" from the decisional authority is that spoliation motions should "be filed as soon as reasonably possible after discovery of the facts that underlie the motion," and suggested filing such a motion during, or soon after the close of, the discovery period. Applying a multifactor test, the court noted that dilatory spoliation motions can interfere with milestone dates, and may be denied on that basis; however, it concluded that on the facts presented, plaintiff's motion was not untimely.

Trigger Date. The court then analyzed the trigger date for the duty to preserve in an unfolding commercial matter. Although defendant had severed all ties with plaintiff in April 1999, an act that may have given rise to the dispute, the parties continued to negotiate, and litigation was not then reasonably foreseeable.

The November 1999 email exchange, where plaintiff complained of potential loss of opportunity, was also deemed insufficient to trigger the duty, based on deposition testimony that did not exclude payment of the "success" fee at that time. The court further held that the March 2000 email, in which plaintiff pointed to "real questions" that may arise in the future, did not objectively put defendant on notice of reasonably foreseeable litigation. A factual dispute over whether the December 2000 telephone conversation included a reference to a release, in exchange for keeping the advanced funds, meant that plaintiff could not show that that discussion was a trigger.

What Was the Triggering Event?

- April 1999: Ties severed
- November 1999: Potential lost opportunity
- March 2000: "Real questions"
- December 2000: Disputed phone call
- January 2001: "May be forced to litigate"
- February 2001: Increased demand

Instead, the court held that the duty to preserve was triggered by plaintiff's January 5, 2001, email stating that he had contacted counsel and would recover substantial sums if "forced to litigate." Even though the message included an effort to suggest settlement, which might not be a trigger, it "openly" threatened litigation.

In short, the escalating tension did not serve as a trigger until it reached a point of reasonable clarity; the court also rejected defendant's assertion that the duty had not been triggered until the February 19, 2001, letter, which increased the plaintiff's demand.

Key Players. The court explained how to identify "key players" once the duty to preserve was triggered, and turned to the application of that concept, and the scope of the duty, vis-à-vis employees and third-party consultants.

The majority of plaintiff's contact was with one of defendant's employees. He also had some limited contacts with two others, and was aware of the role of the third-party consultants.

One of those third-party consultants had not saved his files over the eight-year period, and testified to memory lapses that could have been refreshed by those missing documents. The court noted that "[a] party may be held responsible for the spoliation of relevant evidence done by its agents," and that agency law is directly applicable to a spoliation motion; however, after reviewing the letter agreement with the third consultant, it held that defendant did not have "sufficient legal authority or practical ability to ensure the preservation" of the consultant's file and therefore it had no obligation to preserve documents the consultant prepared.

Duty to Preserve and Employees. On the other hand, the court decided that the duty applied to all three of defendant's employees. Because defendant had not issued a litigation hold, the three employees' computers had been discarded or reimaged, in violation of the duty to preserve. The court rejected the responsive arguments that selective printing of email was sufficient to satisfy the duty to preserve, that the defendant was a "mom and pop" company and should therefore be excused, and that the duty to preserve was only recently coined and therefore not applicable. In short, the employees were deemed key players, and the defendant had breached the duty to preserve.

Duty to Preserve Versus Duty to Produce. The court also rejected plaintiff's contention that defendant's failure to search 280 disaster recovery backup tapes and compact discs was spoliation. The court noted that defendant had preserved that data and plaintiff had not moved to compel a search of it. Thus, defendant fulfilled its duty to preserve the information and had no duty to produce it.

State of Mind Inquiry. Having held that there was a breach of the duty to preserve the computers, the court inquired whether there was a culpable state of mind. Because no court order had been violated, the court analyzed this issue under its inherent powers, not Federal Rule of Civil Procedure 37.

Noting that willful and deliberate acts might not necessarily also be performed in bad faith, the court found that the computers were intentionally destroyed. As to two of the destroyed computers, the movant failed to provide a factual predicate showing that they were used in connection with the project at issue and that they contained relevant information.

The third computer, however, was heavily used in the project. Furthermore, the user generally stored information on the laptop's hard drive, and not the company's networked "i-drive." This willful destruction supported an inference that facts unfavorable to defendant had been destroyed and that defendant had intentionally destroyed evidence, within its control, that it knew to be relevant, and that the destruction occurred after the duty to preserve had been triggered.

Sanctions

Adverse Inference Instruction. Next, the court evaluated the sanction to be imposed. It rejected plaintiff's requests for summary judgment and for fact-specific instructions, noting the absence of authority supporting the latter request and that it would be tantamount to directing a verdict for plaintiff. The request was, therefore, "excessively punitive." Instead, the court determined that an adverse jury instruction would best serve the purpose of "leveling the evidentiary playing field."

Costs. Finally, the court addressed costs and attorney's fees where a sanctions motion was granted in part and denied in part. First, analogizing to Rule 37(a)(5)(C), the court determined that in such a circumstance an award of expenses is discretionary and may be apportioned.

Then, after noting that a pro se litigant could not recover attorney's fees, the court directed filing of an itemized list of expenses, with the goal of compensating plaintiff for costs incurred to obtain the equivalent of the destroyed evidence, that is, an adverse jury instruction, after considering any response and reply to the itemization.

Practical Applications

Request Deadlines. One of many takeaway points from the opinion is that counsel should consider whether to request a deadline for filing spoliation motions as part of a Rule 26(f) conference of the parties and a proposed Rule 16(b) scheduling order. As the court noted, there is a multifactor, common law test to determine the timeliness of such motions. This may leave the matter open to reasonable dispute and introduce a lack of predictability. Absent a milestone deadline, however, spoliation motions should be filed during, or soon after, the close of the discovery period.

Third-Party Preservation. Another important lesson relates to preservation of ESI in the possession of third parties. The defendant escaped sanction for the consultant's failure to preserve because defendant "did not have the sufficient legal authority or practical ability to ensure the preservation" of those documents. The court also noted that the plaintiff knew of the third-party consultants and, in fact, contacted them.

Clarify Intention to File Suit. Additionally, if a disputant intends to rely on a prelitigation "preservation letter" to trigger an opponent's duty to preserve, it is well-advised to make clear in the letter that it intends to litigate, rather than relying on a court to subsequently determine "constructive notice" and when litigation was "reasonably foreseeable." The opinion also demonstrates that the duty to preserve is often broader than the duty to produce. And it shows the necessity for providing a factual predicate in connection with a spoliation motion.

When a spoliation motion arises out of a period of escalating tension, the party seeking sanctions will attempt to advance the trigger date, while the alleged spoliator will argue that litigation was not reasonably foreseeable until late in the process, that the information was not in possession of a key player or within the alleged spoliator's control, that the spoliation motion was untimely, and that there is no prejudice. *Goodman* provides an analytical structure for resolving those issues.

APPENDIX D

TWO COURTS BALANCE BENEFITS AND BURDENS IN DENYING MOTION TO COMPEL ESI: *KAY BEER DISTRIBUTING V. ENERGY BRANDS AND KILPATRICK V. BREG*

By Michael D. Berman

Two judicial decisions demonstrate that, in the words of *Hopson v. Mayor*,[1] "[t]he days when the requesting party can expect to 'get it all' and the producing party to produce whatever they feel like producing are long gone."

This appendix item is based on an article that first appeared in an ABA periodical, Technology for the Litigator.

1. Hopson v. Mayor & City Council of Balt., 232 F.R.D. 228, 245 (D. Md. 2005).

In both *Kay Beer Distributing v. Energy Brands*[2] and *Kilpatrick v. Breg*,[3] courts, while partially granting motions to compel, put the brakes on requests for discovery of electronically stored information (ESI), applying the cost-benefit balancing principles of Rule 26(b)(2)(C) of the Federal Rules of Civil Procedure, as well as traditional concepts defining the scope of discovery, Rule 26(b)(1).

"The decisions reflect the changing tide in the permissible scope of discovery and the judge's more active role in making sure that a balance is struck on the front end of the discovery process," notes Jacqueline Becerra, Miami, Co-Chair of the Section of Litigation's Elevating Your Game Task Force.

Kay Beer sued Energy Brands over an alleged exclusive dealership agreement. At the outset, the parties erroneously predicted to the court that ESI would not be a "significant feature" of the case. Kay served 313 document requests, 52 interrogatories, and 154 requests for admissions.

Energy's electronic search generated five DVDs with 17 gigabytes of data, comprising 56,547 documents and hundreds of thousands of pages, and Energy produced the subset of all email containing "Kay Beer" in the text. Kay, however, demanded production of the DVDs.

The court concluded that the "sheer number" of discovery requests demonstrated "that discovery has spiraled out of control," and that Kay had no right to all potentially discoverable information regardless of the cost and effort needed to gather it. Kay sought access to the DVDs and demanded production with metadata, pointing out that Energy had erroneously represented that it had produced "everything," only to state three days later that there was more to produce.

The court, however, noted that Kay was demanding every email on which any variation of its name (e.g., "Kay Distributing" or "Kay") appeared. It held that the mere fact that Kay's name was in a document did not make the document discoverable, and that Energy had no obligation to turn over nondiscoverable information.

2. 2009 U.S. Dist. Lexis 1773 (E.D. Wisc. Feb. 20, 2009), *subsequent opinion*, 2009 WL 1649592 (June 10, 2009), *subsequent opinion*, 2009 US. Dist. Lexis 49792 (E.D. Wisc. June 12, 2009).

3. Kilpatrick v. Breg, Inc., 2009 U.S. Dist. Lexis 3092 (S D. Fla. Jan. 9, 2009), *subsequent opinion*, 2009 U.S. Dist. Lexis 8480 (S.D. Fla. Jan. 28, 2009), *subsequent opinion*, 2009 U.S. Dist. Lexis S2723 (S.D. Fla. Jun. 22, 2009).

The court expressly noted that Energy had offered to "work with" Kay's counsel in formulating search terms; however, Kay had refused. Considering the nature of the case, "[t]he mere possibility of locating some needle in the haystack" did not warrant the expense Energy would incur in reviewing the DVDs.

Instead, the court ordered only a more thorough search for variants of Kay's name, such as "Kay Distributing," citing Rule 26(g) (discovery responses require "reasonable inquiry").[4]

In *Kilpatrick v. Breg*, the plaintiff sued a manufacturer for alleged injury from a medical device. The court was faced with the assertion, shortly before trial, that recently discovered email showed that Breg had knowledge of facts of which it had previously denied awareness.

The court noted that Breg had failed to produce responsive documents that contradicted depositions of its employees. On the other hand, Kilpatrick's concerns were admittedly circumstantial; the newly discovered information was "not a smoking gun" and was made at the eleventh hour; and granting the motion to compel threatened Breg's trial preparation.

Balancing the potential relevance with the burden and cost of production on the eve of trial, the court permitted Kilpatrick to retain an outside vendor to confirm the completeness of Breg's document production by using a limited methodology (e.g., search of only five backup tapes with limited search terms).

Neither Kilpatrick's circumstantial concerns nor Kay's "needle in a haystack" was sufficient to support a full-scale order compelling discovery of ESI; however, the courts carefully engaged in fact-sensitive, cost-benefit balancing to reach an equitable result.

The courts "got it exactly right in their approach," says Scott J. Atlas, Houston, Section past chair and member of the Section's Federal Practice Task Force. There is a need for courts to be "active referees," balancing discovery costs against the needs of the case, when one side asks for too much, and the other offers too little, especially in the area of e-discovery, Atlas notes.

4. See chapters 20–21.

APPENDIX E

POSTSCRIPT: A HISTORICAL PERSPECTIVE ON THE COMMUNICATIONS REVOLUTION

BY MICHAEL D. BERMAN

Information, itself, has changed.[1] Consequently, the information-based system for litigating disputes has had to adapt. Electronic information has become ubiquitous and many people feel that all discovery is, or soon will be, "e-discovery."

In the movie *Charlie Wilson's War*,[2] the following exchange takes place:

1. G. Paul & J. Baron, *Information Inflation: Can the Legal System Adapt?*, 13 RICH. J. LAW & TECH. 10 (2007).
2. Universal Studios, directed by Mike Nichols (2007).

Gust Avrakotos: There's a little boy and on his 14th birthday he gets a horse . . . and everybody in the village says, "how wonderful. The boy got a horse" And the Zen master says, "we'll see." Two years later, the boy falls off the horse, breaks his leg, and everyone in the village says, "how terrible." And the Zen master says, "we'll see." Then, a war breaks out and all the young men have to go off and fight . . . except the boy can't cause his leg's all messed up. And everybody in the village says, "How wonderful."

Charlie Wilson: Now the Zen master says, "We'll see."

Courts, lawyers, and litigants are, at the beginning of the twenty-first century, still evaluating and "writing the book" on the use of electronic information in litigation. This is partly the case because rules, guidelines, and case law cannot fill all of the gaps, and partly because technology is advancing at a rapid pace.[3] In order to understand issues presented by electronically stored information (ESI), it is important to approach the topic with a historical perspective.

Change is frequently resisted. Consider the following comment: "[T]here is no standard nowadays of elegant letter writing, as there used to be in our time. It is a sort of go as you please development, and the result is atrocious."[4] While this may appear to describe email, it is, in fact, a description of the postcard. Nevertheless, the history of communication is a history of change.[5] In

3. Paul Rice recently noted that "[a]s hardware and software change, the currently inaccessible (or the 'difficult to access'), may become accessible. As a result, the cost-shifting precedent of the past may not be a reliable guide to how courts will rule in the future." ELECTRONIC EVIDENCE: LAW AND PRACTICE 34 (ABA 2d ed. 2008) (citations omitted).

4. B. Yagoda, N.Y. TIMES BOOK REV., Oct. 25, 2009, at 9 (reviewing JOHN FREEMAN, THE TYRANNY OF EMAIL: THE FOUR-THOUSAND-YEAR JOURNEY TO YOUR INBOX (Scribner 2009)).

5. This appendix item borrows heavily from the seminal work on this topic, Paul & Baron, *supra* note 1, as well as an article by Prof. Richard L. Marcus, *E-Discovery & Beyond: Toward Brave New World or 1984?*, 25 REV. LITIG. 633 (2006) (*reprinted in* 236 F.R.D. 598, 614, 618 (2006)) ("The process of adapting to discovery of electronically stored information has gone on for a generation. More than thirty-five years ago, Rule 34 was amended in expectation that discovery of this material would become important. More than twenty-five years ago, major decisions on how to handle discovery of this material began to occur."); *accord* J. Facciola & J. Redgrave, *Asserting and Challenging Privilege Claims in Modern Litigation: The Facciola-Redgrave Framework*, 4 FED. CTS. L. REV. 19, 36 (2009) ("These

the words of Oliver Wendell Holmes, Jr.: "The law embodies the story of a nation's development through many centuries. . . . In order to know what it is, we must know what it has been, and what it tends to become."[6] It has been written that "a new communications technology was developed that allowed people to communicate almost instantly across great distances, in effect shrinking the world faster and further than ever before." That technology "inundated its users with a deluge of information." That technology—called the "highway of thought"—was the telegraph.[7]

1. Those lazy, hazy, crazy days of paper

As we describe these historical changes, we must keep in mind the immediate predecessor of electronically stored information. That ancestor was "paper-based" litigation. While some among us decry the problems of cost, complexity, and technical knowledge presented by voluminous, fragile, and persistent ESI, in order to assess those complaints, we need to take a trip down memory lane.

Those who long for the "good old days" of paper-based discovery look back with selective memories. There was much about what happened that was inefficient, duplicative, costly, and confusing. Legions of attorneys and legal assistants scoured rooms or warehouses filled with boxes of documents, seeking relevant

---

problems are not necessarily new.") (citing Bills v. Kennecott Corp., 108 F.R.D. 459, 462 (D. Utah 1985)).

6. O. HOLMES, COMMON LAW, as cited in W. Shields, *Truth in Legal Practice*, J. PHIL., SCI. & LAW (Nov. 2003), http://www6.miami.edu/ethics/jpsl/archives/newsedit/shieldsA.html. Justice Holmes wrote: "The substance of the law at any given time pretty nearly corresponds, so far as it goes, with what is then understood to be convenient; but its form and machinery, and the degree to which it is able to work out desired results, depend very much upon its past." *Id.* Justice Holmes stated: "At present, in very many cases, if we want to know why a rule of law has taken its particular shape, and more or less if we want to know why it exists at all, we go to tradition. . . . The rational study of law is still to a large extent the study of history. History must be a part of the study, because without it we cannot know the precise scope of rules which it is our business to know." O. Holmes, *The Path of the Law*, 10 HARV. L. REV. 457, 468–69 (1878). He said: "The development of our law has gone on for nearly a thousand years, like the development of a plant, each generation taking the inevitable next step, mind, like matter, simply obeying a law of spontaneous growth." *Id.* at 468. Justice Holmes commented, in 1878, on the explosion of information: "The means of the study are a body of reports, of treatises, and of statutes, in this country and in England, extending back for six hundred years, and *now increasing annually by hundreds.*" *Id.* at 457 (emphasis added).

7. T. STANDAGE, THE VICTORIAN INTERNET xiii—xiv (Walker & Co. 1998, 2007).

information. We examined multiple copies of repetitive documents time and time again, for days on end. Perhaps microfiche was involved. And we may have had to review illegibly scribbled notes, faded and stained documents, and cryptic marginal entries. We may even have been forced to look at paper's version of metadata—through handwriting analysis, fiber samples, watermarks, fingerprints, and the like.[8] We then created a set of documents to Bates number.[9] That set remained pristine, and we next created a "working set." From that set, each attorney and legal assistant created a personal set. We then created a production set for the opponent after, hopefully, removing all privileged and nonresponsive documents. We may have prepared "issue" folders and copied documents for each such folder, as well as a set for a "trial notebook." When it came time to file a motion, draft an affidavit, or prepare a witness, we frantically searched for and copied the key documents to create another set of exhibits. Paper-based litigation was not—despite our fond memories—a paradigm for trouble-free, efficient, cost-proportional discovery.

We also need to remember that in the "paper days," the attorney-client privilege was often waived by inadvertent production of privileged paper documents. And attorneys were sanctioned for failing to preserve information. In the beginning of the twentieth century, a group of Chicago White Sox baseball players was charged with accepting bribes to "throw" the World Series. The celebrated trial, known as the "Black Sox Scandal," ended with an acquittal on August 2, 1921, after several confessions went missing.[10] Roughly eight decades later, Laura Zubulake demonstrated

---

8. An early draft of the Declaration of Independence was recently examined by the Library of Congress, using spectral imaging technology. The document was studied at different wavelengths of light to detect chemical signatures in the ink. M. Kaufman, *Jefferson Changed "Subjects" to "Citizens" in Declaration of Independence*," WASH. POST, July 3, 2010, http://www.washingtonpost.com/wp-dyn/content/article/2010/07/02/AR2010070205525.html. One word in the draft had been obliterated. "Over the smudge, [Thomas] Jefferson then wrote the word 'citizens.'" Scholars wondered what word had been obliterated, and the high-tech analysis showed that the obliterated word was "subjects."

9. For a description of Bates numbering, see R. Losey, *Hash: The New Bates Stamp*, 12 J. TECH. LAW & POLICY 1 (June 2007).

10. G. Hodak, *Baseball's "Black Sox" Acquitted*, ABA J. (Aug. 2008) ("After a two-week trial marked by the revelation of several missing confessions, all eight were acquitted."), http://www.abajournal.com/magazine/article/august_2_1921/.

that UBS Warburg, LLC, had failed to preserve email messages necessary for her case.[11] History provides the needed perspective.

So let us begin our trip down memory lane with a somewhat truncated description of an actual lawsuit. A young boy found a gemstone ring, but he did not know its value. He took the ring to a jeweler for an appraisal. The jeweler returned the setting, without the gem, and declared the gem worthless. The boy sued. The trial judge gave a dreaded "adverse inference" instruction, telling the jury that it was to presume that the missing gem had the highest possible value, because the defendant had failed to preserve the evidence that was essential to resolving the dispute over the true value of the gem. The reason for describing this case in this chapter on ESI is that the case was decided by the King's Bench in England in the year 1722.[12] It seems that the more things change, the more they do stay the same!

We now fast-forward to Iran-Contra and Watergate. In Iran-Contra, during the mid-1980s, the allegations were that Lt. Col. Oliver North destroyed key email, without realizing that copies were maintained on backup tapes.[13] Not long before, the Watergate scandal was characterized by the notorious 18½-minute gap in the tape recordings and the famous photograph of former president Richard M. Nixon's secretary, Rose Mary Woods, assuming a contorted position to explain how she "inadvertently" erased part

11. Zubulake v. UBS Warburg LLC (*Zubulake I*), 217 F.R.D. 309, 313 (S.D.N.Y. 2003) ("In fact, Zubulake knew that there were additional responsive e-mails that UBS had failed to produce because she herself had produced approximately 450 pages of e-mail correspondence. Clearly, numerous responsive e-mails had been created and deleted at UBS, and Zubulake wanted them.").

12. Armory v. Delamirie, Eng. Rep. 664 (K.B. 1722) (described in P. RICE, ELECTRONIC EVIDENCE: LAW AND PRACTICE 81 n.2 (ABA 2d ed. 2008)). It is worthy of note that Justice Holmes wrote, in 1897, "It is the settled law of England that a material alteration of a written contract by a party avoids it as against him." Holmes, *The Path of the Law*, *supra* note 6, at 472. There is, of course, nothing new about the basic concept of the duty to preserve. *E.g.*, Bd. of Justices v. Fennimore, 1 N.J.L., 1794 WL 507 (N.J. 1794) ("The excuse is futile; unless the book is produced, every presumption must be made against the defendant.").

13. It has been asserted that Lt. Col. Oliver North and another person "deleted almost 6,000 email messages—a time-consuming task in the absence of any mass delete option in their primitive email system." The asserted email deletions came to light because Lt. Col. North "didn't realize that the White House Communication Agency kept backup tapes." R. Rosenzweig, *Review, Archives and the Public Good: Accountability and Records in Modern Society*, 66(2) AM. ARCHIVIST, Fall/Winter 2003, http://www.archivists.org/periodicals/aa_v66/review-rosenzweig-aa66_2.asp.

of the tapes in 1973.[14] And just as Judge Sirica rejected the White House contention that nothing wrong had happened because the Special Prosecutor had not requested the tapes,[15] almost 35 years later, another federal judge rejected Qualcomm's contention that Broadcom had not requested "smoking gun" emails in a multimillion-dollar patent dispute.[16] There is truth in the expression that "everything old is new again."

2. The history of writing and its impact on contemporary litigation

Early writing "co-evolved with civilization more than 50 centuries ago."[17] For approximately 5,200 years, writing was a physical act: "From the inception of the invention, molecules were displaced, leaving an original record readable by human beings."[18] Writing progressed through hieroglyphics. Some writing was carved on

14. The concept set forth in the text came from an article by Professor Richard L. Marcus: "Preservation of discoverable material has always been a serious concern. Since Rose Mary Woods became famous [in 1973] due to her reported role in creating an 18 minute gap on a Watergate tape, the risks that technologically stored information might be lost have been clear." Marcus, *supra* note 5, 236 F.R.D. at 614. The photograph of Ms. Woods can be found at http://en.wikipedia.org/wiki/Rose_Mary_Woods.

15. *Time* reported that when President Nixon was told of the erasure of the tapes, he responded: "Don't worry about it. It's not a subpoenaed tape." TIME MAG., Dec. 10, 1973, http://www.time.com/time/magazine/article/0,9171,908267-4,00.html#ixzz0YBm3kMB0. *Time* also reported that "[White House Attorney Buzhardt's] reason, too, for not telling the court about this [18½ minute gap] much sooner was that he thought the Haldeman conversation was not under subpoena. [Judge] Sirica seemed openly skeptical. The subpoena had asked for the tape of a 'meeting of June 20, 1972 in the President's Executive Office Building office involving Richard Nixon, John Ehrlichman and H.R. Haldeman from 10:30 a.m. to noon (time approximate).' [Special Prosecutor Archibald] Cox amended the subpoena on Aug. 13 to make it unmistakably clear. . . ." *Id.* at *5.

16. Qualcomm Inc. v. Broadcom Corp., 2008 WL 66932, at *14 (S.D. Cal. Jan, 7, 2008) ("While all of these attorneys assert that there was a plausible argument that Broadcom did not request these documents, only Bier and Mammen actually read the emails."), *vacated in part*, 2008 WL 638108 (S.D. Cal. Mar. 5, 2008), *reconsideration denied*, 2008 WL 2705161 (S.D. Cal. Jul. 7, 2008), *appeal dismissed*, 327 Fed. Appx. 877 (Fed. Cir. Aug. 18, 2008), *subsequent opinion*, 2008 WL 4858685 (Nov. 7, 2008), *on remand*, 2010 WL 1336937 (S.D. Cal. Apr. 2, 2010), Qualcomm asserted that "the twenty-one unsolicited emails received by Ms. Raveendran from individuals on the avc_ce reflector are not responsive to any valid discovery obligation or commitment." *Id.* at *6.

17. Paul & Baron, *supra* note 1, at 4.

18. *Id.*

stone tablets—it did not present preservation problems, but the duty to produce could be extremely heavy.

Early books were printed from carved wood blocks.[19] Then, there was an information explosion. "Originally from China, the printing press *revolutionized* life in Western Europe during the Renaissance. A German goldsmith by the name of Johannes Gutenberg (1399–1468) was the first European to adapt the Chinese model [of the printing press] for western languages, with the use of movable type."[20] For the first time, the printing press made "mass produced" books available.

"Shorthand" was also developed. Appearing as meaningless dots and squiggles, shorthand meant that for the first time, people could write as rapidly as they spoke.[21] Again, information—in this case paper—was created at an accelerating pace.

Similarly, the invention of the telegraph in the early 1800s[22] meant, for the first time, that information could be transmitted over wire. Short, condensed messages flew over great distances and Samuel Morse asked: "What hath God wrought?"[23] The telegraph was "a technological wonder of its time."[24] It was used to play chess games between towns,[25] and the first online wedding took place by telegraph in the 1800s.[26] Abbreviations, such as

19. *See* Suite 101, West European History: The Printing Press, http://weuropean history.suite101.com/article.cfm/the_printing_press.

20. *Id.* (emphasis added).

21. *See* Wikipedia, Shorthand, http://en.wikipedia.org/wiki/Shorthand. Shorthand is any system of rapid handwriting which can be used to transcribe the spoken word." Omniglot writing systems & language of the world, http://www .omniglot.com/writing/shorthand.htm.

22. *See* Randy H. Katz, What Hath God Wrought: The Electrical Telegraph, http://bnrg.eecs.berkeley.edu/~randy/Courses/CS39C.S97/telegraph/telegraph .html.

23. *Id.* Mr. Morse's invention paled in comparison to the marvel of Alexander Graham Bell. The telephone opened new vistas. Generations of law school students were required to learn the arcane techniques of authenticating telephone messages, just as attorneys now must learn how to authenticate email, SMS, and text messages.

24. STANDAGE, *supra* note 7, at 14. The transatlantic cable was called "the most wonderful achievement of our civilization." *Id.* at 90. It was said that the telegraph "annihilated both space and time in the transmission of intelligence. The breadth of the Atlantic, with all its waves, is as nothing." *Id.*

25. *Id.* at 52.

26. *Id.* at 127–28.

"S F D" for "stop for dinner,"[27] were created, much like today's text messages. And, soon, the telegraph created an "[i]nformation [o]verload" because "[m]essages between New York and Chicago, which had previously taken a month to arrive, could be delivered almost instantly," creating an "increasing flow of information."[28]

The telegraph led to a new device, the stock ticker, in 1867.[29] That machine "offered a continuous printed record of fluctuations in prices of any number of stocks, printed on a paper tape by two wheels."[30] This led to a new, faster device: "[a]utomatic telegraphs—machines that could send messages without the need for skilled operators."[31] In 1858, one of these machines transmitted Morse code messages from a prepunched tape at 400 words per minute.[32] And, in 1886, 1.5 million words were dispatched from the central telegraph station in London.[33] "[I]nstead of charging by the word, messages were charged by the yard of tape."[34]

With the invention of the "duplex," which was "a means of sending messages in both directions over a single wire simultaneously, . . . telegraph companies were suddenly able to send twice as much traffic along a single wire."[35] Later improvements "enabled a single line to carry up to twelve lines' worth of traffic" using a five-unit binary code.[36] Then, the "quadruplex" was developed, "enabl[ing] a single wire to carry four streams of traffic."[37]

27. *Id.* at 65. Chapter 24 discusses authentication of email. In the days of the telegraph: "Early operators could even recognize their friends merely from the style of their Morse code—something that was, apparently, as recognizable as an individual human voice. Each operator had a two-letter signature, or 'sig,' with which to identify themselves on-line. . . ." *Id.* at 130.

28. *Id.* at 164–65.

29. *Id.* at 175.

30. *Id.*

31. *Id.* at 188.

32. *Id.* at 190.

33. *Id.* at 191.

34. *Id.* at 192.

35. *Id.* at 192.

36. *Id.* at 192–93.

37. *Id.* at 194. The telegraph could not compete with the telephone, which permitted faster communication. The average number of words transmitted by the telegraph was 15–20 per minute, while the telephone permitted 100–200 words per minute. *Id.* at 199. "Although it has now faded from view, the telegraph lives on within the communications technologies that have subsequently built upon its foundations: the telephone, the fax machine, and, more recently, the Internet. And, ironically, it is the Internet—despite being regarded as a quintessentially modern means of communication—that has the most in common with its

At about the time of the Civil War, more change occurred, with the invention and widespread use of the typewriter.[38] That mainstay was, itself, eclipsed by the electric typewriter.[39] The electric typewriter soon received competition from the "magnetic card," or "mag card," typewriter, a rudimentary computer capable of generating form letters at what was then considered to be high speed.

There was also a need to make *copies* of what these marvels produced. The "mimeograph" machine used a stencil placed on a round drum to make those copies. "Carbon paper"[40] was frequently used and, if a typographical error occurred, it was necessary to "white out" the original and the copies, or start all over again. Some of the attorneys who now complain of metadata forget the problems of preparing briefs in "the old days."

The invention of the photocopier, however, solved that problem. Suddenly, multiple copies could be printed, quickly and inexpensively, albeit not always in an environmentally friendly way. And the facsimile machine quickly achieved widespread usage.[41] One

---

telegraphic ancestor." *Id.* at 205. "In 1996, Sue Helle and Lynn Bottoms were married on-line by a minister 10 miles away in Seattle, echoing the story of Philip Reade and Clar Choate, who were married by telegraph 120 years earlier by a minister 650 miles away." *Id.* at 209.

38. In C. WELLER, THE EARLY HISTORY OF THE TYPEWRITER (2010), the Secretary of the National Shorthand Reporters Association noted that the typewriter "replaced the painfully slow and tedious method of reducing thought to writing by means of pen and ink" and was "destined in time to create a revolution in the conduct of affairs in all parts of the civilized world."

39. *See* Wikipedia, Typewriter, http://en.wikipedia.org/wiki/Typewriter. Thomas Edison patented an electric typewriter in 1872, but the first workable model was not introduced until the 1920s. In the 1930s IBM introduced a more refined version, the IBM Electromatic. It "greatly increased typing speeds and quickly gained wide acceptance in the business community." *History of Word Processors*, http://www.cs.umd.edu/class/spring2002/cmsc434-0101/MUIseum/applications/wordhistory.html; The Virtual Typewriter Museum, http://www.typewritermuseum.org/history/end_of_history.html.

40. For a description of a decision involving admissibility of carbon copies, see P. Bordman, *Telefacsimile Documents: A Survey of Uses in the Legal Setting*, 36 WAYNE L. REV. 1361, 1368 (1990). The "metadata" that may be mined from a carbon copy was described in that article: "The AGC subpoenaed the carbon copy in order to conduct a laboratory analysis to determine the age of the carbon copy and, thus, whether it had been back-dated." *Id.* at n.125. In an analog to the duty to preserve relevant information, it was asserted that delay would render testing ineffective. *Id.*

41. In a passage reminiscent of an early view of email, a 1990 article noted: "People currently use technologically sophisticated tools such as telefacsimile (facsimile or fax) machines. . . ." P. Bordman, *Telefacsimile Documents: A Survey of*

of the first problems created by these developments was privilege waiver. For example, what happened when the "errant fax" was sent to the adversary whose telephone number was on the speed dial of the fax machine?[42] In one early 1990s case, after selection of a jury, it was learned that defendants' jury selection strategy was misdirected to plaintiffs' counsel by fax. The trial court stated: "I find that the plaintiffs' attorneys have an advantage over the defense attorneys. Specifically, the plaintiffs know pretty

---

Uses in the Legal Setting, 36 Wayne L. Rev. at 1361. In discussing this new digital technology, the author wrote: "Difficult legal issues are surfacing," noting that "legal rules lag behind these innovative tools." *Id.* Fax technology was described in *id.* at n.5.

42. In 1992, the ABA addressed the errant fax issue in Formal Op. 92-368: "This opinion is intended to answer a question which has become increasingly important as the burgeoning of multiparty cases, the availability of xerography and the proliferation of facsimile machines and electronic mail make it technologically ever more likely that through inadvertence, privileged or confidential materials will be produced to opposing counsel by no more than the pushing of the wrong speed dial number on a facsimile machine." The Formal Opinion concluded that "it is the view of the Committee that the receiving lawyer, as a matter of ethical conduct contemplated by the precepts underlying the Model Rules, (a) should not examine the materials once the inadvertence is discovered, (b) should notify the sending lawyer of their receipt and (c) should abide by the sending lawyer's instructions as to their disposition." ABA Formal Op. 92-368, http://www.abanet.org/cpr/nosearch/92_368.pdf. That opinion has been withdrawn. Nevertheless, the problem of inadvertent faxes is well-documented. *E.g.*, Sherman v. State, 128 Wn.2d 164, 175 (Wash. 1995) ("At an April 23, 1990, meeting of the Housestaff Committee, Dr. Richard Zager, a majority member, drafted a concurring opinion that would uphold the termination solely on the basis that Dr. Sherman had failed to properly dispose of the narcotics. Dr. Verhulst suggested that Dr. Zager consider the matter overnight and, if he still wished to concur, to fax a copy to him the next day. The next day, as requested, Dr. Zager instructed his secretary to fax a copy of the draft concurring opinion to Dr. Verhulst. His secretary, however, mistakenly faxed a copy to Dr. Hornbein's office instead (hereinafter the 'errant fax'). As fate would have it, Dr. Peter Colley happened to be waiting for a fax at Dr. Hornbein's fax machine when the errant fax was transmitted. Dr. Colley, who had testified at the Housestaff Committee hearing in opposition to Dr. Sherman's termination, scanned the errant fax and then called Laurie Kinerk, one of Dr. Sherman's attorneys. He informed her that he had seen what appeared to be a copy of the committee's report on Dr. Hornbein's fax machine."); Balt. Scrap Corp. v. David J. Joseph Co., 237 F.3d 394, 398 (4th Cir. 2001) ("Throughout this time, DJJ and Shapiro left no public trace of their involvement in the lawsuit. In late March, however, a so-called 'errant fax' exposed the role of the defendants. This fax was supposed to go to a lawyer working for DJJ and Shapiro, but instead was sent to a friend of Baltimore Scrap's president.").

well which prospective jurors the defense is going to strike. . . . They knew the inner-most thinking of the defense counsel." The judge struck the jury and ordered the entire selection process to begin again.[43] Earlier technological advances raised complex legal problems.

This brings us to the computer age. "Digital computers were invented at the close of World War II, and gradually diffused throughout society as the 'mainframe' of the 1950s, 1960s and 1970s."[44] The first real-time commercial computing system was deployed in 1964.[45] And by the end of the twentieth century, the typewriter was virtually extinct because of the "word processor."[46]

The personal computer, cell phone, personal digital assistant (PDA), and other devices were connected to another innovation, the Internet. "The Web went from 20 host servers in 1992; to 50 as of January 1993; 200 as of August 1993; to 100,000 (post-Netscape) in January 1996; 650,000 in January 1997; and 4.3 million in 1999."[47] Suddenly, information was no longer the tangible object created 5,200 years before.[48] Information was different, and "lawyers must understand that information, as a cultural and technological edifice, has profoundly and irrevocably changed."[49]

Dozens of cases and articles discuss the differences between ESI and paper.[50] While paper may come in boxes and warehouses, ESI comes in terabytes, petabytes, and more,[51] volume that cannot

43. The description in the text is from Baltimore City Personal Injury and Wrongful Death Asbestos Cases, Pretrial Hearing, June 5, 1991, Transcript at 4521, Cir. Court for Balt. City, File No. 89236704, as described in ABA Formal Op. 92-368 (withdrawn).

44. Paul & Baron, *supra* note 1, at 5 n.17.

45. *Id.*

46. *See id.* at 4 n.12.

47. *Id.* at 6 n.24.

48. *Id.*, passim.

49. *Id.* at 1.

50. *E.g.*, M. Crist, *Preserving the Duty to Preserve: The Increasing Vulnerability of Electronic Information*, 58 S.C. L. REV. 7 (2006).

51. SEDONA CONFERENCE GLOSSARY: E-DISCOVERY & DIGITAL INFORMATION (2d ed. Dec. 2007) states: "A Byte is the basic measurement of most computer data and consists of 8 bits. Computer storage capacity is generally measured in bytes. Although characters are stored in bytes, a few bytes are of little use for storing a large amount of data. Therefore, storage is measured in larger increments of bytes. See Kilobyte, Megabyte, Gigabyte, Terabyte, Petabyte, Exabyte, Zettabyte, and Yottabyte (listed here in order of increasing volume)." "Terabyte" is defined as "1,099,511,627,776 bytes—10244 (a trillion bytes)." "Petabyte" means "1,125,899,906,824,624 bytes—10245 (a quadrillion bytes)."

be processed by human minds and hands. While paper has one primary form—you are reading it now—ESI comes in native and static forms, in email, word processing documents, spreadsheets, hard drives, servers, tapes, thumb drives, and removable media. Paper can be remarkably sturdy, while ESI is both fragile and persistent. Paper goes into files, while ESI is dispersed in the "network architecture." While paper may contain differing languages, ESI is dependent on the software program that created it. And while there may be some hidden information in paper, it hardly compares to metadata. Finally, while large volumes of paper stressed litigants and the legal system, the costs of preserving, processing, reviewing, producing, and using ESI can bankrupt the system.

Nevertheless, there is no alternative. While studies and statistics vary, it is clear that more than 90 percent of information is created electronically and only a fraction is printed to paper.[52] Any system that fails to address ESI simply fails to address the overwhelming body of information.

This leads to three salient points elegantly made by others.[53]

- First, "there must be a change in culture among litigation lawyers. The last 30 years have seen truculence, gamesmanship, and a supreme rule of 'volunteer nothing.' . . . Litigators must collaborate far more than they have in the past, particularly concerning the discovery of information systems. If they do not, they act against their own self-interest."
- Second, "[l]itigators can no longer depend on manual review alone. It is too time-consuming and expensive—with costs often exceeding the amount in dispute. . . ."
- Third, "the use of machines to search written records continues to pose a challenge, as language is an ever-evolving, elastic form which has proved notoriously hard to search."

52. *See, e.g.*, C. BALL, MEETING THE CHALLENGE: EMAIL IN CIVIL DISCOVERY 5 (2008) ("well over 95% of all business documents are born digitally and only a tiny fraction are ever printed."), http://www.craigball.com/em2008.pdf (citation omitted).

53. Paul & Baron, *supra* note 1, at 2–3. Each of these points is addressed more fully in chapters 20, 21, and 30.

3. Catalysts of change

The purpose of this book is to provide working tools to those who must deal with ESI at a practical, and cost-effective, level. In order to meet the standards described above, as well as the rigorous requirements of Federal Rules of Civil Procedure 11, 26(f), 26(g), and 37, among others, and to effectuate the "just, speedy, and inexpensive determination" of every action,[54] attorneys must understand the history of communication and the four catalysts of change.

The first catalyst was the change of information from a tangible form to an instantly and inexpensively transferable electronic format.[55] The second was case-by-case development, epitomized by the ground-breaking *Zubulake* decisions.[56] While the common law has many advantages, providing well-reasoned and binding authorities, it also has disadvantages. It can be slow and incremental—the five *Zubulake* decisions centered on backup tapes. And, until the Supreme Court rules, case law can be inconsistent.

The third catalyst has been the Sedona Conference. Sedona is a think tank that "exists to allow leading jurists, lawyers, experts, academics and others, at the cutting edge of issues in the area of . . . complex litigation . . . to come together—in conferences and mini-think tanks (Working Groups)—and engage in true dialogue, not debate, all in an effort to move the law forward in a reasoned and just way."[57] The Sedona Working Group Series "is designed to focus the dialogue on forward-looking principles, best practices and guidelines in specific areas of the law that may have a dearth of guidance or are otherwise at a 'tipping point.' "[58] Thus, Sedona issued its first ESI-related, "best practices" paper in 2003, and it has continued to provide comprehensive, leading-edge guidance in connection with ESI.[59]

The fourth catalyst of change has been rulemaking. The Federal Rules of Civil Procedure were amended to specifically address

54. FED. R. CIV. P. 1. The proportionality rules are discussed in chapter 9.

55. Paul & Baron, *supra* note 1.

56. Zubulake v. UBS Warburg LLC (*Zubulake I*), 217 F.R.D. 309, 313 (S.D.N.Y. 2003). According to Shepard's Citations, *Zubulake I* has been cited more than 450 times.

57. *See* Sedona Conference, TSC Mission, http://www.thesedonaconference.org/content/tsc_mission/show_page_html.

58. *Id.*

59. In the interest of full disclosure, the author is a member of the Sedona Conference Working Group.

ESI (although they previously addressed "data compilations") on December 1, 2006. Many states followed suit. The precise contours of the amended rules are discussed in chapter 2; however, the philosophy of the amendments was to front-load issues related to ESI, and to encourage early discussion, transparency, and cooperation to address and resolve the potentially complex and costly issues presented by that information. The amendments also encouraged judicial attention to ESI issues, early and often. The 2006 amendments have brought about a "paradigm shift" or a "sea change" in litigation.[60] In short: "The days when the requesting party can expect to 'get it all' and the producing party to produce whatever they feel like producing are long gone."[61]

4. Conclusion

"Chronocentricity" is "the egotism that one's own generation is poised on the very cusp of history. Today we are repeatedly told that we are in the midst of a communications revolution. . . . If any generation has the right to claim that it bore the full bewildering, world-shrinking brunt of such a revolution, it is not us—it is our nineteenth-century forebears. Time-traveling Victorians would, no doubt, be unimpressed by the Internet."[62] Practitioners need to place change in historical context in order to continue the dialogue between Bench, Bar, and industries that is required to permit our civil justice system to continue to do what it does so well—foster the "just, speedy, and inexpensive" determination of every action.[63] In the words of Justice Cardozo: "Nothing is stable.

60. Sedona Conference, Best Practice Guidelines and Commentary for Managing Information and Records in the Electronic Age 1 (2d ed. Nov. 2007) ("Yet, laws and policies have been very slow to adapt to this new paradigm involving immense volumes, high volatility and great mobility of electronic information."); Sedona Conference Best Practices Commentary on the Use of Search and Information Retrieval Methods in E-Discovery 193 (Aug. 2007 Public Comment Version) ("But with the digital revolution there has also been a paradigm shift in the review process which is feasible. The shift of information storage to a digital realm has, for a variety of reasons, caused an explosion in the amount of information that resides in any enterprise—profoundly affecting litigation."); Sedona Conference, Commentary on Preservation, Management and Identification of Sources of Information That Are Not Reasonably Accessible 15, Guideline 2 cmt. (July 2008) ("This paradigm shift contemplates greater transparency about preservation issues. . . .").

61. Hopson v. Mayor & City Council of Balt., 232 F.R.D. 228, 245 (D. Md. 2003).

62. Standage, *supra* note 7, at 213.

63. Fed. R. Civ. P. 1.

Nothing absolute. All is fluid and changeable. There is an endless 'becoming.' "[64] Ours is not the first system to face a state of "perpetual flux."[65] "Every new case is an experiment."[66]

64. B. CARDOZO, THE NATURE OF JUDICIAL PROCESS 28 (Yale 1921).

65. *Id.*

66. *Id.* at 23–24 (citations omitted).

REPRINTS

A portion of Chapter 6 ("Introduction to Metadata and Form of Production under Rule 34") is adapted from Craig Ball, "Don't Mess with System Metadata," LAW TECH. NEWS, April 23, 2009. Used by permission of the author.

Chapter 9 ("Proportionality Limits on the Scope of Preservation") is adapted from "Proportionality in the Post-Hoc Analysis of Pre-Litigation Preservation Decisions," by The Hon. Paul W. Grimm, Michael D. Berman, Conor R. Crowley, and Leslie Wharton, 37 U. BALT. L. REV. 381 (2008). Copyright © 2008 The University of Baltimore Law Review. Used by permission.

Chapter 11 ("When Does a Litigation Hold End?") is adapted from an article that first appeared in *Digital Technology and E-Evidence.* Used with permission from Digital Discovery & e-Evidence, 9(10) DIGITAL DISCOVERY & E-EVIDENCE REP., Oct. 1, 2009. Copyright © 2009 by The Bureau of National Affairs, Inc. (800-372-1033), http://www.bna.com.

Chapter 16 ("Are Attorney-Client Communications Imposing a Legal Hold and Implementing Preservation Efforts Privileged?") is adapted from "Discovery About Discovery: Does the Attorney-Client Privilege Protect All Attorney-Client Communications Relating to the Preservation of Potentially Relevant Information?," by The Hon. Paul W. Grimm, Michael D. Berman, Leslie Wharton, Jeanna Beck, and Conor R. Crowley, 37 U. BALT. L. REV. 413 (2008). Copyright © 2008 by the University of Baltimore Law Review. Used by permission.

Portions of Chapter 17 ("Protection from ESI Waiver under FRE 502") were previously published in the ABA's *In-House Litigator.*

Chapter 26 ("Crawling and Indexing: Have Technological Innovations Made Data More Accessible and Bypassed Portions of

Zubulake?") is adapted from an article that first appeared in the 2010 edition of ABA's *Technology for the Litigator.*

Portions of Chapter 29 ("Ethics in E-Discovery") previously appeared in *Digital Discovery and E-Evidence.* Reproduced with permission from 9(8) Digital Discovery & E-Evidence Rep. 240–42 (Aug.1, 2009). Copyright © 2009 by The Bureau of National Affairs, Inc. (800-372-1033), http://www.bna.com.

Chapter 30 ("The Sedona Conference Cooperation Proclamation") is adapted from an article that first appeared in the 2009 publication of the ABA *Technology for the Litigator* newsletter.

Appendix A ("Tips to Avoid Mistakes with ESI Vendors") is adapted from an article that first appeared in the 2009 publication of the ABA *Technology for the Litigator* newsletter.

Appendix B ("Discovery Lapse Could Result in Loss of Privilege") is adapted from an article first published in 34(1) Litig. News, Fall 2008.

Appendix C ("Timing of Spoliation Motions: Goodman v. Praxair Services, Inc.") first appeared as "Magistrate Judge Recommends General Adverse Inference Instruction for Intentional Breach of Duty to Preserve." Reproduced with permission from 9(8) Digital Discovery & E-Evidence Rep. 240–42 (Aug.1, 2009). Copyright © 2009 by The Bureau of National Affairs, Inc. (800-372-1033) http://www.bna.com.

Appendix D ("Two Courts Balance Benefits and Burdens in Denying Motion to Compel ESI") is adapted from an article first published in 35(1) Litig. News, Fall 2009.

TABLE OF CASES

INDEX

ABOUT THE CONTRIBUTORS

The editors wish to thank everyone involved in the project for their gracious contribution of time and efforts. Each author's chapter represents the personal opinions and views of the author, and not the organizations with which they are affiliated or employed, the editors, publisher, or other authors.

Principal Editors

Michael D. Berman is counsel to Rifkin, Livingston, Levitan & Silver, LLC, where he concentrates in commercial litigation and ESI issues. Previously, Mr. Berman spent seven years as the Deputy Chief of Civil Litigation at the Office of the Attorney General of Maryland, was a partner at the Baltimore firms of Tydings & Rosenberg, LLC, and Kaplan, Heyman, Greenberg, Engelman & Belgrad, P.A., and a clerk for the Hon. R. Dorsey Watkins, United States District Court for the District of Maryland. He teaches a three-credit, ESI seminar at the University of Maryland and University of Baltimore Schools of Law, where he is an adjunct professor, and offers ESI mediation services, www.esi-mediation.com.

Mr. Berman is an active member of a Bar Association committee that proposed the Suggested ESI Protocol of the United States District Court for the District of Maryland. He is a Past Co-chair of the Federal District Court Committee, Maryland State and Federal Bar Associations. He is also a Past Chair of the Litigation Section Council, Maryland State Bar Association.

Mr. Berman served four years in the U.S. Army, where he attained the rank of Captain and was a paratrooper. His awards include the Expert Infantry Badge, Army Commendation Medal, Armed Forces Expeditionary Medal, Korea Defense Service Medal, and the National Defense Service Medal.

Mr. Berman's ESI presentations include Panelist, Maryland State Bar Assoc., ESI Presentation (United States Courthouse, 2010);

Moderator, Federal Bar Assoc., MD Chapter, "Electronically Stored Information: A to Z" (United States Courthouse, 2009); Moderator, Maryland State Bar Assoc., Litigation Section Council Regional Meeting Panel Discussion on "ESI and the Maryland Rules" (Nov. 2008); Panelist, E-discovery program at Maryland State Bar Assoc., Annual Meeting (2009); Panelist, "Mastering the Discovery Process for the General Counsel," (Incisive Media, NY Nov. 2008); Participant, "Best Practices for Complex E-Discovery Matters (LexisNexis Applied Discovery, NY 2008); Participant, University of Baltimore ESI Symposium (2008); Presenter, "Electronic Evidence," State Court Judicial Institute of Maryland (Annapolis 2009); Presenter, 5th eDiscovery Workshop (International Quality & Productivity Center, Las Vegas 2008); Presenter, ESI Program, State & Local Government Law Institute, MICPEL (2008); Keynote Speaker, CT Summation Best Practices Summit (Washington 2008); Presenter, "The New Ethics of Discovery," CT Summation Webinar (2008); Presenter, "Rule 26(g) Comes Out of the Shadows," CT Summation Webinar (2008); Presenter, ESI Seminar, Maryland Disability Law Center (2008); Presenter, "Traps for the Unwary," New York Office of the Attorney General (2008); Panelist, Transportation Research Board 46th Annual Workshop, part of the National Research Council, operating under the National Academy of Science (2006 and 2008); Panelist, Trial Expert Webinar, (LexisNexis Discovery Services 2007); and, Panelist, "Discovering Electronic Discovery," (Baltimore City Law Dept. 2007).

Courtney Ingraffia Barton is Senior Counsel for a leading Internet and media company. She manages litigation and complex issues related to litigation preparedness, compliance, legal holds, and electronic discovery processes for both litigation and regulatory matters. Prior to her current position, she was in private practice, where she advised clients, records and information management, technology assessments, cost considerations, ethics, and international and global data issues. Ms. Barton is also an accomplished litigator, specializing in products liability, toxic tort, and environmental matters. She served as a trial attorney with the United States Department of Justice from 2004 to 2005 and she is a Certified Information Privacy Professional (CIPP).

Ms. Barton is a founding Co-Chair of the District of Columbia Bar Association Section of Litigation E-Discovery Committee. She is also an active member in the Sedona Conference, where she is a participant in the Working Groups on Electronic Document Retention and Production and International Electronic Information Management, Discovery and Disclosure. She is also an active member of the ABA and the ACC, and she is a member of the Washington, D.C., and Virginia Chapters of ARMA International. Ms. Barton serves on the Advisory Board for BNA's *Digital Discovery & E-Evidence,* and the Georgetown Advanced E-Discovery Institute. She has served on the ARMA Electronic Discovery Advisory Board and the *E-Discovery Advisor* Editorial Board. She is a prolific writer and frequent speaker on all aspects of e-discovery.

Ms. Barton received her J.D. cum laude from Tulane Law School, an M.P.H. from Harvard University, and her B.A. from Colby College. She is a member of the District of Columbia and Louisiana Bar Associations.

The Hon. Paul W. Grimm serves as a full-time Magistrate Judge for the United States District Court for the District of Maryland. He was appointed in February 1997. He was appointed as Chief Magistrate Judge in May 2006. In September 2009 he was appointed by the Chief Justice of the United States to serve as a member of the Advisory Committee for the Federal Rules of Civil Procedure. Additionally, Judge Grimm is an adjunct professor of law at the University of Baltimore School of Law, where he teaches evidence and a course regarding the discovery of and pretrial practices associated with electronically stored evidence. He also is an adjunct professor of law at the University of Maryland School of Law, where he teaches evidence, and also has taught trial evidence, pretrial civil procedure, and scientific evidence.

Judge Grimm is a frequent lecturer at CLE programs on issues regarding evidence and civil procedure, and he has lectured throughout the United States regarding discovery of electronically stored information and its admissibility in civil and criminal proceedings. He has authored several opinions that have received national attention relating to electronically stored information, including *Thompson v. HUD,* 219 F.R.D. 93 (D. Md. 2003) (discussing the factors that govern the scope of discovery of electronically stored evidence, and the duty to preserve such evidence, as well as spoliation sanctions for failure to do so); *Hopson v. Mayor & City Council of Baltimore,* 232 F.R.D. 228 (D. Md. 2005) (addressing issues of inadvertent waiver of privilege by production of electronically stored evidence with respect to the recent amendments to the

Federal Rules of Civil Procedure); *Lorraine v. Markel American Insurance Co.*, 241 F.R.D. 534 (D. Md. 2007) (comprehensively discussing the evidentiary issues associated with admissibility of electronic evidence); *CNA v. Under Armour, Inc.* 537 F. Supp. 2d 761 (D. Md. 2008) (discussing the circumstances in which inadvertent disclosure of electronically stored information waives privilege and work product protection); *Victor Stanley, Inc. v. Creative Pipe, Inc.*, 250 F.R.D. 251 (D. Md. 2008) (also discussing waiver of privilege regarding inadvertent production of electronically stored information, as well as proper methods of conducting search and information retrieval searches for ESI to fulfill preservation, production and privilege review functions); *Mancia v. Mayflower Textile Services Co.*, 253 F.R.D. 354 (D. Md. 2008) (discussing the duty of counsel and parties to cooperate during the pretrial discovery process to reduce the cost and burden of discovery); and *Victor Stanley, Inc. v. Creative Pipe, Inc.*, 269 F.R.D. 497 (D. Md. 2010) (comprehensively discussing spoliation of ESI evidence). He has authored numerous books, book chapters, and articles on these topics. He also is a frequent lecturer at the Maryland Judicial Institute, the continuing education arm of the Maryland State Judiciary, as well as at programs for the ABA, ALI-ABA, and the United States Department of Justice's National Advocacy Center, where he teaches courses on evidence, civil procedure, and trial advocacy.

In 2002 and 2006 Judge Grimm was awarded the Outstanding Adjunct Professor of the Year Award by the University of Maryland School of Law. In 2001, he was awarded the Maryland Bar Foundation's Professional Excellence Award for the Advancement of Professional Competence. In 1998, he received the Maryland Institute for Continuing Professional Education of Lawyer's Distinguished Service Award, and in 2004 he received the Daily Record Leadership in Law Award.

Before becoming a magistrate judge, Judge Grimm was in private practice in Baltimore for 13 years, during which time he handled commercial litigation. He also served as an Assistant Attorney General for the State of Maryland, an Assistant State's Attorney for Baltimore County, Maryland, and a Captain in the United States Army Judge Advocate General's Corps. In 2001, Judge Grimm retired as a Lieutenant Colonel from the United States Army Reserve.

Judge Grimm is a graduate of the University of California (summa cum laude), and the University of New Mexico School of Law (magna cum laude, Order of the Coif).

Contributing Authors

Members of the Judiciary

The Hon. John M. Facciola was appointed a United States Magistrate Judge in the District of Columbia in 1997. Prior to being appointed to the bench, he served as an Assistant District Attorney in Manhattan from 1969 to 1973, and was in private practice in the District of Columbia from 1974 to 1982. Judge Facciola joined the U.S. Attorney's Office in 1982 and served as Chief of the Special Proceedings section from 1989 until his appointment as Magistrate Judge. Judge Facciola is a frequent lecturer and speaker on the topic of electronic discovery. Judge Facciola is a member of the Sedona Conference Advisory Board and the Georgetown Advanced E-Discovery Institute Advisory Board, and he is also the former Editor-in-Chief of the *Federal Courts Law Review*, the electronic law journal of the Federal Magistrate Judges Association. He has recently been appointed to the Board of Directors of the Federal Judicial Center. His most recent publication is with Jonathan M. Redgrave, *Asserting and Challenging Privilege Claims in Modern Litigation: The Facciola-Redgrave Framework*, 2009 FED. CTS. L. REV. 19 (2009). He received his A.B from the College of the Holy Cross and his J.D. from the Georgetown University Law Center.

The Hon. James C. Francis IV has been a United States Magistrate Judge in the Southern District of New York since October 1985. He received his B.A. from Yale College in 1974, his juris doctor degree from the Yale Law School in 1978, and a master's degree in public policy from Harvard University, also in 1978. Following graduation from law school, Judge Francis clerked for the Honorable Robert L. Carter in the Southern District of New York. He then joined the Civil Appeals and Law Reform Unit of the Legal Aid Society, where he conducted impact litigation in the areas of housing and education and served as director of the Disability Rights Unit. Judge Francis currently serves as an Adjunct Professor at the Fordham University School of Law, where he teaches Constitutional Torts.

In the field of electronic data and the law, Judge Francis is the author of *Rowe Entertainment, Inc. v. William Morris Agency*, 205 F.R.D. 421 (S.D.N.Y. 2002) (allocation of costs), *Convolve, Inc. v. Compaq Computer Corp.*, 223 F.R.D. 162 (S.D.N.Y. 2004) (obligation to preserve ephemeral data), *Treppel v. Biovail Corp.*, 233 F.R.D. 363 (S.D.N.Y. 2006) (standards for preservation orders), *Rozell v. Ross-Holst*, 2006 WL 163143 (S.D.N.Y. Jan. 20, 2006) (relevance of e-mails to claim of computer hacking), *Treppel*, 249 F.R.D. 111 (S.D.N.Y. 2008) (remedies for spoliation of electronically stored information), *Richard Greene (Fine Paintings) v. McClendon*, 2009 WL 2496275 (S.D.N.Y. Aug. 13, 2009) (consequences of destruction of electronically stored information), and *Orbit One Communications, Inc. v. Numerex Corp.*, 2010 WL 4615547 (prerequisites for spoliation sanctions).

The Hon. J. Joseph Murphy, Jr., Court of Appeals of Maryland, graduated from the University of Maryland Law School in 1969, and became a member of the Maryland Bar in December of that year. From 1970 to 1975, Judge Murphy was an Assistant State's Attorney for Baltimore City, and from 1975 to 1976, he was the Deputy State's Attorney. From 1976 to 1984, he was in private practice, specializing in the defense of criminal cases.

Judge Murphy's litigation practice concluded in 1984, when he was appointed to the Circuit Court for Baltimore County. After serving as a trial judge for nine years, he was appointed to the Court of Special Appeals. He was appointed Chief Judge of that court in 1996, and served in that position until December 17, 2007, when he began serving as a judge of the Court of Appeals.

Judge Murphy is a former President of the Maryland Criminal Defense Attorneys Association. He has taught evidence at the University of Baltimore Law School since 1974, and trial practice at the University of Maryland Law School since 1981. He is the author of the *Maryland Evidence Handbook*, the fourth edition of which was published in 2010.

Judge Murphy participated in the Symposium on Advanced Issues in Electronic Discovery: The Impact of the First Year of the Federal Rules and the Adoption of the Maryland Rules, and chaired the Rules Committee when Maryland's e-discovery rules were adopted.

Judge Murphy is the 1990 recipient of the Maryland State Bar Association's Robert C. Heeney Memorial Award, the 2003 recipient of the *Daily Record*'s Top Leadership in Law Award, and the 2008 recipient of the University of Baltimore Law School's Charles Hamilton Houston Award.

The Hon. Barbara Jacobs Rothstein is a United States District Judge for the Western District of Washington and was appointed Director of the Federal Judicial Center in Washington, D.C., by the Board of the Center, chaired by Chief Justice William H. Rehnquist. She was chief judge of the Western District of Washington from 1987-1994. She graduated Phi Beta Kappa from Cornell University and attended Harvard Law School where she was the winning oralist in the Ames Moot Court competition.

After law school Judge Rothstein practiced law with a private firm in Boston, Massachusetts and with the Consumer Protection and Antitrust Division of the State of Washington's Attorney General's office. Judge Rothstein taught trial practice at the University of Washington Law School. Before her appointment to the federal bench in 1980, she served as a King County Superior Court judge for the State of Washington.

Judge Rothstein has trained women judges and lawyers from Afghanistan and Saudi Arabia and many in other countries to help improve the rule of law and the role of an independent judiciary. She has presided over many complex and controversial criminal and civil cases. She has served on a variety of committees including the Federal-State Relations Committee of the United States Judicial Conference and the Ninth Circuit Standing Committee on Gender, Race, Religious and Ethnic Fairness.

Judge Rothstein is a frequent lecturer and is a member of the American Law Institute. She is a Commissioner on the National Historical Publications and Records Commission. She serves on the Judicial Advisory Board of American Society of International Law (ASIL), the Board of the Rule of Law Initiative (ROLI) of the ABA, the Judicial Advisory Board of the Sedona Conference®; the Board of the Institute of Judicial Administration (IJA) at NYU Law School and the Board of the Avon Global Center for Women and Justice at Cornell Law School. She served on the board of EINSHAC, an educational affiliate of the Human Genome Project. She also serves as a member of the National Academy of Science's Committee on Science Technology and Law.

Members of the Bar and ESI Consultants

Jason R. Baron has served since 2000 as Director of Litigation for the National Archives and Records Administration in Washington, D.C. Since 2003, he has represented NARA on The Sedona Conference® Working Group on Electronic Document Retention and Production, and was appointed to the Working Group's steering committee in 2008 and made Co-Chair in 2009. He has served as Editor-in-Chief on three Sedona publications: the *Best Practices Commentary on the Use of Search and Information Retrieval Methods in E-Discovery* (2007), the *Commentary on Achieving Quality in the E-Discovery Process* (2009), and the *Commentary on Finding the Hidden ROI in Information Assets* (2011). Among his many other publications, he is author of "Law in the Age of Exabytes: Some Further Thoughts on 'Information Inflation' And Current Issues in E-Discovery Search," 17 Rich. J.L. & Tech. 9 (2011). He was a founding coordinator of the TREC legal track, and is a founder and organizer of the international DESI (Discovery of ESI) workshop series, held to date in Palo Alto (2007), London (2008), Barcelona (2009), and Pittsburgh (2011). Mr. Baron previously served as a trial lawyer and senior counsel in the Civil Division of the Department of Justice, where he litigated complex litigation, including acting as lead counsel in landmark cases involving the preservation of White House e-mail (including *Armstrong v. Executive Office of the President*). He has been a Visiting Scholar at the University of British Columbia, and is currently an Adjunct Professor at the University of Maryland's Graduate College of Information Studies. Mr. Baron received his B.A., *magna cum laude*, from Wesleyan University, and his J.D. from the Boston University School of Law.

Jeanna Beck is the Career and Professional Development Manager at Arnold & Porter LLP. Ms. Beck provides individualized career development and advancement counseling, oversees the mentoring programs for the associates, and focuses on pro bono litigation. Ms. Beck also develops specialized litigation trainings for all attorneys and CLE trainings for the attorneys in the California offices. Previously, Ms. Beck was a litigation associate in both the Los Angeles and Washington, D.C., offices of Arnold & Porter. Prior to joining the firm, Ms. Beck clerked for Judge James H. Alesia on the U.S. District Court for the Northern District of Illinois. She graduated Order of the Coif from DePaul University College of Law, where she was the Executive Editor of the DePaul Law Review.

Kevin F. Brady is a Litigation Partner at Connolly Bove Lodge & Hutz in Wilmington, Delaware. Mr. Brady is the Chair of the Business Law Group and Chair of the Information Security, Electronic Discovery, and Records Management Group. Prior to joining Connolly Bove, Mr. Brady was Counsel in the Complex Mass Torts and Insurance Group of Skadden Arps Slate Meagher & Flom LLP in Wilmington, Delaware, for almost 20 years. Mr. Brady received his undergraduate degree from the University of Delaware, his M.B.A. from Widener University, and his J.D. from Widener University School of Law.

Mr. Brady is a member of the Advisory Board for the Sedona Conference and a member of the Sedona Conference Working Group on Best Practices for Electronic Document Retention and Production. He is a Co-Chair of the Georgetown University Law Center's Advisory Board for the Advanced E-Discovery Institute and Co-Chair of Georgetown's E-Discovery Training Institute. Mr. Brady is also an Advisory Board member of BNA's Digital Discovery & e-Evidence Report. Mr. Brady is a member of the Ad Hoc Committee for Electronic Discovery of the U.S. District Court of Delaware, a member of the Delaware Court of Chancery Rules Committee and a member of the Delaware Superior Court Rules Committee on Electronic Discovery. Mr. Brady is a Founding Member and current President of the Richard Herrmann Technology and E-Discovery Inn of Court in Delaware, which is the first Inn of Court to focus exclusively on technology and electronic discovery.

David D. Cross is Counsel in the Litigation and E-Discovery and Information Management practice groups in the Washington, D.C., office of Crowell & Moring. Mr. Cross's practice includes antitrust, intellectual property, health care, securities, and general commercial litigation, representing both plaintiffs and defendants in federal and state courts as well as arbitration. His e-discovery experience includes developing and managing all aspects of preservation, collection, processing, review, and production protocols, including designing and negotiating complex e-discovery plans; preparing, defending and examining corporate and percipient witnesses on document retention and discovery efforts; prosecuting and defending spoliation claims; and advising clients regarding document retention policies and practices. Mr. Cross was one of the lead attorneys responsible for the litigation that produced the groundbreaking e-discovery decision *Hopson v. City of Baltimore,* 232. F.R.D. 228 (D. Md. 2005), which gave rise to FRE 502. He co-chairs an E-Discovery Subcommittee for the American Bar Association's Section of Litigation and regularly speaks and publishes on current e-discovery issues.

Mr. Cross holds a J.D. from Columbia University School of Law (2002) and a B.A. from Furman University (1997). At Columbia, he served as an articles editor for the *Journal of Law & Social Problems,* a Moot Court Editor, and a Teaching Fellow for courses in trial practice and negotiations. Mr. Cross clerked for the Honorable Michael B. Mukasey, former Chief Judge of the Southern District of New York and United States Attorney General.

Conor R. Crowley is the founder of the Crowley Law Office, which advises corporate and law firm clients on e-discovery readiness and responsiveness, records and information management, international e-discovery, and data privacy. Mr. Crowley is a member of the Steering Committee for the Sedona Conference Working Group on Best Practices for Electronic Document Retention and Production in addition to being the Editor-in-Chief of *The Sedona Conference Commentary on Proportionality in E-Discovery,* and Senior Editor of a number of the Sedona Conference's publications including *The Sedona Conference Commentary on Legal Holds* and *The Sedona Principles (Second Edition): Best Practices Recommendations & Principles for Addressing Electronic Document Production.* He is an inaugural member of both the Advisory Board for Georgetown University Law Center's Advanced E-Discovery Institute and the Board of Advisors for BNA's Digital Discovery & e-Evidence, and a member of the International Association of Privacy Professionals. Mr. Crowley holds a J.D. from the Columbus School of Law at the Catholic University of America (1997) and a B.Sc. from the Smith Business School at the University of Maryland (1994).

Richard E. Davis is the CEO and Founder of Litigation Logistics, LLC (LitLogix), a New York e-Discovery consulting services provider to law firms, Fortune 1000 corporations, and governmental entities. As a technology diagnostic consultant, Mr. Davis leverages a variety of solutions and designs processes around client-specific

LDLM (Legal Data Lifecycle Management) needs for electronic discovery and document review.

A former IBM systems engineer, Mr. Davis became the Manager of Technical Litigation Support for Cravath, Swaine and Moore LLP shortly after graduating from the Pace University School of Law. His acumen in technology and process design in the LDLM context took him to the IP law firm of Kenyon and Kenyon, LLP, where he founded the firm's first Practice Management Department. While the majority of Mr. Davis's work has been in the United States, he is also experienced in Japan-based multilingual document review pertaining to complex international transactions and litigation, having spent time in Tokyo training several teams of over 100 Tokyo-based Japanese lawyers on U.S.-based FTC second request and privileged document review techniques.

Today, Mr. Davis advises law firms, corporations, and governmental agencies on the selection and implementation of technology that reign in e-discovery costs. His opinions on the direction of e-discovery have been published in the *Wall Street Journal* and his transparent, scalable, and defensible e-discovery cost containment models continue to gain wide acceptance in the e-discovery industry.

Under Mr. Davis's guidance as LitLogix CEO, LitLogix continues to see significant growth as a LDLM advisor to corporate law and IT departments.

Dennis P. Duffy is chair of the labor and employment practice at Baker Botts LLP based in Houston and represents management exclusively in all aspects of labor and employment law. Prior to joining Baker Botts, Mr. Duffy was Vice President and Associate General Counsel for Labor and Employment with Time Warner Inc. Before joining Time Warner, Mr. Duffy was General Counsel of the University of Houston System and the University of Houston from 1997 to 2002. Before joining the University, Mr. Duffy was the first General Counsel of the Office of Compliance, Washington, D.C., responsible for enforcing several labor and employment laws that apply to employment within the U.S. Congress and Legislative Branch entities.

Earlier in his career, Mr. Duffy taught law at the University of Houston Law Center and the University of Virginia. He also was a management labor and employment lawyer with law firms in San Francisco and San Antonio.

Mr. Duffy received his A.B. degree from Princeton University and his J.D. degree from the University of Virginia. He is a member of the California and Texas Bars and is board-certified in labor and employment law by the Texas Board of Legal Specialization.

Mr. Duffy is the author of the *Ethics and Professionalism Handbook for Labor and Employment Lawyers* (6th ed., NELI 2010).

Scott Fischer is Director of Litigation Support Services at US Legal Support. Prior to that, he was an original partner of Array Technology Group, a litigation support firm founded in 1984 and acquired by US Legal Support in 2010. Mr. Fischer is an experienced litigation and e-discovery consultant and has been a featured ESI lecturer at Columbia University School of Law, University of Maryland School of Law, and the University of Baltimore School of Law. Mr. Fischer served as the court-appointed ESI expert for Judge Paul Grimm in *Victor Stanley, Inc. v. Creative Pipe, Inc.*, and was part of the Array team that served as trial consultants in *Zubulake v. UBS Warburg LLC*. He also served on the Committee to write the Suggested Protocol for the Discovery of Electronically Stored Information for the United States District Court for the State of Maryland.

During the course of his long career in litigation support, Mr. Fischer worked on many watershed cases in the use of technology in the litigation, including database creation in the Pan American Lockerbie and United Airlines Sioux City airline disasters, the early silicon breast implant litigation, and various aspects of the tobacco litigation.

Mr. Fischer has been a certified trainer in Summation software for 20 years, Concordance for seven years, and Kazeon for two years. He and his staff currently train and consult throughout the United States and Western Europe on all aspects of technology in litigation.

Melissa E. Goldmeier is a 2010 magna cum laude graduate of the University of Baltimore School of Law, which she attended on a full merit scholarship. She also earned a B.A., summa cum laude, in history from Wright State University in Dayton, Ohio, in 2007. Currently, Ms. Goldmeier serves as a clerk for Susan M. Marzetta, General Equity Master for the Circuit Court for Baltimore City. Ms. Goldmeier's written work has been published in the *University of Baltimore Law Forum*, the Social Science Research Network, and the *Fog Dog Review,* a literary journal affiliated with Wright State University. She is a concert violist and a long-distance runner.

Ronald J. Hedges is the principal of Ronald J. Hedges LLC. Mr. Hedges serves as a special master, mediator, and arbitrator and consults on electronic discovery and records management. He sat as a United States Magistrate Judge in the District of New Jersey from 1986 to 2007. Among other things, Mr. Hedges is a member of the adjunct faculty of Georgetown University Law Center, where he teaches an introduction to electronic discovery and evidence, and of the advisory boards of Georgetown's Advanced E-Discovery Institute and the Sedona Conference. He is also a Visiting Research Collaborator at the Center for Information Technology at Princeton University for the 2010–11 academic year..

Jared S. Hosid is a trial attorney in the U.S. Department of Justice's Criminal Division, where he focuses on issues involving electronic surveillance.* Prior to joining the DOJ, Mr. Hosid was an e-discovery and litigation associate at Crowell & Moring LLP, where he counseled and represented clients in disputes involving the preservation, processing, and production of electronically stored information. He has extensive experience advising clients on records and information management, and has written and presented on various e-discovery topics, particularly with regard to cloud computing. Mr. Hosid began his legal career as a litigation associate at Dechert LLP, and later served as a clerk for Hon. John M. Facciola, U.S. Magistrate Judge for the District Court of the District of Columbia, a thought leader in the field of e-discovery. He holds a J.D. and M.P.P. from Georgetown University (2003), as well as a B.A. (cum laude) from George Washington University (1999).

Sanya Sarich Kerksiek is a senior associate in the Litigation group in the Washington, D.C., office of Crowell & Moring, LLP, where she represents clients in cases involving copyrights, patents, commercial contracts, fraud, and other complex litigation. As part of her practice, she advises clients regarding the processing and production of electronically stored information.

* The Department of Justice, as a matter of policy, disclaims responsibility for any private publication or statement by any of its employees. The views expressed herein are those of Jared S. Hosid and do not reflect the views of the DOJ.

Ms. Kerksiek holds a J.D. from Northwestern University (2003) and a B.A. from University of Illinois at Champaign-Urbana (1999). She clerked for Hon. Geraldine Soat Brown, U.S. Magistrate Judge for the Northern District of Illinois, and for Hon. Oliver W. Wanger, U.S. District Judge for the Eastern District of California.

David J. Kessler is a partner at Fulbright & Jaworski L.L.P. and is co-head of its E-Discovery and Information Management Practice. Mr. Kessler is a commercial and intellectual property litigator who specializes in counseling clients regarding e-discovery, litigation preparedness, records management, data privacy, information security, and cross-border data transfer and discovery. Mr. Kessler is an adjunct professor at the Beasley School of Law at Temple University, where he teaches "E-Discovery," and a member of the Sedona Conference's Working Group's on Record Retention, and Document Production as well as International Discovery. Mr. Kessler is currently assisting in the drafting and publishing the Sedona Conference's Commentary on Database Discovery.

Robert Dale Klein is a name principal in the Annapolis firm of Wharton Levin Ehrmantraut & Klein, P.A., where he focuses on the defense of product liability, mass tort, and other complex litigation matters involving e-discovery issues. A frequent writer and lecturer on product liability and civil procedure topics, Mr. Klein is author of *Maryland Civil Procedure Forms with Practice Commentary*, a well-regarded two-volume treatise that has been in continuous publication since 1984 (3d ed., Matthew Bender & Co.). He has served as a panelist/presenter for the 2008 University of Baltimore Law School Symposium on "Advanced Issues in Electronic Discovery" and in providing continuing legal education teaching on e-discovery issues on behalf of the Maryland State Bar Association. Mr. Klein is a member of the Standing Committee on Rules of Practice and Procedure of the Court of Appeals of Maryland, to which he was first appointed in 1994, and for many years he has chaired its Discovery Subcommittee. In that role, Mr. Klein shepherded the development of the package of e-discovery amendments to the Maryland Rules that took effect January 1, 2008.

Mr. Klein graduated from the Columbia University School of Law School (J.D. 1976), the Massachusetts Institute of Technology (B.S. 1973), and the University of Durham, England (junior year abroad, 1971–72). He has been recognized by his peers as a *Maryland Super Lawyer.*

Michael B. MacWilliams is a partner in the Commercial Litigation practice group in the Baltimore, Maryland, office of Venable LLP, where his practice focuses on the resolution of complex commercial, product liability, and intellectual property disputes, including such areas as copyright infringement, patent infringement, misappropriation of trade secrets and related business torts, and securities and shareholder disputes. He chairs Venable's Electronic Discovery Task Force, plays an active instructional role in the firm's e-discovery CLE program for litigation attorneys, and also serves as Associate Counsel to the Firm.

Mr. MacWilliams holds a J.D. (summa cum laude) from the University of Baltimore School of Law, where he served as Editor-in-Chief of the *Law Review* and was recognized as the law school's outstanding graduate for 1994. Mr. MacWilliams received his bachelor's degree in mechanical engineering from Virginia Tech in 1989, where he was a Marshall Hahn Engineering Scholar.

William A. McComas, a partner at Shapiro Sher Guinot & Sandler and a former software engineer, is a corporate and business transaction attorney who represents corporations and entrepreneurs, as well as investors, within the media, software, and technology sectors. Listed in *The Best Lawyers in America,* Mr. McComas is well-known for his ability to address business challenges and opportunities with a sophisticated understanding of cutting-edge technologies from which those challenges and opportunities arise. He assists companies in creating, protecting, and commercializing technology, and in financing, merging, selling, and/or acquiring those companies. In the mid-1990s, before the concept of e-discovery was widely understood, he led what is believed to be the first large-scale electronically stored information case in the State of Maryland for a major national law firm and subsequently facilitated the development of the e-discovery system and procedures that are still in use today as the e-discovery standard. He has since utilized his expertise in this arena to advise numerous organizations and litigators regarding the development of feasible and rigorous records management practices that mitigate the risks associated with electronically stored information, including litigation and avoiding costly sanctions for inappropriate records management. Mr. McComas is a much-sought-after speaker regarding the issues of technology and law. He teaches a masters course on computer forensics and the law at Stevenson University and has published many articles in periodicals such as the *National Law Journal, Legal Times, Information Week,* and the *Baltimore Business Journal.*

Catherine L. Muir is Counsel in Hunton & Williams's Complex Commercial Litigation eDiscovery and Cyber Investigations practice. Ms. Muir's practice focuses on advising corporate clients on electronic discovery, records and information management, and compliance and litigation preparedness in complex litigation, internal investigations, and class actions, and in responding to cyber security incidents. She previously was Senior Counsel, Director of Electronic Discovery and Records Compliance at Sprint Nextel Corporation.

Ms. Muir is a member of the Sedona Conference Working Group 1 on Electronic Document Retention and Production; Structured Data Drafting Committee, D.C. Bar eDiscovery Committee of the Litigation Section, and Georgetown Law's eDiscovery Practice Support Project. Ms. Muir has divided her years of legal practice between serving as outside and inside counsel. As a result, she has invaluable insight into how to work efficiently with organizations to identify, analyze, and produce information in civil, regulatory, and criminal matters. Ms. Muir received her J.D. from the Vermont Law School and her B.A. from Miami University, Ohio.

Kate Paslin recently joined AccessData Group as Assistant General Counsel following its merger with Summation Litigation Technologies. A former litigator, Kate brings a broad perspective to her support of numerous teams within AccessData as well as clients spanning the corporate, firm and government spaces. Kate supplements her internal role with frequent writing and presentations on the impact of electronic information on disclosure practices and the increasing sophistication of legally defensible technologies.

Prior to joining AccessData Group, Kate regularly used litigation software as a practicing attorney in both California and Texas. Her litigation background includes maritime and admiralty work, securities litigation, corporate fraud and misrepresentation, antitrust and environmental-toxic tort litigation. Kate received her J.D.

from the University of California, Hastings College of the Law and a B.A. from the University of Michigan at Ann Arbor.

Meghan A. Podolny is an associate in the Complex Commercial Litigation and eDiscovery and Cyber-Investigations practice groups in the Richmond, Virginia, office of Hunton & Williams. Ms. Podolny is a veteran of the e-discovery wars. She routinely designs and supervises plans for collection, review, and production of documents for Fortune 500 companies in response to numerous actions, including defending class action claims, and responding to state attorney general investigations. She also has experience preparing and executing response plans to significant government subpoenas and Second Requests. She has served as discovery counsel in large-scale internal investigations of major financial institutions, as well as in responding to related government subpoenas and civil litigation. Ms. Podolny received her J.D. from the College of William & Mary (2007) and her B.A. (summa cum laude) from the University of Notre Dame (2004).

Daniel L. Regard, Managing Director at IDS, is a nationally recognized electronic evidence and case management expert with 20 years of experience in consulting to legal and corporate entities. A programmer and an attorney by training, Mr. Regard has conducted system investigations, created data collections, and managed discovery on some of the highest-profile financial investigations of the last decade. He is responsible for the development and implementation of case and matter strategies that leverage technology to clients' best advantage in both litigations and investigations. Mr. Regard has both national and international experience advising on such issues as electronic discovery, computer forensics, database development, application software, data analysis, and repository services. He has testified and worked as a testifying expert and as a court appointed neutral on issues of electronic discovery.

Prior to founding Intelligent Discovery Solutions, Inc. in December 2007, Mr. Regard was the national director of e-Discovery for LECG. He was also the national director of Electronic Evidence & Consulting for FTI Consulting, and was a national leader of Analytical Dispute Services at Deloitte & Touché, where he managed multinational, multijurisdictional, and multicounsel litigation support projects. He began his career as the founder of a nationwide litigation-support practice.

Mr. Regard holds a bachelor of science degree from the University of Southwestern Louisiana. He holds an MBA and a JD from Tulane University.

Rachel A. Shapiro holds a B.A. (summa cum laude/Phi Beta Kappa) from Tufts University, and a J.D. (magna cum laude/Order of the Coif) from the University of Maryland School of Law, where she served as a Notes and Comments Editor for the Maryland Law Review. Her growing interest in e-discovery stems from a seminar taught by Michael D. Berman in the fall of 2009. Between 2010 and 2011, Ms. Shapiro clerked for the Hon. James R. Eyler, Maryland Court of Special Appeals. In August 2011, she will begin a clerkship for the Hon. Susan Gauvey, United States District Court for the District of Maryland.

Stephanie Weirick is a litigation associate in the Washington, D.C., office of Arnold & Porter LLP. Ms. Weirick has helped clients with a number of e-discovery issues, and took a lead role in implementing a substantial document preservation and collection effort in a multidistrict litigation. She also has contributed to several telecasts and webinars regarding various e-discovery topics. Ms. Weirick graduated magna cum laude from the University of Southern California and earned her J.D. from West Virginia University College of Law, where she was elected to the Order of the Coif.

Leslie Wharton is Senior E-Discovery Counsel in the Office of General Counsel at the Securities and Exchange Commission.* Prior to joining the SEC, she was a partner in the Washington, D.C., office of Arnold & Porter LLP. Ms. Wharton has counseled and represented clients on a variety of e-discovery issues including best practices for satisfying the duty to preserve and the management and protection of privilege claims and has lectured and published numerous articles on these subjects. Ms. Wharton holds a Ph.D. from Princeton University and a J.D. from Harvard Law School.

Bryant L. Young is a principal and co-founder of Hopkins & Young, LLC, formerly B.L. Young, LLC, and serves as of counsel

---

*The Securities and Exchange Commission, as a matter of policy, disclaims responsibility for any private publication or statement by any of its employees. The views expressed herein are those of Leslie Wharton and do not necessarily reflect the views of the Commission or of other staff of the Commission.

with Jordan IP Law, PC. He is also a Scholar in Residence and Chair of Institute Development and Advancement for the Institute for Intellectual Property and Social Justice (IIPSJ) at Howard University School of Law.

Prior to forming Hopkins & Young, LLC, Mr. Young was a Patent Examiner at the U.S. Patent and Trademark Office (USPTO) in Alexandria, VA. He later worked for top ranked patent practices at a few of the *American Lawyer* Top 100 law firms in Washington, DC, area including Finnegan and Oblon Spivak. He also became a Research Chemist/Formulation Engineer at PPG Inc. in Pittsburgh, Pennsylvania after a fellowship in an engineering program at Johns Hopkins University.

Mr. Young has represented clients in the areas of U.S. and foreign patents, trademarks, copyrights, IP counseling, opinions, due diligence, litigation, discovery best practices and strategies, contracts, licensing and commercialization for over a decade. Mr. Young's experience also includes reexamination practice and winning at the Board of Patent Appeals and Interferences at the USPTO.

Mr. Young's technical background includes organic/inorganic chemistry, chemical engineering, cosmetics, polymers, materials science and packaging, coatings, paints, pharmaceutical formulations, and mechanical/device engineering. His diverse experience also includes electrical/software engineering, semiconductors, social media, Internet, and mobile technologies.

Mr. Young earned his Juris Doctorate from the University of Maryland School of Law in December 2004, where he was an Associate Editor of the Maryland Law Review. He earned his bachelor of science degree, summa cum laude, from Morgan State University in 1997. He is a member of the District of Columbia, federal district court, and appellate bars.

In 2010, Mr. Young received a Presidential Award from Morgan State University for his accomplishments and achievements in the fields of law and science.

Visit www.hopkinsyounglaw.com for a listing of Mr. Young's professional licenses, certifications, awards, leadership positions, and publications.